T0188371

MATHEMATICAL ASPECTS OF DEEP LEARNING

In recent years the development of new classification and regression algorithms based on deep learning has led to a revolution in the fields of artificial intelligence, machine learning, and data analysis. The development of a theoretical foundation to guarantee the success of these algorithms constitutes one of the most active and exciting research topics in applied mathematics.

This book presents the current mathematical understanding of deep learning methods from the point of view of the leading experts in the field. It serves both as a starting point for researchers and graduate students in computer science, mathematics, and statistics trying to get into the field and as an invaluable reference for future research.

PHILIPP GROHS is Professor of Applied Mathematics at the University of Vienna and Group Leader of Mathematical Data Science at the Austrian Academy of Sciences.

GITTA KUTYNIOK is Bavarian AI Chair for Mathematical Foundations of Artificial Intelligence at Ludwig-Maximilians-Universität München and Adjunct Professor for Machine Learning at the University of Tromsø.

MATHEMATICAL ASPECTS OF DEEP LEARNING

Edited by

PHILIPP GROHS
Universität Wien, Austria

GITTA KUTYNIOK
Ludwig-Maximilians-Universität München

CAMBRIDGE
UNIVERSITY PRESS

CAMBRIDGE
UNIVERSITY PRESS

University Printing House, Cambridge CB2 8BS, United Kingdom

One Liberty Plaza, 20th Floor, New York, NY 10006, USA

477 Williamstown Road, Port Melbourne, VIC 3207, Australia

314-321, 3rd Floor, Plot 3, Splendor Forum, Jasola District Centre, New Delhi – 110025, India

103 Penang Road, #05–06/07, Visioncrest Commercial, Singapore 238467

Cambridge University Press is part of the University of Cambridge.

It furthers the University's mission by disseminating knowledge in the pursuit of education, learning, and research at the highest international levels of excellence.

www.cambridge.org
Information on this title: www.cambridge.org/9781316516782
DOI: 10.1017/9781009025096

First published 2023

Printed in the United Kingdom by TJ Books Limited, Padstow Cornwall

A catalogue record for this publication is available from the British Library.

ISBN 978-1-316-51678-2 Hardback

Contents

Contributors

Aviad Aberdam   *Electrical Engineering Department, Technion – Israel Institute of Technology, Haifa 32000, Israel*

Leila Arras   *Department of Artificial Intelligence, Fraunhofer Heinrich Hertz Institute, Einsteinufer 37, 10587 Berlin, Germany*

Julius Berner   *Faculty of Mathematics, University of Vienna, Universitätsring 1, 1010 Wien, Austria*

Yoshua Bengio   *University of Montreal, 2900 Edouard Montpetit Blvd, Montreal, QC H3T 1J4, Canada*

Joan Bruna   *Courant Institute and Center for Data Science, New York University, 251 Mercer Street, New York, NY 10012, USA*

Nadav Cohen   *Department of Computer Science and Applied Mathematics Weizmann Institute of Science Rehovot 7610001, Israel*

Alexandros G. Dimakis   *Department of Electrical and Computer Engineering, University of Texas, Austin TX 78712, USA*

Weinan E   *Department of Mathematics, Princeton University, Princeton, NJ 08544–1000, USA.*

Philipp Grohs   *Faculty of Mathematics and Research Platform Data Science, University of Vienna, Oskar Morgenstern Platz 1, 1090 Wien, Austria*

Ingo Gühring   *Institut für Mathematik, Technische Universität Berlin, Straße des 17. Juni 136, 10623 Berlin*

Benjamin D. Haeffele   *Mathematical Institute for Data Science, Department of Biomedical Engineering, Johns Hopkins University, 3400 N. Charles Street, Baltimore MD 21218, USA*

Jiequn Han   *Center for Computational Mathematics, Flatiron Institute, 162 5th Ave. New York, NY 10010, USA*

Leslie Pack Kaelbling   *Massachusetts Institute of Technology, Computer Science & Artificial Intelligence Laboratory, 32 Vassar St., Cambridge, MA 02139, USA*

Kenji Kawaguchi   *Massachusetts Institute of Technology, 77 Massachusetts Ave, Cambridge, MA 02139, USA*

Gitta Kutyniok   *Mathematisches Institut der Universität München, Theresienstraße, 80333 München, Germany*

Yoav Levine   *School of Computer Science and Engineering, The Hebrew University of Jerusalem, 91904 Jerusalem, Israel*

Qianxiao Li   *Department of Mathematics, National University of Singapore, 10 Lower Kent Ridge Road, Singapore 119076.*

Thomas Merkh   *Department of Mathematics and Department of Statistics, UCLA, Los Angeles, CA 90095, USA*

Grégoire Montavon   *Institute of Software Engineering and Theoretical Computer Science, TU Berlin, D-10587 Berlin, Germany*

Guido Montúfar   *Department of Mathematics and Department of Statistics, UCLA, CA 90095, USA and Max Planck Institute for Mathematics in the Sciences, 04103 Leipzig, Germany*

Klaus-Robert Müller   *Institute of Software Engineering and Theoretical Computer Science, TU Berlin, D-10587 Berlin, Germany*

Ahmed Osman   *Department of Artificial Intelligence, Fraunhofer Heinrich Hertz Institute, Einsteinufer 37, 10587 Berlin, Germany*

Philipp Petersen   *Faculty of Mathematics and Research Platform Data Science, University of Vienna, Oskar Morgenstern Platz 1, 1090 Wien, Austria*

Mones Raslan   *Institut für Mathematik, Technische Universität Berlin, Straße des 17. Juni 136, 10623 Berlin, Germany*

Wojciech Samek   *Department of Artificial Intelligence, Fraunhofer Heinrich Hertz Institute, Einsteinufer 37, 10587 Berlin, Germany*

Or Sharir   *School of Computer Science and Engineering, The Hebrew University of Jerusalem, 91904 Jerusalem, Israel*

Amnon Shashua   *School of Computer Science and Engineering, The Hebrew University of Jerusalem, 91904 Jerusalem, Israel*

Jeremias Sulam   *Biomedical Engineering Department & Mathematical Institute for Data Science, Johns Hopkins University, Homewood Campus, Baltimore MD 21218, USA*

René Vidal   *Mathematical Institute for Data Science and Department of Biomedical Engineering, Johns Hopkins University, Clark 302B, 3400 N. Charles Street, Baltimore MD 21218, USA*

Zhihui Zhu   *Department of Electrical & Computer Engineering, University of Denver, 2155 E. Wesley Avenue, Denver CO 80208, USA*

Preface

We currently are witnessing the spectacular success of "deep learning" in both science (for example, in astronomy, biology, and medicine) and the public sector, where autonomous vehicles and robots are already present in daily life. However, the development of a rigorous mathematical foundation for deep learning is at an early stage, and most of the related research is still empirically driven. At the same time, methods based on deep neural networks have already shown their impressive potential in mathematical research areas such as imaging sciences, inverse problems, and the numerical analysis of partial differential equations, sometimes far outperforming classical mathematical approaches for particular classes of problem. This book provides the first comprehensive introduction to the subject, highlighting recent theoretical advances as well as outlining the numerous remaining research challenges.

The model of a deep neural network is inspired by the structure of the human brain, with artificial neurons concatenated and arranged in layers, leading to an (artificial feed-forward) neural network. Because of the structure of artificial neurons, the realization of such a neural network, i.e., the function it provides, consists of compositions of affine linear maps and (non-linear) activation functions $\varrho \colon \mathbb{R} \to \mathbb{R}$. More precisely, the realization of a neural network with L layers, and N_0, N_L, and N_ℓ, $\ell = 1, \ldots, L - 1$, the number of neurons in the input, output, and ℓth hidden layer, as well as weight matrices and bias vectors, $W^{(\ell)} \in \mathbb{R}^{N_\ell \times N_{\ell-1}}$ and $b^{(\ell)} \in \mathbb{R}^{N_\ell}$, respectively, is given by

$$\Phi(x, \theta) = W^{(L)} \rho(W^{(L-1)} \cdots \rho(W^{(1)} x + b^{(1)}) + \cdots + b^{(L-1)}) + b^{(L)}, \qquad x \in \mathbb{R}^{N_0},$$

with free parameters $\theta = \big((W^{(\ell)}, b^{(\ell)})\big)_{\ell=1}^{L}$. Given training data

$$(z^{(i)})_{i=1}^{m} := ((x^{(i)}, y^{(i)}))_{i=1}^{m},$$

which arise from a function $g \colon \mathbb{R}^{N_0} \to \mathbb{R}^{N_L}$, the parameters are then learned by minimizing the empirical risk

$$\frac{1}{m}\sum_{i=1}^{m}\mathcal{L}(\Phi(\cdot,\theta),z^{(i)}),$$

with $\mathcal{L}$ a suitable loss function. This is commonly achieved by stochastic gradient descent, which is a variant of gradient descent accommodating the obstacle that the number of parameters and training samples is typically in the millions. The performance is then measured by the fit of the trained neural network to a test data set.

This leads to three main research directions in the theory of deep learning, namely: (1) expressivity, i.e., studying the error accrued in approximating g by the hypothesis class of deep neural networks; (2) optimization, which studies the algorithmic error using minimization of the empirical risk; and (3) generalization, which aims to understand the out-of-sample error. Expressivity is at present from a theoretical viewpoint the most advanced research direction; a current key question is the impact on the overall performance of various architectural components of neural networks, such as their depth. Optimization has recently seen intriguing new results. However, the main mystery of why stochastic gradient descent converges to good local minima despite the non-convexity of the problem is as yet unraveled. Finally, generalization is the direction that is the least explored so far, and a deep theoretical understanding of, for instance, why highly overparametrized models often do not overfit, is still out of reach. These core theoretical directions are complemented by others such as explainability, fairness, robustness, or safety – sometimes summarized as the reliability of deep neural networks. Interestingly, basically the entire field of mathematics, ranging from algebraic geometry through to approximation theory and then to stochastics is required to tackle these challenges, which often even demand the development of novel mathematics. And, in fact, at a rapidly increasing rate, mathematicians from all areas are joining the field and contributing with their unique expertise.

Apart from the development of a mathematical foundation of deep learning, deep learning has also a tremendous impact on mathematical approaches to other areas such as solving inverse problems or partial differential equations. In fact, it is fair to say that the area of inverse problems, in particular imaging science, has already undergone a paradigm shift towards deep-learning-based approaches. The area of the numerical analysis of partial differential equations has been slower to embrace these novel methodologies, since it was initially not evident what their advantage would be for this field. However, by now there exist various results of both a numerical and a theoretical nature showing that deep neural networks are capable of beating the curse of dimensionality while providing highly flexible and fast solvers. This observation has led to the fact that this area is also currently being swept by deep-learning-type approaches, requiring the development of a theoretical foundation as well.

This book is the first monograph in the literature to provide a comprehensive survey of the mathematical aspects of deep learning. Its potential readers could be researchers in the areas of applied mathematics, computer science, and statistics, or a related research area, or they could be graduate students seeking to learn about the mathematics of deep learning. The particular design of this volume ensures that it can serve as both a state-of-the-art reference for researchers as well as a textbook for students.

The book contains 11 diverse chapters written by recognized leading experts from all over the world covering a large variety of topics. It does not assume any prior knowledge in the field. The chapters are self-contained, covering the most recent research results in the respective topic, and can all be treated independently of the others. A brief summary of each chapter is given next.

Chapter 1 provides a comprehensive introduction to the mathematics of deep learning, and serves as a background for the rest of the book. The chapter covers the key research directions within both the mathematical foundations of deep learning and deep learning approaches to solving mathematical problems. It also discusses why there is a great need for a new theory of deep learning, and provides an overview of the main future challenges.

Chapter 2 provides a comprehensive introduction to generalization properties of deep learning, emphasizing the specific phenomena that are special to deep learning models. Towards analyzing the generalization behavior of deep neural networks, the authors then present generalization bounds based on validation datasets and an analysis of generalization errors based on training datasets.

Chapter 3 surveys a recent body of work related to the expressivity of model classes of neural networks. The chapter covers results providing approximation rates for diverse function spaces as well as those shedding light on the question of why the depth of a neural network is important. The overview not only focuses on feed-forward neural networks, but also includes convolutional, residual, and recurrent ones.

Chapter 4 presents recent advances concerning the algorithmic solution of optimization problems that arise in the context of deep learning, in the sense of analyzing the optimization landscape of neural network training. A specific focus is on linear networks trained with a squared loss and without regularization as well as on deep networks with a parallel structure, positively homogeneous network mapping and regularization, and that have been trained with a convex loss.

Chapter 5 summarizes recent approaches towards rendering deep-learning-based classification decisions interpretable. It first discusses the algorithmic and theoretical aspects of an approach called Layer-wise Relevance Propagation (LRP). This is a propagation-based method, allowing us to derive explanations of the decisions of a variety of ML models. The authors also demonstrate how this method can be applied to a complex model trained for the task of visual question answering.

Chapter 6 introduces stochastic feed-forward neural networks, one prominent example of which is deep belief networks. The authors first review existing expressivity results for this class of networks. They then analyze the question of a universal approximation for shallow networks and present a unified analysis for several classes of such deep networks.

Chapter 7 explores connections between deep learning and sparsity-enforcing algorithms. More precisely, this chapter reviews and builds on previous work on a novel interpretation of deep neural networks from a sparsity viewpoint, namely as pursuit algorithms aiming for sparse representations, provided that the signals belong to a multilayer synthesis sparse model. The authors then present extensions of this conceptual approach and demonstrate the advantage of the resulting algorithms in a specific supervised learning setting, leading to an improvement of performance while retaining the number of parameters.

Chapter 8 provides a comprehensive introduction of the scattering transform. The author presents both mathematical results, showing that geometric stability indeed plays a key role in deep learning representations, and applications to, for instance, computer vision. Also, more general group-invariant feature descriptors in terms of Lie groups and non-Euclidean domains are described.

Chapter 9 focuses on the application of deep neural networks to solving inverse problems. The author provides an introduction to the use of generative deep learning models as priors in the regularization of inverse problems. Also, the specific setting of a compressed sensing problem is studied and both mathematical and numerical results in compressed sensing for deep generative models are presented.

Chapter 10 introduces a reformulation of the training process for residual neural networks as well as a corresponding theory. More precisely, the dynamical systems viewpoint regards the back-propagation algorithm as a simple consequence of variational equations in ordinary differential equations, whereas the control theory viewpoint regards deep learning as one instance of mean-field control where all agents share the same control. The authors finally introduce a new class of algorithms for deep learning as one application of these conceptual viewpoints.

Chapter 11 illuminates the connections between tensor networks and convolutional neural networks. These are established by relating one of the current goals of the field of many-body physics, namely the efficient representation of highly entangled many-particle quantum systems, to the area of deep learning. As one application of this framework, the authors derive a new entanglement-based deep learning design scheme which allows theoretical insight in a wide variety of customarily used network architectures.

1

The Modern Mathematics of Deep Learning

Julius Berner, Philipp Grohs, Gitta Kutyniok and Philipp Petersen

Abstract: We describe the new field of the mathematical analysis of deep learning. This field emerged around a list of research questions that were not answered within the classical framework of learning theory. These questions concern: the outstanding generalization power of overparametrized neural networks, the role of depth in deep architectures, the apparent absence of the curse of dimensionality, a surprisingly successful optimization performance despite the non-convexity of the problem, understanding what features are learned, why deep architectures perform exceptionally well in physical problems, and which fine aspects of an architecture affect the behavior of a learning task in which way. We present an overview of modern approaches that yield partial answers to these questions. For selected approaches, we describe the main ideas in more detail.

1.1 Introduction

Deep learning has undoubtedly established itself as the outstanding machine learning technique of recent times. This dominant position has been claimed through a series of overwhelming successes in widely different application areas.

Perhaps the most famous application of deep learning, and certainly one of the first where these techniques became state-of-the-art, is image classification (LeCun et al., 1998; Krizhevsky et al., 2012; Szegedy et al., 2015; He et al., 2016). In this area, deep learning is nowadays the only method that is seriously considered. The prowess of deep learning classifiers goes so far that they often outperform humans in image-labelling tasks (He et al., 2015).

A second famous application area is the training of deep-learning-based agents to play board games or computer games, such as Atari games (Mnih et al., 2013). In this context, probably the most prominent achievement yet is the development of an algorithm that beat the best human player in the game of Go (Silver et al., 2016, 2017) – a feat that was previously unthinkable owing to the extreme complexity of this game. Moreover, even in multiplayer, team-based games with incomplete information, deep-learning-based agents nowadays outperform world-class human teams (Berner et al., 2019a; Vinyals et al., 2019).

In addition to playing games, deep learning has also led to impressive breakthroughs in the natural sciences. For example, it is used in the development of drugs (Ma et al., 2015), molecular dynamics (Faber et al., 2017), and in high-energy physics (Baldi et al., 2014). One of the most astounding recent breakthroughs in scientific applications is the development of a deep-learning-based predictor for the folding behavior of proteins (Senior et al., 2020). This predictor is the first method to match the accuracy of lab-based methods.

Finally, in the vast field of natural language processing, which includes the subtasks of understanding, summarizing, and generating text, impressive advances have been made based on deep learning. Here, we refer to Young et al. (2018) for an overview. One technique that has recently stood out is based on a so-called transformer neural network (Bahdanau et al., 2015; Vaswani et al., 2017). This network structure has given rise to the impressive GPT-3 model (Brown et al., 2020) which not only creates coherent and compelling texts but can also produce code, such as that for the layout of a webpage according to some instructions that a user inputs in plain English. Transformer neural networks have also been successfully employed in the field of symbolic mathematics (Saxton et al., 2018; Lample and Charton, 2019).

In this chapter, we present and discuss the mathematical foundations of the success story outlined above. More precisely, our goal is to outline the newly emerging field of *the mathematical analysis of deep learning*. To accurately describe this field, a necessary preparatory step is to sharpen our definition of the term deep learning. For the purposes of this chapter, we will use the term in the following narrow sense: *deep learning refers to techniques where deep neural networks*[1] *are trained with gradient-based methods*. This narrow definition helps to make this chapter more concise. We would like to stress, however, that we do not claim in any way that this is the *best* or the *right* definition of deep learning.

Having fixed a definition of deep learning, three questions arise concerning the aforementioned emerging field of mathematical analysis of deep learning. To what extent is a mathematical theory necessary? Is it truly a new field? What are the questions studied in this area?

Let us start by explaining the necessity of a theoretical analysis of the tools described above. From a scientific perspective, the primary reason why deep learning should be studied mathematically is simple curiosity. As we will see throughout this chapter, many practically observed phenomena in this context are not explained

---

[1] We will define the term *neural network* later but, for now, we can view it as a parametrized family of functions with a differentiable parametrization.

theoretically. Moreover, theoretical insights and the development of a comprehensive theory often constitute the driving force underlying the development of new and improved methods. Prominent examples of mathematical theories with such an effect are the theory of fluid mechanics which is fundamental ingredient of the design of aircraft or cars, and the theory of information which affects and shapes all modern digital communication. In the words of Vladimir Vapnik[2]: "Nothing is more practical than a good theory," (Vapnik, 2013, Preface). In addition to being interesting and practical, theoretical insight may also be necessary. Indeed, in many applications of machine learning, such as medical diagnosis, self-driving cars, and robotics, a significant level of control and predictability of deep learning methods is mandatory. Also, in services such as banking or insurance, the technology should be controllable in order to guarantee fair and explainable decisions.

Let us next address the claim that the field of mathematical analysis of deep learning is a newly emerging area. In fact, under the aforementioned definition of deep learning, there are two main ingredients of the technology: deep neural networks and gradient-based optimization. The first artificial neuron was already introduced in McCulloch and Pitts (1943). This neuron was not trained but instead used to explain a biological neuron. The first multi-layered network of such artificial neurons that was also trained can be found in Rosenblatt (1958). Since then, various neural network architectures have been developed. We will discuss these architectures in detail in the following sections. The second ingredient, gradient-based optimization, is made possible by the observation that, owing to the graph-based structure of neural networks, the gradient of an objective function with respect to the parameters of the neural network can be computed efficiently. This has been observed in various ways: see Kelley (1960); Dreyfus (1962); Linnainmaa (1970); Rumelhart et al. (1986). Again, these techniques will be discussed in the upcoming sections. Since then, techniques have been improved and extended. As the rest of the chapter is spent reviewing these methods, we will keep the discussion of literature brief at this point. Instead, we refer to some overviews of the history of deep learning from various perspectives: LeCun et al. (2015); Schmidhuber (2015); Goodfellow et al. (2016); Higham and Higham (2019).

Given the fact that the two main ingredients of deep neural networks have been around for a long time, one might expect that a comprehensive mathematical theory would have been developed that describes why and when deep-learning-based methods will perform well or when they will fail. Statistical learning theory (Anthony and Bartlett, 1999; Vapnik, 1999; Cucker and Smale, 2002; Bousquet et al., 2003; Vapnik, 2013) describes multiple aspects of the performance of general learning methods and in particular deep learning. We will review this theory in the

---

[2] This claim can be found earlier in a non-mathematical context in the works of Kurt Lewin (1943).

context of deep learning in §1.1.2 below. Here, we focus on the classical, deep-learning-related results that we consider to be well known in the machine learning community. Nonetheless, the choice of these results is guaranteed to be subjective. We will find that this classical theory is too general to explain the performance of deep learning adequately. In this context, we will identify the following questions that appear to be difficult to answer within the classical framework of learning theory: *Why do trained deep neural networks not overfit on the training data despite the enormous power of the architecture? What is the advantage of deep compared to shallow architectures? Why do these methods seemingly not suffer from the curse of dimensionality? Why does the optimization routine often succeed in finding good solutions despite the non-convexity, nonlinearity, and often non-smoothness of the problem? Which aspects of an architecture affect the performance of the associated models and how? Which features of data are learned by deep architectures? Why do these methods perform as well as or better than specialized numerical tools in the natural sciences?*

The new field of the mathematical analysis of deep learning has emerged around questions like those listed above. In the remainder of this chapter, we will collect some of the main recent advances towards answering these questions. Because this field of the mathematical analysis of deep learning is incredibly active and new material is added at breathtaking speed, a brief survey of recent advances in this area is guaranteed to miss not only a couple of references but also many of the most essential ones. Therefore we do not strive for a complete overview but, instead, showcase several fundamental ideas on a mostly intuitive level. In this way, we hope to allow readers to familiarize themselves with some exciting concepts and provide a convenient entry-point for further studies.

1.1.1 Notation

We denote by $\mathbb{N}$ the set of natural numbers, by $\mathbb{Z}$ the set of integers, and by $\mathbb{R}$ the field of real numbers. For $N \in \mathbb{N}$, we denote by $[N]$ the set $\{1, \ldots, N\}$. For two functions $f, g \colon X \to [0, \infty)$, we write $f \lesssim g$ if there exists a universal constant c such that $f(x) \le cg(x)$ for all $x \in X$. In a pseudometric space (X, d_X), we define the ball of radius $r \in (0, \infty)$ around a point $x \in X$ by $B_r^{d_X}(x)$, or $B_r(x)$ if the pseudometric d_X is clear from the context. By $\| \cdot \|_p$, $p \in [1, \infty]$, we denote the ℓ^p-norm, and by $\langle \cdot, \cdot \rangle$ the Euclidean inner product of given vectors. By $\| \cdot \|_{\mathrm{op}}$ we denote the operator norm induced by the Euclidean norm and by $\| \cdot \|_F$ the Frobenius norm of given matrices. For $p \in [1, \infty]$, $s \in [0, \infty)$, $d \in \mathbb{N}$, and $X \subset \mathbb{R}^d$, we denote by $W^{s,p}(X)$ the Sobolev–Slobodeckij space, which for $s = 0$ is just a Lebesgue space, i.e., $W^{0,p}(X) = L^p(X)$. For measurable spaces X and $\mathcal{Y}$, we define $\mathcal{M}(X, \mathcal{Y})$ to be the set of measurable functions from X to $\mathcal{Y}$. We denote by $\hat{g}$ the

Fourier transform[3] of a tempered distribution g. For probabilistic statements, we will assume a suitable underlying probability space with probability measure $\mathcal{I}$. For an $\mathcal{X}$-valued random variable X, we denote by $\mathbb{E}[X]$ and $\mathbb{V}[X]$ its expectation and variance and by $\mathcal{I}_X$ the image measure of X on $\mathcal{X}$, i.e., $\mathcal{I}_X(A) = \mathcal{I}(X \in A)$ for every measurable set $A \subset \mathcal{X}$. If possible, we use the corresponding lowercase letter to denote the realization $x \in \mathcal{X}$ of the random variable X for a given outcome. We write I_d for the d-dimensional identity matrix and, for a set A, we write 1_A for the indicator function of A, i.e., $1_A(x) = 1$ if $x \in A$ and $1_A(x) = 0$ otherwise.

1.1.2 Foundations of Learning Theory

Before we describe recent developments in the mathematical analysis of deep learning methods, we will start by providing a concise overview of the classical mathematical and statistical theory underlying machine learning tasks and algorithms that, in their most general form, can be formulated as follows.

Definition 1.1 (Learning – informal). Let $\mathcal{X}$, $\mathcal{Y}$, and $\mathcal{Z}$ be measurable spaces. In a learning task, one is given data in $\mathcal{Z}$ and a loss function $\mathcal{L}\colon \mathcal{M}(\mathcal{X},\mathcal{Y}) \times \mathcal{Z} \to \mathbb{R}$. The goal is to choose a hypothesis set $\mathcal{F} \subset \mathcal{M}(\mathcal{X},\mathcal{Y})$ and to construct a learning algorithm, i.e., a mapping

$$\mathcal{A}\colon \bigcup_{m\in\mathbb{N}} \mathcal{Z}^m \to \mathcal{F},$$

that uses training data $s = (z^{(i)})_{i=1}^{m} \in \mathcal{Z}^m$ to find a model $f_s = \mathcal{A}(s) \in \mathcal{F}$ that performs well on the training data s and also generalizes to unseen data $z \in \mathcal{Z}$. Here, performance is measured via the loss function $\mathcal{L}$ and the corresponding loss $\mathcal{L}(f_s, z)$ and, informally speaking, generalization means that the out-of-sample performance of f_s at z behaves similarly to the in-sample performance on s.

Definition 1.1 is deliberately vague on how to measure generalization performance. Later, we will often study the *expected* out-of-sample performance. To talk about expected performance, a data distribution needs to be specified. We will revisit this point in Assumption 1.10 and Definition 1.11.

For simplicity, we focus on one-dimensional supervised prediction tasks with input features in Euclidean space, as defined in the following.

Definition 1.2 (Prediction task). In a prediction task, we have that $\mathcal{Z} := \mathcal{X} \times \mathcal{Y}$, i.e., we are given training data $s = ((x^{(i)}, y^{(i)}))_{i=1}^{m}$ that consist of input features $x^{(i)} \in \mathcal{X}$ and corresponding labels $y^{(i)} \in \mathcal{Y}$. For one-dimensional regression tasks with $\mathcal{Y} \subset \mathbb{R}$, we consider the quadratic loss $\mathcal{L}(f, (x, y)) = (f(x) - y)^2$ and, for binary

---

[3] Respecting common notation, we will also use the hat symbol to denote the minimizer of the empirical risk $\widehat{f_s}$ in Definition 1.8 but this clash of notation does not involve any ambiguity.

classification tasks with $\mathcal{Y} = \{-1, 1\}$, we consider the 0–1 loss $\mathcal{L}(f, (x, y)) = 1_{(-\infty, 0)}(y f(x))$. We assume that our input features are in Euclidean space, i.e., $\mathcal{X} \subset \mathbb{R}^d$ with input dimension $d \in \mathbb{N}$.

In a prediction task, we aim for a model $f_s : \mathcal{X} \to \mathcal{Y}$, such that, for unseen pairs $(x, y) \in \mathcal{X} \times \mathcal{Y}$, $f_s(x)$ is a good prediction of the true label y. However, note that large parts of the presented theory can be applied to more general settings.

Remark 1.3 (Learning tasks). Apart from straightforward extensions to multi-dimensional prediction tasks and other loss functions, we want to mention that unsupervised and semi-supervised learning tasks are often treated as prediction tasks. More precisely, one transforms unlabeled training data $z^{(i)}$ into features $x^{(i)} = T_1(z^{(i)}) \in \mathcal{X}$ and labels $y^{(i)} = T_2(z^{(i)}) \in \mathcal{Y}$ using suitable transformations $T_1 : \mathcal{Z} \to \mathcal{X}$, $T_2 : \mathcal{Z} \to \mathcal{Y}$. In doing so, one asks for a model f_s approximating the transformation $T_2 \circ T_1^{-1} : \mathcal{X} \to \mathcal{Y}$ which is, for example, made in order to learn feature representations or invariances.

Furthermore, one can consider density estimation tasks, where $\mathcal{X} = \mathcal{Z}$, $\mathcal{Y} := [0, \infty]$, and $\mathcal{F}$ consists of probability densities with respect to some σ-finite reference measure μ on $\mathcal{Z}$. One then aims for a probability density f_s that approximates the density of the unseen data z with respect to μ. One can perform $L^2(\mu)$-approximation based on the discretization $\mathcal{L}(f, z) = -2f(z) + \|f\|_{L^2(\mu)}^2$ or maximum likelihood estimation based on the surprisal $\mathcal{L}(f, z) = -\log(f(z))$.

In deep learning the hypothesis set $\mathcal{F}$ consists of *realizations of neural networks* $\Phi_a(\cdot, \theta)$, $\theta \in \mathcal{P}$, with a given *architecture a* and *parameter set* $\mathcal{P}$. In practice, one uses the term neural network for a range of functions that can be represented by directed acyclic graphs, where the vertices correspond to elementary almost everywhere differentiable functions parametrizable by $\theta \in \mathcal{P}$ and the edges symbolize compositions of these functions. In §1.6, we will review some frequently used architectures; in the other sections, however, we will mostly focus on *fully connected feed-forward* (FC) neural networks as defined below.

Definition 1.4 (FC neural network). A fully connected feed-forward neural network is given by its architecture $a = (N, \varrho)$, where $L \in \mathbb{N}$, $N \in \mathbb{N}^{L+1}$, and $\varrho : \mathbb{R} \to \mathbb{R}$. We refer to ϱ as the activation function, to L as the number of layers, and to N_0, N_L, and N_ℓ, $\ell \in [L-1]$, as the number of neurons in the input, output, and ℓth hidden layer, respectively. We denote the number of parameters by

$$P(N) := \sum_{\ell=1}^{L} N_\ell N_{\ell-1} + N_\ell$$

and define the corresponding realization function $\Phi_a : \mathbb{R}^{N_0} \times \mathbb{R}^{P(N)} \to \mathbb{R}^{N_L}$, which

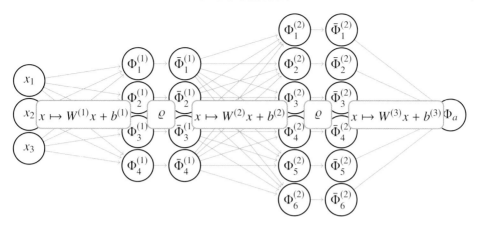

Figure 1.1 Graph (pale gray) and (pre-)activations of the neurons (white) of a deep fully connected feed-forward neural network $\Phi_a : \mathbb{R}^3 \times \mathbb{R}^{53} \mapsto \mathbb{R}$ with architecture $a = ((3,4,6,1), \varrho)$ and parameters $\theta = ((W^{(\ell)}, b^{(\ell)})^3_{\ell=1}$.

satisfies, for every input $x \in \mathbb{R}^{N_0}$ and parameters

$$\theta = (\theta^{(\ell)})^L_{\ell=1} = ((W^{(\ell)}, b^{(\ell)}))^L_{\ell=1} \in \bigtimes_{\ell=1}^{L} (\mathbb{R}^{N_\ell \times N_{\ell-1}} \times \mathbb{R}^{N_\ell}) \cong \mathbb{R}^{P(N)},$$

that $\Phi_a(x, \theta) = \Phi^{(L)}(x, \theta)$, where

$$\begin{aligned}
\Phi^{(1)}(x, \theta) &= W^{(1)}x + b^{(1)}, \\
\bar{\Phi}^{(\ell)}(x, \theta) &= \varrho(\Phi^{(\ell)}(x, \theta)), \quad \ell \in [L-1], \quad \text{and} \\
\Phi^{(\ell+1)}(x, \theta) &= W^{(\ell+1)}\bar{\Phi}^{(\ell)}(x, \theta) + b^{(\ell+1)}, \quad \ell \in [L-1],
\end{aligned}$$
(1.1)

and ϱ is applied componentwise. We refer to $W^{(\ell)} \in \mathbb{R}^{N_\ell \times N_{\ell-1}}$ and $b^{(\ell)} \in \mathbb{R}^{N_\ell}$ as the weight matrices and bias vectors, and to $\bar{\Phi}^{(\ell)}$ and $\Phi^{(\ell)}$ as the activations and pre-activations of the N_ℓ neurons in the ℓth layer. The width and depth of the architecture are given by $\|N\|_\infty$ and L and we call the architecture deep if $L > 2$ and shallow if $L = 2$.

The underlying directed acyclic graph of FC networks is given by compositions of the affine linear maps $x \mapsto W^{(\ell)}x + b^{(\ell)}$, $\ell \in [L]$, with the activation function ϱ intertwined; see Figure 1.1. Typical activation functions used in practice are variants of the *rectified linear unit* (ReLU) given by $\varrho_R(x) := \max\{0, x\}$ and *sigmoidal functions* $\varrho \in C(\mathbb{R})$ satisfying $\varrho(x) \to 1$ for $x \to \infty$ and $\varrho(x) \to 0$ for $x \to -\infty$, such as the logistic function $\varrho_\sigma(x) := 1/(1 + e^{-x})$ (often referred to as *the* sigmoid function). See also Table 1.1 for a comprehensive list of widely used activation functions.

Name	Given as a function of $x \in \mathbb{R}$ by	Plot
linear	x	
Heaviside / step function	$1_{(0,\infty)}(x)$	
logistic / sigmoid	$\frac{1}{1+e^{-x}}$	
rectified linear unit (ReLU)	$\max\{0, x\}$	
power rectified linear unit	$\max\{0, x\}^k$ for $k \in \mathbb{N}$	
parametric ReLU (PReLU)	$\max\{ax, x\}$ for $a \geq 0$, $a \neq 1$	
exponential linear unit (ELU)	$x \cdot 1_{[0,\infty)}(x) +$ $(e^x - 1) \cdot 1_{(-\infty,0)}(x)$	
softsign	$\frac{x}{1+|x|}$	
inverse square root linear unit	$x \cdot 1_{[0,\infty)}(x) +$ $\frac{x}{\sqrt{1+ax^2}} \cdot 1_{(-\infty,0)}(x)$ for $a > 0$	
inverse square root unit	$\frac{x}{\sqrt{1+ax^2}}$ for $a > 0$	
tanh	$\frac{e^x - e^{-x}}{e^x + e^{-x}}$	
arctan	$\arctan(x)$	
softplus	$\ln(1 + e^x)$	
Gaussian	$e^{-x^2/2}$	

Table 1.1 *List of commonly used activation functions.*

Remark 1.5 (Neural networks). If not further specified, we will use the term (neural) network, or the abbreviation NN, to refer to FC neural networks. Note that many of the architectures used in practice (see §1.6) can be written as special cases of Definition 1.4 where, for example, specific parameters are prescribed by constants or shared with other parameters. Furthermore, note that affine linear functions are NNs with depth $L = 1$. We will also consider biasless NNs given by linear mappings without bias vector, i.e., $b^{(\ell)} = 0$, $\ell \in [L]$. In particular, any NN can always be written without bias vectors by redefining

$$x \to \begin{bmatrix} x \\ 1 \end{bmatrix}; \quad (W^{(\ell)}, b^{(\ell)}) \to \begin{bmatrix} W^{(\ell)} & b^{(\ell)} \\ 0 & 1 \end{bmatrix}; \quad \ell \in [L-1]; \quad \text{and}$$

$$(W^{(L)}, b^{(L)}) \to \begin{bmatrix} W^{(L)} & b^{(L)} \end{bmatrix}.$$

To enhance readability we will often not specify the underlying architecture $a = (N, \varrho)$ or the parameters $\theta \in \mathbb{R}^{P(N)}$ but use the term NN to refer to the architecture as well as the realization functions $\Phi_a(\cdot, \theta) \colon \mathbb{R}^{N_0} \to \mathbb{R}^{N_L}$ or $\Phi_a \colon \mathbb{R}^{N_0} \times \mathbb{R}^{P(N)} \to \mathbb{R}^{N_L}$. However, we want to emphasize that one cannot infer the underlying architecture or properties such as the magnitude of parameters solely from these functions, as the mapping $(a, \theta) \mapsto \Phi_a(\cdot, \theta)$ is highly non-injective. As an example, we can set $W^{(L)} = 0$, which implies $\Phi_a(\cdot, \theta) = b^{(L)}$ for all architectures $a = (N, \varrho)$ and all values of $(W^{(\ell)}, b^{(\ell)})_{\ell=1}^{L-1}$.

In view of our considered prediction tasks in Definition 1.2, this naturally leads to the following hypothesis sets of neural networks.

Definition 1.6 (Hypothesis sets of neural networks). Let $a = (N, \varrho)$ be a NN architecture with input dimension $N_0 = d$, output dimension $N_L = 1$, and measurable activation function ϱ. For regression tasks the corresponding hypothesis set is given by

$$\mathcal{F}_a = \{\Phi_a(\cdot, \theta) \colon \theta \in \mathbb{R}^{P(N)}\}$$

and for classification tasks by

$$\mathcal{F}_{a,\text{sgn}} = \{\text{sgn}(\Phi_a(\cdot, \theta)) \colon \theta \in \mathbb{R}^{P(N)}\}, \quad \text{where} \quad \text{sgn}(x) := \begin{cases} 1, & \text{if } x \geq 0, \\ -1, & \text{if } x < 0. \end{cases}$$

Note that we compose the output of the NN with the sign function in order to obtain functions mapping to $\mathcal{Y} = \{-1, 1\}$. This can be generalized to multi-dimensional classification tasks by replacing the sign by an argmax function. Given a hypothesis set, a popular learning algorithm is *empirical risk minimization* (ERM), which minimizes the average loss on the given training data, as described in the next two definitions.

Definition 1.7 (Empirical risk). For training data $s = (z^{(i)})_{i=1}^m \in \mathcal{Z}^m$ and a function $f \in \mathcal{M}(\mathcal{X}, \mathcal{Y})$, we define the empirical risk by

$$\widehat{\mathcal{R}}_s(f) := \frac{1}{m} \sum_{i=1}^m \mathcal{L}(f, z^{(i)}). \tag{1.2}$$

Definition 1.8 (ERM learning algorithm). Given a hypothesis set $\mathcal{F}$, an empirical risk-minimization algorithm $\mathcal{A}^{\mathrm{erm}}$ chooses[4] for training data $s \in \mathcal{Z}^m$ a minimizer $\widehat{f}_s \in \mathcal{F}$ of the empirical risk in $\mathcal{F}$, i.e.,

$$\mathcal{A}^{\mathrm{erm}}(s) \in \operatorname*{argmin}_{f \in \mathcal{F}} \widehat{\mathcal{R}}_s(f). \tag{1.3}$$

Remark 1.9 (Surrogate loss and regularization). Note that, for classification tasks, one needs to optimize over non-differentiable functions with discrete outputs in (1.3). For an NN hypothesis set $\mathcal{F}_{a,\mathrm{sgn}}$ one typically uses the corresponding hypothesis set for regression tasks $\mathcal{F}_a$ to find an approximate minimizer $\widehat{f}_s^{\mathrm{surr}} \in \mathcal{F}_a$ of

$$\frac{1}{m} \sum_{i=1}^m \mathcal{L}^{\mathrm{surr}}(f, z^{(i)}),$$

where $\mathcal{L}^{\mathrm{surr}} \colon \mathcal{M}(\mathcal{X}, \mathbb{R}) \times \mathcal{Z} \to \mathbb{R}$ is a surrogate loss guaranteeing that $\mathrm{sgn}(\widehat{f}_s^{\mathrm{surr}}) \in \operatorname{argmin}_{f \in \mathcal{F}_{a,\mathrm{sgn}}} \widehat{\mathcal{R}}_s(f)$. A frequently used surrogate loss is the logistic loss,[5] given by

$$\mathcal{L}^{\mathrm{surr}}(f, z) = \log\left(1 + e^{-yf(x)}\right).$$

In various learning tasks one also adds regularization terms to the minimization problem in (1.3), such as penalties on the norm of the parameters of the NN, i.e.,

$$\min_{\theta \in \mathbb{R}^{P(N)}} \widehat{\mathcal{R}}_s(\Phi_a(\cdot, \theta)) + \alpha \|\theta\|_2^2,$$

where $\alpha \in (0, \infty)$ is a regularization parameter. Note that in this case the minimizer depends on the chosen parameters θ and not only on the realization function $\Phi_a(\cdot, \theta)$; see also Remark 1.5.

Coming back to our initial, informal description of learning in Definition 1.1, we have now outlined potential learning tasks in Definition 1.2, NN hypothesis sets in Definition 1.6, a metric for the in-sample performance in Definition 1.7, and a

---

[4] For simplicity, we assume that the minimum is attained; this is the case, for instance, if $\mathcal{F}$ is a compact topological space on which $\widehat{\mathcal{R}}_s$ is continuous. Hypothesis sets of NNs $\mathcal{F}_{(N,\varrho)}$ constitute a compact space if, for example, one chooses a compact parameter set $\mathcal{P} \subset \mathbb{R}^{P(N)}$ and a continuous activation function ϱ. One could also work with approximate minimizers: see Anthony and Bartlett (1999).

[5] This can be viewed as cross-entropy between the label y and the output of f composed with a logistic function ϱ_σ. In a multi-dimensional setting one can replace the logistic function with a softmax function.

corresponding learning algorithm in Definition 1.8. However, we are still lacking a mathematical concept to describe the out-of-sample (generalization) performance of our learning algorithm. This question has been intensively studied in the field of statistical learning theory; see §1.1 for various references.

In this field one usually establishes a connection between the unseen data z and the training data $s = (z^{(i)})_{i=1}^m$ by imposing that z and $z^{(i)}$, $i \in [m]$, are realizations of independent samples drawn from the same distribution.

Assumption 1.10 (Independent and identically distributed data)**.** We assume that $z^{(1)}, \ldots, z^{(m)}, z$ are realizations of i.i.d. random variables $Z^{(1)}, \ldots, Z^{(m)}, Z$.

In this formal setting, we can compute the average out-of-sample performance of a model. Recall from our notation in §1.1.1 that we denote by I_Z the image measure of Z on $\mathcal{Z}$, which is the underlying distribution of our training data $S = (Z^{(i)})_{i=1}^m \sim I_Z^m$ and unknown data $Z \sim I_Z$.

Definition 1.11 (Risk)**.** For a function $f \in \mathcal{M}(\mathcal{X}, \mathcal{Y})$, we define[6] the risk by

$$\mathcal{R}(f) := \mathbb{E}\big[\mathcal{L}(f, Z)\big] = \int_{\mathcal{Z}} \mathcal{L}(f, z) \, dI_Z(z). \tag{1.4}$$

Defining $S := (Z^{(i)})_{i=1}^m$, the risk of a model $f_S = \mathcal{A}(S)$ is thus given by $\mathcal{R}(f_S) = \mathbb{E}\big[\mathcal{L}(f_S, Z)|S\big]$.

For prediction tasks, we can write $Z = (X, Y)$ such that the input features and labels are given by an $\mathcal{X}$-valued random variable X and a $\mathcal{Y}$-valued random variable Y, respectively. Note that for classification tasks the risk equals the probability of misclassification

$$\mathcal{R}(f) = \mathbb{E}[1_{(-\infty,0)}(Y f(X))] = I[f(X) \neq Y].$$

For noisy data, there might be a positive lower bound on the risk, i.e., an irreducible error. If the lower bound on the risk is attained, one can also define the notion of an optimal solution to a learning task.

Definition 1.12 (Bayes-optimal function)**.** A function $f^* \in \mathcal{M}(\mathcal{X}, \mathcal{Y})$ achieving the smallest risk, the so-called Bayes risk

$$\mathcal{R}^* := \inf_{f \in \mathcal{M}(\mathcal{X}, \mathcal{Y})} \mathcal{R}(f),$$

is called a Bayes-optimal function.

---

[6] Note that this requires $z \mapsto \mathcal{L}(f, z)$ to be measurable for every $f \in \mathcal{M}(\mathcal{X}, \mathcal{Y})$, which is the case for our considered prediction tasks.

For the prediction tasks in Definition 1.2, we can represent the risk of a function with respect to the Bayes risk and compute the Bayes-optimal function; see, e.g., Cucker and Zhou (2007, Propositions 1.8 and 9.3).

Lemma 1.13 (Regression and classification risk). *For a regression task with* $\mathbb{V}[Y] < \infty$, *the risk can be decomposed as follows:*

$$\mathcal{R}(f) = \mathbb{E}\big[(f(X) - \mathbb{E}[Y|X])^2\big] + \mathcal{R}^*, \quad f \in \mathcal{M}(\mathcal{X}, \mathcal{Y}), \tag{1.5}$$

which is minimized by the regression function $f^*(x) = \mathbb{E}[Y|X = x]$. *For a classification task, the risk can be decomposed as*

$$\mathcal{R}(f) = \mathbb{E}\big[|\mathbb{E}[Y|X]|1_{(-\infty,0)}(\mathbb{E}[Y|X]f(X))\big] + \mathcal{R}^*, \quad f \in \mathcal{M}(\mathcal{X}, \mathcal{Y}), \tag{1.6}$$

which is minimized by the Bayes classifier $f^*(x) = \mathrm{sgn}(\mathbb{E}[Y|X = x])$.

As our model f_S depends on the random training data S, the risk $\mathcal{R}(f_S)$ is a random variable and we might aim[7] for $\mathcal{R}(f_S)$ to be small with high probability or in expectation over the training data. The challenge for the learning algorithm $\mathcal{A}$ is to minimize the risk by using only training data, without knowing the underlying distribution. One can even show that for every learning algorithm there exists a distribution where convergence of the expected risk of f_S to the Bayes risk is arbitrarily slow with respect to the number of samples m (Devroye et al., 1996, Theorem 7.2).

Theorem 1.14 (No free lunch). *Let* $a_m \in (0, \infty)$, $m \in \mathbb{N}$, *be a monotonically decreasing sequence with* $a_1 \leq 1/16$. *Then for every learning algorithm* $\mathcal{A}$ *of a classification task there exists a distribution* $\mathcal{I}_Z$ *such that for every* $m \in \mathbb{N}$ *and training data* $S \sim \mathcal{I}_Z^m$ *it holds true that*

$$\mathbb{E}\big[\mathcal{R}(\mathcal{A}(S))\big] \geq \mathcal{R}^* + a_m.$$

Theorem 1.14 shows the non-existence of a universal learning algorithm for every data distribution $\mathcal{I}_Z$ and shows that useful bounds must necessarily be accompanied by a priori regularity conditions on the underlying distribution $\mathcal{I}_Z$. Such prior knowledge can then be incorporated into the choice of the hypothesis set $\mathcal{F}$. To illustrate this, let $f^*_{\mathcal{F}} \in \mathrm{argmin}_{f \in \mathcal{F}} \mathcal{R}(f)$ be a best approximation in $\mathcal{F}$, such that we can bound the error

$$\begin{aligned}
\mathcal{R}(f_S) &- \mathcal{R}^* \\
&= \mathcal{R}(f_S) - \widehat{\mathcal{R}}_S(f_S) + \widehat{\mathcal{R}}_S(f_S) - \widehat{\mathcal{R}}_S(f^*_{\mathcal{F}}) + \widehat{\mathcal{R}}_S(f^*_{\mathcal{F}}) - \mathcal{R}(f^*_{\mathcal{F}}) + \mathcal{R}(f^*_{\mathcal{F}}) - \mathcal{R}^* \\
&\leq \varepsilon^{\mathrm{opt}} + 2\varepsilon^{\mathrm{gen}} + \varepsilon^{\mathrm{approx}}
\end{aligned} \tag{1.7}$$

---

[7] In order to make probabilistic statements on $\mathcal{R}(f_S)$ we assume that $\mathcal{R}(f_S)$ is a random variable, i.e., measurable. This is, for example, the case if $\mathcal{F}$ constitutes a measurable space and $s \mapsto \mathcal{A}(s)$ and $f \to \mathcal{R}|_{\mathcal{F}}$ are measurable.

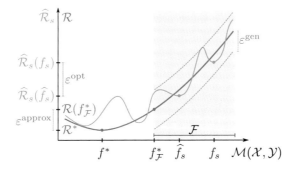

Figure 1.2 Illustration of the errors (A)–(C) in the decomposition (1.7). It shows the exemplary risk $\widehat{\mathcal{R}}$ (blue) and the empirical risk $\widehat{\mathcal{R}}_s$ (red) with respect to the projected space of measurable functions $\mathcal{M}(\mathcal{X}, \mathcal{Y})$. Note that the empirical risk and thus $\varepsilon^{\mathrm{gen}}$ and $\varepsilon^{\mathrm{opt}}$ depend on the realization $s = (z^{(i)})_{i=1}^m$ of the training data $S \sim I_Z^m$.

by

(A) an *optimization error* $\varepsilon^{\mathrm{opt}} := \widehat{\mathcal{R}}_S(f_S) - \widehat{\mathcal{R}}_S(\widehat{f}_S) \geq \widehat{\mathcal{R}}_S(f_S) - \widehat{\mathcal{R}}_S(f_{\mathcal{F}}^*)$, with $\widehat{f}_S$ as in Definition 1.8,

(B) a (uniform[8]) *generalization error*

$$\varepsilon^{\mathrm{gen}} := \sup_{f \in \mathcal{F}} |\mathcal{R}(f) - \widehat{\mathcal{R}}_S(f)| \geq \max\{\mathcal{R}(f_S) - \widehat{\mathcal{R}}_S(f_S), \widehat{\mathcal{R}}_S(f_{\mathcal{F}}^*) - \mathcal{R}(f_{\mathcal{F}}^*)\},$$

and

(C) an *approximation error* $\varepsilon^{\mathrm{approx}} := \mathcal{R}(f_{\mathcal{F}}^*) - \mathcal{R}^*$,

see also Figure 1.2. The approximation error decreases when the hypothesis set is enlarged, but taking $\mathcal{F} = \mathcal{M}(\mathcal{X}, \mathcal{Y})$ prevents control of the generalization error; see also Theorem 1.14. This suggests a sweet-spot for the complexity of our hypothesis set $\mathcal{F}$ and is usually referred to as the *bias–variance trade-off*; see also Figure 1.4 below. In the next sections, we will sketch mathematical ideas to tackle each of the errors in (A)–(C) in the context of deep learning. Observe that we bound the generalization and optimization errors with respect to the empirical risk $\widehat{\mathcal{R}}_S$ and its minimizer $\widehat{f}_S$, motivated by the fact that in deep-learning-based applications one typically tries to minimize variants of $\widehat{\mathcal{R}}_S$.

Optimization

The first error in the decomposition of (1.7) is the optimization error: $\varepsilon^{\mathrm{opt}}$. This error is primarily influenced by the numerical algorithm $\mathcal{A}$ that is used to find the model f_s in a hypothesis set of NNs for given training data $s \in \mathcal{Z}^m$. We will focus on the typical setting, where such an algorithm tries to approximately minimize

---

[8] Although this uniform deviation can be a coarse estimate it is frequently used in order to allow for the application of uniform laws of large numbers from the theory of empirical processes.

the empirical risk $\widehat{\mathcal{R}}_s$. While there are many conceivable methods to solve this minimization problem, by far the most common are gradient-based methods. The main reason for the popularity of gradient-based methods is that for FC networks as in Definition 1.4, the accurate and efficient computation of pointwise derivatives $\nabla_\theta \Phi_a(x,\theta)$ is possible by means of automatic differentiation, a specific form of which is often referred to as the *backpropagation algorithm* (Kelley, 1960; Dreyfus, 1962; Linnainmaa, 1970; Rumelhart et al., 1986; Griewank and Walther, 2008). This numerical scheme is also applicable in general settings, such as those where the architecture of the NN is given by a general directed acyclic graph. Using these pointwise derivatives, one usually attempts to minimize the empirical risk $\widehat{\mathcal{R}}_s$ by updating the parameters θ according to a variant of *stochastic gradient descent* (SGD), which we shall review below in a general formulation.

Algorithm 1.1 Stochastic gradient descent

Input: Differentiable function $r\colon \mathbb{R}^P \to \mathbb{R}$, sequence of step sizes $\eta_k \in (0,\infty)$, $k \in [K]$,
  $\mathbb{R}^P$-valued random variable $\Theta^{(0)}$.
Output: Sequence of $\mathbb{R}^P$-valued random variables $(\Theta^{(k)})_{k=1}^K$.
  for $k = 1,\ldots,K$ **do**
    Let $D^{(k)}$ be a random variable such that $\mathbb{E}[D^{(k)}|\Theta^{(k-1)}] = \nabla r(\Theta^{(k-1)})$ Set $\Theta^{(k)} := \Theta^{(k-1)} - \eta_k D^{(k)}$
  end for

If $D^{(k)}$ is chosen deterministically in Algorithm 1.1, i.e., $D^{(k)} = \nabla r(\Theta^{(k-1)})$, then the algorithm is known as *gradient descent*. To minimize the empirical loss, we apply SGD with $r\colon \mathbb{R}^{P(N)} \to \mathbb{R}$ set to $r(\theta) = \widehat{\mathcal{R}}_s(\Phi_a(\cdot,\theta))$. More concretely, one might choose a *batch-size* $m' \in \mathbb{N}$ with $m' \leq m$ and consider the iteration

$$\Theta^{(k)} := \Theta^{(k-1)} - \frac{\eta_k}{m'} \sum_{z \in S'} \nabla_\theta \mathcal{L}(\Phi_a(\cdot,\Theta^{(k-1)}),z), \tag{1.8}$$

where S' is a so-called *mini-batch* of size $|S'| = m'$ chosen uniformly[9] at random from the training data s. The sequence of step sizes $(\eta_k)_{k\in\mathbb{N}}$ is often called the *learning rate* in this context. Stopping at step K, the output of a deep learning algorithm $\mathcal{A}$ is then given by

$$f_s = \mathcal{A}(s) = \Phi_a(\cdot,\bar\theta),$$

[9] We remark that in practice one typically picks S' by selecting a subset of training data in such a way to cover the full training data after one *epoch* of $\lceil m/m' \rceil$ many steps. This, however, does not necessarily yield an unbiased estimator $D^{(k)}$ of $\nabla_\theta r(\Theta^{(k-1)})$ given $\Theta^{(k-1)}$.

where $\bar{\theta}$ can be chosen to be the realization of the last parameter $\Theta^{(K)}$ of (1.8) or a convex combination of $(\Theta^{(k)})_{k=1}^{K}$ such as the mean.

Algorithm 1.1 was originally introduced in Robbins and Monro (1951) in the context of finding the root of a nondecreasing function from noisy measurements. Shortly afterwards this idea was applied to find the unique global minimum of a Lipschitz-regular function that has no flat regions away from the minimum (Kiefer and Wolfowitz, 1952).

In some regimes, we can guarantee the convergence of SGD at least in expectation. See Nemirovsky and Yudin (1983), Nemirovski et al. (2009), Shalev-Shwartz et al. (2009), Shapiro et al. (2014, Section 5.9), Shalev-Shwartz and Ben-David (2014, Chapter 14). One prototypical convergence guarantee that is found in the aforementioned references in various forms is stated below.

Theorem 1.15 (Convergence of SGD). *Let* $p, K \in \mathbb{N}$ *and let* $r \colon \mathbb{R}^p \supset B_1(0) \to \mathbb{R}$ *be differentiable and convex. Further, let* $(\Theta^{(k)})_{k=1}^{K}$ *be the output of Algorithm 1.1 with initialization* $\Theta^{(0)} = 0$, *step sizes* $\eta_k = K^{-1/2}$, $k \in [K]$, *and random variables* $(D^{(k)})_{k=1}^{K}$ *satisfying* $\|D^{(k)}\|_2 \leq 1$ *almost surely for all* $k \in [K]$. *Then*

$$\mathbb{E}[r(\bar{\Theta})] - r(\theta^*) \leq \frac{1}{\sqrt{K}},$$

where $\bar{\Theta} := \frac{1}{K} \sum_{k=1}^{K} \Theta^{(k)}$ *and* $\theta^* \in \mathrm{argmin}_{\theta \in B_1(0)} r(\theta)$.

Theorem 1.15 can be strengthened to yield a faster convergence rate if the convexity is replaced by strict convexity. If r is not convex then convergence to a global minimum cannot in general be guaranteed. In fact, in that case, stochastic gradient descent may converge to a local, non-global minimum; see Figure 1.3 for an example.

Moreover, gradient descent, i.e., the deterministic version of Algorithm 1.1, will stop progressing if at any point the gradient of r vanishes. This is the case in every stationary point of r. A stationary point is either a local minimum, a local maximum, or a saddle point. One would expect that if the direction of the step $D^{(k)}$ in Algorithm 1.1 is not deterministic then random fluctuations may allow the iterates to escape saddle points. Indeed, results guaranteeing convergence to local minima exist under various conditions on the type of saddle points that r admits (Nemirovski et al., 2009; Ghadimi and Lan, 2013; Ge et al., 2015; Lee et al., 2016; Jentzen et al., 2020).

In addition, many methods that improve convergence by, for example, introducing more elaborate step-size rules or a momentum term have been established. We shall not review these methods here, but instead refer to Goodfellow et al. (2016, Chapter 8) for an overview.

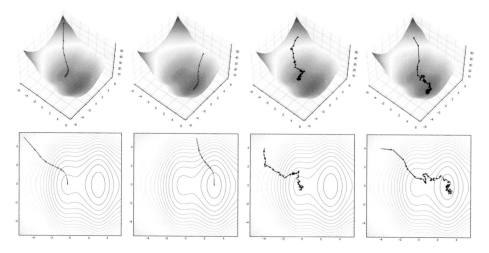

Figure 1.3 Examples of the dynamics of gradient descent (four panels on the left) and stochastic gradient descent (four panels on the right) for an objective function with one non-global minimum next to the global minimum. We see that depending on the initial condition and also on fluctuations in the stochastic part of SGD the algorithm can fail or succeed in finding the global minimum.

Approximation

Generally speaking, NNs, even FC NNs (see Definition 1.4) with only $L = 2$ layers, are universal approximators, meaning that under weak conditions on the activation function ϱ they can approximate any continuous function on a compact set up to arbitrary precision (Cybenko, 1989; Funahashi, 1989; Hornik et al., 1989; Leshno et al., 1993).

Theorem 1.16 (Universal approximation theorem). *Let $d \in \mathbb{N}$, let $K \subset \mathbb{R}^d$ be compact, and let $\varrho \in L^\infty_{\mathrm{loc}}(\mathbb{R})$ be an activation function such that the closure of the points of discontinuity of ϱ is a Lebesgue null set. Further let*

$$\widetilde{\mathcal{F}} := \bigcup_{n \in \mathbb{N}} \mathcal{F}_{((d,n,1),\varrho)}$$

be the corresponding set of two-layer NN realizations. Then it follows that $C(K) \subset \mathrm{cl}(\widetilde{\mathcal{F}})$ (where closure is taken with respect to the topology induced by the $L^\infty(K)$-norm) if and only if there does not exist a polynomial $p \colon \mathbb{R} \to \mathbb{R}$ with $p = \varrho$ almost everywhere.

The theorem can be proven by the Hahn–Banach theorem, which implies that $\widetilde{\mathcal{F}}$ being dense in some real normed vector space $\mathcal{S}$ is equivalent to the following condition: for all non-trivial functionals $F \in \mathcal{S}' \setminus \{0\}$ from the topological dual space of $\mathcal{S}$ there exist parameters $w \in \mathbb{R}^d$ and $b \in \mathbb{R}$ such that

$$F(\varrho(\langle w, \cdot \rangle + b)) \neq 0.$$

In the case $S = C(K)$ we have by the Riesz–Markov–Kakutani representation theorem that S' is the space of signed Borel measures on K; see Rudin (2006). Therefore, Theorem 1.16 holds if ϱ is such that, for a signed Borel measure μ,

$$\int_K \varrho(\langle w, x \rangle + b) \, d\mu(x) = 0 \tag{1.9}$$

for all $w \in \mathbb{R}^d$ and $b \in \mathbb{R}$ implies that $\mu = 0$. An activation function ϱ satisfying this condition is called *discriminatory*. It is not hard to see that any sigmoidal ϱ is discriminatory. Indeed, assume that ϱ satisfies (1.9) for all $w \in \mathbb{R}^d$ and $b \in \mathbb{R}$. Since for every $x \in \mathbb{R}^d$ it follows that $\varrho(ax + b) \to 1_{(0,\infty)}(x) + \varrho(b)1_{\{0\}}(x)$ for $a \to \infty$, we conclude by superposition and passing to the limit that for all $c_1, c_2 \in \mathbb{R}$ and $w \in \mathbb{R}^d$, $b \in \mathbb{R}$,

$$\int_K 1_{[c_1,c_2]}(\langle w, x \rangle + b) \, d\mu(x) = 0.$$

Representing the exponential function $x \mapsto e^{-2\pi i x}$ as the limit of sums of elementary functions yields that $\int_K e^{-2\pi i (\langle w, x \rangle + b)} \, d\mu(x) = 0$ for all $w \in \mathbb{R}^d$, $b \in \mathbb{R}$. Hence, the Fourier transform of μ vanishes, which implies that $\mu = 0$.

Theorem 1.16 addresses the uniform approximation problem on a general compact set. If we are given a finite number of points and care about good approximation only at these points, then one can ask if this approximation problem is potentially simpler. Below we see that, if the number of neurons is larger than or equal to the number of data points, then one can always interpolate, i.e., exactly fit the data to a given finite number of points.

Proposition 1.17 (Interpolation). *Let $d, m \in \mathbb{N}$, let $x^{(i)} \in \mathbb{R}^d$, $i \in [m]$, with $x^{(i)} \neq x^{(j)}$ for $i \neq j$, let $\varrho \in C(\mathbb{R})$, and assume that ϱ is not a polynomial. Then, there exist parameters $\theta^{(1)} \in \mathbb{R}^{m \times d} \times \mathbb{R}^m$ with the following property. For every $k \in \mathbb{N}$ and every sequence of labels $y^{(i)} \in \mathbb{R}^k$, $i \in [m]$, there exist parameters $\theta^{(2)} = (W^{(2)}, 0) \in \mathbb{R}^{k \times m} \times \mathbb{R}^k$ for the second layer of the NN architecture $a = ((d, m, k), \varrho)$ such that*

$$\Phi_a(x^{(i)}, (\theta^{(1)}, \theta^{(2)})) = y^{(i)}, \quad i \in [m].$$

We sketch the proof as follows. First, note that Theorem 1.16 also holds for functions $g \in C(K, \mathbb{R}^m)$ with multi-dimensional output if we approximate each one-dimensional component $x \mapsto (g(x))_i$ and stack the resulting networks. Second, one can add an additional row containing only zeros to the weight matrix $W^{(1)}$ of the approximating neural network as well as an additional entry to the vector $b^{(1)}$. The effect of this is that we obtain an additional neuron with constant output. Since $\varrho \neq 0$, we can choose $b^{(1)}$ such that the output of this neuron is not zero. Therefore, we can include the bias vector $b^{(2)}$ of the second layer in the weight matrix $W^{(2)}$; see also Remark 1.5. Now choose $g \in C(\mathbb{R}^m, \mathbb{R}^m)$ to be a function satisfying

$g(x^{(i)}) = e^{(i)}$, $i \in [m]$, where $e^{(i)} \in \mathbb{R}^m$ denotes the ith standard basis vector. By the discussion above, there exists a neural network architecture $\tilde{a} = ((d, n, m), \varrho)$ and parameters $\tilde{\theta} = ((\widetilde{W}^{(1)}, \tilde{b}^{(1)}), (\widetilde{W}^{(2)}, 0))$ such that

$$\|\Phi_{\tilde{a}}(\cdot, \tilde{\theta}) - g\|_{L^\infty(K)} < \frac{1}{m}, \tag{1.10}$$

where K is a compact set with $x^{(i)} \in K$, $i \in [m]$. Let us abbreviate the output of the activations in the first layer evaluated at the input features by

$$\widetilde{A} := \left[\varrho(\widetilde{W}^{(1)}(x^{(1)}) + \tilde{b}^{(1)})) \cdots \varrho(\widetilde{W}^{(1)}(x^{(m)}) + \tilde{b}^{(1)})) \right] \in \mathbb{R}^{n \times m}. \tag{1.11}$$

The equivalence of the max and operator norm together with (1.10) establish that

$$\|\widetilde{W}^{(2)}\widetilde{A} - I_m\|_{\mathrm{op}} \leq m \max_{i,j \in [m]} \left| (\widetilde{W}^{(2)}\widetilde{A} - I_m)_{i,j} \right| = m \max_{j \in [m]} \|\Phi_{\tilde{a}}(x^{(j)}, \tilde{\theta}) - g(x^{(j)})\|_\infty < 1,$$

where I_m denotes the $m \times m$ identity matrix. Thus, the matrix $\widetilde{W}^{(2)}\widetilde{A} \in \mathbb{R}^{m \times m}$ needs to have full rank and we can extract m linearly independent rows from $\widetilde{A}$, resulting in an invertible matrix $A \in \mathbb{R}^{m \times m}$. Now, we define the desired parameters $\theta^{(1)}$ for the first layer by extracting the corresponding rows from $\widetilde{W}^{(1)}$ and $\tilde{b}^{(1)}$ and the parameters $\theta^{(2)}$ of the second layer by

$$W^{(2)} := \left[y^{(1)} c \ldots y^{(m)} \right] A^{-1} \in \mathbb{R}^{k \times m}.$$

This proves that with any discriminatory activation function we can interpolate arbitrary training data $(x^{(i)}, y^{(i)}) \in \mathbb{R}^d \times \mathbb{R}^k$, $i \in [m]$, using a two-layer NN with m hidden neurons, i.e., $O(m(d + k))$ parameters.

One can also first project the input features onto a one-dimensional line where they are separated and then apply Proposition 1.17 with $d = 1$. For nearly all activation functions, this argument shows that a three-layer NN with only $O(d + mk)$ parameters can interpolate arbitrary training data.[10]

Beyond interpolation results, one can obtain a quantitative version of Theorem 1.16 if one knows additional regularity properties of the Bayes optimal function f^*, such as its smoothness, compositionality, and symmetries. For surveys on such results, we refer the reader to DeVore et al. (2021) and Chapter 3 in this book. For instructive purposes we review one such result, which can be found in Mhaskar (1996, Theorem 2.1), next.

Theorem 1.18 (Approximation of smooth functions). *Let $d, k \in \mathbb{N}$ and $p \in [1, \infty]$. Further, let $\varrho \in C^\infty(\mathbb{R})$ and assume that ϱ is not a polynomial. Then there exists a constant $c \in (0, \infty)$ with the following property. For every $n \in \mathbb{N}$ there exist*

---

[10] To avoid the $m \times d$ weight matrix (without using shared parameters as in Zhang et al., 2017) one interjects an approximate one-dimensional identity (Petersen and Voigtlaender, 2018, Definition 2.5), which can be arbitrarily well approximated by a NN with architecture $a = ((1, 2, 1), \varrho)$, given that $\varrho'(\lambda) \neq 0$ for some $\lambda \in \mathbb{R}$; see (1.12) below.

parameters $\theta^{(1)} \in \mathbb{R}^{n \times d} \times \mathbb{R}^n$ *for the first layer of the NN architecture* $a = ((d, n, 1), \varrho)$
such that for every $g \in W^{k,p}((0,1)^d)$ *it holds true that*

$$\inf_{\theta^{(2)} \in \mathbb{R}^{1 \times n} \times \mathbb{R}} \|\Phi_a(\cdot, (\theta^{(1)}, \theta^{(2)})) - g\|_{L^p((0,1)^d)} \le c n^{-d/k} \|g\|_{W^{k,p}((0,1)^d)}.$$

Theorem 1.18 shows that NNs achieve the same optimal approximation rates that, for example, spline-based approximation yields for smooth functions. The idea behind this theorem is based on a strategy that is employed repeatedly throughout the literature. The strategy involves the re-approximation of classical approximation methods by the use of NNs, thereby transferring the approximation rates of these methods to NNs. In the example of Theorem 1.18, approximation by polynomials is used. Thanks to the non-vanishing derivatives of the activation function,[11] one can approximate every univariate polynomial via divided differences of the activation function. Specifically, accepting unbounded parameter magnitudes, for any activation function $\varrho: \mathbb{R} \to \mathbb{R}$ which is *p-times differentiable* at some point $\lambda \in \mathbb{R}$ with $\varrho^{(p)}(\lambda) \ne 0$, one can approximate the monomial $x \mapsto x^p$ on a compact set $K \subset \mathbb{R}$ up to arbitrary precision by a fixed-size NN via rescaled *p*th-order difference quotients as

$$\lim_{h \to 0} \sup_{x \in K} \left| \sum_{i=0}^{p} \frac{(-1)^i \binom{p}{i}}{h^p \varrho^{(p)}(\lambda)} \varrho\big((p/2 - i)hx + \lambda\big) - x^p \right| = 0. \tag{1.12}$$

Let us end this subsection by clarifying the connection of the approximation results above to the error decomposition of (1.7). Consider, for simplicity, a regression task with quadratic loss. Then, the approximation error $\varepsilon^{\text{approx}}$ equals a common L^2-error:

$$\varepsilon^{\text{approx}} = \mathcal{R}(f_{\mathcal{F}}^*) - \mathcal{R}^* \overset{(*)}{=} \int_X (f_{\mathcal{F}}^*(x) - f^*(x))^2 \, d\mathcal{I}_X(x)$$

$$\overset{(*)}{=} \min_{f \in \mathcal{F}} \|f - f^*\|^2_{L^2(\mathcal{I}_X)}$$

$$\le \min_{f \in \mathcal{F}} \|f - f^*\|^2_{L^\infty(X)},$$

where the identities marked by $(*)$ follow from Lemma 1.13. Hence, Theorem 1.16 postulates that $\varepsilon^{\text{approx}} \to 0$ for increasing NN sizes, whereas Theorem 1.18 additionally explains how fast $\varepsilon^{\text{approx}}$ converges to 0.

Generalization

Towards bounding the generalization error $\varepsilon^{\text{gen}} = \sup_{f \in \mathcal{F}} |\mathcal{R}(f) - \widehat{\mathcal{R}}_S(f)|$, one observes that, for every $f \in \mathcal{F}$, Assumption 1.10 ensures that $\mathcal{L}(f, Z^{(i)})$, $i \in [m]$,

---

[11] The Baire category theorem ensures that for a non-polynomial $\varrho \in C^\infty(\mathbb{R})$ there exists $\lambda \in \mathbb{R}$ with $\varrho^{(p)}(\lambda) \ne 0$ for all $p \in \mathbb{N}$; see, e.g., Donoghue (1969, Chapter 10).

are i.i.d. random variables. Thus, one can make use of concentration inequalities to bound the deviation of the empirical risk $\widehat{R}_S(f) = \frac{1}{m}\sum_{i=1}^m \mathcal{L}(f, Z^{(i)})$ from its expectation $\mathcal{R}(f)$. For instance, assuming boundedness[12] of the loss, Hoeffding's inequality(Hoeffding, 1963) and a union bound directly imply the following generalization guarantee for countable, weighted hypothesis sets $\mathcal{F}$; see, e.g., Bousquet et al. (2003).

Theorem 1.19 (Generalization bound for countable, weighted hypothesis sets). *Let $m \in \mathbb{N}$, $\delta \in (0,1)$ and assume that $\mathcal{F}$ is countable. Further, let p be a probability distribution on $\mathcal{F}$ and assume that $\mathcal{L}(f, Z) \in [0,1]$ almost surely for every $f \in \mathcal{F}$. Then with probability $1 - \delta$ (with respect to repeated sampling of I_Z^m-distributed training data S) it holds true for every $f \in \mathcal{F}$ that*

$$|\mathcal{R}(f) - \widehat{R}_S(f)| \le \sqrt{\frac{\ln(1/p(f)) + \ln(2/\delta)}{2m}}.$$

While the weighting p needs to be chosen before seeing the training data, one could incorporate prior information on the learning algorithm $\mathcal{A}$. For finite hypothesis sets without prior information, setting $p(f) = 1/|\mathcal{F}|$ for every $f \in \mathcal{F}$, Theorem 1.19 implies that, with high probability,

$$\varepsilon^{\text{gen}} \lesssim \sqrt{\frac{\ln(|\mathcal{F}|)}{m}}. \tag{1.13}$$

Again, one notices that, in line with the bias–variance trade-off, the generalization bound increases with the size of the hypothesis set $|\mathcal{F}|$. Although in practice the parameters $\theta \in \mathbb{R}^{P(N)}$ of a NN are discretized according to floating-point arithmetic, the corresponding quantities $|\mathcal{F}_a|$ or $|\mathcal{F}_{a,\text{sgn}}|$ would be huge and we need to find a replacement for the finiteness condition.

We will focus on binary classification tasks and present a main result of VC theory, which to a great extent is derived from the work of Vladimir Vapnik and Alexey Chervonenkis (1971). While in (1.13) we counted the number of functions in $\mathcal{F}$, we now refine this analysis to count the number of functions in $\mathcal{F}$, restricted to a finite subset of X, given by the *growth function*

$$\text{growth}(m, \mathcal{F}) := \max_{(x^{(i)})_{i=1}^m \in X^m} |\{f|_{(x^{(i)})_{i=1}^m} : f \in \mathcal{F}\}|.$$

The growth function can be interpreted as the maximal number of classification patterns in $\{-1,1\}^m$ which functions in $\mathcal{F}$ can realize on m points; thus

---

[12] Note that for our classification tasks in Definition 1.2 it follows that $\mathcal{L}(f, Z) \in \{0,1\}$ for every $f \in \mathcal{F}$. For the regression tasks, one typically assumes boundedness conditions, such as $|Y| \le c$ and $\sup_{f \in \mathcal{F}} |f(X)| \le c$ almost surely for some $c \in (0, \infty)$, which yields that $\sup_{f \in \mathcal{F}} |\mathcal{L}(f, Z)| \le 4c^2$.

growth$(m, \mathcal{F}) \le 2^m$. The asymptotic behavior of the growth function is determined by a single intrinsic dimension of our hypothesis set $\mathcal{F}$, the so-called *VC-dimension*

$$\text{VCdim}(\mathcal{F}) := \sup \left\{ m \in \mathbb{N} \cup \{0\} : \text{ growth}(m, \mathcal{F}) = 2^m \right\},$$

which defines the largest number of points such that $\mathcal{F}$ can realize any classification pattern; see, e.g.,Anthony and Bartlett (1999), Bousquet et al. (2003). There exist various results on the VC-dimensions of NNs with different activation functions; see, for instance, Baum and Haussler (1989), Karpinski and Macintyre (1997), Bartlett et al. (1998), Sakurai (1999). We present the result of Bartlett et al. (1998) for piecewise polynomial activation functions ϱ. It establishes a bound on the VC-dimension of hypothesis sets of NNs for classification tasks $\mathcal{F}_{(N,\varrho),\text{sgn}}$ that scales, up to logarithmic factors, linearly in the number of parameters $P(N)$ and quadratically in the number of layers L.

Theorem 1.20 (VC-dimension of neural network hypothesis sets). *Let ϱ be a piecewise polynomial activation function. Then there exists a constant $c \in (0, \infty)$ such that for every $L \in \mathbb{N}$ and $N \in \mathbb{N}^{L+1}$,*

$$\text{VCdim}(\mathcal{F}_{(N,\varrho),\text{sgn}}) \le c \left(P(N)L \log(P(N)) + P(N)L^2 \right).$$

Given $(x^{(i)})_{i=1}^m \in \mathcal{X}^m$, there exists a partition of $\mathbb{R}^{P(N)}$ such that $\Phi(x^{(i)}, \cdot), i \in [m]$, are polynomials on each region of the partition. The proof of Theorem 1.20 is based on bounding the number of such regions and the number of classification patterns of a set of polynomials.

A finite VC-dimension ensures the following generalization bound (Talagrand, 1994; Anthony and Bartlett, 1999):

Theorem 1.21 (VC-dimension generalization bound). *There exists a constant $c \in (0, \infty)$ with the following property. For every classification task as in Definition 1.2, every $\mathcal{Z}$-valued random variable Z, and every $m \in \mathbb{N}$, $\delta \in (0, 1)$, then, with probability $1 - \delta$ (with respect to the repeated sampling of $\mathcal{I}_Z^m$-distributed training data S), it follows that*

$$\sup_{f \in \mathcal{F}} |\mathcal{R}(f) - \widehat{\mathcal{R}}_S(f)| \le c \sqrt{\frac{\text{VCdim}(\mathcal{F}) + \log(1/\delta)}{m}}.$$

In summary, using NN hypothesis sets $\mathcal{F}_{(N,\varrho),\text{sgn}}$ with a fixed depth and piecewise polynomial activation ϱ for a classification task, with high probability it follows that

$$\varepsilon^{\text{gen}} \lesssim \sqrt{\frac{P(N) \log(P(N))}{m}}. \tag{1.14}$$

In the remainder of this section we will sketch a proof of Theorem 1.21 and, in doing so, present further concepts and complexity measures connected with generalization bounds. We start by observing that McDiarmid's inequality (McDiarmid, 1989) ensures that ε^{gen} is sharply concentrated around its expectation, i.e., with probability $1 - \delta$ it holds true that[13]

$$\left|\varepsilon^{\text{gen}} - \mathbb{E}\big[\varepsilon^{\text{gen}}\big]\right| \lesssim \sqrt{\frac{\log(1/\delta)}{m}}. \tag{1.15}$$

To estimate the expectation of the uniform generalization error we employ a *symmetrization argument* (Giné and Zinn, 1984). Define $\mathcal{G} := \mathcal{L} \circ \mathcal{F} := \{\mathcal{L}(f, \cdot) : f \in \mathcal{F}\}$, let $\widetilde{S} = (\widetilde{Z}^{(i)})_{i=1}^{m} \sim I_Z^m$ be a test data set that is independent of S, and note that $\mathcal{R}(f) = \mathbb{E}[\widehat{\mathcal{R}}_{\widetilde{S}}(f)]$. By properties of the conditional expectation and Jensen's inequality it follows that

$$\mathbb{E}\big[\varepsilon^{\text{gen}}\big] = \mathbb{E}\Big[\sup_{f \in \mathcal{F}} |\mathcal{R}(f) - \widehat{\mathcal{R}}_S(f)|\Big] = \mathbb{E}\Big[\sup_{g \in \mathcal{G}} \frac{1}{m}\Big|\sum_{i=1}^{m} \mathbb{E}\big[g(\widetilde{Z}^{(i)}) - g(Z^{(i)})|S\big]\Big|\Big]$$

$$\leq \mathbb{E}\Big[\sup_{g \in \mathcal{G}} \frac{1}{m}\Big|\sum_{i=1}^{m} g(\widetilde{Z}^{(i)}) - g(Z^{(i)})\Big|\Big]$$

$$= \mathbb{E}\Big[\sup_{g \in \mathcal{G}} \frac{1}{m}\Big|\sum_{i=1}^{m} \tau_i\big(g(\widetilde{Z}^{(i)}) - g(Z^{(i)})\big)\Big|\Big]$$

$$\leq 2\mathbb{E}\Big[\sup_{g \in \mathcal{G}} \frac{1}{m}\Big|\sum_{i=1}^{m} \tau_i g(Z^{(i)})\Big|\Big],$$

where we have used that multiplications with Rademacher variables $(\tau_1, \ldots, \tau_m) \sim \mathcal{U}(\{-1,1\}^m)$ only amount to interchanging $Z^{(i)}$ with $\widetilde{Z}^{(i)}$, which has no effect on the expectation since $Z^{(i)}$ and $\widetilde{Z}^{(i)}$ have the same distribution. The quantity

$$\mathfrak{R}_m(\mathcal{G}) := \mathbb{E}\Big[\sup_{g \in \mathcal{G}} \Big|\frac{1}{m}\sum_{i=1}^{m} \tau_i g(Z^{(i)})\Big|\Big]$$

is called the *Rademacher complexity*[14] of $\mathcal{G}$. One can also prove a corresponding lower bound (van der Vaart and Wellner, 1997), i.e.,

$$\mathfrak{R}_m(\mathcal{G}) - \frac{1}{\sqrt{m}} \lesssim \mathbb{E}\big[\varepsilon^{\text{gen}}\big] \leq \mathfrak{R}_m(\mathcal{G}). \tag{1.16}$$

Now we use a *chaining method* to bound the Rademacher complexity of $\mathcal{F}$ by covering numbers on different scales. Specifically, Dudley's entropy integral (Dudley,

[13] For precise conditions to ensure that the expectation of ε^{gen} is well defined, we refer readers to van der Vaart and Wellner (1997), Dudley (2014).
[14] Due to our decomposition in (1.7), we want to uniformly bound the absolute value of the difference between the risk and the empirical risk. It is also common just to bound $\sup_{f \in \mathcal{F}} \mathcal{R}(f) - \widehat{\mathcal{R}}_S(f)$ leading to a definition of the Rademacher complexity without the absolute values, which can be easier to deal with.

1967; Ledoux and Talagrand, 1991) implies that

$$\Re_m(\mathcal{G}) \lesssim \mathbb{E}\left[\int_0^\infty \sqrt{\frac{\log N_\alpha(\mathcal{G}, d_S)}{m}}\, d\alpha\right], \tag{1.17}$$

where

$$N_\alpha(\mathcal{G}, d_S) := \inf\left\{|G|: G \subset \mathcal{G}, \mathcal{G} \subset \bigcup_{g \in G} B_\alpha^{d_S}(g)\right\}$$

denotes the covering number with respect to the (random) pseudometric given by

$$d_S(f, g) = d_{(Z^{(i)})_{i=1}^m}(f, g) := \sqrt{\frac{1}{m}\sum_{i=1}^m \left(f(Z^{(i)}) - g(Z^{(i)})\right)^2}.$$

For the 0–1 loss $\mathcal{L}(f, z) = 1_{(-\infty, 0)}(y f(x)) = (1 - f(x)y)/2$, we can get rid of the loss function using the fact that

$$N_\alpha(\mathcal{G}, d_S) = N_{2\alpha}(\mathcal{F}, d_{(X^{(i)})_{i=1}^m}). \tag{1.18}$$

The proof is completed by combining the inequalities in (1.15), (1.16), (1.17) and (1.18) with a result of David Haussler (1995) which shows that, for $\alpha \in (0, 1)$, we have

$$\log(N_\alpha(\mathcal{F}, d_{(X^{(i)})_{i=1}^m})) \lesssim \mathrm{VCdim}(\mathcal{F}) \log(1/\alpha). \tag{1.19}$$

We remark that this resembles a typical behavior of covering numbers. For instance, the logarithm of the covering number $\log(N_\alpha(\mathcal{M}))$ of a compact d-dimensional Riemannian manifold $\mathcal{M}$ essentially scales as $d \log(1/\alpha)$. Finally, note that there exists a bound similar to the one in (1.19) for bounded regression tasks that makes use of the so-called *fat-shattering dimension* (Mendelson and Vershynin, 2003, Theorem 1).

1.1.3 Do We Need a New Theory?

Despite the already substantial insight that the classical theories provide, a lot of open questions remain. We will outline these questions below. The remainder of this chapter then collects modern approaches to explain the following issues.

Why do large neural networks not overfit? In §1.1.2, we have observed that three-layer NNs with commonly used activation functions and only $O(d + m)$ parameters can interpolate any training data $(x^{(i)}, y^{(i)}) \in \mathbb{R}^d \times \mathbb{R}, i \in [m]$. While this specific representation might not be found in practice (Zhang et al., 2017), indeed trained convolutional[15] NNs with ReLU activation function and about 1.6 million

---

[15] The basic definition of a convolutional NN will be given in §1.6. In Zhang et al. (2017) more elaborate versions such as an *inception* architecture (Szegedy et al., 2015) are employed.

parameters to achieve zero empirical risk on $m = 50,000$ training images of the CIFAR10 dataset (Krizhevsky and Hinton, 2009) with 32×32 pixels per image, i.e., $d = 1,024$. For such large NNs, generalization bounds scaling with the number of parameters $P(N)$ as the VC-dimension bound in (1.14) are vacuous. However, these workers observed close to state-of-the-art generalization performance.[16]

Generally speaking, NNs are observed in practice to generalize well despite having more parameters than training samples (usually referred to as *overparametrization*) and approximately interpolating the training data (usually referred to as *overfitting*). As we cannot perform any better on the training data, there is no trade-off between the fit to training data and the complexity of the hypothesis set $\mathcal{F}$ happening, seemingly contradicting the classical bias–variance trade-off of statistical learning theory. This is quite surprising, especially given the following additional empirical observations in this regime, see Neyshabur et al. (2014, 2017), Zhang et al. (2017), Belkin et al. (2019b), Nakkiran et al. (2020):

(i) *Zero training error on random labels:* Zero empirical risk can also be achieved for random labels using the same architecture and training scheme with only slightly increased training time. This suggests that the considered hypothesis set of NNs $\mathcal{F}$ can fit arbitrary binary labels, which would imply that $\mathrm{VCdim}(\mathcal{F}) \approx m$ or $\mathfrak{R}_m(\mathcal{F}) \approx 1$, rendering our uniform generalization bounds in Theorem 1.21 and in (1.16) vacuous.

(ii) *Lack of explicit regularization:* The test error depends only mildly on explicit regularization, such as norm-based penalty terms or dropout (see Géron, 2017, for an explanation of different regularization methods). As such regularization methods are typically used to decrease the complexity of $\mathcal{F}$, one might ask if there is any *implicit* regularization (see Figure 1.4), constraining the range of our learning algorithm $\mathcal{A}$ to some smaller, potentially data-dependent, subset, i.e., $\mathcal{A}(s) \in \widetilde{\mathcal{F}}_s \subsetneq \mathcal{F}$.

(iii) *Dependence on the initialization:* The same NN trained to zero empirical risk but starting from different initializations can exhibit different test errors. This indicates that properties of the local minimum at f_s to which gradient descent converges might be correlated with its generalization.

(iv) *Interpolation of noisy training data:* One still observes low test error when training up to approximately zero empirical risk using a regression (or surrogate) loss on noisy training data. This is particularly interesting, as the noise is captured by the model but seems not to hurt the generalization performance.

---

[16] In practice one usually cannot measure the risk $\mathcal{R}(f_s)$ and instead one evaluates the performance of a trained model f_s by $\widehat{\mathcal{R}}_{\tilde{s}}(f_s)$ using test data $\tilde{s}$, i.e., realizations of i.i.d. random variables distributed according to $\mathcal{I}_Z$ and drawn independently of the training data. In this context one often calls $\mathcal{R}_s(f_s)$ the *training error* and $\mathcal{R}_{\tilde{s}}(f_s)$ the *test error*.

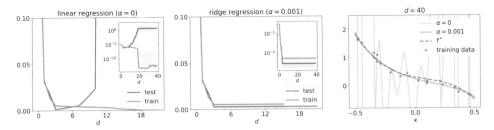

Figure 1.4 The left plot (and its semi-log inset) shows the median and interquartile range of the test and training errors of ten independent linear regressions with $m = 20$ samples, polynomial input features $X = (1, Z, \ldots, Z^d)$ of degree $d \in [40]$, and labels $Y = f^*(Z) + \nu$, where $Z \sim \mathcal{U}([-0.5, 0.5])$, f^* is a polynomial of degree three, and $\nu \sim \mathcal{N}(0, 0.01)$. This clearly reflects the classical ∪-shaped bias–variance curve with a sweet-spot at $d = 3$ and drastic overfitting beyond the interpolation threshold at $d = 20$. However, the middle plot shows that we can control the complexity of our hypothesis set of linear models by restricting the Euclidean norm of their parameters using ridge regression with a small regularization parameter $\alpha = 10^{-3}$, i.e., minimizing the regularized empirical risk $\frac{1}{m} \sum_{i=1}^{m} (\Phi(X^{(i)}, \theta) - Y^{(i)})^2 + \alpha \|\theta\|_2^2$, where $\Phi(\cdot, \theta) = \langle \theta, \cdot \rangle$. Corresponding examples of $\widehat{f}_s$ are depicted in the right plot.

(v) *Further overparametrization improves generalization performance:* Further increasing the NN size can lead to even lower test error. Together with the previous item, this might require a different treatment of models that are complex enough to fit the training data. According to the traditional lore "The training error tends to decrease whenever we increase the model complexity; that is, whenever we fit the data harder. However with too much fitting, the model adapts itself too closely to the training data, and will not generalize well (i.e., it will have a large test error)", (Hastie et al., 2001). While this flawlessly describes the situation for certain machine learning tasks (see Figure 1.4), it seems not to be directly applicable here.

In summary, these observations suggest that the generalization performance of NNs depends on an interplay of the data distribution $\mathcal{I}_Z$ with properties of the learning algorithm $\mathcal{A}$, such as the optimization procedure and its range. In particular, classical uniform bounds as in Item (B) on page 13 of our error decomposition might deliver insufficient explanation; see also Nagarajan and Kolter (2019). The mismatch between the predictions of classical theory and the practical generalization performance of deep NNs is often referred to as the *generalization puzzle*. In §1.2 we will present possible explanations for this phenomenon.

What is the role of depth? We saw in §1.1.2 that NNs can closely approximate every function if they are sufficiently wide (Cybenko, 1989; Funahashi, 1989; Hornik et al., 1989). There are additional classical results that even provide a trade-off between the width and the approximation accuracy (Chui et al., 1994; Mhaskar,

1996; Maiorov and Pinkus, 1999). In these results, the central concept is the width of a NN. In modern applications, however, at least as much focus if not more lies on the depth of the underlying architectures, which can have more than 1000 layers (He et al., 2016). After all, the depth of NNs is responsible for the name "deep learning".

This consideration begs the question of whether there is a concrete mathematically quantifiable benefit of deep architectures over shallow NNs. Indeed, we will see the effects of depth at many places throughout this chapter. However, one aspects of deep learning that is most clearly affected by deep architectures is the approximation-theoretical aspect. In this framework, we will discuss in §1.3 multiple approaches that describe the effect of depth.

Why do neural networks perform well in very high-dimensional environments?
We saw in §1.1.2 and will see in §1.3 that, from the perspective of approximation theory, deep NNs match the performance of the best classical approximation tool in virtually every task. In practice, we observe something that is even more astounding. In fact, NNs seem to perform incredibly well on tasks that no classical, non-specialized approximation method can even remotely handle. The approximation problem that we are talking about here is that of approximation of high-dimensional functions. Indeed, the classical *curse of dimensionality* (Bellman, 1952; Novak and Woźniakowski, 2009) postulates that essentially every approximation method deteriorates exponentially fast with increasing dimension.

For example, for the uniform approximation error of 1-Lipschitz continuous functions on a d-dimensional unit cube in the uniform norm, we have a lower bound of $\Omega(p^{-1/d})$, for $p \to \infty$, when approximating with a continuous scheme[17] of p free parameters (DeVore, 1998).

On the other hand, in most applications the input dimensions are massive. For example, the following datasets are typically used as benchmarks in image classification problems: MNIST (LeCun et al., 1998) with 28×28 pixels per image, CIFAR-10/CIFAR-100 (Krizhevsky and Hinton, 2009) with 32×32 pixels per image, and ImageNet (Deng et al., 2009; Krizhevsky et al., 2012), which contains high-resolution images that are typically down-sampled to 256×256 pixels. Naturally, in real-world applications, the input dimensions may well exceed those of these test problems. However, already for the simplest of the test cases above, the input dimension is $d = 784$. If we use $d = 784$ in the aforementioned lower bound for the approximation of 1-Lipschitz functions, then we require $O(\varepsilon^{-784})$ parameters

---

[17] One can achieve better rates at the cost of discontinuous (with respect to the function to be approximated) parameter assignment. This can be motivated by the use of space-filling curves. In the context of NNs with piecewise polynomial activation functions, a rate of $p^{-2/d}$ can be achieved by very deep architectures (Yarotsky, 2018a; Yarotsky and Zhevnerchuk, 2020).

to achieve a uniform error of $\varepsilon \in (0, 1)$. Even for moderate ε this value will quickly exceed the storage capacity of any conceivable machine in this universe. Considering the aforementioned curse of dimensionality, it is puzzling to see that NNs perform adequately in this regime. In §1.4, we describe three approaches that offer explanations as to why deep NN-based approximation is not rendered meaningless in the context of high-dimensional input dimensions.

Why does stochastic gradient descent converge to good local minima despite the non-convexity of the problem? As mentioned in §1.1.2, a convergence guarantee of stochastic gradient descent to a global minimum can typically be given only if the underlying objective function admits some form of convexity. However, the empirical risk of a NN, i.e., $\widehat{\mathcal{R}}_s(\Phi(\cdot, \theta))$, is typically not a convex function with respect to the parameters θ. For a simple intuitive explanation of why this function fails to be convex, it is instructive to consider the following example.

Example 1.22. Consider the NN

$$\Phi(x, \theta) = \theta_1 \varrho_R(\theta_3 x + \theta_5) + \theta_2 \varrho_R(\theta_4 x + \theta_6), \qquad \theta \in \mathbb{R}^6, \quad x \in \mathbb{R},$$

with the ReLU activation function $\varrho_R(x) = \max\{0, x\}$. It is not hard to see that the two parameter values $\theta = (1, -1, 1, 1, 1, 0)$ and $\bar{\theta} = (-1, 1, 1, 1, 0, 1)$ produce the same realization function,[18] i.e., $\Phi(\cdot, \theta) = \Phi(\cdot, \bar{\theta})$. However, since $(\theta + \bar{\theta})/2 = (0, 0, 1, 1, 1/2, 1/2)$, we conclude that $\Phi(\cdot, (\theta + \bar{\theta})/2) = 0$. Clearly, for the data $s = ((-1, 0), (1, 1))$, we now have that

$$\widehat{\mathcal{R}}_s(\Phi(\cdot, \theta)) = \widehat{\mathcal{R}}_s(\Phi(\cdot, \bar{\theta})) = 0 \quad \text{and} \quad \widehat{\mathcal{R}}_s\left(\Phi(\cdot, (\theta + \bar{\theta})/2)\right) = \frac{1}{2},$$

showing the non-convexity of $\widehat{\mathcal{R}}_s$.

Given this non-convexity, Algorithm 1.1 faces serious challenges. First, there may exist multiple suboptimal local minima. Second, the objective function may exhibit saddle points, some of which may be of higher order, i.e., the Hessian vanishes. Finally, even if no suboptimal local minima exist, there may be extensive areas of the parameter space where the gradient is very small, so that escaping these regions can take a very long time.

These issues are not mere theoretical possibilities, but will almost certainly arise in practice. For example, Auer et al. (1996) and Safran and Shamir (2018) showed the existence of many suboptimal local minima in typical learning tasks. Moreover, for fixed-sized NNs, it was shown by Berner et al. (2019b) and Petersen et al. (2020) that, with respect to L^p-norms, the set of NNs is generally very non-convex and

---

[18] This corresponds to interchanging the two neurons in the hidden layer. In general the realization function of an FC NN is invariant under permutations of the neurons in a given hidden layer.

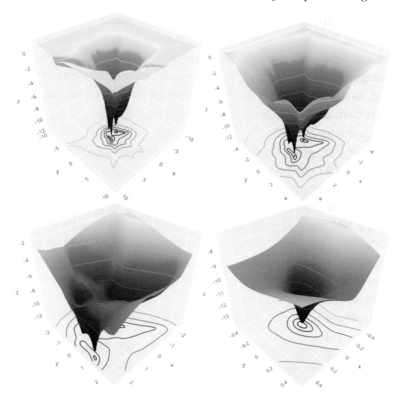

Figure 1.5 Two-dimensional projection of the loss landscape of a neural network with four layers and ReLU activation function on four different scales. From upper left to lower right, we zoom into the global minimum of the landscape.

non-closed. Moreover, the map $\theta \mapsto \Phi_a(\cdot, \theta)$ is not a quotient map, i.e., it is not continuously invertible when its non-injectivity is taken into account. Furthermore, in various situations, finding the global optimum of the minimization problem has been shown to be NP-hard in general (Blum and Rivest, 1989; Judd, 1990; Šíma, 2002). In Figure 1.5 we show the two-dimensional projection of a loss landscape, i.e., a projection of the graph of the function $\theta \mapsto \widehat{\mathcal{R}}_s(\Phi(\cdot, \theta))$. It is apparent from the visualization that the problem exhibits more than one minimum. We also want to add that in practice one neglects the fact that the loss is only almost everywhere differentiable in the case of piecewise-smooth activation functions, such as the ReLU, although one could resort to subgradient methods (Kakade and Lee, 2018).

In view of these considerations, the classical framework presented in §1.1.2 offers no explanation as to why deep learning works in practice. Indeed, in the survey of Orr and Müller (1998, Section 1.4) the state of the art in 1998 was summarized by the following assessment: "There is no formula to guarantee that (1) the NN will converge to a good solution, (2) convergence is swift, or (3) convergence even occurs at all."

Nonetheless, in applications, not only would an explanation of when and why SGD converges be extremely desirable, convergence is also quite often observed even though there is little theoretical explanation for it in the classical set-up. In §1.5 we collect modern approaches explaining why and when convergence occurs and can be guaranteed.

Which aspects of a neural network architecture affect the performance of deep learning? In the introduction to classical approaches to deep learning above, we saw that, in classical results such as in Theorem 1.18, the effect of only a few aspects of the NN architectures are considered. In Theorem 1.18 only the impact of the width of the NN was studied. In further approximation theorems below, for example, in Theorems 1.23 and 1.25, we will additionally have a variable depth of NNs. However, for deeper architectures, there are many additional aspects of the architecture that could potentially affect the performance of the model for the associated learning task. For example, even for a standard FC NN with L layers as in Definition 1.4, there is a lot of flexibility in choosing the number of neurons $(N_1, \ldots, N_{L-1}) \in \mathbb{N}^{L-1}$ in the hidden layers. One would expect that certain choices affect the capabilities of the NNs considerably and that some choices are preferable to others. Note that one aspect of the neural network architecture that can have a profound effect on performance, especially regarding the approximation-theoretic aspects of performance, is the choice of the activation function. For example, in Maiorov and Pinkus (1999) and Yarotsky (2021) activation functions were found that allow the uniform approximation of continuous functions to arbitrary accuracy with fixed-size neural networks. In what follows we will focus, however, on architectural aspects other than the activation function.

In addition, practitioners have invented an immense variety of NN architectures for specific problems. These include NNs with convolutional blocks (LeCun et al., 1998), with skip connections (He et al., 2016), sparse connections (Zhou et al., 2016; Bourely et al., 2017), batch normalization blocks (Ioffe and Szegedy, 2015), and many more. Furthermore, for sequential data, recurrent connections have been used (Rumelhart et al., 1986) and these have often had forget mechanisms (Hochreiter and Schmidhuber, 1997) or other gates (Cho et al., 2014) included in their architectures.

The choice of an appropriate NN architecture is essential to the success of many deep learning tasks. This is so important that frequently an architecture search is applied to find the most suitable one (Zoph and Le, 2017; Pham et al., 2018). In most cases, though, the design and choice of the architecture is based on the intuition of the practitioner.

Naturally, from a theoretical point of view, this situation is not satisfactory.

Instead, it would be highly desirable to have a mathematical theory guiding the choice of NN architectures. More concretely, one would wish for mathematical theorems that identify those architectures that would work for a specific problem and those that would yield suboptimal results. In §1.6, we discuss various results that explain theoretically quantifiable effects of certain aspects, or building blocks, of NN architectures.

Which features of data are learned by deep architectures? It is commonly believed that the neurons of NNs constitute feature extractors at different levels of abstraction that correspond to the layers. This belief is partially grounded in experimental evidence as well as by drawing connections to the human visual cortex; see Goodfellow et al. (2016, Chapter 9.10).

Understanding the features that are learned can be linked, in a way, to understanding the reasoning with which a NN-based model ended up with its result. Therefore, analyzing the features that a NN learns constitutes a data-aware approach to understanding deep learning. Naturally, this falls outside of the scope of the classical theory, which is formulated in terms of optimization, generalization, and approximation errors.

One central obstacle towards understanding these features theoretically is that, at least for practical problems, the data distribution is unknown. However, one often has partial knowledge. One example is that in image classification it appears reasonable to assume that any classifier is translation and rotation invariant as well as invariant under small deformations. In this context, it is interesting to understand under which conditions trained NNs admit the same invariances.

Biological NNs such as the visual cortex are believed to have evolved in a way that is based on sparse multiscale representations of visual information (Olshausen and Field, 1996). Again, a fascinating question is whether NNs trained in practice can be shown to favor such multiscale representations based on sparsity or whether the architecture is theoretically linked to sparse representations. We will discuss various approaches studying the features learned by neural networks in §1.7.

Are neural networks capable of replacing highly specialized numerical algorithms in natural sciences? Shortly after their successes in various data-driven tasks in data science and AI applications, NNs started to be used also as a numerical ansatz for solving highly complex models from the natural sciences that could be combined with data-driven methods. This is *per se* not very surprising as many such models can be formulated as optimization problems where the commonly used deep learning paradigm can be directly applied. What might be considered surprising is that this approach seems to be applicable to a wide range of problems which had previously been tackled by highly specialized numerical methods.

Particular successes include the data-driven solution of ill-posed *inverse problems* (Arridge et al., 2019) which has, for example, led to a fourfold speedup in MRI scantimes (Zbontar et al., 2018) igniting the research project `fastmri.org`. Deep-learning-based approaches have also been very successful in solving a vast array of *partial differential equation* (PDE) models, especially in the high-dimensional regime (E and Yu, 2018; Raissi et al., 2019; Hermann et al., 2020; Pfau et al., 2020) where most other methods would suffer from the curse of dimensionality.

Despite these encouraging applications, the foundational mechanisms governing their workings and limitations are still not well understood. In §§1.4.3 and 1.8 we discuss some theoretical and practical aspects of deep learning methods applied to the solution of inverse problems and PDEs.

1.2 Generalization of Large Neural Networks

In the following we will shed light on the generalization puzzle of NNs as described in §1.1.3. We focus on four different lines of research which, even so, do not cover the wide range of available results. In fact, we had to omit a discussion of a multitude of important works, some of which we reference in the following paragraph.

First, let us mention extensions of the generalization bounds presented in §1.1.2 that make use of *local* Rademacher complexities (Bartlett et al., 2005) or that drop assumptions on boundedness or rapidly decaying tails (Mendelson, 2014). Furthermore, there are approaches to generalization which do not focus on the hypothesis set $\mathcal{F}$, i.e., the range of the learning algorithm $\mathcal{A}$, but on the way in which $\mathcal{A}$ chooses its model f_s. For instance, one can assume that f_s does not depend too strongly on each individual sample (*algorithmic stability*: Bousquet and Elisseeff, 2002, Poggio et al., 2004), but only on a subset of the samples (*compression bounds*: Arora et al., 2018b), or that it satisfies local properties (*algorithmic robustness*: Xu and Mannor, 2012). Finally, we refer the reader to Jiang et al. (2020) and the references mentioned therein for an empirical study of various measures related to generalization.

Note that many results on the generalization capabilities of NNs can still only be proven in simplified settings, for example for deep linear NNs, i.e., $\varrho(x) = x$, or basic linear models, i.e., one-layer NNs. Thus, we start by emphasizing the connection of deep, nonlinear NNs to linear models (operating on features given by a suitable kernel) in the *infinite-width limit*.

1.2.1 Kernel Regime

We consider a one-dimensional prediction setting where the loss $\mathcal{L}(f,(x,y))$ depends on $x \in \mathcal{X}$ only through $f(x) \in \mathcal{Y}$, i.e., there exists a function $\ell : \mathcal{Y} \times \mathcal{Y} \to \mathbb{R}$

such that

$$\mathcal{L}(f,(x,y)) = \ell(f(x),y).$$

For instance, in the case of quadratic loss we have that $\ell(\hat{y},y) = (\hat{y} - y)^2$. Further, let Φ be a NN with architecture $(N,\varrho) = ((d,N_1,\ldots,N_{L-1},1),\varrho)$ and let Θ_0 be a $\mathbb{R}^{P(N)}$-valued random variable. For simplicity, we evolve the parameters of Φ according to the continuous version of gradient descent, so-called *gradient flow*, given by

$$\frac{d\Theta(t)}{dt} = -\nabla_\theta \widehat{\mathcal{R}}_s(\Phi(\cdot,\Theta(t))) = -\frac{1}{m}\sum_{i=1}^{m}\nabla_\theta\Phi(x^{(i)},\Theta(t))D_i(t), \quad \Theta(0) = \Theta_0, \quad (1.20)$$

where

$$D_i(t) := \frac{\partial\ell(\hat{y},y^{(i)})}{\partial\hat{y}}\Big|_{\hat{y}=\Phi(x^{(i)},\Theta(t))}$$

is the derivative of the loss with respect to the prediction at input feature $x^{(i)}$ at time $t \in [0,\infty)$. The chain rule implies the following dynamics of the NN realization

$$\frac{d\Phi(\cdot,\Theta(t))}{dt} = -\frac{1}{m}\sum_{i=1}^{m}K_{\Theta(t)}(\cdot,x^{(i)})D_i(t) \quad (1.21)$$

and of its empirical risk

$$\frac{d\widehat{\mathcal{R}}_s(\Phi(\cdot,\Theta(t)))}{dt} = -\frac{1}{m^2}\sum_{i=1}^{m}\sum_{j=1}^{m}D_i(t)K_{\Theta(t)}(x^{(i)},x^{(j)})D_j(t), \quad (1.22)$$

where K_θ, $\theta \in \mathbb{R}^{P(N)}$, is the so-called *neural tangent kernel* (NTK):

$$K_\theta : \mathbb{R}^d \times \mathbb{R}^d \to \mathbb{R}, \quad K_\theta(x_1,x_2) = \left(\nabla_\theta\Phi(x_1,\theta)\right)^T\nabla_\theta\Phi(x_2,\theta). \quad (1.23)$$

Now let $\sigma_w,\sigma_b \in (0,\infty)$ and assume that the initialization Θ_0 consists of independent entries, where entries corresponding to the weight matrix and bias vector in the ℓth layer follow a normal distribution with zero mean and variances σ_w^2/N_ℓ and σ_b^2, respectively. Under weak assumptions on the activation function, the central limit theorem implies that the pre-activations converge to i.i.d. centered Gaussian processes in the infinite-width limit $N_1,\ldots,N_{L-1} \to \infty$; see Lee et al. (2018) and Matthews et al. (2018). Similarly, K_{Θ_0} also converges to a deterministic kernel K^∞ which stays constant in time and depends only on the activation function ϱ, the depth L, and the initialization parameters σ_w and σ_b (Jacot et al., 2018; Arora et al., 2019b; Yang, 2019; Lee et al., 2020). Thus, within the infinite width limit, gradient flow on the NN parameters as in (1.20) is equivalent to functional gradient flow in the *reproducing kernel Hilbert space* $(\mathcal{H}_{K^\infty}, \|\cdot\|_{K^\infty})$ corresponding to K^∞; see (1.21).

By (1.22), the empirical risk converges to a global minimum as long as the kernel evaluated at the input features, $\bar{K}^\infty := (K^\infty(x^{(i)}, x^{(j)}))_{i,j=1}^m \in \mathbb{R}^{m \times m}$, is positive definite (see, e.g., Jacot et al., 2018, Du et al., 2019, for suitable conditions) and the $\ell(\cdot, y^{(i)})$ are convex and lower bounded. For instance, in the case of quadratic loss the solution of (1.21) is then given by

$$\Phi(\cdot, \Theta(t)) = C(t)(y^{(i)})_{i=1}^m + (\Phi(\cdot, \Theta_0) - C(t)(\Phi(x^{(i)}, \Theta_0))_{i=1}^m), \tag{1.24}$$

where $C(t) := ((K^\infty(\cdot, x^{(i)}))_{i=1}^m)^T (\bar{K}^\infty)^{-1} (I_m - e^{-2\bar{K}^\infty t/m})$. As the initial realization $\Phi(\cdot, \Theta_0)$ constitutes a centered Gaussian process, the second term in (1.24) follows a normal distribution with zero mean at each input. In the limit $t \to \infty$, its variance vanishes on the input features $x^{(i)}$, $i \in [m]$, and the first term converges to the minimum kernel-norm interpolator, i.e., to the solution of

$$\min_{f \in \mathcal{H}_{K^\infty}} \|f\|_{K^\infty} \quad \text{s.t.} \quad f(x^{(i)}) = y^{(i)}.$$

Therefore, within the infinite-width limit, the generalization properties of the NN could be described by the generalization properties of the minimizer in the reproducing kernel Hilbert space corresponding to the kernel K^∞ (Belkin et al., 2018; Liang and Rakhlin, 2020; Liang et al., 2020; Ghorbani et al., 2021; Li, 2021).

This so-called *lazy training*, where a NN essentially behaves like a linear model with respect to the nonlinear features $x \mapsto \nabla_\theta \Phi(x, \theta)$, can already be observed in the non-asymptotic regime; see also §1.5.2. For sufficiently overparametrized $(P(N) \gg m)$ and suitably initialized models, one can show that $K_{\theta(0)}$ is close to K^∞ at initialization and $K_{\theta(t)}$ stays close to $K_{\theta(0)}$ throughout training; see Du et al. (2018b, 2019), Arora et al. (2019b), and Chizat et al. (2019). The dynamics of the NN under gradient flow in (1.21) and (1.22) can thus be approximated by the dynamics of the linearization of Φ at initialization Θ_0, given by

$$\Phi^{\text{lin}}(\cdot, \theta) := \Phi(\cdot, \Theta_0) + \langle \nabla_\theta \Phi(\cdot, \Theta_0), \theta - \Theta_0 \rangle, \tag{1.25}$$

which motivates studying the behavior of linear models in the overparametrized regime.

1.2.2 Norm-Based Bounds and Margin Theory

For piecewise linear activation functions, one can improve upon the VC-dimension bounds in Theorem 1.20 and show that, up to logarithmic factors, the VC-dimension is asymptotically bounded both above and below by $P(N)L$; see Bartlett et al. (2019). The lower bound shows that the generalization bound in Theorem 1.21 can be non-vacuous only if the number of samples m scales at least linearly with the number of NN parameters $P(N)$. However, the heavily overparametrized NNs used in practice seem to generalize well outside of this regime.

One solution is to bound other complexity measures of NNs, taking into account various norms on the parameters, and avoid the direct dependence on the number of parameters (Bartlett, 1998). For instance, we can compute bounds on the Rademacher complexity of NNs with positively homogeneous activation function, where the Frobenius norm of the weight matrices is bounded; see also Neyshabur et al. (2015). Note that, for instance, the ReLU activation is positively homogeneous, i.e., it satisfies that $\varrho_R(\lambda x) = \lambda \varrho_R(x)$ for all $x \in \mathbb{R}$ and $\lambda \in (0, \infty)$.

Theorem 1.23 (Rademacher complexity of neural networks). *Let $d \in \mathbb{N}$, assume that $X = B_1(0) \subset \mathbb{R}^d$, and let ϱ be a positively homogeneous activation function with Lipschitz constant 1. We define the set of all biasless NN realizations with depth $L \in \mathbb{N}$, output dimension 1, and Frobenius norm of the weight matrices bounded by $C \in (0, \infty)$ as*

$$\widetilde{\mathcal{F}}_{L,C} := \{ \Phi_{(N,\varrho)}(\cdot,\theta): N \in \mathbb{N}^{L+1}, N_0 = d, N_L = 1,$$
$$\theta = ((W^{(\ell)},0))_{\ell=1}^L \in \mathbb{R}^{P(N)}, \|W^{(\ell)}\|_F \leq C \}.$$

Then for every $m \in \mathbb{N}$ it follows that

$$\mathfrak{R}_m(\widetilde{\mathcal{F}}_{L,C}) \leq \frac{C(2C)^{L-1}}{\sqrt{m}}.$$

The factor 2^{L-1}, depending exponentially on the depth, can be reduced to $\sqrt{L}$ or completely omitted by invoking the spectral norm of the weight matrices (Golowich et al., 2018). Further, observe that for $L = 1$, i.e., linear classifiers with bounded Euclidean norm, this bound is independent of the input dimension d. Together with (1.16), this motivates why the regularized linear model in Figure 1.4 did perform well in the overparametrized regime.

The proof of Theorem 1.23 is based on the contraction property of the Rademacher complexity (Ledoux and Talagrand, 1991), which establishes that

$$\mathfrak{R}_m(\varrho \circ \widetilde{\mathcal{F}}_{\ell,C}) \leq 2\mathfrak{R}_m(\widetilde{\mathcal{F}}_{\ell,C}), \quad \ell \in \mathbb{N}.$$

We can iterate this together with the fact that for every $\tau \in \{-1,1\}^m$, and $x \in \mathbb{R}^{N_{\ell-1}}$ it follows that

$$\sup_{\|W^{(\ell)}\|_F \leq C} \left\| \sum_{i=1}^m \tau_i \varrho(W^{(\ell)}x) \right\|_2 = C \sup_{\|w\|_2 \leq 1} \left| \sum_{i=1}^m \tau_i \varrho(\langle w, x \rangle) \right|.$$

In summary, we have established that

$$\mathfrak{R}_m(\widetilde{\mathcal{F}}_{L,C}) = \frac{C}{m} \mathbb{E}\left[\sup_{f \in \widetilde{\mathcal{F}}_{L-1,C}} \left\| \sum_{i=1}^m \tau_i \varrho(f(X^{(i)})) \right\|_2 \right] \leq \frac{C(2C)^{L-1}}{m} \mathbb{E}\left[\left\| \sum_{i=1}^m \tau_i X^{(i)} \right\|_2 \right],$$

which by Jensen's inequality yields the claim.

Recall that for classification problems one typically minimizes a surrogate loss $\mathcal{L}^{\text{surr}}$; see Remark 1.9. This suggests that there could be a trade-off happening between the complexity of the hypothesis class $\mathcal{F}_a$ and the underlying regression fit, i.e., the *margin* $M(f, z) := yf(x)$ by which a training example $z = (x, y)$ has been classified correctly by $f \in \mathcal{F}_a$; see Bartlett et al. (2017), Neyshabur et al. (2018), and Jiang et al. (2019). For simplicity, let us focus on the ramp-function surrogate loss with confidence $\gamma > 0$, i.e., $\mathcal{L}_\gamma^{\text{surr}}(f, z) := \ell_\gamma(M(f, z))$, where

$$\ell_\gamma(t) := 1_{(-\infty, \gamma]}(t) - \frac{t}{\gamma} 1_{[0, \gamma]}(t), \quad t \in \mathbb{R}.$$

Note that the ramp function ℓ_γ is $1/\gamma$-Lipschitz continuous. Using McDiarmid's inequality and a symmetrization argument similar to the proof of Theorem 1.21, combined with the contraction property of the Rademacher complexity, yields the following bound on the probability of misclassification. With probability $1 - \delta$ for every $f \in \mathcal{F}_a$ we have

$$I[\text{sgn}(f(X)) \neq Y] \leq \mathbb{E}\left[\mathcal{L}_\gamma^{\text{surr}}(f, Z)\right]$$

$$\lesssim \frac{1}{m} \sum_{i=1}^m \mathcal{L}_\gamma^{\text{surr}}(f, Z^{(i)}) + \mathfrak{R}_m(\mathcal{L}_\gamma^{\text{surr}} \circ \mathcal{F}_a) + \sqrt{\frac{\ln(1/\delta)}{m}}$$

$$\lesssim \frac{1}{m} \sum_{i=1}^m 1_{(-\infty, \gamma)}(Y^{(i)} f(X^{(i)})) + \frac{\mathfrak{R}_m(M \circ \mathcal{F}_a)}{\gamma} + \sqrt{\frac{\ln(1/\delta)}{m}}$$

$$= \frac{1}{m} \sum_{i=1}^m 1_{(-\infty, \gamma)}(Y^{(i)} f(X^{(i)})) + \frac{\mathfrak{R}_m(\mathcal{F}_a)}{\gamma} + \sqrt{\frac{\ln(1/\delta)}{m}}.$$

This shows the trade-off between the complexity of $\mathcal{F}_a$ measured by $\mathfrak{R}_m(\mathcal{F}_a)$ and the fraction of training data classified correctly with a margin of at least γ. In particular this suggests, that (even if we classify the training data correctly with respect to the 0–1 loss) it might be beneficial to increase the complexity of $\mathcal{F}_a$ further, in order to simultaneously increase the margins by which the training data has been classified correctly and thus obtain a better generalization bound.

1.2.3 Optimization and Implicit Regularization

The optimization algorithm, which is usually a variant of SGD, seems to play an important role in generalization performance. Potential indicators for good generalization performance are high speed of convergence (Hardt et al., 2016) or flatness of the local minimum to which SGD converges, which can be characterized by the magnitude of the eigenvalues of the Hessian (or approximately by the robustness of the minimizer to adversarial perturbations on the parameter space); see Keskar et al.

(2017). In Dziugaite and Roy (2017) and Neyshabur et al. (2017) generalization bounds depending on a concept of flatness are established by employing a PAC-Bayesian framework, which can be viewed as a generalization of Theorem 1.19; see McAllester (1999). Further, one can also unite flatness and norm-based bounds by the *Fisher–Rao metric* of information geometry (Liang et al., 2019).

Let us motivate the link between generalization and flatness in the case of simple linear models: We assume that our model takes the form $\langle \theta, \cdot \rangle$, $\theta \in \mathbb{R}^d$, and we will use the abbreviations

$$r(\theta) := \widehat{\mathcal{R}}_s(\langle \theta, \cdot \rangle) \quad \text{and} \quad \gamma(\theta) := \min_{i \in [m]} M(\langle \theta, \cdot \rangle, z^{(i)}) = \min_{i \in [m]} y^{(i)} \langle \theta, x^{(i)} \rangle$$

throughout this subsection to denote the empirical risk and the margin for given training data $s = ((x^{(i)}, y^{(i)}))_{i=1}^m$. We assume that we are solving a classification task with the 0–1 loss and that our training data is linearly separable. This means that there exists a minimizer $\hat{\theta} \in \mathbb{R}^d$ such that $r(\hat{\theta}) = 0$. We observe that δ-robustness in the sense that

$$\max_{\theta \in B_\delta(0)} r(\hat{\theta} + \theta) = r(\hat{\theta}) = 0$$

implies that

$$0 < \min_{i \in [m]} y^{(i)} \left\langle \hat{\theta} - \delta y^{(i)} \frac{x^{(i)}}{\|x^{(i)}\|_2}, x^{(i)} \right\rangle \leq \gamma(\hat{\theta}) - \delta \min_{i \in [m]} \|x^{(i)}\|_2 ;$$

see also Poggio et al. (2017a). This lower bound on the margin $\gamma(\hat{\theta})$ then ensures generalization guarantees, as described in §1.2.2.

Even without explicit[19] control on the complexity of $\mathcal{F}_a$, there do exist results showing that SGD acts as an implicit regularization Neyshabur et al. (2014). This is motivated by linear models where SGD converges to the minimal Euclidean norm solution for a quadratic loss and in the direction of the hard-margin support vector machine solution for the logistic loss on linearly separable data (Soudry et al., 2018). Note that convergence to minimum-norm or maximum-margin solutions in particular decreases the complexity of our hypothesis set and thus improves generalization bounds; see §1.2.2.

While we have seen this behavior of gradient descent for linear regression already in the more general context of kernel regression in §1.2.1, we want to motivate the corresponding result for classification tasks as follows. We focus on the exponential surrogate loss $\mathcal{L}^{\text{surr}}(f, z) = \ell(M(f, z)) = e^{-yf(x)}$ with $\ell(z) = e^{-z}$, but similar observations can be made for the logistic loss defined in Remark 1.9. We assume

---

[19] Note also that different architectures can exhibit vastly different inductive biases (Zhang et al., 2020) and also that, within an architecture, different parameters have different degrees of importance; see Frankle and Carbin (2018), Zhang et al. (2019), and Proposition 1.29.

that the training data is linearly separable, which guarantees the existence of $\hat{\theta} \neq 0$ with $\gamma(\hat{\theta}) > 0$. Then for every linear model $\langle \theta, \cdot \rangle$, $\theta \in \mathbb{R}^d$, it follows that

$$\langle \hat{\theta}, \nabla_\theta r(\theta) \rangle = \frac{1}{m} \sum_{i=1}^{m} \underbrace{\ell'(y^{(i)} \langle \theta, x^{(i)} \rangle)}_{<0} \underbrace{y^{(i)} \langle \hat{\theta}, x^{(i)} \rangle}_{>0} .$$

A critical point $\nabla_\theta r(\theta) = 0$ can therefore be approached if and only if for every $i \in [m]$ we have

$$\ell'(y^{(i)} \langle \theta, x^{(i)} \rangle) = -e^{-y^{(i)} \langle \theta, x^{(i)} \rangle} \to 0,$$

which is equivalent to $\|\theta\|_2 \to \infty$ and $\gamma(\theta) > 0$. Let us now define

$$r_\beta(\theta) := \frac{\ell^{-1}(r(\beta\theta))}{\beta}, \quad \theta \in \mathbb{R}^d, \ \beta \in (0, \infty),$$

and observe that

$$r_\beta(\theta) = -\frac{\log(r(\beta\theta))}{\beta} \to \gamma(\theta), \quad \beta \to \infty. \tag{1.26}$$

Owing to this property, r_β is often referred to as the *smoothed margin* (Lyu and Li, 2019; Ji and Telgarsky, 2019b). We evolve θ according to gradient flow with respect to the smoothed margin r_1, i.e.,

$$\frac{d\theta(t)}{dt} = \nabla_\theta r_1(\theta(t)) = -\frac{1}{r(\theta(t))} \nabla_\theta r(\theta(t)),$$

which produces the same trajectory as gradient flow with respect to the empirical risk r under a rescaling of the time t. Looking at the evolution of the normalized parameters $\tilde{\theta}(t) = \theta(t)/\|\theta(t)\|_2$, the chain rule establishes that

$$\frac{d\tilde{\theta}(t)}{dt} = P_{\tilde{\theta}(t)} \frac{\nabla_\theta r_{\beta(t)}(\tilde{\theta}(t))}{\beta(t)} \quad \text{with } \beta(t) := \|\theta(t)\|_2 \text{ and } P_\theta := \mathrm{I}_d - \theta\theta^T, \ \theta \in \mathbb{R}^d.$$

This shows that the normalized parameters perform projected gradient ascent with respect to the function $r_{\beta(t)}$, which converges to the margin thanks to (1.26) and the fact that $\beta(t) = \|\theta(t)\|_2 \to \infty$ when approaching a critical point. Thus, during gradient flow, the normalized parameters implicitly maximize the margin. See Gunasekar et al. (2018a), Gunasekar et al. (2018b), Lyu and Li (2019), Nacson et al. (2019), Chizat and Bach (2020), and Ji and Telgarsky (2020) for a precise analysis and various extensions, for example, to homogeneous or two-layer NNs and other optimization geometries.

To illustrate one particular research direction, we now present a result by way of example. Let $\Phi = \Phi_{(N,\varrho)}$ be a biasless NN with parameters $\theta = ((W^{(\ell)}, 0))_{\ell=0}^{L}$ and output dimension $N_L = 1$. For given input features $x \in \mathbb{R}^{N_0}$, the gradient

$\nabla_{W^{(\ell)}} \Phi = \nabla_{W^{(\ell)}} \Phi(x, \theta) \in \mathbb{R}^{N_{\ell-1} \times N_\ell}$ with respect to the weight matrix in the ℓth layer satisfies that

$$\nabla_{W^{(\ell)}} \Phi = \varrho(\Phi^{(\ell-1)}) \frac{\partial \Phi}{\partial \Phi^{(\ell+1)}} \frac{\partial \Phi^{(\ell+1)}}{\partial \Phi^{(\ell)}} = \varrho(\Phi^{(\ell-1)}) \frac{\partial \Phi}{\partial \Phi^{(\ell+1)}} W^{(\ell+1)} \operatorname{diag}\left(\varrho'(\Phi^{(\ell)})\right),$$

where the pre-activations $(\Phi^{(\ell)})_{\ell=1}^L$ are as in (1.1). Evolving the parameters according to gradient flow as in (1.20) and using an activation function ϱ with $\varrho(x) = \varrho'(x)x$, such as the ReLU, this implies that

$$\operatorname{diag}\left(\varrho'(\Phi^{(\ell)})\right) W^{(\ell)}(t) \left(\frac{\mathrm{d}W^{(\ell)}(t)}{\mathrm{d}t}\right)^T = \left(\frac{\mathrm{d}W^{(\ell+1)}(t)}{\mathrm{d}t}\right)^T W^{(\ell+1)}(t) \operatorname{diag}\left(\varrho'(\Phi^{(\ell)})\right).$$

$$(1.27)$$

Note that this ensures the conservation of balancedness between the weight matrices of adjacent layers, i.e.,

$$\frac{\mathrm{d}}{\mathrm{d}t} \left(\|W^{(\ell+1)}(t)\|_F^2 - \|W^{(\ell)}(t)\|_F^2 \right) = 0,$$

see Du et al. (2018a). Furthermore, for deep linear NNs, i.e., $\varrho(x) = x$, the property in (1.27) implies conservation of alignment of the left and right singular spaces $W^{(\ell)}$ and $W^{(\ell+1)}$. This can then be used to show the implicit preconditioning and convergence of gradient descent (Arora et al., 2018a, 2019a) and that, under additional assumptions, gradient descent converges to a linear predictor that is aligned with the maximum margin solution (Ji and Telgarsky, 2019a).

1.2.4 Limits of Classical Theory and Double Descent

There is ample evidence that classical tools from statistical learning theory alone, such as Rademacher averages, uniform convergence, or algorithmic stability, may be unable to explain the full generalization capabilities of NNs (Zhang et al., 2017; Nagarajan and Kolter, 2019). It is especially hard to reconcile the classical bias–variance trade-off with the observation of good generalization performance when achieving zero empirical risk on noisy data using a regression loss. On top of that, this behavior of overparametrized models in the interpolation regime turns out not to be unique to NNs. Empirically, one observes for various methods (decision trees, random features, linear models) that the test error decreases even below the sweet-spot in the ∪-shaped bias–variance curve when the number of parameters is increased further (Belkin et al., 2019b; Geiger et al., 2020; Nakkiran et al., 2020). This is often referred to as the *double descent curve* or *benign overfitting*; see Figure 1.6. For special cases, for example linear regression or random feature regression, such behavior can even be proven; see Hastie et al. (2019), Mei and Montanari (2019), Bartlett et al. (2020), Belkin et al. (2020), and Muthukumar et al. (2020).

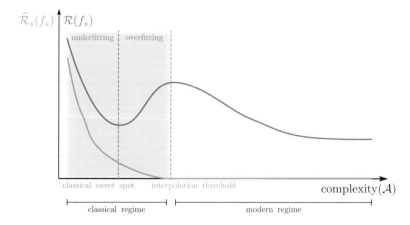

Figure 1.6 This illustration shows the classical, underparametrized regime in green, where the ∪-shaped curve depicts the bias–variance trade-off as explained in §1.1.2. Starting with a complexity of our algorithm $\mathcal{A}$ larger than the interpolation threshold we can achieve zero empirical risk $\widehat{\mathcal{R}}_s(f_s)$ (the training error), where $f_s = \mathcal{A}(s)$. Within this modern interpolation regime, the risk $\mathcal{R}(f_s)$ (the test error) might be even lower than at the classical sweet spot. Whereas complexity($\mathcal{A}$) traditionally refers to the complexity of the hypothesis set $\mathcal{F}$, there is evidence that the optimization scheme and the data also influence the complexity, leading to definitions such as complexity($\mathcal{A}$) := max $\{m \in \mathbb{N} \colon \mathbb{E}\big[\widehat{\mathcal{R}}_S(\mathcal{A}(S))\big] \leq \varepsilon$ with $S \sim \mathcal{I}_Z^m\}$, for suitable $\varepsilon > 0$ (Nakkiran et al., 2020). This illustration is based on Belkin et al. (2019b).

In the following we analyze this phenomenon in the context of linear regression. Specifically, we focus on a prediction task with quadratic loss, input features given by a centered $\mathbb{R}^d$-valued random variable X, and labels given by $Y = \langle \theta^*, X \rangle + v$, where $\theta^* \in \mathbb{R}^d$ and v is a centered random variable that is independent of X. For training data $S = ((X^{(i)}, Y^{(i)}))_{i=1}^m$, we consider the empirical risk minimizer $\widehat{f_S} = \langle \hat{\theta}, \cdot \rangle$ with minimum Euclidean norm of its parameters $\hat{\theta}$ or, equivalently, we can consider the limit of gradient flow with zero initialization. Using (1.5) and a bias–variance decomposition we can write

$$\mathbb{E}[\mathcal{R}(\widehat{f_S})|(X^{(i)})_{i=1}^m] - \mathcal{R}^* = \mathbb{E}[\|\widehat{f_S} - f^*\|_{L^2(\mathcal{I}_X)}|(X^{(i)})_{i=1}^m]$$
$$= (\theta^*)^T P \, \mathbb{E}[XX^T] P\theta^* + \mathbb{E}[v^2] \operatorname{Tr}(\Sigma^+ \mathbb{E}[XX^T]),$$

where $\Sigma := \sum_{i=1}^m X^{(i)}(X^{(i)})^T$, Σ^+ denotes the Moore–Penrose inverse of Σ, and $P := \mathrm{I}_d - \Sigma^+ \Sigma$ is the orthogonal projector onto the kernel of Σ. For simplicity, we focus on the variance $\operatorname{Tr}(\Sigma^+ \mathbb{E}[XX^T])$, which can be viewed as the result of setting $\theta^* = 0$ and $\mathbb{E}[v^2] = 1$. Assuming that X has i.i.d. entries with unit variance and bounded fifth moment, the distribution of the eigenvalues of $\frac{1}{m}\Sigma^+$ in the limit $d, m \to \infty$ with $\frac{d}{m} \to \kappa \in (0, \infty)$ can be described via the Marchenko–Pastur law.

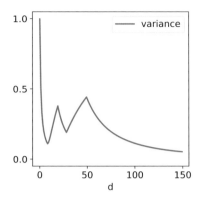

Figure 1.7 The expected variance of the linear regression in (1.29) with $d \in [150]$ and $X_i \sim U(\{-1, 1\})$, $i \in [150]$, where $X_i = X_1$ for $i \in \{10, \ldots, 20\} \cup \{30, \ldots, 50\}$ and all other coordinates are independent.

Therefore, the asymptotic variance can be computed explicitly as

$$\text{Tr}\big(\Sigma^+ \, \mathbb{E}[XX^T]\big) \to \frac{1 - \max\{1 - \kappa, 0\}}{|1 - \kappa|} \quad \text{for} \quad d, m \to \infty \quad \text{with} \quad \frac{d}{m} \to \kappa,$$

almost surely; see Hastie et al. (2019). This shows that despite interpolating the data we can decrease the risk in the overparametrized regime $\kappa > 1$. In the limit $d, m \to \infty$, such benign overfitting can also be shown for more general settings (including lazy training of NNs), some of which even achieve their optimal risk in the overparametrized regime (Mei and Montanari, 2019; Montanari and Zhong, 2020; Lin and Dobriban, 2021).

For normally distributed input features X such that $\mathbb{E}[XX^T]$ has rank larger than m, one can also compute the behavior of the variance in the non-asymptomatic regime (Bartlett et al., 2020). Define

$$k^* := \min \left\{ k \geq 0 : \frac{\sum_{i>k} \lambda_i}{\lambda_{k+1}} \geq cm \right\}, \tag{1.28}$$

where $\lambda_1 \geq \lambda_2 \geq \cdots \geq \lambda_d \geq 0$ are the eigenvalues of $\mathbb{E}[XX^T]$ in decreasing order and $c \in (0, \infty)$ is a universal constant. Assuming that k^*/m is sufficiently small, with high probability we have

$$\text{Tr}\big(\Sigma^+ \, \mathbb{E}[XX^T]\big) \approx \frac{k^*}{m} + \frac{m \sum_{i>k^*} \lambda_i^2}{(\sum_{i>k^*} \lambda_i)^2}.$$

This precisely characterizes the regimes for benign overfitting in terms of the eigenvalues of the covariance matrix $\mathbb{E}[XX^T]$. Furthermore, it shows that adding new input feature coordinates and thus increasing the number of parameters d can lead to either an increase or a decrease in the risk.

To motivate this phenomenon, which is considered in much more depth in Chen et al. (2020), let us focus on a single sample $m = 1$ and features X that take values in $\mathcal{X} = \{-1, 1\}^d$. Then it follows that

$$\Sigma^+ = \frac{X^{(1)}(X^{(1)})^T}{\|X^{(1)}\|^4} = \frac{X^{(1)}(X^{(1)})^T}{d^2}$$

and thus

$$\mathbb{E}\big[\mathrm{Tr}\big(\Sigma^+\mathbb{E}[XX^T]\big)\big] = \frac{1}{d^2}\big\|\mathbb{E}[XX^T]\big\|_F^2. \tag{1.29}$$

In particular, this shows that by incrementing the input feature dimensions via $d \mapsto d + 1$ one can increase or decrease the risk depending on the correlation of the coordinate X_{d+1} with respect to the previous coordinates $(X_i)_{i=1}^d$; see also Figure 1.7.

Generally speaking, overparametrization and the perfect fitting of noisy data does not exclude good generalization performance; see also Belkin et al. (2019a). However, the risk crucially depends on the data distribution and the chosen algorithm.

1.3 The Role of Depth in the Expressivity of Neural Networks

The approximation-theoretic aspect of a NN architecture, which is responsible for the approximation component $\varepsilon^{\mathrm{approx}} := \mathcal{R}(f_{\mathcal{F}}^*) - \mathcal{R}^*$ of the error $\mathcal{R}(f_S) - \mathcal{R}^*$ in (1.7), is probably one of the most well-studied parts of the deep learning pipe-line. The achievable approximation error of an architecture directly describes the power of the architecture.

As mentioned in §1.1.3, many classical approaches study the approximation theory of NNs with only a few layers, whereas modern architectures are typically very deep. A first observation about the effect of depth is that it can often compensate for insufficient width. For example, in the context of the universal approximation theorem, it has been shown that very narrow NNs are still universal if, instead of increasing the width, the number of layers can be chosen arbitrarily (Hanin and Sellke, 2017; Hanin, 2019; Kidger and Lyons, 2020). However, if the width of a NN falls below a critical number, then the universality will no longer hold.

Below, we discuss three additional observations that shed light on the effect of depth on the approximation capacities, or alternative notions of expressivity, of NNs.

1.3.1 Approximation of Radial Functions

One technique to study the impact of depth relies on the construction of specific functions which can be well approximated by NNs of a certain depth, but require significantly more parameters when approximated to the same accuracy by NNs of smaller depth. In the following we present one example of this type of approach, which can be found in Eldan and Shamir (2016).

Theorem 1.24 (Power of depth). *Let $\varrho \in \{\varrho_R, \varrho_\sigma, 1_{(0,\infty)}\}$ be the ReLU, the logistic, or the Heaviside function. Then there exist constants $c, C \in (0, \infty)$ with the following property. For every $d \in \mathbb{N}$ with $d \geq C$ there exist a probability measure μ on $\mathbb{R}^d$, a three-layer NN architecture $a = (N, \varrho) = ((d, N_1, N_2, 1), \varrho)$ with $\|N\|_\infty \leq Cd^5$, and corresponding parameters $\theta^* \in \mathbb{R}^{P(N)}$ with $\|\theta^*\|_\infty \leq Cd^C$ and $\|\Phi_a(\cdot, \theta^*)\|_{L^\infty(\mathbb{R}^d)} \leq 2$ such that for every $n \leq ce^{cd}$ we have*

$$\inf_{\theta \in \mathbb{R}^{P((d,n,1))}} \|\Phi_{((d,n,1),\varrho)}(\cdot, \theta) - \Phi_a(\cdot, \theta^*)\|_{L^2(\mu)} \geq c.$$

In fact, the activation function in Theorem 1.24 is required to satisfy only mild conditions and the result holds, for instance, also for more general sigmoidal functions. The proof of Theorem 1.24 is based on the construction of a suitable radial function $g \colon \mathbb{R}^d \to \mathbb{R}$, i.e., $g(x) = \tilde{g}(\|x\|_2^2)$ for some $\tilde{g} \colon [0, \infty) \to \mathbb{R}$, which can be efficiently approximated by three-layer NNs but for which approximation by only a two-layer NN requires exponentially large complexity, i.e., a width that is exponential in d.

The first observation of Eldan and Shamir (2016) was that g can typically be well approximated on a bounded domain by a three-layer NN, if $\tilde{g}$ is Lipschitz continuous. Indeed, for the ReLU activation function it is not difficult to show that, emulating a linear interpolation, one can approximate a univariate C-Lipschitz function uniformly on $[0, 1]$ up to precision ε by a two-layer architecture of width $O(C/\varepsilon)$. The same holds for smooth, non-polynomial activation functions, owing to Theorem 1.18. This implies that the squared Euclidean norm, as a sum of d univariate functions, i.e., $[0, 1]^d \ni x \mapsto \sum_{i=1}^d x_i^2$, can be approximated up to precision ε by a two-layer architecture of width $O(d^2/\varepsilon)$. Moreover, this shows that the third layer can efficiently approximate $\tilde{g}$, establishing the approximation of g on a bounded domain up to precision ε using a three-layer architecture with the number of parameters polynomial in d/ε.

The second step of Eldan and Shamir (2016) was to choose g in such a way that the realization of any two-layer neural network $\Phi = \Phi_{((d,n,1),\varrho)}(\cdot, \theta)$ with width n and not exponential in d is on average (with respect to the probability measure μ) a constant distance away from g. Their argument is heavily based on ideas from Fourier analysis and will be outlined below. In this context, let us recall that we denote by $\hat{f}$ the Fourier transform of a suitable function, or, more generally, tempered distribution. f.

Assuming that the square root φ of the density function associated with the probability measure μ, as well as Φ and g, are well behaved, the Plancherel theorem

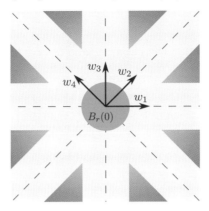

Figure 1.8 This illustration shows the largest possible support (blue) of $\widehat{\Phi\varphi}$, where $\hat{\varphi} = 1_{B_r(0)}$ and Φ is a shallow neural network with architecture $N = (2, 4, 1)$ and weight matrix $W^{(1)} = [w_1 \cdots w_4]^T$ in the first layer. Any radial function with too much of its L^2-mass located at high frequencies (indicated in red) cannot be well approximated by $\Phi\varphi$.

yields

$$\|\Phi - g\|^2_{L^2(\mu)} = \|\Phi\varphi - g\varphi\|^2_{L^2(\mathbb{R}^d)} = \|\widehat{\Phi\varphi} - \widehat{g\varphi}\|^2_{L^2(\mathbb{R}^d)}. \tag{1.30}$$

Next, the specific structure of two-layer NNs is used, which implies that for every $j \in [n]$ there exists $w_j \in \mathbb{R}^d$ with $\|w_j\|_2 = 1$ and $\varrho_j : \mathbb{R} \to \mathbb{R}$ (subsuming the activation function ϱ, the norm of w_j, and the remaining parameters corresponding to the jth neuron in the hidden layer) such that Φ is of the form

$$\Phi = \sum_{j=1}^n \varrho_j(\langle w_j, \cdot \rangle) = \sum_{j=1}^n (\varrho_j \otimes 1_{\mathbb{R}^{d-1}}) \circ R_{w_j}. \tag{1.31}$$

The second equality follows by viewing the action of the jth neuron as a tensor product of ϱ_j and the indicator function $1_{\mathbb{R}^{d-1}}(x) = 1$, $x \in \mathbb{R}^{d-1}$, composed with a d-dimensional rotation $R_{w_j} \in SO(d)$ which maps w_j to the first standard basis vector $e^{(1)} \in \mathbb{R}^d$. Noting that the Fourier transform respects linearity, rotations, and tensor products, we can compute

$$\hat{\Phi} = \sum_{j=1}^n (\hat{\varrho}_j \otimes \delta_{\mathbb{R}^{d-1}}) \circ R_{w_j},$$

where $\delta_{\mathbb{R}^{d-1}}$ denotes the Dirac distribution on $\mathbb{R}^{d-1}$. In particular, the support of $\hat{\Phi}$ has a particular star-like shape, namely $\bigcup_{j=1}^n \text{span}\{w_j\}$, which represent lines passing through the origin.

Now we choose φ to be the inverse Fourier transform of the indicator function of a ball $B_r(0) \subset \mathbb{R}^d$ with $\text{vol}(B_r(0)) = 1$, ensuring that φ^2 is a valid probability density for μ as

$$\mu(\mathbb{R}^d) = \|\varphi^2\|_{L^1(\mathbb{R}^d)} = \|\varphi\|_{L^2(\mathbb{R}^d)}^2 = \|\hat{\varphi}\|_{L^2(\mathbb{R}^d)}^2 = \|1_{B_r(0)}\|_{L^2(\mathbb{R}^d)}^2 = 1.$$

Using the convolution theorem, this choice of φ yields that

$$\text{supp}(\widehat{\Phi\varphi}) = \text{supp}(\hat{\Phi} * \hat{\varphi}) \subset \bigcup_{j=1}^{n} (\text{span}\{w_j\} + B_r(0)).$$

Thus the lines passing through the origin are enlarged to tubes. It is this particular shape which allows the construction of some g such that $\|\widehat{\Phi\varphi} - \widehat{g\varphi}\|_{L^2(\mathbb{R}^d)}^2$ can be suitably lower bounded; see also Figure 1.8. Intriguingly, the peculiar behavior of high-dimensional sets now comes into play. Owing to the well-known concentration of measure principle, the variable n needs to be exponentially large for the set $\bigcup_{j=1}^{n} (\text{span}\{w_j\} + B_r(0))$ not to be sparse. If it is smaller, one can construct a function g such that the main energy content of $\widehat{g\varphi}$ has a certain distance from the origin, yielding a lower bound for $\|\widehat{\Phi\varphi} - \widehat{g\varphi}\|^2$ and hence $\|\Phi - g\|_{L^2(\mu)}^2$; see (1.30). One key technical problem is the fact that such a behavior for $\hat{g}$ does not immediately imply a similar behavior for $\widehat{g\varphi}$, requiring a quite delicate construction of g.

1.3.2 Deep ReLU Networks

Perhaps for no activation function is the effect of depth clearer than for the ReLU activation function $\varrho_R(x) = \max\{0, x\}$. We refer to the corresponding NN architectures (N, ϱ_R) as *ReLU (neural) networks* (ReLU NNs). A two-layer ReLU NN with one-dimensional input and output is a function of the form

$$\Phi(x) = \sum_{i=1}^{n} w_i^{(2)} \varrho_R(w_i^{(1)} x + b_i^{(1)}) + b^{(2)}, \quad x \in \mathbb{R},$$

where $w_i^{(1)}, w_i^{(2)}, b_i^{(1)}, b^{(2)} \in \mathbb{R}$ for $i \in [n]$. It is not hard to see that Φ is a continuous piecewise affine linear function. Moreover, Φ has at most $n + 1$ affine linear pieces. On the other hand, notice that the *hat function*

$$h: [0, 1] \rightarrow [0, 1],$$

$$x \mapsto 2\varrho_R(x) - 4\varrho_R(x - \tfrac{1}{2}) = \begin{cases} 2x, & \text{if } 0 \le x < \tfrac{1}{2}, \\ 2(1 - x), & \text{if } \tfrac{1}{2} \le x \le 1, \end{cases} \tag{1.32}$$

is a NN with two layers and two neurons. Telgarsky (2015) observed that the n-fold convolution $h_n(x) := h \circ \cdots \circ h$ produces a sawtooth function with 2^n spikes. In particular, h_n admits 2^n affine linear pieces with only $2n$ many neurons. In this case, we see that deep ReLU NNs are in some sense exponentially more efficient in generating affine linear pieces.

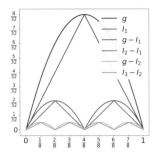

Figure 1.9 Interpolation I_n of $[0, 1] \ni x \mapsto g(x) := x - x^2$ on $2^n + 1$ equidistant points, which can be represented as a sum $I_n = \sum_{k=1}^{n} I_k - I_{k-1} = \sum_{k=1}^{n} h_k / 2^{2k}$ of n sawtooth functions. Each sawtooth function $h_k = h_{k-1} \circ h$ in turn can be written as a k-fold composition of a hat function h. This illustration is based on Elbrächter et al. (2019).

Moreover, it was noted in Yarotsky (2017) that the difference in interpolations of $[0, 1] \ni x \mapsto x - x^2$ at $2^n + 1$ and $2^{n-1} + 1$ equidistant points equals the scaled sawtooth function $h_n / 2^{2n}$; see Figure 1.9. This permits efficient implementation of approximative squaring and, by polarization, also of approximate multiplication using ReLU NNs. Composing these simple functions one can approximate localized Taylor polynomials and thus smooth functions; see Yarotsky (2017). We state below a generalization (Gühring et al., 2020) of Yarotsky's result which includes more general norms, but which for $p = \infty$ and $s = 0$ coincides with his original result.

Theorem 1.25 (Approximation of Sobolev-regular functions). *Let $d, k \in \mathbb{N}$ with $k \geq 2$, let $p \in [1, \infty]$, $s \in [0, 1]$, $B \in (0, \infty)$, and let ϱ be a piecewise-linear activation function with at least one break point. Then there exists a constant $c \in (0, \infty)$ with the following property. For every $\varepsilon \in (0, 1/2)$ there exists a NN architecture $a = (N, \varrho)$ with*

$$P(N) \leq c \varepsilon^{-d/(k-s)} \log(1/\varepsilon)$$

such that for every function $g \in W^{k,p}((0, 1)^d)$ with $\|g\|_{W^{k,p}((0,1)^d)} \leq B$ we have

$$\inf_{\theta \in \mathbb{R}^{P(N)}} \|\Phi_a(\theta, \cdot) - g\|_{W^{s,p}((0,1)^d)} \leq \varepsilon.$$

The ability of deep ReLU neural networks to emulate multiplication has also been employed to reapproximate wide ranges of high-order finite-element spaces. In Opschoor et al. (2020) and Marcati et al. (2020) it was shown that deep ReLU neural networks are capable of achieving the approximation rates of *hp*-finite-element methods. Concretely, this means that for piecewise analytic functions, which appear, for example, as solutions of elliptic boundary and eigenvalue problems with analytic data, exponential approximation rates can be achieved. In other words, the number

depth

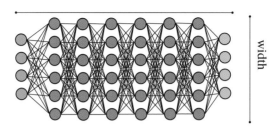

width

Figure 1.10 Standard feed-forward neural network. For certain approximation results, depth and width need to be in a fixed relationship to achieve optimal results.

of parameters of neural networks needed to approximate such a function in the $W^{1,2}$-norm up to an error of ε is logarithmic in ε.

Theorem 1.25 requires the depth of the NN to grow. In fact, it can be shown that the same approximation rate cannot be achieved with shallow NNs. Indeed, there exists a certain optimal number of layers, and if the architecture has fewer layers than optimal then the NNs need to have significantly more parameters to achieve the same approximation fidelity. This has been observed in many different settings in Liang and Srikant (2017), Safran and Shamir (2017), Yarotsky (2017), Petersen and Voigtlaender (2018), andElbrächter et al. (2019). We state here Yarotsky's result:

Theorem 1.26 (Depth–width approximation trade-off). *Let $d, L \in \mathbb{N}$ with $L \geq 2$ and let $g \in C^2([0,1]^d)$ be a function that is not affine linear. Then there exists a constant $c \in (0,\infty)$ with the following property. For every $\varepsilon \in (0,1)$ and every ReLU NN architecture $a = (N, \varrho_R) = ((d, N_1, \ldots, N_{L-1}, 1), \varrho_R)$ with L layers and $\|N\|_1 \leq c\varepsilon^{-1/(2(L-1))}$ neurons it follows that*

$$\inf_{\theta \in \mathbb{R}^{P(N)}} \|\Phi_a(\cdot, \theta) - g\|_{L^\infty([0,1]^d)} \geq \varepsilon.$$

This results is based on the observation that ReLU NNs are piecewise affine linear. The number of pieces they admit is linked to their capacity of approximating functions that have non-vanishing curvature. Using a construction similar to the example at the beginning of this subsection, it can be shown that the number of pieces that can be generated using an architecture $((1, N_1, \ldots, N_{L-1}, 1), \varrho_R)$ scales roughly as $\prod_{\ell=1}^{L-1} N_\ell$.

In the framework of the aforementioned results, we can speak of a depth–width trade-off; see also Figure 1.10. A fine-grained estimate of achievable rates for freely varying depths was also established in Shen (2020).

1.3.3 Alternative Notions of Expressivity

Conceptual approaches to studying the approximation power of deep NNs beyond the classical approximation framework usually aim to relate structural properties of the NN to the "richness" of the set of possibly expressed functions. One early result in this direction was by Montúfar et al. (2014) who described bounds on the number of *affine linear regions* of a ReLU NN $\Phi_{(N,\varrho_R)}(\cdot,\theta)$. In a simplified setting, we already saw estimates on the number of affine linear pieces at the beginning of §1.3.2. Affine linear regions can be defined as the connected components of $\mathbb{R}^{N_0} \setminus H$, where H is the set of non-differentiable parts of the realization[20] $\Phi_{(N,\varrho_R)}(\cdot,\theta)$. A refined analysis on the number of such regions was conducted, for example, by Hinz and van de Geer (2019). It was found that deep ReLU neural networks can exhibit significantly more of such regions than of their shallow counterparts.

The reason for this effectiveness of depth is described by the following analogy. Through the ReLU each neuron $\mathbb{R}^d \ni x \mapsto \varrho_R(\langle x, w \rangle + b)$, $w \in \mathbb{R}^d$, $b \in \mathbb{R}$, splits the space into two affine linear regions separated by the hyperplane

$$\{x \in \mathbb{R}^d : \langle x, w \rangle + b = 0\}. \tag{1.33}$$

A shallow ReLU NN $\Phi_{((d,n,1),\varrho_R)}(\cdot,\theta)$ with n neurons in the hidden layer therefore produces a number of regions defined through n hyperplanes. Using classical bounds on the number of regions defined through hyperplane arrangements (Zaslavsky, 1975), one can bound the number of affine linear regions by $\sum_{j=0}^{d} \binom{n}{j}$. Deepening the neural networks then corresponds to a certain folding of the input space. Through this interpretation it can be seen that composing NNs can lead to a multiplication of the number of regions of the individual NNs, resulting in an exponential efficiency of deep neural networks in generating affine linear regions.[21]

This approach was further developed in Raghu et al. (2017) to a framework to study expressivity that to some extent allows to include the training phase. One central object studied in Raghu et al. (2017) are so-called *trajectory lengths*. In this context, one analyzes how the length of a non-constant curve in the input space changes in expectation through the layers of a NN. The authors found an exponential dependence of the expected curve length on the depth. Let us motivate this in the

---

[20] One can also study the potentially larger set of *activation regions* given by the connected components of $\mathbb{R}^{N_0} \setminus (\bigcup_{\ell=1}^{L-1} \bigcup_{i=1}^{N_\ell} H_{i,\ell})$, where

$$H_{i,\ell} := \{x \in \mathbb{R}^{N_0} : \Phi_i^{(\ell)}(x,\theta) = 0\},$$

with $\Phi_i^{(\ell)}$ as in (1.1), is the set of non-differentiable parts of the activation of the ith neuron in the ℓth layer. In contrast with the linear regions, the activation regions are necessarily convex (Raghu et al., 2017; Hanin and Rolnick, 2019).

[21] However, to exploit this efficiency with respect to the depth, one requires highly oscillating pre-activations snd this in turn can only be achieved with a delicate selection of parameters. In fact, it can be shown that through random initialization the expected number of activation regions per unit cube depends mainly on the number of neurons in the NN, rather than its depth (Hanin and Rolnick, 2019).

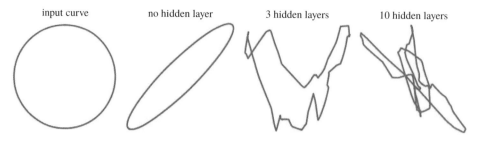

input curve   no hidden layer   3 hidden layers   10 hidden layers

Figure 1.11 Shape of the trajectory $t \mapsto \Phi_{((2,n,\ldots,n,2),\varrho_R)}(\gamma(t), \theta)$ of the output of a randomly initialized network with 0, 3, or 10 hidden layers. The input curve γ is the circle given in the leftmost image. The hidden layers have $n = 20$ neurons and the variance of the initialization is taken as $4/n$.

special case of a ReLU NN with architecture $a = ((N_0, n, \ldots, n, N_L), \varrho_R)$ and depth $L \in \mathbb{N}$.

Given a non-constant continuous curve $\gamma \colon [0, 1] \to \mathbb{R}^{N_0}$ in the input space, the length of the trajectory in the ℓth layer of the NN $\Phi_a(\cdot, \theta)$ is then given by

$$\text{Length}(\bar{\Phi}^{(\ell)}(\gamma(\cdot), \theta)), \quad \ell \in [L-1],$$

where $\bar{\Phi}^{(\ell)}(\cdot, \theta)$ is the activation in the ℓth layer; see (1.1). Here the length of the curve is well defined since $\bar{\Phi}^{(\ell)}(\cdot, \theta))$ is continuous and therefore $\bar{\Phi}^{(\ell)}(\gamma(\cdot), \theta)$ is continuous. Now, let the parameters Θ_1 of the NN Φ_a be initialized independently in such a way that the entries corresponding to the weight matrices and bias vectors follow a normal distribution with zero mean and variances $1/n$ and 1, respectively. It is not hard to see, for example by Proposition 1.17, that the probability that $\bar{\Phi}^{(\ell)}(\cdot, \Theta_1)$ will map γ to a non-constant curve is positive and hence, for fixed $\ell \in [L-1]$,

$$\mathbb{E}\left[\text{Length}(\bar{\Phi}^{(\ell)}(\gamma(\cdot), \Theta_1))\right] = c > 0.$$

Let $\sigma \in (0, \infty)$ and consider a second initialization Θ_σ, where we have changed the variances of the entries corresponding to the weight matrices and bias vectors to σ^2/n and σ^2, respectively. Recall that the ReLU is positively homogeneous, i.e., we have that $\varrho_R(\lambda x) = \lambda \varrho_R(x)$ for all $\lambda \in (0, \infty)$. Then it is clear that

$$\bar{\Phi}^{(\ell)}(\cdot, \Theta_\sigma) \sim \sigma^\ell \bar{\Phi}^{(\ell)}(\cdot, \Theta_1),$$

i.e., the activations corresponding to the two initialization strategies are identically distributed up to the factor σ^ℓ. Therefore, we immediately conclude that

$$\mathbb{E}\left[\text{Length}(\bar{\Phi}^{(\ell)}(\gamma(\cdot), \Theta_\sigma))\right] = \sigma^\ell c.$$

This shows that the expected trajectory length depends exponentially on the depth of the NN, which is in line with the behavior of other notions of expressivity (Poole

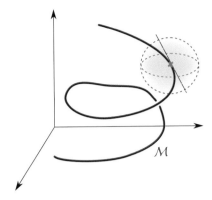

Figure 1.12 Illustration of a one-dimensional manifold $\mathcal{M}$ embedded in $\mathbb{R}^3$. For every point $x \in \mathcal{M}$ there exists a neighborhood in which the manifold can be linearly projected onto its tangent space at x such that the corresponding inverse function is differentiable.

et al., 2016). In Raghu et al. (2017) this result is also extended to a tanh activation function and the constant c is more carefully resolved. Empirically one also finds that the shapes of the trajectories become more complex in addition to becoming longer on average; see Figure 1.11.

1.4 Deep Neural Networks Overcome the Curse of Dimensionality

In §1.1.3, one of the main puzzles of deep learning that we identified was the surprising performance of deep architectures on problems where the input dimensions are very high. This performance cannot be explained in the framework of classical approximation theory, since such results always suffer from the curse of dimensionality (Bellman, 1952; DeVore, 1998; Novak and Woźniakowski, 2009).

In this section, we present three approaches that offer explanations of this phenomenon. As before, we have had to omit certain ideas which have been very influential in the literature to keep the length of this section under control. In particular, an important line of reasoning is that functions to be approximated often have compositional structures which NNs may approximate very well, as reviewed in Poggio et al. (2017b). Note that also a suitable feature descriptor, factoring out invariances, might lead to a significantly reduced effective dimension; see §1.7.1.

1.4.1 Manifold Assumption

A first remedy for the high-dimensional curse of dimensionality is what we call the *manifold assumption*. Here it is assumed that we are trying to approximate a function

$$g: \mathbb{R}^d \supset X \to \mathbb{R},$$

where d is very large. However, we are not seeking to optimize with respect to the uniform norm or a regular L^p space; instead, we consider a measure μ which is supported on a d'-dimensional manifold $\mathcal{M} \subset X$. Then the error is measured in the $L^p(\mu)$-norm. Here we consider the case where $d' \ll d$. This setting is appropriate if the data $z = (x, y)$ of a prediction task is generated from a measure supported on $\mathcal{M} \times \mathbb{R}$.

This set-up or generalizations thereof was fundamental in Chui and Mhaskar (2018), Shaham et al. (2018), Chen et al. (2019), Schmidt-Hieber (2019), Cloninger and Klock (2020), Nakada and Imaizumi (2020). Let us outline an example-based approach, where we consider locally C^k-regular functions and NNs with ReLU activation functions below.

(i) *The regularity of g on the manifold is described.* Naturally, we need to quantify the regularity of the function g restricted to $\mathcal{M}$ in an adequate way. The typical approach would be to make a definition via local coordinate charts. If we assume that $\mathcal{M}$ is an embedded submanifold of X, then locally, i.e., in a neighborhood of a point $x \in \mathcal{M}$, the orthogonal projection of $\mathcal{M}$ onto the d'-dimensional tangent space $T_x\mathcal{M}$ is a diffeomorphism. The situation is depicted in Figure 1.12. Assuming $\mathcal{M}$ to be compact, we can choose a finite set of open balls $(U_i)_{i=1}^p$ that cover $\mathcal{M}$ and on which the local projections γ_i onto the respective tangent spaces as described above exists and are diffeomorphisms. Now we can define the regularity of g via classical regularity. In this example, we say that $g \in C^k(\mathcal{M})$ if $g \circ \gamma_i^{-1} \in C^k(\gamma_i(\mathcal{M} \cap U_i))$ for all $i \in [p]$.

(ii) *Localization and charts are constructed via neural networks.* According to the construction of local coordinate charts in Step (i), we can write g as follows:

$$g(x) = \sum_{i=1}^p \phi_i(x) \left(g \circ \gamma_i^{-1}(\gamma_i(x)) \right) =: \sum_{i=1}^p \tilde{g}_i(\gamma_i(x), \phi_i(x)), \quad x \in \mathcal{M}, \quad (1.34)$$

where ϕ_i is a partition of unity such that $\text{supp}(\phi_i) \subset U_i$. Note that γ_i is a linear map, hence representable by a one-layer NN. Since multiplication is a smooth operation, we have that if $g \in C^k(\mathcal{M})$ then $\tilde{g}_i \in C^k(\gamma_i(\mathcal{M} \cap U_i) \times [0, 1])$.

The partition of unity ϕ_i needs to be emulated by NNs. For example, if the activation function is the ReLU, then such a partition can be efficiently constructed. Indeed, in He et al. (2020) it was shown that such NNs can represent linear finite elements exactly with fixed-size NNs, and hence a partition of unity subordinate to any given covering of $\mathcal{M}$ can be constructed.

(iii) *A classical approximation result is used on the localized functions.* By some form of Whitney's extension theorem (Whitney, 1934), we can extend each $\tilde{g}_i$ to a function $\bar{g}_i \in C^k(X \times [0,1])$ which by classical results can be approximated up to an error of $\varepsilon > 0$ by NNs of size $O(\varepsilon^{-(d'+1)/k})$ for $\varepsilon \to 0$; see Mhaskar (1996), Yarotsky (2017), and Shaham et al. (2018).

(iv) *The compositionality of neural networks is used to build the final network.* We have seen that every component in the representation (1.34), i.e., $\tilde{g}_i$, γ_i, and ϕ_i, can be efficiently represented by NNs. In addition, composition and summation are operations which can directly be implemented by NNs through increasing their depth and widening their layers. Hence (1.34) is efficiently – i.e., with a rate depending only on d' instead of the potentially much larger d – approximated by a NN.

Overall, we see that NNs are capable of learning local coordinate transformations and therefore of reducing the complexity of a high-dimensional problem to the underlying low-dimensional problem given by the data distribution.

1.4.2 Random Sampling

As early as 1992, Andrew Barron showed that, under certain seemingly very natural assumptions on the function to be approximated, a dimension-independent approximation rate by NNs can be achieved (Barron, 1992, 1993). Specifically, the assumption is formulated as a condition on the Fourier transform of a function, and the result is as follows.

Theorem 1.27 (Approximation of Barron-regular functions). *Let $\varrho \colon \mathbb{R} \to \mathbb{R}$ be the ReLU or a sigmoidal function. Then there exists a constant $c \in (0, \infty)$ with the following property. For every $d, n \in \mathbb{N}$, every probability measure μ supported on $B_1(0) \subset \mathbb{R}^d$, and every $g \in L^1(\mathbb{R}^d)$ with $C_g := \int_{\mathbb{R}^d} \|\xi\|_2 |\hat{g}(\xi)| \, d\xi < \infty$ it follows that*

$$\inf_{\theta \in \mathbb{R}^{P((d,n,1))}} \|\Phi_{((d,n,1),\varrho)}(\cdot, \theta) - g\|_{L^2(\mu)} \le \frac{c}{\sqrt{n}} C_g.$$

Note that the L^2-approximation error can be replaced by an L^∞-estimate over the unit ball at the expense of a factor of the order of $\sqrt{d}$ on the right-hand side.

The key idea behind Theorem 1.27 is the following application of the law of large numbers. First, we observe that, as per the assumption, g can be represented via the inverse Fourier transform as

$$g - g(0) = \int_{\mathbb{R}^d} \hat{g}(\xi)(e^{2\pi i \langle \cdot, \xi \rangle} - 1) \, d\xi$$

$$= C_g \int_{\mathbb{R}^d} \frac{1}{\|\xi\|_2} (e^{2\pi i \langle \cdot, \xi \rangle} - 1) \frac{1}{C_g} \|\xi\|_2 \hat{g}(\xi) \, d\xi$$

$$= C_g \int_{\mathbb{R}^d} \frac{1}{\|\xi\|_2} (e^{2\pi i \langle \cdot, \xi \rangle} - 1) \, d\mu_g(\xi), \tag{1.35}$$

where μ_g is a probability measure. Then it was further shown by Barron (1992) that there exist $(\mathbb{R}^d \times \mathbb{R})$-valued random variables $(\Xi, \widetilde{\Xi})$ such that (1.35) can be written as

$$g(x) - g(0) = C_g \int_{\mathbb{R}^d} \frac{1}{\|\xi\|_2} (e^{2\pi i \langle x, \xi \rangle} - 1) \, d\mu_g(\xi) = C_g \mathbb{E}\big[\Gamma(\Xi, \widetilde{\Xi})(x)\big], \quad x \in \mathbb{R}^d,$$
$$\tag{1.36}$$

where for every $\xi \in \mathbb{R}^d, \tilde{\xi} \in \mathbb{R}$, the function $\Gamma(\xi, \tilde{\xi}) \colon \mathbb{R}^d \to \mathbb{R}$ is given by

$$\Gamma(\xi, \tilde{\xi}) := s(\xi, \tilde{\xi})(1_{(0,\infty)}(-\langle \xi/\|\xi\|_2, \cdot \rangle - \tilde{\xi}) - 1_{(0,\infty)}(\langle \xi/\|\xi\|_2, \cdot \rangle - \tilde{\xi}))$$
$$\text{with} \quad s(\xi, \tilde{\xi}) \in \{-1, 1\}.$$

Now, let $((\Xi^{(i)}, \widetilde{\Xi}^{(i)}))_{i \in \mathbb{N}}$ be i.i.d. random variables with $(\Xi^{(1)}, \widetilde{\Xi}^{(1)}) \sim (\Xi, \widetilde{\Xi})$. Then Bienaymé's identity and Fubini's theorem establish that

$$\mathbb{E}\left[\left\| g - g(0) - \frac{C_g}{n} \sum_{i=1}^{n} \Gamma(\Xi^{(i)}, \widetilde{\Xi}^{(i)}) \right\|_{L^2(\mu)}^2 \right]$$

$$= \int_{B_1(0)} \mathbb{V}\left[\frac{C_g}{n} \sum_{i=1}^{n} \Gamma(\Xi^{(i)}, \widetilde{\Xi}^{(i)})(x) \right] d\mu(x)$$

$$= \frac{C_g^2 \int_{B_1(0)} \mathbb{V}\big[\Gamma(\Xi, \widetilde{\Xi})(x)\big] \, d\mu(x)}{n} \le \frac{(2\pi C_g)^2}{n}, \tag{1.37}$$

where the last inequality follows from combining (1.36) with the fact that

$$|e^{2\pi i \langle x, \xi \rangle} - 1| / \|\xi\|_2 \le 2\pi, \quad x \in B_1(0).$$

This implies that there exists a realization $((\xi^{(i)}, \tilde{\xi}^{(i)}))_{i \in \mathbb{N}}$ of the random variables $((\Xi^{(i)}, \widetilde{\Xi}^{(i)}))_{i \in \mathbb{N}}$ that achieves an L^2-approximation error of $n^{-1/2}$. Therefore, it remains to show that NNs can well approximate the functions $((\Gamma(\xi^{(i)}, \tilde{\xi}^{(i)}))_{i \in \mathbb{N}}$. Now it is not hard to see that the function $1_{(0,\infty)}$ and hence functions of the form $\Gamma(\xi, \tilde{\xi})$, $\xi \in \mathbb{R}^d, \tilde{\xi} \in \mathbb{R}$, can be arbitrarily well approximated with a fixed-size, two-layer NN having a sigmoidal or ReLU activation function. Thus, we obtain an approximation rate of $n^{-1/2}$ when approximating functions with one finite Fourier moment by two-layer NNs with n hidden neurons.

It was pointed out in the dissertation of Emmanuel Candès (1998) that the approximation rate of NNs for Barron-regular functions is also achievable by *n*-term approximation with complex exponentials, as is apparent by considering (1.35). However, for deeper NNs, the results also extend to high-dimensional non-smooth functions, where Fourier-based methods are certain to suffer from the curse of dimensionality (Caragea et al., 2020).

In addition, the random sampling idea above was extended in E et al. (2019d, 2020), and E and Wojtowytsch (2020b,c) to facilitate the dimension-independent approximation of vastly more general function spaces. Basically, the idea is to use (1.36) as an inspiration and define a *generalized Barron space* as comprising all functions that may be represented as

$$\mathbb{E}\left[1_{(0,\infty)}(\langle \Xi, \cdot \rangle - \widetilde{\Xi})\right]$$

for any random variable $(\Xi, \widetilde{\Xi})$. In this context, deep and compositional versions of Barron spaces were introduced and studied in Barron and Klusowski (2018), E et al. (2019a), and E and Wojtowytsch (2020a), which considerably extend the original theory.

1.4.3 PDE Assumption

Another structural assumption that leads to the absence of the curse of dimensionality in some cases is that the function we are trying to approximate is given as the solution to a partial differential equation. It is by no means clear that this assumption leads to approximation without the curse of dimensionality, since most standard methods, such as finite elements, sparse grids, or spectral methods, typically do suffer from the curse of dimensionality.

This is not merely an abstract theoretical problem. Very recently, Al-Hamdani et al. (2020) showed that two different gold standard methods for solving the multi-electron Schrödinger equation produce completely different interaction energy predictions when applied to large delocalized molecules. Classical numerical representations are simply not expressive enough to represent accurately complicated high-dimensional structures such as wave functions with long-range interactions.

Interestingly, there exists an emerging body of work that shows that NNs do not suffer from these shortcomings and enjoy superior expressivity properties as compared to standard numerical representations. Such results include, for example, Grohs et al. (2021), Gonon and Schwab (2020), and Hutzenthaler et al. (2020) for (linear and semilinear) parabolic evolution equations, Elbrächter et al. (2019) for stationary elliptic PDEs, Grohs and Herrmann (2021) for nonlinear Hamilton–Jacobi–Bellman equations, and Kutyniok et al. (2019) for parametric PDEs. In all these cases, the absence of the curse of dimensionality in terms of the theoretical approximation power of NNs could be rigorously established.

One way to prove such results is via stochastic representations of the PDE solutions, as well as associated sampling methods. We illustrate the idea for the simple case of linear Kolmogorov PDEs; that is, the problem of representing the function $g\colon \mathbb{R}^d \times [0, \infty) \to \mathbb{R}$ satisfying[22]

$$\frac{\partial g}{\partial t}(x,t) = \frac{1}{2}\mathrm{Tr}\big(\sigma(x,t)[\sigma(x,t)]^*\nabla_x^2 g(x,t)\big) + \langle\mu(x,t),\nabla_x g(x,t)\rangle, \quad g(x,0) = \varphi(x),$$

(1.38)

where the functions

$$\varphi\colon \mathbb{R}^d \to \mathbb{R} \quad \text{(initial condition)} \quad \text{and}$$
$$\sigma\colon \mathbb{R}^d \to \mathbb{R}^{d\times d}, \quad \mu\colon \mathbb{R}^d \to \mathbb{R}^d \quad \text{(coefficient functions)}$$

are continuous and satisfy suitable growth conditions. A stochastic representation of g is given via the Ito processes $(S_{x,t})_{t\geq 0}$ satisfying

$$dS_{x,t} = \mu(S_{x,t})dt + \sigma(S_{x,t})dB_t, \quad S_{x,0} = x,$$

(1.39)

where $(B_t)_{t\geq 0}$ is a d-dimensional Brownian motion. Then g is described via the Feynman–Kac formula, which states that

$$g(x,t) = \mathbb{E}[\varphi(S_{x,t})], \quad x \in \mathbb{R}^d, t \in [0, \infty).$$

(1.40)

Roughly speaking, a NN approximation result can be proven by first approximating, via the law of large numbers, as follows:

$$g(x,t) = \mathbb{E}[\varphi(S_{x,t})] \approx \frac{1}{n}\sum_{i=1}^{n}\varphi(S_{x,t}^{(i)}),$$

(1.41)

where $(S_{x,t}^{(i)})_{i=1}^{n}$ are i.i.d. random variables with $S_{x,t}^{(1)} \sim S_{x,t}$. Care has to be taken to establish such an approximation *uniformly in the computational domain*, for example, for every (x,t) in the unit cube $[0,1]^d \times [0,1]$; see (1.37) for a similar estimate and Grohs et al. (2021) and Gonon and Schwab (2020) for two general approaches to ensure this property. Aside from this issue, (1.41) represents a standard Monte Carlo estimator which can be shown to be free of the curse of dimensionality.

As a next step, one needs to establish that realizations of the processes $(x,t) \mapsto S_{x,t}$ can be efficiently approximated by NNs. This can be achieved by emulating a suitable time-stepping scheme for the SDE (1.39) by NNs; this, roughly speaking, can be done without incurring the curse of dimensionality whenever the coefficient functions μ, σ can be approximated by NNs without incurring the curse of dimensionality and when some growth conditions hold true. In a final step one assumes that the initial condition φ can be approximated by NNs without incurring the curse

---

[22] The natural solution concept to this type of PDEs is the viscosity solution concept, a thorough study of which can be found in Hairer et al. (2015).

of dimensionality which, by the compositionality of NNs and the previous step, directly implies that realizations of the processes $(x,t) \mapsto \varphi(S_{x,t})$ can be approximated by NNs without incurring the curse of dimensionality. By (1.41) this implies a corresponding approximation result for the solution of the Kolmogorov PDE g in (1.38).

Informally, we have discovered a regularity result for linear Kolmogorov equations, namely that (modulo some technical conditions on μ, σ), *the solution g of* (1.38) *can be approximated by NNs without incurring the curse of dimensionality whenever the same holds true for the initial condition φ, as well as for the coefficient functions μ and σ.* In other words, *the property of being approximable by NNs without curse of dimensionality is preserved under the flow induced by the PDE* (1.38). Some comments are in order.

Assumption on the initial condition. One may wonder if the assumption that the initial condition φ can be approximated by NNs without incurring the curse of dimensionality is justified. This is at least the case in many applications in computational finance where the function φ typically represents an option pricing formula and (1.38) represents the famous Black–Scholes model. It turns out that nearly all common option pricing formulas are constructed from iterative applications of linear maps and maximum/minimum functions – in other words, in many applications in computational finance, the initial condition φ can be *exactly* represented by a small ReLU NN.

Generalization and optimization error. The Feynman–Kac representation (1.40) directly implies that $g(\cdot,t)$ can be computed as the Bayes optimal function of a regression task with input features $X \sim \mathcal{U}([0,1]^d)$ and labels $Y = \varphi(S_{X,t})$, which allows for an analysis of the generalization error as well as implementations based on ERM algorithms (Beck et al., 2021; Berner et al., 2020a).

While it is in principle possible to analyze the approximation and generalization errors, the analysis of the computational cost and/or convergence of the corresponding SGD algorithms is completely open. Some promising numerical results exist – see, for instance, Figure 1.13 – but the stable training of NNs approximating PDEs to very high accuracy (which is needed in several applications such as quantum chemistry) remains very challenging. Recent work (Grohs and Voigtlaender, 2021) has even proved several impossibility results in that direction.

Extensions and abstract idea. Similar techniques may be used to prove expressivity results for nonlinear PDEs, for example, using nonlinear Feynman–Kac-type representations of Pardoux and Peng (1992) in place of (1.40) and multilevel Picard sampling algorithms of E et al. (2019c) in place of (1.41).

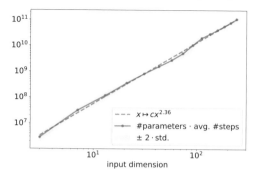

Figure 1.13 Computational complexity as the number of neural network parameters times the number of SGD steps needed to solve heat equations of varying dimensions up to a specified precision. According to the fit above, the scaling is polynomial in the dimension (Berner et al., 2020b).

We can also formulate the underlying idea in an abstract setting (a version of which has also been used in §1.4.2). Assume that a high-dimensional function $g: \mathbb{R}^d \to \mathbb{R}$ admits a probabilistic representation of the form

$$g(x) = \mathbb{E}[Y_x], \quad x \in \mathbb{R}^d, \tag{1.42}$$

for some random variable Y_x which can be approximated by an iterative scheme

$$\mathcal{Y}_x^{(L)} \approx Y_x \quad \text{and} \quad \mathcal{Y}_x^{(\ell)} = T_\ell(\mathcal{Y}_x^{(\ell-1)}), \quad \ell = 1, \ldots, L,$$

with dimension-independent convergence rate. If we can approximate realizations of the initial mapping $x \mapsto \mathcal{Y}_x^0$ and the maps T_ℓ, $\ell \in [L]$, by NNs and if the numerical scheme is stable enough, then we can also approximate $\mathcal{Y}_x^{(L)}$ using compositionality. Emulating a uniform Monte-Carlo approximator of (1.42) then leads to approximation results for g without the curse of dimensionality. In addition, one can choose a $\mathbb{R}^d$-valued random variable X as input features and define the corresponding labels by Y_X to obtain a prediction task, which can be solved by means of ERM.

Other methods. There exist a number of additional works related to the approximation capacities of NNs for high-dimensional PDEs, for example, Elbrächter et al. (2018), Li et al. (2019a), and Schwab and Zech (2019). In most of these works, the proof technique consists of emulating an existing method that does not suffer from the curse of dimensionality. For instance, in the case of first-order transport equations, one can show in some cases that NNs are capable of emulating the method of characteristics, which then also yields approximation results that are free of the curse of dimensionality (Laakmann and Petersen, 2021).

1.5 Optimization of Deep Neural Networks

We recall from §§1.1.3 and 1.1.2 that the standard algorithm to solve the empirical risk minimization problem over the hypothesis set of NNs is stochastic gradient descent. This method would be guaranteed to converge to a global minimum of the objective if the empirical risk were convex, viewed as a function of the NN parameters. However, this function is severely non-convex; it may exhibit (higher-order) saddle points, seriously suboptimal local minima, and wide flat areas where the gradient is very small.

On the other hand, in applications, an excellent performance of SGD is observed. This indicates that the trajectory of the optimization routine somehow misses sub-optimal critical points and other areas that may lead to slow convergence. Clearly, the classical theory does not explain this performance. Below we describe using examples some novel approaches that give partial explanations of this success.

In keeping with the flavor of this chapter, the aim of this section is to present some selected ideas rather than giving an overview of the literature. To give at least some detail about the underlying ideas and to keep the length of this section reasonable, a selection of results has had to be made and some ground-breaking results have had to be omitted.

1.5.1 Loss Landscape Analysis

Given a NN $\Phi(\cdot,\theta)$ and training data $s \in Z^m$, the function $\theta \mapsto r(\theta) := \widehat{\mathcal{R}}_s(\Phi(\cdot,\theta))$ describes, in a natural way through its graph, a high-dimensional surface. This surface may have regions associated with lower values of $\widehat{\mathcal{R}}_s$ which resemble valleys of a landscape if they are surrounded by regions of higher values. The analysis of the topography of this surface is called *loss landscape analysis*. Below we shall discuss a couple of approaches that yield deep insights into the shape of such a landscape.

Spin glass interpretation. One of the first discoveries about the shape of the loss landscape comes from deep results in statistical physics. The Hamiltonian of the *spin glass model* is a random function on the $(n-1)$-dimensional sphere of radius $\sqrt{n}$. Making certain simplifying assumptions, it was shown in Choromanska et al. (2015a) that the loss associated with a NN with random inputs can be considered as the Hamiltonian of a spin glass model, where the inputs of the model are the parameters of the NN.

This connection has far-reaching implications for the loss landscape of NNs because of the following surprising property of the Hamiltonian of spin glass models. Consider the critical points of the Hamiltonian, and associate with each

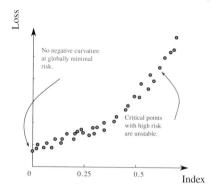

Figure 1.14 The distribution of critical points of the Hamiltonian of a spin glass model.

point an *index* that denotes the percentage of the eigenvalues of the Hessian at that point which are negative. This index corresponds to the relative number of directions in which the loss landscape has negative curvature. Then, with high probability, a picture like that in Figure 1.14 emerges (Auffinger et al., 2013). More precisely, the further away from the optimal loss we are, the more unstable the critical points become. Conversely, if one finds oneself in a local minimum, it is reasonable to assume that the loss is close to the global minimum.

While some of the assumptions establishing the connection between the spin glass model and NNs are unrealistic in practice (Choromanska et al., 2015b), the theoretical distribution of critical points in Figure 1.14 is visible in many practical applications (Dauphin et al., 2014).

Paths and level sets. Another line of research is to understand the loss landscape by analyzing paths through the parameter space, in particular, the existence of paths in parameter space such that the associated empirical risks are monotone along the path. Should there exist a path of non-increasing empirical risk from every point to the global minimum, then we can be certain that no non-global minimum exists, since no such path could escape such a minimum. An even stronger result holds: the existence of such paths shows that the loss landscape has connected level sets (Freeman and Bruna, 2017; Venturi et al., 2019).

A crucial ingredient of the analysis of such paths is *linear substructures*. Consider a biasless two-layer NN Φ of the form

$$\mathbb{R}^d \ni x \mapsto \Phi(x,\theta) := \sum_{j=1}^{n} \theta_j^{(2)} \varrho\left(\left\langle \theta_j^{(1)}, \begin{bmatrix} x \\ 1 \end{bmatrix} \right\rangle\right), \tag{1.43}$$

where $\theta_j^{(1)} \in \mathbb{R}^{d+1}$ for $j \in [n]$, $\theta^{(2)} \in \mathbb{R}^n$, ϱ is a Lipschitz continuous activation function, and we have augmented the vector x by a constant 1 in the last coordinate

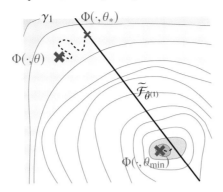

Figure 1.15 Construction of a path from an initial point θ to the global minimum $\theta_{\min}$ that does not have significantly higher risk than the initial point along the way. We depict here the landscape as a function of the neural network realizations rather than of their parametrizations, so that this landscape is convex.

as outlined in Remark 1.5. If we consider $\theta^{(1)}$ to be fixed then it is clear that the space

$$\widetilde{\mathcal{F}}_{\theta^{(1)}} := \{\Phi(\cdot, \theta) \colon \theta = (\theta^{(1)}, \theta^{(2)}), \; \theta^{(2)} \in \mathbb{R}^n\} \tag{1.44}$$

is a linear space. If the risk[23] is convex, as is the case for the widely used quadratic or logistic losses, then this implies that $\theta^{(2)} \mapsto r\big((\theta^{(1)}, \theta^{(2)})\big)$ is a convex map and hence, for every parameter set $\mathcal{P} \subset \mathbb{R}^n$ this map assumes its maximum on $\partial \mathcal{P}$. Therefore, within the vast parameter space, there are many paths one may travel upon that do not increase the risk above the risk of the start and end points.

This idea was used in, for example, Freeman and Bruna (2017) in a way indicated by the following simple sketch. Assume that, for two parameters θ and $\theta_{\min}$, there exists a linear subspace of NNs $\widetilde{\mathcal{F}}_{\hat{\theta}^{(1)}}$ such that there are paths γ_1 and γ_2 connecting $\Phi(\cdot, \theta)$ and $\Phi(\cdot, \theta_{\min})$ respectively to $\widetilde{\mathcal{F}}_{\hat{\theta}^{(1)}}$. Further, assume that these paths are such that, along them, the risk does not significantly exceed $\max\{r(\theta), r(\theta_{\min})\}$. Figure 1.15 shows a visualization of these paths. In this case, a path from θ to $\theta_{\min}$ not significantly exceeding $r(\theta)$ along the way is found by concatenating the path γ_1, a path along $\widetilde{\mathcal{F}}_{\hat{\theta}^{(1)}}$, and the path γ_2. By the previous discussion, we know that only γ_1 and γ_2 determine the extent to which the combined path exceeds $r(\theta)$ along its way. Hence, we need to ask about the existence of an $\widetilde{\mathcal{F}}_{\hat{\theta}^{(1)}}$ that facilitates the construction of appropriate γ_1 and γ_2.

To understand why a good choice of $\widetilde{\mathcal{F}}_{\hat{\theta}^{(1)}}$, such that the risk along γ_1 and γ_2 will

---

[23] As most statements in this subsection are valid for the empirical risk $r(\theta) = \widehat{\mathcal{R}}_s(\Phi(\cdot, \theta))$ as well as the risk $r(\theta) = \mathcal{R}(\Phi(\cdot, \theta))$, given a suitable data distribution of Z, we will just call r the risk.

not rise much higher than $r(\theta)$, is likely to be possible we set[24]

$$\hat{\theta}^{(1)}_j := \begin{cases} \theta^{(1)}_j & \text{for } j \in [n/2], \\ (\theta^{(1)}_{\min})_j & \text{for } j \in [n] \setminus [n/2]. \end{cases} \tag{1.45}$$

In other words, the first half of $\hat{\theta}^{(1)}$ is constructed from $\theta^{(1)}$ and the second from $\theta^{(1)}_{\min}$. If $\theta^{(1)}_j$, $j \in [N]$, are realizations of random variables distributed uniformly on the d-dimensional unit sphere, then, by invoking standard covering bounds of spheres (e.g., Corollary 4.2.13 of Vershynin, 2018), we expect that, for $\varepsilon > 0$ and a sufficiently large number of neurons n, the vectors $(\theta^{(1)}_j)^{n/2}_{j=1}$ already ε-approximate all vectors $(\theta^{(1)}_j)^{n}_{j=1}$. Replacing all vectors $(\theta^{(1)}_j)^{n}_{j=1}$ by their nearest neighbor in $(\theta^{(1)}_j)^{n/2}_{j=1}$ can be done using a linear path in the parameter space, and, given that r is locally Lipschitz continuous and $\|\theta^{(2)}\|_1$ is bounded, this operation will not increase the risk by more than $O(\varepsilon)$. We denote the vector resulting from this replacement procedure by $\theta^{(1)}_*$. Since for all $j \in [n] \setminus [n/2]$ we now have that

$$\varrho\left(\left\langle (\theta^{(1)}_*)_j, \begin{bmatrix} \cdot \\ 1 \end{bmatrix} \right\rangle\right) \in \left\{ \varrho\left(\left\langle (\theta^{(1)}_*)_k, \begin{bmatrix} \cdot \\ 1 \end{bmatrix} \right\rangle\right) : k \in [n/2] \right\},$$

there exists a vector $\theta^{(2)}_*$ with $(\theta^{(2)}_*)_j = 0$, $j \in [n] \setminus [n/2]$, so that

$$\Phi(\cdot, (\theta^{(1)}_*, \theta^{(2)})) = \Phi(\cdot, (\theta^{(1)}_*, \lambda\theta^{(2)}_* + (1 - \lambda)\theta^{(2)})), \quad \lambda \in [0, 1].$$

In particular, this path does not change the risk between $(\theta^{(1)}_*, \theta^{(2)})$ and $(\theta^{(1)}_*, \theta^{(2)}_*)$. Now, since $(\theta^{(2)}_*)_j = 0$ for $j \in [n] \setminus [n/2]$, the realization $\Phi(\cdot, (\theta^{(1)}_*, \theta^{(2)}_*))$ is computed by a subnetwork consisting of the first $n/2$ hidden neurons, and we can replace the parameters corresponding to the other neurons without any effect on the realization function. Specifically, we have

$$\Phi(\cdot, (\theta^{(1)}_*, \theta^{(2)}_*)) = \Phi(\cdot, (\lambda\hat{\theta}^{(1)} + (1 - \lambda)\theta^{(1)}_*, \theta^{(2)}_*)), \quad \lambda \in [0, 1],$$

yielding a path of constant risk between $(\theta^{(1)}_*, \theta^{(2)}_*)$ and $(\hat{\theta}^{(1)}, \theta^{(2)}_*)$. Connecting these paths completes the construction of γ_1 and shows that the risk along γ_1 does not exceed that at θ by more than $O(\varepsilon)$. Of course, γ_2 can be constructed in the same way. The entire construction is depicted in Figure 1.15.

Overall, this derivation shows that for sufficiently wide NNs (appropriately randomly initialized) it is very likely possible to connect a random parameter value to the global minimum with a path which along the way does not need to climb much higher than the initial risk.

In Venturi et al. (2019), a similar approach is taken and the convexity in the last layer is used. However, the authors invoke the concept of intrinsic dimension to

---

[24] We assume, without loss of generality, that n is a multiple of 2.

solve elegantly the nonlinearity of $r((\theta^{(1)}, \theta^{(2)}))$ with respect to $\theta^{(1)}$. Also Safran and Shamir (2016) had already constructed a path of decreasing risk from random initializations. The idea here is that if one starts at a point of sufficiently high risk, one can always find a path to the global optimum with strictly decreasing risk. The intriguing insight behind this result is that if the initialization is sufficiently bad, i.e., worse than that of a NN outputting only zero, then there exist two operations that influence the risk directly. Multiplying the last layer with a number smaller than 1 will decrease the risk, whereas choosing a number larger than 1 will increase it. Using this tuning mechanism, any given potentially non-monotone path from the initialization to the global minimum can be modified so that it is strictly monotonically decreasing. In a similar spirit, Nguyen and Hein (2017) showed that if a deep NN has a layer with more neurons than training data points, then under certain assumptions the training data will typically be mapped to linearly independent points in that layer. Of course, this layer could then be composed with a linear map that maps the linearly independent points to any desirable output, in particular one that achieves vanishing empirical risk; see also Proposition 1.17. As in the case of two-layer NNs, the previous discussion on linear paths shows immediately that in this situation a monotone path to the global minimum exists.

1.5.2 Lazy Training and Provable Convergence of Stochastic Gradient Descent

When training highly overparametrized NNs, one often observes that the parameters of the NNs barely change during training. In Figure 1.16, we show the relative distance traveled by the parameters through the parameter space during the training of NNs of varying numbers of neurons per layer.

The effect described above has been observed repeatedly and has been explained theoretically: see e.g.,Du et al. (2018b, 2019), Li and Liang (2018), Allen-Zhu et al. (2019), and Zou et al. (2020). In §1.2.1, we have already given a high-level overview and, in particular, we discussed the function space perspective of this phenomenon in the infinite-width limit. Below we present a short and highly simplified derivation of this effect and show how it leads to the provable convergence of gradient descent for sufficiently overparametrized deep NNs.

A simple learning model. We consider again the simple NN model of (1.43) with a smooth activation function ϱ which is not affine linear. For a quadratic loss and training data $s = ((x^{(i)}, y^{(i)}))_{i=1}^{m} \in (\mathbb{R}^d \times \mathbb{R})^m$, where $x_i \neq x_j$ for all $i \neq j$, the empirical risk is given by

$$r(\theta) = \widehat{\mathcal{R}}_s(\theta) = \frac{1}{m} \sum_{i=1}^{m} (\Phi(x^{(i)}, \theta) - y^{(i)})^2.$$

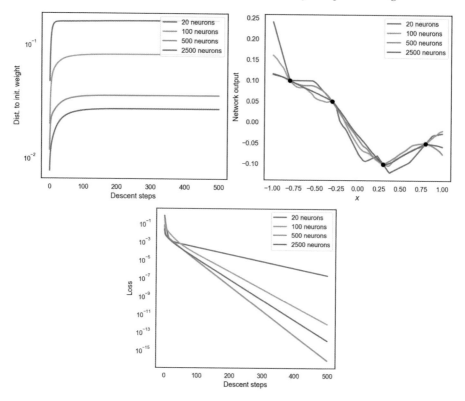

Figure 1.16 Four networks with architecture $((1, n, n, 1), \varrho_R)$ and $n \in \{20, 100, 500, 2500\}$ neurons per hidden layer were trained by gradient descent to fit the four points shown in the top right figure as black dots. We depict on the top left the relative Euclidean distance of the parameters from the initialization through the training process. In the top right, we show the final trained NNs. On the bottom we show the behavior of the training error.

Let us further assume that $\Theta_j^{(1)} \sim \mathcal{N}(0, 1/n)^{d+1}$, $j \in [n]$, and $\Theta_j^{(2)} \sim \mathcal{N}(0, 1/n)$, $j \in [n]$, are independent random variables.

A peculiar kernel. Next we would like to understand what the gradient $\nabla_\theta r(\Theta)$ looks like, with high probability, over the initialization $\Theta = (\Theta^{(1)}, \Theta^{(2)})$. As with Equation (1.22), by restricting the gradient to $\theta^{(2)}$ and applying the chain rule, we have that

$$\|\nabla_\theta r(\Theta)\|_2^2 \geq \frac{4}{m^2} \left\| \sum_{i=1}^{m} \nabla_{\theta^{(2)}} \Phi(x^{(i)}, \Theta)(\Phi(x^{(i)}, \Theta) - y^{(i)}) \right\|_2^2$$

$$= \frac{4}{m^2} \left((\Phi(x^{(i)}, \Theta) - y^{(i)})_{i=1}^{m} \right)^T \bar{K}_\Theta (\Phi(x^{(j)}, \Theta) - y^{(j)})_{j=1}^{m}, \qquad (1.46)$$

where $\bar{K}_\Theta$ is a random $\mathbb{R}^{m \times m}$-valued kernel given by

$$(\bar{K}_\Theta)_{i,j} := \left(\nabla_{\theta^{(2)}} \Phi(x^{(i)}, \Theta)\right)^T \nabla_{\theta^{(2)}} \Phi(x^{(j)}, \Theta), \quad i, j \in [m].$$

This kernel is closely related to the neural tangent kernel in (1.23) evaluated at the features $(x^{(i)})_{i=1}^m$ and the random initialization Θ. It is a slightly simplified version thereof because, in (1.23), the gradient is taken with respect to the full vector θ. This can also be regarded as the kernel associated with a *random features model* (Rahimi et al., 2007).

Note that for our two-layer NN we have that

$$\left(\nabla_{\theta^{(2)}} \Phi(x, \Theta)\right)_k = \varrho\left(\left\langle \Theta_k^{(1)}, \begin{bmatrix} x \\ 1 \end{bmatrix} \right\rangle\right), \quad x \in \mathbb{R}^d, \ k \in [n]. \tag{1.47}$$

Thus, we can write $\bar{K}_\Theta$ as the following sum of (random) rank-1 matrices:

$$\bar{K}_\Theta = \sum_{k=1}^n v_k v_k^T \quad \text{with} \quad v_k = \left(\varrho\left(\left\langle \Theta_k^{(1)}, \begin{bmatrix} x^{(i)} \\ 1 \end{bmatrix} \right\rangle\right)\right)_{i=1}^m \in \mathbb{R}^m, \quad k \in [n]. \tag{1.48}$$

The kernel $\bar{K}_\Theta$ is symmetric and positive semi-definite by construction. It is positive definite if it is non-singular, i.e., if at least m of the n vectors v_k, $k \in [n]$, are linearly independent. Proposition 1.17 shows that for $n = m$ the probability of that event is non-zero, say δ, and is therefore at least $1 - (1 - \delta)^{\lfloor n/m \rfloor}$ for arbitrary n. In other words, the probability increases rapidly with n. It is also clear from (1.48) that $\mathbb{E}[\bar{K}_\Theta]$ scales linearly with n.

From this intuitive derivation we conclude that, for sufficiently large n, with high probability $\bar{K}_\Theta$ is a positive definite kernel with smallest eigenvalue $\lambda_{\min}(\bar{K}_\Theta)$ scaling linearly with n. The properties of $\bar{K}_\Theta$, in particular its positive definiteness, have been studied much more rigorously, as already described in §1.2.1.

Control of the gradient. Applying the expected behavior of the smallest eigenvalue $\lambda_{\min}(\bar{K}_\Theta)$ of $\bar{K}_\Theta$ to (1.46), we conclude that with high probability

$$\|\nabla_\theta r(\Theta)\|_2^2 \geq \frac{4}{m^2} \lambda_{\min}(\bar{K}_\Theta) \|(\Phi(x^{(i)}, \Theta) - y^{(i)})_{i=1}^m\|_2^2 \gtrsim \frac{n}{m} r(\Theta). \tag{1.49}$$

To understand what will happen when applying gradient descent, we first need to understand how the situation changes in a neighborhood of Θ. We fix $x \in \mathbb{R}^d$ and observe that, by the mean value theorem for all $\bar{\theta} \in B_1(0)$, we have

$$\left\|\nabla_\theta \Phi(x, \Theta) - \nabla_\theta \Phi(x, \Theta + \bar{\theta})\right\|_2^2 \lesssim \sup_{\hat{\theta} \in B_1(0)} \left\|\nabla_\theta^2 \Phi(x, \Theta + \hat{\theta})\right\|_{\mathrm{op}}^2, \tag{1.50}$$

where $\|\nabla_\theta^2 \Phi(x, \Theta + \hat{\theta})\|_{\mathrm{op}}$ denotes the operator norm of the Hessian of $\Phi(x, \cdot)$ at $\Theta + \hat{\theta}$.

By inspecting (1.43), it is not hard to see that, for all $i, j \in [n]$ and $k, \ell \in [d+1]$,

$$\mathbb{E}\left[\left(\frac{\partial^2 \Phi(x, \Theta)}{\partial \theta_i^{(2)} \partial \theta_j^{(2)}}\right)^2\right] = 0, \quad \mathbb{E}\left[\left(\frac{\partial^2 \Phi(x, \Theta)}{\partial \theta_i^{(2)} \partial (\theta_j^{(1)})_k}\right)^2\right] \lesssim \delta_{i,j}, \quad \text{and}$$

$$\mathbb{E}\left[\left(\frac{\partial^2 \Phi(x, \Theta)}{\partial (\theta_i^{(1)})_k \partial (\theta_j^{(1)})_\ell}\right)^2\right] \lesssim \frac{\delta_{i,j}}{n},$$

where $\delta_{i,j} = 0$ if $i \neq j$ and $\delta_{i,i} = 1$ for all $i, j \in [n]$. For sufficiently large n, we have that $\nabla_\theta^2 \Phi(x, \Theta)$ is in expectation approximately a block-band matrix with bandwidth $d + 1$. Therefore we conclude that $\mathbb{E}[\|\nabla_\theta^2 \Phi(x, \Theta)\|_{op}^2] \lesssim 1$. Hence we obtain by the concentration of Gaussian random variables that with high probability, $\|\nabla_\theta^2 \Phi(x, \Theta)\|_{op}^2 \lesssim 1$. By the block-banded form of $\nabla_\theta^2 \Phi(x, \Theta)$ we have that, even after perturbation of Θ by a vector $\hat{\theta}$ with norm bounded by 1, the term $\|\nabla_\theta^2 \Phi(x, \Theta + \hat{\theta})\|_{op}^2$ is still bounded, which yields that the right-hand side of (1.50) is bounded with high probability.

Using (1.50), we can extend (1.49), which holds with high probability, to a neighborhood of Θ by the following argument. Let $\bar{\theta} \in B_1(0)$; then

$$\|\nabla_\theta r(\Theta + \bar{\theta})\|_2^2 \geq \frac{4}{m^2}\left\|\sum_{i=1}^{m} \nabla_{\theta^{(2)}} \Phi(x^{(i)}, \Theta + \bar{\theta})(\Phi(x^{(i)}, \Theta + \bar{\theta}) - y^{(i)})\right\|_2^2$$

$$\underset{(1.50)}{=} \frac{4}{m^2}\left\|\sum_{i=1}^{m} (\nabla_{\theta^{(2)}} \Phi(x^{(i)}, \Theta) + O(1))(\Phi(x^{(i)}, \Theta + \bar{\theta}) - y^{(i)})\right\|_2^2$$

$$\underset{(*)}{\geq} \frac{1}{m^2}(\lambda_{min}(\bar{K}_\Theta) + O(1))\|(\Phi(x^{(i)}, \Theta + \bar{\theta}) - y^{(i)})_{i=1}^{m}\|_2^2$$

$$\underset{(*)}{\geq} \frac{n}{m} r(\Theta + \bar{\theta}), \tag{1.51}$$

where the estimate marked by $(*)$ uses the positive definiteness of $\bar{K}_\Theta$ again and only holds for n sufficiently large, so that the $O(1)$ term is negligible.

We conclude that, with high probability over the initialization Θ, on a ball of fixed radius around Θ the squared Euclidean norm of the gradient of the empirical risk is lower bounded by n/m times the empirical risk.

Exponential convergence of gradient descent. For sufficiently small step sizes η, the observation in the previous paragraph yields the following convergence rate for gradient descent as in Algorithm 1.1, specifically (1.8), with $m' = m$ and $\Theta^{(0)} = \Theta$:

if $\|\Theta^{(k)} - \Theta\| \leq 1$ for all $k \in [K + 1]$, then[25]

$$r(\Theta^{(K+1)}) \approx r(\Theta^{(K)}) - \eta\|\nabla_\theta r(\Theta^{(K)})\|_2^2 \leq \left(1 - \frac{c\eta n}{m}\right) r(\Theta^{(K)}) \lesssim \left(1 - \frac{c\eta n}{m}\right)^K, \quad (1.52)$$

for $c \in (0, \infty)$ so that $\|\nabla_\theta r(\Theta^{(k)})\|_2^2 \geq \frac{cn}{m} r(\Theta^{(k)})$ for all $k \in [K]$.

Let us assume without proof that the estimate (1.51) could be extended to an equivalence. In other words, we assume that we additionally have that $\|\nabla_\theta r(\Theta + \bar{\theta})\|_2^2 \lesssim \frac{n}{m} r(\Theta + \bar{\theta})$. This, of course, could have been shown with tools similar to those used for the lower bound. Then we have that $\|\Theta^{(k)} - \Theta\|_2 \leq 1$ for all $k \lesssim \sqrt{m/(\eta^2 n)}$. Setting $t = \sqrt{m/(\eta^2 n)}$ and using the limit definition of the exponential function, i.e., $\lim_{t \to \infty}(1 - x/t)^t = e^{-x}$, yields, for sufficiently small η, that (1.52) is bounded by $e^{-c\sqrt{n/m}}$.

We conclude that, with high probability over the initialization, *gradient descent converges at an exponential rate to an arbitrarily small empirical risk if the width n is sufficiently large. In addition, the iterates of the descent algorithm even stay in a small fixed neighborhood of the initialization during training.* Because the parameters only move very little, this type of training has also been coined lazy training (Chizat et al., 2019).

Ideas similar to those above have led to groundbreaking convergence results of SGD for overparametrized NNs in much more complex and general settings; see, e.g., Du et al. (2018b), Li and Liang (2018), and Allen-Zhu et al. (2019).

In the infinite-width limit, NN training is practically equivalent to kernel regression; see §1.2.1. If we look at Figure 1.16 we see that the most overparametrized NN interpolates the data in the same way as a kernel-based interpolator would. In a sense, which was also highlighted in Chizat et al. (2019), this shows that, while overparametrized NNs in the lazy training regime have very nice properties, they essentially act like linear methods.

1.6 Tangible Effects of Special Architectures

In this section we describe results that isolate the effects of certain aspects of NN architectures. As discussed in §1.1.3, typically only either the depth or the number of parameters is used to study theoretical aspects of NNs. We have seen instances of this throughout §§1.3 and 1.4. Moreover, in §1.5, we saw that wider NNs enjoy certain very favorable properties from an optimization point of view.

Below, we introduce certain specialized NN architectures. We start with one of the most widely used types of NNs, the *convolutional neural network* (CNN). In §1.6.2 we introduce *skip connections* and in §1.6.3 we discuss a specific class

---

[25] Note that the step size η needs to be small enough to facilitate the approximation step in (1.52). Hence, we cannot simply put $\eta = m/(cn)$ in (1.52) and have convergence after one step.

of CNNs equipped with an encoder–decoder structure that is frequently used in image processing techniques. We introduce the *batch normalization block* in §1.6.4. Then, in §1.6.5, we discuss the *sparsely connected* NNs that typically result as an extraction from fully connected NNs. Finally, we briefly comment on recurrent neural networks in §1.6.6.

As we have noted repeatedly throughout this chapter, it is impossible to give a full account of the literature in a short introductory article. In this section this issue is especially severe since the number of special architectures studied in practice is enormous. Therefore, we have had to omit many very influential and widely used neural network architectures. Among those are *graph neural networks*, which handle data from non-Euclidean input spaces. We refer to the survey articles by Bronstein et al. (2017) and Wu et al. (2021) for a discussion. Another highly successful type of architecture comprises *(variational) autoencoders* (Ackley et al., 1985; Hinton and Zemel, 1994). These are neural networks with a bottleneck that enforce a more efficient representation of the data. Similarly, *generative adversarial networks* (Goodfellow et al., 2014), which are composed of two neural networks – one generator and one discriminator – could not be discussed here. Yet another widely used component of architectures used in practice is the so-called *dropout layer*. This layer functions through removing some neurons randomly during training. This procedure empirically prevents overfitting. An in-detail discussion of the mathematical analysis behind this effect is beyond the scope of this chapter. Instead, we refer to Wan et al. (2013), Srivastava et al. (2014), Haeffele and Vidal (2017), and Mianjy et al. (2018). Finally, the very successful *attention mechanism* (Bahdanau et al., 2015; Vaswani et al., 2017), which is the basis of *transformer neural networks*, had to be omitted.

Before we start describing certain effects of special NN architectures, a word of warning is required. The special building blocks that will be presented below have been developed on the basis of a specific need in applications and are used and combined in a very flexible way. To describe these tools theoretically without completely inflating the notational load, some simplifying assumptions need to be made. It is very likely that the building blocks thus simplified do not accurately reflect the practical applications of these tools in all use cases.

1.6.1 Convolutional Neural Networks

Especially for very high-dimensional inputs where the input dimensions are spatially related, fully connected NNs seem to require unnecessarily many parameters. For example, in image classification problems, neighboring pixels very often share information and the spatial proximity should be reflected in the architecture. From this observation, it appears reasonable to have NNs that have local receptive fields in the sense that they collect information jointly from spatially close inputs. In addition, in image processing we are not necessarily interested in a universal hypothesis set. A good classifier is invariant under many operations, such as the translation or rotation of images. It seems reasonable to hard-code such invariances into the architecture.

These two principles suggest that the receptive field of a NN should be the same on different translated patches of the input. In this sense, the parameters of the architecture can be reused. Together, these arguments make up the three fundamental principles of convolutional NNs: local receptive fields, parameter sharing, and equivariant representations, as introduced in LeCun et al. (1989a). We will provide a mathematical formulation of convolutional NNs below and then revisit these concepts.

A convolutional NN corresponds to multiple convolutional blocks, which are special types of layers. For a group G, which typically is either $[d] \cong \mathbb{Z}/(d\mathbb{Z})$ or $[d]^2 \cong (\mathbb{Z}/(d\mathbb{Z}))^2$ for $d \in \mathbb{N}$, depending on whether we are performing one-dimensional or two-dimensional convolutions, the convolution of two vectors $a, b \in \mathbb{R}^G$ is defined as

$$(a * b)_i = \sum_{j \in G} a_j b_{j^{-1}i}, \quad i \in G.$$

Now we can define a *convolutional block* as follows. Let $\widetilde{G}$ be a subgroup of G, let $p: G \to \widetilde{G}$ be a so-called *pooling operator*, and let $C \in \mathbb{N}$ denote the number of channels. Then, for a series of kernels $\kappa_i \in \mathbb{R}^G, i \in [C]$, the output of a convolutional block is given by

$$\mathbb{R}^G \ni x \mapsto x' := (p(x * \kappa_i))_{i=1}^C \in (\mathbb{R}^{\widetilde{G}})^C. \tag{1.53}$$

A typical example of a pooling operator is, for $G = (\mathbb{Z}/(2d\mathbb{Z}))^2$ and $\widetilde{G} = (\mathbb{Z}/(d\mathbb{Z}))^2$, the 2×2 subsampling operator

$$p: \mathbb{R}^G \to \mathbb{R}^{\widetilde{G}}, \quad x \mapsto (x_{2i-1,2j-1})_{i,j=1}^d.$$

Popular alternatives are average pooling or max pooling. These operations then either compute the average or the maximum over patches of similar size. The convolutional kernels correspond to the aforementioned receptive fields. They can be thought of as local if they have small supports, i.e., few non-zero entries.

As explained earlier, a convolutional NN is built by stacking multiple convolutional blocks one after another.[26] At some point, the output can be *flattened*, i.e., mapped to a vector, and is then fed into an FC NN (see Definition 1.4). We depict this set-up in Figure 1.17.

---

[26] We assume that the definition of a convolutional block is suitably extended to input data in the Cartesian product $(\mathbb{R}^G)^C$. For instance, one can take an affine linear combination of C mappings as in (1.53) acting on each coordinate. Moreover, one may also interject an activation function between the blocks.

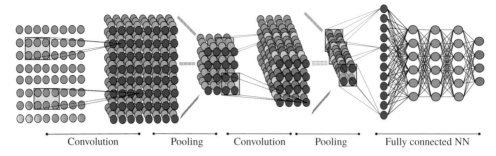

Figure 1.17 Illustration of a convolutional neural network with two-dimensional convolutional blocks and 2×2 subsampling as the pooling operation.

Owing to the fact that convolution is a linear operation, depending on the pooling operation, one may write a convolutional block (1.53) as an FC NN. For example, if $G = (\mathbb{Z}/(2d\mathbb{Z}))^2$ and the 2×2 subsampling pooling operator is used, then the convolutional block could be written as $x \mapsto Wx$ for a block-circulant matrix $W \in \mathbb{R}^{(Cd^2) \times (2d)^2}$. Since we require W to have a special structure, we can interpret a convolutional block as a special, restricted, feed-forward architecture.

After these considerations, it is natural to ask how the restriction of a NN to a pure convolutional structure, i.e., one consisting only of convolutional blocks, will affect the resulting hypothesis set. The first natural question is whether the set of such NNs is still universal in the sense of Theorem 1.16. The answer to this question depends strongly on the type of pooling and convolution that is allowed. If the convolution is performed with padding then the answer is yes (Oono and Suzuki, 2019; Zhou, 2020b). On the other hand, for circular convolutions and without pooling, universality does not hold but the set of translation-equivariant functions can be universally approximated (Yarotsky, 2018b; Petersen and Voigtlaender, 2020). Furthermore, Yarotsky (2018b) illuminates the effect of subsample pooling by showing that if no pooling is applied then universality cannot be achieved, whereas if pooling is applied then universality is possible. The effect of subsampling in CNNs from the viewpoint of approximation theory is further discussed in Zhou (2020a). The role of other types of pooling in enhancing invariances of the hypothesis set will be discussed in §1.7.1 below.

1.6.2 Residual Neural Networks

Let us first illustrate a potential obstacle when training deep NNs. Consider for $L \in \mathbb{N}$ the product operation

$$\mathbb{R}^L \ni x \mapsto \pi(x) = \prod_{\ell=1}^{L} x_\ell.$$

It is clear that

$$\frac{\partial}{\partial x_k} \pi(x) = \prod_{\ell \neq k}^{L} x_\ell, \quad x \in \mathbb{R}^L.$$

Therefore, for sufficiently large L, we expect that $\left|\frac{\partial \pi}{\partial x_k}\right|$ will be exponentially small, if $|x_\ell| < \lambda < 1$ for all $\ell \in [L]$; or exponentially large, if $|x_\ell| > \lambda > 1$ for all $\ell \in [L]$. The output of a general NN, considered as a directed graph, is found by repeatedly multiplying the input with parameters in every layer along the paths that lead from the input to the output neuron. Owing to the aforementioned phenomenon, it is often observed that training the NNs suffers from either an exploding-gradient or a vanishing-gradient problem, which may prevent the lower layers from training at all. The presence of an activation function is likely to exacerbate this effect. The exploding- or vanishing-gradient problem seems to be a serious obstacle to the efficient training of deep NNs.

In addition to the exploding- and vanishing-gradient problems, there is an empirically observed *degradation problem* (He et al., 2016). This phrase describes the fact that FC NNs seem to achieve lower accuracy on both the training and test data when increasing their depth.

From an approximation-theoretic perspective, deep NNs should always be superior to shallow NNs. The reason for this is that NNs with two layers can either exactly represent the identity map or approximate it arbitrarily well. Concretely, for the ReLU activation function ϱ_R we have that $x = \varrho_R(x + b) - b$ for $x \in \mathbb{R}^d$ with $x_i > -b_i$, where $b \in \mathbb{R}^d$. In addition, for any activation function ϱ which is continuously differentiable on a neighborhood of some point $\lambda \in \mathbb{R}$ with $\varrho'(\lambda) \neq 0$ one can approximate the identity arbitrary well; see (1.12). Because of this, extending a NN architecture by one layer can only enlarge the associated hypothesis set.

Therefore, one may expect that the degradation problem is more associated with the optimization aspect of learning. This problem is addressed by a small change to the architecture of a feed-forward NN in He et al. (2016). Instead of defining an FC NN Φ as in (1.1), one can insert a residual block in the ℓth layer by redefining[27]

$$\bar{\Phi}^{(\ell)}(x,\theta) = \varrho(\Phi^{(\ell)}(x,\theta)) + \bar{\Phi}^{(\ell-1)}(x,\theta), \tag{1.54}$$

where we assume that $N_\ell = N_{\ell-1}$. Such a block can be viewed as the sum of a regular FC NN and the identity and is referred to as a skip connection or *residual connection*. A schematic diagram of a NN with residual blocks is shown in Figure 1.18. Inserting a residual block in all layers leads to a so-called *residual NN*.

A prominent approach to analyzing residual NNs is to establish a connection with optimal control problems and dynamical systems (E, 2017; Thorpe and van

---

[27] One can also skip multiple layers – e.g., in He et al. (2016) two or three layers were skipped – use a simple transformation instead of the identity (Srivastava et al., 2015), or randomly drop layers (Huang et al., 2016).

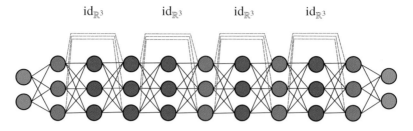

Figure 1.18 Illustration of a neural network with residual blocks.

Gennip, 2018; E et al., 2019b; Li et al., 2019b; Ruthotto and Haber, 2019; Lu et al., 2020). Concretely, if each layer of a NN Φ is of the form (1.54) then we have that

$$\bar{\Phi}^{(\ell)} - \bar{\Phi}^{(\ell-1)} = \varrho(\Phi^{(\ell)}) =: h(\ell, \Phi^{(\ell)}),$$

where for brevity we write $\bar{\Phi}^{(\ell)} = \bar{\Phi}^{(\ell)}(x, \theta)$ and set $\bar{\Phi}^{(0)} = x$. Hence, $(\bar{\Phi}^{(\ell)})_{\ell=0}^{L-1}$ corresponds to an Euler discretization of the ODE

$$\dot{\phi}(t) = h(t, \phi(t)), \qquad \phi(0) = x,$$

where $t \in [0, L-1]$ and h is an appropriate function.

Using this relationship, deep residual NNs can be studied in the framework of the well-established theory of dynamical systems, where strong mathematical guarantees can be derived.

1.6.3 Framelets and U-Nets

One of the most prominent application areas of deep NNs is inverse problems, particularly those in the field of imaging science; see also §1.8.1. A specific architectural design of CNNs, namely so-called *U-nets*, introduced in Ronneberger et al. (2015), seems to perform best for this range of problems. We sketch a U-net in Figure 1.19. However, a theoretical understanding of the success of this architecture was lacking.

Recently, an innovative approach called *deep convolutional framelets* was suggested in Ye et al. (2018), which we now briefly explain. The core idea is to take a frame-theoretic viewpoint, see, e.g., Casazza et al. (2012), and regard the forward pass of a CNN as a decomposition in terms of a frame (in the sense of a generalized basis). A similar approach will be taken in §1.7.2 for understanding the learned kernels using sparse coding. However, based on the analysis and synthesis operators of the corresponding frame, the usage of deep convolutional framelets naturally leads to a theoretical understanding of encoder–decoder architectures, such as U-nets.

Let us describe this approach for one-dimensional convolutions on the group

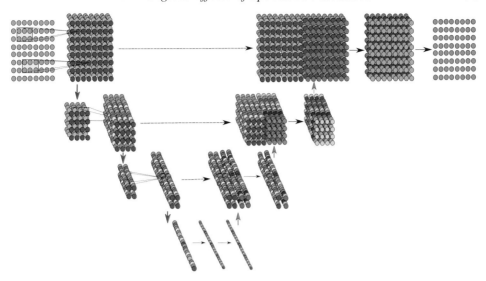

Figure 1.19 Illustration of a simplified U-net neural network. Down arrows stand for pooling, up arrows for deconvolution or upsampling, right-pointing arrows for convolution or fully connected steps. Lines without arrows are skip connections.

$G := \mathbb{Z}/(d\mathbb{Z})$ with kernels defined on the subgroup $H := \mathbb{Z}/(n\mathbb{Z})$, where $d, n \in \mathbb{N}$ with $n < d$; see also §1.6.1. We define the convolution between $u \in \mathbb{R}^G$ and $v \in \mathbb{R}^H$ by zero-padding v, i.e., $g *_{\circ} v := g * \bar{v}$, where $\bar{v} \in \mathbb{R}^G$ is defined by $\bar{v}_i = v_i$ for $i \in H$ and $\bar{v}_i = 0$ else. As an important tool, we consider the Hankel matrix $\mathbb{H}_n(x) = (x_{i+j})_{i \in G, j \in H} \in \mathbb{R}^{d \times n}$ associated with $x \in \mathbb{R}^G$. As one key property, matrix–vector multiplications with Hankel matrices are translated to convolutions via[28]

$$\langle e^{(i)}, \mathbb{H}_n(x)v \rangle = \sum_{j \in H} x_{i+j} v_j = \langle x, e^{(i)} *_{\circ} v \rangle, \quad i \in G, \tag{1.55}$$

where $e^{(i)} := 1_{\{i\}} \in \mathbb{R}^G$ and $v \in \mathbb{R}^H$; see Yin et al. (2017). Further, we can recover the kth coordinate of x by the Frobenius inner product between $\mathbb{H}_n(x)$ and the Hankel matrix associated with $e^{(k)}$, i.e.,

$$\frac{1}{n}\mathrm{Tr}\big(\mathbb{H}_n(e^{(k)})^T \mathbb{H}_n(x)\big) = \frac{1}{n}\sum_{j \in H}\sum_{i \in G} e^{(k)}_{i+j} x_{i+j} = \frac{1}{n}|H|x_k = x_k. \tag{1.56}$$

This allows us to construct global and local bases as follows. Let $p, q \in \mathbb{N}$, let $U = \begin{bmatrix} u_1 \cdots u_p \end{bmatrix} \in \mathbb{R}^{d \times p}$, $V = \begin{bmatrix} v_1 \cdots v_q \end{bmatrix} \in \mathbb{R}^{n \times q}$, $\widetilde{U} = \begin{bmatrix} \tilde{u}_1 \cdots \tilde{u}_p \end{bmatrix} \in \mathbb{R}^{d \times p}$, and

---

[28] Here and in the following we naturally identify elements in $\mathbb{R}^G$ and $\mathbb{R}^H$ with the corresponding vectors in $\mathbb{R}^d$ and $\mathbb{R}^n$.

$\widetilde{V} = \begin{bmatrix} \tilde{v}_1 \cdots \tilde{v}_q \end{bmatrix} \in \mathbb{R}^{n \times q}$, and assume that

$$\mathbb{H}_n(x) = \widetilde{U} U^T \mathbb{H}_n(x) V \widetilde{V}^T. \tag{1.57}$$

For $p \geq d$ and $q \geq n$, this is satisfied if, for instance, U and V constitute frames whose dual frames are respectively $\widetilde{U}$ and $\widetilde{V}$, i.e., $\widetilde{U} U^T = \mathbb{I}_d$ and $V \widetilde{V}^T = \mathbb{I}_n$. As a special case, one can consider orthonormal bases $U = \widetilde{U}$ and $V = \widetilde{V}$ with $p = d$ and $q = n$. In the case $p = q = r \leq n$, where r is the rank of $\mathbb{H}_n(x)$, one can establish (1.57) by choosing the left and right singular vectors of $\mathbb{H}_n(x)$ as $U = \widetilde{U}$ and $V = \widetilde{V}$, respectively. The identity in (1.57) in turn ensures the following decomposition:

$$x = \frac{1}{n} \sum_{i=1}^{p} \sum_{j=1}^{q} \langle x, u_i *_\circ v_j \rangle \tilde{u}_i *_\circ \tilde{v}_j. \tag{1.58}$$

Observing that the vector $v_j \in \mathbb{R}^H$ interacts locally with $x \in \mathbb{R}^G$ owing to the fact that $H \subset G$, whereas $u_i \in \mathbb{R}^G$ acts on the entire vector x, we refer to $(v_j)_{j=1}^q$ as a local basis and $(u_i)_{i=1}^p$ as a global basis. In the context of CNNs, v_i can be interpreted as a local convolutional kernel and u_i as a pooling operation.[29] The proof of (1.58) follows directly from properties (1.55), (1.56), and (1.57):

$$x_k = \frac{1}{n} \mathrm{Tr}\big(\mathbb{H}_n(e^{(k)})^T \mathbb{H}_n(x)\big) = \frac{1}{n} \mathrm{Tr}\big(\mathbb{H}_n(e^{(k)})^T \widetilde{U} U^T \mathbb{H}_n(x) V \widetilde{V}^T\big)$$

$$= \frac{1}{n} \sum_{i=1}^{p} \sum_{j=1}^{q} \langle u_i, \mathbb{H}_n(x) v_j \rangle \langle \tilde{u}_i, \mathbb{H}_n(e^{(k)}) \tilde{v}_j \rangle.$$

The decomposition in (1.58) can now be interpreted as the composition of an encoder and a decoder,

$$x \mapsto C = (\langle x, u_i *_\circ v_j \rangle)_{i \in [p], j \in [q]} \quad \text{and} \quad C \mapsto \frac{1}{n} \sum_{i=1}^{p} \sum_{j=1}^{q} C_{i,j} \tilde{u}_i *_\circ \tilde{v}_j, \tag{1.59}$$

which relates it to CNNs equipped with an encoder–decoder structure such as U-nets; see Figure 1.19. Generalizing this approach to multiple channels, it is possible to stack such encoders and decoders leading to a layered version of (1.58). Ye et al. (2018) show that one can make an informed decision on the number of layers on the basis of the rank of $\mathbb{H}_n(x)$, i.e., the complexity of the input features x. Moreover, an activation function such as the ReLU or bias vectors can also be included. The key question one can then ask is how the kernels can be chosen to obtain sparse coefficients C in (1.59) and a decomposition such as (1.58), i.e., perfect

---

[29] Note that $\langle x, u_i *_\circ v_j \rangle$ can also be interpreted as $\langle u_i, v_j \star x \rangle$, where $\star$ denotes the cross-correlation between the zero-padded v_j and x. This is in line with software implementations for deep learning applications, for example TensorFlow and PyTorch, where typically cross-correlations are used instead of convolutions.

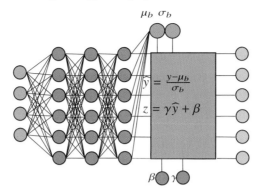

Figure 1.20 A batch normalization block after a fully connected neural network. The parameters μ_b, σ_b are the mean and the standard deviation of the output of the fully connected network computed over a batch s, i.e., a set of inputs. The parameters β, γ are learnable parts of the batch normalization block.

reconstruction. If U and V are chosen as the left and right singular vectors of $\mathbb{H}_n(x)$, one obtains a very sparse, however input-dependent, representation in (1.58) owing to the fact that

$$C_{i,j} = \langle x, u_i *_\circ v_j \rangle = \langle u_i, \mathbb{H}_n(x) v_j \rangle = 0, \quad i \neq j.$$

Finally, using the framework of deep convolutional framelets, theoretical reasons for including skip connections can be derived, since they aid in obtaining a perfect reconstruction.

1.6.4 Batch Normalization

Batch normalization involves a building block of NNs that was invented in Ioffe and Szegedy (2015) with the goal of reducing so-called *internal covariance shift*. In essence, this phrase describes the (undesirable) situation where, during training, each layer receives inputs with different distributions. A batch normalization block is defined as follows. For points $b = (y^{(i)})_{i=1}^m \in (\mathbb{R}^n)^m$ and $\beta, \gamma \in \mathbb{R}$, we define

$$\mathrm{BN}_b^{(\beta,\gamma)}(y) := \gamma \frac{y - \mu_b}{\sigma_b} + \beta, \quad y \in \mathbb{R}^n,$$

$$\text{with} \quad \mu_b = \frac{1}{m} \sum_{i=1}^m y^{(i)} \quad \text{and} \quad \sigma_b^2 = \frac{1}{m} \sum_{i=1}^m (y^{(i)} - \mu_b)^2, \tag{1.60}$$

where all operations are to be understood componentwise; see Figure 1.20.

Such a batch normalization block can be added into a NN architecture. Then b is the output of the previous layer over a batch or the whole training data.[30]

---

[30] In practice, one typically uses a moving average to estimate the mean μ, and the standard deviation σ of the output of the previous layer, over the whole training data by using only batches.

Furthermore, the parameters β, γ are variable and can be learned during training. Note that if one sets $\beta = \mu_b$ and $\gamma = \sigma_b$ then $\mathrm{BN}_b^{(\beta,\gamma)}(y) = y$ for all $y \in \mathbb{R}^n$. Therefore, a batch normalization block does not negatively affect the expressivity of the architecture. On the other hand, batch normalization does have a tangible effect on the optimization aspects of deep learning. Indeed, in Santurkar et al. (2018, Theorem 4.1), the following observation was made.

Proposition 1.28 (Smoothening effect of batch normalization). *Let $m \in \mathbb{N}$ with $m \geq 2$, and for every $\beta, \gamma \in \mathbb{R}$ define $\mathcal{B}^{(\beta,\gamma)} \colon \mathbb{R}^m \to \mathbb{R}^m$ by*

$$\mathcal{B}^{(\beta,\gamma)}(b) = (\mathrm{BN}_b^{(\beta,\gamma)}(y^{(1)}), \ldots, \mathrm{BN}_b^{(\beta,\gamma)}(y^{(m)})), \quad b = (y^{(i)})_{i=1}^m \in \mathbb{R}^m, \qquad (1.61)$$

where $\mathrm{BN}_b^{(\beta,\gamma)}$ is as given in (1.60). Let $\beta, \gamma \in \mathbb{R}$ and let $r \colon \mathbb{R}^m \to \mathbb{R}$ be a differentiable function. Then, for every $b \in \mathbb{R}^m$, we have

$$\|\nabla(r \circ \mathcal{B}^{(\beta,\gamma)})(b)\|_2^2 = \frac{\gamma^2}{\sigma_b^2} \left(\|\nabla r(b)\|^2 - \frac{1}{m}\langle \mathbf{1}, \nabla r(b)\rangle^2 - \frac{1}{m}\langle \mathcal{B}^{(0,1)}(b), \nabla r(b)\rangle^2 \right),$$

where $\mathbf{1} = (1, \ldots, 1) \in \mathbb{R}^m$ and σ_b^2 is as given in (1.60).

For multi-dimensional $y^{(i)} \in \mathbb{R}^n$, $i \in [m]$, the same statement holds for all components as, by definition, the batch normalization block acts componentwise. Proposition 1.28 follows from a convenient representation of the Jacobian of the mapping $\mathcal{B}^{(\beta,\gamma)}$, given by

$$\frac{\partial \mathcal{B}^{(\beta,\gamma)}(b)}{\partial b} = \frac{\gamma}{\sigma_b}\left(\mathrm{I}_m - \frac{1}{m}\mathbf{1}\mathbf{1}^T - \frac{1}{m}\mathcal{B}^{(0,1)}(b)(\mathcal{B}^{(0,1)}(b))^T\right), \quad b \in \mathbb{R}^m,$$

and the fact that $\{\frac{1}{\sqrt{m}}, \frac{1}{\sqrt{m}}\mathcal{B}^{(0,1)}(b)\}$ constitutes an orthonormal set.

Choosing r to mimic the empirical risk of a learning task, Proposition 1.28 shows that, in certain situations – for instance, if γ is smaller than σ_b or if m is not too large – a batch normalization block can considerably reduce the magnitude of the derivative of the empirical risk with respect to the input of the batch normalization block. By the chain rule, this implies that also the derivative of the empirical risk with respect to NN parameters influencing the input of the batch normalization block is reduced.

Interestingly, a similar result holds for second derivatives (Santurkar et al., 2018, Theorem 4.2) if r is twice differentiable. One can conclude that adding a batch normalization block increases the smoothness of the optimization problem. Since the parameters β and γ were introduced, including a batch normalization block also increases the dimension of the optimization problem by 2.

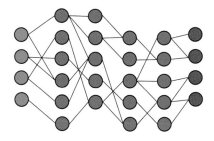

Figure 1.21 A neural network with sparse connections.

1.6.5 Sparse Neural Networks and Pruning

For deep FC NNs, the number of trainable parameters usually scales as the square of the number of neurons. For reasons of computational complexity and memory efficiency, it appears sensible to seek for techniques that reduce the number of parameters or extract *sparse subnetworks* (see Figure 1.21) without much affecting the output of a NN. One way to do it is by *pruning* (LeCun et al., 1989b; Han et al., 2016). Here, certain parameters of a NN are removed after training. This is done by, for example, setting these parameters to zero.

In this context, the *lottery ticket hypothesis* was formulated in Frankle and Carbin (2018). It states that "A randomly-initialized, dense NN contains a subnetwork that is initialized such that – when trained in isolation – it can match the test accuracy of the original NN after training for at most the same number of iterations." In Ramanujan et al. (2020) a similar hypothesis was made and empirically studied. There, it was claimed that, for a sufficiently overparametrized NN, there exists a subnetwork that matches the performance of the large NN after training without being trained itself, i.e., it already does so at initialization.

Under certain simplifying assumptions, the existence of favorable subnetworks is quite easy to prove. We can use a technique that was indirectly used in §1.4.2 – the Carathéodory lemma. This result states the following. Let $n \in \mathbb{N}$, $C \in (0, \infty)$, and $(\mathcal{H}, \| \cdot \|)$ be a Hilbert space. Let $F \subset \mathcal{H}$ with $\sup_{f \in F} \| f \| \leq C$ and let $g \in \mathcal{H}$ be in the convex hull of F. Then there exist $f_i \in F$, $i \in [n]$, and $c \in [0, 1]^n$ with $\|c\|_1 = 1$, such that

$$\left\| g - \sum_{i=1}^{n} c_i f_i \right\| \leq \frac{C}{\sqrt{n}};$$

see, e.g., Vershynin (2018, Theorem 0.0.2).

Proposition 1.29 (Carathéodory pruning). *Let $d, n \in \mathbb{N}$ with $n \geq 100$ and let μ be a probability measure on the unit ball $B_1(0) \subset \mathbb{R}^d$. Let $a = ((d, n, 1), \varrho_R)$ be the architecture of a two-layer ReLU network and let $\theta \in \mathbb{R}^{P((d,n,1))}$ be corresponding* *parameters such that*

$$\Phi_a(\cdot,\theta) = \sum_{i=1}^{n} w_i^{(2)} \varrho_R(\langle w_i^{(1)}, \cdot \rangle + b_i^{(1)}),$$

where $(w_i^{(1)}, b_i^{(1)}) \in \mathbb{R}^d \times \mathbb{R}$, $i \in [n]$, and $w^{(2)} \in \mathbb{R}^n$. Assume that for every $i \in [n]$ it holds true that $\|w_i^{(1)}\|_2 \leq 1/2$ and $b_i^{(1)} \leq 1/2$. Then there exists a parameter $\tilde{\theta} \in \mathbb{R}^{P((d,n,1))}$ with at least 99% of its entries zero such that

$$\|\Phi_a(\cdot,\theta) - \Phi_a(\cdot,\tilde{\theta})\|_{L^2(\mu)} \leq \frac{15\|w^{(2)}\|_1}{\sqrt{n}}.$$

Specifically, there exists an index set $I \subset [n]$ with $|I| \leq n/100$ such that $\tilde{\theta}$ satisfies

$$\tilde{w}_i^{(2)} = 0, \quad \text{if } i \notin I, \qquad \text{and} \qquad (\tilde{w}_i^{(1)}, \tilde{b}_i^{(1)}) = \begin{cases} (w_i^{(1)}, b_i^{(1)}), & \text{if } i \in I, \\ (0,0), & \text{if } i \notin I. \end{cases}$$

The result is clear if $w^{(2)} = 0$. Otherwise, define

$$f_i := \|w^{(2)}\|_1 \varrho_R(\langle w_i^{(1)}, \cdot \rangle + b_i^{(1)}), \quad i \in [n], \tag{1.62}$$

and observe that $\Phi_a(\cdot,\theta)$ is in the convex hull of $\{f_i\}_{i=1}^n \cup \{-f_i\}_{i=1}^n$. Moreover, by the Cauchy–Schwarz inequality, we have

$$\|f_i\|_{L^2(\mu)} \leq \|w^{(2)}\|_1 \|f_i\|_{L^\infty(B_1(0))} \leq \|w^{(2)}\|_1.$$

We conclude with the Carathéodory lemma that there exists $I \subset [n]$ with $|I| = \lfloor n/100 \rfloor \geq n/200$ and $c_i \in [-1,1]$, $i \in I$, such that

$$\left\| \Phi_a(\cdot,\theta) - \sum_{i \in I} c_i f_i \right\|_{L^2(\mu)} \leq \frac{\|w^{(2)}\|_1}{\sqrt{|I|}} \leq \frac{\sqrt{200}\|w^{(2)}\|_1}{\sqrt{n}},$$

which yields the result.

Proposition 1.29 shows that certain, very wide NNs can be approximated very well by sparse subnetworks in which only the output weight matrix needs to be changed. The argument of Proposition 1.29 was inspired by Barron and Klusowski (2018), where a much more refined result is shown for deep NNs.

1.6.6 Recurrent Neural Networks

Recurrent NNs are NNs where the underlying graph is allowed to exhibit cycles, as in Figure 1.22; see Hopfield (1982), Rumelhart et al. (1986), Elman (1990), and Jordan (1990). Above, we excluded cyclic computational graphs. For a feed-forward NN, the computation of internal states is naturally performed step by step through the layers. Since the output of a layer does not affect the previous layers, the order

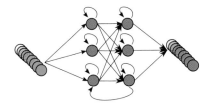

Figure 1.22 Sketch of a recurrent neural network. The cycles in the computational graph incorporate the sequential structure of the input and output.

in which the computations of the NN are performed corresponds to the order of the layers. For recurrent NNs the concept of layers does not exist, and the order of operations is much more delicate. Therefore, one considers time steps. In each time step, all possible computations of the graph are applied to the current state of the NN. This yields a new internal state. Given that time steps arise naturally from the definition of recurrent NNs, this NN type is typically used for sequential data.

If the input to a recurrent NN is a sequence, then every input determines the internal state of the recurrent NN for the following inputs. Therefore, one can claim that these NNs exhibit a memory. This fact is extremely desirable in natural language processing, which is why recurrent NNs are widely used in this application.

Recurrent NNs can be trained in a way similar to regular feed-forward NNs by an algorithm called *backpropagation through time* (Minsky and Papert, 1969; Werbos, 1988; Williams and Zipser, 1995). This procedure essentially unfolds the recurrent structure to yield a classical NN structure. However, the algorithm may lead to very deep structures. Owing to the vanishing- and exploding-gradient problem discussed earlier, very deep NNs are often hard to train. Because of this, special recurrent structures have been introduced that include gates that prohibit too many recurrent steps; these include the widely used long short-term memory gates, LSTMs, (Hochreiter and Schmidhuber, 1997).

The application area of recurrent NNs is typically quite different from that of regular NNs since they are specialized on sequential data. Therefore, it is hard to quantify the effect of a recurrent connection on a fully connected NN. However, it is certainly true that with recurrent connections certain computations can be performed much more efficiently than with feed-forward NN structures. A particularly interesting construction can be found in Bohn and Feischl (2019, Theorem 4.4), where it is shown that a fixed size, recurrent NN with ReLU activation function, can approximate the function $x \mapsto x^2$ to any desired accuracy. The reason for this efficient representation can be seen when considering the self-referential definition of the approximant to $x - x^2$ shown in Figure 1.9.

On the other hand, with feed-forward NNs, it transpires from Theorem 1.26 that the approximation error of fixed-sized ReLU NNs for any non-affine function is greater than a positive lower bound.

1.7 Describing the Features that a Deep Neural Network Learns

This section presents two viewpoints which help in understanding the nature of the features that can be described by NNs. Section 1.7.1 summarizes aspects of the so-called *scattering transform*, which constitutes a specific NN architecture that can be shown to satisfy desirable properties such as translation and deformation invariance. Section 1.7.2 relates NN features to the current paradigm of *sparse coding*.

1.7.1 Invariances and the Scattering Transform

One of the first theoretical contributions to the understanding of the mathematical properties of CNNs was by Mallat (2012). Their approach was to consider specific CNN architectures with *fixed* parameters that result in a stand-alone feature descriptor whose output may be fed into a subsequent classifier (for example, a kernel support vector machine or a trainable FC NN). From an abstract point of view, a feature descriptor is a function Ψ mapping from a signal space, such as $L^2(\mathbb{R}^d)$ or the space of piecewise smooth functions, to a feature space. In an ideal world, such a classifier should "factor" out invariances that are irrelevant to a subsequent classification problem while preserving all other information of the signal. A very simple example of a classifier which is invariant under translations is the Fourier modulus $\Psi: L^2(\mathbb{R}^d) \to L^2(\mathbb{R}^d)$, $u \mapsto |\hat{u}|$. This follows from the fact that a translation of a signal u results in a modulation of its Fourier transform, i.e., $\widehat{u(\cdot - \tau)}(\omega) = e^{-2\pi i \langle \tau, \omega \rangle} \hat{u}(\omega)$, $\tau, \omega \in \mathbb{R}^d$. Furthermore, in most cases – for example, if u is a generic compactly supported function (Grohs et al., 2020), u can be reconstructed up to a translation from its Fourier modulus (Grohs et al., 2020) and an energy conservation property of the form $\|\Psi(u)\|_{L^2} = \|u\|_{L^2}$ holds true. Translation invariance is, for example, typically exhibited by image classifiers, where the label of an image does not change if it is translated.

In practical problems many more invariances arise. Providing an analogous representation that factors out general invariances would lead to a significant reduction in the problem dimensionality and constitutes an extremely promising route towards dealing with the very high dimensionality that is commonly encountered in practical problems (Mallat, 2016). This program was carried out by Mallat (2012) for additional invariances with respect to deformations $u \mapsto u_\tau := u(\cdot - \tau(\cdot))$, where $\tau: \mathbb{R}^d \to \mathbb{R}^d$ is a smooth mapping. Such transformations may occur in practice, for instance, as image warpings. In particular, a feature descriptor Ψ is designed so that, with a suitable norm $\|\cdot\|$ on the image of Ψ, it

(a) is Lipschitz continuous with respect to deformations in the sense that

$$\|\Psi(u) - \Psi(u_\tau)\| \lesssim K(\tau, \nabla\tau, \nabla^2\tau)$$

holds for some K that only mildly depends on τ and essentially grows linearly in $\nabla\tau$ and $\nabla^2\tau$,

(b) is almost (i.e., up to a small and controllable error) invariant under translations of the input data, and

(c) contains all relevant information on the input data in the sense that an energy conservation property

$$\|\Psi(u)\| \approx \|u\|_{L^2}$$

holds true.

Observe that, while the action of translations only represents a d-parameter group, the action of deformations/warpings represents an infinite-dimensional group. Thus, a deformation invariant feature descriptor represents a big potential for dimensionality reduction. Roughly speaking, the feature descriptor Ψ of Mallat (2012) (also coined the *scattering transform*) is defined by collecting features that are computed by iteratively applying a wavelet transform followed by a pointwise modulus nonlinearity and a subsequent low-pass filtering step, i.e.,

$$|||u * \psi_{j_1}| * \psi_{j_2} * \cdots | * \psi_{j_\ell}| * \varphi_J,$$

where ψ_j refers to a wavelet at scale j and φ_J refers to a scaling function at scale J. The collection of all these so-called *scattering coefficients* can then be shown to satisfy the properties listed above in a suitable (asymptotic) sense. The proof of this result relies on a subtle interplay between the "deformation covariance" property of the wavelet transform and the "regularizing" property of the operation of convolution with the modulus of a wavelet. For a much more detailed exposition of the resulting scattering transform, we refer to Chapter 8 in this book. We remark that similar results can be shown also for different systems, such as Gabor frames (Wiatowski et al., 2017; Czaja and Li, 2019).

1.7.2 Hierarchical Sparse Representations

The previous approach modeled the learned features by a specific dictionary, namely wavelets. It is well known that one of the striking properties of wavelets is to provide sparse representations for functions belonging to certain function classes. More generally, we speak of sparse representations with respect to a representation

system. For a vector $x \in \mathbb{R}^d$, a sparsifying representation system $D \in \mathbb{R}^{d \times p}$ –
also called a *dictionary* – is such that $x = D\phi$ where the coefficients $\phi \in \mathbb{R}^p$ are
sparse in the sense that $\|\phi\|_0 := |\operatorname{supp}(\phi)| = |\{i \in [p]: \phi_i \neq 0\}|$ is small compared
with p. A similar definition can be made for signals in infinite-dimensional spaces.
Taking sparse representations into account, the theory of sparse coding provides an
approach to a theoretical understanding of the features that a deep NN learns.

One common method in image processing is the utilization of not the entire
image but overlapping patches of it, coined *patch-based image processing*. Thus
of particular interest are local dictionaries which sparsify those patches but, pre-
sumably, not the global image. This led to the introduction of the *convolutional
sparse coding* (CSC) model, which links such local and global behaviors. Let us
describe this model for one-dimensional convolutions on the group $G := \mathbb{Z}/(d\mathbb{Z})$
with kernels supported on the subgroup $H := \mathbb{Z}/(n\mathbb{Z})$, where $d, n \in \mathbb{N}$ with $n < d$;
see also §1.6.1. The corresponding CSC model is based on the decomposition of a
global signal $x \in (\mathbb{R}^G)^c$ with $c \in \mathbb{N}$ channels as

$$x_i = \sum_{j=1}^{C} \kappa_{i,j} * \phi_j, \quad i \in [c], \tag{1.63}$$

where $\phi \in (\mathbb{R}^G)^C$ is taken to be a sparse representation with $C \in \mathbb{N}$ channels, and
$\kappa_{i,j} \in \mathbb{R}^G$, $i \in [c]$, $j \in [C]$, are local kernels with $\operatorname{supp}(\kappa_{i,j}) \subset H$. Let us consider
a patch $((x_i)_{g+h})_{i \in [c], h \in H}$ of n adjacent entries, starting at position $g \in G$, in each
channel of x. The condition on the support of the kernels $\kappa_{i,j}$ and the representation
in (1.63) imply that this patch is affected only by a stripe of at most $(2n - 1)$ entries
in each channel of ϕ. The local, patch-based sparsity of the representation ϕ can
thus be appropriately measured via

$$\|\phi\|_{0,\infty}^{(n)} := \max_{g \in G} \|((\phi_j)_{g+k})_{j \in [C], k \in [2n-1]}\|_0;$$

see Papyan et al. (2017b). Furthermore, note that we can naturally identify x and
ϕ with vectors in $\mathbb{R}^{dc}$ and $\mathbb{R}^{dC}$ and write $x = D\phi$, where $D \in \mathbb{R}^{dc \times dC}$ is a matrix
consisting of circulant blocks, typically referred to as a *convolutional dictionary*.

The relation between the CSC model and deep NNs is revealed by applying
the CSC model in a layer-wise fashion (Papyan et al., 2017a; Sulam et al., 2018;
Papyan et al., 2018). To see this, let $C_0 \in \mathbb{N}$ and for every $\ell \in [L]$ let $C_\ell, k_\ell \in \mathbb{N}$
and let $D^{(\ell)} \in \mathbb{R}^{dC_{\ell-1} \times dC_\ell}$ be a convolutional dictionary with kernels supported
on $\mathbb{Z}/(n_\ell \mathbb{Z})$. A signal $x = \phi^{(0)} \in \mathbb{R}^{dC_0}$ is said to belong to the corresponding
multi-layered CSC (ML-CSC) *model* if there exist coefficients $\phi^{(\ell)} \in \mathbb{R}^{dC_\ell}$ with

$$\phi^{(\ell-1)} = D^{(\ell)}\phi^{(\ell)} \quad \text{and} \quad \|\phi^{(\ell)}\|_{0,\infty}^{(n_\ell)} \leq k_\ell, \quad \ell \in [L]. \tag{1.64}$$

We now consider the problem of reconstructing the sparse coefficients $(\phi^{(\ell)})_{\ell=1}^{L}$

from a noisy signal $\tilde{x} := x + v$, where the noise $v \in \mathbb{R}^{dC_0}$ is assumed to have small ℓ^2-norm and x is assumed to follow the ML-CSC model in (1.64). In general, this problem is NP-hard. However, under suitable conditions on the ML-CSC model, it can be solved approximately, for instance by a layered thresholding algorithm.

More precisely, for $D \in \mathbb{R}^{dc \times dC}$ and $b \in \mathbb{R}^{dC}$, we define a *soft-thresholding operator* by

$$\mathcal{T}_{D,b}(x) := \varrho_R(D^T x - b) - \varrho_R(-D^T x - b), \quad x \in \mathbb{R}^{dc}, \tag{1.65}$$

where $\varrho_R(x) = \max\{0, x\}$ is applied componentwise. If $x = D\phi$ as in (1.63), we obtain $\phi \approx \mathcal{T}_{D,b}(x)$ roughly under the following conditions. The distance of ϕ from $\psi := D^T x = D^T D\phi$ can be bounded using the local sparsity of ϕ and the mutual coherence and locality of the kernels of the convolutional dictionary D. For a suitable threshold b, the mapping $\psi \mapsto \varrho_R(\psi - b) - \varrho_R(-\psi - b)$ further recovers the support of ϕ by nullifying those entries of ψ with $\psi_i \leq |b_i|$. Utilizing the soft-thresholding operator (1.65) iteratively for corresponding vectors $b^{(\ell)} \in \mathbb{R}^{dC_\ell}$, $\ell \in [L]$, then suggests the following approximations:

$$\phi^{(\ell)} \approx (\mathcal{T}_{D^{(\ell)},b^{(\ell)}} \circ \cdots \circ \mathcal{T}_{D^{(1)},b^{(1)}})(\tilde{x}), \quad \ell \in [L].$$

The resemblance to the realization of a CNN with ReLU activation function is evident. The transposed dictionary $(D^{(\ell)})^T$ can be regarded as modeling the learned convolutional kernels, the threshold $b^{(\ell)}$ models the bias vector, and the soft-thresholding operator $\mathcal{T}_{D^{(\ell)},b^{(\ell)}}$ mimics the application of a convolutional block with an ReLU nonlinearity in the ℓth layer.

Using this model, a theoretical understanding of CNNs from the perspective of sparse coding is now at hand. This novel perspective gives a precise mathematical meaning of the kernels in a CNN as sparsifying dictionaries of an ML-CSC model. Moreover, the forward pass of a CNN can be understood as a layered thresholding algorithm for decomposing a noisy signal $\tilde{x}$. The results derived then have the following flavor. Given a suitable reconstruction procedure such as thresholding or ℓ_1-minimization, the sparse coefficients $(\phi^{(\ell)})_{\ell=1}^L$ of a signal x following an ML-CSC model can be stably recovered from the noisy signal $\tilde{x}$ under certain hypotheses on the ingredients of the ML-CSC model.

1.8 Effectiveness in Natural Sciences

The theoretical insights of the previous sections do not always accurately describe the performance of NNs in applications. Indeed, there often exists a considerable gap between the predictions of approximation theory and the practical performance of NNs (Adcock and Dexter, 2020).

In this section, we consider concrete applications which have been very success-fully solved with deep-learning-based methods. In §1.8.1 we present an overview of deep-learning-based algorithms applied to inverse problems. Section 1.8.2 then continues by describing how NNs can be used as a numerical ansatz for solv-ing PDEs, highlighting their use in the solution of the multi-electron Schrödinger equation.

1.8.1 Deep Neural Networks Meet Inverse Problems

The area of inverse problems, predominantly in imaging, was probably the first class of mathematical methods embracing deep learning with overwhelming success. Let us consider a forward operator $K: \mathcal{Y} \to \mathcal{X}$ where $\mathcal{X}, \mathcal{Y}$ are Hilbert spaces, and the associated inverse problem of finding $y \in \mathcal{Y}$ such that $Ky = x$ for given features $x \in \mathcal{X}$. The classical model-based approach to regularization aims to approximate K by invertible operators, and is hence strongly based on functional analytic prin-ciples. Today, such approaches take the well-posedness of the approximation and its convergence properties, as well as the structure of regularized solutions, into ac-count. The last item allows to incorporate prior information of the original solution such as regularity, sharpness of edges, or – in the case of sparse regularization (Jin et al., 2017a) – a sparse coefficient sequence with respect to a prescribed represen-tation system. Such approaches are typically realized in a variational setting and hence aim to minimize functionals of the form

$$\|Ky - x\|^2 + \alpha R(y), \tag{1.66}$$

where $\alpha \in (0, \infty)$ is a regularization parameter, $R: \mathcal{Y} \to [0, \infty)$ is a regularization term, and $\| \cdot \|$ denotes the norm on $\mathcal{Y}$. As already stated, the regularization term aims to model structural information about the desired solution. However, one main hurdle in this approach is the problem that, typically, solution classes such as images from computed tomography cannot be modeled accurately enough to allow, for instance, reconstruction under the constraint of a significant amount of missing features.

This has opened the door to data-driven approaches, and recently, deep NNs. Solvers of inverse problems that are based on deep learning techniques can be roughly categorized into three classes:

(i) *Supervised approaches.* The most straightforward approach is to train a NN $\Phi(\cdot, \theta): \mathcal{X} \to \mathcal{Y}$ end-to-end, i.e., to completely learn the map from data x to the solution y. More advanced approaches in this direction incorporate information about the operator K into the NN as in Adler and Öktem (2017), Gilton et al. (2019), and Monga et al. (2021). Yet another type of approach aims to combine deep NNs with classical model-based approaches. The first suggestion in this realm was that one should start by applying a standard solver and then use a deep NN, $\Phi(\cdot, \theta) \colon \mathcal{Y} \to \mathcal{Y}$, which serves as a denoiser for specific reconstruction artifacts; e.g., Jin et al. (2017b). This approach was followed by more sophisticated methods such as plug-and-play frameworks for coupling inversion and denoising (Romano et al., 2017).

(ii) *Semi-supervised approaches.* This type of approach aims to encode the regularization by a deep NN $\Phi(\cdot, \theta) \colon \mathcal{Y} \to [0, \infty)$. The underlying idea often requires stronger regularization on those solutions $y^{(i)}$ that are more prone to artifacts or other effects of the instability of the problem. On solutions where typically few artifacts are observed less regularization can be used. Therefore, the learning algorithm requires only a set of labels $(y^{(i)})_{i=1}^{m}$ as well as a method for assessing how hard the inverse problem for this label would be. In this sense, the algorithm can be considered semi-supervised. This idea was followed, for example, in Lunz et al. (2018), and Li et al. (2020). Taking a Bayesian viewpoint, one can also learn prior distributions as deep NNs; this was done in Barbano et al. (2020).

(iii) *Unsupervised approaches.* One highlight of what we might call unsupervised approaches in our problem setting has been the introduction of deep image priors in Dittmer et al. (2020), and Ulyanov et al. (2018). The key idea is to parametrize the solutions y as the output of a NN $\Phi(\xi, \cdot) \colon \mathcal{P} \to \mathcal{Y}$ with parameters in a suitable space $\mathcal{P}$ applied to a fixed input ξ. Then, for given features x, one tries to solve $\min_{\theta \in \mathcal{P}} \|K\Phi(\xi, \theta) - x\|^2$ in order to obtain parameters $\hat{\theta} \in \mathcal{P}$ that yield a solution candidate $y = \Phi(\xi, \hat{\theta})$. Here early stopping is often applied in the training of the network parameters.

As can be seen, one key conceptual question is how to "take the best out of both worlds," in the sense of optimally combining classical (model-based) methods – in particular the forward operator K – with deep learning. This is certainly sensitively linked to all characteristics of the particular application at hand, such as the availability and accuracy of training data, properties of the forward operator, and requirements for the solution. And each of the three classes of hybrid solvers follows a different strategy.

Let us now discuss the advantages and disadvantages of methods from the three categories with a particular focus on a mathematical foundation. *Supervised* approaches suffer on the one hand from the problem that often ground-truth data is not available or only in a very distorted form, leading to the use of synthetic data as a significant part of the training data. Thus the learned NN will mainly perform as well as the algorithm which generated the data, but will not significantly improve on it – except from an efficiency viewpoint. On the other hand, the inversion is often highly ill posed, i.e., the inversion map has a large Lipschitz constant, which negatively affects the generalization ability of the NN. Improved approaches incorporate knowledge about the forward operator K, which helps to circumvent this issue.

One significant advantage of *semi-supervised* approaches is that the underlying mathematical model of the inverse problem is merely augmented by neural-network-based regularization. Assuming that the learned regularizer satisfies natural assumptions, convergence proofs or stability estimates for the resulting regularized methods are still available.

Finally, *unsupervised* approaches have the advantage that the regularization is then fully due to the specific architecture of the deep NN. This makes these methods slightly easier to understand theoretically, although, for instance, the deep prior approach in its full generality is still lacking a profound mathematical analysis.

1.8.2 PDE-Based Models

Besides applications in image processing and artificial intelligence, deep learning methods have recently strongly impacted the field of numerical analysis. In particular, regarding the numerical solution of high-dimensional PDEs. These PDEs are widely used as a model for complex processes and their numerical solution presents one of the biggest challenges in scientific computing. We mention examples from three problem classes.

(i) *Black–Scholes model.* The Nobel award-winning theory of Fischer Black, Robert Merton, and Myron Scholes proposes a linear PDE model for the determination of a fair price of a (complex) financial derivative. The dimensionality of the model corresponds to the number of financial assets, which is typically quite large. The classical linear model, which can be solved efficiently via Monte Carlo methods, is quite limited. In order to take into account more realistic phenomena such as default risk, the PDE that models a fair price becomes nonlinear and much more challenging to solve. In particular (with the notable exception of multi-level Picard algorithms E et al., 2019c) no general algorithm exists that provably scales well with the dimension.

(ii) *Schrödinger equation.* The electronic Schrödinger equation describes the stationary non-relativistic behavior of a quantum mechanical electron system in the electric field generated by the nuclei of a molecule. A numerical solution is required to obtain stable molecular configurations, compute vibrational spectra, or obtain forces governing molecular dynamics. If the number of electrons is large, this is again a high-dimensional problem and to date there exist no satisfactory algorithms for its solution. It is well known that different gold standard methods may produce completely different energy predictions, for example, when applied to large delocalized molecules, rendering these methods useless for those problems.

(iii) *Hamilton–Jacobi–Bellman equation.* The Hamilton–Jacobi–Bellman (HJB) equation models the value function of (deterministic or stochastic) optimal control problems. The underlying dimensionality of the model corresponds to the dimension of the space of states to be controlled and tends to be rather high in realistic applications. This high dimensionality, together with the fact that HJB equations typically tend to be fully nonlinear with non-smooth solutions, renders the numerical solution of HJB equations extremely challenging, and no general algorithms exist for this problem.

Thanks to the favorable approximation results of NNs for high-dimensional functions (see especially §§1.4.3), it might not come as a surprise that a NN ansatz has proven to be quite successful in solving the aforementioned PDE models. Pioneering work in this direction was by Han et al. (2018) who used the backwards SDE reformulation of semi-linear parabolic PDEs to reformulate the evaluation of such a PDE, at a specific point, as an optimization problem that can be solved by the deep learning paradigm. The resulting algorithm proves quite successful in the high-dimensional regime and, for instance, enables the efficient modeling of complex financial derivatives including nonlinear effects such as default risk. Another approach specifically tailored to the numerical solution of HJB equations is Nakamura-Zimmerer et al. (2021). In this work, the Pontryagin principle was used to generate samples of the PDE solution along solutions of the corresponding boundary value problem. Other numerical approaches include the *deep Ritz method* (E and Yu, 2018), where a Dirichlet energy is minimized over a set of NNs; or so-called *physics informed neural networks* (Raissi et al., 2019), where typically the PDE residual is minimized along with some natural constraints, for instance, to enforce boundary conditions.

Deep-learning-based methods arguably work best if they are combined with domain knowledge to inspire NN architecture choices. We would like to illustrate this interplay at the hand of a specific and extremely relevant example: the electronic Schrödinger equation (under the Born–Oppenheimer approximation), which amounts to finding the smallest non-zero eigenvalue of the eigenvalue problem

$$\mathcal{H}_R \psi = \lambda_\psi \psi, \qquad (1.67)$$

for $\psi \colon \mathbb{R}^{3\times n} \to \mathbb{R}$, where the Hamiltonian

$$(\mathcal{H}_R\psi)(r) = -\sum_{i=1}^{n}\frac{1}{2}(\Delta_{r_i}\psi)(r) - \left(\sum_{i=1}^{n}\sum_{j=1}^{p}\frac{Z_j}{\|r_i - R_j\|_2} - \sum_{i=1}^{p-1}\sum_{j=i+1}^{p}\frac{Z_i Z_j}{\|R_i - R_j\|_2}\right.$$
$$\left. -\sum_{i=1}^{n-1}\sum_{j=i+1}^{n}\frac{1}{\|r_i - r_j\|_2}\right)\psi(r)$$

describes the kinetic energy (first term) as well as the Coulomb attraction force between electrons and nuclei (second and third terms) and the Coulomb repulsion force between different electrons (fourth term). Here, the coordinates $R = [R_1,\ldots,R_p] \in \mathbb{R}^{3\times p}$ refer to the positions of the nuclei, $(Z_i)_{i=1}^{p} \in \mathbb{N}^p$ denote the atomic numbers of the nuclei, and the coordinates $r = [r_1,\ldots,r_n] \in \mathbb{R}^{3\times n}$ refer to the positions of the electrons. The associated eigenfunction ψ describes the so-called *wave function*, which can be interpreted in the sense that $|\psi(r)|^2/\|\psi\|_{L^2}^2$ describes the joint probability density of the n electrons to be located at r. The smallest solution λ_ψ of (1.67) describes the *ground state energy* associated with the nuclear coordinates R. It is of particular interest to know the ground state energy for all nuclear coordinates, the so-called *potential energy surface*, whose gradient determines the forces governing the dynamic motions of the nuclei. The numerical solution of (1.67) is complicated by the *Pauli principle*, which states that the wave function ψ must be antisymmetric in all coordinates representing electrons of equal spin. We need to clarify that every electron is defined not only by its location but also by its spin, which may be positive or negative. Depending on whether two electrons have the same spin or not, their interaction changes considerably. This is reflected in the Pauli principle mentioned above. Suppose that electrons i and j have equal spin; then the wave function must satisfy

$$P_{i,j}\psi = -\psi, \tag{1.68}$$

where $P_{i,j}$ denotes the operator that swaps r_i and r_j, i.e.,

$$(P_{i,j}\psi)(r) = \psi(r_1,\ldots,r_j,\ldots,r_i,\ldots,r_n).$$

In particular, no two electrons with the same spin can occupy the same location. The challenges associated with solving the Schrödinger equation inspired the following famous quote of Paul Dirac (1929):

"The fundamental laws necessary for the mathematical treatment of a large part of physics and the whole of chemistry are thus completely known, and the difficulty lies only in the fact that application of these laws leads to equations that are too complex to be solved."

We now describe how deep learning methods might help to mitigate this claim to a certain extent. Let X be a random variable with density $|\psi(r)|^2/\|\psi\|^2_{L^2}$. Using the Rayleigh–Ritz principle, finding the minimal non-zero eigenvalue of (1.67) can be reformulated as minimizing the Rayleigh quotient

$$\frac{\int_{\mathbb{R}^{3\times n}} \overline{\psi(r)}(\mathcal{H}_R\psi)(r)\,dr}{\|\psi\|^2_{L^2}} = \mathbb{E}\left[\frac{(\mathcal{H}_R\psi)(X)}{\psi(X)}\right] \tag{1.69}$$

over all ψ's satisfying the Pauli principle; see Szabo and Ostlund (2012). Since this represents a minimization problem it can in principle be solved via a NN ansatz by generating training data distributed according to X using MCMC sampling.[31] Since the wave function ψ will be parametrized as a NN, the minimization of (1.69) will require the computation of the gradient of (1.69) with respect to the NN parameters (the method in Pfau et al., 2020, even requires second-order derivatives), which, at first sight, might seem to require the computation of third-order derivatives. However, due to the Hermitian structure of the Hamiltonian, one does not need to compute the derivative of the Laplacian of ψ; see, for example Hermann et al. (2020, Equation (8)).

Compared with the other PDE problems we have discussed, an additional complication arises from the need to incorporate structural properties and invariances such as the Pauli principle. Furthermore, empirical evidence shows that it is also necessary to hard-code the so-called *cusp conditions* which describe the asymptotic behavior of nearby electrons and of electrons close to a nucleus into the NN architecture. A first attempt in this direction was made by Han et al. (2019), and significantly improved NN architectures have been developed in Hermann et al. (2020), Pfau et al. (2020), and Scherbela et al. (2021) opening the possibility of accurate ab initio computations for previously intractable molecules. The mathematical properties of this exciting line of work remain largely unexplored. We briefly describe the main ideas behind the NN architecture of Hermann et al. (2020); Scherbela et al. (2021). Standard numerical approaches (notably the multireference Hartree–Fock method; see Szabo and Ostlund, 2012) use a low-rank approach to minimize (1.69). Such an approach would approximate ψ by sums of products of *one-electron orbitals* $\prod_{i=1}^n \varphi_i(r_i)$ but clearly this would not satisfy the Pauli principle (1.68). In order to accommodate the Pauli principle, one constructs so-called *Slater determinants* from one-electron orbitals with equal spin. More precisely, suppose that the first n_+ electrons with coordinates $r_1,\ldots,r_{n_+}$ have positive spin and the last $n - n_+$ electrons have negative spin. Then any function of the form

$$\det\left(\left(\varphi_i(r_j)\right)_{i,j=1}^{n_+}\right) \times \det\left(\left(\varphi_i(r_j)\right)_{i,j=n_++1}^{n}\right) \tag{1.70}$$

---

[31] Observe that for such sampling methods one can just use the unnormalized density $|\psi(r)|^2$ and thus avoid the computation of the normalization $\|\psi\|^2_{L^2}$.

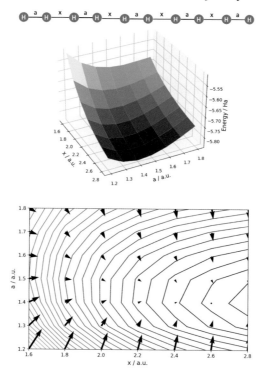

Figure 1.23 By sharing layers across different nuclear geometries one can efficiently compute different geometries in one single training step (Scherbela et al., 2021). Top: potential energy surface of an H_{10} chain computed by the deep-learning-based algorithm from Scherbela et al. (2021). The lowest energy is achieved when pairs of H atoms enter into a covalent bond to form five H_2 molecules. Bottom: the method of Scherbela et al. (2021) is capable of accurately computing forces between nuclei, which allows for molecular dynamics simulations from first principles.

satisfies (1.68) and is typically called a Slater determinant. While the Pauli principle establishes a (non-classical) interaction between electrons of equal spin, the so-called *exchange correlation*, in the representation (1.70) electrons with opposite spins are uncorrelated. In particular, (1.70) ignores interactions between electrons that arise through Coulomb forces, implying that no non-trivial wave function can be accurately represented by a single Slater determinant. To capture the physical interactions between different electrons, one needs to use sums of Slater determinants as an ansatz. However, it turns out that the number of such determinants that are needed to guarantee a given accuracy scales very badly with the system size n (to our knowledge the best currently known approximation results are contained in Yserentant (2010), where an n-independent error rate is shown; however, the implicit constant in this rate depends at least exponentially on the system size n).

We would like to highlight the approach of Hermann et al. (2020), whose main idea was to use NNs to incorporate interactions into Slater determinants of the form (1.70) using what is called the *backflow trick* (Ríos et al., 2006). The basic building blocks would now consist of functions of the form

$$\det\left(\left(\varphi_i(r_j)\Psi_j(r,\theta_j)\right)_{i,j=1}^{n_+}\right) \times \det\left(\left(\varphi_i(r_j)\Psi_j(r,\theta_j)\right)_{i,j=n_++1}^{n}\right), \qquad (1.71)$$

where the $\Psi_k(\cdot,\theta_k)$, $k \in [n]$, are NNs. If these are arbitrary NNs, it is easy to see that the Pauli principle (1.68) will not be satisfied. However, if we require the NNs to be symmetric, for example, in the sense that for $i,j,s \in [n_+]$ it holds true that

$$P_{i,j}\Psi_k(\cdot,\theta_k) = \begin{cases} \Psi_k(\cdot,\theta_k), & \text{if } k \notin \{i,j\}, \\ \Psi_i(\cdot,\theta_i), & \text{if } k = j, \\ \Psi_j(\cdot,\theta_j), & \text{if } k = i, \end{cases} \qquad (1.72)$$

and analogous conditions hold for $i,j,k \in [n] \setminus [n_+]$, the expression (1.71) does actually satisfy (1.68). The construction of such symmetric NNs can be achieved by using a modification of the so-called *SchNet architecture* (Schütt et al., 2017) which can be considered as a specific residual NN.

We describe a simplified construction inspired by Han et al. (2019) and used in a slightly more complex form in Scherbela et al. (2021). We restrict ourselves to the case of positive spin (for example, the first n_+ coordinates), the case of negative spin being handled in the same way. Let $\Upsilon(\cdot,\theta_{emb}^+)$ be a univariate NN (with possibly multivariate output) and denote

$$\text{Emb}_k(r,\theta_{emb}^+) := \sum_{i=1}^{n_+} \Upsilon(\|r_k - r_i\|_2, \theta_{emb}^+), \qquad k \in [n_+],$$

as the kth *embedding layer*. For $k \in [n_+]$, we can now define

$$\Psi_k(r,\theta_k) = \Psi_k\left(r,(\theta_{k,fc},\theta_{emb}^+)\right) = \Gamma_k\left((\text{Emb}_k(r,\theta_{emb}^+),(r_{n_++1},\dots,r_n)),\theta_{k,fc}\right),$$

where $\Gamma_k(\cdot,\theta_{k,fc})$ denotes a standard FC NN with input dimension equal to the output dimension of Ψ^+ plus the dimension of the negative-spin electrons. The networks Ψ_k, $k \in [n] \setminus [n_+]$, are defined analogously using different parameters θ_{emb}^- for the embeddings. It is straightforward to check that the NNs Ψ_k, $k \in [n]$, satisfy (1.72) so that the backflow determinants (1.71) satisfy the Pauli principle (1.68).

In Hermann et al. (2020) the backflow determinants (1.71) are further augmented by a multiplicative correction term, the so-called *Jastrow factor*, which is also represented by a specific symmetric NN, as well as a correction term that ensures the validity of the cusp conditions. The results of Hermann et al. (2020) show that this ansatz (namely using linear combinations of backflow determinants (1.71) instead of plain Slater determinants (1.70)) is vastly more efficient in terms of the number of determinants needed to obtain chemical accuracy. The full architecture provides a general purpose NN architecture to represent complicated wave functions. A distinct advantage of this approach is that some parameters (for example, regarding the embedding layers) may be shared across different nuclear geometries $R \in \mathbb{R}^{3 \times P}$, which allows for the efficient computation of potential energy surfaces (Scherbela et al., 2021); see Figure 1.23.

Finally, we would like to highlight the need for customized NN design that incorporates physical invariances, domain knowledge (for example, in the form of cusp conditions), and existing numerical methods, all of which are required for the method to reach its full potential.

Acknowledgments

The research of JB was supported by the Austrian Science Fund (FWF) under grant I3403-N32. GK acknowledges support from DFG-SPP 1798 Grants KU 1446/21-2 and KU 1446/27-2, DFG-SFB/TR 109 Grant C09, BMBF Grant MaGriDo, and NSF-Simons Foundation Grant SIMONS 81420. The authors would like to thank Héctor Andrade Loarca, Dennis Elbrächter, Adalbert Fono, Pavol Harar, Lukas Liehr, Duc Anh Nguyen, Mariia Seleznova, and Frieder Simon for their helpful feedback on an early version of this chapter. In particular, Dennis Elbrächter provided help for several theoretical results.

References

Ackley, David H., Hinton, Geoffrey E., and Sejnowski, Terrence J. 1985. A learning algorithm for Boltzmann machines. *Cognitive Science*, **9**(1), 147–169.

Adcock, Ben, and Dexter, Nick. 2020. The gap between theory and practice in function approximation with deep neural networks. ArXiv preprint arXiv:2001.07523.

Adler, Jonas, and Öktem, Ozan. 2017. Solving ill-posed inverse problems using iterative deep neural networks. *Inverse Problems*, **33**(12), 124007.

Al-Hamdani, Yasmine S., Nagy, Péter R., Barton, Dennis, Kállay, Mihály, Brandenburg, Jan Gerit, and Tkatchenko, Alexandre. 2020. Interactions between large molecules: Puzzle for reference quantum-mechanical methods. ArXiv preprint arXiv:2009.08927.

Allen-Zhu, Zeyuan, Li, Yuanzhi, and Song, Zhao. 2019. A convergence theory for deep learning via over-parameterization. Pages 242–252 of: *Proc. International Conference on Machine Learning*.

Anthony, Martin, and Bartlett, Peter L. 1999. *Neural Network Learning: Theoretical Foundations*. Cambridge University Press.

Arora, Sanjeev, Cohen, Nadav, and Hazan, Elad. 2018a. On the optimization of deep networks: Implicit acceleration by overparameterization. Pages 372–389 of: *Proc. International Conference on Machine Learning*.

Arora, Sanjeev, Ge, Rong, Neyshabur, Behnam, and Zhang, Yi. 2018b. Stronger generalization bounds for deep nets via a compression approach. Pages 254–263 of: *Proc. International Conference on Machine Learning*.

Arora, Sanjeev, Cohen, Nadav, Golowich, Noah, and Hu, Wei. 2019a. A convergence analysis of gradient descent for deep linear neural networks. In: *International Conference on Learning Representations*.

Arora, Sanjeev, Du, Simon S., Hu, Wei, Li, Zhiyuan, Salakhutdinov, Ruslan, and Wang, Ruosong. 2019b. On exact computation with an infinitely wide neural net. Pages 8139–8148 of: *Advances in Neural Information Processing Systems*.

Arridge, Simon, Maass, Peter, Öktem, Ozan, and Schönlieb, Carola-Bibiane. 2019. Solving inverse problems using data-driven models. *Acta Numerica*, **28**, 1–174.

Auer, Peter, Herbster, Mark, and Warmuth, Manfred K. 1996. Exponentially many local minima for single neurons. Page 316–322 of: *Advances in Neural Information Processing Systems*.

Auffinger, Antonio, Arous, Gérard Ben, and Černỳ, Jiří. 2013. Random matrices and complexity of spin glasses. *Communications on Pure and Applied Mathematics*, **66**(2), 165–201.

Bahdanau, Dzmitry, Cho, Kyunghyun, and Bengio, Yoshua. 2015. Neural machine translation by jointly learning to align and translate. In: *Proc. International Conference on Learning Representations*.

Baldi, Pierre, Sadowski, Peter, and Whiteson, Daniel. 2014. Searching for exotic particles in high-energy physics with deep learning. *Nature Communications*, **5**(1), 1–9.

Barbano, Riccardo, Zhang, Chen, Arridge, Simon, and Jin, Bangti. 2020. Quantifying model uncertainty in inverse problems via Bayesian deep gradient descent. ArXiv preprint arXiv:2007.09971.

Barron, Andrew R. 1992. Neural net approximation. Pages 69–72 of: *Proc. Yale Workshop on Adaptive and Learning Systems*, vol. 1.

Barron, Andrew R. 1993. Universal approximation bounds for superpositions of a sigmoidal function. *IEEE Transactions on Information Theory*, **39**(3), 930–945.

Barron, Andrew R., and Klusowski, Jason M. 2018. Approximation and estimation for high-dimensional deep learning networks. ArXiv preprint arXiv:1809.03090.

Bartlett, Peter L. 1998. The sample complexity of pattern classification with neural networks: The size of the weights is more important than the size of the network. *IEEE Transactions on Information Theory*, **44**(2), 525–536.

Bartlett, Peter L, Maiorov, Vitaly, and Meir, Ron. 1998. Almost linear VC-dimension bounds for piecewise polynomial networks. *Neural Computation*, **10**(8), 2159–2173.

Bartlett, Peter L., Bousquet, Olivier, and Mendelson, Shahar. 2005.   Local
    Rademacher complexities. *Annals of Statistics*, **33**(4), 1497–1537.
Bartlett, Peter L., Foster, Dylan J., and Telgarsky, Matus. 2017.   Spectrally-
    normalized margin bounds for neural networks. Pages 6240–6249 of: *Ad-
    vances in Neural Information Processing Systems*.
Bartlett, Peter L., Harvey, Nick, Liaw, Christopher, and Mehrabian, Abbas. 2019.
    Nearly-tight VC-dimension and pseudodimension bounds for piecewise linear
    neural networks. *Journal of Machine Learning Research*, **20**, 63–1.
Bartlett, Peter L., Long, Philip M., Lugosi, Gábor, and Tsigler, Alexander. 2020.
    Benign overfitting in linear regression. *Proceedings of the National Academy
    of Sciences*, **117**(48), 30063–30070.
Baum, Eric B., and Haussler, David. 1989. What size net gives valid generalization?
    Neural Computation, **1**(1), 151–160.
Beck, Christian, Becker, Sebastian, Grohs, Philipp, Jaafari, Nor, and Jentzen, Ar-
    nulf. 2021. Solving the Kolmogorov PDE by means of deep learning. *Journal
    of Scientific Computing*, **83**(3), 1–28.
Belkin, Mikhail, Ma, Siyuan, and Mandal, Soumik. 2018. To understand deep
    learning we need to understand kernel learning. Pages 541–549 of: *Proc.
    International Conference on Machine Learning*.
Belkin, Mikhail, Rakhlin, Alexander, and Tsybakov, Alexandre B. 2019a. Does
    data interpolation contradict statistical optimality? Pages 1611–1619 of: *Proc.
    International Conference on Artificial Intelligence and Statistics*.
Belkin, Mikhail, Hsu, Daniel, Ma, Siyuan, and Mandal, Soumik. 2019b. Rec-
    onciling modern machine-learning practice and the classical bias–variance
    trade-off. *Proceedings of the National Academy of Sciences*, **116**(32), 15849–
    15854.
Belkin, Mikhail, Hsu, Daniel, and Xu, Ji. 2020. Two models of double descent for
    weak features. *SIAM Journal on Mathematics of Data Science*, **2**(4), 1167–
    1180.
Bellman, Richard. 1952. On the theory of dynamic programming. *Proceedings of
    the National Academy of Sciences*, **38**(8), 716.
Berner, Christopher, Brockman, Greg, Chan, Brooke, Cheung, Vicki, Debiak, Prze-
    myslaw, Dennison, Christy, Farhi, David, Fischer, Quirin, Hashme, Shariq,
    and Hesse, Chris. 2019a. Dota 2 with large scale deep reinforcement learning.
    ArXiv preprint arXiv:1912.06680.
Berner, Julius, Elbrächter, Dennis, and Grohs, Philipp. 2019b. How degenerate is
    the parametrization of neural networks with the ReLU activation function?
    Pages 7790–7801 of: *Advances in Neural Information Processing Systems*.
Berner, Julius, Grohs, Philipp, and Jentzen, Arnulf. 2020a. Analysis of the general-
    ization error: Empirical risk minimization over deep artificial neural networks
    overcomes the curse of dimensionality in the numerical approximation of
    Black–Scholes partial differential equations. *SIAM Journal on Mathematics
    of Data Science*, **2**(3), 631–657.

Berner, Julius, Dablander, Markus, and Grohs, Philipp. 2020b. Numerically solving parametric families of high-dimensional Kolmogorov partial differential equations via deep learning. Pages 16615–16627 of: *Advances in Neural Information Processing Systems*.

Blum, Avrim, and Rivest, Ronald L. 1989. Training a 3-node neural network is NP-complete. Pages 494–501 of: *Advances in Neural Information Processing Systems*.

Bohn, Jan, and Feischl, Michael. 2019. Recurrent neural networks as optimal mesh refinement strategies. ArXiv preprint arXiv:1909.04275.

Bourely, Alfred, Boueri, John Patrick, and Choromonski, Krzysztof. 2017. Sparse neural networks topologies. ArXiv preprint arXiv:1706.05683.

Bousquet, Olivier, and Elisseeff, André. 2002. Stability and generalization. *Journal of Machine Learning Research*, **2**(March), 499–526.

Bousquet, Olivier, Boucheron, Stéphane, and Lugosi, Gábor. 2003. Introduction to statistical learning theory. Pages 169–207 of: *Proc. Summer School on Machine Learning*.

Bronstein, Michael M, Bruna, Joan, LeCun, Yann, Szlam, Arthur, and Vandergheynst, Pierre. 2017. Geometric deep learning: Going beyond euclidean data. *IEEE Signal Processing Magazine*, **34**(4), 18–42.

Brown, Tom, Mann, Benjamin, Ryder, Nick, Subbiah, Melanie, Kaplan, Jared D, Dhariwal, Prafulla, Neelakantan, Arvind, Shyam, Pranav, Sastry, Girish, Askell, Amanda, Agarwal, Sandhini, Herbert-Voss, Ariel, Krueger, Gretchen, Henighan, Tom, Child, Rewon, Ramesh, Aditya, Ziegler, Daniel, Wu, Jeffrey, Winter, Clemens, Hesse, Chris, Chen, Mark, Sigler, Eric, Litwin, Mateusz, Gray, Scott, Chess, Benjamin, Clark, Jack, Berner, Christopher, McCandlish, Sam, Radford, Alec, Sutskever, Ilya, and Amodei, Dario. 2020. Language models are few-shot learners. Pages 1877–1901 of: *Advances in Neural Information Processing Systems*.

Candès, Emmanuel J. 1998. *Ridgelets: Theory and Applications*. Ph.D. thesis, Stanford University.

Caragea, Andrei, Petersen, Philipp, and Voigtlaender, Felix. 2020. Neural network approximation and estimation of classifiers with classification boundary in a Barron class. ArXiv preprint arXiv:2011.09363.

Casazza, Peter G., Kutyniok, Gitta, and Philipp, Friedrich. 2012. Introduction to finite frame theory. Pages 1–53 of: *Finite Frames: Theory and Applications*. Birkhäuser Boston.

Chen, Lin, Min, Yifei, Belkin, Mikhail, and Karbasi, Amin. 2020. Multiple descent: Design your own generalization curve. ArXiv preprint arXiv:2008.01036.

Chen, Minshuo, Jiang, Haoming, Liao, Wenjing, and Zhao, Tuo. 2019. Efficient approximation of deep ReLU networks for functions on low dimensional manifolds. Pages 8174–8184 of: *Advances in Neural Information Processing Systems*.

Chizat, Lenaic, and Bach, Francis. 2020. Implicit bias of gradient descent for wide two-layer neural networks trained with the logistic loss. Pages 1305–1338 of: *Proc. Conference on Learning Theory.*

Chizat, Lenaic, Oyallon, Edouard, and Bach, Francis. 2019. On lazy training in differentiable programming. Pages 2937–2947 of: *Advances in Neural Information Processing Systems.*

Cho, Kyunghyun, van Merriënboer, Bart, Gulcehre, Caglar, Bahdanau, Dzmitry, Bougares, Fethi, Schwenk, Holger, and Bengio, Yoshua. 2014. Learning phrase representations using RNN encoder–decoder for statistical machine translation. Pages 1724–1734 of: *Proc. 2014 Conference on Empirical Methods in Natural Language Processing.*

Choromanska, Anna, Henaff, Mikael, Mathieu, Michael, Arous, Gérard Ben, and LeCun, Yann. 2015a. The loss surfaces of multilayer networks. Pages 192–204 of: *Proc. International Conference on Artificial Intelligence and Statistics.*

Choromanska, Anna, LeCun, Yann, and Arous, Gérard Ben. 2015b. Open problem: rhe landscape of the loss surfaces of multilayer networks. Pages 1756–1760 of: *Proc. Conference on Learning Theory.*

Chui, Charles K., and Mhaskar, Hrushikesh N. 2018. Deep nets for local manifold learning. *Frontiers in Applied Mathematics and Statistics*, **4**, 12.

Chui, Charles K., Li, Xin, and Mhaskar, Hrushikesh N. 1994. Neural networks for localized approximation. *Mathematics of Computation*, **63**(208), 607–623.

Cloninger, Alexander, and Klock, Timo. 2020. ReLU nets adapt to intrinsic dimensionality beyond the target domain. ArXiv preprint arXiv:2008.02545.

Cucker, Felipe, and Smale, Steve. 2002. On the mathematical foundations of learning. *Bulletin of the American Mathematical Society*, **39**(1), 1–49.

Cucker, Felipe, and Zhou, Ding-Xuan. 2007. *Learning Theory: An Approximation Theory Viewpoint.* Cambridge University Press.

Cybenko, George. 1989. Approximation by superpositions of a sigmoidal function. *Mathematics of Control, Signals and Systems*, **2**(4), 303–314.

Czaja, Wojciech, and Li, Weilin. 2019. Analysis of time–frequency scattering transforms. *Applied and Computational Harmonic Analysis*, **47**(1), 149–171.

Dauphin, Yann N., Pascanu, Razvan, Gulcehre, Caglar, Cho, Kyunghyun, Ganguli, Surya, and Bengio, Yoshua. 2014. Identifying and attacking the saddle point problem in high-dimensional non-convex optimization. Pages 2933–2941 of: *Advances in Neural Information Processing Systems.*

Deng, Jia, Dong, Wei, Socher, Richard, Li, Li-Jia, Li, Kai, and Fei-Fei, Li. 2009. Imagenet: A large-scale hierarchical image database. Pages 248–255 of: *Proc. IEEE Conference on Computer Vision and Pattern Recognition.*

DeVore, Ronald A. 1998. Nonlinear approximation. *Acta Numerica*, **7**, 51–150.

DeVore, Ronald, Hanin, Boris, and Petrova, Guergana. 2021. Neural network approximation. *Acta Numerica*, **30**, 327–444.

Devroye, Luc, Györfi, László, and Lugosi, Gábor. 1996. *A Probabilistic Theory of Pattern Recognition.* Springer.

Dirac, Paul Adrien Maurice. 1929. Quantum mechanics of many-electron systems. *Proceedings of the Royal Society of London. Series A, Containing Papers of a Mathematical and Physical Character*, **123**(792), 714–733.

Dittmer, Sören, Kluth, Tobias, Maass, Peter, and Baguer, Daniel Otero. 2020. Regularization by architecture: A deep prior approach for inverse problems. *Journal of Mathematical Imaging and Vision*, **62**(3), 456–470.

Donoghue, William F. 1969. *Distributions and Fourier Transforms*. Academic Press.

Dreyfus, Stuart. 1962. The numerical solution of variational problems. *Journal of Mathematical Analysis and Applications*, **5**(1), 30–45.

Du, Simon S., Hu, Wei, and Lee, Jason D. 2018a. Algorithmic regularization in learning deep homogeneous models: Layers are automatically balanced. Pages 384–395 of: *Advances in Neural Information Processing Systems*.

Du, Simon S., Zhai, Xiyu, Poczos, Barnabas, and Singh, Aarti. 2018b. Gradient descent provably optimizes over-parameterized neural networks. In: *Proc. International Conference on Learning Representations*.

Du, Simon S., Lee, Jason D., Li, Haochuan, Wang, Liwei, and Zhai, Xiyu. 2019. Gradient descent finds global minima of deep neural networks. Pages 1675–1685 of: *Proc. International Conference on Machine Learning*.

Dudley, Richard M. 1967. The sizes of compact subsets of Hilbert space and continuity of Gaussian processes. *Journal of Functional Analysis*, **1**(3), 290–330.

Dudley, Richard M. 2014. *Uniform Central Limit Theorems*. Cambridge University Press.

Dziugaite, Gintare Karolina, and Roy, Daniel M. 2017. Computing nonvacuous generalization bounds for deep (stochastic) neural networks with many more parameters than training data. In: *Proc. Conference on Uncertainty in Artificial Intelligence*.

E, Weinan. 2017. A proposal on machine learning via dynamical systems. *Communications in Mathematics and Statistics*, **5**(1), 1–11.

E, Weinan, and Wojtowytsch, Stephan. 2020a. On the Banach spaces associated with multi-layer ReLU networks: Function representation, approximation theory and gradient descent dynamics. ArXiv preprint arXiv:2007.15623.

E, Weinan, and Wojtowytsch, Stephan. 2020b. A priori estimates for classification problems using neural networks. ArXiv preprint arXiv:2009.13500.

E, Weinan, and Wojtowytsch, Stephan. 2020c. Representation formulas and point-wise properties for Barron functions. ArXiv preprint arXiv:2006.05982.

E, Weinan, and Yu, Bing. 2018. The deep Ritz method: A deep learning-based numerical algorithm for solving variational problems. *Communications in Mathematics and Statistics*, **6**(1), 1–12.

E, Weinan, Ma, Chao, and Wu, Lei. 2019a. Barron spaces and the compositional function spaces for neural network models. ArXiv preprint arXiv:1906.08039.

E, Weinan, Han, Jiequn, and Li, Qianxiao. 2019b. A mean-field optimal control formulation of deep learning. *Research in the Mathematical Sciences*, **6**(1), 1–41.

E, Weinan, Hutzenthaler, Martin, Jentzen, Arnulf, and Kruse, Thomas. 2019c. On multilevel Picard numerical approximations for high-dimensional nonlinear parabolic partial differential equations and high-dimensional nonlinear back-ward stochastic differential equations. *Journal of Scientific Computing*, **79**(3), 1534–1571.

E, Weinan, Ma, Chao, and Wu, Lei. 2019d. A priori estimates of the population risk for two-layer neural networks. *Communications in Mathematical Sciences*, **17**(5), 1407–1425.

E, Weinan, Ma, Chao, Wojtowytsch, Stephan, and Wu, Lei. 2020. Towards a mathematical understanding of neural network-based machine learning: what we know and what we don't. ArXiv preprint arXiv:2009.10713.

Elbrächter, Dennis, Grohs, Philipp, Jentzen, Arnulf, and Schwab, Christoph. 2018. DNN expression rate analysis of high-dimensional PDEs: Application to option pricing. ArXiv preprint arXiv:1809.07669.

Elbrächter, Dennis, Perekrestenko, Dmytro, Grohs, Philipp, and Bölcskei, Hel-mut. 2019. Deep neural network approximation theory. ArXiv preprint arXiv:1901.02220.

Eldan, Ronen, and Shamir, Ohad. 2016. The power of depth for feedforward neural networks. Pages 907–940 of: *Proc. Conference on Learning Theory*, vol. 49.

Elman, Jeffrey L. 1990. Finding structure in time. *Cognitive Science*, **14**(2), 179–211.

Faber, Felix A., Hutchison, Luke, Huang, Bing, Gilmer, Justin, Schoenholz, Samuel S., Dahl, George E., Vinyals, Oriol, Kearnes, Steven, Riley, Patrick F., and Von Lilienfeld, O. Anatole. 2017. Prediction errors of molecular machine learning models lower than hybrid DFT error. *Journal of Chemical Theory and Computation*, **13**(11), 5255–5264.

Frankle, Jonathan, and Carbin, Michael. 2018. The lottery ticket hypothesis: Find-ing sparse, trainable neural networks. In: *proc. International Conference on Learning Representations*.

Freeman, Daniel C., and Bruna, Joan. 2017. Topology and geometry of half-rectified network optimization. In: *Proc. International Conference on Learning Representations*.

Funahashi, Ken-Ichi. 1989. On the approximate realization of continuous mappings by neural networks. *Neural Networks*, **2**(3), 183–192.

Ge, Rong, Huang, Furong, Jin, Chi, and Yuan, Yang. 2015. Escaping from saddle points – online stochastic gradient for tensor decomposition. Pages 797–842 of: *Proc. Conference on Learning Theory*.

Geiger, Mario, Jacot, Arthur, Spigler, Stefano, Gabriel, Franck, Sagun, Levent, d'Ascoli, Stéphane, Biroli, Giulio, Hongler, Clément, and Wyart, Matthieu. 2020. Scaling description of generalization with number of parameters in deep learning. *Journal of Statistical Mechanics: Theory and Experiment*, **2**(2), 023401.

Géron, Aurelien. 2017. *Hands-On Machine Learning with Scikit-Learn and Tensor-Flow: Concepts, Tools, and Techniques to Build Intelligent Systems*. O'Reilly Media.

Ghadimi, Saeed, and Lan, Guanghui. 2013. Stochastic first- and zeroth-order methods for nonconvex stochastic programming. *SIAM Journal on Optimization*, **23**(4), 2341–2368.

Ghorbani, Behrooz, Mei, Song, Misiakiewicz, Theodor, and Montanari, Andrea. 2021. Linearized two-layers neural networks in high dimension. *Annals of Statistics*, **49**(2), 1029–1054.

Gilton, Davis, Ongie, Greg, and Willett, Rebecca. 2019. Neumann networks for linear inverse problems in imaging. *IEEE Transactions on Computational Imaging*, **6**, 328–343.

Giné, Evarist, and Zinn, Joel. 1984. Some limit theorems for empirical processes. *Annals of Probability*, 929–989.

Golowich, Noah, Rakhlin, Alexander, and Shamir, Ohad. 2018. Size-independent sample complexity of neural networks. Pages 297–299 of: *Proc. Conference On Learning Theory*.

Gonon, Lukas, and Schwab, Christoph. 2020. Deep ReLU network expression rates for option prices in high-dimensional, exponential Lévy models. ETH Zurich SAM Research Report.

Goodfellow, Ian, Pouget-Abadie, Jean, Mirza, Mehdi, Xu, Bing, Warde-Farley, David, Ozair, Sherjil, Courville, Aaron, and Bengio, Yoshua. 2014. Generative adversarial nets. Pages 2672–2680 of: *Advances in Neural Information Processing Systems*.

Goodfellow, Ian, Bengio, Yoshua, and Courville, Aaron. 2016. *Deep Learning*. MIT Press.

Griewank, Andreas, and Walther, Andrea. 2008. *Evaluating Derivatives: Principles and Techniques of Algorithmic Differentiation*. SIAM.

Grohs, Philipp, and Herrmann, Lukas. 2021. Deep neural network approximation for high-dimensional parabolic Hamilton–Jacobi–Bellman equations. ArXiv preprint arXiv:2103.05744.

Grohs, Philipp, and Voigtlaender, Felix. 2021. Proof of the theory-to-practice gap in deep learning via sampling complexity bounds for neural network approximation spaces. ArXiv preprint arXiv:2104.02746.

Grohs, Philipp, Koppensteiner, Sarah, and Rathmair, Martin. 2020. Phase retrieval: Uniqueness and stability. *SIAM Review*, **62**(2), 301–350.

Grohs, Philipp, Hornung, Fabian, Jentzen, Arnulf, and von Wurstemberger, Philippe. 2021. A proof that artificial neural networks overcome the curse of dimensionality in the numerical approximation of Black–Scholes partial differential equations. *Memoirs of the American Mathematical Society*, to appear.

Gühring, Ingo, Kutyniok, Gitta, and Petersen, Philipp. 2020. Error bounds for approximations with deep ReLU neural networks in $W^{s,p}$ norms. *Analysis and Applications*, **18**(05), 803–859.

Gunasekar, Suriya, Lee, Jason D., Soudry, Daniel, and Srebro, Nathan. 2018a. Characterizing implicit bias in terms of optimization geometry. Pages 1832–1841 of: *Proc. International Conference on Machine Learning*.

Gunasekar, Suriya, Lee, Jason D., Soudry, Daniel, and Srebro, Nathan. 2018b. Implicit bias of gradient descent on linear convolutional networks. Pages 9461–9471 of: *Advances in Neural Information Processing Systems*.

Haeffele, Benjamin D., and Vidal, René. 2017. Global optimality in neural network training. Pages 7331–7339 of: *Proc. IEEE Conference on Computer Vision and Pattern Recognition*.

Hairer, Martin, Hutzenthaler, Martin, and Jentzen, Arnulf. 2015. Loss of regularity for Kolmogorov equations. *Annals of Probability*, **43**(2), 468–527.

Han, Song, Mao, Huizi, and Dally, William J. 2016. Deep compression: compressing deep neural network with pruning, trained quantization and Huffman coding. In: *Proc. International Conference on Learning Representations*.

Han, Jiequn, Jentzen, Arnulf, and E, Weinan. 2018. Solving high-dimensional partial differential equations using deep learning. *Proceedings of the National Academy of Sciences*, **115**(34), 8505–8510.

Han, Jiequn, Zhang, Linfeng, and E, Weinan. 2019. Solving many-electron Schrödinger equation using deep neural networks. *Journal of Computational Physics*, **399**, 108929.

Hanin, Boris. 2019. Universal function approximation by deep neural nets with bounded width and ReLU activations. *Mathematics*, **7**(10), 992.

Hanin, Boris, and Rolnick, David. 2019. Deep ReLU networks have surprisingly few activation patterns. Pages 359–368 of: *Advances in Neural Information Processing Systems*.

Hanin, Boris, and Sellke, Mark. 2017. Approximating continuous functions by ReLU nets of minimal width. ArXiv preprint arXiv:1710.11278.

Hardt, Moritz, Recht, Ben, and Singer, Yoram. 2016. Train faster, generalize better: Stability of stochastic gradient descent. Pages 1225–1234 of: *Proc. International Conference on Machine Learning*.

Hastie, Trevor, Tibshirani, Robert, and Friedman, Jerome. 2001. *The Elements of Statistical Learning: Data Mining, Inference, and Prediction*. Springer.

Hastie, Trevor, Montanari, Andrea, Rosset, Saharon, and Tibshirani, Ryan J. 2019. *Surprises in high-dimensional ridgeless least squares interpolation*. ArXiv preprint arXiv:1903.08560.

Haussler, David. 1995. Sphere packing numbers for subsets of the Boolean n-cube with bounded Vapnik–Chervonenkis dimension. *Journal of Combinatorial Theory, Series A*, **2**(69), 217–232.

He, Juncai, Li, Lin, Xu, Jinchao, and Zheng, Chunyue. 2020. ReLU deep neural networks and linear finite elements. *Journal of Computational Mathematics*, **38**(3), 502–527.

He, Kaiming, Zhang, Xiangyu, Ren, Shaoqing, and Sun, Jian. 2015. Delving deep into rectifiers: surpassing human-level performance on imagenet classification. Pages 1026–1034 of: *Proc. IEEE International Conference on Computer Vision*.

He, Kaiming, Zhang, Xiangyu, Ren, Shaoqing, and Sun, Jian. 2016. Deep residual learning for image recognition. Pages 770–778 of: *Proc. IEEE Conference on Computer Vision and Pattern Recognition*.

Hermann, Jan, Schätzle, Zeno, and Noé, Frank. 2020. Deep-neural-network solution of the electronic Schrödinger equation. *Nature Chemistry*, **12**(10), 891–897.

Higham, Catherine F., and Higham, Desmond J. 2019. Deep learning: An introduction for applied mathematicians. *SIAM Review*, **61**(4), 860–891.

Hinton, Geoffrey E., and Zemel, Richard S. 1994. Autoencoders, minimum description length, and Helmholtz free energy. *Advances in Neural Information Processing Systems*, **6**, 3–10.

Hinz, Peter, and van de Geer, Sara. 2019. A framework for the construction of upper bounds on the number of affine linear regions of ReLU feed-forward neural networks. *IEEE Transactions on Information Theory*, **65**, 7304–7324.

Hochreiter, Sepp, and Schmidhuber, Jürgen. 1997. Long short-term memory. *Neural Computation*, **9**(8), 1735–1780.

Hoeffding, Wassily. 1963. Probability inequalities for sums of bounded random variables. *Journal of the American Statistical Association*, **58**(301), 13–30.

Hopfield, John J. 1982. Neural networks and physical systems with emergent collective computational abilities. *Proceedings of the National Academy of Sciences*, **79**(8), 2554–2558.

Hornik, Kurt, Stinchcombe, Maxwell, and White, Halbert. 1989. Multilayer feedforward networks are universal approximators. *Neural Networks*, **2**(5), 359–366.

Huang, Gao, Sun, Yu, Liu, Zhuang, Sedra, Daniel, and Weinberger, Kilian Q. 2016. Deep networks with stochastic depth. Pages 646–661 of: *Proc. European Conference on Computer Vision*.

Hutzenthaler, Martin, Jentzen, Arnulf, Kruse, Thomas, and Nguyen, Tuan Anh. 2020. A proof that rectified deep neural networks overcome the curse of dimensionality in the numerical approximation of semilinear heat equations. *SN Partial Differential Equations and Applications*, **1**(2), 1–34.

Ioffe, Sergey, and Szegedy, Christian. 2015. Batch normalization: Accelerating deep network training by reducing internal covariate shift. Pages 448–456 of: *Proc. International Conference on Machine Learning*.

Jacot, Arthur, Gabriel, Franck, and Hongler, Clément. 2018. Neural tangent kernel: Convergence and generalization in neural networks. Pages 8571–8580 of: *Advances in Neural Information Processing Systems*.

Jentzen, Arnulf, Kuckuck, Benno, Neufeld, Ariel, and von Wurstemberger, Philippe.

2020. Strong error analysis for stochastic gradient descent optimization algorithms. *IMA Journal of Numerical Analysis*, **41**(1), 455–492.

Ji, Ziwei, and Telgarsky, Matus. 2019a. Gradient descent aligns the layers of deep linear networks. In: *Proc. International Conference on Learning Representations*.

Ji, Ziwei, and Telgarsky, Matus. 2019b. A refined primal–dual analysis of the implicit bias. ArXiv preprint arXiv:1906.04540.

Ji, Ziwei, and Telgarsky, Matus. 2020. Directional convergence and alignment in deep learning. Pages 17176–17186 of: *Advances in Neural Information Processing Systems*.

Jiang, Yiding, Krishnan, Dilip, Mobahi, Hossein, and Bengio, Samy. 2019. Predicting the generalization gap in deep networks with margin distributions. In: *Proc. International Conference on Learning Representations*.

Jiang, Yiding, Neyshabur, Behnam, Mobahi, Hossein, Krishnan, Dilip, and Bengio, Samy. 2020. Fantastic generalization measures and where to find them. In: *International Conference on Learning Representations*.

Jin, Bangti, Maaß, Peter, and Scherzer, Otmar. 2017a. Sparsity regularization in inverse problems. *Inverse Problems*, **33**(6), 060301.

Jin, Kyong Hwan, McCann, Michael T., Froustey, Emmanuel, and Unser, Michael. 2017b. Deep convolutional neural network for inverse problems in imaging. *IEEE Transactions on Image Processing*, **26**(9), 4509–4522.

Jordan, Michael I. 1990. Attractor dynamics and parallelism in a connectionist sequential machine. Pages 112–127 of: *Artificial Neural Networks: Concept Learning*. IEEE Press.

Judd, Stephen J. 1990. *Neural Network Design and the Complexity of Learning*. MIT Press.

Kakade, Sham M., and Lee, Jason D. 2018. Provably correct automatic subdifferentiation for qualified programs. Pages 7125–7135 of: *Advances in Neural Information Processing Systems*.

Karpinski, Marek, and Macintyre, Angus. 1997. Polynomial bounds for VC dimension of sigmoidal and general Pfaffian neural networks. *Journal of Computer and System Sciences*, **54**(1), 169–176.

Kelley, Henry J. 1960. Gradient theory of optimal flight paths. *Ars Journal*, **30**(10), 947–954.

Keskar, Nitish Shirish, Mudigere, Dheevatsa, Nocedal, Jorge, Smelyanskiy, Mikhail, and Tang, Ping Tak Peter. 2017. On large-batch training for deep learning: Generalization gap and sharp minima. In: *Proc. International Conference on Learning Representations*.

Kidger, Patrick, and Lyons, Terry. 2020. Universal approximation with deep narrow networks. Pages 2306–2327 of: *Proc. Conference on Learning Theory*.

Kiefer, Jack, and Wolfowitz, Jacob. 1952. Stochastic estimation of the maximum of a regression function. *Annals of Mathematical Statistics*, **23**(3), 462–466.

Krizhevsky, Alex, and Hinton, Geoffrey. 2009. Learning multiple layers of features from tiny images. Technical Report. University of Toronto.

Krizhevsky, Alex, Sutskever, Ilya, and Hinton, Geoffrey E. 2012. ImageNet classification with deep convolutional neural networks. Pages 1097–1105 of: *Advances in Neural Information Processing Systems*.

Kutyniok, Gitta, Petersen, Philipp, Raslan, Mones, and Schneider, Reinhold. 2019. A theoretical analysis of deep neural networks and parametric PDEs. ArXiv preprint arXiv:1904.00377.

Laakmann, Fabian, and Petersen, Philipp. 2021. Efficient approximation of solutions of parametric linear transport equations by ReLU DNNs. *Advances in Computational Mathematics*, **47**(1), 1–32.

Lample, Guillaume, and Charton, François. 2019. Deep learning For symbolic mathematics. In: *Proc. International Conference on Learning Representations*.

LeCun, Yann, Boser, Bernhard, Denker, John S., Henderson, Donnie, Howard, Richard E., Hubbard, Wayne, and Jackel, Lawrence D. 1989a. Backpropagation applied to handwritten zip code recognition. *Neural Computation*, **1**(4), 541–551.

LeCun, Yann, Denker, John S., and Solla, Sara A. 1989b. Optimal brain damage. Pages 598–605 of: *Advances in Neural Information Processing Systems*.

LeCun, Yann, Bottou, Léon, Bengio, Yoshua, and Haffner, Patrick. 1998. Gradient-based learning applied to document recognition. *Proceedings of the IEEE*, **86**(11), 2278–2324.

LeCun, Yann, Bengio, Yoshua, and Hinton, Geoffrey. 2015. Deep learning. *Nature*, **521**(7553), 436–444.

Ledoux, Michel, and Talagrand, Michel. 1991. *Probability in Banach Spaces: Isoperimetry and Processes*. Springer Science & Business Media.

Lee, Jason D., Simchowitz, Max, Jordan, Michael I., and Recht, Benjamin. 2016. Gradient descent only converges to minimizers. Pages 1246–1257 of: *Proc. Conference on Learning Theory*.

Lee, Jaehoon, Bahri, Yasaman, Novak, Roman, Schoenholz, Samuel S., Pennington, Jeffrey, and Sohl-Dickstein, Jascha. 2018. Deep neural networks as Gaussian processes. In: *Proc. International Conference on Learning Representations*.

Lee, Jaehoon, Xiao, Lechao, Schoenholz, Samuel S., Bahri, Yasaman, Novak, Roman, Sohl-Dickstein, Jascha, and Pennington, Jeffrey. 2020. Wide neural networks of any depth evolve as linear models under gradient descent. *Journal of Statistical Mechanics: Theory and Experiment*, **2020**(12), 124002.

Leshno, Moshe, Lin, Vladimir Ya., Pinkus, Allan, and Schocken, Shimon. 1993. Multilayer feedforward networks with a nonpolynomial activation function can approximate any function. *Neural Networks*, **6**(6), 861–867.

Lewin, Kurt. 1943. Psychology and the process of group living. *The Journal of Social Psychology*, **17**(1), 113–131.

Li, Bo, Tang, Shanshan, and Yu, Haijun. 2019a. Better approximations of high-dimensional smooth functions by deep neural networks with rectified power units. *Communications in Computational Physics*, **27**(2), 379–411.

Li, Housen, Schwab, Johannes, Antholzer, Stephan, and Haltmeier, Markus. 2020. NETT: Solving inverse problems with deep neural networks. *Inverse Problems*, **36**(6), 065005.

Li, Qianxiao, Lin, Ting, and Shen, Zuowei. 2019b. Deep learning via dynamical systems: An approximation perspective. ArXiv preprint arXiv:1912.10382.

Li, Weilin. 2021. Generalization error of minimum weighted norm and kernel interpolation. *SIAM Journal on Mathematics of Data Science*, **3**(1), 414–438.

Li, Yuanzhi, and Liang, Yingyu. 2018. Learning overparameterized neural networks via stochastic gradient descent on structured data. Pages 8157–8166 of: *Advances in Neural Information Processing Systems*.

Liang, Shiyu, and Srikant, R. 2017. Why deep neural networks for function approximation? In: *Proc. International Conference on Learning Representations*.

Liang, Tengyuan, and Rakhlin, Alexander. 2020. Just interpolate: Kernel "ridgeless" regression can generalize. *Annals of Statistics*, **48**(3), 1329–1347.

Liang, Tengyuan, Poggio, Tomaso, Rakhlin, Alexander, and Stokes, James. 2019. Fisher–Rao metric, geometry, and complexity of neural networks. Pages 888–896 of: *Proc. International Conference on Artificial Intelligence and Statistics*.

Liang, Tengyuan, Rakhlin, Alexander, and Zhai, Xiyu. 2020. On the multiple descent of minimum-norm interpolants and restricted lower isometry of kernels. Pages 2683–2711 of: *Proc. Conference on Learning Theory*.

Lin, Licong, and Dobriban, Edgar. 2021. What causes the test error? Going beyond bias-variance via anova. *Journal of Machine Learning Research*, **22**(155), 1–82.

Linnainmaa, Seppo. 1970. *Alogritmin Kumulatiivinen Pyöristysvirhe Yksittäisten Pyöristysvirheiden Taylor-Kehitelmänä*. M.Phil. thesis, University of Helsinki.

Lu, Yiping, Ma, Chao, Lu, Yulong, Lu, Jianfeng, and Ying, Lexing. 2020. A mean field analysis of deep ResNet and beyond: Towards provable optimization via overparameterization from depth. Pages 6426–6436 of: *Proc. International Conference on Machine Learning*.

Lunz, Sebastian, Öktem, Ozan, and Schönlieb, Carola-Bibiane. 2018. Adversarial regularizers in inverse problems. Pages 8507–8516 of: *Advances in Neural Information Processing Systems*.

Lyu, Kaifeng, and Li, Jian. 2019. Gradient descent maximizes the margin of homogeneous neural networks. In: *Proc. International Conference on Learning Representations*.

Ma, Junshui, Sheridan, Robert P., Liaw, Andy, Dahl, George E., and Svetnik, Vladimir. 2015. Deep neural nets as a method for quantitative structure–activity relationships. *Journal of Chemical Information and Modeling*, **55**(2), 263–274.

Maiorov, Vitaly, and Pinkus, Allan. 1999. Lower bounds for approximation by MLP neural networks. *Neurocomputing*, **25**(1-3), 81–91.

Mallat, Stéphane. 2012. Group invariant scattering. *Communications on Pure and Applied Mathematics*, **65**(10), 1331–1398.

Mallat, Stéphane. 2016. Understanding deep convolutional networks. *Philosophical Transactions of the Royal Society A: Mathematical, Physical and Engineering Sciences*, **374**(2065), 20150203.

Marcati, Carlo, Opschoor, Joost, Petersen, Philipp, and Schwab, Christoph. 2020. Exponential ReLU neural network approximation rates for point and edge singularities. ETH Zurich SAM Research Report.

Matthews, Alexander G. de G., Hron, Jiri, Rowland, Mark, Turner, Richard E., and Ghahramani, Zoubin. 2018. Gaussian process behaviour in wide deep neural networks. In: *Proc. International Conference on Learning Representations*.

McAllester, David A. 1999. PAC-Bayesian model averaging. Pages 164–170 of: *Prc. Conference on Learning Theory*.

McCulloch, Warren S., and Pitts, Walter. 1943. A logical calculus of the ideas immanent in nervous activity. *Bulletin of Mathematical Biophysics*, **5**(4), 115–133.

McDiarmid, Colin. 1989. On the method of bounded differences. Pages 148–188 of: *Surveys in Combinatorics*. London Mathematical Society Lecture Notes, vol. 141. Cambridge University Press.

Mei, Song, and Montanari, Andrea. 2019. The generalization error of random features regression: Precise asymptotics and double descent curve. ArXiv preprint arXiv:1908.05355.

Mendelson, Shahar. 2014. Learning without concentration. Pages 25–39 of: *Proc. Conference on Learning Theory*.

Mendelson, Shahar, and Vershynin, Roman. 2003. Entropy and the combinatorial dimension. *Inventiones Mathematicae*, **152**(1), 37–55.

Mhaskar, Hrushikesh N. 1996. Neural networks for optimal approximation of smooth and analytic functions. *Neural Computation*, **8**(1), 164–177.

Mianjy, Poorya, Arora, Raman, and Vidal, Rene. 2018. On the implicit bias of dropout. Pages 3540–3548 of: *Proc. International Conference on Machine Learning*.

Minsky, Marvin, and Papert, Seymour A. 1969. *Perceptrons*. MIT Press.

Mnih, Volodymyr, Kavukcuoglu, Koray, Silver, David, Graves, Alex, Antonoglou, Ioannis, Wierstra, Daan, and Riedmiller, Martin. 2013. Playing Atari with deep reinforcement learning. ArXiv preprint arXiv:1312.5602.

Monga, Vishal, Li, Yuelong, and Eldar, Yonina C. 2021. Algorithm unrolling: Interpretable, efficient deep learning for signal and image processing. *IEEE Signal Processing Magazine*, **38**(2), 18–44.

Montanari, Andrea, and Zhong, Yiqiao. 2020. The interpolation phase transition in neural networks: Memorization and generalization under lazy training. ArXiv preprint arXiv:2007.12826.

Montúfar, Guido, Pascanu, Razvan, Cho, Kyunghyun, and Bengio, Yoshua. 2014. On the number of linear regions of deep neural networks. Pages 2924–2932 of: *Advances in Neural Information Processing Systems.*

Muthukumar, Vidya, Vodrahalli, Kailas, Subramanian, Vignesh, and Sahai, Anant. 2020. Harmless interpolation of noisy data in regression. *IEEE Journal on Selected Areas in Information Theory*, **1**(1), 67–83.

Nacson, Mor Shpigel, Lee, Jason D., Gunasekar, Suriya, Savarese, Pedro Henrique Pamplona, Srebro, Nathan, and Soudry, Daniel. 2019. Convergence of gradient descent on separable data. Pages 3420–3428 of: *International Conference on Artificial Intelligence and Statistics.*

Nagarajan, Vaishnavh, and Kolter, J. Zico. 2019. Uniform convergence may be unable to explain generalization in deep learning. Pages 11615–11626 of: *Advances in Neural Information Processing Systems.*

Nakada, Ryumei and Imaizumi, Masaaki. 2020. Adaptive approximation and generalization of deep neural network with intrinsic dimensionality. *Journal of Machine Learning Research*, **21**(174), 1–38.

Nakamura-Zimmerer, Tenavi, Gong, Qi, and Kang, Wei. 2021. Adaptive deep learning for high-dimensional Hamilton–Jacobi–Bellman equations. *SIAM Journal on Scientific Computing*, **43**(2), A1221–A1247.

Nakkiran, Preetum, Kaplun, Gal, Bansal, Yamini, Yang, Tristan, Barak, Boaz, and Sutskever, Ilya. 2020. Deep double descent: Where bigger models and more data hurt. In: *Proc. International Conference on Learning Representations.*

Nemirovski, Arkadi, Juditsky, Anatoli, Lan, Guanghui, and Shapiro, Alexander. 2009. Robust stochastic approximation approach to stochastic programming. *SIAM Journal on Optimization*, **19**(4), 1574–1609.

Nemirovsky, Arkadi Semenovich, and Yudin, David Borisovich. 1983. *Problem Complexity and Method Efficiency in Optimization.* Wiley-Interscience Series in Discrete Mathematics. Wiley.

Neyshabur, Behnam, Tomioka, Ryota, and Srebro, Nathan. 2014. In search of the real inductive bias: On the role of implicit regularization in deep learning. ArXiv preprint arXiv:1412.6614.

Neyshabur, Behnam, Tomioka, Ryota, and Srebro, Nathan. 2015. Norm-based capacity control in neural networks. Pages 1376–1401 of: *Proc. Conference on Learning Theory.*

Neyshabur, Behnam, Bhojanapalli, Srinadh, McAllester, David, and Srebro, Nati. 2017. Exploring generalization in deep learning. Pages 5947–5956 of: *Advances in Neural Information Processing Systems.*

Neyshabur, Behnam, Bhojanapalli, Srinadh, and Srebro, Nathan. 2018. A PAC-Bayesian approach to spectrally-normalized margin bounds for neural networks. In: *Proc. International Conference on Learning Representations.*

Nguyen, Quynh, and Hein, Matthias. 2017. The loss surface of deep and wide neural networks. Pages 2603–2612 of: *Proc. International Conference on Machine Learning.*

Novak, Erich, and Woźniakowski, Henryk. 2009. Approximation of infinitely differentiable multivariate functions is intractable. *Journal of Complexity*, **25**(4), 398–404.

Olshausen, Bruno A., and Field, David J. 1996. Sparse coding of natural images produces localized, oriented, bandpass receptive fields. *Nature*, **381**(60), 609.

Oono, Kenta, and Suzuki, Taiji. 2019. Approximation and non-parametric estimation of ResNet-type convolutional neural networks. Pages 4922–4931 of: *Proc. International Conference on Machine Learning*.

Opschoor, Joost, Petersen, Philipp, and Schwab, Christoph. 2020. Deep ReLU networks and high-order finite element methods. *Analysis and Applications*, 1–56.

Orr, Genevieve B, and Müller, Klaus-Robert. 1998. *Neural Networks: Tricks of the Trade*. Springer.

Papyan, Vardan, Romano, Yaniv, and Elad, Michael. 2017a. Convolutional neural networks analyzed via convolutional sparse coding. *Journal of Machine Learning Research*, **18**(1), 2887–2938.

Papyan, Vardan, Sulam, Jeremias, and Elad, Michael. 2017b. Working locally thinking globally: Theoretical guarantees for convolutional sparse coding. *IEEE Transactions on Signal Processing*, **65**(21), 5687–5701.

Papyan, Vardan, Romano, Yaniv, Sulam, Jeremias, and Elad, Michael. 2018. Theoretical foundations of deep learning via sparse representations: A multilayer sparse model and its connection to convolutional neural networks. *IEEE Signal Processing Magazine*, **35**(4), 72–89.

Pardoux, Etienne, and Peng, Shige. 1992. Backward stochastic differential equations and quasilinear parabolic partial differential equations. Pages 200–217 of: *Stochastic Partial Differential Equations and Their Applications*. Springer.

Petersen, Philipp, and Voigtlaender, Felix. 2018. Optimal approximation of piecewise smooth functions using deep ReLU neural networks. *Neural Networks*, **108**, 296–330.

Petersen, Philipp, and Voigtlaender, Felix. 2020. Equivalence of approximation by convolutional neural networks and fully-connected networks. *Proceedings of the American Mathematical Society*, **148**(4), 1567–1581.

Petersen, Philipp, Raslan, Mones, and Voigtlaender, Felix. 2020. Topological properties of the set of functions generated by neural networks of fixed size. *Foundations of Computational Mathematics*, **21**, 375–444.

Pfau, David, Spencer, James S., Matthews, Alexander G. D. G., and Foulkes, W. M. C. 2020. Ab initio solution of the many-electron Schrödinger equation with deep neural networks. *Physical Review Research*, **2**(3), 033429.

Pham, Hieu, Guan, Melody, Zoph, Barret, Le, Quoc, and Dean, Jeff. 2018. Efficient neural architecture search via parameters sharing. Pages 4095–4104 of: *Proc. International Conference on Machine Learning*.

Poggio, Tomaso, Rifkin, Ryan, Mukherjee, Sayan, and Niyogi, Partha. 2004. General conditions for predictivity in learning theory. *Nature*, **428**(6981), 419–422.

Poggio, Tomaso, Kawaguchi, Kenji, Liao, Qianli, Miranda, Brando, Rosasco, Lorenzo, Boix, Xavier, Hidary, Jack, and Mhaskar, Hrushikesh N. 2017a. Theory of deep learning III: explaining the non-overfitting puzzle. ArXiv preprint arXiv:1801.00173.

Poggio, Tomaso, Mhaskar, Hrushikesh N., Rosasco, Lorenzo, Miranda, Brando, and Liao, Qianli. 2017b. Why and when can deep – but not shallow – networks avoid the curse of dimensionality: a review. *International Journal of Automation and Computing*, **14**(5), 503–519.

Poole, Ben, Lahiri, Subhaneil, Raghu, Maithra, Sohl-Dickstein, Jascha, and Ganguli, Surya. 2016. Exponential expressivity in deep neural networks through transient chaos. Pages 3368–3376 of: *Advances in Neural Information Processing Systems*.

Raghu, Maithra, Poole, Ben, Kleinberg, Jon, Ganguli, Surya, and Sohl-Dickstein, Jascha. 2017. On the expressive power of deep neural networks. Pages 2847–2854 of: *Proc. International Conference on Machine Learning*.

Rahimi, Ali, Recht, Benjamin, et al. 2007. Random features for large-scale kernel machines. Pages 1177–1184 of: *Advances in Neural Information Processing Systems*.

Raissi, Maziar, Perdikaris, Paris, and Karniadakis, George E. 2019. Physics-informed neural networks: A deep learning framework for solving forward and inverse problems involving nonlinear partial differential equations. *Journal of Computational Physics*, **378**, 686–707.

Ramanujan, Vivek, Wortsman, Mitchell, Kembhavi, Aniruddha, Farhadi, Ali, and Rastegari, Mohammad. 2020. What's hidden in a randomly weighted neural network? Pages 11893–11902 of: *Proc. IEEE Conference on Computer Vision and Pattern Recognition*.

Ríos, P. López, Ma, Ao, Drummond, Neil D., Towler, Michael D., and Needs, Richard J. 2006. Inhomogeneous backflow transformations in quantum Monte Carlo calculations. *Physical Review E*, **74**(6), 066701.

Robbins, Herbert, and Monro, Sutton. 1951. A stochastic approximation method. *Annals of Mathematical Statistics*, 400–407.

Romano, Yaniv, Elad, Michael, and Milanfar, Peyman. 2017. The little engine that could: Regularization by denoising (RED). *SIAM Journal on Imaging Sciences*, **10**(4), 1804–1844.

Ronneberger, Olaf, Fischer, Philipp, and Brox, Thomas. 2015. U-net: convolutional networks for biomedical image segmentation. Pages 234–241 of: *Proc. International Conference on Medical image Computing and Computer-Assisted Intervention*.

Rosenblatt, Frank. 1958. The perceptron: a probabilistic model for information storage and organization in the brain. *Psychological Review*, **65**(6), 386.

Rudin, Walter. 2006. *Real and Complex Analysis*. McGraw-Hill.

Rumelhart, David E., Hinton, Geoffrey E., and Williams, Ronald J. 1986. Learning representations by back-propagating errors. *Nature*, **323**(6088), 533–536.

Ruthotto, Lars, and Haber, Eldad. 2019. Deep neural networks motivated by partial differential equations. *Journal of Mathematical Imaging and Vision*, 1–13.

Safran, Itay, and Shamir, Ohad. 2016. On the quality of the initial basin in over-specified neural networks. Pages 774–782 of: *Proc. International Conference on Machine Learning*.

Safran, Itay, and Shamir, Ohad. 2017. Depth–width tradeoffs in approximating natural functions with neural networks. Pages 2979–2987 of: *Proc. International Conference on Machine Learning*.

Safran, Itay, and Shamir, Ohad. 2018. Spurious local minima are common in two-layer ReLU neural networks. Pages 4433–4441 of: *Proc. International Conference on Machine Learning*.

Sakurai, Akito. 1999. Tight bounds for the VC-dimension of piecewise polynomial networks. Pages 323–329 of: *Advances in Neural Information Processing Systems*.

Santurkar, Shibani, Tsipras, Dimitris, Ilyas, Andrew, and Madry, Aleksander. 2018. How does batch normalization help optimization? Pages 2488–2498 of: *Advances in Neural Information Processing Systems*.

Saxton, David, Grefenstette, Edward, Hill, Felix, and Kohli, Pushmeet. 2018. Analysing mathematical reasoning abilities of neural models. In: *Proc. International Conference on Learning Representations*.

Scherbela, Michael, Reisenhofer, Rafael, Gerard, Leon, Marquetand Philipp, and Grohs, Philipp. 2021. Solving the electronic Schrödinger equation for multiple nuclear geometries with weight-sharing deep neural network. ArXiv preprint arXiv:2105.08351.

Schmidhuber, Jürgen. 2015. Deep learning in neural networks: An overview. *Neural Networks*, **61**, 85–117.

Schmidt-Hieber, Johannes. 2019. Deep ReLU network approximation of functions on a manifold. ArXiv preprint arXiv:1908.00695.

Schütt, Kristof T., Kindermans, Pieter-Jan, Sauceda, Huziel E., Chmiela, Stefan, Tkatchenko, Alexandre, and Müller, Klaus-Robert. 2017. Schnet: A continuous-filter convolutional neural network for modeling quantum interactions. Pages 992–1002 of: *Advances in Neural Information Processing Systems*.

Schwab, Christoph, and Zech, Jakob. 2019. Deep learning in high dimension: Neural network expression rates for generalized polynomial chaos expansions in UQ. *Analysis and Applications*, **17**(01), 19–55.

Senior, Andrew W., Evans, Richard, Jumper, John, Kirkpatrick, James, Sifre, Laurent, Green, Tim, Qin, Chongli, Žídek, Augustin, Nelson, Alexander W. R., and Bridgland, Alex. 2020. Improved protein structure prediction using potentials from deep learning. *Nature*, **577**(7792), 706–710.

Shaham, Uri, Cloninger, Alexander, and Coifman, Ronald R. 2018. Provable approximation properties for deep neural networks. *Applied and Computational Harmonic Analysis*, **44**(3), 537–557.

Shalev-Shwartz, Shai, and Ben-David, Shai. 2014. *Understanding Machine Learning: From Theory to Algorithms.* Cambridge University Press.

Shalev-Shwartz, Shai, Shamir, Ohad, Srebro, Nathan, and Sridharan, Karthik. 2009. Stochastic convex optimization. In: *Proc. Conference on Learning Theory.*

Shapiro, Alexander, Dentcheva, Darinka, and Ruszczyński, Andrzej. 2014. *Lectures on Stochastic Programming: Modeling and Theory.* SIAM.

Shen, Zuowei. 2020. Deep network approximation characterized by number of neurons. *Communications in Computational Physics*, **28**(5), 1768–1811.

Silver, David, Huang, Aja, Maddison, Chris J., Guez, Arthur, Sifre, Laurent, Van Den Driessche, George, Schrittwieser, Julian, Antonoglou, Ioannis, Panneershelvam, Veda, and Lanctot, Marc. 2016. Mastering the game of Go with deep neural networks and tree search. *Nature*, **529**(7587), 484–489.

Silver, David, Schrittwieser, Julian, Simonyan, Karen, Antonoglou, Ioannis, Huang, Aja, Guez, Arthur, Hubert, Thomas, Baker, Lucas, Lai, Matthew, and Bolton, Adrian. 2017. Mastering the game of Go without human knowledge. *Nature*, **550**(7676), 354–359.

Šíma, Jiří. 2002. Training a single sigmoidal neuron is hard. *Neural Computation*, **14**(11), 2709–2728.

Soudry, Daniel, Hoffer, Elad, Nacson, Mor Shpigel, Gunasekar, Suriya, and Srebro, Nathan. 2018. The implicit bias of gradient descent on separable data. *Journal of Machine Learning Research*, **19**, 1–57.

Srivastava, Nitish, Hinton, Geoffrey, Krizhevsky, Alex, Sutskever, Ilya, and Salakhutdinov, Ruslan. 2014. Dropout: a simple way to prevent neural networks from overfitting. *Journal of Machine Learning Research*, **15**(1), 1929–1958.

Srivastava, Rupesh Kumar, Greff, Klaus, and Schmidhuber, Jürgen. 2015. Training very deep networks. Pages 2377–2385 of: *Advances in Neural Information Processing Systems.*

Sulam, Jeremias, Papyan, Vardan, Romano, Yaniv, and Elad, Michael. 2018. Multilayer convolutional sparse modeling: Pursuit and dictionary learning. *IEEE Transactions on Signal Processing*, **66**(15), 4090–4104.

Szabo, Attila, and Ostlund, Neil S. 2012. *Modern Quantum Chemistry: Introduction to Advanced Electronic Structure Theory.* Courier Corporation.

Szegedy, Christian, Liu, Wei, Jia, Yangqing, Sermanet, Pierre, Reed, Scott, Anguelov, Dragomir, Erhan, Dumitru, Vanhoucke, Vincent, and Rabinovich, Andrew. 2015. Going deeper with convolutions. Pages 1–9 of: *Proc. IEEE Conference on Computer Vision and Pattern Recognition.*

Talagrand, Michel. 1994. Sharper bounds for Gaussian and empirical processes. *Annals of Probability*, 28–76.

Telgarsky, Matus. 2015. Representation benefits of deep feedforward networks. ArXiv preprint arXiv:1509.08101.

Thorpe, Matthew, and van Gennip, Yves. 2018. Deep limits of residual neural networks. ArXiv preprint arXiv:1810.11741.

Ulyanov, Dmitry, Vedaldi, Andrea, and Lempitsky, Victor. 2018. Deep image prior. Pages 9446–9454 of: *Proc. IEEE Conference on Computer Vision and Pattern Recognition*.

van der Vaart, Aad W., and Wellner, Jon A. 1997. Weak convergence and empirical processes with applications to statistics. *Journal of the Royal Statistical Society Series A: Statistics in Society*, **160**(3), 596–608.

Vapnik, Vladimir. 1999. An overview of statistical learning theory. *IEEE Transactions on Neural Networks*, **10**(5), 988–999.

Vapnik, Vladimir. 2013. *The Nature of Statistical Learning Theory*. Springer Science & Business Media.

Vapnik, Vladimir, and Chervonenkis, Alexey. 1971. On the uniform convergence of relative frequencies of events to their probabilities. *Theory of Probability & its Applications*, **16**(2), 264–280.

Vaswani, Ashish, Shazeer, Noam, Parmar, Niki, Uszkoreit, Jakob, Jones, Llion, Gomez, Aidan N., Kaiser, Łukasz, and Polosukhin, Illia. 2017. Attention is all you need. Pages 5998–6008 of: *Advances in Neural Information Processing Systems*.

Venturi, Luca, Bandeira, Alfonso S., and Bruna, Joan. 2019. Spurious valleys in one-hidden-layer neural network optimization landscapes. *Journal of Machine Learning Research*, **20**(133), 1–34.

Vershynin, Roman. 2018. *High-Dimensional Probability: An Introduction with Applications in Data Science*. Cambridge University Press.

Vinyals, Oriol, Babuschkin, Igor, Czarnecki, Wojciech M., Mathieu, Michaël, Dudzik, Andrew, Chung, Junyoung, Choi, David H., Powell, Richard, Ewalds, Timo, and Georgiev, Petko. 2019. Grandmaster level in StarCraft II using multi-agent reinforcement learning. *Nature*, **575**(7782), 350–354.

Wan, Li, Zeiler, Matthew, Zhang, Sixin, Le Cun, Yann, and Fergus, Rob. 2013. Regularization of neural networks using dropconnect. Pages 1058–1066 of: *Proc. International Conference on Machine Learning*.

Werbos, Paul J. 1988. Generalization of backpropagation with application to a recurrent gas market model. *Neural Networks*, **1**(4), 339–356.

Whitney, Hassler. 1934. Analytic extensions of differentiable functions defined in closed sets. *Transactions of the American Mathematical Society*, **36**(1), 63–89.

Wiatowski, Thomas, Grohs, Philipp, and Bölcskei, Helmut. 2017. Energy propagation in deep convolutional neural networks. *IEEE Transactions on Information Theory*, **64**(7), 4819–4842.

Williams, Ronald J., and Zipser, David. 1995. Gradient-based learning algorithms for recurrent networks and their computational complexity. Pages 433–486 of: *Backpropagation: Theory, Architectures, and Applications*, Psychology Press.

Wu, Zonghan, Pan, Shirui, Chen, Fengwen, Long, Guodong, Zhang, Chengqi, and Philip, S. Yu. 2021. A comprehensive survey on graph neural networks. *IEEE Transactions on Neural Networks and Learning Systems*, **32**(1), 4–24.

Xu, Huan, and Mannor, Shie. 2012. Robustness and generalization. *Machine learning*, **86**(3), 391–423.

Yang, Greg. 2019. Scaling limits of wide neural networks with weight sharing: Gaussian process behavior, gradient independence, and neural tangent kernel derivation. ArXiv preprint arXiv:1902.04760.

Yarotsky, Dmitry. 2017. Error bounds for approximations with deep ReLU networks. *Neural Networks*, **94**, 103–114.

Yarotsky, Dmitry. 2018a. Optimal approximation of continuous functions by very deep ReLU networks. Pages 639–649 of: *Proc. Conference on Learning Theory*.

Yarotsky, Dmitry. 2018b. Universal approximations of invariant maps by neural networks. ArXiv preprint arXiv:1804.10306.

Yarotsky, Dmitry. 2021. Elementary superexpressive activations. ArXiv preprint arXiv:2102.10911.

Yarotsky, Dmitry, and Zhevnerchuk, Anton. 2020. The phase diagram of approximation rates for deep neural networks. In: *Advances in Neural Information Processing Systems*, vol. 33.

Ye, Jong Chul, Han, Yoseob, and Cha, Eunju. 2018. Deep convolutional framelets: A general deep learning framework for inverse problems. *SIAM Journal on Imaging Sciences*, **11**(2), 991–1048.

Yin, Rujie, Gao, Tingran, Lu, Yue M., and Daubechies, Ingrid. 2017. A tale of two bases: Local–nonlocal regularization on image patches with convolution framelets. *SIAM Journal on Imaging Sciences*, **10**(2), 711–750.

Young, Tom, Hazarika, Devamanyu, Poria, Soujanya, and Cambria, Erik. 2018. Recent trends in deep learning based natural language processing. *IEEE Computational Intelligence Magazine*, **13**(3), 55–75.

Yserentant, Harry. 2010. *Regularity and Approximability of Electronic Wave Functions*. Springer.

Zaslavsky, Thomas. 1975. *Facing up to Arrangements: Face-Count Formulas for Partitions of Space by Hyperplanes*. Memoirs of the American Mathematical Society. American Mathematical Society.

Zbontar, Jure, Knoll, Florian, Sriram, Anuroop, Murrell, Tullie, Huang, Zhengnan, Muckley, Matthew J., Defazio, Aaron, Stern, Ruben, Johnson, Patricia, Bruno, Mary, Parente, Marc, Geras, Krzysztof J., Katsnelson, Joe, Chandarana, Hersh, Zhang, Zizhao, Drozdzal, Michal, Romero, Adriana, Rabbat, Michael, Vincent, Pascal, Yakubova, Nafissa, Pinkerton, James, Wang, Duo, Owens, Erich, Zitnick, C. Lawrence, Recht, Michael P., Sodickson, Daniel K., and Lui, Yvonne W. 2018. fastMRI: An open dataset and benchmarks for accelerated MRI. ArXiv preprint arXiv:1811.08839.

Zhang, Chiyuan, Bengio, Samy, Hardt, Moritz, Recht, Benjamin, and Vinyals, Oriol. 2017. Understanding deep learning requires rethinking generalization. In: *Proc. International Conference on Learning Representations*.

Zhang, Chiyuan, Bengio, Samy, and Singer, Yoram. 2019. Are all layers created equal? ArXiv preprint arXiv:1902.01996.

Zhang, Chiyuan, Bengio, Samy, Hardt, Moritz, Mozer, Michael C., and Singer, Yoram. 2020. Identity crisis: Memorization and generalization under extreme overparameterization. In: *Proc. International Conference on Learning Representations*.

Zhou, Ding-Xuan. 2020a. Theory of deep convolutional neural networks: Downsampling. *Neural Networks*, **124**, 319–327.

Zhou, Ding-Xuan. 2020b. Universality of deep convolutional neural networks. *Applied and Computational Harmonic Analysis*, **48**(2), 787–794.

Zhou, Hao, Alvarez, Jose M., and Porikli, Fatih. 2016. Less is more: Towards compact CNNs. Pages 662–677 of: *Proc. European Conference on Computer Vision*.

Zoph, Barret, and Le, Quoc V. 2017. Neural architecture search with reinforcement learning. In: *Proc.Dobriban International Conference on Learning Representations*.

Zou, Difan, Cao, Yuan, Zhou, Dongruo, and Gu, Quanquan. 2020. Gradient descent optimizes over-parameterized deep ReLU networks. *Machine Learning*, **109**(3), 467–492.

2

Generalization in Deep Learning

K. Kawaguchi, Y. Bengio, and L. Kaelbling

Abstract: This chapter provides theoretical insights into why and how deep learning can generalize well, despite its large capacity, complexity, possible algorithmic instability, non-robustness, and sharp minima. This chapter forms a response to an open question in the literature. We also discuss approaches to provide non-vacuous generalization guarantees for deep learning. On the basis of theoretical observations, we propose new open problems.

2.1 Introduction

Deep learning has seen significant practical success and has had a profound impact on the conceptual bases of machine learning and artificial intelligence. Along with its practical success, the theoretical properties of deep learning have been a subject of active investigation. For the *expressivity* of neural networks, there are classical results regarding their universality (Leshno et al., 1993) and their exponential advantages over hand-crafted features (Barron, 1993). Another series of theoretical studies has considered how *trainable* (or optimizable) deep hypothesis spaces are, revealing structural properties that may enable non-convex optimization (Choromanska et al., 2015; Kawaguchi, 2016b). However, merely having an *expressive* and *trainable* hypothesis space does not guarantee good performance in predicting the values of future inputs, because of possible over-fitting to training data. This leads to the study of *generalization*, which is the focus of this chapter.

Some classical theory work attributes generalization ability to the use of a low-capacity class of hypotheses (Vapnik, 1998; Mohri et al., 2012). From the viewpoint of compact representation, which is related to small capacity, it has been shown that deep hypothesis spaces have an exponential advantage over shallow hypothesis spaces for representing some classes of natural target functions (Pascanu et al., 2014; Montufar et al., 2014; Livni et al., 2014; Telgarsky, 2016; Poggio et al., 2017). In other words, when some assumptions implicit in the hypothesis space (e.g., the

112

deep composition of piecewise linear transformations) are approximately satisfied by the target function, one can achieve very good generalization, compared with methods that do not rely on that assumption. However, a recent paper (Zhang et al., 2017) showed empirically that successful deep hypothesis spaces have sufficient capacity to memorize random labels. This observation has been called an "apparent paradox" and has led to active discussion by many researchers (Arpit et al., 2017; Krueger et al., 2017; Hoffer et al., 2017; Wu et al., 2017; Dziugaite and Roy, 2017; Dinh et al., 2017). Zhang et al. (2017) concluded with an open problem stating that understanding such observations requires the rethinking of generalization, while Dinh et al. (2017) stated that explaining why deep learning models can generalize well, despite their overwhelming capacity, is an open area of research.

In §2.3 we illustrate that, even in the case of linear models, hypothesis spaces with overwhelming capacity can result in arbitrarily small test errors and expected risks. Here, the *test error* is the error of a learned hypothesis on data on which it was not trained, but which is often drawn from the same distribution. Test error is a measure of how well the hypothesis generalizes to new data. We will examine this phenomenon closely, extending the original open problem from previous papers (Zhang et al., 2017; Dinh et al., 2017) into a new open problem that strictly includes the original. We reconcile an apparent paradox by checking theoretical consistency and identifying a difference in the underlying assumptions. Considering the differences in focus of theory and practice, we outline possible practical roles that generalization theory can play.

Towards addressing these issues, §2.4 presents generalization bounds based on validation datasets, which can provide non-vacuous and numerically-tight generalization guarantees for deep learning in general. Section 2.5 analyzes generalization errors based on training datasets, focusing on a specific case of feed-forward neural networks with ReLU units and max pooling. Under these conditions, the developed theory provides quantitatively tight theoretical insights into the generalization behavior of neural networks.

2.2 Background

Let $\mathcal{R}[f]$ be the expected risk of a function f, $\mathcal{R}[f] = \mathbb{E}_{X,Y \sim \mathbb{P}_{(X,Y)}}[\mathcal{L}(f(X),Y)]$, where X and Y are a input and a target, $\mathcal{L}$ is a loss function, and $\mathbb{P}_{(X,Y)}$ is the true distribution. Let $\hat{f}_{\mathcal{A},S} \colon \mathcal{X} \to \mathcal{Y}$ be a model learned by a learning algorithm $\mathcal{A}$ (including random seeds for simplicity) using a training dataset $S = ((X^{(i)}, Y^{(i)}))_{i=1}^{m}$ of size m. Let $\mathcal{R}_S[f]$ be the empirical risk of f as $\mathcal{R}_S[f] = \frac{1}{m} \sum_{i=1}^{m} \mathcal{L}(f(X^{(i)}), Y^{(i)})$ with $\{(X^{(i)}, Y^{(i)})\}_{i=1}^{m} = S$. Let $\mathcal{F}$ be a set of functions endowed with some structure, i.e., a *hypothesis space*. All vectors are *column* vectors in this chapter. For any given variable v, let d_v be its dimensionality.

A goal in machine learning is typically framed as the minimization of the expected risk $\mathcal{R}[\hat{f}_{\mathcal{A},S}]$. We typically aim to minimize the non-computable expected risk $\mathcal{R}[\hat{f}_{\mathcal{A},S}]$ by minimizing the computable empirical risk $\mathcal{R}_S[\hat{f}_{\mathcal{A},S}]$ (i.e., empirical risk minimization). One goal of generalization theory is to explain and justify when and how minimizing $\mathcal{R}_S[\hat{f}_{\mathcal{A},S}]$ is a sensible approach to minimizing $\mathcal{R}[\hat{f}_{\mathcal{A},S}]$ by analyzing

$$\text{the generalization gap} := \mathcal{R}[\hat{f}_{\mathcal{A},S}] - \mathcal{R}_S[\hat{f}_{\mathcal{A},S}].$$

In this section only, we use the typical assumption that S is generated by independent and identically distributed (i.i.d.) draws according to the true distribution $\mathbb{P}_{(X,Y)}$; the following sections of this chapter do not utilize this assumption. Under this assumption, a primary challenge of analyzing the generalization gap stems from the *dependence* of $\hat{f}_{\mathcal{A},S}$ on the same dataset S as that used in the definition of $\mathcal{R}_S$. Several approaches in *statistical learning theory* have been developed to handle this dependence.

The *hypothesis-space complexity* approach handles this dependence by decoupling $\hat{f}_{\mathcal{A},S}$ from the particular dataset S by considering the worst-case gap for functions in the hypothesis space as

$$\mathcal{R}[\hat{f}_{\mathcal{A},S}] - \mathcal{R}_S[\hat{f}_{\mathcal{A},S}] \leq \sup_{f \in \mathcal{F}} \mathcal{R}[f] - \mathcal{R}_S[f],$$

and by carefully analyzing the right-hand side. Because the cardinality of $\mathcal{F}$ is typically (uncountably) infinite, a direct use of the union bound over all elements in $\mathcal{F}$ yields a vacuous bound, leading to the need to consider different quantities for characterizing $\mathcal{F}$, e.g., Rademacher complexity and the Vapnik–Chervonenkis (VC) dimension. For example, if the codomain of $\mathcal{L}$ is in $[0,1]$, we have (Mohri et al., 2012, Theorem 3.1) that for any $\delta > 0$, with probability at least $1 - \delta$,

$$\sup_{f \in \mathcal{F}} \mathcal{R}[f] - \mathcal{R}_S[f] \leq 2\mathfrak{R}_m(\mathcal{F}) + \sqrt{\frac{\ln \frac{1}{\delta}}{2m}},$$

where $\mathfrak{R}_m(\mathcal{F})$ is the Rademacher complexity of the set $\{(X,Y) \mapsto \mathcal{L}(f(X),Y) : f \in \mathcal{F}\}$ and is defined by

$$\mathfrak{R}_m(\mathcal{F}) = \mathbb{E}_{S,\xi}\left[\sup_{f \in \mathcal{F}} \frac{1}{m} \sum_{i=1}^m \xi_i \mathcal{L}(f(X^{(i)}), Y^{(i)})\right],$$

where $\xi = (\xi_1, \ldots, \xi_n)$ and $\xi_1, \ldots, \xi_n$ are independent uniform random variables taking values in $\{-1, +1\}$ (i.e., Rademacher variables). For the deep-learning hypothesis spaces $\mathcal{F}$, there are several well-known bounds on $\mathfrak{R}_m(\mathcal{F})$, including those with explicit exponential dependence on depth (Sun et al., 2016; Neyshabur et al.,

2015a; Xie et al., 2015) and explicit linear dependence on the number of trainable parameters (Shalev-Shwartz and Ben-David, 2014). There has been significant work on improving the bounds in this approach, but all existing solutions with this approach still depend on the complexity of a hypothesis space or a sequence of hypothesis spaces, resulting in vacuous, and numerically too loose, generalization bounds.

The *stability* approach deals with the dependence of $\hat{f}_{\mathcal{A},S}$ on the dataset S by considering the *stability* of algorithm $\mathcal{A}$ with respect to different datasets. The considered stability is a measure of how much changing a data point in S can change $\hat{f}_{\mathcal{A},S}$. For example, an algorithm $\mathcal{A}$ is said to have uniform stability β (w.r.t. $\mathcal{L}$) if we have that for all $S \in (X \times \mathcal{Y})^m$, all $i \in \{1, \dots, m\}$, and all $(X,Y) \in X \times \mathcal{Y}$,

$$|\mathcal{L}(\hat{f}_{\mathcal{A},S}(X), Y) - \mathcal{L}(\hat{f}_{\mathcal{A},S^{\setminus i}}(X), Y)| \le \beta,$$

where $S^{\setminus i} = ((X^{(1)}, Y^{(1)}), \dots, (X^{(i-1)}, Y^{(i-1)}), (X^{(i+1)}, Y^{(i+1)}), \dots, (X^{(m)}, Y^{(m)}))$ ($S^{\setminus i}$ is S with the ith sample being removed). If the algorithm $\mathcal{A}$ has uniform stability β (w.r.t. $\mathcal{L}$) and if the codomain of $\mathcal{L}$ is in $[0, M]$, we have (Bousquet and Elisseeff, 2002) that for any $\delta > 0$, with probability at least $1 - \delta$,

$$\mathcal{R}[\hat{f}_{\mathcal{A},S}] - \mathcal{R}_S[\hat{f}_{\mathcal{A},S}] \le 2\beta + (4m\beta + M)\sqrt{\frac{\ln \frac{1}{\delta}}{2m}}.$$

On the basis of previous work on stability (e.g., Hardt et al., 2016; Kuzborskij and Lampert, 2017; Gonen and Shalev-Shwartz, 2017), one may conjecture some reason for generalization in deep learning.

The *robustness* approach avoids dealing with certain details of the dependence of $\hat{f}_{\mathcal{A},S}$ on S by considering the robustness of algorithm $\mathcal{A}$ for all possible datasets. In contrast with stability, robustness is the measure of how much the loss value can vary with respect to the *space* of the values of (X, Y). More precisely, an algorithm $\mathcal{A}$ is said to be $(|\Omega|, \zeta(\cdot))$-robust if $X \times \mathcal{Y}$ can be partitioned into $|\Omega|$ disjoint sets $\Omega_1, \dots, \Omega_{|\Omega|}$, such that, for all $S \in (X \times \mathcal{Y})^m$, all $(X, Y) \in S$, all $(X', Y') \in X \times \mathcal{Y}$, and all $i \in \{1, \dots, |\Omega|\}$, if $(X, Y), (X', Y') \in \Omega_i$ then

$$|\mathcal{L}(\hat{f}_{\mathcal{A},S}(X), Y) - \mathcal{L}(\hat{f}_{\mathcal{A},S}(X'), Y')| \le \zeta(S).$$

If algorithm $\mathcal{A}$ is $(\Omega, \zeta(\cdot))$-robust and the codomain of $\mathcal{L}$ is upper-bounded by M, given a dataset S we have (Xu and Mannor, 2012) that for any $\delta > 0$, with probability at least $1 - \delta$,

$$|\mathcal{R}[\hat{f}_{\mathcal{A},S}] - \mathcal{R}_S[\hat{f}_{\mathcal{A},S}]| \le \zeta(S) + M\sqrt{\frac{2|\Omega| \ln 2 + 2 \ln \frac{1}{\delta}}{m}}.$$

The robustness approach requires an *a priori known and fixed* partition of the input space such that the number of sets in the partition is $|\Omega|$ and the change of loss values in each set of the partition is bounded by $\zeta(S)$ *for all S* (Definition 2 and the proof of Theorem 1 in Xu and Mannor, 2012). In classification, if the *margin* is ensured to be large, we can fix the partition with balls of radius corresponding to this large margin, filling the input space. Recently, this idea was applied to deep learning (Sokolic et al., 2017a,b), producing insightful and effective generalization bounds while still suffering from the curse of the dimensionality of the a priori known and fixed input manifold.

With regard to the above approaches, *flat minima* can be viewed as the concept of low variation in the *parameter space*; i.e., a small perturbation in the parameter space around a solution results in a small change in the loss surface. Several studies have provided arguments for generalization in deep learning based on flat minima (Keskar et al., 2017). However, Dinh et al. (2017) showed that flat minima in practical deep-learning hypothesis spaces can be turned into sharp minima via re-parameterization without affecting the generalization gap, indicating that this requires further investigation.

There have been investigations into the connection between generalization and stochastic gradient descent (SGD) based on the Rademacher complexity, stability, and flat minima. For the Rademacher complexity, we can define the hypothesis space $\mathcal{F}$ explored by SGD, and could argue that the Rademacher complexity of it is somehow small; e.g., SGD with an appropriate initialization finds a minimal-norm solution (Poggio et al., 2018). The stability of SGD has been also analyzed (e.g., Hardt et al., 2016), but it is known that the existing bounds quickly become too loose and vacuous as the training time increases, even in the practical regime of the training time where a neural network can still generalize well. One can also argue that SGD prefers flat minima and degenerate minima, resulting in better generalization (Keskar et al., 2017; Banburski et al., 2019). Stochastic gradient descent with added noise has been also studied, but its convergence rate grows exponentially as the number of parameters increases (Raginsky et al., 2017). For all these approaches, there is yet no theoretical proof with a non-vacuous and numerically tight generalization bound on the practical regime of deep learning.

2.3 Rethinking Generalization

Zhang et al. (2017) demonstrated empirically that several deep hypothesis spaces can memorize random labels, while having the ability to produce zero training error and small test errors for particular natural datasets (e.g., CIFAR-10). They also observed empirically that regularization on the norm of weights seemed to be unnecessary to obtain small test errors, in contradiction to conventional wisdom. These observations suggest the following open problem.

Open Problem 1. How to tightly characterize the expected risk $\mathcal{R}[f]$ or the generalization gap $\mathcal{R}[f] - \mathcal{R}_S[f]$ with a sufficiently complex deep-learning hypothesis space $\mathcal{F} \ni f$, to produce theoretical insights and distinguish the case of "natural" problem instances $(\mathbb{P}_{(X,Y)}, S)$ (e.g., images with natural labels) from the case of other problem instances $(\mathbb{P}'_{(X,Y)}, S')$ (e.g., images with random labels).

In support of and extending the empirical observations by Zhang et al. (2017), we provide a theorem (Theorem 2.1) stating that the hypothesis space of over-parameterized linear models can memorize any training data *and* decrease the training and test errors arbitrarily close to zero (including zero itself) *with* arbitrarily large parameters norms, *even when* the parameters are arbitrarily far from the ground-truth parameters. Furthermore, Corollary 2.2 shows that conventional wisdom regarding the norms of the parameters w can fail to explain generalization, even in linear models that might seem not to be over-parameterized. All proofs for this chapter are presented in the appendix.

Theorem 2.1. *Consider a linear model with the training prediction* $\hat{Y}(w) = \Phi w \in \mathbb{R}^{m \times s}$, *where* $\Phi \in \mathbb{R}^{m \times n}$ *is a fixed feature matrix of the training inputs. Let* $\hat{Y}_{\text{test}}(w) = \Phi_{\text{test}} w \in \mathbb{R}^{m_{\text{test}} \times s}$ *be the test prediction, where* $\Phi_{\text{test}} \in \mathbb{R}^{m_{\text{test}} \times n}$ *is a fixed feature matrix of the test inputs. Let* $M = [\Phi^\top, \Phi_{\text{test}}^\top]^\top$. *Then, if* $n > m$ *and if* $\text{rank}(\Phi) = m$ *and* $\text{rank}(M) < n$,

(i) *for any* $Y \in \mathbb{R}^{m \times s}$, *there exists a parameter* w' *such that* $\hat{Y}(w') = Y$, *and*

(ii) *if there exists a ground truth* w^* *satisfying* $Y = \Phi w^*$ *and* $Y_{\text{test}} = \Phi_{\text{test}} w^*$ *then, for any* $\epsilon, \delta \geq 0$, *there exists a parameter* w *such that*

    (a) $\hat{Y}(w) = Y + \epsilon A$ *for some matrix* A *with* $\|A\|_F \leq 1$, *and*

    (b) $\hat{Y}_{\text{test}}(w) = Y_{\text{test}} + \epsilon B$ *for some matrix* B *with* $\|B\|_F \leq 1$, *and*

    (c) $\|w\|_F \geq \delta$ *and* $\|w - w^*\|_F \geq \delta$.

Corollary 2.2. *If* $n \leq m$ *and if* $\text{rank}(M) < n$, *then statement* (ii) *in Theorem 2.1 holds.*

Whereas Theorem 2.1 and Corollary 2.2 concern test errors rather than the expected risk (in order to be consistent with empirical studies), Proposition 2.3 below shows the same phenomena for the expected risk for general machine learning models not limited to deep learning and linear hypothesis spaces; i.e., Proposition 2.3 shows that, regarding small capacity, low complexity, stability, robustness, and flat minima, none of these is *necessary* for generalization in machine learning for any given problem instance $(\mathbb{P}_{(X,Y)}, S)$, although one of them can be *sufficient* for generalization. This statement does not contradict the necessary conditions and the no-free-lunch theorem from previous learning theory, as will be explained later in the chapter.

Proposition 2.3. *Given a pair* $(\mathbb{P}_{(X,Y)}, S)$ *and a desired* $\epsilon > \inf_{f \in \mathcal{Y}^{\mathcal{X}}} \mathcal{R}[f] - \mathcal{R}_S[f]$, *let* f_ϵ^* *be a function such that* $\epsilon \geq \mathcal{R}[f_\epsilon^*] - \mathcal{R}_S[f_\epsilon^*]$. *Then,*

(i) *for any hypothesis space* $\mathcal{F}$ *whose hypothesis-space complexity is large enough to memorize any dataset and which includes* f_ϵ^* *possibly at an arbitrarily sharp minimum, there exist learning algorithms* $\mathcal{A}$ *such that the generalization gap of* $\hat{f}_{\mathcal{A},S}$ *is at most* ϵ, *and*

(ii) *there exist arbitrarily unstable and arbitrarily non-robust algorithms* $\mathcal{A}$ *such that the generalization gap of* $\hat{f}_{\mathcal{A},S}$ *is at most* ϵ.

Proposition 2.3 is a direct consequence of the following remark which captures the essence of all the above observations (see Appendix A5 for the proof of Proposition 2.3).

Remark 2.4. The expected risk $\mathcal{R}[f]$ and the generalization gap $\mathcal{R}[f] - \mathcal{R}_S[f]$ of a hypothesis f with a true distribution $\mathbb{P}_{(X,Y)}$ and a dataset S are completely determined by the tuple $(\mathbb{P}_{(X,Y)}, S, f)$, independently of other factors, such as the hypothesis space $\mathcal{F}$ (and hence its properties such as capacity, Rademacher complexity, and flat-minima) or the properties of random datasets different from the given S (e.g., the stability and robustness of the learning algorithm $\mathcal{A}$). In contrast, conventional wisdom states that these other factors are what matter. This has created the "apparent paradox" in the literature.

From these observations, we propose the following open problem.

Open Problem 2. To tightly characterize the expected risk $\mathcal{R}[f]$ or the generalization gap $\mathcal{R}[f] - \mathcal{R}_S[f]$ of a hypothesis f with a pair $(\mathbb{P}_{(X,Y)}, S)$ of a true distribution and a dataset, *so as to produce theoretical insights* based only on properties of the hypothesis f and the pair $(\mathbb{P}_{(X,Y)}, S)$.

Solving Open Problem 2 for deep learning implies solving Open Problem 1, but not vice versa. Open Problem 2 encapsulates the essence of Open Problem 1 and all the issues from our Theorem 2.1, Corollary 2.2, and Proposition 2.3.

2.3.1 Consistency of Theory

The empirical observations in Zhang et al. (2017) and our results above may seem to contradict the results of statistical learning theory. However, there is no contradiction, and the apparent inconsistency arises from the misunderstanding and misuse of the precise meanings of the theoretical statements.

Statistical learning theory can be considered to provide two types of statements relevant to the scope of this chapter. The first type (which comes from upper bounds) is logically in the form of "*p* implies *q*," where *p* := "the hypothesis-space complexity is small" (or another statement about stability, robustness, or flat minima), and *q* := "the generalization gap is small." Notice that "*p* implies *q*" does not imply "*q* implies *p*." Thus, based on statements of this type, it is entirely possible that the generalization gap is small even when the hypothesis-space complexity is large or the learning mechanism is unstable, non-robust, or subject to sharp minima.

The second type of statement (which comes from lower bounds) is, logically, in the following form. In a set U_{all} of all possible problem configurations, there exists a subset $U \subseteq U_{all}$ such that "*q* implies *p*" in U (with the same definitions of *p* and *q* as in the previous paragraph). For example, Mohri et al. (2012, Section 3.4) derived lower bounds on the generalization gap by showing the existence of a "bad" distribution that characterizes U. Similarly, the classical no-free-lunch theorems are the results that give a worst-case distribution for each algorithm. However, if the problem instance at hand (e.g., object classification with MNIST or CIFAR-10) is not in such a subset U in the proofs (e.g., if the data distribution is not among the "bad" ones considered in the proofs), *q* does not necessarily imply *p*. Thus, it is still naturally possible that the generalization gap is small with large hypothesis-space complexity, instability, non-robustness, and sharp minima. Therefore, there is no contradiction or paradox.

2.3.2 Differences in Assumptions and Problem Settings

Under certain assumptions, many results in statistical learning theory have been shown to be tight and insightful (e.g., Mukherjee et al., 2006; Mohri et al., 2012). Hence, the need to rethink generalization comes partly from differences in the assumptions and problem settings.

Figure 2.1 illustrates the differences between the assumptions in statistical learning theory and in some empirical studies. On the one hand, in statistical learning theory a distribution $\mathbb{P}_{(X,Y)}$ and a dataset S are usually unspecified except that $\mathbb{P}_{(X,Y)}$ is in some set $\mathcal{P}$ and the dataset $S \in D$ is drawn randomly according to $\mathbb{P}_{(X,Y)}$ (typically with the i.i.d. assumption). On the other hand, in most empirical studies and in our theoretical results (Theorem 2.1 and Proposition 2.3), the distribution $\mathbb{P}_{(X,Y)}$ is still unknown, yet specified (e.g., via a real-world process), and the dataset S is specified and usually known (e.g., CIFAR-10 or ImageNet). Intuitively, whereas statistical learning theory needs to consider a set $\mathcal{P} \times D$ because of weak assumptions, some empirical studies can focus on a specified point $(\mathbb{P}_{(X,Y)}, S)$ in a set $\mathcal{P} \times D$ because of stronger assumptions. Therefore, by using the same terminology such as "expected risk" and "generalization" in both cases, we are susceptible to confusion and apparent contradiction.

Lower bounds, necessary conditions, and tightness in statistical learning theory

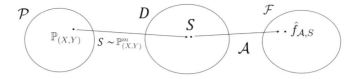

Figure 2.1 An illustration of differences in assumptions. Statistical learning theory analyzes the generalization behaviors of $\hat{f}_{\mathcal{A},S}$ over randomly drawn *unspecified* datasets $S \in D$ according to some *unspecified* distribution $\mathbb{P}_{(X,Y)} \in \mathcal{P}$. Intuitively, statistical learning theory is concerned more with questions regarding the set $\mathcal{P} \times D$ because of the *unspecified* nature of $(\mathbb{P}_{(X,Y)}, S)$, whereas certain empirical studies (e.g., Zhang et al., 2017) can focus on questions regarding each *specified* point $(\mathbb{P}_{(X,Y)}, S) \in \mathcal{P} \times D$.

are typically defined via a worst-case distribution $\mathbb{P}^{\text{worst}}_{(X,Y)} \in \mathcal{P}$. For instance, classical "no-free-lunch" theorems and certain lower bounds on the generalization gap (e.g., Mohri et al., 2012, Section 3.4) have actually been proven *for* the worst-case distribution $\mathbb{P}^{\text{worst}}_{(X,Y)} \in \mathcal{P}$. Therefore, "tight" and "necessary" typically mean "tight" and "necessary" for the set $\mathcal{P} \times D$ (e.g., through the worst or average case), but *not* for each particular point $(\mathbb{P}_{(X,Y)}, S) \in \mathcal{P} \times D$. From this viewpoint, we can understand that even if the quality of the set $\mathcal{P} \times D$ is "bad" overall, there may exist a "good" point $(\mathbb{P}_{(X,Y)}, S) \in \mathcal{P} \times D$.

Several approaches to statistical learning theory, such as the data-dependent and Bayesian ones (Herbrich and Williamson, 2002; Dziugaite and Roy, 2017), use further assumptions on the set $\mathcal{P} \times D$ to take advantage of more prior and posterior information; these have the ability to tackle Open Problem 1. However, these approaches do not apply to Open Problem 2 as they still depend on factors other than the given $(\mathbb{P}_{(X,Y)}, S, f)$. For example, data-dependent bounds with the *luckiness framework* (Shawe-Taylor et al., 1998; Herbrich and Williamson, 2002) and *empirical* Rademacher complexity (Koltchinskii and Panchenko, 2000; Bartlett et al., 2002) still depend on the concept of hypothesis spaces (or the sequence of hypothesis spaces), and the robustness approach (Xu and Mannor, 2012) depends on datasets different from a given S via the definition of robustness (i.e., in §2.2, $\zeta(S)$ is a data-dependent term, but the definition of ζ itself and Ω depend on datasets other than S).

We note that analyzing a set $\mathcal{P} \times D$ is of significant interest for its own merits and is a natural task in the field of computational complexity (e.g., categorizing a set of problem instances into subsets with or without polynomial solvability). Indeed, a situation where theory theory focuses on a set whereas many practical studies focus on each element in the set is prevalent in computer science (see the discussion in Appendix A2 for more detail).

2.3.3 Practical Role of Generalization Theory

From the discussions above, we can see that there is a *logically expected* difference between the scope of theory and the focus in practice; it is logically expected that there are problem instances where theoretical bounds are pessimistic. In order for generalization theory to have maximal impact in practice, we must be clear on the set of different roles it can play regarding practice, and then work to extend and strengthen it in each of these roles. We have identified the following practical roles for a theory:

Role 1 To provide guarantees on expected risk.
Role 2 To guarantee that the generalization gap:

> **Role 2.1** is small for a given fixed S, and/or
> **Role 2.2** approaches zero for *a fixed model class* as m increases.

Role 3 To provide theoretical insights to guide the search over model classes.

2.4 Generalization Bounds via Validation

In practical deep learning, we typically adopt the training–validation paradigm, usually with a held-out validation set. We then search over hypothesis spaces by changing architectures (and other hyper-parameters) to obtain a low validation error. In this view we can conjecture the reason why deep learning can sometimes generalize well to be as follows: it is partially because we can obtain a good model via search using a validation dataset. Indeed, Proposition 2.5 states that if the validation error of a hypothesis is small, it is guaranteed to generalize well regardless of its capacity, Rademacher complexity, stability, robustness, or flat minima. Let $S^{(\text{val})}$ be a held-out validation dataset, of size m_{val}, which is independent of the training dataset S.

Proposition 2.5. (Generalization guarantee via validation error) *Assume that $S^{(\text{val})}$ is generated by i.i.d. draws according to a true distribution $\mathbb{P}_{(X,Y)}$. Let $\kappa_{f,i} = \mathcal{R}[f] - \mathcal{L}(f(X^{(i)}), Y^{(i)})$ for $(X^{(i)}, Y^{(i)}) \in S^{(\text{val})}$. Suppose that $\mathbb{E}[\kappa_{f,i}^2] \leq \gamma^2$ and $|\kappa_{f,i}| \leq C$ almost surely, for all $(f,i) \in \mathcal{F}_{\text{val}} \times \{1, \ldots, m_{\text{val}}\}$. Then, for any $\delta > 0$, with probability at least $1 - \delta$, the following holds for all $f \in \mathcal{F}_{\text{val}}$:*

$$\mathcal{R}[f] \leq \mathcal{R}_{S^{(\text{val})}}[f] + \frac{2C \ln(|\mathcal{F}_{\text{val}}|/\delta)}{3m_{\text{val}}} + \sqrt{\frac{2\gamma^2 \ln(|\mathcal{F}_{\text{val}}|/\delta)}{m_{\text{val}}}}.$$

Here, $\mathcal{F}_{\text{val}}$ is defined as a set of models f that is independent of a held-out validation dataset $S^{(\text{val})}$. Importantly, $\mathcal{F}_{\text{val}}$ *can, however, depend on the training dataset S,* because a dependence on S does not imply a dependence on $S^{(\text{val})}$. For example, $\mathcal{F}_{\text{val}}$ can contain a set of models f such that each f is a model, obtained at the end of training, with at least 99.5% *training* accuracy. In this example, $|\mathcal{F}_{\text{val}}|$ equals at most the number of end epochs times the cardinality of the set of possible hyper-parameter settings, and it is likely to be much smaller than that because of the 99.5% training accuracy criterion and the fact that a space of many hyper-parameters is narrowed down by using the training dataset as well as other datasets from different tasks. If a hyper-parameter search depends on the validation dataset, $\mathcal{F}_{\text{val}}$ will be the possible space of the search instead of the space actually visited by the search. We can also use a sequence $(\mathcal{F}_{\text{val}}^{(j)})_j$ to obtain validation-data-dependent bounds (see Appendix A6).

The bound in Proposition 2.5 is non-vacuous and tight enough to be practically meaningful. For example, consider a classification task with 0–1 loss. Set $m_{\text{val}} = 10,000$ (e.g., as in MNIST and CIFAR-10) and $\delta = 0.1$. Then, even in the worst case, with $C = 1$ and $\gamma^2 = 1$, and even with $|\mathcal{F}_{\text{val}}| = 1,000,000,000$, we have, with probability at least 0.9, that $\mathcal{R}[f] \le \mathcal{R}_{S^{(\text{val})}}[f] + 6.94\%$ for all $f \in \mathcal{F}_{\text{val}}$. In a non-worst-case scenario, for example, with $C = 1$ and $\gamma^2 = (0.05)^2$, we can replace 6.94% by 0.49%. With a larger validation set (e.g., as in ImageNet) and/or more optimistic C and γ^2 values, we can obtain much better bounds.

Although Proposition 2.5 poses the concern of increasing that the generalization bound will be increased when one is using a single validation dataset with too large a value of $|\mathcal{F}_{\text{val}}|$, the rate of increase goes as only $\ln|\mathcal{F}_{\text{val}}|$ and $\sqrt{\ln|\mathcal{F}_{\text{val}}|}$. We can also avoid dependence on the cardinality of $\mathcal{F}_{\text{val}}$ by using Remark 2.6.

Remark 2.6. Assume that $S^{(\text{val})}$ is generated by i.i.d. draws according to $\mathbb{P}_{(X,Y)}$. By applying Mohri et al. (2012, Theorem 3.1) to $\mathcal{F}_{\text{val}}$, if the codomain of $\mathcal{L}$ is in $[0,1]$, with probability at least $1 - \delta$, then, for all $f \in \mathcal{F}_{\text{val}}$,

$$\mathcal{R}[f] \le \mathcal{R}_{S^{(\text{val})}}[f] + 2\mathfrak{R}_m(\mathcal{F}_{\text{val}}) + \sqrt{(\ln 1/\delta)/m_{\text{val}}}.$$

Unlike the standard use of Rademacher complexity with a training dataset, the set $\mathcal{F}_{\text{val}}$ cannot depend on the validation set S but can depend on the training dataset S in any manner, and hence $\mathcal{F}_{\text{val}}$ differs significantly from the typical hypothesis space defined by the parameterization of models. We can thus end up with a very different effective capacity and hypothesis complexity (as selected by model search using the validation set) depending on whether the training data are random or have interesting structure which the neural network can capture.

2.5 Direct Analyses of Neural Networks

Unlike the previous section, this section analyzes the generalization gap with a training dataset S. In §2.3, we extended Open Problem 1 to Open Problem 2, and identified the different assumptions in theoretical and empirical studies. Accord-

Table 2.1 *Additional notation for DAG in Section 2.5*

Description	Notation
pre-activation output of the lth hidden layer given (X, w)	$z^{[l]}(X, w)$
component of an input $X^{(i)}$ used for the jth path	$\bar{X}_j^{(i)}$
path activation for the jth path given $X^{(i)}$ and $(X^{(i)}, w)$	$\bar{\sigma}_j(X^{(i)}, w)$
vector of trainable parameters	w
the jth path weight for the kth output unit	$\bar{w}_{k,j}$
vector of parameters trained with $(\mathcal{A}, S)$	w^S
vector of parameters frozen in two-phase training	w_σ
weight matrix connecting the $(l-1)$th layer to the lth layer	$W^{[l]}$
weight matrix connecting the l'th layer to the lth layer	$W^{(l,l')}$

ingly, this section aims to address these problems, to some extent, both in the case of particular specified datasets and the case of random unspecified datasets. To achieve this goal, this section presents a *direct analysis* of neural networks, rather than deriving results about neural networks from more generic theories based on capacity, Rademacher complexity, stability, or robustness.

Sections 2.5.2 and 2.5.3 deal with the squared loss, while §2.5.4 considers 0–1 loss with multi-labels. Table 2.1 summarizes the notation used in this section for a directed acyclic graph (DAG).

2.5.1 *Model Description via Deep Paths*

We consider general neural networks of any depth that have the structure of a DAG with ReLU nonlinearity and/or max pooling. This includes a feedforward network of any structure and with convolutional and/or fully connected layers, potentially with skip connections. For pedagogical purposes, we first discuss our model description for layered networks without skip connections, and then describe it for DAGs.

Layered nets without skip connections. Let $z^{[l]}(X, w) \in \mathbb{R}^{n_l}$ be the pre-activation vector of the lth hidden layer, where n_l is the width of the lth hidden layer and w represents the trainable parameters. Let $L - 1$ be the number of hidden layers. For layered networks without skip connections, the pre-activation (or pre-nonlinearity) vector of the lth layer can be written as

$$z^{[l]}(X, w) = W^{[l]} \sigma^{(l-1)} \left(z^{[l-1]}(X, w) \right),$$

with a boundary definition $\sigma^{(0)} \left(z^{[0]}(X, w) \right) \equiv X$, where $\sigma^{(l-1)}$ represents nonlinearity via ReLU and/or max pooling at the $(l-1)$th hidden layer, and $W^{[l]} \in \mathbb{R}^{n_l \times n_{l-1}}$

is a matrix of weight parameters connecting the $(l-1)$th layer to the lth layer. Here, $W^{[l]}$ can have *any* structure (e.g., shared and sparse weights to represent a convolutional layer). Let $\dot{\sigma}^{[l]}(X, w)$ be a vector, each of whose elements is 0 or 1, such that $\sigma^{[l]}\left(z^{[l]}(X, w)\right) = \dot{\sigma}^{[l]}(X, w) \circ z^{[l]}(X, w)$, which is an elementwise product of the vectors $\dot{\sigma}^{[l]}(X, w)$ and $z^{[l]}(X, w)$. Then we can write the pre-activation of the kth output unit at the last layer $l = L$ as

$$z_k^{[L]}(X, w) = \sum_{j_{L-1}=1}^{n_{L-1}} W_{kj_{L-1}}^{[L]} \dot{\sigma}_{j_{L-1}}^{(L-1)}(X, w) z_{j_{L-1}}^{[L-1]}(X, w).$$

By expanding $z^{[l]}(X, w)$ repeatedly and exchanging the sum and product via the distributive law of multiplication, we obtain

$$z_k^{[L]}(X, w) = \sum_{j_{L-1}=1}^{n_{L-1}} \sum_{j_{L-2}=1}^{n_{L-2}} \cdots \sum_{j_0=1}^{n_0} \overline{W}_{kj_{L-1}j_{L-2}\cdots j_0} \dot{\sigma}_{j_{L-1}j_{L-2}\cdots j_1}(X, w) X_{j_0},$$

where

$$\overline{W}_{kj_{L-1}j_{L-2}\cdots j_0} = W_{kj_{L-1}}^{[L]} \prod_{l=1}^{L-1} W_{j_l j_{l-1}}^{[l]}$$

and

$$\dot{\sigma}_{j_{L-1}j_{L-2}\cdots j_1}(X, w) = \prod_{l=1}^{L-1} \dot{\sigma}_{j_l}^{[l]}(X, w).$$

By merging the indices $j_0, \ldots, j_{L-1}$ into j with some bijection between

$$\{1, \ldots, n_0\} \times \cdots \times \{1, \ldots, n_{L-1}\} \ni (j_0, \ldots, j_{L-1}) \quad \text{and} \quad \{1, \ldots, n_0 n_1 \cdots n_{L-1}\} \ni j,$$

we have

$$z_k^{[L]}(X, w) = \sum_j \bar{w}_{k,j} \bar{\sigma}_j(X, w) \bar{X}_j,$$

where $\bar{w}_{k,j}, \bar{\sigma}_j(X, w)$ and $\bar{X}_j$ represent $\overline{W}_{kj_{L-1}j_{L-2}\cdots j_0}, \dot{\sigma}_{j_{L-1}j_{L-2}\cdots j_1}(X, w)$ and X_{j_0}, respectively with the change of indices (i.e., $\sigma_j(X, w)$ and $\bar{X}_j$, respectively, contain the n_0 numbers and $n_1 \cdots n_{L-1}$ numbers of the same copy of each $\dot{\sigma}_{j_{L-1}j_{L-2}\cdots j_1}(X, w)$ and X_{j_0}). Note that $\sum_j$ represents summation over all the paths from the input X to the kth output unit.

DAGs. Remember that every DAG has at least one topological ordering, which can be used to to create a layered structure with possible skip connections (e.g., see Healy and Nikolov, 2001; Neyshabur et al., 2015a). In other words, we consider

DAGs such that the pre-activation vector of the *l*th layer can be written as

$$z^{[l]}(X, w) = \sum_{l'=0}^{l-1} W^{(l,l')} \sigma^{[l']} \left(z^{[l']}(X, w) \right)$$

with a boundary definition $\sigma^{(0)} \left(z^{[0]}(X, w) \right) \equiv X$, where $W^{(l,l')} \in \mathbb{R}^{n_l \times n_{l'}}$ is a matrix of weight parameters connecting the *l'*th layer to the *l*th layer. Again, $W^{(l,l')}$ can have *any* structure. Thus, in the same way as with layered networks without skip connections, for all $k \in \{1, \ldots, d_y\}$,

$$z_k^{[L]}(X, w) = \sum_j \bar{w}_{k,j} \bar{\sigma}_j(X, w) \bar{X}_j,$$

where $\sum_j$ represents summation over all paths from the input X to the kth output unit; i.e., $\bar{w}_{k,j} \bar{\sigma}_j(X, w) \bar{X}_j$ is the contribution from the jth path to the kth output unit. Each of $\bar{w}_{k,j}$, $\bar{\sigma}_j(X, w)$, and $\bar{X}_j$ is defined in the same manner as in the case of layered networks without skip connections. In other words, the jth path weight $\bar{w}_{k,j}$ is the product of the weight parameters in the jth path, and $\bar{\sigma}_j(X, w)$ is the product of the 0–1 activations in the jth path, corresponding to ReLU nonlinearity and max pooling; $\bar{\sigma}_j(X, w) = 1$ if all units in the jth path are active, and $\bar{\sigma}_j(X, w) = 0$ otherwise. Also, $\bar{X}_j$ is the input used in the jth path. Therefore, for DAGs, including layered networks without skip connections,

$$z_k^{[L]}(X, w) = [\bar{X} \circ \bar{\sigma}(X, w)]^\top \bar{w}_k, \tag{2.1}$$

where $[\bar{X} \circ \bar{\sigma}(X, w)]_j = \bar{X}_j \bar{\sigma}_j(X, w)$ and $(\bar{w}_k)_j = \bar{w}_{k,j}$ are vectors whose size is the number of paths.

2.5.2 *Theoretical Insights via Tight Theory for Every Pair* $(\mathbb{P}, S)$

Theorem 2.7 below solves Open Problem 2 (and hence Open Problem 1) for neural networks with squared loss by stating that the generalization gap of a trainable parameter vector w with respect to a problem $(\mathbb{P}_{(X,Y)}, S)$ is tightly analyzable with theoretical insights, based only on the quality of w and the pair $(\mathbb{P}_{(X,Y)}, S)$. We do *not* assume that S is generated randomly on the basis of some relationship with $\mathbb{P}_{(X,Y)}$; the theorem holds for any dataset, regardless of how it was generated. Let w^S and $\bar{w}_k^S$ be the parameter vectors w and $\bar{w}_k$ learned with a dataset S and $\mathcal{A}$. Let $\mathcal{R}[w^S]$ and $\mathcal{R}_S[w^S]$ be the expected risk and empirical risk of the model with the learned parameter w^S. Let $z_i = [\bar{X}^{(i)} \circ \bar{\sigma}(X^{(i)}, w^S)]$. Let $G = \mathbb{E}_{X,Y \sim \mathbb{P}_{(X,Y)}}[zz^\top] - \frac{1}{m} \sum_{i=1}^m z_i z_i^\top$ and $v = \frac{1}{m} \sum_{i=1}^m Y_k^{(i)} z_i - \mathbb{E}_{X,Y \sim \mathbb{P}_{(X,Y)}}[Y_k z]$. Given a matrix M, let $\lambda_{\max}(M)$ be the largest eigenvalue of M.

Theorem 2.7. *Let $\{\lambda_j\}_j$ and be a set of eigenvalues and $\{u_j\}_j$ the corresponding* *orthonormal set of eigenvectors of G. Let* $\theta^{(1)}_{\bar{w}_k,j}$ *be the angle between* u_j *and* $\bar{w}_k$. *Let* $\theta^{(2)}_{\bar{w}_k}$ *be the angle between* v *and* $\bar{w}_k$. *Then (deterministically),*

$$\mathcal{R}[w^s] - \mathcal{R}_S[w^s] - c_y = \sum_{k=1}^{s}\left(2\|v\|_2\|\bar{w}^s_k\|_2 \cos\theta^{(2)}_{\bar{w}^s_k} + \|\bar{w}^s_k\|_2^2 \sum_j \lambda_j \cos^2\theta^{(1)}_{\bar{w}^s_k,j}\right)$$

$$\leq \sum_{k=1}^{s}\left(2\|v\|_2\|\bar{w}^s_k\|_2 + \lambda_{\max}(G)\|\bar{w}^s_k\|_2^2\right),$$

where $c_y = \mathbb{E}_Y[\|Y\|_2^2] - \frac{1}{m}\sum_{i=1}^{m}\|Y^{(i)}\|_2^2$.

Proof Idea   From Equation (2.1) with squared loss, we can decompose the generalization gap into three terms:

$$\mathcal{R}[w^s] - \mathcal{R}_S[w^s] = \sum_{k=1}^{s}\left[(\bar{w}^s_k)^\top\left(\mathbb{E}[zz^\top] - \frac{1}{m}\sum_{i=1}^{m}z_i z_i^\top\right)\bar{w}^s_k\right]$$

$$+ 2\sum_{k=1}^{s}\left[\left(\frac{1}{m}\sum_{i=1}^{m}Y^{(i)}_k z_i^\top - \mathbb{E}[Y_k z^\top]\right)\bar{w}^s_k\right]$$

$$+ \mathbb{E}[Y^\top Y] - \frac{1}{m}\sum_{i=1}^{m}(Y^{(i)})^\top Y^{(i)}. \qquad (2.2)$$

By manipulating each term, we obtain the desired statement. See Appendix C3 for a complete proof.   □

In Theorem 2.7, there is no issue of a vacuous or too loose a bound. Instead, it indicates that if the norm of the weights $\|\bar{w}^s_k\|_2$ is small then the generalization gap is small, with the tightest bound (i.e., equality) having no dependence on the hypothesis space.

Importantly, in Theorem 2.7, there are two other significant factors in addition to the norm of the weights $\|\bar{w}^s_k\|_2$. First, the eigenvalues of G and v measure the concentration of the given dataset S with respect to the (unknown) $\mathbb{P}_{(X,Y)}$ in the space of the learned representation $z_i = [\bar{X}^{(i)} \circ \bar{\sigma}(X^{(i)}, w^s)]$. Here, we can see the benefit of deep learning from the viewpoint of "deep-path" feature learning: even if a given S is not concentrated in the original space, optimizing w can result in concentrating it in the space of z. Similarly, c_y measures the concentration of $\|Y\|_2^2$, but c_y is independent of w and remains unchanged after a pair $(\mathbb{P}_{(X,Y)}, S)$ is given. Second, the $\cos\theta$ terms measure the similarity between $\bar{w}^s_k$ and these concentration terms. Because the norm of the weights $\|\bar{w}^s_k\|_2$ is multiplied by these other factors, the generalization gap can remain small, even if $\|\bar{w}^s_k\|_2$ is large, as long as some of the other factors are small.

On the basis of a generic bound-based theory, Neyshabur et al. (2015b) and

Neyshabur et al. (2015a) proposed controlling the norm of the *path* weights $\|\bar{w}_k\|_2$, which is consistent with our direct bound-less result (and which is as computationally tractable as a standard forward–backward pass[1]). Unlike the previous results, we do *not* require a predefined bound on $\|\bar{w}_k\|_2$ over different datasets, but require only its final value for each S in question, in addition to tighter insights (besides the norm) via equality as discussed above. In addition to the predefined norm bound, these previous results have an explicit exponential dependence on the depth of the network, which does not appear in our Theorem 2.7. Similarly, some previous results specific to layered networks without skip connections (Sun et al., 2016; Xie et al., 2015) contain the 2^{L-1} factor *and* a bound on the product of the norms of weight matrices, $\prod_{l=1}^{L} \|W^{(l)}\|$, rather than on $\sum_k \|\bar{w}_k^s\|_2$. Here, $\sum_k \|\bar{w}_k\|_2^2 \leq \prod_{l=1}^{L} \|W^{(l)}\|_F^2$ because the latter contains all the same terms as the former as well as additional non-negative additive terms after expanding the sums in the definition of the norms.

Therefore, unlike previous bounds, Theorem 2.7 generates these new theoretical insights from a *the tight equality* (in the first line of the equation in Theorem 2.7). Notice that, without manipulating the generalization gap, we can always obtain equality. However, the question answered here is whether or not we can obtain competitive theoretical insights (the path norm bound) via equality instead of inequality. From a practical view point, if the insights obtained are the same (e.g., they regularize the norm), then equality-based theory has the obvious advantage of being more precise.

2.5.3 Probabilistic Bounds over Random Datasets

While the previous subsection tightly analyzed each given point $(\mathbb{P}_{(X,Y)}, S)$, this subsection considers the set $\mathcal{P} \times D \ni (\mathbb{P}_{(X,Y)}, S)$, where D is the set of possible datasets S endowed with an i.i.d. product measure $\mathbb{P}_{(X,Y)}^m$ where $\mathbb{P}_{(X,Y)} \in \mathcal{P}$ (see §2.3.2).

In Equation (2.2), the generalization gap is decomposed into three terms, each containing the difference between a sum of *dependent* random variables and its expectation. The dependence comes from the fact that the $z_i = [\bar{X}^{(i)} \circ \bar{\sigma}(X^{(i)}, w^s)]$ are dependent on the sample index i, because of the dependence of w^s on the entire dataset S. We then observe the following: in $z_k^{[L]}(X, w) = [\bar{X} \circ \bar{\sigma}(X, w)]^\top \bar{w}$, the derivative of $z = [\bar{X} \circ \bar{\sigma}(X, w)]$ with respect to w is zero everywhere (except for the measure-zero set, where the derivative does not exist). Therefore, each step of the (stochastic) gradient descent greedily chooses the best direction in terms of $\bar{w}$ (with the current $z = [\bar{X} \circ \bar{\sigma}(X, w)]$), but not in terms of the w in $z = [\bar{X} \circ \bar{\sigma}(X, w)]$

---

[1] From the derivation of Equation (2.1), one can compute $\|\bar{w}_k^s\|_2^2$ with a single forward pass using element-wise squared weights, an identity input, and no nonlinearity. One can also follow (Neyshabur et al., 2015b) for this computation.

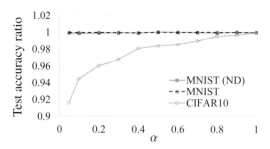

Figure 2.2 Test accuracy ratio (two-phase/base). Notice that the y-axis starts with high initial accuracy, even with a very small dataset size, αm, for learning w_σ.

(see Appendix A3 for more detail). This observation leads to a conjecture that the dependence of $z_i = [\bar{X}^{(i)} \circ \bar{\sigma}(X^{(i)}, w^s)]$, via the training process on the whole dataset S, is not entirely "bad" in terms of the concentration of the sum of the terms involving z_i.

Empirical Observations

As a first step in investigating the dependences of z_i, we evaluated the following novel *two-phase* training procedure which explicitly breaks the dependence of z_i on the sample index i. We first train a network in a standard way, but only using a *partial* training dataset $S_{\alpha m} = \{(X^{(1)}, Y^{(1)}), \ldots, (X^{(\alpha m)}, Y^{(\alpha m)})\}$ of size αm, where $\alpha \in (0,1)$ (this is the standard phase of the procedure). We then assign the value of $w^{S_{\alpha m}}$ to a new placeholder $w_\sigma := w^{S_{\alpha m}}$ and freeze w_σ, meaning that, as w changes, w_σ does not change. At this point, we have that $z_k^{[L]}(X, w^{S_{\alpha m}}) = [\bar{X} \circ \bar{\sigma}(X, w_\sigma)]^\top \bar{w}_k^{S_{\alpha m}}$. We then keep training only the $\bar{w}_k^{S_{\alpha m}}$ part with the entire training dataset of size m (the freeze phase), yielding the final model via this two-phase training procedure as

$$\bar{z}_k^{[L]}(X, w^S) = [\bar{X} \circ \bar{\sigma}(X, w_\sigma)]^\top \bar{w}_k^S. \tag{2.3}$$

Note that the vectors $w_\sigma = w^{S_{\alpha m}}$ and $\bar{w}_k^S$ contain the untied parameters in $\bar{z}_k^{[L]}(X, w^S)$. See Appendix A4 for a simple implementation of this two-phase training procedure that requires at most (approximately) twice as much computational cost as the normal training procedure.

We implemented the two-phase training procedure with the MNIST and CIFAR-10 datasets. The test accuracies of the standard training procedure (the base case) were 99.47% for MNIST (ND), 99.72% for MNIST, and 92.89% for CIFAR-10. Here MNIST (ND) indicates MNIST with no data augmentation. The experimental details are given in Appendix B.

Our source code is available at:

> http://lis.csail.mit.edu/code/gdl.html

Figure 2.2 presents the test accuracy ratios for varying α: the test accuracy of the two-phase training procedure divided by the test accuracy of the standard (base) training procedure. The plot in Figure 2.2 begins with $\alpha = 0.05$, for which $\alpha m = 3000$ in MNIST and $\alpha m = 2500$ in CIFAR-10. Somewhat surprisingly, using a much smaller dataset for learning w_σ still resulted in a competitive performance. A dataset from which we could more easily obtain a better generalization (i.e., MNIST) allowed us to use a smaller value of αm to achieve a competitive performance, which is consistent with our discussion above.

Theoretical Results

We now prove a probabilistic bound for the hypotheses resulting from the two-phase training algorithm. Let $\tilde{z}_i = [\bar{X}^{(i)} \circ \bar{\sigma}(X^{(i)}, w_\sigma)]$ where $w_\sigma := w^{S_{\alpha m}}$, as defined in the two-phase training procedure above. Our two-phase training procedure forces $\tilde{z}_{\alpha m+1}, \ldots, \tilde{z}_m$ over samples to be independent random variables (each $\tilde{z}_i$ is dependent over coordinates, which is taken care of in our proof), while maintaining the competitive practical performance of the output model $\tilde{z}_k^{[L]}(\cdot, w^S)$. As a result, we obtain the following bound on the generalization gap for the practical deep models $\tilde{z}_k^{[L]}(\cdot, w^S)$. Let $m_\sigma = (1 - \alpha)m$. Given a matrix M, let $\|M\|_2$ be the spectral norm of M.

Assumption 2.8. Let $G^{(i)} = \mathbb{E}_X[\tilde{z}\tilde{z}^\top] - \tilde{z}_i\tilde{z}_i^\top$, $V_{kk'}^{(i)} = Y_k^{(i)}\tilde{z}_{i,k'} - \mathbb{E}_{X,Y}[Y_k\tilde{z}_{k'}]$, and $c_y^{(i)} = \mathbb{E}_Y[\|Y\|_2^2] - \|Y^{(i)}\|_2^2$. Assume that, for all $i \in \{\alpha m + 1, \ldots, m\}$:

- $C_{zz} \geq \lambda_{\max}(G^{(i)})$ and $\gamma_{zz}^2 \geq \|\mathbb{E}_X[(G^{(i)})^2]\|_2$;
- $C_{yz} \geq \max_{k,k'} |V_{kk'}^{(i)}|$ and $\gamma_{yz}^2 \geq \max_{k,k'} \mathbb{E}_X[(V_{kk'}^{(i)})^2])$;
- $C_y \geq |c_y^{(i)}|$ and $\gamma_y^2 \geq \mathbb{E}_X[(c_y^{(i)})^2]$.

Theorem 2.9. *Suppose that Assumption 2.8 holds. Assume that $S \setminus S_{\alpha m}$ is generated by i.i.d. draws according to the true distribution $\mathbb{P}_{(X,Y)}$. Assume further that $S \setminus S_{\alpha m}$ is independent of $S_{\alpha m}$. Let $\hat{f}_{\mathcal{A},S}$ be the model learned by the two-phase training procedure with S. Then, for each $w_\sigma := w^{S_{\alpha m}}$, for any $\delta > 0$, with probability at least $1 - \delta$,*

$$\mathcal{R}[\hat{f}_{\mathcal{A},S}] - \mathcal{R}_{S \setminus S_{\alpha m}}[\hat{f}_{\mathcal{A},S}] \leq \beta_1 \sum_{k=1}^s \|\bar{w}_k^S\|_1 + 2\beta_2 \sum_{k=1}^s \|\bar{w}_k^S\|_2^2 + \beta_3,$$

where

$$\beta_1 = \frac{2C_{zz}}{3m_\sigma} \ln \frac{3d_z}{\delta} + \sqrt{\frac{2\gamma_{zz}^2}{m_\sigma} \ln \frac{3d_z}{\delta}},$$

$$\beta_2 = \frac{2C_{yz}}{3m_\sigma} \ln \frac{6d_y d_z}{\delta} + \sqrt{\frac{\gamma_{yz}^2}{m_\sigma} \ln \frac{6d_y d_z}{\delta}},$$

and

$$\beta_2 = \frac{2C_y}{3m_\sigma} \ln \frac{3}{\delta} + \sqrt{\frac{2\gamma_y^2}{m_\sigma} \ln \frac{3}{\delta}}.$$

Our proof does *not* require independence of the coordinates of $\tilde{z}_i$ from the entries of the random matrices $\tilde{z}_i \tilde{z}_i^\top$ (see the proof of Theorem 2.9).

The bound in Theorem 2.9 is data dependent because the norms of the weights $\bar{w}_k^S$ depend on each particular S. As with Theorem 2.7, the bound in Theorem 2.9 does not contain a predetermined bound on the norms of weights and can be independent of the choice of hypothesis space, if desired; i.e., Assumption 2.8 can be also satisfied without referencing a hypothesis space of w, because $\tilde{z} = [\bar{X}^{(i)} \circ \bar{\sigma}(X^{(i)}, w_\sigma)]$ with $\bar{\sigma}_j(X^{(i)}, w_\sigma) \in \{0, 1\}$. However, unlike Theorem 2.7, Theorem 2.9 *implicitly* contains the properties of datasets different from a given S, via the predefined bounds in Assumption 2.8. This is expected since Theorem 2.9 makes claims about the set of random datasets S rather than about each instantiated S. Therefore, while Theorem 2.9 presents a strongly data-dependent bound (over random datasets), Theorem 2.7 is tighter for each given S; indeed, the main equality of Theorem 2.7 is as tight as possible.

Theorems 2.7 and 2.9 provide generalization bounds for practical deep learning models that do not necessarily have an explicit dependence on the number of weights or an exponential dependence on depth or the effective input dimensionality. Although the size of the vector $\bar{w}_k^S$ can be exponentially large in the depth of the network, the norms of the vector need not be. Because $\tilde{z}_k^{[L]}(X, w^S) = \|\bar{X} \circ \bar{\sigma}(X, w_\sigma)\|_2 \|\bar{w}_k^S\|_2 \cos\theta$, we have that $\|\bar{w}_k^S\|_2 = z_k^{[L]}(X, w)/(\|\bar{X} \circ \bar{\sigma}(X, w_\sigma)\|_2 \cos\theta)$ (unless the denominator is zero), where θ is the angle between $\bar{X} \circ \bar{\sigma}(X, w_\sigma)$ and $\bar{w}_k^S$. Additionally, as discussed in §2.5.2, $\sum_k \|\bar{w}_k\|_2^2 \le \prod_{l=1}^L \|W^{(l)}\|_F^2$.

2.5.4 Probabilistic Bound for 0–1 Loss with Multi-Labels

For a 0–1 loss with multi-labels, the two-phase training procedure in §2.5.3 yields the generalization bound in Theorem 2.10. Similarly to the bounds in Theorems 2.7 and 2.9, the generalization bound in Theorem 2.10 does not necessarily have a dependence on the number of weights, or an exponential dependence on depth, or effective input dimensionality.

Theorem 2.10. *Assume that $S \setminus S_{am}$ is generated by i.i.d. draws according to a true distribution $\mathbb{P}_{(X,Y)}$. Assume also that $S \setminus S_{am}$ is independent of S_{am}. Fix $\rho > 0$ and w_σ. Let $\mathcal{F}$ be the set of models with the two-phase training procedure. Suppose that $\mathbb{E}_X[\|\bar{X} \circ \bar{\sigma}(X, w_\sigma)\|_2^2] \le C_\sigma^2$ and $\max_k \|\bar{w}_k\|_2 \le C_w$ for all $f \in \mathcal{F}$. Then, for* *any $\delta > 0$, with probability at least $1 - \delta$, the following holds for all $f \in \mathcal{F}$:*

$$R[f] \leq R_{S \backslash S_{am}}^{(\rho)}[f] + \frac{2d_y^2(1-\alpha)^{-1/2}C_\sigma C_w}{\rho\sqrt{m_\sigma}} + \sqrt{\frac{\ln\frac{1}{\delta}}{2m_\sigma}}.$$

Here, the empirical margin loss $R_S^{(\rho)}[f]$ is defined as

$$R_S^{(\rho)}[f] = \frac{1}{m} \sum_{i=1}^{m} \mathcal{L}_{\text{margin},\rho}(f(X^{(i)}), Y^{(i)}),$$

where $\mathcal{L}_{\text{margin},\rho}$ is defined as follows:

$$\mathcal{L}_{\text{margin},\rho}(f(X),Y) = \mathcal{L}_{\text{margin},\rho}^{(2)}(\mathcal{L}_{\text{margin},\rho}^{(1)}(f(X),Y)),$$

with

$$\mathcal{L}_{\text{margin},\rho}^{(1)}(f(X),Y) = z_y^{[L]}(X) - \max_{y \neq y'} z_{y'}^{[L]}(X) \in \mathbb{R}$$

and

$$\mathcal{L}_{\text{margin},\rho}^{(2)}(t) = \begin{cases} 0 & \text{if } \rho \leq t, \\ 1 - t/\rho & \text{if } 0 \leq t \leq \rho, \\ 1 & \text{if } t \leq 0. \end{cases}$$

2.6 Discussions and Open Problems

It is very difficult to make a detailed characterization of how well a specific hypothesis generated by a certain learning algorithm will generalize in the absence of detailed information about the given problem instance. Traditional learning theory addresses this very difficult question and has developed bounds that are as tight as possible given the generic information available. In this chapter, we have worked toward drawing stronger conclusions by developing theoretical analyses tailored for the situations with more detailed information, including actual neural network structures, and actual performance on a validation set.

Optimization and generalization in deep learning are closely related via the following observation: if we make optimization easier by changing the model architecture, the generalization performance can be degraded, and vice versa. Hence, the non-pessimistic generalization theory discussed in this chapter might allow more architectural choices and assumptions in optimization theory.

We now note an additional important open problem designed to address the gap between learning theory and practice: for example, theoretically motivated algorithms can degrade actual performances when compared with heuristics. Define the partial order of problem instances $(\mathbb{P}, S, f)$ as

$$(\mathbb{P}, S, f) \leq (\mathbb{P}', S', f') \quad \Leftrightarrow \quad \mathcal{R}_{\mathbb{P}}[f] - \mathcal{R}_S[f] \leq \mathcal{R}_{\mathbb{P}'}[f'] - \mathcal{R}_{S'}[f'],$$

where $\mathcal{R}_{\mathbb{P}}[f]$ is the expected risk with probability measure $\mathbb{P}$. Then, any theoretical insights without partial order preservation can be misleading as they can change the preference ranking of $(\mathbb{P}, S, f)$. For example, theoretically motivated algorithms can be worse than heuristics, if the theory does not preserve the partial order of $(\mathbb{P}, S, f)$. This observation suggests the following open problem.

Open Problem 3. Tightly characterize the expected risk $\mathcal{R}[f]$ or the generalization gap $\mathcal{R}[f] - \mathcal{R}_S[f]$ of a hypothesis f together with a pair $(\mathbb{P}, S)$, producing theoretical insights while partially yet provably preserving the partial order of $(\mathbb{P}, S, f)$.

Theorem 2.7 addresses Open Problem 3 by preserving the exact ordering via equality without bounds, *while producing the same and more tight practical insights* (e.g., regularizing the norm) when compared with existing bound-based theory. However, it would be beneficial also to consider a weaker notion of order preservation in order to gain analyzability with more useful insights, as stated in Open Problem 3.

Our discussion of Proposition 2.5 and Remark 2.6 suggests another open problem: analyzing the role and influence of *human intelligence* on generalization. For example, human intelligence often seems to be able to find good architectures (and other hyper-parameters) that get low validation errors (without non-exponentially large $|\mathcal{F}_{\text{val}}|$ as in Proposition 2.5, or a low complexity of $\mathcal{F}_{\text{val}}$ as in Remark 2.6). A close look at the deep learning literature seems to suggest that this question is fundamentally related to the progress of science and engineering, because many successful architectures have been designed based on the physical properties and engineering priors of the problems at hand (e.g., their hierarchical nature, convolution, and architecture for motion, such as that considered by Finn et al., 2016, memory networks, and so on). While this further open problem is a hard question, understanding it would be beneficial for further automating the role of human intelligence towards the goal of artificial intelligence.

Acknowledgements

We gratefully acknowledge support from NSF grants 1420316, 1523767, and 1723381, from AFOSR FA9550-17-1-0165, from ONR grant N00014-14-1-0486, and from ARO grant W911 NF1410433, as well as support from the NSERC, CIFAR, and Canada Research Chairs. Any opinions, findings, and conclusions or recommendations expressed in this material are those of the authors and do not necessarily reflect the views of our sponsors.

Appendix A Additional Discussions

This appendix contains additional results and discussions.

A1 Simple Regularization Algorithm

In general, theoretical bounds from statistical learning theory can be too loose to be directly used in practice. In addition, many theoretical results in statistical learning theory end up simply suggesting the regularization of some notion of smoothness of a hypothesis class. Indeed, by upper-bounding a distance between two functions (e.g., a hypothesis and the ground-truth function corresponding to the expected true labels), one can immediately see *without statistical learning theory* that regularizing the smoothness of the hypothesis class helps guarantees on generalization. Then, by an Occam's razor argument, one might prefer a simpler (yet still rigorous) theory and a corresponding simpler algorithm.

Accordingly, this subsection examines another simple regularization algorithm that directly regularizes the smoothness of the learned hypothesis. In this subsection we focus on multi-class classification problems with d_y classes, such as object classification with images. Accordingly, we analyze the expected risk with 0–1 loss as $\mathcal{R}[f] = \mathbb{E}_X[\mathbb{1}\{f(X) = Y\}]$, where $f(X) = \text{argmax}_{k \in \{1,\dots,d_y\}}(z_k^{[L]}(X))$ is the model prediction and $Y \in \{1,\dots,d_y\}$ is the true label of X.

This subsection proposes the following family of simple regularization algorithms: given any architecture and method, add a new regularization term for each training mini-batch as

$$\text{loss} = \text{original loss} + \frac{\lambda}{\bar{m}}\left|\max_k \sum_{i=1}^{\bar{m}} \xi_i z_k^{[L]}(X^{(i)})\right|,$$

where $X^{(i)}$ is drawn from some distribution approximating the true distribution of X, $\xi_1, \dots, \xi_{\bar{m}}$ are independently and uniformly drawn from $\{-1, 1\}$, $\bar{m}$ is the mini-batch size, and λ is a hyper-parameter. Importantly, the distribution approximating the true distribution of X is used only for regularization purposes and hence need not be precisely accurate (as long as it plays its role in regularization). For example, the true distribution can be approximated by populations generated by a generative neural network and/or an extra data augmentation process. For simplicity, we refer to this family of methods as directly approximately regularizing complexity (DARC).

In this chapter, as a first step, we evaluated only a very simple version of the proposed family of methods. That is, our experiments employed the following

Table A.2 *Test error (%)*

Method	MNIST	CIFAR-10
Baseline	0.26	3.52
DARC1	0.20	3.43

Table A.3 *Test error ratio (DARC1/Base)*

	MNIST (ND)		MNIST		CIFAR-10	
	mean	stdv	mean	stdv	mean	stdv
Ratio	0.89	0.61	0.95	0.67	0.97	0.79

Table A.4 *Values of* $\frac{1}{m}\left(\max_k \sum_{i=1}^m |z_k^{[L]}(X^{(i)})|\right)$

Method	MNIST (ND)		MNIST		CIFAR-10	
	mean	stdv	mean	stdv	mean	stdv
Base	17.2	2.40	8.85	0.60	12.2	0.32
DARC1	1.30	0.07	1.35	0.02	0.96	0.01

simple and easy-to-implement method, called DARC1:

$$\text{loss} = \text{original loss} + \frac{\lambda}{\bar{m}}\left(\max_k \sum_{i=1}^{\bar{m}} |z_k^{[L]}(X^{(i)})|\right), \tag{A.1}$$

where $X^{(i)}$ is the ith sample in the training mini-batch. The additional computational cost and programming effort due to this new regularization is almost negligible because $z_k^{[L]}(X^{(i)})$ is already used in computing the original loss. This simplest version was derived by approximating the true distribution of X by the empirical distribution of the training data.

We evaluated the proposed method (DARC1) by simply adding the new regularization term in (A.1) to the existing standard codes for MNIST and CIFAR-10. Standard variants of LeNet (LeCun et al., 1998) and ResNeXt-29(16 × 64d) (Xie et al., 2017) were used for MNIST and CIFAR-10, and compared with the addition of the studied regularizer. For all the experiments, we fixed $(\lambda/\bar{m}) = 0.001$ with $\bar{m} = 64$. We used a single model without ensemble methods. The experimental details are given in Appendix B. The source code is available at

    http://lis.csail.mit.edu/code/gdl.html

Table A.2 shows the error rates in comparison with previous results. To the best of our knowledge, the previous state-of-the-art classification error is 0.23% for MNIST with a single model (Sato et al., 2015) (and 0.21% with an ensemble, by Wan et al., 2013). To further investigate the improvement, we ran 10 random trials with computationally less expensive settings, to gather the mean and standard deviation (stdv). For MNIST, we used fewer epochs with the same model. For CIFAR-10, we used a smaller model class (pre-activation ResNet with only 18 layers). Table A.3 summarizes the improvement ratio, i.e., the new model's error divided by the base model's error. We observed improvements in all cases. The test errors (standard deviations) of the base models were 0.53 (0.029) for MNIST (ND), 0.28 (0.024) for MNIST, and 7.11 (0.17) for CIFAR-10 (all in %).

Table A.4 contains the values of the regularization term $\frac{1}{m}(\max_k \sum_{i=1}^{m} |z_k^{[L]}(X^{(i)})|)$ for each obtained model. The models learned with the proposed method were significantly different from the base models in terms of this value. Interestingly, a comparison of the base cases for MNIST (ND) and MNIST shows that data augmentation by itself *implicitly* regularized what we explicitly regularized in the proposed method.

A2 Relationship to Other Fields

The situation where theoretical studies focus on a set of problems and practical applications are concerned with each element in a set is prevalent in the machine learning and computer science literature, and is not limited to the field of learning theory. For example, for each practical problem instance $q \in Q$, the size of the set Q that had been analyzed in theory for optimal exploration in Markov decision processes (MDPs) was demonstrated to be frequently too pessimistic, and a methodology to partially mitigate the issue was proposed (Kawaguchi, 2016a). Bayesian optimization would suffer from a pessimistic set Q regarding each problem instance $q \in Q$, the issue of which had been partially mitigated (Kawaguchi et al., 2015).

Moreover, characterizing a set of problems Q only via a worst-case instance $q' \in Q$ (i.e., worst-case analysis) is known to have several issues in theoretical computer science, and so-called *beyond worst-case analysis* (e.g., smoothed analysis) is an active area of research to mitigate these issues.

A3 SGD Chooses Direction in Terms of $\bar{w}$

Recall that

$$z_k^{[L]}(X, w) = z^\top \bar{w} = [\bar{X} \circ \bar{\sigma}(X, w)]^\top \bar{w}.$$

Note that $\sigma(X, w)$ is 0 or 1 for max pooling and/or ReLU nonlinearity. Thus, the derivative of $z = [\bar{X} \circ \bar{\sigma}(X, w)]$ with respect to w is zero everywhere (except at the measure-zero set, where the derivative does not exists). Thus, by the chain rule (and power rule), the gradient of the loss with respect to w contains only a contribution from the derivative of $z_k^{[L]}$ with respect to $\bar{w}$, but not from that with respect to w in z.

A4 Simple Implementation of Two-Phase Training Procedure

Directly implementing Equation (2.3) requires a summation over all paths, which can be computationally expensive. To avoid thi, we implemented it by creating two deep neural networks, one of which defines $\bar{w}$ paths hierarchically, the other defining w_σ paths hierarchically, resulting in a computational cost at most (approximately) twice as much as the original cost of training standard deep learning models. We tied w_σ and $\bar{w}$ in the two networks during the standard phase, and untied them during the freeze phase.

Our source code is available at http://lis.csail.mit.edu/code/gdl.html

The computation of the standard network without skip connection can be re-written as

$$z^{[l]}(X,w) = \sigma^{[l]}(W^{[l]}z^{[l-1]}(X,w))$$
$$= \dot{\sigma}^{[l]}(W^{[l]}z^{[l-1]}(X,w)) \circ W^{[l]}z^{[l-1]}(X,w)$$
$$= \dot{\sigma}^{[l]}(W_\sigma^{[l]}z_\sigma^{[l-1]}(X,w)) \circ W^{[l]}z^{[l-1]}(X,w),$$

where

$$W_\sigma^{[l]} := W^{[l]}, \qquad z_\sigma^{[l-1]} := \sigma(W_\sigma^{[l]}z_\sigma^{[l-1]}(X,w))$$

and

$$\dot{\sigma}_j^{[l]}(W^{[l]}z^{[l-1]}(X,w)) = \begin{cases} 1 & \text{if the } j\text{th unit at the } l\text{th layer is active,} \\ 0 & \text{otherwise.} \end{cases}$$

Note that because $W_\sigma^{[l]} = W^{[l]}$, we have that $z_\sigma^{[l-1]} = z^{[l]}$ in the standard phase and standard models.

In the two-phase training procedure, we created two networks for $W_\sigma^{[l]}z_\sigma^{[l-1]}(X,w)$ and $W^{[l]}z^{[l-1]}(X,w)$ separately. We then set $W_\sigma^{[l]} = W^{[l]}$ during the standard phase, and froze $W_\sigma^{[l]}$ and just trained $W^{[l]}$ during the freeze phase. By following the same derivation of Equation (2.1), we can see that this defines the desired computation without explicitly computing the summation over all paths. By the same token, this applies to DAGs.

A5 On Proposition 2.3

Proposition 2.3 is a direct consequence of Remark 2.4. Consider statement (i). Given such an $\mathcal{F}$, consider any tuples $(\mathcal{A},\mathcal{F},S)$ such that $\mathcal{A}$ takes $\mathcal{F}$ and S as input and outputs f_ϵ^*. Clearly, there are many such tuples $(\mathcal{A}, \mathcal{F}, S)$ because of Remark 2.4. This establishes statement (i).

Consider statement (ii). Given any dataset S', consider any algorithm $\mathcal{A}'$ that happens to output f_ϵ^* if $S = S'$ and outputs any f' otherwise, such that f' is arbitrarily non-robust and $|\mathcal{L}(f_\epsilon^*(X), Y) - \mathcal{L}(f'(X), Y)|$ is arbitrarily large (i.e., arbitrarily non-stable). This proves statement (ii). Note that although this particular A' suffices to prove statement (ii), there are clearly many other tuples $(\mathcal{A}, \mathcal{F}, \mathbb{P}_{(X,Y)}, S)$ that could be used to prove statement (ii) because of Remark 2.4.

A6 On Extensions

Theorem 2.7 addresses Open Problem 2 with limited applicability, i.e., to certain neural networks with squared loss. In contrast, a parallel study (Kawaguchi et al., 2018) presented a novel generic learning theory to address Open Problem 2 for general cases in machine learning. It would be beneficial to explore both a generic analysis (Kawaguchi et al., 2018) and a concrete analysis in deep learning to get theoretical insights that are tailored for each particular case.

For previous bounds with a hypothesis space $\mathcal{F}$, if we try different such spaces then $\mathcal{F}$, depending on S, the basic proof breaks down. An easy recovery at the cost of an extra quantity in a bound is achieved by taking a union bound over all possible $\mathcal{F}_j$ for $j = 1, 2, \ldots$, where we pre-decide $(\mathcal{F}_j)_j$ without dependence on S (because simply considering the "largest" $\mathcal{F} \supseteq \mathcal{F}_j$ can result in a very loose bound for each $\mathcal{F}_j$). Then, after training with a dataset S, if we have $\hat{f}_{\mathcal{A}, S} \in \mathcal{F}_j$, we can use the complexity of $\mathcal{F}_j$ without using the complexity of other $\mathcal{F}_i$ with $i \neq j$. Because the choice of $\mathcal{F}_j$ (out of $(\mathcal{F}_j)_j$) depends on S, it is called a data-dependent bound and indeed this is the idea behind data-dependent bounds in statistical learning theory.

Similarly, if we need to try many $w_\sigma := w^{S_{am}}$ depending on the whole of S in Theorem 2.9, we can take a union bound over $w_\sigma^{(j)}$ for $j = 1, 2, \ldots$, where we pre-determine $\{w_\sigma^{(j)}\}_j$ without dependence on $S \setminus S_{am}$ but with dependence on S_{am}. We can do the same with Proposition 2.5 and Remark 2.6 to use many different $\mathcal{F}_{\text{val}}$ depending on the validation dataset $S^{(\text{val})}$ with a predefined sequence.

Appendix B Experimental Details

For MNIST: We used the following fixed architecture:

(i) Convolutional layer with 32 filters with filter size 5 by 5, followed by max pooling of size 2 by 2 and ReLU.
(ii) Convolution layer with 32 filters with filter size 5 by 5, followed by max pooling of size 2 by 2 and ReLU.

(iii) Fully connected layer with output 1024 units, followed by ReLU and Dropout with its probability set to 0.5.

(iv) Fully connected layer with output 10 units.

Layer (iv) outputs $z^{[L]}$ in our notation. For training purpose, we used the softmax of $z^{[L]}$. Also, $f(X) = \text{argmax}(z^{[L]}(X))$ was taken as the label prediction.

We fixed the learning rate to be 0.01, the momentum coefficient to be 0.5, and the optimization algorithm to be the standard stochastic gradient descent (SGD). We fixed the data augmentation process as: a random crop with size 24, a random rotation up to ±15 degrees, and scaling of 15%. We used 3000 epochs for Table A.2, and 1000 epochs for Tables A.3 and A.4.

For CIFAR-10: For data augmentation, we used a random horizontal flip with probability 0.5 and a random crop of size 32 with padding of size 4.

For Table A.2, we used ResNeXt-29(16×64d) (Xie et al., 2017). We set the initial learning rate to be 0.05, decreasing it to 0.005 at 150 epochs and to 0.0005 at 250 epochs. We fixed the momentum coefficient to be 0.9, the weight decay coefficient to be 5×10^{-4}, and the optimization algorithm to be stochastic gradient descent (SGD) with Nesterov momentum. We stopped the training at 300 epochs.

For Tables A.3 and A.4, we used pre-activation ResNet with only 18 layers (pre-activation ResNet-18) (He et al., 2016). We fixed learning rate to be 0.001 and momentum coefficient to be 0.9, and optimization algorithm to be (standard) stochastic gradient descent (SGD). We used 1000 epochs.

Appendix C Proofs

We will use the following lemma in the proof of Theorem 2.7.

Lemma 2.11. (Matrix Bernstein inequality: corollary to Theorem 1.4 in Tropp, 2012) *Consider a finite sequence $\{M_i\}$ of independent, random, self-adjoint matrices with dimension d. Assume that each random matrix satisfies that $\mathbb{E}[M_i] = 0$ and $\lambda_{\max}(M_i) \leq R$ almost surely. Let $\gamma^2 = \|\sum_i \mathbb{E}[M_i^2]\|_2$. Then, for any $\delta > 0$, with probability at least $1 - \delta$,*

$$\lambda_{\max}\left(\sum_i M_i\right) \leq \frac{2R}{3}\ln\frac{d}{\delta} + \sqrt{2\gamma^2 \ln\frac{d}{\delta}}.$$

Proof   Theorem 1.4 of Tropp (2012) states that, for all $t \geq 0$,

$$\mathbb{P}\left[\lambda_{\max}\left(\sum_i M_i\right) \geq t\right] \leq d \cdot \exp\left(\frac{-t^2/2}{\gamma^2 + Rt/3}\right).$$

Setting $\delta = d \exp\left(-\frac{t^2/2}{\gamma^2 + Rt/3}\right)$ implies

$$-t^2 + \frac{2}{3}R(\ln d/\delta)t + 2\gamma^2 \ln d/\delta = 0.$$

Solving for t with the quadratic formula and bounding the solution using the sub-additivity of square roots of non-negative terms (i.e., $\sqrt{a+b} \le \sqrt{a} + \sqrt{b}$ for all $a, b \ge 0$), gives

$$t \le \frac{2}{3}R(\ln d/\delta) + 2\gamma^2 \ln d/\delta. \qquad \square$$

C1 Proof of Theorem 2.1

Proof For any matrix M, let $\mathrm{Col}(M)$ and $\mathrm{Null}(M)$ be the column space and null space of M. Since $\mathrm{rank}(\Phi) \ge m$ and $\Phi \in \mathbb{R}^{m \times n}$, the set of its columns spans $\mathbb{R}^m$, which proves statement (i). Let $w^* = w_1^* + w_2^*$ where $\mathrm{Col}(w_1^*) \subseteq \mathrm{Col}(M^T)$ and $\mathrm{Col}(w_2^*) \subseteq \mathrm{Null}(M)$. For statement (ii), set the parameter as $w := w_1^* + \epsilon C_1 + \alpha C_2$ where $\mathrm{Col}(C_1) \subseteq \mathrm{Col}(M^T)$, $\mathrm{Col}(C_2) \subseteq \mathrm{Null}(M)$, $\alpha \ge 0$, and $C_2 = \frac{1}{\alpha}w_2^* + \bar{C}_2$. Since $\mathrm{rank}(M) < n$, $\mathrm{Null}(M) \ne \{0\}$ and there exist non-zero $\bar{C}_2$. Then

$$\hat{\mathbf{Y}}(w) = \mathbf{Y} + \epsilon\Phi C_1$$

and

$$\hat{\mathbf{Y}}_{\mathrm{test}}(w) = \mathbf{Y}_{\mathrm{test}} + \epsilon\Phi_{\mathrm{test}}C_1.$$

Setting $A = \Phi C_1$ and $B = \Phi_{\mathrm{test}}C_1$ with a proper normalization of C_1 yields (ii)(a) and (ii)(b) in statement (ii) (note that C_1 has an arbitrary freedom in the bound on its scale because the only condition on it is $\mathrm{Col}(C_1) \subseteq \mathrm{Col}(M^T)$). At the same time, with the same parameter, since $\mathrm{Col}(w_1^* + \epsilon C_1) \perp \mathrm{Col}(C_2)$ we have

$$\|w\|_F^2 = \|w_1^* + \epsilon C_1\|_F^2 + \alpha^2\|C_2\|_F^2$$

and

$$\|w - w^*\|_F^2 = \|\epsilon C_1\|_F^2 + \alpha^2\|\bar{C}_2\|_F^2,$$

which grows unboundedly as $\alpha \to \infty$ without changing A and B, proving (ii)(c) in statement (ii). $\qquad \square$

C2 Proof of Corollary 2.2

Proof This follows the fact that the proof in Theorem 2.1 uses the assumption of $n > m$ and $\mathrm{rank}(\Phi) \ge m$ only for statement (i). $\qquad \square$

C3 Proof of Theorem 2.7

Proof From Equation (2.1), the squared loss of the deep models for each point (X, Y) can be rewritten as

$$\sum_{k=1}^{s} (z^\top \bar{w}_k - Y_k)^2 = \sum_{k=1}^{s} \bar{w}_k^\top (zz^\top) \bar{w}_k - 2 Y_k z^\top \bar{w}_k + Y_k^2.$$

Thus, from Equation (2.1) for a squared loss, we can decompose the generalization gap into three terms as

$$\mathcal{R}[w^s] - \mathcal{R}_S[w^s] = \sum_{k=1}^{s} \left[(\bar{w}_k^s)^\top \left(\mathbb{E}[zz^\top] - \frac{1}{m} \sum_{i=1}^{m} z_i z_i^\top \right) \bar{w}_k^s \right]$$
$$+ 2 \sum_{k=1}^{s} \left[\left(\frac{1}{m} \sum_{i=1}^{m} Y_k^{(i)} z_i^\top - \mathbb{E}[Y_k z^\top] \right) \bar{w}_k^s \right]$$
$$+ \left(\mathbb{E}[Y^\top Y] - \frac{1}{m} \sum_{i=1}^{m} (Y^{(i)})^\top Y^{(i)} \right).$$

As G, defined before Theorem 2.7, is a real symmetric matrix, we can write an eigendecomposition of G as $G = U \Lambda U^\top$ where the diagonal matrix Λ contains eigenvalues $\Lambda_{jj} = \lambda_j$ with corresponding orthogonal eigenvector matrix U; u_j is the jth column of U. Then

$$(\bar{w}_k^s)^\top G \bar{w}_k^s = \sum_j \lambda_j (u_j^\top \bar{w}_k^s)^2 = \|\bar{w}_k^s\|_2^2 \sum_j \lambda_j \cos^2 \theta_{\bar{w}_k^s, j}^{(1)}$$

and

$$\sum_j \lambda_j (u_j^\top \bar{w}_k^s)^2 \le \lambda_{\max}(G) \|U^\top \bar{w}_k^s\|_2^2 = \lambda_{\max}(G) \|\bar{w}_k^s\|_2^2.$$

Also,

$$v^\top \bar{w}_k^s = \|v\|_2 \|\bar{w}_k^s\|_2 \cos \theta_{\bar{w}_k^s}^{(2)} \le \|v\|_2 \|\bar{w}_k^s\|_2.$$

Using these expressions we obtain

$$\mathcal{R}[w^s] - \mathcal{R}_S[w^s] - c_y$$
$$= \sum_{k=1}^{s} \left(2 \|v\|_2 \|\bar{w}_k^s\|_2 \cos \theta_{\bar{w}_k^s}^{(2)} + \|\bar{w}_k^s\|_2^2 \sum_j \lambda_j \cos^2 \theta_{\bar{w}_k^s, j}^{(1)} \right)$$
$$\le \sum_{k=1}^{s} \left(2 \|v\|_2 \|\bar{w}_k^s\|_2 + \lambda_{\max}(G) \|\bar{w}_k^s\|_2^2 \right) \qquad \qquad \square$$

as required.

C4 Proof of Theorem 2.9

Proof We do *not* require independence of the coordinates of $\tilde{z}_i$ and the entries of the random matrices $\tilde{z}_i \tilde{z}_i^\top$ because of the definition of independence required for the matrix Bernstein inequality (for $\frac{1}{m_\sigma} \sum_{i=1}^{m_\sigma} \tilde{z}_i \tilde{z}_i^\top$); see, e.g., Section 2.2.3 of Tropp *et al.*, 2015) and because of the union bound over the coordinates (for $\frac{1}{m_\sigma} \sum_{i=1}^{m_\sigma} Y_k^{(i)} \tilde{z}_i$). We use the fact that $\tilde{z}_{\alpha m+1}, \ldots, \tilde{z}_m$ are independent random variables *over the sample index* (although dependent on the coordinates), because each $w_\sigma := w^{S_{\alpha m}}$ is fixed and independent of $X^{(\alpha m+1)}, \ldots, X^{(m)}$.

From Equation (2.2), with the definition of induced matrix norm and the Cauchy–Schwarz inequality,

$$
\mathcal{R}[\hat{f}_{\mathcal{A},S}] - \mathcal{R}_{S\backslash S_{\alpha m}}[\hat{f}_{\mathcal{A},S}]
$$

$$
\leq \sum_{k=1}^{s} \left\| \bar{w}_k^S \right\|_2^2 \lambda_{\max} \left(\mathbb{E}[\tilde{z}\tilde{z}^\top] - \frac{1}{m_\sigma} \sum_{i=\alpha m+1}^{m} \tilde{z}_i \tilde{z}_i^\top \right)
$$

$$
+ 2 \sum_{k=1}^{s} \left\| \bar{w}_k^S \right\|_1 \left\| \frac{1}{m_\sigma} \sum_{i=\alpha m+1}^{m} Y_k^{(i)} \tilde{z}_i - \mathbb{E}[Y_k \tilde{z}] \right\|_\infty
$$

$$
+ \left(\mathbb{E}[Y^\top Y] - \frac{1}{m_\sigma} \sum_{i=\alpha m+1}^{m} (Y^{(i)})^\top Y^{(i)} \right). \tag{C.1}
$$

In what follows, we bound each term on the right-hand side with concentration inequalities.

For the first term: The matrix Bernstein inequality (Lemma 2.11) states that for any $\delta > 0$, with probability at least $1 - \delta/3$,

$$
\lambda_{\max} \left(\mathbb{E}[\tilde{z}\tilde{z}^\top] - \frac{1}{m_\sigma} \sum_{i=\alpha m+1}^{m} \tilde{z}_i \tilde{z}_i^\top \right) \leq \frac{2C_{zz}}{3m_\sigma} \ln \frac{3d_z}{\delta} + \sqrt{\frac{2\gamma_{zz}^2}{m_\sigma} \ln \frac{3d_z}{\delta}}.
$$

Here, the matrix Bernstein inequality was applied as follows. Let $M_i = (\frac{1}{m_\sigma} G^{(i)})$. Then $\sum_{i=\alpha m+1}^{m} M_i = \mathbb{E}[\tilde{z}\tilde{z}^\top] - \frac{1}{m_\sigma} \sum_{i=\alpha m+1}^{m} \tilde{z}_i \tilde{z}_i^\top$. We have that $\mathbb{E}[M_i] = 0$ for all i. Also, $\lambda_{\max}(M_i) \leq \frac{1}{m_\sigma} C_{zz}$ and $\| \sum_i \mathbb{E}[M_i^2] \|_2 \leq \frac{1}{m_\sigma} \gamma_{zz}^2$.

For the second term: To each $(k, k') \in \{1, \ldots, s\} \times \{1, \ldots, d_z\}$ we apply the matrix Bernstein inequality and take the union bound over $d_y d_z$ events, obtaining that for any $\delta > 0$, with probability at least $1 - \delta/3$, for all $k \in \{1, 2, \ldots, s\}$,

$$
\left\| \frac{1}{m_\sigma} \sum_{i=\alpha m+1}^{m} Y_k^{(i)} \tilde{z}_i - \mathbb{E}[Y_k \tilde{z}] \right\|_\infty \leq \frac{2C_{yz}}{3m_\sigma} \ln \frac{6d_y d_z}{\delta} + \sqrt{\frac{\gamma_{yz}^2}{m_\sigma} \ln \frac{6d_y d_z}{\delta}}.
$$

For the third term: From the matrix Bernstein inequality, with probability at least

$1 - \delta/3$,

$$\mathbb{E}[Y^\top Y] - \frac{1}{m_\sigma} \sum_{i=\alpha m+1}^{m} (Y^{(i)})^\top Y^{(i)} \le \frac{2C_y}{3m} \ln \frac{3}{\delta} + \sqrt{\frac{2\gamma_{\bar{y}}^2}{m} \ln \frac{3}{\delta}}.$$

Putting it all together: Pulling all this together, for a fixed (or frozen) w_σ, with probability (over $S \setminus S_{\alpha m} = \{(X^{(\alpha m+1)}, Y^{(\alpha m+1)}), \dots, (X^{(m)}, Y^{(m)})\}$) at least $1 - \delta$, we have that

$$\lambda_{\max}\left(\mathbb{E}[\bar{z}\bar{z}^\top] - \frac{1}{m_\sigma} \sum_{i=\alpha m+1}^{m} \bar{z}_i \bar{z}_i^\top\right) \le \beta_1,$$

$$\left\|\frac{1}{m_\sigma} \sum_{i=\alpha m+1}^{m} Y_k^{(i)} \bar{z}_i - \mathbb{E}[Y_k \bar{z}]\right\|_\infty \le \beta_2 \quad \text{(for all } k\text{)},$$

and

$$\mathbb{E}[Y^\top Y] - \frac{1}{m_\sigma} \sum_{i=\alpha m+1}^{m} (Y^{(i)})^\top Y^{(i)} \le \beta_3.$$

Since Equation (C.1) always hold deterministically (with or without such a dataset), the desired statement of this theorem follows. □

C5 Proof of Theorem 2.10

Proof Define S_{m_σ} as

$$S_{m_\sigma} = S \setminus S_{\alpha m} = \{(X^{(\alpha m+1)}, Y^{(\alpha m+1)}), \dots, (X^{(m)}, Y^{(m)})\}.$$

Recall the following fact: using the result of Koltchinskii and Panchenko (2002), we have that for any $\delta > 0$, with probability at least $1 - \delta$, the following holds for all $f \in \mathcal{F}$:

$$\mathcal{R}[f] \le \mathcal{R}_{S_{m_\sigma}, \rho}[f] + \frac{2d_y^2}{\rho m_\sigma} \mathfrak{R}'_{m_\sigma}(\mathcal{F}) + \sqrt{\frac{\ln \frac{1}{\delta}}{2m_\sigma}},$$

where $\mathfrak{R}'_{m_\sigma}(\mathcal{F})$ is the Rademacher complexity, defined as

$$\mathfrak{R}'_{m_\sigma}(\mathcal{F}) = \mathbb{E}_{S_{m_\sigma}, \xi}\left[\sup_{k,w} \sum_{i=1}^{m_\sigma} \xi_i z_k^{[L]}(X^{(i)}, w)\right].$$

Here, ξ_i is the Rademacher variable, and the supremum is taken over all $k \in \{1, \dots, s\}$ and all w allowed in $\mathcal{F}$. Then, for our parameterized hypothesis spaces, with any frozen w_σ,

$$\mathfrak{R}'_{m_\sigma}(\mathcal{F}) = \mathbb{E}_{S_{m_\sigma},\xi}\left[\sup_{k,\bar{w}_k}\sum_{i=1}^{m_\sigma}\xi_i[\bar{X}^{(i)}\circ\bar{\sigma}(X^{(i)},w_\sigma)]^\top\bar{w}_k\right]$$

$$\leq \mathbb{E}_{S_{m_\sigma},\xi}\left[\sup_{k,\bar{w}_k}\left\|\sum_{i=1}^{m_\sigma}\xi_i[\bar{X}^{(i)}\circ\bar{\sigma}(X^{(i)},w_\sigma)]\right\|_2 \|\bar{w}_k\|_2\right]$$

$$\leq C_w\mathbb{E}_{S_{m_\sigma},\xi}\left[\left\|\sum_{i=1}^{m_\sigma}\xi_i[\bar{X}^{(i)}\circ\bar{\sigma}(X^{(i)},w_\sigma)]\right\|_2\right].$$

Because the square root is concave in its domain, by using Jensen's inequality and linearity of expectation, we obtain

$$\mathbb{E}_{S_{m_\sigma},\xi}\left[\left\|\sum_{i=1}^{m_\sigma}\xi_i[\bar{X}^{(i)}\circ\bar{\sigma}(X^{(i)},w_\sigma)]\right\|_2\right]$$

$$\leq \left(\mathbb{E}_{S_{m_\sigma}}\sum_{i=1}^{m_\sigma}\sum_{j=1}^{m_\sigma}\mathbb{E}_\xi[\xi_i\xi_j][\bar{X}^{(i)}\circ\bar{\sigma}(X^{(i)},w_\sigma)]^\top[\bar{X}_j\circ\bar{\sigma}(X_j,w_\sigma)]\right)^{1/2}$$

$$= \left(\sum_{i=1}^{m_\sigma}\mathbb{E}_{S_{m_\sigma}}\left[\left\|[\bar{X}^{(i)}\circ\bar{\sigma}(X^{(i)},w_\sigma)]\right\|_2^2\right]\right)^{1/2}$$

$$\leq C_\sigma\sqrt{m_\sigma}.$$

Putting it all together, we find $\mathfrak{R}'_m(\mathcal{F}) \leq C_\sigma C_w\sqrt{m_\sigma}$. $\qquad\qquad\qquad\square$

C6 Proof of Proposition 2.5

Proof Consider a fixed $f \in \mathcal{F}_{\text{val}}$. Because $\mathcal{F}_{\text{val}}$ is independent of the validation dataset $S^{(\text{val})}$, it follows that $\kappa_{f,1},\ldots,\kappa_{f,m_{\text{val}}}$ are independent zero-mean random variables, given, as above, a fixed $f \in \mathcal{F}_{\text{val}}$ (note that we can make $\mathcal{F}_{\text{val}}$ dependent on S because we are considering $S^{(\text{val})}$ here, resulting in the requirement that $\mathcal{F}_{\text{val}}$ is independent of $S^{(\text{val})}$, instead of S). Thus, we can apply the matrix Bernstein inequality, yielding

$$\mathbb{P}\left(\frac{1}{m_{\text{val}}}\sum_{i=1}^{m_{\text{val}}}\kappa_{f,i} > \epsilon\right) \leq \exp\left(-\frac{\epsilon^2 m_{\text{val}}/2}{\gamma^2 + \epsilon C/3}\right).$$

By taking the union bound over all elements in $\mathcal{F}_{\text{val}}$, we find

$$\mathbb{P}\left(\bigcup_{f\in\mathcal{F}_{\text{val}}}\left\{\frac{1}{m_{\text{val}}}\sum_{i=1}^{m_{\text{val}}}\kappa_{f,i} > \epsilon\right\}\right) \leq |\mathcal{F}_{\text{val}}|\exp\left(-\frac{\epsilon^2 m_{\text{val}}/2}{\gamma^2 + \epsilon C/3}\right).$$

Setting $\delta = |\mathcal{F}_{\text{val}}| \exp\left(-\frac{\epsilon^2 m_{\text{val}}/2}{\gamma^2 + \epsilon C/3}\right)$ and solving for ϵ gives (via the quadratic formula),

$$\epsilon = \frac{2C \ln(\frac{|\mathcal{F}_{\text{val}}|}{\delta})}{6m_{\text{val}}} \pm \frac{1}{2} \sqrt{\left(\frac{2C \ln(\frac{|\mathcal{F}_{\text{val}}|}{\delta})}{3m_{\text{val}}}\right)^2 + \frac{8\gamma^2 \ln(\frac{|\mathcal{F}_{\text{val}}|}{\delta})}{m_{\text{val}}}}.$$

Noticing that the solution of ϵ with the minus sign results in $\epsilon < 0$, which is invalid for the matrix Bernstein inequality, we obtain the valid solution, the one with with the plus sign. Then we have

$$\epsilon \le \frac{2C \ln(\frac{|\mathcal{F}_{\text{val}}|}{\delta})}{3m_{\text{val}}} + \sqrt{\frac{2\gamma^2 \ln(\frac{|\mathcal{F}_{\text{val}}|}{\delta})}{m_{\text{val}}}},$$

where we have used $\sqrt{a+b} \le \sqrt{a} + \sqrt{b}$. By taking the negation of the statement, we obtain that, for any $\delta > 0$, with probability at least $1 - \delta$, for all $f \in \mathcal{F}_{\text{val}}$,

$$\frac{1}{m_{\text{val}}} \sum_{i=1}^{m_{\text{val}}} \kappa_{f,i} \le \frac{2C \ln(\frac{|\mathcal{F}_{\text{val}}|}{\delta})}{3m_{\text{val}}} + \sqrt{\frac{2\gamma^2 \ln(\frac{|\mathcal{F}_{\text{val}}|}{\delta})}{m}},$$

where

$$\frac{1}{m_{\text{val}}} \sum_{i=1}^{m_{\text{val}}} \kappa_{f,i} = \mathcal{R}[f] - \mathcal{R}_{S^{(\text{val})}}[f]. \qquad \square$$

References

Arpit, Devansh, Jastrzebski, Stanislaw, Ballas, Nicolas, Krueger, David, Bengio, Emmanuel, Kanwal, Maxinder S., Maharaj, Tegan, Fischer, Asja, Courville, Aaron, Bengio, Yoshua, et al. 2017. A Closer Look at Memorization in Deep Networks. In: *Proc. International Conference on Machine Learning.*

Banburski, Andrzej, Liao, Qianli, Miranda, Brando, Rosasco, Lorenzo, Liang, Bob, Hidary, Jack, and Poggio, Tomaso. 2019. Theory III: Dynamics and Generalization in Deep Networks. *Massachusetts Institute of Technology CBMM Memo No. 90.*

Barron, Andrew R. 1993. Universal Approximation Bounds for Superpositions of a Sigmoidal Function. *IEEE Transactions on Information theory*, **39**(3), 930–945.

Bartlett, Peter L., Boucheron, Stéphane, and Lugosi, Gábor. 2002. Model Selection and Error Estimation. *Machine Learning*, **48**(1), 85–113.

Bousquet, Olivier, and Elisseeff, André. 2002. Stability and Generalization. *Journal of Machine Learning Research*, **2**(Mar), 499–526.

Choromanska, Anna, Henaff, Mikael, Mathieu, Michael, Ben Arous, Gerard, and LeCun, Yann. 2015. The Loss Surfaces of Multilayer Networks. Pages 192–204 of: *Proc. 18th International Conference on Artificial Intelligence and Statistics*.

Dinh, Laurent, Pascanu, Razvan, Bengio, Samy, and Bengio, Yoshua. 2017. Sharp Minima Can Generalize for Deep Nets. In: *International Conference on Machine Learning*.

Dziugaite, Gintare Karolina, and Roy, Daniel M. 2017. Computing Nonvacuous Generalization Bounds for Deep (Stochastic) Neural Networks with Many More Parameters than Training Data. In: *Proc. 33rd Conference on Uncertainty in Artificial Intelligence*.

Finn, Chelsea, Goodfellow, Ian, and Levine, Sergey. 2016. Unsupervised Learning for Physical Interaction through Video Prediction. Pages 64–72 of: *Advances in Neural Information Processing Systems*.

Gonen, Alon, and Shalev-Shwartz, Shai. 2017. Fast Rates for Empirical Risk Minimization of Strict Saddle Problems. Pages 1043–1063 of: *Proc. Conference on Learning Theory*.

Hardt, Moritz, Recht, Ben, and Singer, Yoram. 2016. Train Faster, Generalize Better: Stability of Stochastic Gradient Descent. Pages 1225–1234 of: *proc. International Conference on Machine Learning*.

He, Kaiming, Zhang, Xiangyu, Ren, Shaoqing, and Sun, Jian. 2016. Identity Mappings in Deep Residual Networks. Pages 630–645 of: *Proc. European Conference on Computer Vision*. Springer.

Healy, Patrick, and Nikolov, Nikola S. 2001. How to Layer a Directed Acyclic Graph. Pages 16–30 of: *proc. International Symposium on Graph Drawing*. Springer.

Herbrich, Ralf, and Williamson, Robert C. 2002. Algorithmic Luckiness. *Journal of Machine Learning Research*, **3**, 175–212.

Hoffer, Elad, Hubara, Itay, and Soudry, Daniel. 2017. Train Longer, Generalize Better: Closing the Generalization Gap in Large Batch Training of Neural Networks. Pages 1731–1741 of: *Advances in Neural Information Processing Systems*.

Kawaguchi, Kenji. 2016a. Bounded Optimal Exploration in MDP. In: *Proc. 30th AAAI Conference on Artificial Intelligence*.

Kawaguchi, Kenji. 2016b. Deep Learning without Poor Local Minima. In: *Advances in Neural Information Processing Systems*.

Kawaguchi, Kenji, Bengio, Yoshua, Verma, Vikas, and Kaelbling, Leslie Pack. 2018. Generalization in Machine Learning via Analytical Learning Theory. Massachusetts Institute of Technology, Report MIT-CSAIL-TR-2018-019.

Kawaguchi, Kenji, Kaelbling, Leslie Pack, and Lozano-Pérez, Tomás. 2015. Bayesian Optimization with Exponential Convergence. In: *Advances in Neural Information Processing*.

Keskar, Nitish Shirish, Mudigere, Dheevatsa, Nocedal, Jorge, Smelyanskiy, Mikhail, and Tang, Ping Tak Peter. 2017. On Large-Batch Training for Deep Learning: Generalization Gap and Sharp Minima. In: *Proc. International Conference on Learning Representations.*

Koltchinskii, Vladimir, and Panchenko, Dmitriy. 2000. Rademacher Processes and Bounding the Risk of Function Learning. Pages 443–457 of: *High Dimensional Probability II.* Springer.

Koltchinskii, Vladimir, and Panchenko, Dmitry. 2002. Empirical Margin Distributions and Bounding the Generalization Error of Combined Classifiers. *Annals of Statistics*, 1–50.

Krueger, David, Ballas, Nicolas, Jastrzebski, Stanislaw, Arpit, Devansh, Kanwal, Maxinder S., Maharaj, Tegan, Bengio, Emmanuel, Fischer, Asja, and Courville, Aaron. 2017. Deep Nets Don't Learn via Memorization. In: *proc. Workshop Track of International Conference on Learning Representations.*

Kuzborskij, Ilja, and Lampert, Christoph. 2017. Data-Dependent Stability of Stochastic Gradient Descent. ArXiv preprint arXiv:1703.01678.

LeCun, Yann, Bottou, Léon, Bengio, Yoshua, and Haffner, Patrick. 1998. Gradient-Based Learning Applied to Document Recognition. *Proc. IEEE*, **86**(11), 2278–2324.

Leshno, Moshe, Lin, Vladimir Ya., Pinkus, Allan, and Schocken, Shimon. 1993. Multilayer Feedforward Networks with a Nonpolynomial Activation Function can Approximate Any Function. *Neural Networks*, **6**(6), 861–867.

Livni, Roi, Shalev-Shwartz, Shai, and Shamir, Ohad. 2014. On the Computational Efficiency of Training Neural Networks. Pages 855–863 of: *Advances in Neural Information Processing Systems.*

Mohri, Mehryar, Rostamizadeh, Afshin, and Talwalkar, Ameet. 2012. *Foundations of Machine Learning.* MIT Press.

Montufar, Guido F., Pascanu, Razvan, Cho, Kyunghyun, and Bengio, Yoshua. 2014. On the Number of Linear Regions of Deep Neural Networks. Pages 2924–2932 of: *Advances in Neural Information Processing Systems.*

Mukherjee, Sayan, Niyogi, Partha, Poggio, Tomaso, and Rifkin, Ryan. 2006. Learning Theory: Stability is Sufficient for Generalization and Necessary and Sufficient for Consistency of Empirical Risk Minimization. *Advances in Computational Mathematics*, **25**(1), 161–193.

Neyshabur, Behnam, Tomioka, Ryota, and Srebro, Nathan. 2015a. Norm-Based Capacity Control in Neural Networks. Pages 1376–1401 of: *Proc. 28th Conference on Learning Theory.*

Neyshabur, Behnam, Salakhutdinov, Ruslan R., and Srebro, Nati. 2015b. Path-SGD: Path-Normalized Optimization in Deep Neural Networks. Pages 2422–2430 of: *Advances in Neural Information Processing Systems.*

Pascanu, Razvan, Montufar, Guido, and Bengio, Yoshua. 2014. On the Number of Response Regions of Deep Feed Forward Networks with Piece-Wise Linear Activations. In: *Proc. International Conference on Learning Representations.*

Poggio, Tomaso, Kawaguchi, Kenji, Liao, Qianli, Miranda, Brando, Rosasco, Lorenzo, Boix, Xavier, Hidary, Jack, and Mhaskar, Hrushikesh. 2018. Theory of Deep Learning III: Explaining the Non-overfitting Puzzle. Massachusetts Institute of Technology CBMM Memo No. 73.

Poggio, Tomaso, Mhaskar, Hrushikesh, Rosasco, Lorenzo, Miranda, Brando, and Liao, Qianli. 2017. Why and When Can Deep – But not Shallow – Networks Avoid the Curse of Dimensionality: A Review. *International Journal of Automation and Computing*, **14**, 1–17.

Raginsky, Maxim, Rakhlin, Alexander, and Telgarsky, Matus. 2017. Non-Convex Learning via Stochastic Gradient Langevin Dynamics: A Nonasymptotic Analysis. Pages 1674–1703 of: *Proc. Conference on Learning Theory*.

Sato, Ikuro, Nishimura, Hiroki, and Yokoi, Kensuke. 2015. Apac: Augmented Pattern Classification with Neural Networks. ArXiv preprint arXiv:1505.03229.

Shalev-Shwartz, Shai, and Ben-David, Shai. 2014. *Understanding Machine Learning: From Theory to Algorithms*. Cambridge University Press.

Shawe-Taylor, John, Bartlett, Peter L., Williamson, Robert C., and Anthony, Martin. 1998. Structural Risk Minimization over Data-Dependent Hierarchies. *IEEE Transactions on Information Theory*, **44**(5), 1926–1940.

Sokolic, Jure, Giryes, Raja, Sapiro, Guillermo, and Rodrigues, Miguel. 2017a. Generalization Error of Invariant Classifiers. Pages 1094–1103 of: *Artificial Intelligence and Statistics*.

Sokolic, Jure, Giryes, Raja, Sapiro, Guillermo, and Rodrigues, Miguel R. D. 2017b. Robust Large Margin Deep Neural Networks. *IEEE Transactions on Signal Processing*, **65**(16), 4265–4280.

Sun, Shizhao, Chen, Wei, Wang, Liwei, Liu, Xiaoguang, and Liu, Tie-Yan. 2016. On the Depth of Deep Neural Networks: A Theoretical View. Pages 2066–2072 of: *Proc. 30th AAAI Conference on Artificial Intelligence*. AAAI Press.

Telgarsky, Matus. 2016. Benefits of Depth in Neural Networks. Pages 1517–1539 of: *Proc. 29th Annual Conference on Learning Theory*.

Tropp, Joel A. 2012. User-Friendly Tail Bounds for Sums of Random Matrices. *Foundations of Computational Mathematics*, **12**(4), 389–434.

Tropp, Joel A., et al. 2015. An Introduction to Matrix Concentration Inequalities. *Foundations and Trends® in Machine Learning*, **8**(1-2), 1–230.

Vapnik, Vladimir. 1998. *Statistical Learning Theory*. Vol. 1. Wiley.

Wan, Li, Zeiler, Matthew, Zhang, Sixin, Cun, Yann L., and Fergus, Rob. 2013. Regularization of Neural Networks using Dropconnect. Pages 1058–1066 of: *Proc. 30th International Conference on Machine Learning*.

Wu, Lei, Zhu, Zhanxing, et al. 2017. Towards Understanding Generalization of Deep Learning: Perspective of Loss Landscapes. ArXiv preprint arXiv:1706.10239.

Xie, Pengtao, Deng, Yuntian, and Xing, Eric. 2015. On the Generalization Error Bounds of Neural Networks under Diversity-Inducing Mutual Angular Regularization. ArXiv preprint arXiv:1511.07110.

Xie, Saining, Girshick, Ross, Dollár, Piotr, Tu, Zhuowen, and He, Kaiming. 2017. Aggregated Residual Transformations for Deep Neural Networks. Pages 1492–1500 of: *Proc. IEEE Conference on Computer Vision and Pattern Recognition*.

Xu, Huan, and Mannor, Shie. 2012. Robustness and Generalization. *Machine Learning*, **86**(3), 391–423.

Zhang, Chiyuan, Bengio, Samy, Hardt, Moritz, Recht, Benjamin, and Vinyals, Oriol. 2017. Understanding Deep Learning Requires Rethinking Generalization. In: *Proc. International Conference on Learning Representations*.

3

Expressivity of Deep Neural Networks

Ingo Gühring, Mones Raslan, and Gitta Kutyniok

Abstract: In this chapter, we give a comprehensive overview of the large variety of approximation results for neural networks. The approximation rates for classical function spaces as well as the benefits of deep neural networks over shallow ones for specifically structured function classes are discussed. While the main body of existing results applies to general feedforward architectures, we also review approximation results for convolutional, residual and recurrent neural networks.

3.1 Introduction

While many aspects of the success of deep learning still lack a comprehensive mathematical explanation, the approximation properties[1] of neural networks have been studied since around 1960 and are relatively well understood. *Statistical learning theory* formalizes the problem of approximating – in this context also called *learning* – a function from a finite set of samples. Next to statistical and algorithmic considerations, approximation theory plays a major role in the analysis of statistical learning problems. We will clarify this in the following by introducing some fundamental notions.[2]

Assume that X is an *input space*, $\mathcal{Y}$ is a *target space*, $\mathcal{L}\colon \mathcal{Y} \times \mathcal{Y} \to [0,\infty]$ is a *loss function*, and $\mathbb{P}_{(X,\mathcal{Y})}$ a (usually unknown) *probability distribution* on some σ-algebra of $X \times \mathcal{Y}$. We then aim at finding a minimizer of the risk functional[3]

$$\mathcal{R}\colon \mathcal{Y}^X \to [0,\infty], \ f \mapsto \int_{X \times \mathcal{Y}} \mathcal{L}\left(f(x), y\right) \mathrm{d}\mathbb{P}_{(X,\mathcal{Y})}(x, y),$$

induced by $\mathcal{L}$ and $\mathbb{P}_{(X,\mathcal{Y})}$ (where $\mathcal{Y}^X$ denotes the set of all functions from X to $\mathcal{Y}$).

---

[1] Throughout the chapter, we will interchangeably use the term *approximation* theory and *expressivity* theory.
[2] Cucker and Zhou (2007) provides a concise introduction to statistical learning theory from the point of view of approximation theory.
[3] With the convention that $\mathcal{R}(f) = \infty$ if the integral is not well defined.

That means we are looking for a function $\hat{f}$ with

$$\hat{f} = \operatorname{argmin} \{\mathcal{R}(f): f \in \mathcal{Y}^{\mathcal{X}}\}\,.$$

In the overwhelming majority of practical applications, however, this optimization problem turns out to be infeasible for three reasons:

(i) The set $\mathcal{Y}^{\mathcal{X}}$ is simply too large, so one usually fixes a priori some *hypothesis class* $\mathcal{H} \subset \mathcal{Y}^{\mathcal{X}}$ and instead searches for

$$\hat{f}_{\mathcal{H}} = \operatorname{argmin} \{\mathcal{R}(f): f \in \mathcal{H}\}\,.$$

In the context of deep learning, the set $\mathcal{H}$ consists of *deep neural networks*, which we will introduce later.

(ii) Since $\mathbb{P}_{(\mathcal{X},\mathcal{Y})}$ is unknown, one cannot compute the risk of a given function f. Instead, we are given a *training set* $S = ((x_i, y_i))_{i=1}^m$, which consists of $m \in \mathbb{N}$ i.i.d. samples drawn from $\mathcal{X} \times \mathcal{Y}$ with respect to $\mathbb{P}_{(\mathcal{X},\mathcal{Y})}$. Thus, we can only hope to find the minimizer of the *empirical risk* $\mathcal{R}_S(f) = \frac{1}{m}\sum_{i=1}^m \mathcal{L}(f(x_i), y_i))$, given by

$$\hat{f}_{\mathcal{H},S} = \operatorname{argmin} \{\mathcal{R}_S(f): f \in \mathcal{H}\}\,.$$

(iii) In the case of deep learning one needs to solve a complicated non-convex optimization problem to find $\hat{f}_{\mathcal{H},S}$; this is called *training* and can only be done approximately.

Denoting the approximate solution by $\hat{f}^*_{\mathcal{H},S} \in \mathcal{H}$, the overall error is (see Figure 3.1)

$$\left|\mathcal{R}(\hat{f}) - \mathcal{R}(\hat{f}^*_{\mathcal{H},S})\right| \leq \underbrace{\left|\mathcal{R}(\hat{f}^*_{\mathcal{H},S}) - \mathcal{R}(\hat{f}_{\mathcal{H},S})\right|}_{\text{training error}}$$

$$+ \underbrace{\left|\mathcal{R}(\hat{f}_{\mathcal{H},S}) - \mathcal{R}(\hat{f}_{\mathcal{H}})\right|}_{\text{estimation error}}$$

$$+ \underbrace{\left|\mathcal{R}(\hat{f}_{\mathcal{H}}) - \mathcal{R}(\hat{f})\right|}_{\text{approximation error}}\,.$$

The results discussed in this chapter deal with estimating the approximation error if the set $\mathcal{H}$ consists of deep neural networks. However, the observant reader will notice that practically all the results presented below ignore the dependence on the unknown probability distribution $\mathbb{P}_{(\mathcal{X},\mathcal{Y})}$. This can be justified by various strategies (see also Cucker and Zhou, 2007) one of which we will describe here.

Under suitable conditions it is possible to bound the approximation error by

$$\left|\mathcal{R}(\hat{f}_{\mathcal{H}}) - \mathcal{R}(\hat{f})\right| \leq \operatorname{error}(\hat{f}_{\mathcal{H}} - \hat{f}),$$

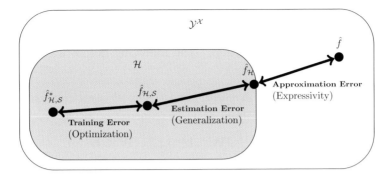

Figure 3.1 Decomposition of the overall error into training error, estimation error and approximation error.

where error($\cdot$) is an expression (e.g. the $\| \cdot \|_\infty$ norm) that is independent of $\mathbb{P}_{(X,Y)}$. As an example, assume that $\mathcal{Y} \subset \mathbb{R}$ and that the loss function $\mathcal{L}(\cdot, y)$ is Lipschitz continuous for all $y \in \mathcal{Y}$ with uniform Lipschitz constant $\text{Lip}(\mathcal{L})$. We then get

$$\left| \mathcal{R}(\hat{f}_\mathcal{H}) - \mathcal{R}(\hat{f}) \right| \leq \text{Lip}(\mathcal{L}) \cdot \left\| \hat{f}_\mathcal{H} - \hat{f} \right\|_\infty, \tag{3.1}$$

and hence the upper bound of $\| \hat{f}_\mathcal{H} - \hat{f} \|_\infty$ can be used to upper-bound the approximation error.

The *universal approximation theorem* (see Funahashi, 1989; Cybenko, 1989; Hornik et al., 1989; Hornik, 1991), which is the starting point of approximation theory of neural networks, states:

> *For every $\hat{f} \in C(K)$ with $K \subset \mathbb{R}^d$ compact and every $\epsilon > 0$ there exists a neural network $\hat{f}_{\mathcal{H},\epsilon}$ such that $\| \hat{f}_\mathcal{H} - \hat{f} \|_\infty \leq \epsilon$.*

Utilizing the fact that neural networks are universal approximators, we can now see from Equation (3.1) that for $\mathcal{H} = C(K)$ the approximation error can be made arbitrarily small. In practice, we are faced with a finite memory and computation budget, which shows the importance of results similar to the theorem above that additionally quantify the complexity of $\hat{f}_\mathcal{H}$.

We now proceed by introducing the notion of neural networks, considered throughout this chapter, in mathematical terms.

3.1.1 Neural Networks

We now give a mathematical definition of feedforward neural networks, which were first introduced in McCulloch and Pitts (1943). More refined architectures, such as convolutional, residual and recurrent neural networks, are defined in later sections (see §3.8).

In most cases it makes the exposition simpler to differentiate between a neural network considered as a collection of weights and biases, and the corresponding function, referred to as its realization.[4] The following notion was introduced in Petersen and Voigtlaender (2018).

Definition 3.1. Let $d, s, L \in \mathbb{N}$. A *neural network* Φ *with input dimension* d, *output dimension* s *and* L *layers* (see Figure 3.2) is a sequence of matrix–vector tuples

$$\Phi = ((\mathbf{W}^{[1]}, \mathbf{b}^{[1]}), (\mathbf{W}^{[2]}, \mathbf{b}^{[2]}), \ldots, (\mathbf{W}^{[L]}, \mathbf{b}^{[L]})),$$

where $n_0 = d$, $n_L = s$ and $n_1, \ldots, n_{L-1} \in \mathbb{N}$, and where each $\mathbf{W}^{[\ell]}$ is an $n_\ell \times n_{\ell-1}$ matrix and $\mathbf{b}^{[\ell]} \in \mathbb{R}^{n_\ell}$.

If Φ is a neural network as above, $K \subset \mathbb{R}^d$, and if $\sigma \colon \mathbb{R} \to \mathbb{R}$ is arbitrary then we define the associated *realization of* Φ *with activation function* σ *over* K (in short, the σ-*realization of* Φ *over* K) as the map $R_\sigma(\Phi) \colon K \to \mathbb{R}^s$ such that

$$R_\sigma(\Phi)(x) = \mathbf{x}^{[L]},$$

where $\mathbf{x}^{[L]}$ results from the following scheme:

$$\mathbf{x}^{[0]} := x,$$
$$\mathbf{x}^{[\ell]} := \sigma(\mathbf{W}^{[\ell]} \mathbf{x}^{[\ell-1]} + \mathbf{b}^{[\ell]}), \qquad \text{for } \ell = 1, \ldots, L-1,$$
$$\mathbf{x}^{[L]} := \mathbf{W}^{[L]} \mathbf{x}^{[L-1]} + \mathbf{b}^{[L]},$$

and where σ acts componentwise; that is, $\sigma(v) = (\sigma(v_1), \ldots, \sigma(v_m))$ for every $v = (v_1, \ldots, v_m) \in \mathbb{R}^m$.

We call $N(\Phi) := d + \sum_{j=1}^{L} n_j$ the *number of neurons of the neural network* Φ and $L = L(\Phi)$ the *number of layers*. For $\ell \leq L$ we call $M_\ell(\Phi) := \|\mathbf{W}^{[\ell]}\|_0 + \|\mathbf{b}^{[\ell]}\|_0$ the *number of weights in the* ℓth *layer* and we define $M(\Phi) := \sum_{\ell=1}^{L} M_\ell(\Phi)$, which we call the *number of weights of* Φ. Finally, we denote by $\max\{N_1, \ldots, N_{L-1}\}$ the *width* of Φ.

Although the activation can be chosen arbitrarily, a variety of particularly useful activation functions has been used in the context of deep learning. We refer to Table 3.1, which is an adapted version of Petersen et al. (2021, Table 1), for an overview of frequently used activation functions.

Many research results give a relation between the approximation accuracy and the *complexity* of a neural network Φ, which is measured in terms of the number of neurons $N(\Phi)$, the number of non-zero weights and biases $M(\Phi)$ and the number of layers $L(\Phi)$.

Before we proceed, let us fix the following notions concerning the set of all (realizations of) neural networks.

---

[4] However, if it is clear from the context, in the following we denote by the term "neural networks" both the parameter collections as well as their corresponding realizations.

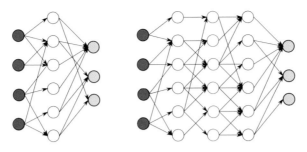

Figure 3.2 Visualization of (left) a shallow and (right) a deep (feedforward) neural network with input dimension $d = 4$ and output dimension $s = 3$.

Name	Given by
rectified linear unit (ReLU)	$\max\{0, x\}$
a-leaky ReLU	$\max\{ax, x\}$ for some $a \geq 0$, $a \neq 1$
exponential linear unit	$x \cdot \chi_{x \geq 0}(x) + (\exp(x) - 1) \cdot \chi_{x < 0}(x)$
softsign	$\dfrac{x}{1 + \|x\|}$
a-inverse square root linear unit	$x \cdot \chi_{x \geq 0}(x) + \dfrac{x}{\sqrt{1 + ax^2}} \cdot \chi_{x < 0}(x)$ for $a > 0$
a-inverse square root unit	$\dfrac{x}{\sqrt{1 + ax^2}}$ for $a > 0$
sigmoidal (type)	$\lim_{x \to \infty} \sigma(x) = 1$ and $\lim_{x \to -\infty} \sigma(x) = 0$.
sigmoid / logistic	$\dfrac{1}{1 + \exp(-x)}$
tanh	$\dfrac{\exp(x) - \exp(-x)}{\exp(x) + \exp(-x)}$
arctan	$\arctan(x)$
softplus	$\ln(1 + \exp(x))$

Table 3.1 *Commonly used activation functions.*

Definition 3.2. Let $d = n_0, n_1, \ldots, n_{L-1}, s = n_L \in \mathbb{N}$ for some $L \in \mathbb{N}$ and $\sigma : \mathbb{R} \to \mathbb{R}$. Then we set

$$\mathcal{N}_{(d, n_1, \ldots, n_{L-1}, s)} := \{\Phi \text{ neural network with } L \text{ layers, } n_\ell \text{ neurons in layer } \ell\}$$

as well as

$$\mathcal{RN}_{(d, n_1, \ldots, n_{L-1}, s), \sigma} := \{R_\sigma(\Phi) : \Phi \in \mathcal{N}_{(d, n_1, \ldots, n_{L-1}, s)}\}.$$

In the following, if not stated otherwise, we fix an input dimension $d \in \mathbb{N}$ as well as an output dimension $s \in \mathbb{N}$.

3.1.2 Goal and Outline of this Chapter

The aim of this chapter is to provide a comprehensive overview of the area of approximation theory for neural networks. In §3.2, we start with the universal approximation theorem for *shallow* neural networks. These were the main types of neural networks studied until the 1990s. We then relate the approximation accuracy of neural networks to their complexity. It turns out that for many well-known classical function spaces one can derive upper and lower complexity bounds in terms of the number of weights, neurons and layers.

Since 2012, *deep* neural networks have been remarkably successful in various fields of applications. In §3.3, we transfer universality results for shallow neural networks to their deep counterparts. We then proceed with finding approximation rates of deep neural networks for classes of smooth functions in §3.4 and piecewise smooth functions in §3.5. Function classes for which the so-called *curse of dimensionality* can be overcome will be discussed in §3.6. Another important line of research aims to explain the benefit of *deep* neural networks over *shallow* ones. This will be the focus of §3.7.

Finally, there exists a large variety of different network architectures, each adapted to specific applications. It remains an interesting question how architectural design choices influence expressivity. In §3.8, we will present results that cover this question for *convolutional* neural networks, which have shown tremendous successes in computer vision, *residual* neural networks, which have allowed the use of much deeper models and, lastly, *recurrent* neural networks, which can be viewed as dynamical systems.

3.1.3 Notation

We denote by $\mathbb{N} = \{1, 2, \dots\}$ the set of all *natural numbers* and define $\mathbb{N}_0 := \mathbb{N} \cup \{0\}$. For $a \in \mathbb{R}$ we set $\lfloor a \rfloor := \max\{b \in \mathbb{Z}: b \leq a\}$ and $\lceil a \rceil := \min\{b \in \mathbb{Z}: b \geq a\}$. For two real-valued functions f, g we say that $f \lesssim g$ if there exists some constant $C > 0$ such that $f \leq Cg$. Conversely, we write $f \gtrsim g$ if $g \lesssim f$ and $f \sim g$ if $f \lesssim gb$ and $f \gtrsim g$.

For two sets A, B such that $A \subset B$ we denote by $\mathbf{1}_A$ the *indicator function of A in B*. Moreover, $|A|$ denotes the *cardinality* of A. If $(B, \mathcal{T})$ is a topological space, we denote by ∂A the *boundary of A* and by $\overline{A}$ its closure.

For $x \in \mathbb{R}^n$ we denote by $|x|$ its *Euclidean norm* and by $\|x\|_p$ its *p-norm*, $p \in [1, \infty]$. If $(V, \| \cdot \|_V)$ is a normed vector space, we denote by $(V^*, \| \cdot \|_{V^*})$ the *topological dual space of V*, i.e. the set of all scalar-valued, linear, continuous functions equipped with the *operator norm*.

Let $d, s \in \mathbb{N}$. For a measurable set $K \subset \mathbb{R}^d$ we denote by $C^n(K, \mathbb{R}^s)$, for $n \in \mathbb{N}_0 \cup \{\infty\}$, the spaces of n *times continuously differentiable functions with values in* $\mathbb{R}^s$. Equipped with $\|f\|_{C^n} = \max_{\|\alpha\|_1 \le n} \|D^\alpha f\|_\infty$ these spaces are Banach spaces if K is compact. We denote by $C_0^\infty(K)$ the *set of infinitely many times differentiable functions with compact support in K*. In the case $s = 1$, we simply write $C(K) := C(K, \mathbb{R})$. Let $\beta = (n, \zeta)$ for some $n \in \mathbb{N}_0$, $\zeta \in (0, 1]$, and let $K \subset \mathbb{R}^d$ be compact. Then, for $f \in C^n(K)$, we write

$$\|f\|_{C^\beta} := \max \left\{ \max_{\|\alpha\|_1 \le n} \|D^\alpha f\|_\infty, \max_{\|\alpha\|_1 = n} \mathrm{Lip}_\zeta(D^\alpha f) \right\} \in [0, \infty],$$

where

$$\mathrm{Lip}_\zeta(f) = \sup_{x, y \in K, \ x \ne y} \frac{|f(x) - f(y)|}{|x - y|^\zeta}.$$

We denote by $C^\beta(K) := \{f \in C^n(K) \colon \|f\|_{C^\beta} < \infty\}$ the *space of all β-Hölder continuous functions*. For an *n*-times differentiable function $f \colon K \subset \mathbb{R} \to \mathbb{R}$ we denote by $f^{(n)}$ its *n*th derivative.

For a measure space $(K, \mathcal{G}, \mu)$ we denote by $\mathcal{L}_p(K; \mu)$, for $p \in [1, \infty]$, the spaces of equivalence classes of $\mathcal{G}$-measurable real-valued functions $f \colon K \to \mathbb{R}$ which coincide μ-almost everywhere and for which $\|f\|_p < \infty$, where

$$\|f\|_p := \begin{cases} \left(\int_K |f(x)|^p \, d\mu(x) \right)^{1/p}, & \text{if } p < \infty, \\ \mathrm{ess\,sup}_{x \in K} |f(x)|, & \text{if } p = \infty. \end{cases}$$

If λ is the Lebesgue measure on the Lebesgue σ-algebra of $K \subset \mathbb{R}^d$ then we will simply write $\mathcal{L}_p(K) = \mathcal{L}_p(K; \lambda)$ as well as $dx = d\lambda(x)$.

Let $W^{n,p}(K)$ be the *Sobolev space* of order n consisting of $f \in \mathcal{L}_p(K)$ satisfying $D^\alpha f \in \mathcal{L}_p(K)$ for all multi-indices $\|\alpha\|_1 \le n$, where $D^\alpha f \in \mathcal{L}_p(K)$ denotes the weak derivative. Finally, we denote by $F^p_{n,d}$ the *unit ball* in $W^{n,p}([0,1]^d)$.

3.2 Shallow Neural Networks

In this section we examine expressivity results for *shallow* neural networks, which form the groundwork for a variety of results connected with deep neural networks. After reviewing their universality properties in §3.2.1, we examine lower complexity bounds in §3.2.2 and upper complexity bounds in §3.2.3.

3.2.1 Universality of Shallow Neural Networks

The most famous type of expressivity result for neural networks states that shallow neural networks are *universal approximators*. This means that, for a wide variety of relevant function classes C, every function $f \in C$ can be arbitrarily well approximated by a shallow neural network. In mathematical terms the statement reads as follows.

> For every $f \in C$ and every $\epsilon > 0$ as well as different types of activation functions $\sigma : \mathbb{R} \to \mathbb{R}$ there exists some $N \in \mathbb{N}$ and some neural network $\Phi_{f,\epsilon} \in \mathcal{N}_{(d,N,s)}$ such that
>
> $$\left\| f - R_\sigma \left(\Phi_{f,\epsilon} \right) \right\|_C \leq \epsilon.$$

For all commonly used activation functions σ and many relevant function classes C, the widths N of the approximating neural networks $\Phi_{f,\epsilon}$ do not remain uniformly bounded over C and ϵ but grow with increasing approximation accuracy.

Within a very short period of time three papers containing results in this direction appeared. The first one, Funahashi (1989), established the universality of shallow neural networks with non-constant, bounded and monotonically increasing continuous activation functions for the space $C(K)$, with $K \subset \mathbb{R}^d$ compact. The idea of the proof is based on Fourier theory, Paley–Wiener theory and an integral formula from Irie and Miyake (1988).

A slightly different set of activation functions (monotonically increasing, sigmoidal) was considered in Hornik et al. (1989), where universality was established for $C = C(K)$ and $C = \mathcal{L}_p(\mathbb{R}^d ; \mu)$,. There, μ is a probability measure defined on the Borel σ-algebra of $\mathbb{R}^d$. The main idea behind the proof is based on the Stone–Weierstrass theorem.

Shortly afterwards, the universality of continuous sigmoidal functions was proved in Cybenko (1989) for the function space $C = C(K)$, where $K \subset \mathbb{R}^d$ is compact. The proof, whose main ideas we will sketch in Theorem 3.4, is based on an elegant application of the Hahn–Banach theorem combined with a measure-theoretic version of the Riesz representation theorem.

An extension of this result for discrete choices of scaling weights and biases wasgiven in Chui and Li (1992). We note that the statements given in Funahashi (1989), Hornik et al. (1989), Cybenko (1989) and Chui and Li (1992) are all applicable to sigmoidal activation functions, which were commonly used in practice at that time. The result of Cybenko considers the more general activation function class of *discriminatory functions* (see Definition 3.3) with which he was able to establish the universality of shallow neural networks for $C = \mathcal{L}_1(K)$. Moreover, the universality of shallow neural networks with a sigmoidal activation function for

$C = \mathcal{L}_2(K)$ based on so-called *Fourier networks* was demonstrated in Gallant and White (1988) and, closely related to this result, in Hecht-Nielsen (1989). Another universal result for the space $C = \mathcal{L}_2(K)$ for continuous sigmoidal activation functions employing the Radon transform was given in Carroll and Dickinson (1989). In Hornik et al. (1990) and Hornik (1991) universality for functions with high-order derivatives was examined. In this case C is given by the Sobolev space $W^{n,p}(K)$ or the space $C^n(K)$, and σ is a sufficiently smooth function.

Further advances under milder conditions on the activation function were made in Leshno et al. (1993). Again, their result is based on an application of the Stone–Weierstrass theorem. The precise statement along with the main proof idea are depicted in Theorem 3.5.

In the following we present a selection of elegant proof strategies for universal approximation theorems. We start by outlining a proof strategy utilizing the Riesz representation theorem for measures (see Theorem 6.19 of Rudin, 1987).

Definition 3.3 (Cybenko, 1989). Let $K \subset \mathbb{R}^d$ be compact. A measurable function $f: \mathbb{R} \to \mathbb{R}$ is *discriminatory with respect to K* if, for every finite, signed, regular Borel measure μ on K we have that

$$\left(\int_K f(\mathbf{W}x + \mathbf{b}) d\mu(x) = 0, \text{ for all } \mathbf{W} \in \mathbb{R}^{1 \times d} \text{ and } \mathbf{b} \in \mathbb{R} \right) \implies \mu = 0.$$

In fact, in Cybenko (1989, Lemma 1) it was demonstrated that every sigmoidal function is indeed discriminatory with respect to closed cubes in $\mathbb{R}^d$. The universal approximation result for discriminatory functions now reads as follows.

Theorem 3.4 (Cybenko, 1989). *Let $\sigma \in C(\mathbb{R})$ be discriminatory with respect to a compact set $K \subset \mathbb{R}^d$. Then $\mathcal{RN}_{(d,\infty,1),\sigma} := \cup_{N \in \mathbb{N}} \mathcal{RN}_{(d,N,1),\sigma}$ is dense in $C(K)$.*

Proof We restrict ourselves to the case $s = 1$. Towards a contradiction, assume that the linear subspace $\mathcal{RN}_{(d,\infty,1),\sigma}$ is not dense in $C(K)$. Set $\overline{\mathcal{RN}} := \overline{\mathcal{RN}_{(d,\infty,1),\sigma}}$. Then there exists some $f \in C(K) \setminus \overline{\mathcal{RN}}$. By the Hahn–Banach theorem, there exists some $\kappa \in C(K)^*$ with $\kappa(f) \neq 0$ and $\kappa|_{\overline{\mathcal{RN}}} = 0$. Invoking the Riesz representation theorem (see Theorem 6.19 of Rudin, 1987), there exists some finite, non-zero, signed Borel measure μ such that

$$\kappa(f) = \int_K f(x) d\mu(x), \quad \text{for all } f \in C(K).$$

Notice that, for all $\mathbf{W} \in \mathbb{R}^{1 \times d}$ and all $\mathbf{b} \in \mathbb{R}$, we have that $\sigma(\mathbf{W}(\cdot) + \mathbf{b}) \in \mathcal{RN}_{(d,\infty,1),\sigma}$. This implies that

$$0 = \kappa(\sigma(\mathbf{W}(\cdot) + \mathbf{b})) = \int_K \sigma(\mathbf{W}x + \mathbf{b}) d\mu(x), \quad \text{for all } \mathbf{W} \in \mathbb{R}^{1 \times d}, \mathbf{b} \in \mathbb{R}.$$

But since σ is a discriminatory function, $\mu = 0$, which is a contradiction. □

Now we proceed by describing the universality result given in Leshno et al. (1993), which is based on an application of the Stone–Weierstrass theorem.

Theorem 3.5 (Leshno et al., 1993). *Let $K \subset \mathbb{R}^d$ be a compact set and $\sigma : \mathbb{R} \to \mathbb{R}$ be continuous and not a polynomial. Then $\mathcal{RN}_{(d,\infty,s),\sigma}$ is dense in $C(K)$.*

Sketch of Proof   We consider only the case $s = 1$. Moreover, by Leshno et al. (1993, Proof of Theorem 1, Step 2), we can restrict ourselves to the case $d = 1$. This follows from the fact that if $\mathcal{RN}_{(1,\infty,1),\sigma}$ is dense in $C(\tilde{K})$ for all compact $\tilde{K} \subset \mathbb{R}$ then $\mathcal{RN}_{(d,\infty,1),\sigma}$ is dense in $C(K)$ for all compact $K \subset \mathbb{R}^d$.

In the following, we will write that $f \in \overline{M}^{C(\mathbb{R})}$ for some $M \subset C(\mathbb{R})$ if for every compact set $K \subset \mathbb{R}$ and every $\epsilon > 0$ there exists some $g \in M$ such that $\|f|_K - g|_K\|_\infty \leq \epsilon$. Hence, the claim follows if we can show that $\overline{\mathcal{RN}_{(1,\infty,1),\sigma}}^{C(\mathbb{R})} = C(\mathbb{R})$.

Step 1 (Activation $\sigma \in C^\infty(\mathbb{R})$):   Assume that $\sigma \in C^\infty(\mathbb{R})$. Since for every $\mathbf{W}, \mathbf{b} \in \mathbb{R}$, $h \in \mathbb{R} \setminus \{0\}$, we know

$$\frac{\sigma((\mathbf{W} + h) \cdot + \mathbf{b}) - \sigma(\mathbf{W} \cdot + \mathbf{b})}{h} \in \mathcal{RN}_{(1,\infty,1)},$$

we obtain that $\frac{d}{d\mathbf{W}}\sigma(\mathbf{W} \cdot + \mathbf{b}) \in \overline{\mathcal{RN}_{(1,\infty,1)}}^{C(\mathbb{R})}$. By an inductive argument, we obtain $\frac{d^k}{d\mathbf{W}^k}\sigma(\mathbf{W} \cdot + \mathbf{b}) \in \overline{\mathcal{RN}_{(1,\infty,1)}}^{C(\mathbb{R})}$ for every $k \in \mathbb{N}_0$. Moreover,

$$\frac{d^k}{d\mathbf{W}^k}\sigma(\mathbf{W} \cdot + \mathbf{b}) = (\cdot)^k \sigma^{(k)}(\mathbf{W} \cdot + \mathbf{b}).$$

Since σ is not a polynomial, for every $k \in \mathbb{N}_0$ there exists some $\mathbf{b}_k \in \mathbb{R}$ such that $\sigma^{(k)}(\mathbf{b}_k) \neq 0$. Hence, $(\cdot)^k \cdot \sigma^{(k)}(\mathbf{b}_k) \in \overline{\mathcal{RN}_{(1,\infty,1)}}^{C(\mathbb{R})} \setminus \{0\}$ for all $k \in \mathbb{N}_0$ and $\overline{\mathcal{RN}_{(1,\infty,1),\sigma}}^{C(\mathbb{R})}$ contains all monomials and hence also all polynomials. Since polynomials are dense in $C(\mathbb{R})$ by the Weierstrass theorem, $\overline{\mathcal{RN}_{(1,\infty,1),\sigma}}^{C(\mathbb{R})} = C(\mathbb{R})$.

Step 2 (Activation $\sigma \in C(\mathbb{R})$):   Now assume that $\sigma \in C(\mathbb{R})$ and σ is not a polynomial. Step 1 is used via a mollification argument by showing that, for $z \in C_0^\infty(\mathbb{R})$,

$$\sigma * z = \int_{\mathbb{R}} \sigma(\cdot - y)z(y)\,dy \in \overline{\mathcal{RN}_{(1,\infty,1)}}^{C(\mathbb{R})},$$

holds by an approximation of the integral by a Riemann series. If $\sigma * z$ is not a polynomial then by invoking Step 1 we conclude that

$$\overline{\mathcal{RN}_{(1,\infty,1),\sigma}}^{C(\mathbb{R})} = C(\mathbb{R}).$$

Finally, using standard arguments from functional analysis, it can be shown that, for every $\sigma \in C(\mathbb{R})$ for which σ is not a polynomial, there exists some $z \in C_0^\infty(\mathbb{R})$ such that $\sigma * z$ is not a polynomial. This yields the claim. $\qquad\qquad\qquad\square$

As mentioned before, these universality results do not yield an estimate of the width of a neural network necessary to achieve a certain approximation accuracy. However, due to hardware-induced constraints on the network size, such an analysis is imperative.

We will see in the following, that many of the subsequent results suffer from the infamous *curse of dimensionality* (Bellman, 1952), i.e. the number of parameters of the approximating networks grows exponentially in the input dimension. To be more precise, for a variety of function classes $C \subset \{f : \mathbb{R}^d \to \mathbb{R}^s\}$, in order to obtain

$$\left\| f - R_\sigma \left(\Phi_{f,\epsilon} \right) \right\|_C \leq \epsilon,$$

for an unspecified $f \in C$, the width of $\Phi_{f,\epsilon}$ needs to scale asymptotically as $\epsilon^{-d/C}$ for a constant $C = C(C) > 0$ as $\epsilon \searrow 0$. In other words, the complexity of the networks in question grows exponentially in the input dimension with increasing approximation accuracy.

3.2.2 Lower Complexity Bounds

We now look at answering the following question: Given a function space C and an approximation accuracy ε, how many (unspecified) weights and neurons are necessary for a neural network such that its realizations are potentially able to achieve approximation accuracy ϵ for an arbitrary function $f \in C$? We start by presenting results for classical function spaces C where the curse of dimensionality can in general not be avoided.

The first lower bounds have been deduced by a combination of two arguments in Maiorov et al. (1999) and Maiorov and Pinkus (1999) for the case where no restrictions on the parameter selection process are imposed. It was also shown in Maiorov et al. (1999) that the set of functions such that this lower bound is attained is of large measure.

Theorem 3.6 (Maiorov et al., 1999; Maiorov and Pinkus, 1999). *Let $\sigma \in C(\mathbb{R})$, $d \geq 2$, $\varepsilon > 0$ and $N \in \mathbb{N}$ such that, for each $f \in F_{n,d}^2$, there exists a neural network $\Phi_{f,\epsilon} \in \mathcal{N}_{(d,N,s)}$ satisfying*

$$\left\| R_\sigma \left(\Phi_{f,\varepsilon} \right) - f \right\|_2 \leq \varepsilon.$$

Then $N \gtrsim \varepsilon^{-(d-1/n)}$.

The next theorem can be used to derive lower bounds if the parameter selection is required to depend continuously on the function to be approximated. We will state the theorem in full generality and draw out the connection to neural networks afterwards.

Theorem 3.7 (DeVore et al., 1989). *Let $\varepsilon > 0$ and $1 \leq p \leq \infty$. For $M \in \mathbb{N}$, let $\phi \colon \mathbb{R}^M \to \mathcal{L}_p([0,1]^d)$ be an arbitrary function. Suppose there is a continuous function $\mathcal{P} \colon F_{n,d}^p \to \mathbb{R}^M$ such that $\|f - \phi(\mathcal{P}(f))\|_p \leq \epsilon$ for all $f \in F_{n,d}^p$. Then $M \gtrsim \epsilon^{-d/n}$.*

In Yarotsky (2017) it was observed that, when taking M as the number of weights and ϕ as a function mapping from the weight space to functions realized by neural networks, one can directl obtain a lower complexity bound. We note that the increased regularity (expressed in terms of n) of the function to be approximated implies a potentially better approximation rate, something which is also apparent in many results to follow.

3.2.3 Upper Complexity Bounds

Now we turn our attention to results examining the sharpness of the deduced lower bounds by deriving upper bounds. In principle, it was proved in Maiorov and Pinkus (1999) that there do indeed exist sigmoidal, strictly increasing, activation functions $\sigma \in C^\infty(\mathbb{R})$ for which the bound $N \lesssim \epsilon^{-(d-1)/n}$ of Theorem 3.6 is attained. However, the construction of such an activation function is based on the separability of the space $C([-1,1])$ and hence is not useful in practice. A more relevant upper bound is given in Mhaskar (1996).

Theorem 3.8 (Mhaskar, 1996). *Let $n \in \mathbb{N}$ and $p \in [1, \infty]$. Moreover, let $\sigma \colon \mathbb{R} \to \mathbb{R}$ be a function such that $\sigma|_I \in C^\infty(I)$ for some open interval $I \subset \mathbb{R}$ and $\sigma^{(k)}(x_0) \neq 0$ for some $x_0 \in I$ and all $k \in \mathbb{N}_0$. Then, for every $f \in F_{n,d}^p$ and every $\epsilon > 0$, there exists a shallow neural network $\Phi_{f,\epsilon} \in \mathcal{N}_{(d,N,1)}$ such that*

$$\|f - R_\sigma(\Phi_{f,\epsilon})\|_p \leq \epsilon,$$

and $N \lesssim \epsilon^{-d/n}$.

We note that this rate is optimal if one assumes a *continuous* dependence of the parameters on the approximating function (see Theorem 3.7). This is fulfilled in the proof of the upper bounds of Theorem 3.8, since it is based on the approximation of Taylor polynomials by realizations of shallow neural networks. It was mentioned in Mhaskar (1996, Section 4) that this rate can be improved if the function f is analytic.

The aforementioned lower and upper bounds suffer from the curse of dimensionality. This can for example be avoided if the function class under consideration is assumed to have strong regularity. As an example we state a result given in Barron (1993, 1994) and Makovoz (1996), where finite Fourier moment conditions are used.

Theorem 3.9 (Barron, 1993, 1994; Makovoz, 1996). *Let σ be a bounded, measurable, and sigmoidal function. Then, for every*

$$f \in \left\{ g : \mathbb{R}^d \to \mathbb{R}, \ \int_{\mathbb{R}^d} |\xi| \cdot |\mathcal{F}g(\xi)| \, d\xi < \infty \right\},$$

where $\mathcal{F}g$ denotes the Fourier transform of g, and for every $\epsilon > 0$, there exists a shallow neural network $\Phi_{f,\epsilon} \in \mathcal{N}_{(d,N,1)}$ with

$$\left\| f - R_\sigma \left(\Phi_{f,\epsilon} \right) \right\|_2 \le \epsilon,$$

and $N \lesssim \epsilon^{-2d/(d+1)}$.

Although the dimension appears in the underlying rate, the curse of dimensionality is absent.

Lastly, we present a result where a complexity bound is derived for approximations of a *finite* set of test points. It was shown in Sontag (1992a) that if $\sigma : \mathbb{R} \to \mathbb{R}$ is sigmoidal and differentiable at one point $x \in \mathbb{R}$ with non-zero derivative, and if $(x_1, y_1), \ldots, (x_{2N+1}, y_{2N+1}) \in \mathbb{R} \times \mathbb{R}$ for some $N \in \mathbb{N}$ is a set of test points, then, for every $\epsilon > 0$, there exists a neural network $\Phi_\epsilon \in \mathcal{N}_{(1,N+1,1)}$ such that

$$\sup_{i=1,\ldots,2N+1} |R_\sigma \left(\Phi_\epsilon \right)(x_i) - y_i| \le \epsilon.$$

This concludes our examination of shallow neural networks. Because of the multitude of existing results we could only discuss a representative selection. For a more comprehensive overview focusing solely on shallow neural networks we refer to Pinkus (1999).

3.3 Universality of Deep Neural Networks

So far, our focus has been entirely on shallow neural networks. Recently, however, the use of *deep* neural networks, i.e. networks with $L > 2$ layers, has become significant.

Early attempts to study the expressivity of deep neural networks were based on the *Kolmogorov superposition theorem* (see, for instance, Kolmogorov, 1957, 1961). A variant of this theorem (see Sprecher, 1965) states that every continuous function $f\colon [0,1]^d \to \mathbb{R}$ can be *exactly* represented as

$$f(x_1,\ldots,x_d) = \sum_{i=1}^{2d+1} g\left(\sum_{j=1}^{d} k_j \phi_i(x_j) \right). \tag{3.2}$$

Here, $k_j > 0$, for $j = 1,\ldots,d$, such that $\sum_{j=1}^{d} k_j \le 1$; $\phi_i\colon [0,1] \to [0,1]$, $i = 1,\ldots,2d+1$, is strictly increasing, and $g \in C([0,1])$ are functions depending on f. In Hecht-Nielsen (1987), Equation (3.2) was interpreted in the context of (a general version of) a neural network. It yields that every continuous function can be exactly represented by a 3-layer neural network with width $2d^2 + d$ and different activation functions in each neuron depending on the function to be approximated. However, quoting Hecht-Nielsen (1987), the "direct usefulness of this result is doubtful", since it is not known how to construct the functions $g, \phi_1,\ldots,\phi_{2d+1}$, which play the roles of the activation functions. Furthermore, Girosi and Poggio (1989) pointed out that the dependence of the activation functions on f makes this approach hardly usable in practice. We refer to their paper for a more detailed discussion about the suitability of the Kolmogorov superposition theorem in this context.

Subsequent contributions focused on more practical neural network architectures, where the activation functions were fixed a priori and only the parameters of the affine maps were adjusted. Under these assumptions, however, the capability of representing every function in $C([0,1]^d)$ in an exact way is lost. Consequently, the expressivity of neural networks with a fixed activation function has been studied in terms of their approximative power for specific function classes C. We note that the universality results for shallow neural networks from the last section in general also hold for *deep* neural networks with a fixed number of layers (see Funahashi, 1989; Hornik et al., 1989). In Hornik et al. (1989, Corollary 2.7) universality for shallow networks in $C(K)$ was transferred to the multi-layer case via Lemma A.6 of the same paper. It states that if $F, G \subset C(\mathbb{R})$ are such that $F|_K, G|_K$ are dense sets for every compact subset $K \subset \mathbb{R}$ then also $\{f \circ g\colon f \in F, g \in G\}$ is dense in $C(K)$.

In contrast with the lower bounds in Theorem 3.6, for the case of three layer neural networks it is possible to show the existence of a pathological (i.e. in practice unusable) activation function σ such that the set $\mathcal{RN}_{(d,2d+1,4d+3,1),\sigma}$ is dense in $C([-1,1]^d)$ (see Maiorov and Pinkus, 1999). As in the case of Equation (3.2), the remarkable independence of the complexity from the approximation error and its mere linear dependence on d (implying that the curse of dimensionality can be circumvented) is due to the choice of the activation function. However, for practically used activation functions such as the ReLU, parametric ReLU, exponential linear unit, softsign and tanh, universality in $C(K)$ does not hold (Remark 2.3 in Petersen et al., 2021).

The dual problem of considering neural networks with *fixed depth* and *unbounded width*, is to explore expressivity of neural networks with *fixed width* and *unrestricted depth*. In Hanin and Sellke (2017) and Hanin (2019) it is shown that the set of ReLU neural networks with width $\geq d + n$ and unrestricted depth is an universal approximator for the function class $C = C([0,1]^d, \mathbb{R}^n)$. In the case $n = 1$, the lower bound on the width is sharp. For $C = \mathcal{L}_1(\mathbb{R}^d)$, Lu et al. (2017) established universality of deep ReLU neural networks with width $\geq d + 4$. The necessary width for ReLU neural networks to yield universal approximators is bounded from below by d.

3.4 Approximation of Classes of Smooth Functions

In this chapter, we examine approximation rates of *deep* neural networks for functions characterized by smoothness properties. This chapter can be seen as a counterpart of §§3.2.2 and 3.2.3 with three major differences. We now focus on deep neural networks (instead of shallow ones); most of these results were shown after the rise of deep learning in 2012; currently used activation functions (such as, e.g., the ReLU[5]) are analyzed.

A ground-laying result was given in Yarotsky (2017). There it was shown that, for each $\epsilon > 0$ and for each function f in $F_{n,d}^\infty$, there exists a ReLU neural network with $L \lesssim \log_2(1/\varepsilon)$ layers, as well as $M, N \lesssim \varepsilon^{-d/n} \log_2(1/\varepsilon)$ weights and neurons capable of approximating f with $\mathcal{L}_\infty$-approximation error ϵ. A generalization of this result for functions from $F_{n,d}^p$ with error measured in the $W^{r,p}$-norm[6] for $0 \leq r \leq 1$ was obtained in Gühring et al. (2019). Arbitrary Sobolev norms and general activation functions were examined in Gühring and Raslan (2021). These results show that the error can also be measured in norms that include the distance of the derivative and that there is a trade-off between the regularity r used in the approximating norm and the complexity of the network. The following theorem summarizes the findings of Yarotsky (2017)[7] and Gühring et al. (2019).

Theorem 3.10 (Yarotsky, 2017; Gühring et al., 2019). *For every $f \in F_{n,d}^p$ there exists a neural network $\Phi_{f,\varepsilon}$ whose realization is capable of approximating f with error ε in the $W^{r,p}$-norm ($0 \leq r \leq 1$), with*

---

[5] The first activation function that was used was the *threshold function* $\sigma = \mathbf{1}_{[0,\infty)}$ (see McCulloch and Pitts, 1943). This was biologically motivated and constitutes a mathematical interpretation of the fact that "a neuron fires if the incoming signal is strong enough". Since this function is not differentiable everywhere and its derivative is zero almost everywhere, smoothed versions (sigmoidal functions) have been employed to allow for the usage of the backpropagation algorithm. These functions, however, are subject to the *vanishing gradient problem*, which is not as common for the ReLU (see Glorot et al., 2011). Another advantage of the ReLU is that it is easy to compute and promotes sparsity in data representation (see Bengio et al., 2013).

[6] Here, $W^{r,p}$ for $r \in (0,1)$ denotes the Sobolev–Slobodeckij spaces as considered in Gühring et al. (2019, Definition 3.3).

[7] The results are presented in a slightly modified version. The neural networks considered in Yarotsky (2017) are allowed to have skip connections possibly linking a layer to all its successors. The rates obtained are equal, except that the square power of the logarithm needs to be removed.

(i) $M(\Phi_{f,\varepsilon}) \lesssim \epsilon^{-d/(n-r)} \cdot \log_2^2\left(\varepsilon^{-n/(n-r)}\right)$, *and*

(ii) $L(\Phi_{f,\varepsilon}) \lesssim \log_2\left(\varepsilon^{-n/(n-r)}\right)$.

Remark 3.11. The depth scales logarithmically in the approximation accuracy. This is due to the ReLU, which renders the approximation of the map $x \mapsto x^2$ difficult. For activation functions σ with $\sigma(x_0)$, $\sigma'(x_0)$, $\sigma''(x_0) \neq 0$, for some $x_0 \in \mathbb{R}$ it is possible to approximate $x \mapsto x^2$ by a neural network with a fixed number of weights and $L = 2$ (see Rolnick and Tegmark, 2018).

A common tool for deducing upper complexity bounds is based on the approximation of suitable representation systems. Smooth functions, for instance, can be locally described by (Taylor) polynomials, i.e.

$$f \approx \sum_{\|\alpha\|_1 \leq k}^{n} c_k(\cdot - x_0)^\alpha \quad \text{locally.}$$

Approximating monomials by neural networks then yields an approximation of f.[8] The proof strategy employed by Yarotsky is also based on this idea. It has been picked up in several follow-up works (Gühring et al., 2019; Petersen and Voigtlaender, 2018) and we describe it here in more detail.

Proof sketch The core of the proof is an approximation of the square function $x \mapsto x^2$ by a piecewise linear interpolation that can be expressed by ReLU neural networks (see Figure 3.3 for a visualization). First, we define $g : [0,1] \to [0,1]$, by $g(x) := \min\{2x, 2 - 2x\}$. Notice that the hat function g is representable by a ReLU neural network. Multiple compositions of g with itself result in saw-tooth functions (see Figure 3.3). We set, for $m \in \mathbb{N}$, $g_1 := g$ and $g_{m+1} := g \circ g_m$. It was demonstrated in Yarotsky (2017) that

$$x^2 = \lim_{n \to \infty} f_n(x) := \lim_{n \to \infty} x - \sum_{m=1}^{n} \frac{g_m(x)}{2^{2m}}, \quad \text{for all } x \in [0,1].$$

Hence, there exist neural networks $\Phi_{x^2,\epsilon}$ the ReLU realizations of which approximate $x \mapsto x^2$ uniformly on $[0,1]$ up to an error ϵ. It can be shown that $M(\Phi_{x^2,\epsilon})$, $L(\Phi_{x^2,\epsilon})$, $N(\Phi_{x^2,\epsilon}) \lesssim \log_2(1/\epsilon)$. From this a neural network Φ_{mult} is constructed via the polarization identity

$$xy = \frac{1}{2}\left((x+y)^2 - x^2 - y^2\right) \quad \text{for } x, y \in \mathbb{R},$$

the ReLU realizations of which locally approximates the multiplication map $(x, y) \mapsto xy$. It is now straight-forward to approximate arbitrary polynomials by realizations

---

[8] For shallow neural networks this ansatz was used, for example, in Mhaskar (1996).

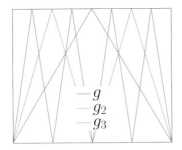 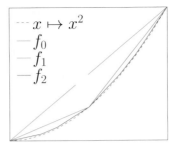

Figure 3.3 Visualization of the approximation of the square function $x \mapsto x^2$ by ReLU realizations of neural networks as in Yarotsky (2017).

of neural networks with $L \lesssim \log_2(1/\epsilon)$ layers and $M \lesssim \text{polylog}(1/\epsilon)$ weights.[9] In order to approximate f globally, a partition of unity is constructed with ReLU neural networks and combined with approximate polynomials. Since the domain needs to be partitioned into roughly $\varepsilon^{-d/n}$ patches, the curse of dimensionality occurs in these bounds. □

From Theorem 3.7 we can deduce that, under the hypothesis of a continuous dependence of weights and biases on the function f to be approximated, the upper bound shown in Theorem 3.10 for the case $r = 0$ is tight (up to a log factor). Dropping the assumption of continuous weight dependency, Yarotsky derived a bound for the case $r = 0$, $p = \infty$ and in Gühring et al. (2019) the case $r = 1, p = \infty$ was covered. Both cases are combined in the next theorem. For its exposition we need to introduce additional notation. Analogously to Yarotsky (2017), we denote by $\mathcal{A}$ a neural network with unspecified non-zero weights and call it a neural network architecture. We say that *the architecture $\mathcal{A}$ is capable of approximating a function f with error ε and activation function σ, if this can be achieved by the σ-realization of some weight assignment.*

Theorem 3.12 (Yarotsky, 2017; Gühring et al., 2019). *Let $\epsilon > 0$ and $r \in \{0, 1\}$. If $\mathcal{A}_\varepsilon$ is a neural network architecture that is capable of approximating every function from $F_{n,d}^\infty$ with error ε in $W^{r,\infty}$-norm and with activation function ReLU, then*

$$M(\mathcal{A}_\varepsilon) \gtrsim \varepsilon^{-d/2(n-r)}.$$

Remark 3.13. The gap between the upper bound $M_\varepsilon \lesssim \epsilon^{-d/n}$ of Theorem 3.10 and the lower bound $M_\varepsilon \gtrsim \epsilon^{-d/2n}$ for $r = 0$ is discussed in Yarotsky (2018) and Yarotsky and Zhevnerchuk (2019). It is an instance of the benefit of deep (in this case very) over shallow neural networks. It was shown that for every $\zeta \in [d/(2n), d/n)$

---

[9] In Telgarsky (2017), approximation rates for polynomials are extended to rational functions. It is shown that one can locally uniformly approximate rational functions $f: [0, 1]^d \to \mathbb{R}$ up to an error $\epsilon > 0$ by ReLU realizations of neural networks $\Phi_{f,\epsilon}$ of size $M(\Phi_{f,\epsilon}) \lesssim \text{poly}(d) \cdot \text{polylog}(1/\epsilon)$.

there exist neural networks with $M_\varepsilon \lesssim \epsilon^{-\zeta}$ non-zero weights and $L_\varepsilon \lesssim \epsilon^{-d/(r(\zeta-1))}$ layers that uniformly ε-approximate functions in $F_{n,d}^\infty$.

Proof sketch   We prove the statement only for $r = 0$. The case $r = 1$ is proven similarly. The proof provides a general way of showing lower complexity bounds based on the *Vapnik–Chervonenkis dimension* (VCdim) Vapnik and Chervonenkis (2015). The quantity VCdim measures the expressiveness of a set of binary-valued functions H defined on some set A, and is itself defined by

$$\text{VCdim}(H) := \sup \left\{ m \in \mathbb{N}: \begin{array}{l} \text{there exist } x_1, \ldots, x_m \in A \text{ such that} \\ \text{for every } y \in \{0,1\}^m \text{ there is a function} \\ h \in H \text{ with } h(x_i) = y_i \text{ for } i = 1, \ldots, m \end{array} \right\}.$$

We define the set of thresholded realizations of neural networks

$$H := \left\{ \mathbf{1}_{(-\infty,a]} \circ R_\sigma\left(\Phi_\theta\right) : \theta \in \mathbb{R}^{M(\Phi)} \right\},$$

for some (carefully chosen) $a \in \mathbb{R}$, and derive the chain of inequalities

$$c \cdot \varepsilon^{-d/n} \leq \text{VCdim}(H) \leq C \cdot M(\Phi_\varepsilon)^2. \tag{3.3}$$

The upper bound on VCdim(H) in Equation (3.3) was given in Anthony and Bartlett (2009, Theorem 8.7).

To establish the lower bound, set $N := \lfloor \varepsilon^{-1/n} \rfloor$ and let

$$x_1, \ldots, x_{N^d} \in [0,1]^d \quad \text{such that} \quad |x_m - x_n| \geq 1/N$$

for all $m, n = 1, \ldots, N^d$ with $m \neq n$. For arbitrary $y = (y_1, \ldots, y_{N^d}) \in \{0,1\}^{N^d}$, Yarotsky constructed a function $f_y \in F_{n,d}^\infty$ with $f_y(x_m) = y_m \cdot N^{-n}$ for $m = 1, \ldots, N^d$. Now let Φ_{f_y} be a neural network such that $R_\sigma\left(\Phi_{f_y}\right)$ ε-approximates f_y; then we have for a thresholded neural network realization $\mathbf{1}_{(-\infty,a]} \circ R_\sigma\left(\Phi_{f_y}\right)$ that $R_\sigma\left(\Phi_{f_y}\right)(x_m) = y_m$ (see Figure 3.4).

Figure 3.4   The function f_y in $d = 2$ dimensions.

Using the definition of VCdim it is easy to see that

$$c \cdot \varepsilon^{-d/n} \leq N^d \leq \text{VCdim}(H),$$

which is the lower bound in the inequality (3.3). The theorem now follows easily from (3.3).   □

Approximations in the $\mathcal{L}_p$-norm for β-Hölder-continuous functions were considered in Schmidt-Hieber (2017) and Petersen and Voigtlaender (2018). In contrast with Yarotsky (2017) and Gühring et al. (2019), the depth of the networks involved remains fixed and does not depend on the approximation accuracy. Additionally in Petersen and Voigtlaender (2018), the weights are required to be encodable.[10] We summarize their findings in the following theorem.

Theorem 3.14 (Petersen and Voigtlaender, 2018). *Let $\beta = (n, \zeta)$ for $n \in \mathbb{N}_0$, $\zeta \in (0, 1]$ and $p \in (0, \infty)$. Then, for every $\epsilon > 0$ and every $f \in C^\beta([-1/2, 1/2]^d)$ with $\|f\|_{C^\beta} \leq 1$, there exist ReLU neural networks $\Phi_{f,\epsilon}$ with encodable weights, $L(\Phi_{f,\epsilon}) \lesssim \log_2((n+\zeta))\cdot(n+\zeta)/d$ layers and $M(\Phi_{f,\epsilon}) \lesssim \epsilon^{-d/(n+\zeta)}$ non-zero weights such that*

$$\left\| f - R_\sigma\left(\Phi_{f,\epsilon}\right) \right\|_p \leq \epsilon.$$

There also exist results based on the approximation of B-splines (Mhaskar, 1993) or finite elements (He et al., 2018; Opschoor et al., 2020). It is shown in those works that neural networks perform as well as the underlying approximation procedure.

Finally, instead of examining the approximation rates of deep neural networks for specific function classes, one could also ask the following question. *Which properties does the set of* all *functions that can be approximated by deep neural networks at a given rate fulfil?* This question was discussed extensively in Gribonval et al. (2019). Among other results, it was shown that, under certain assumptions on the neural network architecture, these sets of functions can be embedded into classical function spaces, such as Besov spaces, of a certain degree of smoothness.

3.5 Approximation of Piecewise Smooth Functions

When modelling real-world phenomena one often assumes only *piecewise* smoothness. A prominent example is given by *cartoon-like functions* (see Donoho, 2001),

$$\mathcal{E}^n([0,1]^d) := \left\{ f_1 + \mathbf{1}_B f_2 : \begin{array}{l} f_1, f_2 \in C^n([0,1]^d), \, B \subset (0,1)^d, \, \partial B \in C^n \\ \text{and } \|g\|_{C^n} \leq 1 \text{ for } g = f_1, f_2, \partial B \end{array} \right\},$$

which are commonly used as a mathematical model for images. Figure 3.5 provides an illustration for the case $d = 2$.

The first expressivity results in this direction were deduced in Bölcskei et al. (2019) for neural networks with weights of restricted complexity.[11] To present this result, we first need to introduce some notions from information theory.

---

[10] Tha is, the weights are representable by no more than $\sim \log_2(1/\epsilon)$ bits.
[11] Note that computers can also only store weights of restricted complexity.

Figure 3.5 Illustration of a cartoon-like function on $[0,1]^2$.

The *minimax code length* describes the necessary length of bitstrings of an encoded representation of functions from a function class $C \subset \mathcal{L}_2(K)$ such that it can be decoded with an error smaller then $\varepsilon > 0$. The precise definition is given as follows.

Definition 3.15 (see Bölcskei et al. (2019) and the references therein). Let $K \subset \mathbb{R}^d$ be measurable, and let $C \subset \mathcal{L}_2(K)$ be compact. For each $\ell \in \mathbb{N}$, we denote by

$$\mathfrak{E}^\ell := \{E \colon C \to \{0,1\}^\ell\}$$

the set of *binary encoders mapping elements of C to bit strings of length ℓ*, and we let

$$\mathfrak{D}^\ell := \{D \colon \{0,1\}^\ell \to \mathcal{L}_2(K)\},$$

be the set of *binary decoders mapping bit strings of length ℓ to elements of $\mathcal{L}_2(K)$*.

An encoder–decoder pair $(E^\ell, D^\ell) \in \mathfrak{E}^\ell \times \mathfrak{D}^\ell$ is said to *achieve distortion $\epsilon > 0$ over the function class C* if

$$\sup_{f \in C} \left\| D^\ell(E^\ell(f)) - f \right\|_2 \leq \epsilon.$$

Finally, for $\epsilon > 0$ the *minimax code length* $L(\epsilon, C)$ is

$$L(\epsilon, C) := \min \left\{ \begin{array}{l} \ell \in \mathbb{N} \colon \exists \, (E^\ell, D^\ell) \in \mathfrak{E}^\ell \times \mathfrak{D}^\ell \colon \\ \sup_{f \in C} \left\| D^\ell(E^\ell(f)) - f \right\|_2 \leq \epsilon \end{array} \right\},$$

with the interpretation $L(\epsilon, C) = \infty$ if $\sup_{f \in C} \left\| D^\ell(E^\ell(f)) - f \right\|_2 > \epsilon$ for all $(E^\ell, D^\ell) \in \mathfrak{E}^\ell \times \mathfrak{D}^\ell$ and arbitrary $\ell \in \mathbb{N}$.

We are particularly interested in the asymptotic behavior of $L(\epsilon, C)$, which can be quantified by the *optimal exponent*.

Definition 3.16. Let $K \subset \mathbb{R}^d$ and $C \subset \mathcal{L}_2(K)$. Then, the *optimal exponent* $\gamma^*(C)$ is defined by

$$\gamma^*(C) := \inf \left\{ \gamma \in \mathbb{R} \colon L(\epsilon, C) \lesssim \epsilon^{-\gamma}, \text{ as } \epsilon \searrow 0 \right\}.$$

The optimal exponent $\gamma^*(C)$ describes how fast $L(\epsilon, C)$ tends to infinity as ϵ decreases. For function classes C_1 and C_2, the relation $\gamma^*(C_1) < \gamma^*(C_2)$ indicates that asymptotically, i.e., for $\epsilon \searrow 0$, the necessary length of the encoding bit string for C_2 is larger than that for C_1. In other words, a smaller exponent indicates a smaller description complexity.

Example 3.17. For many function classes the optimal exponent is well known (see Bölcskei et al. (2019) and the references therein). Let $n \in \mathbb{N}$, $1 \leq p, q \leq \infty$; then

(i) $\gamma^* \left(\{ f \in C^n([0,1]^d) : \|f\|_{C^n} \leq 1 \} \right) = d/n$,
(ii) if $n \in \{1, 2\}$ then $\gamma^*(\mathcal{E}^n([0,1]^d)) = 2(d-1)/n$.

The next theorem connects the description complexity of a function class with the necessary complexity of neural network approximations with encodable weights. It shows that, at best, one can hope for an asymptotic growth governed by the optimal exponent.

Theorem 3.18 (Bölcskei et al., 2019). *Let $K \subset \mathbb{R}^d$, $\sigma \colon \mathbb{R} \to \mathbb{R}$, $c > 0$, and $C \subset \mathcal{L}_2(K)$. Let $\epsilon \in (0, \frac{1}{2})$ and $M_{\mathcal{E}} \in \mathbb{N}$. If for every $f \in C$ there exists a neural network $\Phi_{\varepsilon, f}$ with weights encodable with $\lceil c \log_2(\frac{1}{\epsilon}) \rceil$ bits and if $\| f - R_\sigma (\Phi_{\varepsilon, f}) \|_{\mathcal{L}_2} \leq \varepsilon$ and $M(\Phi_{\varepsilon, f}) \leq M_{\mathcal{E}}$ then*

$$M_{\mathcal{E}} \gtrsim \varepsilon^{-\gamma}$$

for all $\gamma < \gamma^*(C)$.

We will now consider the deduction of optimal upper bounds. We have seen already, in many instances, that one of the main ideas behind establishing approximation rates for neural networks is to demonstrate how other function systems, often polynomials, can be emulated by them. In Shaham et al. (2018), a similar approach was followed by demonstrating that neural networks can reproduce wavelet-like functions (instead of polynomials) and thereby also sums of wavelets. This observation lets us transfer *M-term approximation rates* with wavelets to *M*-weight approximation rates with neural networks. In Bölcskei et al. (2019) this route is taken for general affine systems. An *affine system* is constructed by applying affine linear transformations to a *generating function*. We will not give the precise definition of an affine system here (see e.g. Bölcskei et al., 2019) but intend to build some intuition by considering *shearlets* in $\mathbb{R}^2$ as an example.

Shearlet systems (Kutyniok and Labate, 2012) are representation systems used mainly in signal and image processing. As with the Fourier transform, which expands a function in its frequencies, a shearlet decomposition allows an expansion associated with different location, direction and resolution levels. To construct a shearlet system $\mathcal{SH}$, one needs a *parabolic scaling* operation, defined by the matrix

$$A_j := \begin{bmatrix} 2^j & 0 \\ 0 & 2^{j/2} \end{bmatrix},$$

and a *shearing* operation, defined by

$$S_k := \begin{bmatrix} 1 & k \\ 0 & 1 \end{bmatrix},$$

together with the translation operation. These operations are applied to a generating function $\psi \in L_2(\mathbb{R}^2)$ (satisfying some technical conditions) to obtain a *shearlet system*

$$\mathcal{SH} := \left\{ 2^{3j/4} \psi(S_k A_j(\cdot) - n) : j \in \mathbb{Z}, k \in \mathbb{Z}, n \in \mathbb{Z}^2 \right\}.$$

Shearlet systems are particularly well suited for the class of cartoon-like functions. To make this statement rigorous, we first need the following definition.

Definition 3.19. For a normed space V and a system $(\phi_i)_{i \in I} \subset V$ we define the *error of best M-term approximation* of a function $f \in V$ as

$$\Sigma_M(f) := \inf_{\substack{I_M \subset I, |I_M| = M, \\ (c_i)_{i \in I_M}}} \left\| \sum_{i \in I_M} c_i \phi_i - f \right\|_V.$$

For $C \subset V$, the system $(\phi_i)_{i \in I}$ yields an *M-term approximation rate* of M^{-r} for $r \in \mathbb{R}^+$ if

$$\sup_{f \in C} \Sigma_M(f) =\lesssim M^{-r} \text{ for } M \to \infty.$$

It is possible to show that certain shearlet systems yield almost optimal M-term approximation rates[12] for the class of cartoon-like functions $\mathcal{E}^n([0,1]^2)$ (see, for instance, Kutyniok and Lim, 2010).

In Bölcskei et al. (2019, Theorem. 6.8), (optimal) M-term approximation rates of shearlets are transferred to M-weight approximations with neural networks. It is shown that with certain assumptions on the activation function σ one can emulate a generating function ψ with a fixed-size neural network Φ_ψ such that $\psi \approx R_\sigma(\Phi_\psi)$. As a consequence, for every element ϕ_i of the system $\mathcal{SH}$ there exists a corresponding fixed-size neural network Φ_i with $\phi_i \approx R_\sigma(\Phi_i)$. An M-term approximation $\sum_{i \in I_M} c_i(f)\phi_i$ of a function f can then be approximated by a parallelization of networks Φ_i with $\lesssim M$ weights. This line of argument was first

---

[12] The optimal M-term approximation rate is the best rate that can be achieved under some restrictions on the representation system and the selection procedure of the coefficients. See Donoho (2001) for optimal M-term approximation rates for cartoon-like functions.

used in Shaham et al. (2018) and also works for general affine systems. This is made precise in the next theorem.

Theorem 3.20 (Bölcskei et al., 2019). *Let $K \subset \mathbb{R}^d$ be bounded and $\mathcal{D} = (\varphi_i)_{i \in \mathbb{N}} \subset L_2(K)$ be an affine system with generating function $\psi \in L_2(K)$. Suppose that for an activation function $\sigma : \mathbb{R} \to \mathbb{R}$ there exists a constant $C \in \mathbb{N}$ such that for all $\epsilon > 0$ and all $D > 0$ there is a neural network $\Phi_{D,\epsilon}$, with at most C non-zero weights, satisfying*

$$\| \psi - R_\sigma \left(\Phi_{D,\epsilon} \right) \|_{L_2([-D,D]^d)} \leq \epsilon.$$

Then, if $\epsilon > 0$, $M \in \mathbb{N}$, $g \in L_2(K)$ such that there exist $(d_i)_{i=1}^M$ satisfying

$$\left\| g - \sum_{i=1}^M d_i \varphi_i \right\|_2 \leq \epsilon,$$

there exists a neural network Φ with $\lesssim M$ non-zero weights such that

$$\| g - R_\sigma \left(\Phi \right) \|_2 \leq 2\epsilon.$$

Consequently, if shearlet systems yield a certain M-term approximation rate for a function class C then neural networks produce at least that error rate in terms of weights. We can conclude from Theorem 3.20 that neural networks yield an optimal M-weight approximation rate of $\lesssim M^{-n/2}$. On the other hand, we saw in Example 3.17 that $\gamma^*(\mathcal{E}^n([0,1]^2)) = 2/n$, so Theorem 3.18 demonstrates that $\lesssim M^{-n/2}$ is also the optimal approximation rate. Similar results were deduced in Grohs et al. (2019).

An extension to functions $f \in \mathcal{L}_p([-1/2, 1/2]^d)$, $p \in (0, \infty)$, that are C^β-smooth apart from C^β-singularity hypersurfaces is derived in Petersen and Voigtlaender (2020). It is shown that the Heaviside function can be approximated by a shallow ReLU neural networks with five weights (Lemma A.2. in Petersen and Voigtlaender, 2018). Combining this with Theorem 3.14 then yields the next theorem.

Theorem 3.21 (Petersen and Voigtlaender, 2018). *Let $\beta = (n, \zeta)$, $n \in \mathbb{N}_0$, $\zeta \in (0, 1]$ and $p \in (0, \infty)$. Let $f = \mathbf{1}_K \cdot g$, where we assume that $g \in C^{\beta'}([-1/2, 1/2]^d)$ for $\beta' = (d\beta)/(p(d-1))$ with $\|g\|_{C^{\beta'}} \leq 1$ and that $K \subset [-1/2, 1/2]^d$ with $\partial K \in C^\beta$. Moreover, let $\sigma = \mathrm{ReLU}$.*

Then, for every $\epsilon > 0$, there exists a neural network $\Phi_{f,\epsilon}$ with encodable weights, $L(\Phi_{f,\varepsilon}) \lesssim \log_2((n + \zeta)) \cdot (n + \zeta)/d$ layers as well as $M(\Phi_{f,\epsilon}) \lesssim \epsilon^{-p(d-1)/(n+\zeta)}$ non-zero weights such that

$$\| f - R_\sigma \left(\Phi_{f,\epsilon} \right) \|_p \leq \varepsilon.$$

This rate can also be shown to be optimal. We note that approximation rates for piecewise-Hölder functions in $\mathcal{L}_2$ were proven in Imaizumi and Fukumizu (2019) and more general spaces, such as Besov spaces, wereconsidered in Suzuki (2019).

Some remarks on the role of depth for the results presented above can be found in §3.7.

3.6 Assuming More Structure

We have seen in the last sections that even approximations by deep neural networks face the curse of dimensionality for classical function spaces. How to avoid this by assuming more structured function spaces is the topic of this section. We start in §3.6.1 by assuming a hierarchical structure for which deep neural networks overcome the curse of dimensionality but shallow ones do not. Afterwards, we review approximations of high-dimensional functions lying on a low-dimensional set in §3.6.2. Of a similar flavor are the results of §3.6.3, where we examine specifically structured solutions of (parametric) partial differential equations.

3.6.1 Hierachical Structure

Tight approximation rates for smooth functions

$$f: [0,1]^d \to \mathbb{R}, \qquad x \mapsto g_1 \circ g_2 \circ \cdots \circ g_k \circ l(x)$$

with a hierarchical structure, where l is a multivariate polynomial and $g_1, \ldots, g_k$ are sufficiently smooth univariate functions, were derived in Liang and Srikant (2016). Achieving a uniform approximation error $\epsilon > 0$ with $L \lesssim 1$ layers requires $N \gtrsim \text{poly}(1/\epsilon)$ neurons, whereas neural networks with $L \sim 1/\epsilon$ layers only require $N \lesssim \text{polylog}(1/\epsilon)$ neurons. The proof idea is again based on approximation by Taylor polynomials.

Similarly to Liang and Srikant (2016), superior deep neural network approximation rates for high-dimensional functions with a compositional structure were deduced by Mhaskar et al. (2016, 2017), Mhaskar and Poggio (2016), and Poggio et al. (2017). They argued that computations on, for example, images should reflect properties of image statistics such as locality and shift invariance, which naturally leads to a compositional structure. As an example, consider a function $f: [-1,1]^d \to \mathbb{R}$ with input dimension $d = 8$ such that

$$f(x_1, \ldots, x_8) = f_3\big(f_{21}(f_{11}(x_1, x_2), f_{12}(x_3, x_4)), f_{22}(f_{13}(x_5, x_6), f_{14}(x_7, x_8))\big),$$

where each function $f_3, f_{21}, f_{22}, f_{11}, f_{12}, f_{13}, f_{14}$ is bivariate and in $W^{n,\infty}([-1,1]^2)$ (see Figure 3.6 for a visualization). Efficient approximations can be constructed in two steps. First, each bivariate function is approximated by a shallow neural network with smooth, non-polynomial activation function and size $M \lesssim \epsilon^{-2/n}$. Then, the

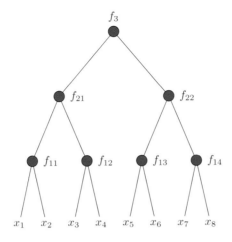

Figure 3.6 A visualization of the hierarchically structured function f.

neural networks are concatenated in a suitable way by allowing depth $L \lesssim \log_2(d)$. The resulting neural network has $M \lesssim (d-1)\epsilon^{-2/n}$ weights (see Theorem 2 in Poggio et al., 2017). In contrast, shallow neural networks with the same activation function require $M \gtrsim \epsilon^{-d/n}$ parameters (see Theorem 1 in Poggio et al., 2017). Moreover, if the components f_{ij} of f are simply assumed to be Lipschitz continuous, then shallow ReLU neural networks in general require $M \gtrsim \epsilon^{-d}$ parameters. On the other hand, deep ReLU neural networks with $L \lesssim \log_2(d)$ layers require only $M \lesssim (d-1)\epsilon^{-2}$ non-zero weights (see Theorem 4 in Poggio et al., 2017).

In Montanelli and Du (2019), neural network approximations for the *Korobov spaces*

$$\mathcal{K}_{2,p}([0,1]^d) = \left\{ f \in \mathcal{L}_p([0,1]^d) \colon f|_{\partial[0,1]^d} = 0, D^\alpha f \in \mathcal{L}_p([0,1]^d), \|\alpha\|_\infty \le 2 \right\},$$

for $p \in [2,\infty]$, are considered. We note that $\mathcal{K}_{2,p}([0,1]^d) \subset W^{2,p}([0,1]^d)$ holds trivially. These functions admit a hierarchical representation (similar to a wavelet decomposition) with respect to basis functions obtained from *sparse grids* (see Bungartz and Griebel, 2004). By emulating these basis functions, the authors were able to show that, for every $f \in \mathcal{K}_{2,p}([0,1]^d)$ and every $\epsilon > 0$, there exists a neural network $\Phi_{f,\epsilon}$ with

$$L(\Phi_{f,\epsilon}) \lesssim \log_2(1/\epsilon) \log_2(d)$$

layers as well as

$$N(\Phi_{f,\epsilon}) \lesssim \epsilon^{-1/2} \cdot \log_2(1/\epsilon)^{\frac{3}{2}(d-1)+1} \log_2(d)$$

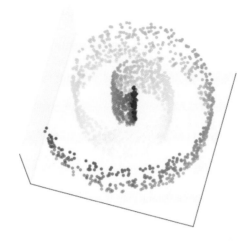

Figure 3.7 Visualization of the Swiss roll data manifold.

neurons such that

$$\left\| f - R_\sigma \left(\Phi_{f,\epsilon} \right) \right\|_\infty \leq \epsilon,$$

where $\sigma = \text{ReLU}$. The curse of dimensionality is significantly lessened since it appears only in the log factor.

3.6.2 Assumptions on the Data Manifold

A typical assumption is that high-dimensional data actually reside on a much lower dimensional manifold. A standard example is provided in Figure 3.7. One may consider the set of images with 128×128 pixels as being in $\mathbb{R}^{128 \times 128}$: certainly, most elements in this high-dimensional space are not perceived as an image by a human being, so images are a proper subset of $\mathbb{R}^{128 \times 128}$. Moreover, images are governed by edges and faces and, thus, form a highly structured set. This motivates the idea that the set of images in $\mathbb{R}^{128 \times 128}$ can be described by a lower-dimensional manifold.

In Shaham et al. (2018) the approximation rates of ReLU neural networks for functions $f \in \mathcal{L}_2(K)$ residing on a d-dimensional manifold $K \subset \mathbb{R}^D$, possibly with $d \ll D$, were shown to depend only weakly on D. In particular, the following theorem was proved.

Theorem 3.22 (Shaham et al., 2018). *Let $K \subset \mathbb{R}^D$ be a smooth d-dimensional manifold, and $f \in \mathcal{L}_2(K)$. Then there exists a depth-4 neural network $\Phi_{f,N}$ with $M(\Phi_{f,N}) \lesssim DC_K + dC_K N$ whose* ReLU *realization computes a wavelet approxi-*

mation of f with N wavelet terms. The constant C_K depends only on the curvature of K.

Note that the underlying dimension D scales with C_K, whereas the number of wavelet terms that influences the approximation accuracy scales only with d. Additional assumptions on how well f can be approximated by wavelets can, with Theorem 3.22, be transferred directly to approximation rates by neural networks. The following corollaries provide two examples for different assumptions on the wavelet representation.

Corollary 3.23. *If f has wavelet coefficients in ℓ_1 then, for every $\varepsilon > 0$, there exists a depth-4 network $\Phi_{f,\varepsilon}$ with $M(\Phi_{f,\varepsilon}) \lesssim DC_K + dC_K^2 M_f \varepsilon^{-1}$ such that*

$$\|f - R_\sigma\left(\Phi_{f,\varepsilon}\right)\|_{\mathcal{L}_2(K)} \leq \varepsilon,$$

where M_f is some constant depending on f and $\sigma =$ ReLU.

Corollary 3.24. *If $f \in C^2(K)$ has bounded Hessian matrix then, for every $\varepsilon > 0$, there exists a depth-4 neural network $\Phi_{f,\varepsilon}$ with $M(\Phi_{f,\varepsilon}) \lesssim DC_K + dC_K \varepsilon^{-d/2}$ satisfying*

$$\|f - R_\sigma\left(\Phi_{f,\varepsilon}\right)\|_{\mathcal{L}_\infty(K)} \leq \varepsilon,$$

where $\sigma =$ ReLU.

Lastly, we mention a result shown in Petersen and Voigtlaender (2018, Theorem 5.4). There, functions of the type $f = g \circ h$, where $h \colon [-1/2, 1/2]^D \to [-1/2, 1/2]^d$ is a smooth dimension-reduction map and $g \colon [-1/2, 1/2]^d \to \mathbb{R}$ is piecewise smooth, are examined. They showed that the approximation rate is primarily governed by the reduced dimension d.

3.6.3 Expressivity of Deep Neural Networks for Solutions of PDEs

Recently, neural-network-based algorithms have shown promising results for the numerical solution of partial differential equations (PDEs): see for instance Lagaris et al. (1998), E et al. (2017), E and Yu (2018), Sirignano and Spiliopoulos (2018), Han et al. (2018), Beck et al. (2018), Han and E (2016), Beck et al. (2019), Khoo et al. (2017), Hesthaven and Ubbiali (2018), Lee and Carlberg (2020), Yang and Perdikaris (2018), Raissi (2018), and Lu et al. (2019).

There also exist several results showing that specifically structured solutions of PDEs admit an approximation by neural networks that does not suffer from the curse of dimensionality: see Grohs et al. (2018), Elbrächter et al. (2018), Berner et al. (2018), Jentzen and Welti (2018), Reisinger and Zhang (2019), and Hutzenthaler et al. (2019, 2020).

The key idea behind these contributions is a stochastic interpretation of a deterministic PDE.[13] As an example, we consider the *Black–Scholes equation*, which models the price of a financial derivative. For $T > 0$, $a < b$, the Black–Scholes equation (a special case of the *linear Kolmogorov equation*) is given by

$$\begin{cases} \partial_t u(t,x) = \frac{1}{2}\text{trace}\big(\kappa(x)\kappa(x)^*(\text{Hessian}_x u)(t,x)\big) + \langle \tilde{\kappa}(x),(\nabla_x u)(t,x)\rangle, \\ u(0,x) = \varphi(x), \end{cases} \tag{3.4}$$

where

(i) $\varphi \in C(\mathbb{R}^d)$ is the *initial value*,[14]

(ii) $\kappa \in C(\mathbb{R}^d,\mathbb{R}^{d\times d})$, $\tilde{\kappa} \in C(\mathbb{R}^d,\mathbb{R}^d)$ are assumed to be affine, and

(iii) $u \in C([0,T]\times\mathbb{R}^d)$ is the solution.

In Berner et al. (2018) the goal is to find a neural network (of moderate complexity) that $\mathcal{L}_2$-approximates the end value of the solution $[a,b]^d \ni x \mapsto u(T,\cdot)$. Using the Feynman–Kac formula (Grohs et al., 2018, Section 2), the deterministic PDE (3.4) can be associated with a stochastic PDE of the form

$$dS_t^x = \kappa(S_t^x)dB_t + \tilde{\kappa}(S_t^x)dt, \quad S_0^x = x, \tag{3.5}$$

on some probability space $(\Omega,\mathcal{G},\mathbb{P})$, where $x \in [a,b]^d$, $(B_t)_{t\in[0,T]}$ is a d-dimensional Brownian motion, and $(S_t^x)_{t\in[0,T]}$ is the stochastic process that solves (3.5). Define $Y := \varphi(S_t^x)$. Then the terminal state $u(T,x)$ has an integral representation with respect to the solution of (3.5) given by $u(T,x) = \mathbb{E}(Y)$. Using this relation, standard estimates on Monte Carlo sampling and the special structure of $\kappa, \tilde{\kappa}$ (Berner et al., 2018) obtained the following statement. *For each $i \in \mathbb{N}$, there exist affine maps* $\mathbf{W}_i(\cdot) + \mathbf{b}_i : \mathbb{R}^d \to \mathbb{R}$ *such that*

$$\frac{1}{(b-a)^d}\left\|u(T,\cdot) - \frac{1}{n}\sum_{i=1}^{n}\varphi(\mathbf{W}_i(\cdot)+\mathbf{b}_i)\right\|_2^2 \lesssim \frac{d^{1/2}}{n}.$$

This implies that $u(T,\cdot)$ can be approximated in $\mathcal{L}_2$ by ReLU neural networks $\Phi_{u,\epsilon}$ with $M(\Phi_{u,\epsilon}) \lesssim \text{poly}(d,1/\epsilon)$. Thus, the curse of dimensionality is avoided.

In the setting of parametric PDEs one is interested in computing solutions u_y of a family of PDEs parametrized by $y \in \mathbb{R}^p$. Such PDEs are typically modelled as operator equations in their variational form:

$$b_y(u_y,v) = f_y(v), \quad \text{for all } v \in \mathcal{H}, \ y \in \mathcal{P} \quad \text{(the parameter set)},$$

where, for every $y \in \mathcal{P} \subset \mathbb{R}^p$, with $p \in \mathbb{N} \cup \{\infty\}$,

---

[13] This stochastic point of view can also be utilized to estimate the generalization error in such a setting (Berner et al., 2018).

[14] The initial value is typically either exactly representable or well-approximable by a small ReLU neural network.

(i) the maps $b_y \colon \mathcal{H} \times \mathcal{H} \to \mathbb{R}$ are parameter-dependent bilinear forms (derived from the PDE) defined on some Hilbert space $\mathcal{H} \subset L^\infty(K)$ for $K \subset \mathbb{R}^n$,

(ii) $f_y \in \mathcal{H}^*$ is the parameter-dependent right-hand side, and

(iii) $u_y \in \mathcal{H}$ is the parameter-dependent solution.

The parameter $y \in \mathbb{R}^p$ models uncertainties in real-world phenomena such as geometric properties of the domain and physical quantities such as elasticity coefficients or the distribution of sources. Parametric PDEs occur for instance in the context of multi-query applications and in the framework of uncertainty quantification.

In the context of deep learning, the goal is, for a given $\epsilon > 0$, to substitute the solution map $y \mapsto u_y$ by a neural network Φ_ϵ such that

$$\sup_{y \in \mathcal{P}} \left\| R_\sigma\left(\Phi_\epsilon(y, \cdot)\right) - u_y \right\|_{\mathcal{H}} \leq \epsilon. \tag{3.6}$$

A common observation is that the *solution manifold* $\{u_y \colon y \in \mathcal{P}\}$ is low dimensional for many parametric problems. More precisely, there exist $(\varphi_i)_{i=1}^d \subset \mathcal{H}$, where d is comparatively small compared with the ambient dimension, such that for every $y \in \mathcal{Y}$ there exists some coefficient vector $(c_i(y))_{i=1}^d$ with

$$\left\| u_y - \sum_{i=1}^d c_i(y)\varphi_i \right\|_{\mathcal{H}} \leq \epsilon.$$

For analytic solution maps $y \mapsto u_y$ Schwab and Zech (2019) constructed neural networks with smooth or ReLU activation functions that fulfill (3.6). Exploiting a sparse Taylor decomposition of the solution with respect to the parameters y, they were able to avoid the curse of dimensionality in the complexity of the approximating networks.

In Kutyniok et al. (2019) the following oberservation was made. If the forward maps $y \mapsto b_y(u, v)$, $y \mapsto f_y(v)$, are well-approximable by neural networks for all $u, v \in \mathcal{H}$, then the map $y \mapsto (c_i(y))_{i=1}^d$ is also approximable by ReLU neural networks $\Phi_{c,\epsilon}$ with $M(\Phi_{c,\epsilon}) \lesssim \mathrm{poly}(d) \cdot \mathrm{polylog}(1/\epsilon)$. Since in many cases $d \lesssim \log_2(1/\epsilon)^p$ and for some cases one can even completely avoid the dependence of d on p, the curse of dimensionality is either significantly lessened or completely overcome. The main idea behind the computation of the coefficients by neural networks lies in the efficient approximation of the map $y \mapsto ((b_y(\varphi_j, \varphi_i))_{i=1}^d)^{-1}$. This is done via a Neumann series representation of the matrix inverse, which possesses a hierarchical structure.

3.7 Deep Versus Shallow Neural Networks

Deep neural networks have advanced the state of the art in many fields of application. We have already seen a number of results highlighting differences between the expressivity of shallow and deep neural networks throughout the chapter. In this section, we present advances made in approximation theory explicitly aiming at revealing the role of depth.

First of all, we note that basically all the upper bounds given in §§3.4 and 3.5 use $L > 2$ layers. Furthermore, in Yarotsky (2017, Section 4.4) andPetersen and Voigtlaender (2018, Section 4.2), it is shown that the upper bound of non-zero weights in Theorems 3.10, 3.14 and 3.21 *cannot* be achieved by shallow networks. For a fixed number of layers, Petersen and Voigtlaender (2018) showed that the number of layers in Theorems 3.14 and 3.21 is optimal up to the involved log factors.

A common strategy in many works that compare the expressive power of very deep over moderately deep neural networks is to construct functions that are efficiently approximable by *deep* neural networks, whereas far more complex *shallow* neural networks are needed to obtain the same approximation accuracy. The first results in this direction dealt with the approximation of Boolean functions by *Boolean circuits*: see, e.g., Sipser (1983) or Håstad (1986). In the latter, the existence of function classes that can be computed with Boolean circuits of polynomial complexity and depth k is proven. In contrast, if the depth is restricted to $k - 1$, an exponential complexity is required. Later works such as Håstad and Goldmann (1991), Hajnal et al. (1993), Martens and Medabalimi (2014) and the references therein, focused on the representation and approximation of Boolean functions by deep neural networks where the activation is the threshold function $\sigma = \mathbf{1}_{[0,\infty)}$.[15]

In Delalleau and Bengio (2011), networks built from sum and product neurons, called *sum–product* networks, were investigated. A sum neuron computes a weighted sum[16] of its inputs, and a product neuron computes the product of its inputs. The identity function is used as activation function and layers of product neurons are alternated with layers of sum neurons. The authors then considered functions implemented by deep sum–product networks with input dimension d, depth $L \lesssim \log_2(d)$ and $N \lesssim d$ neurons that can be represented only by shallow sum–product networks with at least $N \gtrsim 2^{\sqrt{d}}$ neurons. Thus, the complexity of the shallow representations grows exponentially in $\sqrt{d}$. Similar statements were shown for slightly different settings.

Rolnick and Tegmark (2018) examined the approximation rates of neural networks with smooth activation functions for polynomials. It was shown that in order to approximate a polynomial by a shallow neural network, one needs exponentially more parameters than with a corresponding deep counterpart.

In Telgarsky (2016) neural networks with L layers are compared with networks

---

[15] These are called *deep threshold circuits*.
[16] as in the standard setting

with L^3 layers. Telgarsky showed that there exist functions $f : \mathbb{R}^d \to \mathbb{R}$ which can be represented by neural networks with $\sim L^3$ layers and with $\sim L^3$ neurons but which, in $\mathcal{L}_1$, cannot be arbitrarily well approximated by neural networks with $\lesssim L$ layers and $\lesssim 2^L$ neurons. This result is valid for a large variety of activation functions such as piecewise polynomials. The main argument of Telgarsky (2016) is based on the representation and approximation of functions with oscillations. First, it is shown that functions with a small number of oscillations cannot approximate functions with a large number of oscillations arbitrarily well. Afterwards, it is shown that functions computed by neural networks with a small number of layers can have only a small number of oscillations, whereas functions computed by deeper neural networks can have many oscillations. A combination of both arguments leads to the result. Eldan and Shamir (2016) and Safran and Shamir (2017) showed similar results for a larger variety of activation functions[17] in which the $\mathcal{L}_2$-approximation of certain radial basis functions[18] requires $M \lesssim 2^d$ weights, whereas three-layered networks can represent these functions exactly with $M \lesssim \text{poly}(d)$ weights. Extensions and improvements of the results of Telgarsky (2016) were derived in Chatziafratis et al. (2020a,b).

In Pascanu et al. (2013); Montúfar et al. (2014) it is shown that deep ReLU neural networks have the capability of dividing the input domain into an exponentially larger number of linear regions than shallow ones.[19] A ReLU neural network with input dimension d, width $n \geq d$, and L layers is capable of computing functions with number of linear regions less than $(n/d)^{(L-1)d} n^d$, whereas ReLU neural networks with input dimension d, two layers and width Ln are only able to divide the input domain into $L^d n^d$ linear regions. Similarly, Raghu et al. (2017) gave corresponding upper bounds on the number of linear regions representable by deep ReLU neural networks. It was shown that ReLU neural networks with input dimension d, width n, and L layers are only able to represent $\lesssim n^{Ld}$ linear regions. Improved estimates on the number of linear regions werederived in Serra et al. (2018) and Serra and Ramalingam (2020).

Results comparable with those of the aforementioned papers can be found in Arora et al. (2018). In particular, Theorem 3.1of that paper establishes that for every $L \in \mathbb{N}$, $K \geq 2$, there exists a function $f : \mathbb{R} \to \mathbb{R}$ which is representable by ReLU neural networks with $L + 1$ layers, and $K \cdot L$ neurons. Moreover, if f is also representable by the ReLU realization of a neural network $\tilde{\Phi}$ with $\tilde{L} + 1 \leq L + 1$ layers, then the number of neurons of $\tilde{\Phi}$ is bounded from below by $\gtrsim \tilde{L} K^{L/\tilde{L}}$. Bianchini and Scarselli (2014) connected the approximative power of deep neural networks to a topological complexity measure based on Betti numbers: for shallow

---

[17] including the ReLU and sigmoidal functions
[18] i.e. functions of the form $f : \mathbb{R}^d \to \mathbb{R}$, where $f(x) = g(\|x\|_1)$ for some univariate function g
[19] A *linear region* of a function $f : \mathbb{R}^d \to \mathbb{R}^s$ is a maximally connected subset A of $\mathbb{R}^d$ such that $f|_A$ is linear.

neural networks, the representation power grows polynomially in the numbers of parameters whereas it grows exponentially for deep neural networks. They also drew connections to complexity measures based on VC-dimensions.

3.8 Special Neural Network Architectures and Activation Functions

So far we have focused entirely on general *feedforward* neural network architectures. But since neural networks are used for many different types of data in various problem settings, there exists a plethora of architectures, each adapted to a specific task. In the following we cover expressivity results for three prominent architectures: *convolutional neural networks*, *residual neural networks*, and *recurrent neural networks*. Since explaining the architectures and their applications in detail is beyond the scope of this chapter we will just review the basics and give references for the interested reader.[20]

3.8.1 Convolutional Neural Networks

Convolutional neural networks were first introduced in Lecun (1989) and since then have led to tremendous success, particularly in computer vision tasks. As an example, consider the popular ILSVR[21] challenge (see Russakovsky et al., 2015), an image recognition task on the ImageNet database (see Deng et al., 2009) containing variable-resolution images that are to be classified into categories. In 2012 a convolutional neural network called *AlexNet* (see Krizhevsky et al., 2012) achieved a top-five error of 16.4%, realizing a 10% error rate drop compared with the winner of the previous year. The winners of all annual ILSVR challenges since then have been convolutional neural networks; see Zeiler and Fergus (2014), Simonyan and Zisserman (2015), Szegedy et al. (2015), He et al. (2016),. . . .

We now start with a brief explanation of the basic building blocks of a convolutional neural network and recommend Goodfellow et al. (2016, Chapter 9) for an extensive and in-depth introduction.

Instead of vectors in $\mathbb{R}^d$, the input of a convolutional neural network potentially consists of tensors $\mathbf{x}^{[0]} \in \mathbb{R}^{d_1 \times \cdots \times d_n}$ where $n = 2$ or $n = 3$ for the case of images described above. The main characteristic of convolutional neural networks is the use of *convolutional layers*. The input $\mathbf{x}^{[i-1]}$ of layer i is subject to an affine

---

[20] Note that in this section we sometimes deviate from the notation used so far in this chapter. For instance, in the case of convolutional neural networks, we no longer differentiate between the network as a collection of weights and biases and the function realized by it. Such a distinction would make the exposition of the statements in these cases unnecessarily technical. Moreover, we stick closely to the conventional notation for recurrent neural networks, where the indices of the layers are expressed in terms of discrete time steps t.

[21] The abbreviation *ILSRC* stands for *ImageNet Large Scale Visual Recognition Challenge*.

transformation of the form

$$\mathbf{z}^{[i]} = \mathbf{w}^{[i]} * \mathbf{x}^{[i-1]} + \mathbf{b}^{[i]},$$

where $\mathbf{w}^{[i]}$ denotes the *convolution filter* and $\mathbf{b}^{[i]}$ the *bias*. In fact, the application of a convolution can be rewritten as an affine transformation of the form $\mathbf{z}^{[i]} = \mathbf{W}^{[i]}\mathbf{x}^{[i-1]} + \mathbf{b}^{[i]}$, where $\mathbf{W}^{[i]}$ is a matrix with a specific structure and potentially many zero entries (depending on the size of the filter). Convolutional layers enforce *locality*, in the sense that neurons in a specific layer are connected only to neighboring neurons in the preceeding layer, as well as *weight sharing*, i.e. different neurons in a given layer share weights with neurons in other parts of the layer. The application of convolutions results in *translation equivariant* outputs in the sense that $\mathbf{w}^{[i]} * (T\mathbf{x}^{[i-1]}) = T(\mathbf{w}^{[i]} * \mathbf{x}^{[i-1]})$, where T is a translation (or shift) operator.

As in the case of feedforward neural networks, the convolution is followed by a nonlinear activation function $\sigma \colon \mathbb{R} \to \mathbb{R}$, which is applied coordinate-wise to $\mathbf{z}^{[i]}$. Hence, a convolutional layer corresponds to a standard layer in a feedforward neural network with a particular structure of the corresponding affine map.

Often the nonlinearity is followed by a *pooling layer*, which can be seen as a dimension-reduction step. Popular choices for pooling operations include *max pooling*, where only the maxima of certain regions in $\sigma(\mathbf{z}^{[i]})$ are kept, or *average pooling*, where the average over certain regions is taken. In contrast with convolutions, pooling often induces *translation invariance* in the sense that a small translation of the input $\mathbf{x}^{[i-1]}$ does not change the output of the pooling stage.

Stacking several convolutional and pooling layers results in a deep convolutional neural network. After an architecture has been fixed, the goal is to learn the convolutional filters $\mathbf{w}^{[i]}$ and the biases $\mathbf{b}^{[i]}$.

We now turn our attention to the expressivity results of convolutional neural networks. Motivated by classification tasks, Cohen et al. (2016) compared the expressivity of deep and shallow *convolutional arithmetic circuits* for the representation of *score functions*. A convolutional arithmetic circuit can be interpreted as a convolutional neural network with linear activation function, product pooling, and convolutional layers consisting of 1×1 convolutions. We consider a classification task of the following form. For an observation $X = (\mathbf{x}_1, \ldots, \mathbf{x}_m) \in \mathbb{R}^{dm}$, where X could be an image represented by a collection of vectors, find a suitable classification $n \in Y = \{1, \ldots, N\}$, where Y is a set of possible labels. This can be modeled by per-label score functions $\{h_n\}_{n \in \{1, \ldots, N\}}$, with $h_n \colon \mathbb{R}^{dm} \to \mathbb{R}$. The label corresponding to X is then denoted by $\operatorname{argmax}_{n \in Y} h_n(X)$. It is assumed that these score functions have a tensor decomposition of the form

$$h_n(\mathbf{x}_1, \ldots, \mathbf{x}_m) = \sum_{i_1, \ldots, i_m = 1}^{r} c^n_{i_1, \ldots, i_m} \prod_{j=1}^{m} f_{i_j}(\mathbf{x}_i),$$

for some representation functions $f_1, \ldots, f_r : \mathbb{R}^d \to \mathbb{R}$ and a coefficient tensor $\mathbf{c}^n$. Hence every h_n is representable by a *shallow* convolutional arithmetic circuit with, however, a *potentially large number* of parameters. Using hierarchichal tensor decompositions the main result states, roughly speaking, that it is with high probability not possible to significantly reduce the complexity of the shallow convolutional arithmetic circuit in order to approximate or represent the underlying score function. However, *deep* convolutional arithmetic circuits *are* able to represent score functions exactly with exponentially fewer parameters. This is yet another instance of the benefit of deep over shallow neural networks, this time for a larger function class rather than just for special instances of functions such as those considered in §3.7. The main proof ideas rely on tools from matrix algebra, tensor analysis, and measure theory.

In Yarotsky (2019) the classification task is approached by directly approximating the classification function $f : \mathcal{L}_2(\mathbb{R}^2) \to \mathbb{R}$, which maps an image to a real number. Here, images are modelled as elements of the function space $\mathcal{L}_2(\mathbb{R}^2)$ (see also §3.5, where images are modelled by cartoon-like functions). In order to deal with a non-discrete input (in this case elements of $\mathcal{L}_2$), the neural networks considered in that paper consist of a discretization step $\mathcal{L}_2(\mathbb{R}^2) \to V$ (where V is isometrically isomorphic to $\mathbb{R}^{D_\varepsilon}$ for some $D_\varepsilon < \infty$) followed by convolutional layers and downsampling operations, which replace pooling. The following theorem (Yarotsky, 2019, Theorem 3.2) was proved.

Theorem 3.25. *Let $f : \mathcal{L}_2(\mathbb{R}^2) \to \mathbb{R}$. Then the following conditions are equivalent.*

(i) *The function f is continuous (in the norm topology).*
(ii) *For every $\varepsilon > 0$ and every compact set $K \subset \mathcal{L}_2(\mathbb{R}^2)$ there exists a convolutional neural network (in the above sense, with downsampling) $\Phi_{K,\varepsilon}$ that approximates f uniformly on K, i.e.*

$$\sup_{\xi \in K} |f(\xi) - \Phi_{K,\varepsilon}(\xi)| \le \varepsilon.$$

A second setting considered in Yarotsky (2019) deals with approximating translation equivariant image-to-image mappings. Think for example of a segmentation task where an image (e.g. of a cell) is mapped to another image (e.g. the binary segmentation mask). Translating the input image should result in a translation of the predicted segmentation mask, which means in mathematical terms that the mapping is translation equivariant. To make the convolutional neural networks also translation equivariant, no downsampling is applied. The next theorem (Yarotsky, 2019, Theorem 3.1) addresses the second setting.

Theorem 3.26 (simplified). *Let $f : \mathcal{L}_2(\mathbb{R}^2) \to \mathcal{L}_2(\mathbb{R}^2)$. Then the following conditions are equivalent.*

(i) *The function f is continuous (in the norm topology) and translation equivariant, i.e.* $f(\xi(\cdot - \tau)) = f(\xi)(\cdot - \tau)$ *for all* $\tau \in \mathbb{R}^2$.
(ii) *For every* $\varepsilon > 0$ *and every compact set* $K \subset \mathcal{L}_2(\mathbb{R}^2)$, *there exists a convolutional neural network (in the above sense)* $\Phi_{K,\varepsilon}$, *which approximates f uniformly on K, i.e.*

$$\sup_{\xi \in K} \|f(\xi) - \Phi_{K,\varepsilon}(\xi)\|_{\mathcal{L}_2} \le \varepsilon.$$

We note that Yarotsky (2019, Theorem 3.1) considers equivariances with respect to more general transformations, including rotations of the function domain.

A result of similar flavor to Theorem 3.26 for functions $f : \mathbb{R}^d \to \mathbb{R}^s$ that are equivariant with respect to finite groups was given in Petersen and Voigtlaender (2020). In that paper, it was established that every fully connected neural network can be expressed by a convolutional neural network without pooling and with periodic padding (in order to preserve equivariance) with a comparable number of parameters, and vice versa. This result can then be used to transfer approximation rates of fully connected neural networks for a function class C to convolutional neural networks approximating a subclass C^{equi} containing equivariant functions. As an example, we consider translation equivariant Hölder functions $f \in C^{\mathrm{equi}} = C^\beta([-1/2, 1/2]^d)$ with $\beta = (n, \zeta)$. By Petersen and Voigtlaender (2020, Proposition 4.3), there exist convolutional neural networks $\Phi_{f,\epsilon}$ that ϵ-approximate f in $\mathcal{L}_p([-1/2, 1/2]^d)$ and have $M \lesssim \epsilon^{-d/(n+\zeta)}$ parameters and $L \lesssim \log_2((n+\zeta)) \cdot (n+\zeta)/d$ layers. Note that this rate coincides with that provided by Theorem 3.14.

Zhou (2020) mainly derives two types of results. The first, Theorem A therein, establishes the universality of deep purely convolutional networks (i.e. no pooling is applied) mapping from $\mathbb{R}^d \to \mathbb{R}$ for functions in $C(K)$, with $K \subset \mathbb{R}^d$ compact. To be more precise, it is shown that, for every $f \in C(K)$ and every $\epsilon > 0$, there exist an $L \in \mathbb{N}$ and a convolutional neural network $\Phi_{f,\epsilon}$ equipped with L convolutional layers and the ReLU activation function, such that

$$\|f - \Phi_{f,\varepsilon}\|_\infty \le \varepsilon.$$

Note that, in contrast with most classical universality results, the depth does not remain uniformly bounded over the whole function class $C(K)$.

The second result, Theorem B, establishes approximation *rates* for Sobolev functions by convolutional neural networks, which we present in a simplified form.

Theorem 3.27 (Zhou, 2020). *Let* $r > d/2 + 2$. *Then, for every* $\varepsilon > 0$ *and every* $f \in F_{r,d}^2$, *there exists a convolutional neural network* $\Phi_{f,\varepsilon}$ *(without pooling layers) with depth* $L \lesssim \varepsilon^{-1/d}$ *such that*

$$\|f - \Phi_{f,\varepsilon}\|_\infty \le \varepsilon.$$

In contrast with most expressivity results considered before, Nguyen and Hein (2018) examined the ability of deep convolutional neural networks to fit a *finite* set of n samples $(X, Y) \in \mathbb{R}^{d \times n} \times \mathbb{R}^{s \times n}$ for some $n \in \mathbb{N}$. It was shown that for such a dataset there exist over-parametrized convolutional neural networks (in this case the number of neurons in one of the layers is larger than the size of the data set n) $\Phi_{(X,Y)}$ equipped with max pooling and rather generic activation functions such that

$$\sum_{i=1}^{n} |Y_i - \Phi_{(X,Y)}(X_i)|^2 = 0.$$

Further expressivity results for convolutional neural networks can be found in Oono and Suzuki (2018).

3.8.2 Residual Neural Networks

Driven by the observation that the performance of a neural network very much benefits from its depth, architectures with an increasing number of layers have been tested. However, in Srivastava et al. (2015), He and Sun (2015), and He et al. (2016) the observation was made that after adding a certain number of layers the test and training accuracy decreases again. He et al. (2016) argued that that the drop in performance caused by adding more and more layers is not related to overfitting, for otherwise the training accuracy should still increase while only the test accuracy degrades. Knowing that deeper models should perform at least as well as shallower ones, since the additional stacked layers could learn an identity mapping, the authors concluded that the performance drop is caused by the optimization algorithm not finding a suitable weight configuration.

Motivated by those findings, a new network architecture called *residual neural network (ResNet)* was proposed in He et al. (2016). It incorporates identity shortcuts such that the network only needs to learn a residual. These networks were shown to yield excellent performance (winning several challenges) by employing a large number of layers. One of the popular models, called ResNet-152, employs 152 layers, but ResNets with even more layers have been used. To be precise, ResNets are composed of blocks of stacked layers (see Figure 3.8(a)) having a shortcut identity connection from the input of the block to the output (Figure 3.8(b)). In detail, the function implemented by such a block can be parametrized by weight matrices $\mathbf{V}$ and $\mathbf{W} \in \mathbb{R}^{k \times k}$ with bias vector $\mathbf{b} \in \mathbb{R}^k$ and is given by

$$\mathbf{z} \colon \mathbb{R}^k \to \mathbb{R}^k \quad \text{with} \quad \mathbf{z}(x) = \mathbf{V}\sigma(\mathbf{W}x + \mathbf{b}) + x.$$

Assume that those two layers are intended to learn a function $F \colon \mathbb{R}^k \to \mathbb{R}^k$; then the block is forced to learn the residual $H(x) := F(x) - x$. The function implemented by a ResNet now results from composing the residual blocks $\mathbf{z}^{[i]}$, $i = 1, \ldots, L$:

$$\text{ResNet}: \mathbb{R}^k \to \mathbb{R}^k \quad \text{with} \quad \text{ResNet}(x) = \mathbf{z}^{[L]} \circ \sigma(\mathbf{z}^{[L-1]}) \circ \cdots \cdots \circ \sigma(\mathbf{z}^{[1]}x). \quad (3.7)$$

Even if the idea behind the residual learning framework is to make the optimization process easier, in this chapter we will focus only on the approximation properties of the proposed architecture.

In Hardt and Ma (2016), the ability of ResNets to fit a finite set of training samples perfectly is shown. The authors considered the case where the input data consists of pairs (x_i, y_i) with $x_i \in \mathbb{R}^d$ and $y_i \in \{e_1, \ldots, e_s\}$ for $i = 1, \ldots, n$. Here, e_j denotes the jth unit vector in $\mathbb{R}^s$ such that s can be interpreted as the number of classes in a classification task. The ResNet architecture considered in Hardt and Ma (2016) slightly differs from the one in Equation (3.7), in that no activation function is used after the residual blocks and some of the matrices are of different shapes to allow for inputs and outputs of different dimensions. Under mild additional assumptions on the training set the following theorem was shown.

Theorem 3.28 (Hardt and Ma, 2016). *Let $n, s \in \mathbb{N}$ and $(x_1, y_1), \ldots, (x_n, y_n)$ be a set of training samples as above. Then there exists a ResNet Φ with $M \lesssim n \log n + s^2$ weights such that*

$$\Phi(x_i) = y_i, \quad \text{for all} \quad i = 1, \ldots, n.$$

In Lin and Jegelka (2018) it was shown that ResNets are universal approximators for functions from $\mathcal{L}_1(\mathbb{R}^d)$. This is of particular interest, since the width of the ResNets considered in that paper is bounded by the input dimension d, and it is shown in Hanin (2019) and Lu et al. (2017) that standard feedforward neural networks with width bounded by d are not universal approximators (see also §3.3). The idea of the proof relies on a re-approximation of step functions (which are dense in $\mathcal{L}_1$).

Instead of forcing skip connections to encode an identity function, one can also consider more general skip connections linking earlier layers to deeper layers with connections that are learned in the training process. Such networks have been considered in, for instance, Yarotsky (2017) and Gühring et al. (2019). Slightly better approximation rates for those architectures in contrast with the standard feedforward case are shown for functions from $F_{n,d}^p$. In more detail, when allowing skip connections, the upper approximation bounds shown in Theorem 3.10 can be improved by dropping the square of the log terms.

3.8.3 Recurrent Neural Networks

Until now we have considered only feedforward network architectures that were able to deal with a fixed input and output dimensions. However, in many applications it is

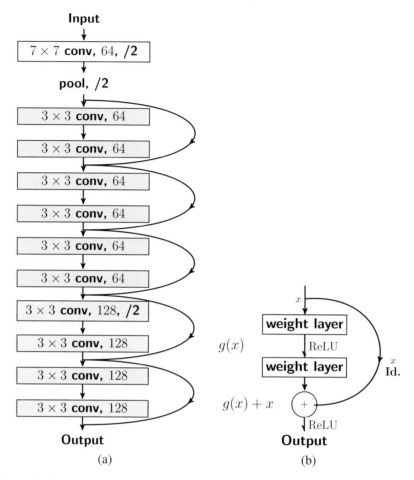

Figure 3.8 Visualizations of CNNs and ResNet. (a) Stacked block architecture of a convolutional neural network of ResNet type. (b) Building block of ResNet with identity shortcut connection.

desirable to use a neural network that can handle sequential data with varying length as input/output. This is for example often the case for natural language processing tasks where one might be interested in predicting the topic of a sentence or text (varying input dimension, fixed output) or in producing an image caption for a given image (fixed input dimension, varying output dimension).

Recurrent neural networks are specialized for those tasks. In its vanilla form, a recurrent neural network computes a hidden state $h_t = f_\theta(h_{t-1}, x_t)$ from the current input x_t and, using a *recurrent* connection, the previous hidden state h_{t-1}. The hidden state h_t can then be used in a second step to compute an output $y_t = g_\theta(h_t)$ enabling the network to memorize features from previous inputs until time t, such that the output y_t depends on $x_0, \dots, x_t$ (see Figure 3.9). It it important to note that the same functions f_θ and g_θ, parametrized by the weight vector θ, are used in each time step. For an in-depth treatment of recurrent neural networks we refer to Goodfellow et al. (2016, Chapter 10).

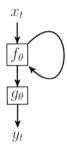

Figure 3.9 Visualization of the architecture of a recurrent neural network.

Recurrent neural networks can be viewed as dynamical systems (Sontag, 1992b). Hence, it is natural to ask whether the universal approximation capacity of feedforward neural networks can be transferred to recurrent neural networks regarded as dynamical systems. Discrete-time dynamical systems of the form

$$h_{t+1} = f(h_t, x_t),$$
$$y_t = g(h_t),$$

where $f: \mathbb{R}^n \times \mathbb{R}^m \to \mathbb{R}^n$ and $g: \mathbb{R}^n \to \mathbb{R}^p$, and $x_t \in \mathbb{R}^n$, $h_t \in \mathbb{R}^m$, $y_t \in \mathbb{R}^p$, were considered in Sontag (1992b). We call the tuple $\Sigma = (n, m, p, f, g)$ a *time-discrete dynamical system* and say that n is the *dimension of the hidden state* of Σ, m its *input dimension* and p its *output dimension*. Moreover, we call $x_0, \ldots, x_T$ the *inputs of the system until time* $T \in \mathbb{N}$ and h_0 the *initial state*. With these tools at hand we can now formally define a shallow sequence-to-sequence recurrent neural network.

Definition 3.29. Let $\Sigma = (n, m, p, f, g)$ be a dynamical system and $\sigma: \mathbb{R} \to \mathbb{R}$. Then Σ is a *shallow sequence-to-sequence recurrent neural network with activation function* σ if, for matrices $\mathbf{A} \in \mathbb{R}^{n \times n}$, $\mathbf{B} \in \mathbb{R}^{m \times n}$, and $\mathbf{C} \in \mathbb{R}^{n \times p}$, the functions f and g are of the form

$$f(h, x) = \sigma(\mathbf{A}h + \mathbf{B}x) \quad \text{and} \quad g(x) = \mathbf{C}x.$$

It was then shown in Sontag (1992b) that recurrent neural networks of the form described above are able to approximate time-discrete dynamical systems (with only weak assumptions on f and g) arbitrarily well. To formalize this claim, we first describe how the closeness of two dynamical systems is measured by the authors. For this, we introduce the following definition from Sontag (1992b).

Definition 3.30. Let $\Sigma = (n, m, p, f, g)$ and $\tilde{\Sigma} = (\tilde{n}, m, p, \tilde{f}, \tilde{g})$ be two discrete-time dynamical systems as introduced in Definition 3.29. Furthermore, let $K_1 \subset \mathbb{R}^n$ and $K_2 \subset \mathbb{R}^m$ be compact, $T \in \mathbb{N}$, and $\varepsilon > 0$. Then we say $\tilde{\Sigma}$ *approximates* Σ *with accuracy* ε *on* K_1 *and* K_2 *in time* T, *if the following holds.*

There exist continuous functions $\alpha \colon \mathbb{R}^{\tilde{n}} \to \mathbb{R}^n$ *and* $\beta \colon \mathbb{R}^n \to \mathbb{R}^{\tilde{n}}$ *such that, for all initial states* $h_0 \in K_1$ *and* $\beta(h_0)$ *for* Σ *and* $\tilde{\Sigma}$, *respectively, and all inputs* $x_0, \ldots, x_T \in K_2$ *for* Σ *and* $\tilde{\Sigma}$, *we have*

$$\|h_t - \alpha(\tilde{h}_t)\|_2 < \varepsilon \quad \text{for} \quad t = 0, \ldots, T$$

and

$$\|y_t - \tilde{y}_t\|_2 < \varepsilon \quad \text{for} \quad t = 1, \ldots, T.$$

Note that while input and output dimensions of Σ and $\tilde{\Sigma}$ coincide, the dimension of the hidden states might differ. Using the universal approximation theorem for shallow feedforward neural networks (see §3.2.1), a universality result for recurrent neural networks with respect to dynamical systems can be derived.

Theorem 3.31 (Sontag, 1992b). *Let* $\sigma \colon \mathbb{R} \to \mathbb{R}$ *be an activation function for which the universal approximation theorem holds. Let* $\Sigma = (n, m, p, f, g)$ *be a discrete-time dynamical system with* f, g *continuously differentiable. Furthermore, let* $K_1 \subset \mathbb{R}^n$, $K_2 \subset \mathbb{R}^m$ *be compact and* $T \in \mathbb{N}$. *Then, for each* $\varepsilon > 0$, *there exist* $\tilde{n} \in \mathbb{N}$ *and matrices* $\mathbf{A} \in \mathbb{R}^{\tilde{n} \times \tilde{n}}$, $\mathbf{B} \in \mathbb{R}^{m \times \tilde{n}}$, $\mathbf{C} \in \mathbb{R}^{\tilde{n} \times p}$ *such that the shallow recurrent neural network* $\tilde{\Sigma} = (\tilde{n}, m, p, \tilde{f}, \tilde{g})$ *with activation function* σ,

$$\tilde{f}(h, x) = \sigma(\mathbf{A}h + \mathbf{B}x) \quad \text{and} \quad \tilde{g}(x) = \mathbf{C}x,$$

approximates Σ *with accuracy* ε *on* K_1 *and* K_2 *in time* T.

Similar results also based on the universality of shallow feedforward neural networks were shown in Schäfer and Zimmermann (2006) and in Doya (1993). In Doya (1993) and Polycarpou and Ioannou (1991), the case of continuous dynamical systems was additionally included.

Discrete-time fading-memory systems are dynamical systems that asymptotically "forget" inputs that were fed into the system earlier in time. Matthews (1993) showed the universality of recurrent neural networks for these types of systems.

The above results cover the case of recurrent neural networks that realize sequence-to-sequence mappings. As mentioned in the introduction to this section, recurrent neural networks are also used in practice to map sequences of varying length to scalar outputs, thus (for $\mathbb{R}^m$-valued sequences) realizing functions mapping from $\bigcup_{i \geq 0}(\mathbb{R}^m)^i \to \mathbb{R}$. In Hammer (2000b), the capacity of such recurrent neural networks to approximate arbitrary measurable functions $f \colon \bigcup_{i \geq 0}(\mathbb{R}^m)^i \to \mathbb{R}$ with high probability was shown. Note that in contrast with approximation results for time-discrete dynamical systems, where the system to be approximated naturally displays a recursive structure (as does the recurrent neural network), no such assumption was used. It was furthermore shown that recurrent neural networks are not capable of universally approximating such functions with respect to the sup norm.

For the rest of this section we denote by $(\mathbb{R}^m)^* := \bigcup_{i \geq 0}(\mathbb{R}^m)^i$ the set of finite sequences with elements in $\mathbb{R}^m$. To present the aforementioned results in more detail, we start with a formal introduction to the type of recurrent neural network considered in Hammer (2000b, Definition 1).

Definition 3.32. Any function $f: \mathbb{R}^n \times \mathbb{R}^m \to \mathbb{R}^n$ and initial state $h_0 \in \mathbb{R}^n$ recursively induce a mapping $\tilde{f}_{h_0}: (\mathbb{R}^m)^* \to \mathbb{R}^n$ as follows:

$$\tilde{f}_{h_0}([x_1, \ldots, x_i]) = \begin{cases} h_0, & \text{if } i = 0, \\ f(\tilde{f}_{h_0}([x_1, \ldots, x_{i-1}]), x_i), & \text{otherwise.} \end{cases}$$

A *shallow sequence-to-vector recurrent neural network with initial state* $h_0 \in \mathbb{R}^n$ *and activation function* $\sigma: \mathbb{R} \to \mathbb{R}$ is a mapping from $(\mathbb{R}^m)^*$ to $\mathbb{R}^p$ of the form

$$x \mapsto \mathbf{C} \cdot \tilde{f}_{h_0}(x).$$

Here, $\mathbf{C} \in \mathbb{R}^{n \times p}$ is a matrix and f is the realization of a shallow feedforward neural network with no hidden layer and nonlinearity σ (applied coordinatewise) in the output layer, i.e. $f: \mathbb{R}^n \times \mathbb{R}^m \to \mathbb{R}^n$ is of the form

$$f(h, x) = \sigma(\mathbf{A}h + \mathbf{B}x) \quad \text{for} \quad h \in \mathbb{R}^n, x \in \mathbb{R}^m,$$

where $\mathbf{A} \in \mathbb{R}^{n \times n}$ and $\mathbf{B} \in \mathbb{R}^{m \times n}$.

In simpler terms, a sequence-to-vector recurrent neural network is a sequence-to-sequence recurrent neural network where only the last output is used.

Next, we need the definition of approximation in probability from Hammer (2000b).

Definition 3.33. Let $\mathbb{P}$ be a probability measure on $(\mathbb{R}^m)^*$ and $f_1, f_2: (\mathbb{R}^m)^* \to \mathbb{R}^p$ be two measurable functions. Then f_1 *approximates* f_2 *with accuracy* $\varepsilon > 0$ *and probability* $\delta > 0$ if

$$\mathbb{P}(|f_1 - f_2| > \varepsilon) < \delta.$$

The next theorem establishes the universal approximation capacity in probability of recurrent neural networks for real-valued functions with real-valued sequences of arbitrary length as input.

Theorem 3.34 (Hammer, 2000b). *Let* $\sigma: \mathbb{R} \to \mathbb{R}$ *be an activation function for* which the universal approximation theorem holds and $\varepsilon, \delta > 0$. Then every measurable function $f: (\mathbb{R}^m)^* \to \mathbb{R}^n$ can be approximated with accuracy ε and probability δ by a shallow recurrent neural network.

Interestingly, even though Theorem 3.31 deals only with approximations of dynamical systems in finite time, it can still be utilized for a proof of Theorem 3.34. Hammer (2000b) outlined a proof based on this idea,[22] which we will present here to underline the close connections between the theorems. The main ingredient is the observation that $\mathbb{P}(\bigcup_{i > i_0}(\mathbb{R}^m)^i)$ converges to zero for $i_0 \to \infty$. As a consequence, one needs to approximate a function $f: (\mathbb{R}^m)^* \to \mathbb{R}^n$ only on sequences up to a certain length in order to achieve approximation in probability. The first step of the proof now consists of approximating f by the output of a dynamical system for input sequences up to a certain length. In the second step one can make use of Theorem 3.31 to approximate the dynamical system by a recurrent neural network.

In Khrulkov et al. (2017) the expressive power of certain recurrent neural networks, where a connection to a tensor train decomposition can be made is analyzed.

Network architectures dealing with more structured inputs, such as trees or graphs, that also make use of recurrent connections and can thus be seen as a generalization of recurrent neural networks, were considered in Hammer (1999), Hammer (2000a, Ch. 3), Bianchini et al. (2005) and Scarselli et al. (2008).

Acknowledgements.

The authors would like to thank Philipp Petersen for valuable comments that improve this manuscript. Moreover, they would like to thank Mark Cheng for creating most of the figures and Johannes von Lindheim for providing Figure 3.7.

I.G. acknowledges support from the Research Training Group "Differential Equation- and Data-Driven Models in Life Sciences and Fluid Dynamics: An Interdisciplinary Research Training Group (DAEDALUS)" (GRK 2433) funded by the German Research Foundation (DFG). G.K. acknowledges partial support by the Bundesministerium für Bildung und Forschung (BMBF) through the Berliner Zentrum for Machine Learning (BZML), Project AP4, by the Deutsche Forschungsgemeinschaft (DFG), through grants CRC 1114 "Scaling Cascades in Complex Systems", Project B07, CRC/TR 109 "Discretization in Geometry and Dynamics", Projects C02 and C03, RTG DAEDALUS (RTG 2433), Projects P1 and P3, RTG BIOQIC (RTG 2260), Projects P4 and P9, and SPP 1798 "Compressed Sensing in Information Processing", Coordination Project and Project Massive MIMO-I/II, by

---

[22] The actual proof given in Hammer (2000b) is not based on Theorem 3.31, so the authors are able to draw some conclusions about the complexity necessary for the recurrent neural network in special situations.

the Berlin Mathematics Research Center MATH+, and Projects EF1-1, and EF1-4, by the Einstein Foundation Berlin.

References

Anthony, M., and Bartlett, P. 2009. *Neural Network Learning: Theoretical Foundations*. Cambridge University Press.

Arora, R., Basu, A., Mianjy, P., and Mukherjee, A. 2018. Understanding deep neural networks with rectified linear units. In: *Proc. 2018 International Conference on Learning Representations (ICLR)*.

Barron, A. R. 1993. Universal approximation bounds for superpositions of a sigmoidal function. *IEEE Trans. Inf. Theory*, **39**(3), 930–945.

Barron, A. R. 1994. Approximation and estimation bounds for artificial neural networks. *Mach. Learn.*, **14**(1), 115–133.

Beck, C., Becker, S., Grohs, P., Jaafari, N., and Jentzen, A. 2018. Solving stochastic differential equations and Kolmogorov equations by means of deep learning. ArXiv preprint arXiv:1806.00421.

Beck, C., Becker, S., Cheridito, P., Jentzen, A., and Neufeld, A. 2019. Deep splitting method for parabolic PDEs. ArXiv preprint arXiv:1907.03452.

Bellman, R. 1952. On the theory of dynamic programming. *Proc. Natl. Acad. SciA.*, **38**(8), 716.

Bengio, Y., Courville, A., and Vincent, P. 2013. Representation learning: A review and new perspectives. *IEEE Trans. Pattern Anal. Mach. Intell.*, **35**(8), 1798–1828.

Berner, J., Grohs, P., and Jentzen, A. 2018. Analysis of the generalization error: Empirical risk minimization over deep artificial neural networks overcomes the curse of dimensionality in the numerical approximation of Black–Scholes partial differential equations. ArXiv preprint arXiv:1809.03062.

Bianchini, M., and Scarselli, F. 2014. On the complexity of neural network classifiers: A comparison between shallow and deep architectures. *IEEE Trans. Neural Netw. Learn. Syst.*, **25**(8), 1553–1565.

Bianchini, M., Maggini, M., Sarti, L., and Scarselli, F. 2005. Recursive neural networks for processing graphs with labelled edges: Theory and applications. *Neural Netw.*, **18**(8), 1040–1050.

Bölcskei, H., Grohs, P., Kutyniok, G., and Petersen, P. C. 2019. Optimal approximation with sparsely connected deep neural networks. *SIAM J. Math. Data Sci.*, **1**, 8–45.

Bungartz, H., and Griebel, M. 2004. Sparse grids. *Acta Numer.*, **13**, 147–269.

Carroll, S., and Dickinson, B. 1989. Construction of neural nets using the Radon transform. Pages 607–611 of: *Proc. International 1989 Joint Conference on Neural Networks*, vol. 1.

Chatziafratis, Vaggos, Nagarajan, Sai Ganesh, and Panageas, Ioannis. 2020a. Better depth–width trade-offs for neural networks through the lens of dynamical systems. ArXiv preprint arxiv:2003.00777.

Chatziafratis, Vaggos, Nagarajan, Sai Ganesh, Panageas, Ioannis, and Wang, Xiao. 2020b. Depth–width trade-offs for ReLU networks via Sharkovsky's theorem. In: *Proc. International Conference on Learning Representations.*

Chui, C. K., and Li, X. 1992. Approximation by ridge functions and neural networks with one hidden layer. *J. Approx. Theory*, **70**(2), 131 – 141.

Cohen, N., Sharir, O., and Shashua, A. 2016. On the expressive power of deep learning: A tensor analysis. Pages 698–728 of: *Proc. 29th Annual Conference on Learning Theory.*

Cucker, F., and Zhou, D. 2007. *Learning Theory: An Approximation Theory Viewpoint.* Cambridge Monographs on Applied and Computational Mathematics, vol. 24. Cambridge University Press.

Cybenko, G. 1989. Approximation by superpositions of a sigmoidal function. *Math. Control Signals Systems*, **2**(4), 303–314.

Delalleau, O., and Bengio, Y. 2011. Shallow vs. deep sum–product networks. Pages 666–674 of: *Advances in Neural Information Processing Systems* vol. 24.

Deng, J., Dong, W., Socher, R., Li, L., Li, K., and Fei-Fei, L. 2009. ImageNet: A large-scale hierarchical image database. Pages 248–255 of: *Proc. 2009 IEEE Conference on Computer Vision and Pattern Recognition (CVPR).*

DeVore, R., Howard, R., and Micchelli, C. 1989. Optimal nonlinear approximation. *Manuscripta Math.*, **63**(4), 469–478.

Donoho, D. L. 2001. Sparse components of images and optimal atomic decompositions. *Constr. Approx.*, **17**(3), 353–382.

Doya, K. 1993. Universality of fully connected recurrent neural networks. technical Report, Deptment of Biology, UCSD.

E, W., and Yu, B. 2018. The Deep Ritz method: A deep learning-based numerical algorithm for solving variational problems. *Commun. Math. Statistics*, **6**(1), 1–12.

E, W., Han, J., and Jentzen, A. 2017. Deep learning-based numerical methods for high-dimensional parabolic partial differential equations and backward stochastic differential equations. *Commun. Math. Statistics*, **5**(4), 349–380.

Elbrächter, D., Grohs, P., Jentzen, A., and Schwab, C. 2018. DNN Expression rate analysis of high-dimensional PDEs: Application to option pricing. ArXiv preprint arXiv:1809.07669.

Eldan, R., and Shamir, O. 2016. The power of depth for feedforward neural networks. Pages 907–940 of: *Proc. 29th Annual Conference on Learning Theory.*

Funahashi, K. 1989. On the approximate realization of continuous mappings by neural networks. *Neural Netw.*, **2**(3), 183 – 192.

Gallant, A. R., and White, H. 1988. There exists a neural network that does not make avoidable mistakes. Pages 657–664 of: *Proc. IEEE 1988 International Conference on Neural Networks*, vol. 1.

Girosi, F., and Poggio, T. 1989. Representation properties of networks: Kolmogorov's theorem is irrelevant. *Neural Comp.*, **1**(4), 465–469.

Glorot, X., Bordes, A., and Bengio, Y. 2011. Deep sparse rectifier neural networks. Pages 315–323 of: *Proc. 14th International Conference on Artificial Intelligence and Statistics*.

Goodfellow, I., Bengio, Y., and Courville, A. 2016. *Deep Learning*. MIT Press.

Gribonval, R., Kutyniok, G., Nielsen, M., and Voigtlaender, F. 2019. Approximation spaces of deep neural networks. ArXiv preprint arXiv:1905.01208.

Grohs, P., Hornung, F., Jentzen, A., and von Wurstemberger, P. 2018. A proof that artificial neural networks overcome the curse of dimensionality in the numerical approximation of Black–Scholes partial differential equations. ArXiv preprint arXiv:1809.02362.

Grohs, P., Perekrestenko, D., Elbrächter, D., and Bölcskei, H. 2019. Deep neural network approximation theory. ArXiv preprint arXiv:1901.02220.

Gühring, I., and Raslan, M. 2021. Approximation rates for neural networks with encodable weights in smoothness spaces. *Neural Netw.*, **134**, 107–130.

Gühring, I., Kutyniok, G., and Petersen, P. 2019. Error bounds for approximations with deep ReLU neural networks in $W^{s,p}$ norms. *Anal. Appl. (Singap.)*, 1–57.

Hajnal, A., Maass, W., Pudlák, P., Szegedy, M., and Turán, G. 1993. Threshold circuits of bounded depth. *J. Comput. Syst. Sci.*, **46**(2), 129–154.

Hammer, B. 1999. Approximation capabilities of folding networks. Pages 33–38 of: *Proc. 7th European Symposium on Artificial Neural Networks*.

Hammer, B. 2000a. *Learning with Recurrent Neural Networks*. Lecture Notes in Control and Information Sciences, vol. 254. Springer.

Hammer, B. 2000b. On the approximation capability of recurrent neural networks. *Neurocomputing*, **31**(1-4), 107–123.

Han, J., and E, W. 2016. Deep learning approximation for stochastic control problems. ArXiv preprint arXiv:1611.07422.

Han, J., Jentzen, A., and E, W. 2018. Solving high-dimensional partial differential equations using deep learning. *Proc. Natl. Acad. Sci.*, **115**(34), 8505–8510.

Hanin, B. 2019. Universal function approximation by deep neural nets with bounded width and ReLU activations. *Mathematics*, **7**(10), 992.

Hanin, B., and Sellke, M. 2017. Approximating continuous functions by ReLU nets of minimal width. ArXiv preprint arXiv:1710.11278.

Hardt, M., and Ma, T. 2016. Identity matters in deep learning. ArXiv preprint arXiv:1611.04231.

Håstad, J. 1986. Almost optimal lower bounds for small depth circuits. Page 6–20 of: *Proc. 18th Annual ACM Symposium on Theory of Computing*.

Håstad, J., and Goldmann, M. 1991. On the power of small-depth threshold circuits. *Comput. Compl.*, **1**(2), 113–129.

He, J., Li, L., Xu, J., and Zheng, C. 2018. ReLU deep neural networks and linear finite elements. ArXiv preprint arXiv:1807.03973.

He, K., and Sun, J. 2015. Convolutional neural networks at constrained time cost. Pages 5353–5360 of: *Proc. IEEE Conference on Computer Vision and Pattern Recognition.*

He, K., Zhang, X., Ren, S., and Sun, J. 2016. Deep residual learning for image recognition. Pages 770–778 of: *Proc. IEEE Conference on Computer Vision and Pattern Recognition.*

Hecht-Nielsen, R. 1987. Kolmogorov's mapping neural network existence theorem. Pages 11–13 of: *Proc. IEEE First International Conference on Neural Networks*, vol. III.

Hecht-Nielsen, R. 1989. Theory of the backpropagation neural network. Pages 593–605 of: *Proc. International 1989 Joint Conference on Neural Networks*, vol. 1.

Hesthaven, J. S., and Ubbiali, S. 2018. Non-intrusive reduced order modeling of nonlinear problems using neural networks. *J. Comput. Phys.*, **363**, 55–78.

Hornik, K. 1991. Approximation capabilities of multilayer feedforward networks. *Neural Netw.*, **4**(2), 251–257.

Hornik, K., Stinchcombe, M., and White, H. 1989. Multilayer feedforward networks are universal approximators. *Neural Netw.*, **2**(5), 359–366.

Hornik, K., Stinchcombe, M., and White, H. 1990. Universal approximation of an unknown mapping and its derivatives using multilayer feedforward networks. *Neural Netw.*, **3**(5), 551–560.

Hutzenthaler, M., Jentzen, A., and von Wurstemberger, P. 2019. Overcoming the curse of dimensionality in the approximative pricing of financial derivatives with default risks. ArXiv preprint arXiv:1903.05985.

Hutzenthaler, M., Jentzen, A., Kruse, T., and Nguyen, T.A. 2020. A proof that rectified deep neural networks overcome the curse of dimensionality in the numerical approximation of semilinear heat equations. *SN Partial Differ. Equ. Appl.*, **1**(10).

Imaizumi, M., and Fukumizu, K. 2019. Deep neural networks learn non-smooth functions effectively. Pages 869–878 of: *Proc. Machine Learning Research*, vol. 89.

Irie, B., and Miyake, S. 1988. Capabilities of three-layered perceptrons. Pages 641–648 of: *IProc. EEE 1988 International Conference on Neural Networks*, vol. 1.

Jentzen, A., Salimova D., and Welti, T. 2018. A proof that deep artificial neural networks overcome the curse of dimensionality in the numerical approximation of Kolmogorov partial differential equations with constant diffusion and nonlinear drift coefficients. ArXiv preprint arXiv:1809.07321.

Khoo, Y., Lu, J., and Ying, L. 2017. Solving parametric PDE problems with artificial neural networks. ArXiv preprint arXiv:1707.03351.

Khrulkov, V., Novikov, A., and Oseledets, I. 2017. Expressive power of recurrent neural networks. ArXiv preprint arXiv:1711.00811.

Kolmogorov, A. N. 1957. On the representation of continuous functions of many variables by superposition of continuous functions of one variable and addition. *Doklady Akademii Nauk*, **114**, 953–956.

Kolmogorov, A. N. 1961. On the representation of continuous functions of several variables by superpositions of continuous functions of a smaller number of variables. *Amer. Math. Soc. Transl. (2)*, **17**, 369–373.

Krizhevsky, A., Sutskever, I., and Hinton, G. 2012. ImageNet classification with deep convolutional neural networks. Pages 1097–1105 of: *Advances in Neural Information Processing Systems*, vol. 25.

Kutyniok, G., and Labate, D. 2012. *Shearlets: Multiscale Analysis for Multivariate Data*. Birkhäuser.

Kutyniok, G., and Lim, W.-Q. 2010. Compactly supported shearlets are optimally sparse. *J. Approx. Theory*, **163**, 1564–1589.

Kutyniok, G., Petersen, P. C., Raslan, M., and Schneider, R. 2019. A theoretical analysis of deep neural networks and parametric PDEs. ArXiv preprint, arXiv:1904.00377.

Lagaris, I.E., Likas, A., and Fotiadis, D.I. 1998. Artificial neural networks for solving ordinary and partial differential equations. *IEEE Trans. Neural Netw.*, **9**(5), 987–1000.

Lecun, Y. 1989. Generalization and network design strategies. In: *Connectionism in Perspective*, Pfeifer, R., Schreter, Z., Fogelman, F., and Steels, L. (eds). Elsevier.

Lee, K., and Carlberg, K. 2020. Model reduction of dynamical systems on nonlinear manifolds using deep convolutional autoencoders. *J. Comput. Phys.*, **404**, 108973.

Leshno, M., Lin, V. Ya., Pinkus, A., and Schocken, S. 1993. Multilayer feedforward networks with a nonpolynomial activation function can approximate any function. *Neural Netw.*, **6**(6), 861–867.

Liang, S., and Srikant, R. 2016. Why deep neural networks for function approximation? ArXiv preprint arXiv:1610.04161.

Lin, H., and Jegelka, S. 2018. ResNet with one-neuron hidden layers is a Universal Approximator. Pages 6172–6181 of: *Advances in Neural Information Processing Systems*, vol. 32.

Lu, L., Meng, X., Mao, T., and Karniadakis, G. 2019. DeepXDE: A deep learning library for solving differential equations. ArXiv preprint arXiv:1907.04502.

Lu, Z., Pu, H., Wang, F., Hu, Z., and Wang, L. 2017. The expressive power of neural networks: A view from the width. Pages 6231–6239 of: *Advances in Neural Information Processing Systems*, vol. 30.

Maiorov, V., and Pinkus, A. 1999. Lower bounds for approximation by MLP neural networks. *Neurocomputing*, **25**(1–3), 81–91.

Maiorov, V., Meir, R., and Ratsaby, J. 1999. On the approximation of functional classes equipped with a uniform measure using ridge functions. *J. Approx. Theory*, **99**(1), 95 – 111.

Makovoz, Y. 1996. Random approximants and neural networks. *J. Approx. Theory*, **85**(1), 98–109.

Martens, J., and Medabalimi, V. 2014. On the expressive efficiency of sum product networks. ArXiv preprint arXiv:1411.7717.

Matthews, M. 1993. Approximating nonlinear fading-memory operators using neural network models. *Circuits, Systems, and Signal Processing*, **12**(2), 279–307.

McCulloch, W., and Pitts, W. 1943. A logical calculus of ideas immanent in nervous activity. *Bull. Math. Biophys.*, **5**, 115–133.

Mhaskar, H. 1993. Approximation properties of a multilayered feedforward artificial neural network. *Adv. Comput. Math.*, **1**(1), 61–80.

Mhaskar, H. 1996. Neural networks for optimal approximation of smooth and analytic functions. *Neural Comp.*, **8**(1), 164–177.

Mhaskar, H., and Poggio, T. 2016. Deep vs. shallow networks: An approximation theory perspective. *Anal. Appl.*, **14**(06), 829–848.

Mhaskar, H., Liao, Q., and Poggio, T. 2016. Learning functions: When is deep better than shallow? ArXiv preprint arXiv:1603.00988.

Mhaskar, H., Liao, Q., and Poggio, T. 2017. When and why are deep networks better than shallow ones? Pages 2343–2349 of: *Proc. 31st AAAI Conference on Artificial Intelligence*.

Montanelli, H., and Du, Q. 2019. New error bounds for deep ReLU networks using sparse grids. *SIAM J. Math. Data Sci.*, **1**(1), 78–92.

Montúfar, G.F., Pascanu, R., Cho, K., and Bengio, Y. 2014. On the number of linear regions of deep neural networks. Pages 2924–2932 of: *Advances in Neural Information Processing Systems*, vol. 27.

Nguyen, Q., and Hein, M. 2018. The loss surface and expressivity of deep convolutional neural networks. In: *Proc. 6th International Conference on Learning Representations*.

Oono, K., and Suzuki, T. 2018. Approximation and non-parametric estimation of ResNet-type convolutional neural networks via block-sparse fully-connected neural networks. ArXiv preprint arXiv:1903.10047.

Opschoor, J. A. A., Petersen, P. C., and Schwab, C. 2020. Deep ReLU networks and high-order finite element methods. *Anal. Appl.*, **18**(05), 715–770.

Pascanu, R., Montúfar, G., and Bengio, Y. 2013. On the number of response regions of deep feed forward networks with piece-wise linear activations. ArXiv preprint arXiv:1312.6098.

Petersen, P. C., and Voigtlaender, F. 2018. Optimal approximation of piecewise smooth functions using deep ReLU neural networks. *Neural Netw.*, **180**, 296–330.

Petersen, P. C., and Voigtlaender, F. 2020. Equivalence of approximation by convolutional neural networks and fully-connected networks. *Proc. Amer. Math. Soc.*, **148**, 1567–1581.

Petersen, P., Raslan, M., and Voigtlaender, F. 2021. Topological properties of the set of functions generated by neural networks of fixed size. *Found. Comp. Math.*, **21**, 275–444.

Pinkus, A. 1999. Approximation theory of the MLP model in neural networks. *Acta Numer.*, **8**, 143–195.

Poggio, T., Mhaskar, H., Rosasco, L., Miranda, B., and Liao, Q. 2017. Why and when can deep – but not shallow – networks avoid the curse of dimensionality: A review. *Int. J. Autom. Comput.*, **14**(5), 503–519.

Polycarpou, M., and Ioannou, P. 1991. *Identification and Control of Nonlinear Systems using Neural Network Models: Design and Stability Analysis*. University of Southern California.

Raghu, M., Poole, B., Kleinberg, J., Ganguli, S., and Sohl-Dickstein, J. 2017. On the expressive power of deep neural networks. Pages 2847–2854 of: *Proc. 34th International Conference on Machine Learning*.

Raissi, M. 2018. Deep hidden physics models: Deep learning of nonlinear partial differential equations. *J. Mach. Learn. Res.*, **19**(1), 932–955.

Reisinger, C., and Zhang, Y. 2019. Rectified deep neural networks overcome the curse of dimensionality for nonsmooth value functions in zero-sum games of nonlinear stiff systems. ArXiv preprint arXiv:1903.06652.

Rolnick, D., and Tegmark, M. 2018. The power of deeper networks for expressing natural functions. In: *Proc. International Conference on Learning Representations*.

Rudin, W. 1987. *Real and Complex Analysis*. Third edition. McGraw–Hill.

Russakovsky, O., Deng, J., Su, H., Krause, J., Satheesh, S., Ma, S., Huang, Z., Karpathy, A., Khosla, A., Bernstein, M., Berg, A., and Fei-Fei, L. 2015. ImageNet large scale visual recognition challenge. *Int. J. Comput. Vis.*, **115**(3), 211–252.

Safran, I., and Shamir, O. 2017. Depth-Width Tradeoffs in Approximating Natural Functions with Neural Networks. Pages 2979–2987 of: *Proceedings of the 34th International Conference on Machine Learning*.

Scarselli, F., Gori, M., Tsoi, A., Hagenbuchner, M., and Monfardini, G. 2008. Computational capabilities of graph neural networks. *IEEE Trans. Neural Netw.*, **20**(1), 81–102.

Schäfer, A., and Zimmermann, H. 2006. Recurrent neural networks are universal approximators. Pages 632–640 of: *Proc. Conference on Artificial Neural Networks*.

Schmidt-Hieber, J. 2017. Nonparametric regression using deep neural networks with ReLU activation function. ArXiv preprint arXiv:1708.06633.

Schwab, C., and Zech, J. 2019. Deep learning in high dimension: Neural network expression rates for generalized polynomial chaos expansions in UQ. *Anal. Appl. (Singapore)*, **17**(1), 19–55.

Serra, Thiago, and Ramalingam, Srikumar. 2020. Empirical bounds on linear regions of deep rectifier networks. Pages 5628–5635 of: *Proc. 34th AAAI Conference on Artificial Intelligence.*

Serra, Thiago, Tjandraatmadja, Christian, and Ramalingam, Srikumar. 2018. Bounding and counting linear regions of deep neural networks. Pages 4558–4566 of: *Proc. 35th International Conference on Machine Learning.*

Shaham, U., Cloninger, A., and Coifman, R. R. 2018. Provable approximation properties for deep neural networks. *Appl. Comput. Harmon. Anal.,* **44**(3), 537–557.

Simonyan, K., and Zisserman, A. 2015. Very deep convolutional networks for large-scale image recognition. In: *Proc. 3rd International Conference on Learning Representations.*

Sipser, M. 1983. A complexity-theoretic approach to randomness. Pages 330–335 of: *Proc. 15th Annual ACM Symposium on Theory of Computing.*

Sirignano, J., and Spiliopoulos, K. 2018. DGM: A deep learning algorithm for solving partial differential equations. *J. Comput. Syst. Sci.,* **375**, 1339–1364.

Sontag, E. 1992a. Feedforward nets for interpolation and classification. *J. Comput. Syst. Sci.,* **45**(1), 20–48.

Sontag, E. 1992b. Neural nets as systems models and controllers. Pages 73–79 of: *Proc. 7th Yale Workshop on Adaptive and Learning Systems.*

Sprecher, D. 1965. On the structure of continuous functions of several variables. *Trans. Amer. Math. Soc.,* **115**, 340–355.

Srivastava, R., Greff, K., and Schmidhuber, J. 2015. Highway networks. ArXiv preprint arXiv:1505.00387.

Suzuki, T. 2019. Adaptivity of deep ReLU network for learning in Besov and mixed smooth Besov spaces: Optimal rate and curse of dimensionality. In: *Proc. 7th International Conference on Learning Representations.*

Szegedy, C., Liu, W., Jia, Y., Pierre, S., Reed, S., Anguelov, D., Erhan, D., Vanhoucke, V., and Rabinovich, A. 2015. Going deeper with convolutions. Pages 1–9 of: *Proc. IEEE Conference on Computer Vision and Pattern Recognition.*

Telgarsky, M. 2016. Benefits of depth in neural networks. Pages 1517–1539 of: *Proc. 29th Annual Conference on Learning Theory.*

Telgarsky, M. 2017. Neural networks and rational functions. Pages 3387–3393 of: *Proc. 34th International Conference on Machine Learning.*

Vapnik, V.N., and Chervonenkis, A. Y. 2015. On the uniform convergence of relative frequencies of events to their probabilities. Pages 11–30 of *Measures of Complexities*, Vladimir Vovk, Harris Papadopoulos and Alexander Gammerman (eds). Springer.

Yang, Y., and Perdikaris, P. 2018. Physics-informed deep generative models. ArXiv preprint arXiv:1812.03511.

Yarotsky, D. 2017. Error bounds for approximations with deep ReLU networks. *Neural Netw.,* **94**, 103–114.

Yarotsky, D. 2018. Optimal approximation of continuous functions by very deep ReLU networks. Pages 639–649 of: *Proc. 31st Conference On Learning Theory*.

Yarotsky, D. 2019. Universal approximations of invariant maps by neural networks. ArXiv preprint arXiv:1804.10306.

Yarotsky, D., and Zhevnerchuk, A. 2019. The phase diagram of approximation rates for deep neural networks. ArXiv preprint arXiv:1906.09477.

Zeiler, M. D., and Fergus, R. 2014. Visualizing and understanding convolutional networks. Pages 818–833 of: *Proc. ECCV*.

Zhou, D.-X. 2020. Universality of deep convolutional neural networks. *Appl. Comput. Harmon. Anal.*, **48**(2), 787–794.

4

Optimization Landscape of Neural Networks

René Vidal, Zhihui Zhu, and Benjamin D. Haeffele

Abstract: Many tasks in machine learning involve solving a convex optimization problem which significantly facilitates the analysis of properties of the resulting algorithms, such as their optimality, robustness, and generalization. An important challenge in training neural networks occurs when the associated optimization problem is non-convex; this complicates the analysis because global optima can be difficult to characterize and the optimization landscape can also include spurious local minima and saddle points. As a consequence, different algorithms might attract different weights depending on initialization, parameter tuning, etc. Despite this challenge, in practice existing algorithms routinely converge to good solutions, which suggests that the landscape might be simpler than expected, at least for certain classes of networks.

This chapter summarizes recent advances in the analysis of optimization landscapes in neural network training. We first review classical results for linear networks trained with a squared loss and without regularization. Such results show that, under certain conditions on the input–output data, spurious local minima are guaranteed not to exist, i.e. critical points are either saddle points or global minima. Moreover, globally optimal weights can be found by factorizing certain matrices obtained from the input–output covariance matrices. We then review recent results for deep networks with a parallel structure, positively homogeneous network mapping and regularization, and trained with a convex loss. Such results show that a non-convex objective on the weights can be lower-bounded by a convex objective on the network mapping. Moreover, when the network is sufficiently wide, local minima of the non-convex objective that satisfy a certain condition yield global minima of both the non-convex and convex objectives, and that there is always a non-increasing path to a global minimizer from any initialization.

4.1 Introduction

Many machine learning tasks involve solving an optimization problem of the form

$$\min_{\mathbf{W}} \mathcal{L}(\Phi(\mathbf{X}, \mathbf{W}), \mathbf{Y}) + \lambda \Theta(\mathbf{W}). \tag{4.1}$$

For example, in the case of classification, $\mathcal{L}(\Phi(\mathbf{X}, \mathbf{W}), \mathbf{Y})$ is a *loss function* that measures the agreement between the true matrix of labels, $\mathbf{Y}$, and the predicted matrix of labels, $\Phi(\mathbf{X}, \mathbf{W})$, where $\mathbf{X}$ is the input data matrix, $\mathbf{W}$ represents the classifier parameters, $\Theta(\mathbf{W})$ is a *regularization function* designed to prevent overfitting,[1] and $\lambda > 0$ is a parameter that controls the trade-off between the loss function and the regularization function. Another example is regression, where the setting is essentially the same, except that $\mathbf{Y}$ is typically continuous-valued, while in classification $\mathbf{Y}$ is categorical.

Some machine learning problems, such as linear regression, support vector machines, ℓ_1 minimization, and nuclear norm minimization, involve solving a *convex optimization problem*, where both the loss and the regularization functions are assumed to be convex functions of $\mathbf{W}$. For example, in linear regression with a squared loss and Tikhonov regularization we have[2]

$$\mathcal{L}(\Phi(\mathbf{X}, \mathbf{W}), \mathbf{Y}) = \|\mathbf{Y} - \mathbf{W}^\top \mathbf{X}\|_F^2 \qquad \text{and} \qquad \Theta(\mathbf{W}) = \|\mathbf{W}\|_F^2. \tag{4.2}$$

When the optimization problem is convex, non-global local minima and saddle points are guaranteed not to exist, which significantly facilitates the analysis of optimization algorithms, especially the study of their convergence to a global minimizer. In addition, convexity allows one to analyze properties of the resulting machine learning algorithm, such as robustness and generalization, without having to worry about the particulars of the optimization method, such as initialization, step size (learning rate), etc., as the global optima are easily characterized and many optimization schemes exist which provide guaranteed convergence to a global minimizer.[3]

Unfortunately, many other machine learning problems, particularly those that seek to learn an appropriate representation of features directly from the data – with principal component analysis (PCA), non-negative matrix factorization, sparse dictionary learning, tensor factorization, and deep learning being well-known examples

---

[1] Note that Θ could also depend on $\mathbf{X}$, but we will omit this for notational simplicity.

[2] The squared loss between vectors $\mathbf{y}$ and $\mathbf{z}$ is $\mathcal{L}(\mathbf{y}, \mathbf{z}) = \|\mathbf{y} - \mathbf{z}\|_2^2$. Here we consider a dataset $(\mathbf{X}, \mathbf{Y})$ with m training examples arranged as columns of a matrix $(\mathbf{X}, \mathbf{Y}) = \left([\mathbf{x}^{(1)}, \dots, \mathbf{x}^{(m)}], [\mathbf{y}^{(1)}, \dots, \mathbf{y}^{(m)}]\right)$. The sum of the squared losses over the training examples $\sum_{i=1}^{m} \|\mathbf{y}^{(i)} - \mathbf{z}^{(i)}\|_2^2$ becomes the Frobenius norm $\|\mathbf{Y} - \mathbf{Z}\|_F^2$.

[3] For convex learning problems, the convergence of the optimization method to a global minimum does depend on initialization and parameter tuning, but the analysis of generalization does not.

– involve solving a *non-convex optimization problem* of the form:

$$\min_{\{\mathbf{W}^{[l]}\}_{l=1}^L} \mathcal{L}(\Phi(\mathbf{X}, \mathbf{W}^{[1]}, \ldots, \mathbf{W}^{[L]}), \mathbf{Y}) + \lambda\Theta(\mathbf{W}^{[1]}, \ldots, \mathbf{W}^{[L]}), \qquad (4.3)$$

where Φ is an arbitrary convexity-destroying mapping. In PCA, for example, the goal is to factorize a given data matrix $\mathbf{Y}$ as the product of two matrices $\mathbf{W}^{[1]}$ and $\mathbf{W}^{[2]}$, subject to the constraint that the columns of $\mathbf{W}^{[1]}$ are orthonormal. In that case, $\Phi(\mathbf{X}, \mathbf{W}^{[1]}, \mathbf{W}^{[2]}) = \mathbf{W}^{[1]}\mathbf{W}^{[2]\top}$ and Θ enforces the orthogonality constraints $\mathbf{W}^{[1]\top}\mathbf{W}^{[1]} = \mathbf{I}$, both of which make the optimization problem non-convex. Similarly, in deep neural network training, the output of the network is typically generated by applying an alternating series of linear and non-linear functions to the input data:

$$\Phi(\mathbf{X}, \mathbf{W}^{[1]}, \ldots, \mathbf{W}^{[L]}) = \psi_L(\mathbf{W}^{[L]}\psi_{L-1}(\mathbf{W}^{[L-1]} \cdots \psi_2(\mathbf{W}^{[2]}\psi_1(\mathbf{W}^{[1]}\mathbf{X})) \cdots)), (4.4)$$

where each $\mathbf{W}^{[l]}$ is an appropriately sized matrix that contains the connection weights between layers $l - 1$ and l of the network, and the $\psi_l(\cdot)$ functions apply some form of non-linearity after each matrix multiplication, e.g., a sigmoid function, a rectified linear unit (ReLU), or max-pooling.[4]

For a very small number of non-convex problems, e.g., PCA, one is fortunate, and a global minimizer can be found in closed form. For other problems, e.g., ℓ_0 minimization, rank minimization, and low-rank matrix completion, one can replace the non-convex objective by a convex surrogate and show that under certain conditions the solutions to both problems are the same.[5] In most cases, however, the optimal solutions cannot be computed in closed form, and a good convex surrogate may not be easy to find. This presents significant challenges to existing optimization algorithms – including (but certainly not limited to) alternating minimization, gradient descent, stochastic gradient descent, block coordinate descent, back propagation, and quasi-Newton methods – which are typically guaranteed only to converge to a critical point of the objective function (Mairal et al., 2010; Rumelhart et al., 1986; Wright and Nocedal, 1999; Xu and Yin, 2013). As the set of critical points for non-convex problems includes not only global minima but also spurious (non-global) local minima, local maxima, saddle points, and saddle plateaus, as illustrated in Figure 4.1, the non-convexity of such a problem leaves the model somewhat ill-posed in the sense that it is not just the model formulation that is important but also the implementation details, such as how the model is initialized and particulars of the optimization algorithm, which can have a significant impact on the performance of the model.

Despite these challenges, optimization methods that combine backpropagation

---

[4] Here we have shown the linear operation as simple matrix multiplication to simplify notation, but this easily generalizes to other linear operators (e.g., convolution) and affine operators (i.e., those using bias terms).

[5] See e.g. Donoho (2006) and Candès and Tao (2010) for the relationships between ℓ_0 and ℓ_1 minimization.

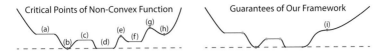

Figure 4.1 Example critical points of a non-convex function (shown in red). (a,c) Plateaus. (b,d) Global minima. (e,g) Local maxima. (f,h) Local minima. © 2017 IEEE. Reprinted, with permission, from Haeffele and Vidal (2017).

(Werbos, 1974) with variants of stochastic gradient descent (Robbins and Monro, 1951), such as Nesterov accelerated gradient (Nesterov, 1983), Adam (Kingma and Ba, 2014), and Adagrad (Duchi et al., 2017), appear to routinely yield good solutions for training deep networks. Recent work attempting to understand this phenomenon can be broadly classified into three main themes.

(i) *Benign optimization landscape*: While the optimization problem in (4.3) is not convex for deep network training, there are certain classes of networks for which there are no spurious local minima (Baldi and Hornik, 1989; Kawaguchi, 2016; Haeffele and Vidal, 2017), local minima concentrate near the global optimum (Choromanska et al., 2015), or critical points are more likely to be saddle points rather than spurious local minima Dauphin et al. (2014). A similar benign landscape has also been observed for non-convex problems arising in phase retrieval (Sun et al., 2018), dictionary learning (Sun et al., 2017), and blind deconvolution (Zhang et al., 2018).

(ii) *Optimization dynamics lead to global optima*: In addition to study of the landscape of the learning objective, there has also been work focused on how specific algorithms (largely gradient-descent-based) perform when optimizing neural networks. For example, Gori and Tesi (1991, 1992) showed that gradient descent generally finds a global minimizer for linearly separable data. More generally, work has also shown that if the optimization landscape satisfies the *strict saddle property* (where the Hessian evaluated at every saddle point has a sufficiently negative eigenvalue) then gradient descent and many other first-order descent techniques are guaranteed to converge to a local minimum and not get stuck in saddle points (Ge et al., 2015; Lee et al., 2019). Using these results, it has been shown that gradient descent converges to a global minimum (Kawaguchi, 2016; Nouiehed and Razaviyayn, 2018; Zhu et al., 2020) for linear neural networks that satisfy the strict saddle conditions. Unfortunately, however, the strict saddle property does not typically hold for non-linear neural networks. Nevertheless, several recent studies have shown that if the network is sufficiently large then, under certain conditions, gradient descent will converge at a linear rate to global minimizers. However, the necessary conditions are potentially quite strict. Moreover, it is unclear whether such results can be generalized to other formulations that include regularization on the network parameters (Du et al., 2019; Allen-Zhu et al., 2019).

(iii) *Implicit bias of the optimization algorithm*: Another possible explanation for the observed success of deep learning is that the optimization algorithm either explores only a subset of the landscape (depending on properties of the data or initialization of the algorithm) or automatically induces a regularizer that avoids spurious local minima. For example, Gunasekar et al. (2017, 2018a,b) showed that gradient descent applied to certain classes of linear networks automatically induces a bias towards solutions that minimize a certain norm. Further, Arora et al. (2019) extended this idea to deep linear models, arguing that depth in linear networks trained with gradient descent induces a low-rank regularization through the dynamics of gradient descent. Further, other optimization techniques such as dropout (Srivastava et al., 2014), which adds stochastic noise by randomly setting the output of neurons to zero during training, have been shown to induce low-rank structures in the solution (Cavazza et al., 2018; Mianjy et al., 2018; Pal et al., 2020).

This chapter concentrates on the first theme by presenting an overview of the optimization landscape of neural network training. In §4.3 we study the landscape of linear networks. Specifically, in §4.3.1 we review classical results from Baldi and Hornik (1989) for single-hidden-layer linear networks trained using a squared loss, which show that under certain conditions on the network width and the input–output data, every critical point is either a global minimum or a saddle point. We also review recent results from Nouiehed and Razaviyayn (2018) and Zhu et al. (2020) which show that all saddle points are strict (i.e., at least one eigenvalue of the Hessian is negative). Moreover, Baldi and Hornik (1989), Nouiehed and Razaviyayn (2018), and Zhu et al. (2020) have also shown that globally optimal weights can be found by factorizing a certain matrix obtained from the input–output covariance matrices. Then, in §4.3.2 we review the work of Kawaguchi (2016), which extends these results to networks of any depth and width by showing that critical points are also either global minima or saddle points. In the same paper Kawaguchi also shows that saddle points of networks with one hidden layer are strict, but networks with two or more layers can have "bad" (non-strict) saddle points.

In §4.4 we study the landscape of nonlinear networks. Specifically, we review recent results from Haeffele and Vidal (2017, 2019) that study the conditions under which the optimization landscape for the non-convex optimization problem in (4.3) is such that *all critical points are either global minimizers or saddle points or plateaus*, as shown in Figure 4.2. Their results show that if the network size is large enough and the functions Φ and Θ are *sums of positively homogeneous functions of*

Figure 4.2 Guaranteed properties of the proposed framework. Starting from any initialization, a non-increasing path exists to a global minimizer. Starting from points on a plateau, a simple "sliding" method exists to find the edge of the plateau (green points). © 2017 IEEE. Reprinted, with permission, from Haeffele and Vidal (2017).

the same degree then a monotonically decreasing path to a global minimizer exists from every point.

4.2 Basics of Statistical Learning

Let $(\mathbf{x}, \mathbf{y}) \in \mathcal{X} \times \mathcal{Y}$ be a pair of random variables drawn from an unknown distribution $\mathbb{P}_{(\mathbf{x},\mathbf{y})}$, where $\mathcal{X}$ is the input space and $\mathcal{Y}$ the output space. Assume we wish to predict $\mathbf{y}$ from an observation about $\mathbf{x}$ by finding a hypothesis $\hat{f} \in \mathcal{Y}^{\mathcal{X}}$, i.e. $\hat{f} \colon \mathcal{X} \to \mathcal{Y}$, that minimizes the *expected loss* or *risk*, $\mathcal{R}(f)$; i.e. we want to find

$$\min_{f \in \mathcal{F}} \left[\mathcal{R}(f) \doteq \mathbb{E}_{\mathbf{x},\mathbf{y}}[\mathcal{L}(f(\mathbf{x}), \mathbf{y})] \right]. \tag{4.5}$$

Here $\mathcal{F} \subset \mathcal{Y}^{\mathcal{X}}$ is the space of hypotheses (e.g., the space of linear functions or the space of measurable functions from $\mathcal{X}$ to $\mathcal{Y}$) and $\mathcal{L} \colon \mathcal{Y} \times \mathcal{Y} \to [0, \infty]$ is a loss function, where $\mathcal{L}(f(\mathbf{x}), \mathbf{y})$ gives the cost of predicting $\mathbf{y}$ as $f(\mathbf{x})$ (e.g., the zero-one loss $1_{\mathbf{y} \neq f(\mathbf{x})}$ for classification or the squared loss $\|\mathbf{y} - f(\mathbf{x})\|_2^2$ for regression). The smallest expected risk $\mathcal{R}(\hat{f})$ is called the *Bayes error*.

Since $\mathbb{P}_{(\mathbf{x},\mathbf{y})}$ is unknown, $\hat{f}$ and $\mathcal{R}(\hat{f})$ cannot be computed. Instead, we assume we are given a training set $\mathcal{S} = \{(\mathbf{x}^{(i)}, \mathbf{y}^{(i)})\}_{i=1}^{m}$ of i.i.d. samples from $\mathbb{P}_{(\mathbf{x},\mathbf{y})}$ and seek to find a hypothesis $\hat{f}_{\mathcal{F},\mathcal{S}}$ that minimizes the *empirical risk*

$$\min_{f \in \mathcal{F}} \left[\mathcal{R}_S(f) \doteq \frac{1}{m} \sum_{i=1}^{m} \mathcal{L}(f(\mathbf{x}^{(i)}), \mathbf{y}^{(i)}) \right]. \tag{4.6}$$

Since the objective functions in (4.5) and (4.6) are different, a priori there is no guarantee that $\hat{f}_{\mathcal{F},\mathcal{S}}$ or its risk, $\mathcal{R}(\hat{f}_{\mathcal{F},\mathcal{S}})$, will be close to $\hat{f}$ or $\mathcal{R}(\hat{f})$, respectively. This leads to the question of *generalization*, which seeks to understand the performance of $\hat{f}_{\mathcal{F},\mathcal{S}}$ not just on the training set $\mathcal{S}$ but on the entire population. In principle, we could use the error $\mathcal{R}(\hat{f}_{\mathcal{F},\mathcal{S}}) - \mathcal{R}(\hat{f})$ to assess the quality of $\hat{f}_{\mathcal{F},\mathcal{S}}$. However, $\hat{f}_{\mathcal{F},\mathcal{S}}$ depends on the data $\mathcal{S}$, so $\hat{f}_{\mathcal{F},\mathcal{S}}$ is a random function and $\mathcal{R}(\hat{f}_{\mathcal{F},\mathcal{S}})$ is a random variable. While we could use the expectation of $\mathcal{R}(\hat{f}_{\mathcal{F},\mathcal{S}})$ with respect to the data,

$\mathbb{E}_S[\mathcal{R}(\hat{f}_{\mathcal{F},S}) - \mathcal{R}(\hat{f})]$, or verify that $\hat{f}_{\mathcal{F},S}$ is *universally consistent*, i.e. check that

$$\lim_{m \to \infty} \mathcal{R}(\hat{f}_{\mathcal{F},S}) = \mathcal{R}(\hat{f}) \qquad \text{almost surely,} \qquad (4.7)$$

both approaches are difficult to implement because $\mathbb{P}_{(\mathbf{x},\mathbf{y})}$ is unknown.

To address this issue, a common practice is to decompose the error as

$$\mathcal{R}(\hat{f}_{\mathcal{F},S}) - \mathcal{R}(\hat{f}) = \left(\mathcal{R}(\hat{f}_{\mathcal{F},S}) - \mathcal{R}_S(\hat{f}_{\mathcal{F},S})\right) + \left(\mathcal{R}_S(\hat{f}_{\mathcal{F},S}) - \mathcal{R}_S(\hat{f})\right)$$
$$+ \left(\mathcal{R}_S(\hat{f}) - \mathcal{R}(\hat{f})\right) \qquad (4.8)$$

and use the fact that the second group of terms is nonpositive and the third group of terms has zero expectation to arrive at an upper bound on the expected error

$$\mathbb{E}_S[\mathcal{R}(\hat{f}_{\mathcal{F},S}) - \mathcal{R}(\hat{f})] \le \mathbb{E}_S[\mathcal{R}(\hat{f}_{\mathcal{F},S}) - \mathcal{R}_S(\hat{f}_{\mathcal{F},S})]$$
$$\le \mathbb{E}_S[\sup_{f \in \mathcal{F}} \mathcal{R}(f) - \mathcal{R}_S(f)]. \qquad (4.9)$$

As the bound on the right-hand side may not be easily computable, a typical approach is to derive an easier-to-compute upper bound, say $\Theta(f)$, and then solve the *regularized empirical risk minimization* problem

$$\min_{f \in \mathcal{F}}[\mathcal{R}_S(f) + \Theta(f)]. \qquad (4.10)$$

In other words, rather than minimizing the empirical risk, $\mathcal{R}_S(f)$, we usually minimize the regularized empirical risk, $\mathcal{R}_S(f) + \Theta(f)$, in the hope of controlling the error $\mathbb{E}_S[\mathcal{R}(\hat{f}_{\mathcal{F},S}) - \mathcal{R}(\hat{f})]$.

Therefore, this chapter will focus on understanding the landscape of the optimization problem in (4.10), although we will also make connections with the optimization problem in (4.5) whenever possible (e.g., for single-hidden-layer linear networks trained with a squared loss). We refer the reader to other chapters in this book for a study of the generalization properties.

4.3 Optimization Landscape of Linear Networks

In this section we study the landscape of linear networks trained using a squared loss. In §4.3.1 we show that under certain conditions every critical point of a single-hidden-layer linear network is either a global minimum or a strict saddle point and that globally optimal weights can be obtained using linear-algebraic methods. In §4.3.2 we show that the critical points of linear networks with more than two layers are either global minima or saddle points, but such saddle points may not be strict.

4.3.1 Single-Hidden-Layer Linear Networks with Squared Loss and Fixed Size Regularization

Let us first consider the case of linear networks with n_0 inputs, n_2 outputs, and a single hidden layer with n_1 neurons. In this case, the hypothesis space $\mathcal{F}$ can be parametrized by the network weights $(\mathbf{W}^{[1]}, \mathbf{W}^{[2]}) = (\mathbf{U}, \mathbf{V})$ as[6]

$$\mathcal{F} = \{f \in \mathcal{Y}^{\mathcal{X}} : f(\mathbf{x}) = \mathbf{U}\mathbf{V}^{\top}\mathbf{x}, \text{ where } \mathbf{U} \in \mathbb{R}^{n_2 \times n_1} \text{ and } \mathbf{V} \in \qquad (4.11)$$
$$\mathbb{R}^{n_0 \times n_1}\}. \qquad (4.12)$$

In this section, we study the optimization landscape for single-hidden-layer linear networks trained using a squared loss, $\mathcal{L}(\mathbf{z}, \mathbf{y}) = \|\mathbf{y} - \mathbf{z}\|_2^2$. No regularization on the network weights is assumed, except that the network size n_1 is assumed to be known and sufficiently small relative to the input–output dimensions, i.e., $n_1 \leq \min\{n_0, n_2\}$. Under these assumptions, the problem of minimizing the expected risk reduces to[7]

$$\min_{\mathbf{U},\mathbf{V}} \left[\mathcal{R}(\mathbf{U}, \mathbf{V}) \doteq \mathbb{E}_{\mathbf{x},\mathbf{y}}[\|\mathbf{y} - \mathbf{U}\mathbf{V}^{\top}\mathbf{x}\|_2^2] \right]. \qquad (4.13)$$

Letting $\mathbf{\Sigma}_{\mathbf{xx}} = \mathbb{E}[\mathbf{xx}^{\top}] \in \mathbb{R}^{n_0 \times n_0}$, $\mathbf{\Sigma}_{\mathbf{xy}} = \mathbb{E}[\mathbf{xy}^{\top}] \in \mathbb{R}^{n_0 \times n_2}$, $\mathbf{\Sigma}_{\mathbf{yx}} = \mathbb{E}[\mathbf{yx}^{\top}] = \mathbf{\Sigma}_{\mathbf{xy}}^{\top} \in \mathbb{R}^{n_2 \times n_0}$, and $\mathbf{\Sigma}_{\mathbf{yy}} = \mathbb{E}[\mathbf{yy}^{\top}] \in \mathbb{R}^{n_2 \times n_2}$, the expected risk can be rewritten as:

$$\mathcal{R}(\mathbf{U}, \mathbf{V}) = \text{trace}(\mathbf{\Sigma}_{\mathbf{yy}} - 2\mathbf{\Sigma}_{\mathbf{yx}}\mathbf{V}\mathbf{U}^{\top} + \mathbf{U}\mathbf{V}^{\top}\mathbf{\Sigma}_{\mathbf{xx}}\mathbf{V}\mathbf{U}^{\top}). \qquad (4.14)$$

Consider now the empirical-risk-minimization problem

$$\min_{\mathbf{U},\mathbf{V}} \left[\mathcal{R}_S(\mathbf{U}, \mathbf{V}) = \frac{1}{m} \sum_{i=1}^{m} \|\mathbf{y}^{(i)} - \mathbf{U}\mathbf{V}^{\top}\mathbf{x}^{(i)}\|_2^2 = \frac{1}{m}\|\mathbf{Y} - \mathbf{U}\mathbf{V}^{\top}\mathbf{X}\|_F^2 \right], \qquad (4.15)$$

where $S = \{(\mathbf{x}^{(i)}, \mathbf{y}^{(i)})\}_{i=1}^{m}$ is the training set and $\mathbf{X} = [\mathbf{x}^{(1)}, \dots, \mathbf{x}^{(m)}]$ and $\mathbf{Y} = [\mathbf{y}^{(1)}, \dots, \mathbf{y}^{(m)}]$ are the input and output data matrices. It is easy to see that the empirical risk $\mathcal{R}_S(\mathbf{U}, \mathbf{V})$ is equal to $\mathcal{R}(\mathbf{U}, \mathbf{V})$ if the covariance matrices $\mathbf{\Sigma}_{\mathbf{xx}}, \mathbf{\Sigma}_{\mathbf{xy}}$, and $\mathbf{\Sigma}_{\mathbf{yy}}$ are substituted by their empirical estimates $\frac{1}{m}\mathbf{XX}^{\top}, \frac{1}{m}\mathbf{XY}^{\top}$, and $\frac{1}{m}\mathbf{YY}^{\top}$, respectively. Therefore, in this case, analysis of the optimization landscape for both the expected and empirical risk can be done by analyzing the landscape of $\mathcal{R}(\mathbf{U}, \mathbf{V})$.

To motivate the analysis of the landscape of $\mathcal{R}(\mathbf{U}, \mathbf{V})$, let us first analyze the landscape of the risk as a function of the product of the weights, i.e., $\mathbf{Z} = \mathbf{U}\mathbf{V}^{\top}$, which is given by $\mathcal{R}(\mathbf{Z}) = \text{trace}(\mathbf{\Sigma}_{\mathbf{yy}} - 2\mathbf{\Sigma}_{\mathbf{yx}}\mathbf{Z}^{\top} + \mathbf{Z}\mathbf{\Sigma}_{\mathbf{xx}}\mathbf{Z}^{\top})$. When there is no constraint on $\mathbf{Z}$ (e.g. when $\mathbf{U}$ and $\mathbf{V}$ are full column rank), the risk is a convex function of $\mathbf{Z}$ and the first-order condition for optimality is given by $\mathbf{Z}\mathbf{\Sigma}_{\mathbf{xx}} = \mathbf{\Sigma}_{\mathbf{yx}}$. Thus, if $\mathbf{\Sigma}_{\mathbf{xx}}$ is invertible, the global minimum is unique and is given by $\mathbf{Z}^* = \mathbf{U}^*\mathbf{V}^{*\top} = \mathbf{\Sigma}_{\mathbf{yx}}\mathbf{\Sigma}_{\mathbf{xx}}^{-1}$. Of course, this provides a characterization of the optimal $\mathbf{Z}$, but

---

[6] For simplicity of notation, if we only have two groups of parameters we will use $(\mathbf{U}, \mathbf{V})$ rather than $(\mathbf{W}^{[1]}, \mathbf{W}^{[2]})$.
[7] With an abuse of notation, we will write the risk as a function of the network weights, i.e., $\mathcal{R}(\mathbf{U}, \mathbf{V})$, rather than as a function of the input–output map, i.e., $\mathcal{R}(f)$.

not of the optimal $\mathbf{U}$ and $\mathbf{V}$. The challenge in characterizing the landscape of $\mathcal{R}(\mathbf{U}, \mathbf{V})$ is hence to understand the effect of the low-rank constraint $n_1 \leq \min\{n_0, n_2\}$, i.e. to consider the possibility that critical points for $\mathbf{U}$ or $\mathbf{V}$ might not be low-rank.

The following lemma characterizes properties of the critical points of $\mathcal{R}(\mathbf{U}, \mathbf{V})$. The original statements and proofs for these results can be found in Baldi and Hornik (1989). Here we provide a unified treatment for both the expected and empirical risk, as well as alternative derivations.

Lemma 4.1. *If* $(\mathbf{U}, \mathbf{V})$ *is a critical point of* $\mathcal{R}$ *then*

$$\mathbf{U}\mathbf{V}^\top\Sigma_{xx}\mathbf{V} = \Sigma_{yx}\mathbf{V} \quad \text{and} \quad \Sigma_{xx}\mathbf{V}\mathbf{U}^\top\mathbf{U} = \Sigma_{xy}\mathbf{U}. \tag{4.16}$$

Moreover, if Σ_{xx} *is invertible then the following three properties hold.*

(i) *If* $\mathbf{V}$ *is full column rank then* $\mathbf{U} = \Sigma_{yx}\mathbf{V}(\mathbf{V}^\top\Sigma_{xx}\mathbf{V})^{-1}$.
(ii) *If* $\mathbf{U}$ *is full column rank then* $\mathbf{V} = \Sigma_{xx}^{-1}\Sigma_{xy}\mathbf{U}(\mathbf{U}^\top\mathbf{U})^{-1}$.
(iii) *Let* $\Sigma = \Sigma_{yx}\Sigma_{xx}^{-1}\Sigma_{xy}$. *If* $\mathbf{U}$ *is full column rank and* $\mathbf{P}_\mathbf{U} = \mathbf{U}(\mathbf{U}^\top\mathbf{U})^{-1}\mathbf{U}^\top$ *then* $\Sigma\mathbf{P}_\mathbf{U} = (\Sigma\mathbf{P}_\mathbf{U})^\top = \mathbf{P}_\mathbf{U}\Sigma$.

Proof   The gradient of $\mathcal{R}$ with respect to $\mathbf{U}$ is given by

$$\frac{\partial\mathcal{R}}{\partial\mathbf{U}} = -2(\Sigma_{yx} - \mathbf{U}\mathbf{V}^\top\Sigma_{xx})\mathbf{V} = 0 \implies \mathbf{U}\mathbf{V}^\top\Sigma_{xx}\mathbf{V} = \Sigma_{yx}\mathbf{V}. \tag{4.17}$$

Therefore, when Σ_{xx} is invertible and $\mathbf{V}$ is full column rank, we have

$$\mathbf{U} = \Sigma_{yx}\mathbf{V}(\mathbf{V}^\top\Sigma_{xx}\mathbf{V})^{-1}, \tag{4.18}$$

as claimed in 4.1(i). On the other hand, the gradient of $\mathcal{R}$ with respect to $\mathbf{V}$ is given by

$$\frac{\partial\mathcal{R}}{\partial\mathbf{V}} = -2(\Sigma_{xy} - \Sigma_{xx}\mathbf{V}\mathbf{U}^\top)\mathbf{U} = 0 \implies \Sigma_{xx}\mathbf{V}\mathbf{U}^\top\mathbf{U} = \Sigma_{xy}\mathbf{U}. \tag{4.19}$$

Therefore, when Σ_{xx} is invertible and $\mathbf{U}$ is full column rank, we have

$$\mathbf{V} = \Sigma_{xx}^{-1}\Sigma_{xy}\mathbf{U}(\mathbf{U}^\top\mathbf{U})^{-1}, \tag{4.20}$$

as claimed in 4.1(ii). Moreover, notice that

$$\mathbf{U}\mathbf{V}^\top = \mathbf{U}(\mathbf{U}^\top\mathbf{U})^{-1}\mathbf{U}^\top\Sigma_{yx}\Sigma_{xx}^{-1} = \mathbf{P}_\mathbf{U}\Sigma_{yx}\Sigma_{xx}^{-1}. \tag{4.21}$$

Combining this with the first equation in (4.16) we obtain

$$\mathbf{U}\mathbf{V}^\top\Sigma_{xx}\mathbf{V}\mathbf{U}^\top = \Sigma_{yx}\mathbf{V}\mathbf{U}^\top, \tag{4.22}$$

$$\mathbf{P}_\mathbf{U}\Sigma_{yx}\Sigma_{xx}^{-1}\Sigma_{xx}\Sigma_{xx}^{-1}\Sigma_{xy}\mathbf{P}_\mathbf{U} = \Sigma_{yx}\Sigma_{xx}^{-1}\Sigma_{xy}\mathbf{P}_\mathbf{U}, \tag{4.23}$$

$$\mathbf{P}_\mathbf{U}\Sigma\mathbf{P}_\mathbf{U} = \Sigma\mathbf{P}_\mathbf{U}. \tag{4.24}$$

As a consequence, $\Sigma\mathbf{P}_\mathbf{U} = (\Sigma\mathbf{P}_\mathbf{U})^\top = \mathbf{P}_\mathbf{U}\Sigma$, as claimed in 4.1(iii).   □

Baldi and Hornik (1989) used these properties to show that, under certain conditions, the expected loss has a unique global minimum (up to an equivalence) and that all other critical points are saddle points. Recently, Nouiehed and Razaviyayn (2018) and Zhu et al. (2020) extended such results to show that all saddle points are strict. Recall that a critical point is a strict saddle if the Hessian evaluated at this point has a strictly negative eigenvalue, indicating that not only it is not a local minimum, but also the objective function has a negative curvature at this point. The following theorem characterizes the landscape of the risk functional for single-hidden-layer linear networks.

Theorem 4.2. *Assume Σ_{xx} is invertible and $\Sigma = \Sigma_{yx}\Sigma_{xx}^{-1}\Sigma_{xy}$ is full rank with n_2 distinct eigenvalues $\lambda_1 > \lambda_2 > \cdots > \lambda_{n_2}$. Let $\Sigma = Q\Lambda Q^{\top}$ be the eigendecomposition of Σ, where the columns of $Q \in \mathbb{R}^{n_2 \times n_2}$ contain the corresponding eigenvectors. Let $Q_{\mathcal{J}}$ denote the submatrix of Q whose columns are indexed by $\mathcal{J}$. Then the following holds.*

- *If U is full column rank, the set of critical points of $\mathcal{R}(U, V)$ is given by*

$$U = Q_{\mathcal{J}}C \quad and \quad V = \Sigma_{xx}^{-1}\Sigma_{xy}Q_{\mathcal{J}}C^{-\top}, \tag{4.25}$$

  where $\mathcal{J}$ is an ordered subset of $[n_2]$ of cardinality n_1, i.e. $\mathcal{J} \subset [n_2]$ and $|\mathcal{J}| = n_1$, and $C \in \mathbb{R}^{n_1 \times n_1}$ is an arbitrary invertible matrix.
- *If U is full column rank, then critical points with $\mathcal{J} \neq [n_1]$ are strict saddles, i.e., the Hessian evaluated at these points has a strictly negative eigenvalue, while critical points with $\mathcal{J} = [n_1]$ are global minima. Specifically, the set of global minima (U, V) of the risk $\mathcal{R}$ is given by*

$$U = Q_{1 : n_1}C,$$
$$V = \Sigma_{xx}^{-1}\Sigma_{xy}Q_{1 : n_1}C^{-\top}, \tag{4.26}$$
$$UV^{\top} = Q_{1 : n_1}Q_{1 : n_1}^{\top}\Sigma_{yx}\Sigma_{xx}^{-1},$$

  where C is an arbitrary invertible matrix.
- *If U is rank deficient then any critical point is a strict saddle.*

Proof The proof of part (i) is based on Baldi and Hornik (1989), while the proofs of parts (ii) and (iii) are based on Nouiehed and Razaviyayn (2018) and Zhu et al. (2020). For part (i), note that

$$P_{Q^{\top}U} = Q^{\top}U(U^{\top}QQ^{\top}U)^{-1}U^{\top}Q = Q^{\top}U(U^{\top}U)^{-1}U^{\top}Q = Q^{\top}P_UQ,$$

which together with Lemma 4.1(iii) gives

$$P_{Q^{\top}U}\Lambda = Q^{\top}P_UQ\Lambda Q^{\top}Q = Q^{\top}P_U\Sigma Q = Q^{\top}\Sigma P_UQ = \Lambda P_{Q^{\top}U}.$$

Since Λ is a diagonal matrix with diagonal entries $\lambda_1 > \lambda_2 > \cdots > \lambda_{n_2} > 0$, it follows that $\mathbf{P_{Q^\top U}}$ is also a diagonal matrix. Notice that $\mathbf{P_{Q^\top U}}$ is an orthogonal projector of rank n_1, i.e., it has n_1 eigenvalues equal to 1 and $n_2 - n_1$ eigenvalues equal to 0. Therefore $\mathbf{P_{Q^\top U}} = \mathbf{I}_{\mathcal{J}}\mathbf{I}_{\mathcal{J}}^\top$, where $\mathcal{J} \subset [n_2]$ is an ordered subset of $[n_2]$ with cardinality $|\mathcal{J}| = n_1$. Here we denote by $\mathbf{I}_{\mathcal{J}}$ the submatrix of the identity matrix $\mathbf{I}$ obtained by keeping only the columns indexed by $\mathcal{J}$. It follows that

$$\mathbf{P_U} = \mathbf{Q}\mathbf{P_{Q^\top U}}\mathbf{Q}^\top = \mathbf{Q}\mathbf{I}_{\mathcal{J}}\mathbf{I}_{\mathcal{J}}^\top\mathbf{Q}^\top = \mathbf{Q}_{\mathcal{J}}\mathbf{Q}_{\mathcal{J}}^\top,$$

which implies that $\mathbf{U}$ and $\mathbf{Q}_{\mathcal{J}}$ have the same column spaces. Thus, there exists an invertible $n_1 \times n_1$ matrix $\mathbf{C}$ such that $\mathbf{U} = \mathbf{Q}_{\mathcal{J}}\mathbf{C}$. Now according to Lemma 4.1(ii), we have $\mathbf{V} = \mathbf{\Sigma}_{\mathbf{xx}}^{-1}\mathbf{\Sigma}_{\mathbf{xy}}\mathbf{Q}_{\mathcal{J}}\mathbf{C}^{-\top}$.

We now prove the first statement in part (ii), i.e., for any $\mathcal{J} \neq [n_1]$, the corresponding critical point has strictly negative curvature. Towards that goal, standard computations give the Hessian quadrature form[8]

$$\nabla^2\mathcal{R}(\mathbf{U}, \mathbf{V})[\Delta, \Delta] = \|(\mathbf{U}\Delta_{\mathbf{V}}^\top + \Delta_{\mathbf{U}}\mathbf{V}^\top)\mathbf{\Sigma}_{\mathbf{xx}}^{1/2}\|_F^2 + 2\langle \Delta_{\mathbf{U}}\Delta_{\mathbf{V}}^\top, \mathbf{U}\mathbf{V}^\top\mathbf{\Sigma}_{\mathbf{xx}} - \mathbf{\Sigma}_{\mathbf{yx}}\rangle. \quad (4.27)$$

for any $\Delta = (\Delta_{\mathbf{U}}, \Delta_{\mathbf{V}}) \in \mathbb{R}^{n_2 \times n_1} \times \mathbb{R}^{n_0 \times n_1}$.

Since $\mathcal{J} \neq [n_1]$, there exists $k \leq n_1$ such that $k \notin \mathcal{J}$. Let J be the largest element of $\mathcal{J}$, and choose $\Delta_{\mathbf{U}} = \mathbf{q}_k\mathbf{e}_{n_1}^\top\mathbf{C}$ and $\Delta_{\mathbf{V}} = \mathbf{\Sigma}_{\mathbf{xx}}^{-1}\mathbf{\Sigma}_{\mathbf{xy}}\mathbf{q}_k\mathbf{e}_{n_1}^\top\mathbf{C}^{-\top}$, where $\mathbf{q}_k$ is the kth column of $\mathbf{Q}$ and $\mathbf{e}_{n_1}$ is the n_1th standard basis vector of appropriate dimension, i.e. all entries of $\mathbf{e}_{n_1} \in \mathbb{R}^{n_1}$ are zero except for the last entry, which is equal to 1. The first term in (4.27) reduces to

$$\|(\mathbf{U}\Delta_{\mathbf{V}}^\top + \Delta_{\mathbf{U}}\mathbf{V}^\top)\mathbf{\Sigma}_{\mathbf{xx}}^{1/2}\|_F^2 = \|\mathbf{Q}_{\mathcal{J}}\mathbf{e}_{n_1}\mathbf{q}_k^\top\mathbf{\Sigma}_{\mathbf{yx}}\mathbf{\Sigma}_{\mathbf{xx}}^{-1/2} + \mathbf{q}_k\mathbf{e}_{n_1}^\top\mathbf{Q}_{\mathcal{J}}^\top\mathbf{\Sigma}_{\mathbf{yx}}\mathbf{\Sigma}_{\mathbf{xx}}^{-1/2}\|_F^2$$
$$= \|\mathbf{q}_J\mathbf{q}_k^\top\mathbf{\Sigma}_{\mathbf{yx}}\mathbf{\Sigma}_{\mathbf{xx}}^{-1/2}\|_F^2 + \|\mathbf{q}_k\mathbf{q}_J^\top\mathbf{\Sigma}_{\mathbf{yx}}\mathbf{\Sigma}_{\mathbf{xx}}^{-1/2}\|_F^2$$
$$\leq \|\mathbf{q}_k^\top\mathbf{\Sigma}_{\mathbf{yx}}\mathbf{\Sigma}_{\mathbf{xx}}^{-1/2}\|_2^2 + \|\mathbf{q}_J^\top\mathbf{\Sigma}_{\mathbf{yx}}\mathbf{\Sigma}_{\mathbf{xx}}^{-1/2}\|_2^2$$
$$= \lambda_k + \lambda_J.$$

Similarly, the second term in (4.27) can be computed as

$$\langle \Delta_{\mathbf{U}}\Delta_{\mathbf{V}}^\top, \mathbf{U}\mathbf{V}^\top\mathbf{\Sigma}_{\mathbf{xx}} - \mathbf{\Sigma}_{\mathbf{yx}}\rangle = \langle \mathbf{q}_k\mathbf{q}_k^\top\mathbf{\Sigma}_{\mathbf{yx}}\mathbf{\Sigma}_{\mathbf{xx}}^{-1}, \mathbf{Q}_{\mathcal{J}}\mathbf{Q}_{\mathcal{J}}^\top\mathbf{\Sigma}_{\mathbf{yx}} - \mathbf{\Sigma}_{\mathbf{yx}}\rangle$$
$$= -\langle \mathbf{q}_k\mathbf{q}_k^\top\mathbf{\Sigma}_{\mathbf{yx}}\mathbf{\Sigma}_{\mathbf{xx}}^{-1}, \mathbf{\Sigma}_{\mathbf{yx}}\rangle = -\lambda_k.$$

---

[8] For a scalar function $f(\mathbf{W}): \mathbb{R}^{m \times n} \to \mathbb{R}$, its Hessian $\nabla^2 f(\mathbf{W})$ is a 4D tensor, or an $(mn) \times (mn)$ matrix if we vectorize the variable $\mathbf{W}$. Alternatively, we can represent the Hessian by a bilinear form defined via $[\nabla^2 f(\mathbf{W})](\mathbf{A}, \mathbf{B}) = \sum_{i,j,k,l} \frac{\partial^2 f(\mathbf{W})}{\partial W_{ij} \partial W_{kl}} A_{ij} B_{kl}$ for any $\mathbf{A}, \mathbf{B} \in \mathbb{R}^{m \times n}$. When $n = 1$, i.e., $\nabla^2 f(\mathbf{W}) \in \mathbb{R}^{m \times m}$ and $\mathbf{A}$ and $\mathbf{B}$ are vectors, this bilinear form reduces to the standard matrix-vector multiplication $[\nabla^2 f(\mathbf{W})](\mathbf{A}, \mathbf{B}) = \mathbf{A}^\top \nabla^2 f(\mathbf{W})\mathbf{B}$. Thus, using this bilinear form lets us represent the Hessian in a simple way even when the variable is a matrix. Also, without explicitly computing the eigenvalues of $\nabla^2 f(\mathbf{W})$, we know that it has a strictly negative eigenvalue if we can find a direction $\Delta \in \mathbb{R}^{m \times n}$ such that $[\nabla^2 f(\mathbf{W})](\Delta, \Delta) < 0$. Note that this quadratic form appears naturally in the Taylor expansion $f(\mathbf{W} + \Delta) = f(\mathbf{W}) + \langle \nabla f(\mathbf{W}), \Delta \rangle + \frac{1}{2}[\nabla^2 f(\mathbf{W})](\Delta, \Delta) + \cdots$, which indeed provides a simple but very useful trick for computing $[\nabla^2 f(\mathbf{W})](\Delta, \Delta)$, as long as $f(\mathbf{W} + \Delta)$ can be easily expanded. For example, when $f(\mathbf{W}) = \frac{1}{2}\|\mathbf{Y} - \mathbf{W}\|_F^2$, we have $f(\mathbf{W} + \Delta) = \frac{1}{2}\|\mathbf{Y} - \mathbf{W} - \Delta\|_F^2 = \frac{1}{2}\|\mathbf{Y} - \mathbf{W}\|_F^2 + \langle \mathbf{W} - \mathbf{Y}, \Delta \rangle + \frac{1}{2}\|\Delta\|_F^2$, which implies that $[\nabla^2 f(\mathbf{W})](\Delta, \Delta) = \|\Delta\|_F^2$.

Therefore, since $k \leq n_1$ and $J > n_1$, we have

$$\nabla^2 \mathcal{R}(\mathbf{U}, \mathbf{V})[\Delta, \Delta] = \lambda_k + \lambda_J - 2\lambda_k = \lambda_J - \lambda_k < 0.$$

As a consequence, all critical points with $\mathcal{J} \neq [n_1]$ are strict saddles, and all critical points with $\mathcal{J} = [n_1]$ are global minima.

To show part (iii), notice that when $\mathrm{rank}(\mathbf{U}) < n_1$, there exists a non-zero vector $\mathbf{a} \in \mathbb{R}^{n_1}$ such that $\mathbf{Ua} = 0$. Since $\boldsymbol{\Sigma}_{\mathbf{xx}}$ and $\boldsymbol{\Sigma} = \boldsymbol{\Sigma}_{\mathbf{yx}}\boldsymbol{\Sigma}_{\mathbf{xx}}^{-1}\boldsymbol{\Sigma}_{\mathbf{xy}}$ are assumed to be invertible, $\boldsymbol{\Sigma}_{\mathbf{xy}}$ must have full column rank n_2, hence $n_2 \leq n_0$. Since the rank of $\mathbf{UV}^\top\boldsymbol{\Sigma}_{\mathbf{xx}}$ is at most the rank of $\mathbf{U}$ and $\boldsymbol{\Sigma}_{\mathbf{yx}}$ has rank n_2, we know that $\mathbf{UV}^\top\boldsymbol{\Sigma}_{\mathbf{xx}} - \boldsymbol{\Sigma}_{\mathbf{yx}} \neq 0$. Without loss of generality, we assume its (i, j)th entry is non-zero and choose $\Delta_{\mathbf{U}} = \mathbf{e}_i\mathbf{a}^\top$ and $\Delta_{\mathbf{V}} = \alpha\tilde{\mathbf{e}}_j\mathbf{a}^\top$, where $\mathbf{e}_i \in \mathbb{R}^{n_2}$ and $\tilde{\mathbf{e}}_j \in \mathbb{R}^{n_0}$ are the standard basis vectors, whose entries are equal to zero except for their ith and jth elements, respectively. With this, we compute the first term in (4.27) as

$$\|(\mathbf{U}\Delta_{\mathbf{V}}^\top + \Delta_{\mathbf{U}}\mathbf{V}^\top)\boldsymbol{\Sigma}_{\mathbf{xx}}^{1/2}\|_F^2 = \|(\alpha\mathbf{Ua}\tilde{\mathbf{e}}_j^\top + \mathbf{e}_i\mathbf{a}^\top\mathbf{V}^\top)\boldsymbol{\Sigma}_{\mathbf{xx}}^{1/2}\|_F^2 = \|\mathbf{e}_i\mathbf{a}^\top\mathbf{V}^\top\boldsymbol{\Sigma}_{\mathbf{xx}}^{1/2}\|_F^2$$

and the second term in (4.27) by writing

$$\langle \Delta_{\mathbf{U}}\Delta_{\mathbf{V}}^\top, \mathbf{UV}^\top\boldsymbol{\Sigma}_{\mathbf{xx}} - \boldsymbol{\Sigma}_{\mathbf{yx}} \rangle = \langle \alpha\|\mathbf{a}\|^2\mathbf{e}_i\tilde{\mathbf{e}}_j^\top, \mathbf{UV}^\top\boldsymbol{\Sigma}_{\mathbf{xx}} - \boldsymbol{\Sigma}_{\mathbf{yx}} \rangle$$
$$= \alpha\|\mathbf{a}\|^2(\mathbf{UV}^\top\boldsymbol{\Sigma}_{\mathbf{xx}} - \boldsymbol{\Sigma}_{\mathbf{yx}})_{ij},$$

from which it follows that

$$\nabla^2 \mathcal{R}(\mathbf{U}, \mathbf{V})[\Delta, \Delta] = \|\mathbf{e}_i\mathbf{a}^\top\mathbf{V}^\top\boldsymbol{\Sigma}_{\mathbf{xx}}^{1/2}\|_F^2 + 2\alpha\|\mathbf{a}\|^2(\mathbf{UV}^\top\boldsymbol{\Sigma}_{\mathbf{xx}} - \boldsymbol{\Sigma}_{\mathbf{yx}})_{ij},$$

where the right-hand side can always be made negative by choosing an appropriate α. Thus, $\mathcal{R}$ has negative curvature when $\mathbf{U}$ is rank deficient. $\square$

Theorem 4.2 implies that, under certain conditions on the input-output covariance matrices, $\boldsymbol{\Sigma}_{\mathbf{xx}}$, $\boldsymbol{\Sigma}_{\mathbf{yx}}$ and $\boldsymbol{\Sigma}_{\mathbf{yy}}$, both the expected and empirical risk of a single-hidden layer linear neural network with the squared loss have no spurious local minima and the saddle points are strict. This benign geometry ensures that a number of local search algorithms (such as gradient descent) converge to a global minimum when training a single-hidden layer linear neural network (Ge et al., 2015; Lee et al., 2019).

But what if the conditions in Theorem 4.2 are violated? When $\boldsymbol{\Sigma}_{\mathbf{xx}}$ is invertible but $\boldsymbol{\Sigma}$ is rank deficient, a more sophisticated analysis shows that one can still characterize the set of critical points with full column rank $\mathbf{U}$ as in (4.25) but with a slightly different form (Zhu et al., 2020). Then, following the sequence of arguments in the proof of Theorem 4.2, one can show that a critical point $(\mathbf{U}, \mathbf{V})$ that is not a global minimum has strictly negative curvature, by finding a direction (which depends on whether $\mathbf{U}$ is full column rank) such that the corresponding Hessian quadrature form is strictly negative.

When $\mathbf{\Sigma_{xx}}$ is not invertible, it seems difficult to characterize all the critical points as in (4.25). Nevertheless, by exploiting the *local openness* property of the risk $\mathcal{R}(\mathbf{U}, \mathbf{V})$, Nouiehed and Razaviyayn (2018) showed that any local minimum is a global minimum for all possible input–output covariance matrices, $\mathbf{\Sigma_{xx}}$, $\mathbf{\Sigma_{yx}}$, and $\mathbf{\Sigma_{yy}}$. We summarize these results in the following theorem, but we refer to Nouiehed and Razaviyayn (2018) and Zhu et al. (2020) for the full proof.

Theorem 4.3 (Nouiehed and Razaviyayn, 2018; Zhu et al., 2020). *Any local minimum of $\mathcal{R}$ is a global minimum. Moreover, if $\mathbf{\Sigma_{xx}}$ is invertible then any critical point of $\mathcal{R}$ that is not a global minimum is a strict saddle point.*

4.3.2 Deep Linear Networks with Squared Loss

We now extend the analysis of the optimization landscape of single-hidden-layer linear networks, trained using an unregularized squared loss, to deep linear networks. We consider a network with dimensions $n_0, n_1, \ldots, n_L$, where n_0 is the input dimension, n_L is the output dimension, $n_1, \ldots, n_{L-1}$ are the hidden-layer dimensions, $\mathbf{W}^{[l]} \in \mathbb{R}^{n_l \times n_{l-1}}$ is the matrix of weights between layers $l-1$ and l, and L is the number of weight layers. The hypothesis space $\mathcal{F}$ can be parametrized in terms of the network weights $\mathbf{W} = \{\mathbf{W}^{[l]}\}_{l=1}^L$ as

$$\mathcal{F} = \{f \in \mathcal{Y}^{\mathcal{X}} : f(\mathbf{x}) = \mathbf{W}^{[L]}\mathbf{W}^{[L-1]} \cdots \mathbf{W}^{[1]}\mathbf{x}, \text{ where } \mathbf{W}^{[l]} \in \mathbb{R}^{n_l \times n_{l-1}}\}. \quad (4.28)$$

Therefore, the problem of minimizing the expected risk becomes

$$\min_{\{\mathbf{W}^{[l]}\}_{l=1}^L} \left[\mathcal{R}(\mathbf{W}) \doteq \mathbb{E}_{\mathbf{x},\mathbf{y}}[\|\mathbf{y} - \mathbf{W}^{[L]}\mathbf{W}^{[L-1]} \cdots \mathbf{W}^{[1]}\mathbf{x}\|_2^2] \right]. \quad (4.29)$$

Similarly to the single-hidden-layer case in (4.14), the expected risk can be rewritten as

$$\mathcal{R}(\mathbf{W}) = \text{trace}(\mathbf{\Sigma_{yy}} - 2\mathbf{\Sigma_{yx}}\mathbf{W}_{1:L}^\top + \mathbf{W}_{1:L}\mathbf{\Sigma_{xx}}\mathbf{W}_{1:L}^\top), \quad (4.30)$$

where $\mathbf{W}_{L:1} = \mathbf{W}^{[L]}\mathbf{W}^{[L-1]} \cdots \mathbf{W}^{[1]}$. As with to the single-hidden-layer case in (4.15), the problem of minimizing the empirical risk

$$\min_{\{\mathbf{W}^{[l]}\}_{l=1}^L} \left[\mathcal{R}_S(\mathbf{W}) \doteq \frac{1}{m}\|\mathbf{Y} - \mathbf{W}_{L:1}\mathbf{X}\|_F^2 \right], \quad (4.31)$$

where $\mathbf{X}$ and $\mathbf{Y}$ are the input and output data matrices, is equivalent to minimizing $\mathcal{R}(\mathbf{W})$, except that $\mathbf{\Sigma_{xx}}$, $\mathbf{\Sigma_{xy}}$ and $\mathbf{\Sigma_{yy}}$ need to be substituted by their empirical estimates $\frac{1}{m}\mathbf{X}\mathbf{X}^\top$, $\frac{1}{m}\mathbf{X}\mathbf{Y}^\top$, and $\frac{1}{m}\mathbf{Y}\mathbf{Y}^\top$, respectively. Thus, the analysis of the optimization landscape of both the expected risk and the empirical risk can be done by analyzing the landscape of $\mathcal{R}(\mathbf{W})$. As discussed in §4.3.1, when there is no constraint on $\mathbf{W}_{L:1}$ (e.g., when the dimensions of the hidden layers is sufficiently large) and $\Sigma_{\mathbf{xx}}$ is invertible, the optimal input–output weight matrix is given by $\mathbf{W}^*_{L:1} = \Sigma_{\mathbf{yx}}\Sigma_{\mathbf{xx}}^{-1}$. However, this result does not provide a characterization of the optimal weight matrices $\mathbf{W}^{[l]}$ for each layer. Thus, the challenge in characterizing the landscape of $\mathcal{R}(\mathbf{W})$ is to understand the effect of the low-rank constraint $n_l \leq \min\{n_0, n_L\}$ or to consider the possibility that critical points for $\mathbf{W}^{[l]}$ might not be low-rank.

Recent work by Kawaguchi (2016) provided a formal analysis of the optimization landscape of $\mathcal{R}(\mathbf{W})$. In particular, by using a purely deterministic approach that exploits both first-order and second-order information at critical points (as also used in the proof of Theorem 4.2), Kawaguchi characterized the following properties of critical points of $\mathcal{R}(\mathbf{W})$.

Theorem 4.4 (Kawaguchi, 2016). *Assume that $\Sigma_{\mathbf{xx}}$ and $\Sigma_{\mathbf{xy}}$ are of full rank with $n_L \leq n_0$ and that $\Sigma = \Sigma_{\mathbf{yx}}\Sigma_{\mathbf{xx}}^{-1}\Sigma_{\mathbf{xy}}$ is of full rank with n_L distinct eigenvalues. Then $\mathcal{R}(\mathbf{W})$ has the following properties:*

- *Any local minimum is a global minimum.*
- *Every critical point that is not a global minimum is a saddle point.*
- *A saddle point $\mathbf{W}$ such that $\mathrm{rank}(\mathbf{W}^{[L-1]}\cdots\mathbf{W}^{[2]}) = \min_{1\leq l\leq L-1} n_l$ is strict, i.e., the Hessian of $\mathcal{R}$ at $\mathbf{W}$ has a strictly negative eigenvalue.*
- *A saddle point $\mathbf{W}$ such that $\mathrm{rank}(\mathbf{W}^{[L-1]}\cdots\mathbf{W}^{[2]}) < \min_{1\leq l\leq L-1} n_l$ may not be strict, i.e., the Hessian at $\mathbf{W}$ may not have any negative eigenvalues.*

On the one hand, similarly to Theorem 4.2 for one-hidden-layer linear networks, Theorem 4.4 guarantees that, under similar conditions on $\Sigma_{\mathbf{xx}}$ and $\Sigma_{\mathbf{xy}}$, any local minimum of the risk is a global minimum. On the other hand, unlike the results for single-hidden-layer linear networks where every saddle point is strict, Theorem 4.4 shows that networks with two or more hidden layers can have "bad" (non-strict) saddle points, which are also referred to as degenerate saddle points or higher-order saddle points, since the first- and second-order derivatives cannot distinguish them from local optima. To illustrate why depth introduces degenerate saddle points, consider the simplest case where $L = 3$ and $n_0 = n_1 = n_2 = n_3 = 1$. The risk then becomes

$$\mathcal{R}(w^{[1]}, w^{[2]}, w^{[3]}) = \sigma_{\mathbf{yy}} - 2\sigma_{\mathbf{yx}}w^{[1]}w^{[2]}w^{[3]} + \sigma_{\mathbf{xx}}(w^{[1]}w^{[2]}w^{[3]})^2. \qquad (4.32)$$

By computing the gradient (first-order derivatives) and Hessian (second-order derivatives), it is easy to see that $(0,0,0)$ is a critical point but the Hessian is the zero matrix, which has no negative eigenvalues. This also holds true for general deep linear networks. Intuitively, when the network has more layers, the objective function tends to be flatter at the origin, making the origin a higher-order saddle. This is similar to the fact that 0 is a critical point of both the functions $(1 - u^2)^2$ and

$(1 - u^3)^2$: the former has a negative second-order derivative at 0, while the latter has a zero second-order derivative at 0.

We end our discussion of deep linear networks by noting that there is recent work that improves upon Theorem 4.4, mostly with weaker conditions to guarantee the absence of spurious local minima. For example, to show that any local minimum is a global minimum, Lu and Kawaguchi (2017) require Σ_{xx} and Σ_{xy} to be of full rank, while Laurent and Brecht (2018) require only that the size of the hidden layers be larger than or equal to the input or output dimensions, i.e., $n_1, \ldots, n_{L-1} \geq \min\{n_0, n_L\}$, which could potentially help guide the design of network architectures.

4.4 Optimization Landscape of Nonlinear Networks

In this section, we review work by Haeffele and Vidal (2015, 2017) on the analysis of the landscape of a class of nonlinear networks with positively homogeneous activation functions, such as rectified linear units (ReLU), max-pooling, etc. Critical to the analysis tools that are employed is to consider networks regularized by a function that is also positively homogeneous and of the same degree as the network mapping. These results apply to a class of deep networks whose output is formed as the sum of the outputs of multiple positively homogeneous subnetworks connected in parallel (see the right-hand panel in Figure 4.3), where the architecture of a subnetwork can be arbitrary provided that the overall mapping of the subnetwork is a positively homogeneous function of the network parameters. Specifically, we show that, when the network is sufficiently wide, a path to a global minimizer always exists from any initialization (i.e., local minima which require one to increase the objective in order to escape are guaranteed not to exist).

As a motivating example, before considering the case of deep positively homogeneous networks, in §4.4.1 we revisit the case of shallow linear networks discussed in §4.3.1, as this simple case conveys the key insights behind the more general cases discussed in §4.4.2. The primary difference from the case of shallow linear networks discussed in §4.3.1 is that, rather than fixing the number of columns in $(\mathbf{U}, \mathbf{V})$ a priori, we constrain the hypothesis space using Tykhonov regularization on $(\mathbf{U}, \mathbf{V})$ while allowing the number of columns in $(\mathbf{U}, \mathbf{V})$ to be variable. As we will see, the Tykhonov regularization results in the promotion of low-rank solutions even though we do not place an explicit constraint on the number of columns in $(\mathbf{U}, \mathbf{V})$. The extension of these results to deep positively homogeneous networks will highlight the importance of using similar explicit regularization to constrain the overall size of the network.

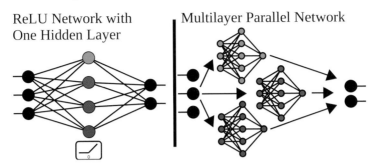

ReLU Network with
One Hidden Layer

Multilayer Parallel Network

Figure 4.3 Example networks. (Left panel) ReLU network with a single hidden layer with the mapping Φ_{n_1} described by the equation in (4.45) with ($n_1 = 4$). Each color corresponds to one element of the elemental mapping $\phi(\mathbf{X}, \mathbf{W}_i^{[1]}, \mathbf{W}_i^{[2]})$. The colored hidden units have rectifying nonlinearities, while the black units are linear. (Right panel) Multilayer ReLU network with three fully connected parallel subnetworks ($r = 3$), where each color corresponds to the subnetwork described by the elemental mapping $\phi(\mathbf{X}, \mathbf{W}_i^{[1]}, \mathbf{W}_i^{[2]}, \mathbf{W}_i^{[3]}, \mathbf{W}_i^{[4]})$. © 2017 IEEE. Reprinted, with permission, from Haeffele and Vidal (2017).

4.4.1 Motivating Example

Consider the empirical risk minimization problem in (4.15) for a single-hidden-layer linear network with n_0 inputs, n_1 hidden neurons, and n_2 outputs, which is equivalent to

$$\min_{\mathbf{U},\mathbf{V}} \tfrac{1}{2}\|\mathbf{Y} - \mathbf{U}\mathbf{V}^\top\mathbf{X}\|_F^2, \tag{4.33}$$

where $\mathbf{U} \in \mathbb{R}^{n_2 \times n_1}$ and $\mathbf{V} \in \mathbb{R}^{n_0 \times n_1}$ are the network weights. We showed in §4.3.1 that, under certain conditions, this problem has no spurious local minima and all saddle points are strict. In particular, we assumed that the number of hidden neurons is fixed and limited by the input and output dimensions, specifically, $n_1 \leq \min\{n_0, n_2\}$.

In what follows, we relax this constraint on the network size and optimize over both the network size and weights. Arguably, this requires some form of regularization on the network weights that allows us to control the growth of the network size. A commonly used regularizer is weight decay, $\Theta(\mathbf{U}, \mathbf{V}) = \|\mathbf{U}\|_F^2 + \|\mathbf{V}\|_F^2$, also known as Tykhonov regularization. Here, we use weight decay to regularize (4.33) in the particular case where $\mathbf{X} = \mathbf{I}$ for simplicity of presentation,[9]

$$\min_{n_1 \in \mathbb{N}^+} \min_{\substack{\mathbf{U} \in \mathbb{R}^{n_2 \times n_1} \\ \mathbf{V} \in \mathbb{R}^{n_0 \times n_1}}} \left[\frac{1}{2}\|\mathbf{Y} - \mathbf{U}\mathbf{V}^\top\|_F^2 + \frac{\lambda}{2}(\|\mathbf{U}\|_F^2 + \|\mathbf{V}\|_F^2)\right], \tag{4.34}$$

where $\lambda > 0$ is a regularization parameter.

---

[9] Note that with this simplification the problem becomes an unsupervised learning problem (matrix factorization) instead of the original supervised learning problem (linear network training).

There are several reasons for considering this particular case. First, (4.34) can be understood as a matrix factorization problem where, given a matrix $\mathbf{Y} \in \mathbb{R}^{n_2 \times n_0}$, the goal is to factorize it as $\mathbf{Y} \approx \mathbf{U}\mathbf{V}^\top$, where $\mathbf{U} \in \mathbb{R}^{n_2 \times n_1}$ and $\mathbf{V} \in \mathbb{R}^{n_0 \times n_1}$. Second, it is known that weight decay is closely connected to the nuclear norm of the product of the factorized matrices $\mathbf{Z} = \mathbf{U}\mathbf{V}^\top$; recall that the nuclear norm $\|\mathbf{Z}\|_*$ is the sum of the singular values of a matrix $\mathbf{Z}$, from the so-called variational form of the nuclear norm (Srebro et al., 2004):

$$\|\mathbf{Z}\|_* = \min_{n_1 \in \mathbb{N}^+} \min_{\substack{\mathbf{U},\mathbf{V}: \\ \mathbf{U}\mathbf{V}^\top = \mathbf{Z}}} \frac{1}{2}(\|\mathbf{U}\|_F^2 + \|\mathbf{V}\|_F^2), \tag{4.35}$$

where the above equation states that, given a matrix $\mathbf{Z}$, if one considers all possible factorizations of $\mathbf{Z}$ into $\mathbf{U}\mathbf{V}^\top$ then a factorization $\mathbf{Z} = \mathbf{U}\mathbf{V}^\top$ which minimizes the Tykhonov regularization on $(\mathbf{U}, \mathbf{V})$ will be equal to the nuclear norm of $\mathbf{Z}$. Third, recall that the nuclear norm is a convex relaxation of the rank of the matrix which is known to encourage low-rank solutions. As a result, this allows us to control the network width, n_1, and ensure capacity control via matrix factorization techniques without placing explicit constraints on n_1. Indeed, owing to the variational definition of the nuclear norm in (4.35), the objective problem in (4.34) is closely related to a *convex* optimization problem with nuclear norm regularization:

$$\min_{\mathbf{Z}} \left[\frac{1}{2} \|\mathbf{Y} - \mathbf{Z}\|_F^2 + \lambda \|\mathbf{Z}\|_* \right]. \tag{4.36}$$

The strong similarity between (4.35) and the regularizer in (4.34) suggest we look at the *convex* problem in (4.36), whose solution can be found in closed form from the SVD of $\mathbf{Y}$. Specifically, if $\mathbf{Y} = \mathbf{U_Y}\boldsymbol{\Sigma_Y}\mathbf{V_Y^\top}$ is the SVD of $\mathbf{Y}$ then the global minimizer of (4.36) is given by the singular value thresholding operator $\mathbf{Z} = \mathcal{D}_\lambda(\mathbf{Y}) = \mathbf{U_Y}(\boldsymbol{\Sigma_Y} - \lambda\mathbf{I})_+\mathbf{V_Y^\top}$, where the singular vectors of $\mathbf{Y}$ (the columns of $\mathbf{U_Y}$ and $\mathbf{V_Y}$) are maintained while the singular values of $\mathbf{Y}$ (the diagonal entries of $\boldsymbol{\Sigma_Y}$) are shrunk by λ and then thresholded at zero, i.e., $a_+ = \max(a, 0)$.

But how do these results for the convex problem in (4.36) relate to solutions to the non-convex problem in (4.34)? First, observe that (4.35) implies that the convex problem provides a global lower bound for the non-convex problem. Specifically, for any $(\mathbf{U}, \mathbf{V}, \mathbf{Z})$ such that $\mathbf{Z} = \mathbf{U}\mathbf{V}^\top$, (4.35) implies that

$$\frac{1}{2}\|\mathbf{Y} - \mathbf{Z}\|_F^2 + \lambda\|\mathbf{Z}\|_* \leq \frac{1}{2}\|\mathbf{Y} - \mathbf{U}\mathbf{V}^\top\|_F^2 + \frac{\lambda}{2}(\|\mathbf{U}\|_F^2 + \|\mathbf{V}^2\|_F^2). \tag{4.37}$$

Additionally, this lower bound is always tight once n_1 becomes sufficiently large, in the sense that for any $\mathbf{Z}$ one can find a $(\mathbf{U}, \mathbf{V})$ such that $\mathbf{Z} = \mathbf{U}\mathbf{V}^\top$ and the inequality above becomes an equality. As a result, a global minimum $(\mathbf{U}, \mathbf{V})$ of the non-convex problem (4.34) gives a global minimum $\mathbf{Z} = \mathbf{U}\mathbf{V}^\top$ for the convex problem (4.36), and owing to the global lower bound in (4.37), this further implies that we have a global minimum of both the convex and non-convex problems, as we show next.

Theorem 4.5. *Let* $\mathbf{u}_i$ *and* $\mathbf{v}_i$ *be the* ith *columns of* $\mathbf{U}$ *and* $\mathbf{V}$, *respectively. If* $(\mathbf{U}, \mathbf{V}, n_1)$ *is a local minimum of* (4.34) *such that for some* $i \in [n_1]$ *we have* $\mathbf{u}_i = \mathbf{0}$ *and* $\mathbf{v}_i = \mathbf{0}$ *then*

(i) $\mathbf{Z} = \mathbf{U}\mathbf{V}^\top$ *is a global minimum of* (4.36) *and*

(ii) $(\mathbf{U}, \mathbf{V}, n_1)$ *is a global minimum of* (4.34) *and* (4.35).

Proof Recall that the Fenchel conjugate of a function Ω is defined as $\Omega^*(\mathbf{Q}) = \sup_{\mathbf{Z}} \langle \mathbf{Q}, \mathbf{Z} \rangle - \Omega(\mathbf{Z})$, leading to Fenchel's inequality $\langle \mathbf{Q}, \mathbf{Z} \rangle \le \Omega(\mathbf{Z}) + \Omega^*(\mathbf{Q})$. Also recall that the subgradient of a convex function Ω at $\mathbf{Z}$ is defined as

$$\partial \Omega(\mathbf{Z}) = \{\mathbf{Q} \colon \Omega(\bar{\mathbf{Z}}) \ge \Omega(\mathbf{Z}) + \langle \mathbf{Q}, \bar{\mathbf{Z}} - \mathbf{Z} \rangle, \text{ for all } \bar{\mathbf{Z}}\}$$
$$= \{\mathbf{Q} \colon \langle \mathbf{Q}, \mathbf{Z} \rangle = \Omega(\mathbf{Z}) + \Omega^*(\mathbf{Q})\}.$$

Applying this to the nuclear norm $\Omega(\mathbf{Z}) = \|\mathbf{Z}\|_*$ and using (4.35), we obtain

$$\Omega^*(\mathbf{Q}) = \sup_{\mathbf{Z}} \langle \mathbf{Q}, \mathbf{Z} \rangle - \|\mathbf{Z}\|_* = \sup_{n_1 \in \mathbb{N}^+} \sup_{\tilde{\mathbf{U}}, \tilde{\mathbf{V}}} \langle \mathbf{Q}, \tilde{\mathbf{U}}\tilde{\mathbf{V}}^\top \rangle - \frac{1}{2}(\|\tilde{\mathbf{U}}\|_F^2 + \|\tilde{\mathbf{V}}\|_F^2)$$

$$= \sup_{n_1 \in \mathbb{N}^+} \sup_{\tilde{\mathbf{U}}, \tilde{\mathbf{V}}} \sum_{i=1}^{n_1} \left(\tilde{\mathbf{u}}_i^\top \mathbf{Q} \tilde{\mathbf{v}}_i - \frac{1}{2}(\|\tilde{\mathbf{u}}_i\|_2^2 + \|\tilde{\mathbf{v}}_i\|_2^2) \right)$$

$$= \begin{cases} 0 & \text{if } \mathbf{u}^\top \mathbf{Q} \mathbf{v} \le \frac{1}{2}(\|\mathbf{u}\|_2^2 + \|\mathbf{v}\|_2^2) \text{ for all } (\mathbf{u}, \mathbf{v}) \\ \infty & \text{else,} \end{cases} \tag{4.38}$$

which then implies that

$$\partial \|\mathbf{Z}\|_* = \left\{ \mathbf{Q} \colon \langle \mathbf{Q}, \mathbf{Z} \rangle = \|\mathbf{Z}\|_* \text{ and } \mathbf{u}^\top \mathbf{Q} \mathbf{v} \le \tfrac{1}{2}(\|\mathbf{u}\|_2^2 + \|\mathbf{v}\|_2^2) \text{ for all}(\mathbf{u}, \mathbf{v}) \right\}. \tag{4.39}$$

To prove (i), we need to show that $0 \in \mathbf{Z} - \mathbf{Y} + \lambda \partial \|\mathbf{Z}\|_*$ or $\mathbf{Y} - \mathbf{Z} \in \lambda \partial \|\mathbf{Z}\|_*$. Let us first show that $\mathbf{Q} = \frac{\mathbf{Y} - \mathbf{Z}}{\lambda}$ satisfies the inequality in (4.39). Assume, without loss of generality, that the last columns of $\mathbf{U}$ and $\mathbf{V}$ are zero, choose any $\mathbf{u} \in \mathbb{R}^{n_2}$, $\mathbf{v} \in \mathbb{R}^{n_0}$, and $\epsilon > 0$, and let $\mathbf{U}_\epsilon = \mathbf{U} + \epsilon^{1/2}\mathbf{u}\mathbf{e}_{n_1}^\top$ and $\mathbf{V}_\epsilon = \mathbf{V} + \epsilon^{1/2}\mathbf{v}\mathbf{e}_{n_1}^\top$, so that $\mathbf{Z}_\epsilon = \mathbf{U}_\epsilon \mathbf{V}_\epsilon^\top = \mathbf{U}\mathbf{V}^\top + \epsilon \mathbf{u}\mathbf{v}^\top = \mathbf{Z} + \epsilon \mathbf{u}\mathbf{v}^\top$. Since $(\mathbf{U}, \mathbf{V}, n_1)$ is a local minimum of (4.34), for all $(\mathbf{u}, \mathbf{v})$ there exists $\delta > 0$ such that for all $\epsilon \in (0, \delta)$ we have:

$$\frac{1}{2}\|\mathbf{Y} - \mathbf{Z}_\epsilon\|_F^2 + \frac{\lambda}{2}(\|\mathbf{U}_\epsilon\|_F^2 + \|\mathbf{V}_\epsilon\|_F^2) - \frac{1}{2}\|\mathbf{Y} - \mathbf{Z}\|_F^2 - \frac{\lambda}{2}(\|\mathbf{U}\|_F^2 + \|\mathbf{V}\|_F^2) \ge 0,$$

$$\frac{1}{2}(-2\langle \mathbf{Y}, \mathbf{Z}_\epsilon - \mathbf{Z} \rangle + \langle \mathbf{Z}_\epsilon + \mathbf{Z}, \mathbf{Z}_\epsilon - \mathbf{Z} \rangle) + \frac{\lambda}{2}(\|\mathbf{U}_\epsilon\|_F^2 - \|\mathbf{U}\|_F^2 + \|\mathbf{V}_\epsilon\|_F^2 - \|\mathbf{V}\|_F^2) \ge 0,$$

$$\frac{\epsilon}{2}(-2\langle \mathbf{Y}, \mathbf{u}\mathbf{v}^\top \rangle + \langle 2\mathbf{Z} + \epsilon \mathbf{u}\mathbf{v}^\top, \mathbf{u}\mathbf{v}^\top \rangle) + \frac{\lambda\epsilon}{2}(\|\mathbf{u}\|_2^2 + \|\mathbf{v}\|_2^2) \ge 0,$$

$$\mathbf{u}^\top(\mathbf{Z} - \mathbf{Y})\mathbf{v} + \frac{\epsilon}{2}\|\mathbf{u}\|_2^2\|\mathbf{v}\|_2^2 + \frac{\lambda}{2}(\|\mathbf{u}\|_2^2 + \|\mathbf{v}\|_2^2) \ge 0.$$

Letting $\epsilon \searrow 0$, gives

$$\mathbf{u}^\top \frac{(\mathbf{Y}-\mathbf{Z})}{\lambda} \mathbf{v} \le \frac{1}{2}(\|\mathbf{u}\|_2^2 + \|\mathbf{v}\|_2^2), \text{ for all } (\mathbf{u}, \mathbf{v})$$

as claimed.

Let us now demonstrate that $\mathbf{Q} = \frac{\mathbf{Y}-\mathbf{Z}}{\lambda}$ satisfies the equality in (4.39). Because the inequality in (4.39) holds, we know that $\Omega^*(\mathbf{Q}) = 0$, which together with Fenchel's inequality gives $\langle \mathbf{Q}, \mathbf{Z} \rangle \le \|\mathbf{Z}\|_*$. Then, since $\mathbf{Z} = \mathbf{U}\mathbf{V}^\top$, it follows from (4.35) that $\|\mathbf{Z}\|_* \le \frac{1}{2}(\|\mathbf{U}\|_F^2 + \|\mathbf{V}\|_F^2)$. Therefore, to show that $\langle \mathbf{Q}, \mathbf{Z} \rangle = \|\mathbf{Z}\|_*$ it suffices to show that $\langle \mathbf{Q}, \mathbf{Z} \rangle = \frac{1}{2}(\|\mathbf{U}\|_F^2 + \|\mathbf{V}\|_F^2)$. For this particular problem it is possible to prove that this equality holds simply by considering the first-order optimality conditions, which must be satisfied since $(\mathbf{U}, \mathbf{V}, n_1)$ is a local minimum:

$$-(\mathbf{Y} - \mathbf{U}\mathbf{V}^\top)\mathbf{V} + \lambda\mathbf{U} = 0 \quad \text{and} \quad -(\mathbf{Y} - \mathbf{U}\mathbf{V}^\top)^\top\mathbf{U} + \lambda\mathbf{V} = 0. \tag{4.40}$$

It follows that

$$\mathbf{U}^\top(\mathbf{Y} - \mathbf{U}\mathbf{V}^\top)\mathbf{V} = \lambda\mathbf{U}^\top\mathbf{U} \quad \text{and} \quad \mathbf{U}^\top(\mathbf{Y} - \mathbf{U}\mathbf{V}^\top)\mathbf{V}^\top = \lambda\mathbf{V}^\top\mathbf{V}. \tag{4.41}$$

Summing, taking the trace, and dividing by λ gives the desired result:

$$\langle \tfrac{\mathbf{Y}-\mathbf{U}\mathbf{V}^\top}{\lambda}, \mathbf{U}\mathbf{V}^\top \rangle = \frac{1}{2}(\|\mathbf{U}\|_F^2 + \|\mathbf{V}\|_F^2) = \|\mathbf{Z}\|_*. \tag{4.42}$$

As a consequence, $\mathbf{W} \in \partial\|\mathbf{Z}\|_*$ and hence $\mathbf{Z} = \mathbf{U}\mathbf{V}^\top$ is a global minimum of the convex problem in (4.36), thus concluding the proof of (i).

As an alternative to the above approach, to develop an intuition for more general results, we will also provide a different proof of the equality in (4.42) without relying on the objective being differentiable with respect to $(\mathbf{U}, \mathbf{V})$ but only requiring the loss function to be differentiable with respect to $\mathbf{Z} = \mathbf{U}\mathbf{V}^\top$. In particular, let $\mathbf{U}_\tau = (1 + \tau)^{1/2}\mathbf{U}$, $\mathbf{V}_\tau = (1 + \tau)^{1/2}\mathbf{V}$, and $\mathbf{Z}_\tau = \mathbf{U}_\tau\mathbf{V}_\tau^\top = (1 + \tau)\mathbf{U}\mathbf{V}^\top = (1 + \tau)\mathbf{Z}$. Again, since $(\mathbf{U}, \mathbf{V}, n_1)$ is a local minimum for $\tau > 0$ sufficiently small we have:

$$\frac{1}{2}\|\mathbf{Y} - \mathbf{Z}_\tau\|_F^2 + \frac{\lambda}{2}(\|\mathbf{U}_\tau\|_F^2 + \|\mathbf{V}_\tau\|_F^2) - \frac{1}{2}\|\mathbf{Y} - \mathbf{Z}\|_F^2 - \frac{\lambda}{2}(\|\mathbf{U}\|_F^2 + \|\mathbf{V}\|_F^2) \ge 0,$$

$$\frac{1}{2}\|\mathbf{Y} - (1 + \tau)\mathbf{Z}\|_F^2 - \frac{1}{2}\|\mathbf{Y} - \mathbf{Z}\|_F^2 + \frac{\lambda}{2}(\tau\|\mathbf{U}\|_F^2 + \tau\|\mathbf{V}\|_F^2) \ge 0,$$

$$\frac{1}{\tau}\left(\frac{1}{2}\|\mathbf{Y} - \mathbf{Z} - \tau\mathbf{Z}\|_F^2 - \frac{1}{2}\|\mathbf{Y} - \mathbf{Z}\|_F^2\right) \ge -\frac{\lambda}{2}(\|\mathbf{U}\|_F^2 + \|\mathbf{V}\|_F^2).$$

Taking the limit $\tau \searrow 0$ (recalling that the above limit on the left-hand side is the directional derivative of the loss in the direction $\mathbf{Z}$) gives:

$$\langle \mathbf{Z} - \mathbf{Y}, \mathbf{Z} \rangle \ge -\frac{\lambda}{2}(\|\mathbf{U}\|_F^2 + \|\mathbf{V}\|_F^2) \implies \langle \tfrac{\mathbf{Y}-\mathbf{U}\mathbf{V}^\top}{\lambda}, \mathbf{U}\mathbf{V}^\top \rangle \le \frac{1}{2}(\|\mathbf{U}\|_F^2 + \|\mathbf{V}\|_F^2).$$

If we let $\overline{\mathbf{U}}_\tau = (1 - \tau)^{1/2}\mathbf{U}$, $\overline{\mathbf{V}}_\tau = (1 - \tau)^{1/2}\mathbf{V}$, and $\overline{\mathbf{Z}}_\tau = \overline{\mathbf{U}}_\tau\overline{\mathbf{V}}_\tau^\top = (1 - \tau)\mathbf{Z}$ then, by repeating an identical set of arguments to those above, we obtain the opposite inequality:

$$\frac{1}{2}\|\mathbf{Y}-\bar{\mathbf{Z}}_\tau\|_F^2 + \frac{\lambda}{2}(\|\bar{\mathbf{U}}_\tau\|_F^2 + \|\bar{\mathbf{V}}_\tau\|_F^2) - \frac{1}{2}\|\mathbf{Y}-\mathbf{Z}\|_F^2 - \frac{\lambda}{2}(\|\mathbf{U}\|_F^2 + \|\mathbf{V}\|_F^2) \geq 0,$$

$$\frac{1}{2}\|\mathbf{Y}-(1-\tau)\mathbf{Z}\|_F^2 - \frac{1}{2}\|\mathbf{Y}-\mathbf{Z}\|_F^2 - \frac{\lambda}{2}(\tau\|\mathbf{U}\|_F^2 + \tau\|\mathbf{V}\|_F^2) \geq 0,$$

$$\frac{1}{\tau}\left(\frac{1}{2}\|\mathbf{Y}-\mathbf{Z}+\tau\mathbf{Z}\|_F^2 - \frac{1}{2}\|\mathbf{Y}-\mathbf{Z}\|_F^2\right) \geq \frac{\lambda}{2}(\|\mathbf{U}\|_F^2 + \|\mathbf{V}\|_F^2).$$

Taking the limit $\tau \searrow 0$ implies

$$\langle \mathbf{Z}-\mathbf{Y},-\mathbf{Z}\rangle \geq \frac{\lambda}{2}(\|\mathbf{U}\|_F^2 + \|\mathbf{V}\|_F^2) \implies \langle \tfrac{\mathbf{Y}-\mathbf{U}\mathbf{V}^\top}{\lambda}, \mathbf{U}\mathbf{V}^\top\rangle \geq \frac{1}{2}(\|\mathbf{U}\|_F^2 + \|\mathbf{V}\|_F^2).$$

Thus we have again shown that (4.42) must be true, without relying on the differentiability of the objective with respect to $(\mathbf{U}, \mathbf{V})$, but only on the differentiablity of the loss function with respect to $\mathbf{Z}$ when we take the limits as $\tau \searrow 0$.

Finally, to see that claim (ii) is true, observe that the equality on the right-hand side of (4.42) implies that $(\mathbf{U}, \mathbf{V}, n_1)$ is an optimal factorization, i.e. a global minimum of (4.35). Finally, since the convex problem in (4.36) is a global lower bound for the non-convex problem in (4.34) and since $\mathbf{Z} = \mathbf{U}\mathbf{V}^\top$ is a global minimum of the convex problem, it follows that $(\mathbf{U}, \mathbf{V}, n_1)$ must be a global minimum of the non-convex problem. □

In summary, we have shown that the non-convex matrix-factorization problem in $(\mathbf{U}, \mathbf{V})$ admits a global lower bound in the product space $\mathbf{Z} = \mathbf{U}\mathbf{V}^\top$. Moreover, the lower bound is a convex function of $\mathbf{Z}$ and the global minima agree, i.e. if $(\mathbf{U}, \mathbf{V}, n_1)$ is a global minimum of the non-convex problem then $\mathbf{U}\mathbf{V}^\top$ is a global minimum of the convex problem. In addition, Theorem 4.5 provides a characterization of the local minima of the non-convex problem which are also global: they are the local minima with one column of $\mathbf{U}$ and the corresponding column of $\mathbf{V}$ equal to zero. Such a statement can be easily extended to local minima $(\mathbf{U}, \mathbf{V}, n_1)$ that are rank deficient, i.e. there exists $\mathbf{e} \neq 0$ such that $\mathbf{U}\mathbf{e} = 0$ and $\mathbf{V}\mathbf{e} = 0$, since the only part of the proof that depends on columns of $\mathbf{U}$ and $\mathbf{V}$ being zero is the definition of $\mathbf{U}_\epsilon$ and $\mathbf{V}_\epsilon$, which can be readily replaced by $\mathbf{U}_\epsilon = \mathbf{U} + \epsilon^{1/2}\mathbf{u}\mathbf{e}^\top$ and $\mathbf{V}_\epsilon = \mathbf{V} + \epsilon^{1/2}\mathbf{v}\mathbf{e}^\top$ with $\|\mathbf{e}\|_2 = 1$. In addition, observe that the proof of Theorem 4.5 relies only on the following necessary and sufficient conditions for the global optimality of any $(\mathbf{U}, \mathbf{V}, n_1)$.

Corollary 4.6. $(\mathbf{U}, \mathbf{V}, n_1)$ *is a global minimum of* (4.34) *if and only if it satisfies the following conditions:*

(i) $\langle \mathbf{Y} - \mathbf{U}\mathbf{V}^\top, \mathbf{U}\mathbf{V}^\top\rangle = \frac{\lambda}{2}(\|\mathbf{U}\|_F^2 + \|\mathbf{V}\|_F^2);$

(ii) $\mathbf{u}^{\top}(\mathbf{Y} - \mathbf{U}\mathbf{V}^{\top})\mathbf{v} \leq \frac{\lambda}{2}(\|\mathbf{u}\|_2^2 + \|\mathbf{v}\|_2^2)$ *for all* $(\mathbf{u}, \mathbf{v})$.

Recall that the global minimum of the convex problem (4.36) is given by the singular value thresholding of $\mathbf{Y}$, $\mathbf{Z} = \mathcal{D}_{\lambda}(\mathbf{Y}) = \mathbf{U}_{\mathbf{Y}}(\boldsymbol{\Sigma}_{\mathbf{Y}} - \lambda\mathbf{I})_+\mathbf{V}_{\mathbf{Y}}^{\top}$, where $\mathbf{Y} = \mathbf{U}_{\mathbf{Y}}\boldsymbol{\Sigma}_{\mathbf{Y}}\mathbf{V}_{\mathbf{Y}}^{\top}$ is the SVD of $\mathbf{Y}$. It follows that a global minimum of (4.34) can be obtained as $\mathbf{U} = \mathbf{U}_{\mathbf{Y}}(\boldsymbol{\Sigma}_{\mathbf{Y}} - \lambda\mathbf{I})_+^{1/2}$ and $\mathbf{V} = \mathbf{V}_{\mathbf{Y}}(\boldsymbol{\Sigma}_{\mathbf{Y}} - \lambda\mathbf{I})_+^{1/2}$.

In practice, while a globally optimal solution to (4.36) can be found using linear algebraic techniques, computing the SVD of $\mathbf{Y}$ is highly inefficient for large matrices $\mathbf{Y}$. Therefore, we may still be interested in solving (4.36) using, e.g., gradient descent. In this case, we may need to use Corollary 4.6 to check that a global minimum has been found. Observe from the proof of Theorem 4.5 that condition (i) is satisfied by any first-order point and that optimization methods are often guaranteed to converge to first-order points. Therefore, condition (ii) is the important one to check. It can be shown that that condition is equivalent to $\sigma_{\max}(\mathbf{Y}-\mathbf{U}\mathbf{V}^{\top}) \leq \lambda$, which involves computing only the largest singular value of a matrix. But what if condition (ii) is violated? In this case, one might wonder whether condition (ii) may be used to escape the non-global local minimum. Indeed, if condition (ii) is violated, then there exists $(\mathbf{u}, \mathbf{v})$ such that

$$\mathbf{u}^{\top}(\mathbf{Y} - \mathbf{U}\mathbf{V}^{\top})\mathbf{v} > \tfrac{\lambda}{2}(\|\mathbf{u}\|_2^2 + \|\mathbf{v}\|_2^2).$$

Then it follows from the proof of Theorem 4.5 that, if we choose $\mathbf{U}_{\epsilon} = [\mathbf{U}\ \epsilon^{1/2}\mathbf{u}]$ and $\mathbf{V}_{\epsilon} = [\mathbf{V}\ \epsilon^{1/2}\mathbf{v}]$ for ϵ small enough, then we can reduce the objective problem. This suggest an algorithm for minimizing (4.34) which consists of the following two steps.

(i) For a fixed n_1, use a local descent strategy to minimize (4.34) with respect to $\mathbf{U}$ and $\mathbf{V}$ until convergence to a first-order point occurs.

(ii) Check whether condition (ii) is satisfied, which is equivalent to solving the following optimization problem (called the polar problem):

$$\max_{\mathbf{u},\mathbf{v}} \frac{\mathbf{u}^{\top}(\mathbf{Y} - \mathbf{U}\mathbf{V}^{\top})\mathbf{v}}{\|\mathbf{u}\|_2^2 + \|\mathbf{v}\|_2^2} \leq \frac{\lambda}{2} \iff \max_{\mathbf{u},\mathbf{v}} \frac{\mathbf{u}^{\top}(\mathbf{Y} - \mathbf{U}\mathbf{V}^{\top})\mathbf{v}}{\|\mathbf{u}\|_2\|\mathbf{v}\|_2} \leq \lambda. \quad (4.43)$$

If the condition holds then a global minimum has been found. If not, let $(\mathbf{u}, \mathbf{v})$ be a solution to the polar problem,[10] augment $\mathbf{U}$ and $\mathbf{V}$ with one additional column to give $\mathbf{U}_{\epsilon} = [\mathbf{U}\ \epsilon^{1/2}\mathbf{u}]$ and $\mathbf{V}_{\epsilon} = [\mathbf{V}\ \epsilon^{1/2}\mathbf{v}]$ for some $\epsilon > 0$, and go to (i).

We refer the reader to Haeffele and Vidal (2019) for a more precise and detailed description of this meta-algorithm.

---

[10] Note that a solution to the polar problem is given by the left and right singular vectors of $\mathbf{Y} - \mathbf{U}\mathbf{V}^{\top}$ associated with its largest singular value.

4.4.2 *Positively Homogeneous Networks*

The above discussion on matrix factorization can be extended to neural networks with one hidden layer by adjusting the definitions of the maps Φ and Θ appropriately. In the above matrix-factorization example (returning to the use of $\mathbf{W}$ to notate the model parameters), Φ and Θ can be rewritten as

$$\Phi(\mathbf{X}, \mathbf{W}^{[1]}, \mathbf{W}^{[2]}) = \mathbf{W}^{[2]}(\mathbf{W}^{[1]})^\top = \sum_{i=1}^{n_1} \mathbf{w}_i^{[2]}(\mathbf{w}_i^{[1]})^\top, \qquad \text{and}$$

$$\Theta(\mathbf{W}^{[1]}, \mathbf{W}^{[2]}) = \frac{1}{2}(\|\mathbf{W}^{[1]}\|_F^2 + \|\mathbf{W}^{[2]}\|_F^2) = \sum_{i=1}^{n_1} \frac{1}{2}(\|\mathbf{w}_i^{[1]}\|_2^2 + \|\mathbf{w}_i^{[2]}\|_2^2),$$

(4.44)

where $\mathbf{w}_i^{[1]}$ and $\mathbf{w}_i^{[2]}$ are the ith columns of $\mathbf{W}^{[1]}$ and $\mathbf{W}^{[2]}$, respectively. A key observation is that the map Φ and regularization Θ decompose as sums of functions over the columns of $\mathbf{W}^{[1]}$ and $\mathbf{W}^{[2]}$. Further, these functions are both positively homogeneous[11] with degree 2.

Turning to single-hidden-layer neural networks, if we again let n_1 denote the number of neurons in the hidden layer this motivates the following more general definitions for Φ and Θ:

$$\Phi_{n_1}(\mathbf{X}, \mathbf{W}^{[1]}, \mathbf{W}^{[2]}) = \sum_{i=1}^{n_1} \phi(\mathbf{X}, \mathbf{w}_i^{[1]}, \mathbf{w}_i^{[2]}), \qquad \text{and}$$

$$\Theta_{n_1}(\mathbf{W}^{[1]}, \mathbf{W}^{[2]}) = \sum_{i=1}^{n_1} \theta(\mathbf{w}_i^{[1]}, \mathbf{w}_i^{[2]}),$$

(4.45)

where $\phi(\mathbf{X}, \mathbf{w}^{[1]}, \mathbf{w}^{[2]})$ and $\theta(\mathbf{w}^{[1]}, \mathbf{w}^{[2]})$ are functions which are both positively homogeneous and of the same degree $p > 0$ with respect to $(\mathbf{w}^{[1]}, \mathbf{w}^{[2]})$. Clearly, $\phi(\mathbf{X}, \mathbf{w}^{[1]}, \mathbf{w}^{[2]}) = \mathbf{w}^{[1]}(\mathbf{w}^{[2]})^\top$ and $\theta(\mathbf{w}^{[1]}, \mathbf{w}^{[2]}) = \frac{1}{2}(\|\mathbf{w}^{[1]}\|_2^2 + \|\mathbf{w}^{[2]}\|_2^2)$ satisfy this property, with $p = 2$. But notice that it is also satisfied, for example, by the map $\phi(\mathbf{X}, \mathbf{w}^{[1]}, \mathbf{w}^{[2]}) = \mathbf{w}^{[2]}\text{ReLU}((\mathbf{w}^1)^\top\mathbf{X})$, where we recall that $\text{ReLU}(z) = \max(z, 0)$ is a ReLU applied to each entry of $(\mathbf{w}^{[1]})^\top\mathbf{X}$. The fundamental observation is that both linear transformations and ReLU nonlinearities[12] are positively homogeneous functions, and so the composition of such functions is also positively homogeneous. With these definitions, it is easy to see that the output of a two-layer neural network with ReLU nonlinearity on the hidden units, such as the network illustrated in the left-hand panel of Figure 4.3, can be expressed by the map Φ in (4.45).

This same approach can be generalized beyond single-hidden-layer networks to

---

[11] Recall that a function f is said to be **positively homogeneous with degree-p** if, for all $\alpha \geq 0$ one has $f(\alpha x) = \alpha^p f(x)$.

[12] Notice that many other neural network operators such as max-pooling, leaky ReLUs, ones that raise to a polynomial power, and convolution are also positively homogeneous.

the more general multi-layer parallel network shown in the right-hand panel of Figure 4.3, by considering more general ϕ and θ functions. In particular, we define the mapping of the multi-layer parallel network and its corresponding regularization function as the sum of the corresponding mappings and regularization functions for r parallel subnetworks with identical architectures but possibly different weights. Specifically, we define the mapping of the multi-layer parallel network and its regularization function as

$$\Phi_r(\mathbf{X}, \mathbf{W}^{[1]}, \ldots, \mathbf{W}^{[L]}) = \sum_{i=1}^{r} \phi(\mathbf{X}, \mathbf{W}_i^{[1]}, \ldots, \mathbf{W}_i^{[L]}), \quad \text{and}$$

$$\Theta_r(\mathbf{W}^{[1]}, \ldots, \mathbf{W}^{[L]}) = \sum_{i=1}^{r} \theta(\mathbf{W}_i^{[1]}, \ldots, \mathbf{W}_i^{[L]}),$$

(4.46)

where $\mathbf{W}_i^{[l]}$ denotes the weight parameters for the lth layer of the ith subnetwork, $\mathbf{W}^{[l]} = \{\mathbf{W}_i^{[l]}\}_{i=1}^{r}$ is the set of weight parameters for the lth layer of all r subnetworks, and the network mapping $\phi(\mathbf{X}, \mathbf{W}_i^{[1]}, \ldots, \mathbf{W}_i^{[L]})$ and regularization function $\theta(\mathbf{W}_i^{[1]}, \ldots, \mathbf{W}_i^{[L]})$ are positively homogeneous functions of degree $p > 0$ on the weights of the ith subnetwork $(\mathbf{W}_i^{[1]}, \ldots, \mathbf{W}_i^{[L]})$.[13] Therefore we can write the training problem for a network which consists of the sum of parallel subnetworks (where we also search over the number of subnetworks, r) as

$$\min_{r \in \mathbb{N}^+} \min_{\mathbf{W}^{[1]}, \ldots, \mathbf{W}^{[L]}} \left(\mathcal{L}(\mathbf{Y}, \Phi_r(\mathbf{X}, \mathbf{W}^{[1]}, \ldots, \mathbf{W}^{[L]})) + \lambda \Theta_r(\mathbf{W}^{[1]}, \ldots, \mathbf{W}^{[L]}) \right). \quad (4.47)$$

Note that this problem is typically non-convex owing to the mapping Φ_r, regardless of the choice of loss and regularization functions, $\mathcal{L}$ and Θ, respectively. Therefore, to analyze this non-convex problem, we define a generalization of the variational form of the nuclear norm in (4.35) for neural networks which consist of the sum of parallel subnetworks as:

$$\Omega_{\phi,\theta}(\mathbf{Z}) = \min_{r \in \mathbb{N}^+} \min_{\mathbf{W}^{[1]}, \ldots, \mathbf{W}^{[L]}: \Phi_r(\mathbf{X}, \mathbf{W}^{[1]}, \ldots, \mathbf{W}^{[L]})=\mathbf{Z}} \Theta_r(\mathbf{W}^{[1]}, \ldots, \mathbf{W}^{[L]}), \quad (4.48)$$

with the additional condition that $\Omega_{\phi,\theta}(\mathbf{Z}) = \infty$ if $\Phi_r(\mathbf{X}, \mathbf{W}^{[1]}, \ldots, \mathbf{W}^{[L]}) \neq \mathbf{Z}$ for all $(\mathbf{W}^{[1]}, \ldots, \mathbf{W}^{[L]}, r)$. The intuition behind the above problem is that, given an output $\mathbf{Z}$ generated by the network for some input $\mathbf{X}$, we wish to find the number of subnetworks (or the number of hidden units in the single-hidden-layer case) and weights $(\mathbf{W}^{[1]}, \ldots, \mathbf{W}^{[L]})$ that produce the output $\mathbf{Z}$. Then, among all possible choices of sizes and weights, we prefer those that minimize $\Theta_r(\mathbf{W}^{[1]}, \ldots, \mathbf{W}^{[L]})$.

Note that the function $\Omega_{\phi,\theta}$ is completely specified once one chooses the functions

[13] Note that θ could additionally depend on $\mathbf{X}$, but we omit that possibility here for notational simplicity.

ϕ and θ in (4.46), so for $\Omega_{\phi,\theta}$ to be well-posed, ϕ and θ must satisfy the following conditions.[14]

Definition 4.7. We will say that (ϕ,θ) is a **nondegenerate pair** if for any set of weights for one subnetwork $(\overline{\mathbf{W}}^{[1]},\ldots,\overline{\mathbf{W}}^{[L]})$ the functions satisfy the following three conditions:

(i) Both ϕ and θ are positively homogeneous functions of the weights with the same degree $p > 0$: $\phi(\mathbf{X},\alpha\overline{\mathbf{W}}^{[1]},\ldots,\alpha\overline{\mathbf{W}}^{[L]}) = \alpha^p\phi(\mathbf{X},\overline{\mathbf{W}}^{[1]},\ldots,\overline{\mathbf{W}}^{[L]})$ and $\theta(\alpha\overline{\mathbf{W}}^{[1]},\ldots,\alpha\overline{\mathbf{W}}^{[L]}) = \alpha^p\theta(\overline{\mathbf{W}}^{[1]},\ldots,\overline{\mathbf{W}}^{[L]})$ for all $\alpha \geq 0$.

(ii) θ is positive semidefinite: $\theta(\overline{\mathbf{W}}^{[1]},\ldots,\overline{\mathbf{W}}^{[L]}) \geq 0$.

(iii) The set $\{\phi(\mathbf{X},\overline{\mathbf{W}}^{[1]},\ldots,\overline{\mathbf{W}}^{[L]}) : \theta(\overline{\mathbf{W}}^{[1]},\ldots,\overline{\mathbf{W}}^{[L]}) \leq 1\}$ is compact.

As a concrete example, choosing $\phi(\mathbf{X},\mathbf{w}^{[1]},\mathbf{w}^{[2]}) = \mathbf{w}^{[2]}\mathrm{ReLU}((\mathbf{w}^{[1]})^\top\mathbf{X})$ as above and $\theta(\mathbf{w}^{[1]},\mathbf{w}^{[2]}) = \frac{1}{2}(\|\mathbf{w}^{[1]}\|_2^2 + \|\mathbf{w}^{[2]}\|_2^2)$ satisfies the above requirements and corresponds to a single-hidden-layer fully connected network (as $\Phi_{n_1}(\mathbf{X},\mathbf{W}^{[1]},\mathbf{W}^{[2]}) = \mathbf{W}^{[2]}\mathrm{ReLU}((\mathbf{W}^{[1]})^\top\mathbf{X}))$ with ℓ_2 weight decay on the parameters. From these preliminaries, one can show that $\Omega_{\phi,\theta}$ satisfies the following properties.

Proposition 4.8 (Haeffele and Vidal, 2015, 2017). *Given a nondegenerate pair of functions (ϕ,θ) then $\Omega_{\phi,\theta}(\mathbf{Z})$ has the following properties:*

(i) *It is positive definite: $\Omega_{\phi,\theta}(\mathbf{Z}) > 0$ for all $\mathbf{Z} \neq \mathbf{0}$, and $\Omega_{\phi,\theta}(\mathbf{0}) = 0$.*

(ii) *It is positively homogeneous with degree 1: $\Omega_{\phi,\theta}(\alpha\mathbf{Z}) = \alpha\Omega_{\phi,\theta}(\mathbf{Z})$, for all $\alpha \geq 0$ and $\mathbf{Z}$.*

(iii) *It satisfies the triangle inequality: $\Omega_{\phi,\theta}(\mathbf{Q} + \mathbf{Z}) \leq \Omega_{\phi,\theta}(\mathbf{Q}) + \Omega_{\phi,\theta}(\mathbf{Z})$, for all $\mathbf{Q}$ and $\mathbf{Z}$.*

(iv) *It is convex with respect to $\mathbf{Z}$.*

(v) *The infimum in (4.48) can be achieved with $r \leq \mathrm{card}(\mathbf{Z})$, for all $\mathbf{Z}$.*

Further, if, for any choice of weights for one subnetwork $\overline{\mathbf{W}}^{[1]},\ldots,\overline{\mathbf{W}}^{[L]}$, there exists a vector $\mathbf{s} = \{-1,1\}^L$ such that

$$\phi(\mathbf{X},s_1\overline{\mathbf{W}}^{[1]},\ldots,s_L\overline{\mathbf{W}}^{[L]}) = -\phi(\mathbf{X},\overline{\mathbf{W}}^{[1]},\ldots,\overline{\mathbf{W}}^{[L]}) \quad and$$

$$\theta(s_1\overline{\mathbf{W}}^{[1]},\ldots,s_L\overline{\mathbf{W}}^{[L]}) = \theta(\overline{\mathbf{W}}^{[1]},\ldots,\overline{\mathbf{W}}^{[L]})$$

then $\Omega_{\phi,\theta}(\mathbf{Z})$ is also a norm on $\mathbf{Z}$.

Note that regardless of whether $\Omega_{\phi,\theta}$ is a norm or not, we always have that $\Omega_{\phi,\theta}(\mathbf{Z})$ is convex on $\mathbf{Z}$. Therefore, if the loss $\mathcal{L}$ is convex on $\mathbf{Z}$, so is the problem

$$\min_{\mathbf{Z}} \mathcal{L}(\mathbf{Y},\mathbf{Z}) + \lambda\Omega_{\phi,\theta}(\mathbf{Z}). \tag{4.49}$$

---

[14] The first two conditions are typically easy to verify, while the third condition is needed to avoid trivial situations such as $\Omega_{\phi,\theta}(\mathbf{Z}) = 0$, for all $\mathbf{Z}$.

Further, just as in the previous matrix factorization example, we have that for any $(\mathbf{Z}, \mathbf{W}^{[1]}, \ldots, \mathbf{W}^{[L]})$ such that $\mathbf{Z} = \Phi_r(\mathbf{X}, \mathbf{W}^{[1]}, \ldots, \mathbf{W}^{[L]})$ the following global lower bound exists:

$$\mathcal{L}(\mathbf{Y}, \mathbf{Z}) + \lambda\Omega_{\phi,\theta}(\mathbf{Z}) \leq \mathcal{L}(\mathbf{Y}, \Phi_r(\mathbf{X}, \mathbf{W}^{[1]}, \ldots, \mathbf{W}^{[L]})) + \lambda\Theta_r(\mathbf{W}^{[1]}, \ldots, \mathbf{W}^{[L]}),$$
(4.50)

and the lower bound is tight in the sense that for any $\mathbf{Z}$ such that $\Omega_{\phi,\theta}(\mathbf{Z}) \neq \infty$ there exists $(\mathbf{W}^{[1]}, \ldots, \mathbf{W}^{[L]}, r)$ such that $\mathbf{Z} = \Phi_r(\mathbf{X}, \mathbf{W}^{[1]}, \ldots, \mathbf{W}^{[L]})$ and the above inequality becomes an equality. As a result, using a very similar analysis as that used to prove Theorem 4.5, one can show the following result.

Theorem 4.9 (Haeffele and Vidal, 2015, 2017). *Given a nondegenerate pair of functions (ϕ, θ), if $(\mathbf{W}^{[1]}, \ldots, \mathbf{W}^{[L]}, r)$ is a local minimum of (4.47) such that for some $i \in [r]$ we have $\mathbf{W}_i^{[1]} = 0, \ldots, \mathbf{W}_i^{[L]} = 0$, then*

(i) $\mathbf{Z} = \Phi_r(\mathbf{X}, \mathbf{W}^{[1]}, \ldots, \mathbf{W}^{[L]})$ *is a global minimum of (4.49) and*
(ii) $(\mathbf{W}^{[1]}, \ldots, \mathbf{W}^{[L]}, r)$ *is a global minimum of (4.47) and (4.48).*

We refer to Haeffele and Vidal (2015, 2017) for the full proof, but it closely follows the sequences of arguments from the proof of Theorem 4.5. In particular, we note that the key property which is needed to generalize the proof of Theorem 4.5 is that ϕ and θ are positively homogeneous functions of the same degree.

Additionally, building on the discussion of the meta-algorithm from §4.4.1, it can also be shown (in combination with Theorem 4.9) that if the network is sufficiently large (as measured by the number of subnetworks, r) then there always exists a path from any initialization to a global minimizer which does not require the value of the objective to be increased.

Theorem 4.10 (Haeffele and Vidal, 2015, 2017). *Given a nondegenerate pair of functions (ϕ, θ), let $|\phi|$ denote the number of elements in the output of the function ϕ. Then if $r > |\phi|$ for the optimization problem*

$$\min_{\mathbf{W}^{[1]}, \ldots, \mathbf{W}^{[L]}} (\mathcal{L}(\mathbf{Y}, \Phi_r(\mathbf{X}, \mathbf{W}^{[1]}, \ldots, \mathbf{W}^{[L]})) + \lambda\Theta_r(\mathbf{W}^{[1]}, \ldots, \mathbf{W}^{[L]})), \quad (4.51)$$

a nonincreasing path to a global minimizer will always exist from any initialization.

Again we refer to Haeffele and Vidal (2015, 2017) for the complete proof, but the key idea is that once one arrives at a local minimum if either the condition of Theorem 4.9 is satisfied or the outputs of the subnetworks are linearly dependent. As a result, by positive homogeneity, one can traverse a flat surface of the objective landscape until reaching a point that does satisfy the condition of Theorem 4.9. This point is either a local minimum (and hence a global minimum from the theorem) or else a descent direction must exist.

4.5 Conclusions

We have studied the optimization landscape of neural network training for two classes of networks: linear networks trained with a squared loss and without regularization, and positively homogeneous networks with parallel structure trained with a convex loss and positively homogeneous regularization. In the first case, we derived conditions on the input–output covariance matrices under which all critical points are either global minimizers or saddle points. In the second case, we showed that when the networks is sufficiently wide, the non-convex objective on the weights can be lower bounded by a convex objective on the network mapping, and we derived conditions under which local minima of the non-convex objective yield global minima of both objectives. Future avenues for research include extending the results presented here to other classes of deep architectures. In particular, the current results are limited to parallel architectures whose size is measured by the number of parallel subnetworks of fixed depth and width. This motivates extending the framework to cases in which both the depth and width of the network are varied. Moreover, the landscape of the objective is only one ingredient for explaining the role of optimization in deep learning. As discussed in the introduction, other ingredients are the development of efficient algorithms for finding a global minimum and the study of the implicit regularization and generalization performance of such algorithms. We refer the reader to other chapters in this book for recent results on these fascinating subjects.

Acknowledgments

The authors acknowledge partial support by the NSF-Simons Research Collaborations on the Mathematical and Scientific Foundations of Deep Learning (NSF grant 2031985), the NSF HDR TRIPODS Institute for the Foundations of Graph and Deep Learning (NSF grant 1934979), NSF grants 1704458 and 2008460, and ARO grant MURI W911NF-17-1-0304.

References

Allen-Zhu, Zeyuan, Li, Yuanzhi, and Song, Zhao. 2019. A convergence theory for deep learning via over-parameterization. Pages 242–252 of: *Proc. International Conference on Machine Learning*.

Arora, Sanjeev, Cohen, Nadav, Hu, Wei, and Luo, Yuping. 2019. Implicit regularization in deep matrix factorization. Pages 7413–7424 of: *Proc. Neural Information Processing Systems*.

Baldi, P., and Hornik, K. 1989. Neural networks and principal component analysis: Learning from examples without local minima. *Neural Networks*, **2**(1), 53–58.

Candès, E., and Tao, T. 2010. The power of convex relaxation: Near-optimal matrix completion. *IEEE Transactions on Information Theory*, **56**(5), 2053–2080.

Cavazza, Jacopo, Haeffele, Benjamin D., Lane, Connor, Morerio, Pietro, Murino, Vittorio, and Vidal, Rene. 2018. Dropout as a low-rank regularizer for matrix factorization. Pages 435–444 of: *Proc. International Conference on Artificial Intelligence and Statistics*, vol. 84.

Choromanska, Anna, Henaff, Mikael, Mathieu, Michael, Ben Arous, Gerard, and LeCun, Yann. 2015. The loss surfaces of multilayer networks. Pages 192–204 of: *Proc. International Conference on Artificial Intelligence and Statistics*.

Dauphin, Yann N., Pascanu, Razvan, Gulcehre, Caglar, Cho, Kyunghyun, Ganguli, Surya, and Bengio, Yoshua. 2014. Identifying and attacking the saddle point problem in high-dimensional non-convex optimization. Pages 2933–2941 of: *Proc. Neural Information Processing Systems*.

Donoho, David L. 2006. For most large underdetermined systems of linear equations the minimal ℓ^1-norm solution is also the sparsest solution. *Communications on Pure and Applied Mathematics*, **59**(6), 797–829.

Du, Simon, Lee, Jason, Li, Haochuan, Wang, Liwei, and Zhai, Xiyu. 2019. Gradient descent finds global minima of deep neural networks. Pages 1675–1685 of: *Proc. International Conference on Machine Learning*.

Duchi, J., Hazan, E., and Singer, Y. 2017. Adaptive subgradient methods of online learning and stochastic optimization. *Journal of Machine Learning Research*, **12**, 2121–2159.

Ge, Rong, Huang, Furong, Jin, Chi, and Yuan, Yang. 2015. Escaping from saddle points – online stochastic gradient for tensor decomposition. Pages 797–842 of: *Proc. Conference on Learning Theory*.

Gori, M., and Tesi, A. 1991. Backpropagation converges for multi-layered networks and linearly-separable patterns. Page 896 of: *Proc. International Joint Conference on Neural Networks*, vol. 2.

Gori, M., and Tesi, A. 1992. On the problem of local minima in backpropagation. *IEEE Transactions on Pattern Analysis and Machine Intelligence*, **14**(1), 76–86.

Gunasekar, Suriya, Woodworth, Blake E., Bhojanapalli, Srinadh, Neyshabur, Behnam, and Srebro, Nati. 2017. Implicit regularization in matrix factorization. Pages 6151–6159 of: *Proc. Neural Information Processing Systems*.

Gunasekar, Suriya, Lee, Jason, Soudry, Daniel, and Srebro, Nathan. 2018a. Characterizing implicit bias in terms of optimization geometry. In: *Proc. International Conference on Machine Learning*.

Gunasekar, Suriya, Lee, Jason D., Soudry, Daniel, and Srebro, Nati. 2018b. Implicit bias of gradient descent on linear convolutional networks. Pages 9461–9471 of: *Advances in Neural Information Processing Systems*.

Haeffele, Benjamin D., and Vidal, René. 2015. Global optimality in tensor factorization, deep learning, and beyond. ArXiv preprint arXiv:1506.07540.

Haeffele, Benjamin D., and Vidal, Rene. 2017. Global optimality in neural network training. Pages 7331–7339 of: *Proc. IEEE Conference on Computer Vision and Pattern Recognition*.

Haeffele, Benjamin D., and Vidal, Rene. 2019. Structured low-rank matrix factorization: Global optimality, algorithms, and applications. *IEEE Transactions on Pattern Analysis and Machine Intelligence*, **42**(6), 1468–1482.

Kawaguchi, Kenji. 2016. Deep learning without poor local minima. Pages 586–594 of: *Proc. Neural Information Processing Systems*.

Kingma, Diederik, and Ba, Jimmy. 2014. Adam: A method for stochastic optimization. *Proc. International Conference on Learning Representations*.

Laurent, Thomas, and Brecht, James. 2018. Deep linear networks with arbitrary loss: All local minima are global. Pages 2902–2907 of: *Proc. International Conference on Machine Learning*.

Lee, Jason D., Panageas, Ioannis, Piliouras, Georgios, Simchowitz, Max, Jordan, Michael I., and Recht, Benjamin. 2019. First-order methods almost always avoid strict saddle points. *Mathematical Programming*, **176**, 311–337.

Lu, Haihao, and Kawaguchi, Kenji. 2017. Depth creates no bad local minima. ArXiv preprint arXiv:1702.08580.

Mairal, Julien, Bach, Francis, Ponce, Jean, and Sapiro, Guillermo. 2010. Online learning for matrix factorization and sparse coding. *Journal of Machine Learning Research*, **11**, 19–60.

Mianjy, Poorya, Arora, Raman, and Vidal, René. 2018. On the implicit bias of dropout. In: *Proc. International Conference on Machine Learning*.

Nesterov, Y. 1983. A method of solving a convex programming problem with convergence rate $O(1/k^2)$. *Soviet Math. Doklady*, **27**(2), 372–376.

Nouiehed, Maher, and Razaviyayn, Meisam. 2018. Learning deep models: Critical points and local openness. ArXiv preprint arXiv:1803.02968.

Pal, Ambar, Lane, Connor, Vidal, René, and Haeffele, Benjamin D. 2020. On the regularization properties of structured dropout. Pages 7671–7679 of: *Proc. IEEE Conference on Computer Vision and Pattern Recognition*.

Robbins, H., and Monro, S. 1951. A stochastic approximation method. *Annals of Mathematical Statistics*, **22**, 400–407.

Rumelhart, David E., Hinton, Geoffrey E., and Williams, Ronald J. 1986. Learning representations by back-propagating errors. *Nature*, **323**, 533–536.

Srebro, Nathan, Rennie, Jason D. M., and Jaakkola, Tommi S. 2004. Maximum-margin matrix factorization. Pages 1329–1336 of: *Proc. Neural Information Processing Systems*, vol. 17.

Srivastava, N., Hinton, G., Krizhevsky, A., Sutskever, I., and Salakhutdinov, R. 2014. Dropout: A simple way to prevent neural networks from overfitting. *Journal of Machine Learning Research*, **15**(1), 1929–1958.

Sun, Ju, Qu, Qing, and Wright, John. 2017. Complete dictionary recovery over the sphere I: Overview and the geometric picture. *IEEE Transactions on Information Theory*, **63**(2), 853–884.

Sun, Ju, Qu, Qing, and Wright, John. 2018. A geometric analysis of phase retrieval. *Found. Comput. Math.*, **18**, 1131–1198.

Werbos, P.J. 1974. *Beyond Regression: New Tools for Predictions and Analysis in the Behavioral Sciences*. Ph.D. thesis, Harvard University.

Wright, Stephen J., and Nocedal, Jorge. 1999. *Numerical Optimization*, vol. 2. Springer.

Xu, Yangyang, and Yin, Wotao. 2013. A block coordinate descent method for regularized multiconvex optimization with applications to nonnegative tensor factorization and completion. *SIAM Journal on Imaging Sciences*, **6**(3), 1758–1789.

Zhang, Yuqian, Kuo, Han-Wen, and Wright, John. 2018. Structured local minima in sparse blind deconvolution. Pages 2322–2331 of: *Advances in Neural Information Processing Systems*.

Zhu, Zhihui, Soudry, Daniel, Eldar, Yonina C., and Wakin, Michael B. 2020. The global optimization geometry of shallow linear neural networks. *Journal of Mathematical Imaging and Vision*, **62**, 279–292.

5

Explaining the Decisions of Convolutional and Recurrent Neural Networks

Wojciech Samek, Leila Arras, Ahmed Osman, Grégoire Montavon,
Klaus-Robert Müller

Abstract: The ability to explain and understand the prediction behaviour of complex machine learning (ML) models such as deep neural networks is of great interest to developers, users and researchers. It allows them to verify the system's decision making and gain new insights into the data and the model, including the detection of any malfunctioning. Moreover, it can also help to improve the overall training process, e.g., by removing detected biases. However, owing to the large complexity and highly nested structure of deep neural networks, it is non-trivial to obtain these interpretations for most of today's models. This chapter describes layer-wise relevance propagation (LRP), a propagation-based explanation technique that can explain the decisions of a variety of ML models, including state-of-the-art convolutional and recurrent neural networks. As the name suggests, LRP implements a propagation mechanism that redistributes the prediction outcome from the output to the input, layer by layer through the network. Mathematically, the LRP algorithm can be embedded into the framework of deep Taylor decomposition and the propagation process can be interpreted as a succession of first-order Taylor expansions performed locally at each neuron. The result of the LRP computation is a *heatmap* visualizing how much each input variable (e.g., pixel) has contributed to the prediction. This chapter will discuss the algorithmic and theoretical under-pinnings of LRP, apply the method to a complex model trained for the task of visual question answering (VQA) and demonstrate that it produces meaningful explanations, revealing interesting details about the model's reasoning. We conclude the chapter by commenting on the general limitations of the current explanation techniques and interesting future directions.

5.1 Introduction

Over the years machine learning (ML) models have steadily grown in complexity, gaining predictivity often at the expense of interpretability. Deep neural networks are a prime example of this development. These models typically contain millions of parameters and tens or even hundreds of non-linearly interwoven layers of increasing abstraction. After being fed with vast amounts of data, these models can achieve record performances on complex tasks such as vision (Cireşan et al., 2011; Lu and Tang, 2015), language understanding (Bahdanau et al., 2014; Devlin et al., 2018), strategic game playing (Mnih et al., 2015; Silver et al., 2017; Moravčík et al., 2017), medical diagnosis (Esteva et al., 2017; Hannun et al., 2019; Jurmeister et al., 2019) and scientific data analysis (Baldi et al., 2014; Mayr et al., 2016; Schütt et al., 2017). The complexity of state-of-the-art convolutional neural networks (CNNs) can be illustrated by the popular VGG-16 model (Simonyan and Zisserman, 2014). This model consists of 16 layers of increasing abstraction and 138 million weight parameters; moreover, it requires 15.5 billion elementary operations (MACs) to classify a single 224×224 image. Clearly, for such a large model it becomes very difficult to *explain* why and how it arrived at its decision, i.e., to find the relevant parts in the input (e.g., pixels) which have triggered an individual decision. Such an analysis becomes even more complicated for models with an internal state, e.g., long short-term memory (LSTM) networks (Hochreiter and Schmidhuber, 1997), which are often used to process time series data or textual input, because the internal state influences the model's decision making in complex ways. Unsurprisingly, until recently, state-of-the-art CNNs, LSTMs and deep models in general have been commonly regarded as "black boxes".

Although the wish to understand and interpret the decision-making process of an AI system is as old as the technology itself, the field of explainable AI (XAI) has seen a significant revival in the last years. With the many advances in the area of deep learning, various methods have been proposed recently to make these models more interpretable (Samek et al., 2019). While some of these methoda aim to construct and train ML models that are by design more interpretable, e.g., by incorporating sparsity priors or disentangling the learned representation, other methods have been proposed that are capable of explaining a given (trained) ML model post hoc. This chapter will focus exclusively on the latter methods. We will consider the problem of visual question answering (VQA), where a deep model is trained to answer questions about a given image. In order to do so, the model needs to consist of LSTM and CNN parts, which process the question and the image, respectively. Thus, explaining decisions of the VQA model requires an XAI technique which can explain both types of models. In this chapter we will introduce such a technique, termed layer-wise relevance propagation (LRP) (Bach et al., 2015); it is a generic method for explaining individual predictions of ML models by meaningfully redistributing the decisions backwards onto the input variables. The result of this explanation process is a "heatmap", visualizing how much each input variable has contributed to the prediction. In the context of VQA, LRP will thus highlight the relevant words in the question and the part in the image which is relevant for answering the question. Analysing and interpreting these explanations allows us to get insights into the functioning of the VQA model, and in particular helps us to understand its failure modes.

In the remainder of this chapter we motivate the need for explainability (§5.2), formalize the explanation problem for simple linear models and discuss the difficulties occurring when extending this concept to deep neural networks (§5.3). Then, in §5.4 we introduce LRP for convolutional neural networks, demonstrate that it can be theoretically embedded into the framework of deep Taylor decomposition (Montavon et al., 2017), and present extensions of the method suited for LSTM architectures. In §5.5 we demonstrate experimentally that LRP provides meaningful explanations and helps to understand the reasoning of a model that was trained on a visual question answering task. We conclude the chapter in §5.6 with a discussion of the limitations of current explanation techniques and open research questions.

5.2 Why Explainability?

This section motivates the need for explainability in machine learning and shows that being able to explain and understand the reasoning of an ML model is highly beneficial for at least three different reasons. For a detailed discussion on the risks and challenges of transparency we refer the interested reader to Weller (2019).

5.2.1 Practical Advantages of Explainability

Explanations can be seen as an additional tool for inspecting and debugging ML models. In this role they help us to identify models which are malfunctioning or have learned a strategy which does not match our expectations. In the extreme case, this may lead to an unmasking of "Clever Hans" predictors,[1] i.e., models that rely on spurious correlations and artifacts in the data and do not solve the task they were trained for (Lapuschkin et al., 2019). Such models appear to perform well, but would fail if put to a real test. The use of explanations facilitates quickly identifying such invalid prediction strategies and finding biases in the training data (Anders et al., 2020), which would be very cumbersome or even practically impossible if one were using standard performance metrics such as cross-validation. Overall, being able to explain predictions is of high value to ML practitioners.

---

[1] Clever Hans was a horse that was supposed to be able to perform simple calculations. However, as it turned out, Hans was not doing the math, but selecting the correct answers by watching the body language of the human who asked the questions and presented the candidate answers. Similar behaviours have been reported for a competition-winning ML model, which turned out to classify images of a horse by the presence of a copyright tag (Lapuschkin et al., 2016a); since then, many further Clever Hans incidents have been observed across the board of various deep learning and other ML models (Lapuschkin et al., 2019).

5.2.2 *Social and Legal Role of Explainability*

The acceptance of AI technology in sensitive domains such as medicine or autonomous driving may depend very much on the ability of the AI to explain its decisions. Not only may users (e.g., patients) mistrust a decision or feel uncomfortable if confronted with a black box system: for experts (e.g., medical doctors) also, comprehending the reasoning of an AI-based assistant system and being able to verify its prediction is an important requirement for accepting new technologies, in particular if it is they who are ultimately responsible. But, even for a perfect AI system, explanations are very valuable simply because they are an integral part of human–machine interaction and enable the users to make informed decisions. Also, from a legal perspective, explainability is of utmost importance because it concerns anti-discrimination and fairness aspects. For instance, explanations are a direct way to check that the model does not base its predictions on certain features (e.g., age or social status) or that it implements consistent prediction strategies for different groups (e.g., men and women). The EU's General Data Protection Regulation (GDPR) explicitly mentions the *right to explanation* for users subjected to decisions of an automated processing system (Goodman and Flaxman, 2017).

5.2.3 *Theoretical Insights Through Explainability*

Explanations also provide new insights into the data and the model. For instance, Lapuschkin et al. (2019) analysed the neural network training process on a reinforcement learning task (the Atari Breakout game) and found that the depth of the architecture and the size of the replay memory both have a strong effect on the effectivity of the network to learn to focus on the relevant elements (i.e., the ball and paddle) of the game. Apart from providing insights into the learned strategies of a model, explanations also allow us to better understand the data. For instance, knowing that the network is focusing on particular features (e.g., genes) when predicting the survival times of a patient may help us discover unknown causal relationships between these two. The ability of machine learning to uncover such hidden patterns in data has been demonstrated in the past, e.g., in the context of the game of Go (Silver et al., 2016). Since explanations make learned prediction strategies accessible for human experts, they have the potential to lead to new scientific insights. Therefore, XAI methods have already been used in various scientific disciplines (e.g., Thomas et al., 2019; Horst et al., 2019; Schütt et al., 2017; von Lilienfeld et al., 2020; Reyes et al., 2018).

5.3 From Explaining Linear Models to General Model Explainability

This section will introduce the problem of explanation and discuss a simple and mathematically well founded technique for explaining the predictions of linear (and mildly nonlinear) ML models. After explaining why the generalization of this simple XAI technique to deep neural networks fails, we will conclude this section with a brief review of state-of-the-art explanation techniques for deep learning models.

5.3.1 Explainability of Linear Models

Let us consider a simple binary classification setting. Assume we are given a trained ML model with parameters θ, i.e.,

$$f_\theta : \mathbb{R}^d \to \mathbb{R}, \qquad (5.1)$$

which estimates the class membership of a given input vector $X = [x_1, \ldots, x_d]^\top \in \mathbb{R}^d$ by the sign of the output, i.e., inputs with $f_\theta(X) > 0$ are classified as "class 1" and other inputs are classified as "class 2". In the following, we assume that f_θ is a linear classifier trained to solve the binary classification task. Thus, f_θ has the form

$$f_\theta(X) = \sum_{i=1}^{d} w_i x_i + b, \qquad (5.2)$$

with parameters $\theta = (w_1, \ldots, w_d, b) \in \mathbb{R}^{d+1}$.

Problem of wxplanation. Explaining the prediction of the model for a specific input X means of determining how much the ith input feature x_i (e.g., pixel) has contributed to the classification decision $f_\theta(X)$. Thus, an *explanation* (or heatmap) is a collection of relevance values having the same dimensionality as the input, i.e., $[R_1, \ldots, R_d] \in \mathbb{R}^d$. We want explanations to have some *faithfulness* (Swartout and Moore, 1993; Samek et al., 2017) with respect to the function $f_\theta(X)$: in other words, each *relevance value* $R_i \in \mathbb{R}$ should indicate how much the ith input feature x_i has contributed to the overall classification decision $f_\theta(X)$. Although there may be different ways to measure such a contribution, the explanation must identify and highlight the features actually used by the model. Consequently, for faithful explanations we may assume that a perturbation of the relevant features has a detrimental effect on the model's prediction (Samek et al., 2017). Specific quantifiable aspects of the explanation that relate to faithfulness are as follows.

(i) **Conservation**. The conservation property, e.g. Bach et al. (2015), establishes a connection between the explanation and the model's output. Thus, a conservative explanation lets us interpret the summed relevance values as the total evidence at the output of the network:

$$\sum_{i=1}^{d} R_i \approx f_\theta(X).$$ (5.3)

Note that the approximate, rather than strict, equality accounts for potentially unexplainable elements of the function such as biases in the linear model in Eq. (5.2).

(ii) **Model–data interaction**. Furthermore, an explanation should reflect the interaction between a feature and its usage by the model. That means that for one data point $X^{(1)}$ the ith feature may be present and used by the model (i.e., it is relevant to the decision) whereas for another data point $X^{(2)}$ it may be present but not used by the model (i.e., it is irrelevant to the decision). Thus, in contrast to feature selection (Guyon and Elisseeff, 2003), an input feature cannot *per se* be regarded as relevant or irrelevant. This property leads to *individual* explanations.

(iii) **Signed relevance**. Finally, we want relevance values to have a meaningful sign. More precisely, a positive value of R_i should indicate a feature x_i which is relevant to the prediction whereas a negative R_i should mark a feature contradicting the decision. For example, when classifying images as urban or non-urban, visual features such as buildings, cars, and pedestrians would be assigned positive relevance scores, whereas trees or wild animals would be assigned negative scores as they would tend to contradict the predicted class.

For linear models we can easily find an explanation that fulfills all the above properties if we define the contribution of the ith feature as the ith summand in (5.2), i.e.,

$$R_i = w_i x_i.$$ (5.4)

Numerous other desirable properties of explanations have been proposed in the literature (Swartout and Moore, 1993; Baehrens et al., 2010; Shrikumar et al., 2016; Montavon et al., 2018; Robnik-Šikonja and Bohanec, 2018); however, a commonly accepted mathematical definition of what explanations are and which axioms they need to fulfil is still lacking. Therefore, we do not aim to introduce a rigorous axiomatic definition of an explanation in this chapter. However, we would like to note that many popular explanation techniques do not fulfill the properties described above, even for linear models. For instance, sensitivity analysis (e.g., Baehrens et al., 2010; Simonyan et al., 2013) computes values R_i indicating how much changes in an input feature translate into changes in the output. For linear models the sensitivity score for the ith input feature is simply w_i, i.e., it is constant with respect to the input X. Thus, sensitivity-based explanations neither reflect the interaction between the feature and the model nor are they conservative or providing a meaningful interpretation of the sign.

5.3.2 Generalizing Explainability to Nonlinear Models

Practical machine learning models are often nonlinear. For example, kernel machines expose the input features through a nonlinear feature map and deep neural networks interleave linear projections with nonlinear activation functions. The resulting output is a complex, interwoven mixture of those input features that are more capable of learning the prediction task.

When the function is nonlinear but remains locally linear, explanations can be obtained using the well-known Taylor expansion. The latter offers a generic tool for decomposing the prediction in terms of elements of a linear sum. If the function $f_\theta : \mathbb{R}^d \to \mathbb{R}$ is twice continuously differentiable at the reference point $\widetilde{X} \in \mathbb{R}^d$, then it can be decomposed as follows:

$$f_\theta(X) = f_\theta(\widetilde{X}) + \sum_{i=1}^{d} \underbrace{(x_i - \widetilde{x}_i) \cdot [\nabla f_\theta(\widetilde{X})]_i}_{R_i} + \varepsilon \tag{5.5}$$

$$\text{with} \quad \varepsilon = O(\|X - \widetilde{X}\|^2) \text{ as } X \to \widetilde{X}, \tag{5.6}$$

where the relevance contributions R_i can be identified from the first-order terms, and where ε denotes the higher-order terms. For a well-chosen reference point with $f_\theta(\widetilde{X}) = 0$ (i.e., the root point) and small enough higher-order terms, we can explain the predictions of the nonlinear model in terms of R_i, while retaining approximately the conservation property

$$f_\theta(X) \approx \sum_{i=1}^{d} R_i, \tag{5.7}$$

which we also had for the linear case (up to the linear function's bias term). Note that the solution in (5.4) can be regarded as a special case of the Taylor-based decomposition with reference point $\widetilde{X} = \mathbf{0}$.

Thus, Taylor expansion offers a generic mathematical tool to decompose a prediction into dimension-wise contributions. But does this method produce meaningful explanations for any nonlinear function? Unfortunately this is not the case. The Taylor approach provides meaningful decompositions only for simple (e.g., locally linear) nonlinear models. It fails to produce meaningful explanations for functions which are highly nonlinear.

For example, the function $f(x, y) = x \cdot y$ is dominated by second-order terms near the origin (x and y only matter jointly). Also, for piecewise-linear models, e.g., deep neural networks with ReLU activations, this naive Taylor-based decomposition has been shown to provide low-quality explanations (Montavon et al., 2018; Samek et al., 2020). The first problem arises from the complexity of the neural network function and the high-dimensional space to which it is applied. In these high dimensions many root points $\widetilde{X}$ are potentially reachable; however, only a few of them are truly meaningful (those that are close enough to the input data point to explain X, lying on the data manifold etc.). Deep neural networks are known to lack robustness to inputs lying outside the data manifold (i.e., "adversarial" examples); thus, selecting a reference point which lies even slightly outside this complex manifold can lead to unintended behaviour of the model, resulting in noisy and uninformative explanations. For ReLU-based networks without bias, choosing a reference point $\widetilde{X} = \delta X$ is valid[2] for any positive value of δ, and the non-explainable zero-order term vanishes in the limit $\delta \to 0$, hence leading to an explanation that satisfies conservation. We note however that the reference point is in most cases quite far from the input sample X, and hence does not sufficiently contextualize the prediction, causing spurious negative relevance scores. Furthermore, owing to the multiscale and distributed nature of a neural network representation, its predictions are a combination of local and global effects. The combination of the two effects introduces a nonlinearity that is impossible to capture in one single linear expansion. Finally, the high complexity of today's deep models often results in a shattered-gradients effect (Balduzzi et al., 2017). Thus, methods relying on gradients (as the Taylor expansion in (5.5)) will systematically produce noisy explanations.

In summary, one can say that Taylor-based decomposition provides a principled way to decompose a function into dimension-wise contributions, but it only works well for relatively simple (nonlinear) functions.

5.3.3 Short Survey on Explanation Methods

To address the challenge of explaining nonlinear models and to overcome the difficulties mentioned above, a number of approaches have been proposed. We now give a brief overview of the different approaches proposed in the context of deep neural networks. As in Samek and Müller (2019) we categorize the methods into three classes: surrogate-based, perturbation-based, and propagation-based explanation methods.

We saw in §5.3.1 that simple linear classifiers are intrinsically explainable, because they can readily be decomposed as a sum over individual dimensions. Surrogate-based XAI methods utilize this property and explain the predictions of complex classifiers by locally approximating them with a simple surrogate func-

---

[2] The resulting reference point $\widetilde{X}$ lies on the same linear region as the point X (Montavon et al., 2018).

tion that is interpretable. Local interpretable model-agnostic explanations (LIME) (Ribeiro et al., 2016) is the most popular explanation technique falling into this category. While LIME has the advantage of being model-agnostic, i.e., it applies to any black-box model without requiring access to its internal structure, one needs to collect a sample of input–output pairs to build the surrogate. This can be computationally expensive and the result may depend on the sample.

The second class of XAI methods constructs explanations from the model's response to local changes, e.g. to some coarse perturbations (Zeiler and Fergus, 2014; Zintgraf et al., 2017; Lundberg and Lee, 2017), or directly to chnages in the gradient, which can be computed cheaply (Baehrens et al., 2010; Simonyan et al., 2013; Shrikumar et al., 2016). To address the gradient noise and its locality, averaging approaches such as SmoothGrad (Smilkov et al., 2017) or integrated gradients (Sundararajan et al., 2017) have been proposed that improve explanation quality compared with a sole gradient, although averaging incurs an additional computational cost. Additionally, the perturbation approach can also be expressed as an optimization problem (Fong and Vedaldi, 2017; Chang et al., 2018; Macdonald et al., 2019), for example by trying to identify a minimal set of relevant input features, such as features that leave the expected classifier score nearly constant when randomizing the remaining (non-relevant) features.

Finally, propagation-based methods, such as layer-wise relevance [ropagation (Bach et al., 2015) and its deep Taylor decomposition theoretical framework (Montavon et al., 2017) explain decisions of neural networks by utilizing the internal structure of the model, specifically, by running a purpose-designed backward pass in the network. They give robust explanations and can be computed quickly in a time of the order of a single backward pass. Furthermore, they overcome many disadvantages of the other explanation techniques, e.g., they do not require sampling and do not have the problem of gradient shattering. The price to pay for these advantageous properties is the reliance on the structure of the model (i.e., these methods are not model-agnostic and require careful design of the backward pass to take into account the specificity of each layer in the network). More recent work has focused on systematizing the design of the backward pass (Montavon et al., 2017, 2019) and on extending the approach beyond neural networks classifiers (Kauffmann et al., 2019, 2020; Eberle et al., 2021; Ruff et al., 2021).

Besides developing novel explanation methods, several works have also focused on comparing existing XAI techniques using objective evaluation criteria. For instance, Samek et al. (2017) measured the quality of explanations using "pixel flipping". Some authors have considered proxy tasks for evaluation (Doshi-Velez and Kim, 2017), e.g., using an explanation for localization tasks (Zhang et al., 2018). Other authors have evaluated explanations using ground-truth information from a synthetic dataset (Osman et al., 2020). Yet other works assess explanation methods based on the fulfilment of certain axioms (Sundararajan et al., 2017; Lundberg and Lee, 2017; Montavon, 2019). Although the evaluation of XAI is still an ongoing research topic, propagation-based explanation techniques have already demonstrated their strength in various practical settings.

A recent trend is also to move from individual explanations to *dataset-wide* explanations, which are presented to the user in a way that provides insight into the internal representation or the set of learned behaviours of the classifier. For instance, Lapuschkin et al. (2019) proposed a technique for (semi-)automatically searching for interesting patterns in a set of explanations. Other works project explanations of the neural network onto more abstract semantic concepts that can be understood by a human (Bau et al., 2017; Kim et al., 2018) or strive for an interaction with the human user (e.g. Baehrens et al., 2010; Hansen et al., 2011).

5.4 Layer-Wise Relevance Propagation: Faithful Explanations by Leveraging Structure

Layer-wise relevance propagation (LRP) (Bach et al., 2015; Montavon et al., 2019) is an XAI method which assumes that the ML model has a layered neural network structure, and leverages this structure to produce robust explanations at low computational cost. The LRP method implements a reverse propagation procedure from the output of the network to the input features (Lapuschkin et al., 2016b; Alber et al., 2019). The propagation is implemented as a collection of redistribution rules applied at each layer of the network. In contrast with many other XAI methods, which rely on sampling or optimization, LRP computes explanations in a time of the order of one backward pass. This allows for fast GPU-based implementations (Alber et al., 2019), where hundreds of explanations can be computed per second. Furthermore, as we will see in §5.4.2, the propagation procedure used by LRP can be embedded in the framework of deep Taylor decomposition (Montavon et al., 2017), which views the backward pass as performing a multitude of Taylor expansions at each layer. Each of these Taylor expansions is simple and tractable, and consequently this procedure conceptually overcomes the various difficulties (of finding good reference points or of gradient shattering) that are encountered with the global Taylor expansion approach presented in §5.3.2.

By viewing LRP from the perspective of Taylor expansions, it is natural that certain desirable properties of an explanation such as *conservation* will be inherited. In fact, LRP propagation rules will be shown to enforce the conservation *locally* at each neuron and, by extension, this also ensures conservation at a coarser level, e.g., between two consecutive layers, and more globally from the neural network output to the neural network input.[3] Thus, LRP ensures that the total evidence for the

---

[3] In practice, conservation holds only approximately owing to the possible presence of bias terms at each

decision taken by the model is redistributed, i.e., no evidence is added or removed through the propagation process. Mathematically, we can express this layer-wise conservation property of LRP as

$$f(X) \approx \sum_{k=1}^{n_L} R_k^{[L]} \approx \cdots \approx \sum_{i=1}^{n_0} R_i^{[0]}, \tag{5.8}$$

where $[l]$ and n_l denote the superscript index and input dimension of the considered layer l, for $l = 0, \ldots, L$. In the following we will show how this redistribution process is implemented in convolutional and recurrent neural networks and how it can be embedded in the framework of deep Taylor decomposition.

5.4.1 LRP in Convolutional Neural Networks

Figure 5.1 illustrates the propagation procedure implemented by LRP for a convolutional neural network. First, the neural network classifies the input, e.g., an image of a rooster. In order to do so, it passes the individual pixel values through a set of convolutional layers, before the resulting activation pattern is classified using fully connected layers. At every layer i, activations are computed as

$$x_k^{[i]} = \sigma\left(\sum_{j=1}^{n_{i-1}} x_j^{[i-1]} w_{jk}^{[i]} + b_k^{[i]}\right), \tag{5.9}$$

where $\sigma(x) = \max(0, x)$ is the ReLU activation function and the sum runs over all lower-layer activations $x_j^{[i-1]}$, plus an extra bias term $b_k^{[i]}$. The activation(s) at the output layer can be interpreted as the total evidence for the presence of a given class. If we aim to explain the network's decision, then the prediction output (pre-softmax) is used to initialize the last layer's relevance value $R_k^{[L]}$. If the network's prediction is wrong or if we want to investigate the model's view on alternative decisions (e.g., identify features $R_i^{[0]} > 0$ speaking for the presence of a specific class), it may be useful to initialize the last layer's relevance value in a different way (e.g., by using the ground-truth label). In the example illustrated in Figure 5.1 the classification decision is correct ("rooster"), thus we initialize the last layer's relevance value with the pre-softmax value of the neuron associated with the class "rooster".

In the next step, the backward-propagation procedure starts, i.e., the relevance values from the upper-layer neurons are redistributed to the lower-layer ones. The

---

layer. The latter receive some share of the redistributed evidence (we could explicitly represent the relevance assigned to the biases at each layer by adding a 0th summation index in (5.8), resulting in an exact conservation throughout layers). Also, a certain LRP rule dissipates relevance by design to improve the signal-to-noise ratio of the explanation (the LRP-ϵ rule; the details are given later).

LRP method redistributes the relevance values proportionally to the contribution of neurons in the forward pass, i.e.,

$$R_j^{[i-1]} = \sum_{k=1}^{n_i} \frac{z_{jk}^{[i]}}{\sum_{l=1}^{n_{i-1}} z_{lk}^{[i]} + b_k^{[i]}} R_k^{[i]}, \qquad (5.10)$$

where $R_k^{[i]}$ denotes the relevance values of the upper-layer neurons (which are already known) and $R_j^{[i-1]}$ stands for the newly computed relevance values of the lower-layer neurons. In this generic formula $z_{jk}^{[i]}$ represents the extent to which neuron j from layer $i-1$ has contributed to make neuron k at layer i relevant.

The abstract redistribution rule described in (5.10) is general enough to be applicable to almost any ML model, including convolutional and recurrent neural networks. In practice, the choice of propagation rule must be made carefully for the explanation method to handle the different layer types properly (Montavon et al., 2018, 2019). Table 5.1 summarizes the different redistribution rules proposed for CNNs. Since the last two layers of the network depicted in Figure 5.1 are fully connected layers, we instantiate the general formulation with the LRP-ϵ redistribution rule. Additionally, for the lower convolutional layers we use a different redistribution rule, namely the LRP-$\alpha\beta$ rule with $\alpha = 1$ and $\beta = 0$. A justification of this layer-type specificity of LRP will be provided in §5.4.2. The result of the redistribution process is a *heatmap* highlighting the pixels which have contributed the most to the model's decision that the image belongs to the class "rooster". We see that the rooster's head and comb are the most relevant features for this decision. In the following we will discuss specific instances of the redistribution rule for different layer types (fc, conv, input layer) of a convolutional neural network. Section 5.4.3 will separately treat the redistribution of relevance through product layers, which are present in LSTM networks.

The basic rule (LRP-0) and epsilon rule (LRP-ϵ) (Bach et al., 2015) redistribute the relevance in proportion to two factors, namely the activations of lower-layer neurons and the connection strengths (weights). The intuition behind these rules is that the neurons that are more activated during prediction encode something about the input, e.g., features present in the image such as the rooster's comb, and should therefore receive a larger share of relevance than neurons which are not activated (note that with ReLU nonlinearities activations are positive or zero). Since the activation patterns will vary for different inputs, these redistribution rules will produce individual explanations for each input. However, since features may be present but irrelevant for the task, activations are not the only criterion to guide the relevance redistribution process. The connections between neurons (the weights) reflect the integration of the encoded low-level features into higher-level concepts (and finally into the prediction) and should be therefore also taken into account

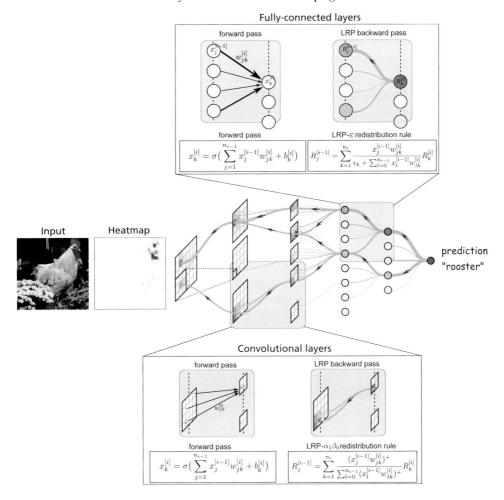

Figure 5.1 Illustration of the LRP procedure for a CNN. Each neuron redistributes as much relevance to the lower layer as it has received from the higher layer, i.e., no relevance is lost or artificially added in the explanation process.

when explaining model decisions. Therefore, both rules redistribute relevance in proportion to the activations of lower-layer neurons and the connection strengths (the model–data–interaction). The LRP-ϵ rule includes a small non-zero term ϵ in the denominator. This additional term stabilizes the redistribution process by absorbing some relevance when the contributions to the activation of neuron k are weak or contradictory.

Two rules which distinguish between the supporting (positive relevance) and contradicting (negative relevance) explanatory factors are LRP-$\alpha\beta$ (Bach et al., 2015) and LRP-γ (Montavon et al., 2019). These rules are also based on the strength of the activations and the weight values. By setting the α, β, and γ parameters appropriately, we can control how much positive relevance is redistributed relative to the negative relevance (and vice versa). Note that as the γ parameter goes to infinity, LRP-γ approaches LRP-$\alpha\beta$ with $\alpha = 1$ and $\beta = 0$.

The other rules shown in Table 5.1 are flat redistribution and two redistribution rules satisfying different requirements on the first layer. While the flat redistribution rule can be used to reduce the spatial resolution of heatmaps (by simply uniformly redistributing relevance from some intermediate layer onto the input), the $z^{\mathcal{B}}$-rule and w^2-rule are derived from the deep Taylor decomposition framework (DTD) (Montavon et al., 2017). Almost all the redistribution rules in Table 5.1 can be embedded into the DTD framework and interpreted as performing a local Taylor decomposition with specific assumptions on the reference point (see §5.4.2). This theoretical foundation of LRP is a strength of the method, because it allows one to design specific rules for different neural network layers (see the discussion in Montavon et al., 2019, and Kohlbrenner et al., 2020). Finally, there are two types of layers that are also commonly encountered in practical convolutional neural networks: pooling layers and batch normalization layers. For max-pooling layers, we can redistribute on the basis of a simple winner-take-all scheme. For average pooling layers, we note that they are a particular instance of a linear layer with positive constant weights and, therefore, the rules that have been defined for linear layers can also be used. Batch-normalization layers are typically treated by fusing them with the fully connected or convolution layer to which they connect (Montavon et al., 2019). This fusing is done after training but before applying LRP, so that LRP sees only an alternation of convolution or fully connected, ReLU and pooling layers.

5.4.2 Theoretical Interpretation of the LRP Redistribution Process

We now present the embedding of LRP into the theoretical framework of deep Taylor decomposition (DTD) (Montavon et al., 2017) and show that the redistribution rules introduced above correspond to a particular Taylor expansion performed locally at the neuron. This match between the algorithmic view (LRP) and the theoretical view (DTD) on the explanation problem gives us the possibility to design redistribution rules tailored to each specific layer type of the CNN.

We have seen that Taylor expansion lets us represent a function as a sum of zeroth-, first- and higher-order terms (cf. Eq. (5.5)). If the reference point $\widetilde{X}$ is chosen wisely, one can use the expansion to decompose the function value in terms of dimension-wise contributions (Eq. (5.7)). However, as discussed in §5.3.2 most of such Taylor decompositions are unreliable for deep neural networks owing to the gradient-shattering problem, to a combination of local and global effects and to the difficulty of finding a good reference point. Thus, although Taylor decomposition

Table 5.1 *Overview of different LRP redistribution rules for CNNs. For better readability we include a 0th-index term with $x_0^{[i-1]} := 1$ and $w_{0k}^{[i]} := b_k^{[i]}$. We use the notation $(x)^+ = \max(0, x)$ and $(x)^- = \min(0, x)$. L_i and H_i denote the minimum and maximum pixel values.*

Name	Redistribution Rule	Usage	DTD
LRP-0 (Bach et al., 2015)	$R_j^{[i-1]} = \sum_{k=1}^{n_i} \dfrac{x_j^{[i-1]} w_{jk}^{[i]}}{\sum_{l=0}^{n_{i-1}} x_l^{[i-1]} w_{lk}^{[i]}} R_k^{[i]}$	fc layers	✓
LRP-ϵ (Bach et al., 2015)	$R_j^{[i-1]} = \sum_{k=1}^{n_i} \dfrac{x_j^{[i-1]} w_{jk}^{[i]}}{\epsilon_k + \sum_{l=0}^{n_{i-1}} x_l^{[i-1]} w_{lk}^{[i]}} R_k^{[i]}$	fc layers	✓
LRP-γ (Montavon et al., 2019)	$R_j^{[i-1]} = \sum_{k=1}^{n_i} \dfrac{x_j^{[i-1]} (w_{jk}^{[i]} + \gamma (w_{jk}^{[i]})^+)}{\sum_{l=0}^{n_{i-1}} x_l^{[i-1]} (w_{lk}^{[i]} + \gamma (w_{lk}^{[i]})^+)} R_k^{[i]}$	conv layers	✓
LRP-$\alpha\beta$ (s.t. $\alpha - \beta = 1$) (Bach et al., 2015)	$R_j^{[i-1]} = \sum_{k=1}^{n_i} \left(\alpha \dfrac{(x_j^{[i-1]} w_{jk}^{[i]})^+}{\sum_{l=0}^{n_{i-1}} (x_l^{[i-1]} w_{lk}^{[i]})^+} - \beta \dfrac{(x_j^{[i-1]} w_{jk}^{[i]})^-}{\sum_{l=0}^{n_{i-1}} (x_l^{[i-1]} w_{lk}^{[i]})^-} \right) R_k^{[i]}$	conv layers	✗ (except $\alpha = 1, \beta = 0$)
flat (Lapuschkin et al., 2019)	$R_j^{[i-1]} = \sum_{k=1}^{n_i} \dfrac{1}{n_{i-1}} R_k^{[i]}$	decrease resolution	✗
w^2-rule (Montavon et al., 2017)	$R_i^{[0]} = \sum_{j=1}^{n_1} \dfrac{(w_{ij}^{[1]})^2}{\sum_{l=1}^{n_0} (w_{lj}^{[1]})^2} R_j^{[1]}$	first layer ($\mathbb{R}^d$)	✓
$z^{\mathcal{B}}$-rule (Montavon et al., 2017)	$R_i^{[0]} = \sum_{j=1}^{n_1} \dfrac{x_i^{[0]} w_{ij}^{[1]} - L_i \cdot (w_{ij}^{[1]})^+ - H_i \cdot (w_{ij}^{[1]})^-}{\sum_{l=1}^{n_0} x_l^{[0]} w_{lj}^{[1]} - L_i \cdot (w_{lj}^{[1]})^+ - H_i \cdot (w_{lj}^{[1]})^-} R_j^{[1]}$	first layer (pixels)	✓

is an appropriate mathematical tool for determining dimension-wise contributions, it does not work reliably when we are trying to explain the deep neural network function in one step, i.e., when trying to linearly approximate its complex input–output relation.

The DTD method makes use of Taylor expansions, but leverages the deep layered structure of the model. Specifically, DTD uses Taylor expansions not to attribute directly the network output to its input (which we have shown to be unstable) but at each layer to attribute the relevance scores $R_k^{[i]}$ to the neurons $\mathbf{x}^{[i-1]}$ in the layer just below. This local attribution task can be interpreted as providing relevance messages that flow between the neurons of the two consecutive layers.

Technically, DTD provides the theoretical framework for LRP in the following ways:

(1) the relevance $R_k^{[i]}$ at each layer is mainly driven by local activations and we can therefore approximate it locally using a relevance function $R_k^{[i]} = \widehat{r}_k(\mathbf{x}^{[i-1]})$;

(2) a first-order Taylor expansion of the relevance function leads to a layer-wise redistribution scheme that corresponds to various LRP rules for appropriate choices of reference points.

These two aspects of DTD are described in detail now.

Relevance Function

The relevance $R_k^{[i]}$ of neuron k at layer i is a deterministic function r_k of the activations $\mathbf{x}^{[i-1]}$ at the lower-level layer, $i-1$, i.e.,

$$R_k^{[i]} = r_k(\mathbf{x}^{[i-1]}). \tag{5.11}$$

This expresses the fact that both the forward propagation through the neural network as well as the backward relevance redistribution are deterministic processes. We need to know only the activations at layer $i-1$ in order to compute all the activations and relevance values from layer i to the output layer L.

As discussed in §5.3.2, Taylor decomposition offers a principled way to determine the dimension-wise contributions of the neurons at layer $i-1$ to the relevance value $R_k^{[i]}$. However, Taylor-based redistribution works reliably only for simple functions $r_k(\mathbf{x}^{[i-1]})$. The function $r_k(\mathbf{x}^{[i-1]})$ is in fact quite complex, because it includes the forward propagation from layer i to the output layer L as well as the relevance redistribution from the output layer L to layer i.

A key insight of DTD is that the relevance function $r_k(\mathbf{x}^{[i-1]})$ can be approximated locally by the simple relevance model $\widehat{r}_k(\mathbf{x}^{[i-1]})$ defined as

$$\widehat{r}_k(\mathbf{x}^{[i-1]}) = x_k^{[i]} \cdot c_k^{[i]}$$

$$= \max\left(0, \sum_{j=1}^{n_{i-1}} x_j^{[i-1]} w_{jk}^{[i]} + b_k^{[i]}\right) \cdot c_k^{[i]}, \tag{5.12}$$

where $c_k^{[i]}$ is a constant. This approximation holds for the last layer L, where the relevance of the output neuron is initialized to be the prediction (pre-softmax) output ($R_k^{[L]} = x_k^{[L]}$). Here the constant $c_k^{[L]}$ is simply 1. Thus, for the last layer we can safely use the Taylor-based redistribution approach.

The question arises whether the approximation still holds for the lower layers, assuming that we have applied LRP in the higher layers. Take for example the LRP-γ rule. If the approximation holds in the layer above, the application of LRP-γ results in the following relevance scores:

$$R_j^{[i-1]} = \sum_{k=1}^{n_i} \frac{x_j^{[i-1]}\left(w_{jk}^{[i]} + \gamma\left(w_{jk}^{[i]}\right)^+\right)}{\sum_{l=0}^{n_{i-1}} x_l^{[i-1]}\left(w_{lk}^{[i]} + \gamma\left(w_{lk}^{[i]}\right)^+\right)} R_k^{[i]}$$

$$= x_j^{[i-1]} \sum_{k=1}^{n_i} \left(w_{jk}^{[i]} + \gamma\left(w_{jk}^{[i]}\right)^+\right) \frac{\max\left(0, \sum_{l=0}^{n_{i-1}} x_l^{[i-1]} w_{lk}^{[i]}\right)}{\sum_{l=0}^{n_{i-1}} x_l^{[i-1]}\left(w_{lk}^{[i]} + \gamma\left(w_{lk}^{[i]}\right)^+\right)} c_k^{[i]}$$

where we observe that the activation $x_j^{[i-1]}$ is multiplied by a factor whose dependence on activations is diluted by two nested sums. This argument supports the
modelling of that term as constant in that lower layer as well. Then, by induction,
the approximation continues to hold at each layer. A similar argument can be made
for other propagation rules, e.g., LRP-0 and LRP-ϵ, as well as for LRP-$\alpha\beta$ with
$\alpha = 0$ and $\beta = 1$.

Taylor-Based Redistribution and LRP Rules

Having shown that the application of LRP at each layer produces the desired
relevance structure, we now focus on the attribution of this relevance to the layer
below by means of a Taylor expansion. The relevance function $\widehat{r}_k(\mathbf{x}^{[i-1]})$ shown in
Eq. (5.12) is a rescaled ReLU neuron taking the lower-layer activations as input.
Hence, it consists of two linear pieces corresponding to the activated and deactivated
domains. For the deactivated domain, there is no relevance to redistribute. For the
activated domain, we consider some reference point $\widetilde{\mathbf{x}}^{[i-1]}$ (also on the activated
domain), and a Taylor expansion at this point gives

$$R_k^{[i]} \approx \widehat{r}_k(\mathbf{x}^{[i-1]}) = \widehat{r}_k(\widetilde{\mathbf{x}}^{[i-1]}) + \underbrace{\sum_{j=1}^{n_{i-1}} (x_j^{[i-1]} - \widetilde{x}_j^{[i-1]}) \cdot [\nabla \widehat{r}_k(\widetilde{\mathbf{x}}^{[i-1]})]_j}_{R_{k \to j}^{[i] \to [i-1]}} + \underbrace{\epsilon}_{0}.$$

$$(5.13)$$

The first-order terms, $R_{k \to j}^{[i] \to [i-1]}$, determine how much of $R_k^{[i]}$ should be redistributed
to the neuron j of the lower layer. Thus, this formulation is equivalent to that in
Eq. (5.5); however, here we are determining how the relevance should be redistributed between two adjacent layers (i and $i-1$) whereas in (5.5) we tried to
determine how the relevance should be redistributed between the output and input
of the network. The redistribution process between two adjacent layers turns out
to be much simpler than that between output and input (i.e., there is no gradient
shattering, the root point is easy to find, etc.). Note that, because of the linearity of
the ReLU function on its activated domain (see (5.12)), higher-order terms vanish
(i.e., $\epsilon = 0$). It can be easily seen that the first-order terms reduce to

$$R_{k \to j}^{[i] \to [i-1]} = (x_j^{[i-1]} - \widetilde{x}_j^{[i-1]}) \cdot w_{jk}^{[i]} c_k^{[i]}.$$

Finally to obtain the relevance of neuron j in the lower-layer $i-1$, one needs only
to pool all incoming relevance messages from layer i:

$$R_j^{[i-1]} = \sum_{k=1}^{n_i} R_{k \to j}^{[i] \to [i-1]}.$$

From this equation, various LRP propagation rules can be recovered. For example, choosing the reference point $\widetilde{\mathbf{x}}^{[i-1]} = \delta \cdot \mathbf{x}^{[i-1]}$, with δ a small positive number, gives the LRP-ϵ rule with $\delta = \epsilon(x_k^{[i]} + \epsilon)^{-1}$ (Montavon et al., 2019): we recover the LRP-0 rule in the limit $\delta \to 0$. The LRP-γ rule is obtained by searching the root point on the line $\{\mathbf{x}^{[i-1]} - t\mathbf{x}^{[i-1]} \odot (\mathbf{1} + \gamma\mathbf{1}_{w_k^{[i]} \geq \mathbf{0}}), t \in \mathbb{R}\}$, where $\odot$ denotes point-wise multiplication (Montavon et al., 2019).

This connection between the LRP propagation rules and the choice of root points in the DTD framework gives a different perspective on how to choose propagation rules at each layer. These LRP rules no longer appear to be heuristically defined. For example, we can show that LRP-0/ϵ/γ all correspond to a reference point whose components are positive. Hence, these rules can be justified as being suitable for use in layers that receive positive quantities, e.g., ReLU activations, as input. Furthermore, LRP rules can be designed directly from the DTD framework, e.g., by choosing root points that satisfy membership of particular domains. For example, the $z^{\mathcal{B}}$-rule and the w^2-rule (shown in Table 5.1) were originally derived from the DTD framework, where the root point is chosen in the first case to satisfy pixel-value boxconstraints, or, in the second case, to be not subject to any domain constraint. More details on DTD, including proofs, can be found in (Montavon et al., 2017), where different LRP rules were derived for ReLU-activated neural networks with negative biases.

Choosing LRP Rules in Practice

The LRP-0 rule (Bach et al., 2015) is the simplest provided by LRP. It is conservative (except for biases) and gives equal treatment to positive and negative contributions. In practice, LRP-0 leads to explanations that closely follow the function and its gradient (see also Shrikumar et al., 2016 or Montavon, 2019). When the network becomes complex and deep, however, LRP-0 becomes exposed to the problem of shattered gradients, which causes the explanation to become noisy. In the DTD framework, such noisy behaviour can be explained by LRP-0 being associated with a root point at the origin, which is far from the actual data point, and thus is likely to bring irrelevant factors into the explanation. Hence, LRP-0 should be reserved for simple functions only (e.g., the very top layers of a CNN).

The LRP-ϵ rule (Bach et al., 2015) stabilizes the redistribution process by adding a constant to the denominator. This has a sparsification effect, where the relevance of neurons with weak net contributions is driven to zero by the stabilization term. We have observed that LRP-ϵ works well for redistribution in the fully connected layers present in the top layers of the neural network and also in the topmost convolution layers. In the DTD framework, the gain in stability can be explained by the fact that the root point lies now closer to the data point and thus provides a better contextualization for the explanation.

The convolutional layers of a CNN exhibit strong levels of nonlinearity, especially due to the stacking of many of these layers. In practice, it can be difficult to fully identify the individual positive or negative effects of each pixel. Instead, it is more practical to assign relevance to a collection of pixels, modelling their combined relevance. This behaviour of the explanation can be induced by imposing a preference for positive contributions over negative ones. Two rules that impose a different treatment between the positive and negative contributions are LRP-$\alpha\beta$ (Bach et al., 2015) and LRP-γ (Montavon et al., 2019), and they are both suitable for these lower-level layers; LRP-γ in particular has a DTD interpretation and the corresponding root point is at the ReLU hinge and relatively close to the data point. Hence, as with LRP-ϵ, the benefit of LRP-γ can again be understood as a better contextualization of the explanation.

The LRP-γ and LRP-$\alpha\beta$ rules assume positive inputs. This is the case for most convolution layers building on ReLU neurons, but not in the first layer where the input can be, e.g., pixel scores, which potentially are negative. For these special input layers, purpose-designed propagation rules, such as the w^2-rule or the $z^{\mathcal{B}}$-rule (Montavon et al., 2017) (see Table 5.1), are more suitable. Finally, if we simply want to highlight a receptive field rather than the contributing features within the receptive field, the "flat" redistribution rule (Lapuschkin et al., 2019) is appropriate.

Now, while here and in §5.4.1 we have highlighted the layer-specific application of the LRP rules on a typical CNN for image classification (according to Montavon et al., 2019 and Kohlbrenner et al., 2020), another configuration of LRP rules might be more appropriate for other network architectures or tasks.

For example, the LRP-ϵ rule was found to work well on a word-embedding-based CNN for text classification (Arras et al., 2017b). Furthermore, while LRP-$\alpha_1\beta_0$ tends to produce explanations with a selectivity that is somewhat too low on a typical CNN for image classification, the same rule has been shown to work very well in the context of the explanation-based pruning of CNNs (Yeom et al., 2019), as well as for the CNN-based relation network model (Osman et al., 2020) used for visual question answering in our experimental section, §5.5.

More generally, when faced with a novel neural network model or task, and if the network is built upon ReLU activations, a default configuration that can be tried is to apply the LRP-$\alpha_1\beta_0$ rule in every hidden layer. The LRP-$\alpha\beta$ rule, with parameters fixed as $\alpha = 1$ and $\beta = 0$, considers only positively contributing neurons and delivers positive-valued relevances; compared with LRP-ϵ and LRP-γ it has the advantage of having no free hyperparameter. Furthermore, if an objective assessment of explanation quality is available for a given task then it is possible to try various combinations of LRP rules and hyperparameters and run an actual hyperparameter selection procedure to optimize explanation for that particular task.

In that sense, the multiple hyperparameters provided by LRP can prove very useful to address the exact application's needs.

We now turn to the application of LRP to LSTM networks.

5.4.3 Extending LRP to LSTM Networks

Long short-term memory (LSTM) (Hochreiter and Schmidhuber, 1997) networks are popular deep models for processing sequential inputs such as biomedical time series, genetic sequences, or textual data. These models consist of a *memory cell* storing an internal state. Figure 5.2 displays such an LSTM memory cell. In the forward pass this cell processes the input and sends it through the input gate,

$$\mathbf{z}_t = g\left(\mathbf{W}_\mathbf{z}\mathbf{x}_t + \mathbf{U}_\mathbf{z}\mathbf{y}_{t-1} + \mathbf{b}_\mathbf{z}\right) \qquad \text{cell input,} \qquad (5.14)$$

$$\mathbf{i}_t = \sigma\left(\mathbf{W}_\mathbf{i}\mathbf{x}_t + \mathbf{U}_\mathbf{i}\mathbf{y}_{t-1} + \mathbf{b}_\mathbf{i}\right) \qquad \text{input gate,} \qquad (5.15)$$

where $\mathbf{x}_t$ is the input vector at time t and $\mathbf{z}_t$ and $\mathbf{i}_t$ are the corresponding cell input and input gate activations, respectively. The input gate, together with the forget gate, control, and update, the cell state,

$$\mathbf{f}_t = \sigma\left(\mathbf{W}_\mathbf{f}\mathbf{x}_t + \mathbf{U}_\mathbf{f}\mathbf{y}_{t-1} + \mathbf{b}_\mathbf{f}\right) \qquad \text{forget gate,} \qquad (5.16)$$

$$\mathbf{c}_t = \mathbf{i}_t \odot \mathbf{z}_t + \mathbf{f}_t \odot \mathbf{c}_{t-1} \qquad \text{cell state,} \qquad (5.17)$$

and the cell state itself has an influence on the output of the LSTM cell:

$$\mathbf{o}_t = \sigma\left(\mathbf{W}_\mathbf{o}\mathbf{x}_t + \mathbf{U}_\mathbf{o}\mathbf{y}_{t-1} + \mathbf{b}_\mathbf{o}\right) \qquad \text{output gate,} \qquad (5.18)$$

$$\mathbf{y}_t = \mathbf{o}_t \odot h\left(\mathbf{c}_t\right) \qquad \text{cell output.} \qquad (5.19)$$

Thus, the LSTM output $\mathbf{y}_t$ depends on the actual input $\mathbf{x}_t$ as well as on the cell state $\mathbf{c}_t$. Both factors are connected through point-wise multiplication (denoted as $\odot$). The activation functions g, h are typically tanh or sigmoid, and the gate activation, σ, is a sigmoid.

For applying the LRP propagation principle to LSTMs, the same redistribution rules which were proposed for convolutional neural networks with ReLU activation (as introduced in Table 5.1) can also be employed in the LSTM to redistribute the relevance through linear layers followed by an element-wise activation (even though the LSTM network typically uses activation functions that differ from ReLU). In particular, previous works have relied on the LRP-ϵ rule for that purpose (Arras et al., 2017a; Ding et al., 2017; Arjona-Medina et al., 2019), i.e., the rule which is recommended for dense layers in CNNs and which provides a signed relevance. This means that in practice linear layers *redirect* the higher-layer relevance proportionally to the neuron forward-pass contributions (i.e., the neuron's activated value times the connection weight), while through element-wise activation layers the relevance

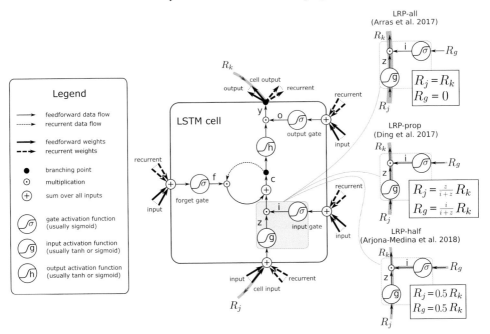

Figure 5.2 Illustration of the LRP procedure for an LSTM. Each neuron, including the product neurons, redistributes to the input neurons as much as it has received from the higher layer (schematic diagram of the LSTM cell from Arras et al., 2019b, reprinted with permission of Springer Nature).

is backward propagated identically (there is no relevance *redirection* through such layers).

Besides, a novel challenge arises when trying to explain LSTM networks (as well as other gated recurrent networks): it comes from the point-wise multiplicative connections. To handle such nonlinearities in the LRP backward redistribution process, authors have proposed several redistribution rules verifying the layer-wise relevance conservation property of LRP (Arras et al., 2017a; Ding et al., 2017; Arjona-Medina et al., 2019). Denoting by x_k such a product neuron in the forward pass, we note that it has the form

$$x_k = x_g \cdot x_j, \tag{5.20}$$

where x_g denotes a sigmoid activated *gate* neuron and x_j, the remaining neuron, is a *signal* neuron. As per the design of the LSTM network (Hochreiter and Schmidhuber, 1997), the role of the gate is to control the flow of information in the LSTM cell (let the information pass if open, or refuse passage if closed), while the signal neuron carries the information itself; this information is either conveyed by the cell input or stored in the LSTM cell's memory via the cell state. A similar configuration for products can also be found in other popular gated recurrent networks such as GRUs (Cho et al., 2014).

Given the upper-layer relevance R_k of the neuron x_k, three alternatives rules can be used to redistribute this quantity onto the input neurons x_g and x_j. These rules are illustrated at the right Figure 5.2 for the particular case of the product between input gate i and cell input z.

LRP-all: One rule proposed by Arras et al. (2017a) assigns all the relevance to the signal neuron, i.e., it sets $R_j = R_k$ and $R_g = 0$. This redistribution follows a signal-take-all strategy. It is based on the idea that gates could be considered as connection weights (although their value is not constant). Accordingly, they influence the LRP redistribution process through the computation of R_k (which, via the relevance redistribution in the next higher linear layer, is proportional to x_k and thus also depends on x_g), but they do not get a relevance value assigned *per se*, since their expected role in the LSTM forward pass is only to reweight the value of the signal x_j.

LRP-prop: The rule proposed by Ding et al. (2017) redistributes the relevance proportionally to the neurons' activated values, i.e., $R_j = \frac{x_j}{x_j+x_g} R_k$ and $R_g = \frac{x_g}{x_j+x_g} R_k$.

LRP-half: A rule proposed by Arjona-Medina et al. (2019) redistributes the relevance equally, i.e., $R_j = R_g = 0.5 R_k$.

Arras et al. (2019a,b) carefully compared these three redistribution rules in simulations and experiments with real-world natural language processing (NLP) data on commonly used LSTMs (Greff et al., 2017) that follow the structure given by equations (5.14)–(5.19) and that use the tanh nonlinearity for the cell input and output (the functions g and h in (5.14) and (5.19)). The qualitative and quantitative results showed a clear superiority of the LRP-all rule[4] (Arras et al., 2017a) over LRP-prop and LRP-half. Independent works also successfully applied the LRP-all redistribution rule to LSTMs on a synthetic task, in the medical domain (Yang et al., 2018), as well as in NLP (Poerner et al., 2018) and in computer security (Warnecke et al., 2020), demonstrating the resulting LRP explanations are superior to other explanation methods for recurrent neural networks.

DTD Interpretation

In the following we will show that the LRP-all rule can be further motivated under the theoretical framework of deep Taylor decomposition (Montavon et al., 2017),

---

[4] Note, though, that on non-standard customized LSTM models, as were introduced in Arjona-Medina et al. (2019); Arras et al. (2019b), other LRP rules for product neurons can become advantageous over LRP-all.

as was proposed in Arras et al. (2019b). Let us introduce the neuron pre-activations z_g and z_j, for neurons x_g and x_j, respectively, and consider a product of neurons where the signal is tanh activated:

$$x_k = \text{sigm}(z_g) \cdot \text{tanh}(z_j).$$

Suppose the relevance of the product neuron $R_k(z_g, z_j)$, as a function of the pre-activations, can be approximated by a simple relevance model of the form

$$\widehat{R}_k(z_g, z_j) = \text{sigm}(z_g) \cdot \text{tanh}(z_j) \cdot c_k = x_k \cdot c_k,$$

where c_k is a constant, such that $R_k(z_g, z_j) = \widehat{R}_k(z_g, z_j)$ locally. This is the generic relevance form assumed by the DTD framework (Montavon et al., 2017). By performing a Taylor expansion of this relevance model at a root point $(\widetilde{z}_g, \widetilde{z}_j)$, we obtain

$$
\begin{aligned}
\widehat{R}_k(z_g, z_j) = &\widehat{R}_k(\widetilde{z}_g, \widetilde{z}_j) & (= 0) \\
&+ \text{sigm}'(\widetilde{z}_g) \cdot \text{tanh}(\widetilde{z}_j) \cdot c_k \cdot (z_g - \widetilde{z}_g) & (= R_g) \\
&+ \text{sigm}(\widetilde{z}_g) \cdot \text{tanh}'(\widetilde{z}_j) \cdot c_k \cdot (z_j - \widetilde{z}_j) & (= R_j) \\
&+ \epsilon.
\end{aligned}
$$

Using the nearest root point in the space of pre-activations (Arras et al., 2019b), which is given by $\widetilde{z}_j = 0$ and $\widetilde{z}_g = z_g$, it follows the LRP-all rule: $R_g = 0$ and $R_j = \widehat{R}_k$. Moreover, using this root point, higher-order terms of the form $(z_g - \widetilde{z}_g)^k$ as well as the interaction terms $(z_g - \widetilde{z}_g)^{\cdots}(z_j - \widetilde{z}_j)^{\cdots}$ vanish; thus the error term ϵ depends only on the signal variable z_j. In other words, if the tanh activation is working near its linear regime then the error term ϵ in the LRP decomposition is negligible (no matter whether the gate's sigmoid activation is saturated or not). Lastly, if instead of using a tanh activation for the signal neuron, one used a ReLU activation, for example, then the approximation error would be exactly zero in this case (i.e., $\epsilon = 0$). For more details on the various DTD relevance models for different signal activation functions we refer to Arras et al. (2019b).

5.5 Explaining a Visual Question Answering Model

This section demonstrates the ability of LRP to explain the decisions of a complex model trained for visual question answering (VQA) with the CLEVR dataset (Johnson et al., 2017a). Visual question answering is a multi-modal task at the intersection between nature language processing and computer vision: the model is fed with an image and a textual question about that image, and is asked to predict the answer to that question, either with a single word or in free-form text.

Dataset and Model

The CLEVR dataset is a synthetic VQA task which was proposed by Johnson et al. (2017a) to avoid the biases present in VQA benchmarks based on real-world images (Antol et al., 2015; Goyal et al., 2017): its primary goal was to diagnose the visual reasoning capabilities of state-of-the-art VQA models. It is based on images of 3D rendered objects – more precisely, geometric shapes positioned on a plane surface with a grey background. Each object has four types of attributes (spread among eight colours, two materials, two sizes, and three shapes). The questions are designed to test the following reasoning abilities: spatial relationships between objects, comparison and recognition of object attributes, object counting, and the comparison of object sets sizes. The data consists of 70,000/15,000/15,000 training/validation/test images, and respectively 699,989/149,991/149,988 questions (i.e., there are roughly 10 questions per image). The prediction problem is framed as a 28-way classification task (the output is a single word among a vocabulary of size 28).

Early work on this task used complex models, e.g., with stacked attention (Yang et al., 2016) or with an explicit representation of the question-generation program (Johnson et al., 2017b), but Santoro et al. (2017) proposed a simpler architecture based on a relation network (RN) that performs even better in terms of prediction accuracy. We re-implemented their model and trained it as described in Santoro et al. (2017). Our trained model reaches a test accuracy of 93.3% on the CLEVR dataset (the original authors reported a performance of 95.5%).

The model architecture is displayed in Figure 5.3. It consists of a four-layer CNN to extract feature maps from the image, a LSTM network to process the question, and a pairwise concatenation of visual "objects" together with the question representation to fuse the visual and textual information. Here the "objects" are simply pixels in the CNN last-layer feature maps. Each layer of the CNN has the following structure: `conv` → `relu` → `batchnorm`, with 24 kernels of size 3×3 and stride 2 (no padding). The LSTM part of the network is a unidirectional LSTM with word embeddings of size 32, and a hidden layer of size 128. The paired representations (the object pair concatenated with the LSTM final hidden state) are passed to a RN, which is made of a four-layer MLP of fully connected layers of size 256, each followed by ReLU activation, and a final element-wise summation layer. The resulting representation is passed to a three-layer MLP with fully connected layers of size 256, each followed by ReLU activation. The output layer is a fully connected layer of size 28. For preprocessing the questions, we removed punctuation and performed lower-casing; the resulting input vocabulary has size 80. For preprocessing the images, we resized them to 128×128 pixels and rescaled the pixel values to the range $[0, 1]$. Training was done with the Adam optimizer.

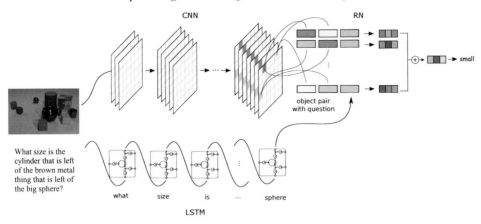

Figure 5.3 VQA model from Santoro et al. (2017) used in our experiments.

Methods for Explaining VQA

In order to get insights into the model's prediction strategies, we computed relevance values for the question (explaining the LSTM part of the model) and the image (explaining the CNN part of the model) using LRP. For the LSTM part of the network, we employed the LRP-all rule for product layers, and the LRP-ϵ rule (with $\epsilon = 0.001$) for the remaining layers. For the CNN and RN parts of the network (i.e., on the image-processing side), we used the LRP-$\alpha\beta$ rule with $\alpha = 1$ and $\beta = 0$, as this variant was shown to perform better, according to quantitative experiments performed in Osman et al. (2020), compared with a composite application of the LRP-$\alpha\beta$/LRP-ϵ rules for different layers.

In addition, we computed relevances using two simple baseline methods, namely Gradient × Input (Shrikumar et al., 2016) and Occlusion (Li et al., 2016). The first method computes the relevance of an input feature by simply using the partial derivative of the prediction function (pre-softmax) multiplied by the feature's value, i.e., $R_i^{[0]} = \frac{\partial f_c}{\partial x_i^{[0]}}(\mathbf{x}^{[0]}) \cdot x_i^{[0]}$ (where f_c is the prediction function for the target class c, and $\mathbf{x}^{[0]}$ is the input), whereas the latter method computes the relevance value using a difference of probabilities $R_i^{[0]} = P_c(\mathbf{x}^{[0]}) - P_c(\mathbf{x}_{|x_i^{[0]}=0})$ (where P_c are the predicted softmax probabilities, respectively, for the original unmodified input and for the input where the feature of interest $x_i^{[0]}$ has been set to zero).

For all methods we explained the decision for the model's *predicted* class. For the question heatmaps, in order to get one relevance value per word, we summed the relevances over the word embedding dimensions and took the absolute value for visualization. For the image heatmaps, we summed the relevances across the channels, took the absolute value, and applied gaussian blurring (with standard deviation 0.02 times the image size) for visualization of the original image overlayed

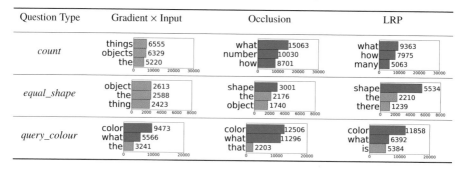

Figure 5.4 The most important words for three CLEVR question types, sorted by decreasing frequency over the validation set. A word is chosen as important if it appears in the top three relevant words of a question.

with the heatmap. For raw heatmap visualization we just summed the relevances across the channels.

Results and Insights

In order to see which words are the most relevant per question type, we performed a word relevance statistic over the CLEVR validation set. For each question we identified the three most relevant words, and compiled the selected words by question type. Then we retrieved the words with the highest frequencies for a few question types in Figure 5.4. We manually highlighted words that were directly related to the question type, regardless of the image, in green. Note that the network does not have access to the question types during prediction.

One can see that the nouns `shape` and `colour` have been identified (except by Gradient × Input) as being relevant to answer questions about the shape or colour of objects. For the question type *count*, where the goal is to count objects in a set, Occlusion and LRP both selected meaningful words, while Gradient × Input attributed high relevance to generic words such as `the`, `things`, `objects`. Similar words were selected by Gradient × Input for the question type *equal_shape*, which suggests that the latter method is less suited to find important words related to the question type.

Additionally, we visualized relevance heatmaps for individual data points in Figures 5.5 and 5.6, using Gradient × Input and LRP (we did not compute heatmaps for Occlusion, since this method is very expensive to compute on the image side). The exemplary data points were automatically selected in the following way: we conducted a search over both correctly and falsely predicted CLEVR validation points with specific question types, and retrieved the three points with the highest predicted probabilities, i.e., the points where the model is very confident with its prediction. Indeed we expected the corresponding explanations to be more focused and insightful on such data points, while on data points where the model is hesitating the heatmaps might be more diffuse and less informative. For correctly predicted data points (Figure 5.5), we considered all questions that query an object's attribute, i.e., we used the question types *query_material*, *query_colour*, *query_size*, *query_shape*. For falsely predicted data points (Figure 5.6) we used only the question type *query_colour*.

From the heatmap visualizations of the textual questions in Figure 5.5 and Fig. 5.6 we could not make a clear-cut statement about which explanation method was qualitatively better. Both methods seem to deliver equally sparse explanations. When the questions are about an object's material (Figure 5.5), the word `material` is often highlighted (except in the last question for LRP); when they are about a colour (Figure 5.6), the word `colour` is always highlighted by LRP, and highlighted once by Gradient × Input. However, it seems that Gradient × Input attributes higher relevances to the last words in the question compared with those at the beginning of the question (which is probably due to a vanishing-gradient effect induced by the forget gate in the unidirectional LSTM), while LRP is able to assign a high relevance, e.g., to the word `colour` (Figure 5.6), even when it appears at the beginning of the question.

On the image side however, we clearly see that the LRP heatmaps in Figures 5.5 and 5.6 are qualitatively better than those delivered by Gradient × Input: the LRP explanations are generally less noisier, more concentrated on objects, and provide pertinent clues to the model's visual reasoning (as we will see below), while Gradient × Input seems to attribute (partly) spurious relevances to background areas.

Let us take a closer look at the LRP heatmaps in Figure 5.5. In the first question, the target object of the question is the grey metal sphere at the top left of the scene. In the VQA question this object is referenced through its spatial location relatively to the brown sphere. And correspondingly, the LRP visual explanation both highlights the target object, as well as the referring object of the question. The second question has a similar pattern, where the target object is the yellow cube, and the referring object is the small blue sphere. Again the LRP heatmap reveals the two important objects of the question. In contrast, the Gradient × Input heatmaps are not helpful for understanding the model's decisions for question 1 and 2. Finally, in the third question, the target object of the VQA question is the red cylinder. Here the spatial relationships formulated in the VQA question are more intricate and involve multiple objects, including a big cyan cube and a small rubber sphere. Thus the LRP explanation is more diffuse: it highlights several objects, namely the two cyan cubes as well as all objects on their right. Intuitively it makes sense that the model is focusing on all these objects to answer the given more complex question.

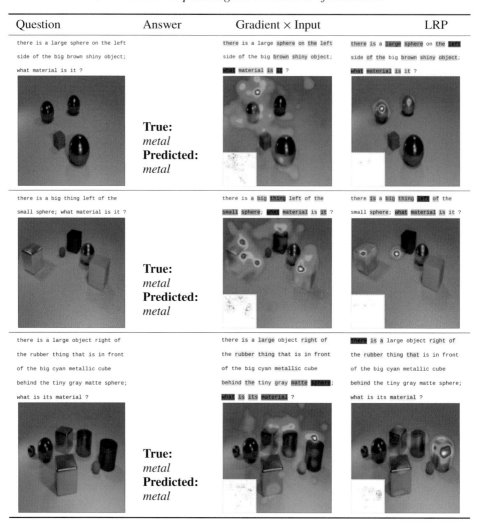

Figure 5.5 Heatmaps for three CLEVR questions which are correctly predicted. On the image side, we visualizeed the heatmap overlayed with the original image, as well as the raw heatmap (at bottom left of the images). In the top row, the VQA question is a query about the material (metal vs. rubber) of the grey sphere situated in the top left of the scene, and on the left side from the brown sphere. In the middle row, the queried object is the yellow cube, which is situated left of the small blue rubber sphere. In the bottom question, the query is about the material of the red cylinder, which is referenced with respect to the small grey rubber sphere and the cyan cube in the background of the scene. In all cases, we observe that the generated LRP explanations are informative and consistently highlight the important objects of the VQA question that the model relies on to predict the correct answer, while the gradient input heatmaps are noisier and less helpful for understanding the predictions.

Also the target object of the question (the red cylinder) is identified by the LRP heatmap.

Question	Answer	Gradient × Input	LRP

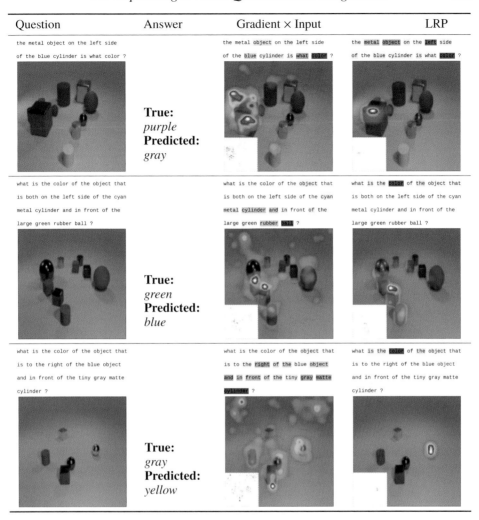

Row 1:

Question: the metal object on the left side of the blue cylinder is what color ?

Answer: True: *purple* Predicted: *gray*

Gradient × Input: the metal object on the left side of the blue cylinder is what color ?

LRP: the metal object on the left side of the blue cylinder is what color ?

Row 2:

Question: what is the color of the object that is both on the left side of the cyan metal cylinder and in front of the large green rubber ball ?

Answer: True: *green* Predicted: *blue*

Gradient × Input: what is the color of the object that is both on the left side of the cyan metal cylinder and in front of the large green rubber ball ?

LRP: what is the color of the object that is both on the left side of the cyan metal cylinder and in front of the large green rubber ball ?

Row 3:

Question: what is the color of the object that is to the right of the blue object and in front of the tiny gray matte cylinder ?

Answer: True: *gray* Predicted: *yellow*

Gradient × Input: what is the color of the object that is to the right of the blue object and in front of the tiny gray matte cylinder ?

LRP: what is the color of the object that is to the right of the blue object and in front of the tiny gray matte cylinder ?

Figure 5.6 Heatmaps for three CLEVR questions which were falsely predicted. On the image side, we visualized the heatmap overlayed with the original image, as well as the raw heatmap (at bottom left of the images). In the top question, the query is about the colour of the purple cylinder located left from the blue cylinder, and both of these objects are largely occluded by the big grey cube. Here the model obviously mistakenly interpreted the grey cube as being the target object of the question, as it provided "gray" as an answer, while the correct answer was "purple". In the middle row, the queried object is the small green rubber cube, which is both situated left from the small cyan cylinder and in front of the big green rubber sphere. Here the model also made a mistake, and identified the little blue metal cube as the target object. Lastly in the bottom question, the queried object is the grey metal ball, which is situated on the right of the blue cube and in front of the grey cylinder, however the model mistakenly identified the yellow sphere as being the target object of the question. In all cases, the LRP heatmaps are coherent with the model's predicted wrong answers, while the gradient input heatmaps are more diffuse and less helpful for understanding the model's decisions.

Other useful insights can be revealed by the LRP explanations in order to understand misclassified examples in Figure 5.6. In these questions the colour of a given object is asked. And, in all cases, the object with the highest relevance, as identified by the LRP heatmap, is consistent with the model's predicted answer, while the Gradient × Input heatmaps are less distinct. In the first question, the target object of the question (the small purple object to the left of the grey cube), as well as the referring object (the small blue object behind the grey cube) are highly occluded by the grey cube, which explains why the model did not correctly identify the target object of the question and made a false prediction by focusing on the grey cube instead, as revealed by the LRP heatmap. In the second question the target object of the VQA question was the green cube; however, according to the LRP heatmap, the model identified instead the blue cube as being the target object of the question. Thus, the model mistakenly interpreted the spatial relationships defined by the VQA question. A similar phenomenon can be observed in the third question: the target object of the VQA question is the grey metal sphere, but the LRP heatmap reveals that the model instead identified the yellow metal sphere as being the target object, which again confirms that the model has some difficulty in catching subtle spatial relationships: here it obviously did not correctly recognize the "in front of" relationship.

Overall, the LRP visual explanations helped to understand *why* the VQA model generated a particular answer. A further interesting point to note is that the neural network model we use – which is based on a relation network (Santoro et al., 2017) – does not contain any explicit attention mechanism in its architecture. Still, the LRP heatmaps were able to reveal image regions that are important to the model's decision, and that resemble typical attention heatmaps (as provided, e.g., by highly customized models for the CLEVR dataset such as the model from Mascharka et al., 2018).

5.6 Discussion

This chapter has presented LRP as a powerful technique for explaining predictions of complex ML models such as convolutional and recurrent neural networks. The redistribution rules of LRP were derived from first principles using the deep Taylor decomposition framework. It was shown that a careful choice of the redistribution rules (respectively, root points in DTD) is very important when applying LRP to composite architectures, i.e., models that combine layers with different properties. A naive choice of redistribution rule, e.g., LRP-ϵ for all layers of an image classification CNN, or LRP-prop for a standard LSTM model, can produce poor results. However, when applied properly, LRP can produce meaningful explanations and lead to interesting insights, even for complex and multimodal models such as that used for the VQA task.

As well as the successful application of LRP to different scenarios, progress has recently been made on the development of criteria to objectively assess the quality and utility of explanations (Samek et al., 2017; Lundberg and Lee, 2017; Montavon, 2019; Osman et al., 2020). Here, several metrics as well as axiomatic approaches have been developed, yet many challenges remain. For instance, while several general frameworks for XAI have been developed, e.g., based on deep Taylor decomposition (Montavon et al., 2017), Shapley values (Lundberg and Lee, 2017) or rate-distortion theory (Macdonald et al., 2019), a unified theory of explanation is still lacking.

A limitation of today's methods is the low semantic level of explanations. For instance, heatmaps do let us distinguish whether a group of features is jointly relevant for a given classification decision or whether each feature in this group contributes individually. Also, pixel-level heatmaps do not provide any information about the underlying concepts in the data, e.g., objects in the image. The resulting interpretation gap (i.e., relating relevant pixels to the relevant object) has to be closed by the recipient of the explanations, which can be difficult and erroneous. Furthermore, the vulnerability of explanations to adversarial manipulations (Dombrowski et al., 2019) is a serious challenge, because it may undermine trust in the explanation results.

Promising future research topics in the field of XAI are the use of explanations beyond interpretability. For instance, Yeom et al. (2019) demonstrated that LRP relevance scores can be used to prune a neural network. Other applications of XAI, e.g., in the detection of adversarial attacks or general model improvement (e.g., by self-supervision) are interesting future research directions. Also, the field of human–machine interaction offers various opportunities for explainability research. For instance, questions such as "what type of explanation is most useful for humans", "how can we move towards interactive explainability" or "how can we prevent misleading explanations from harming performance" need to be investigated in order to allow for reliable and efficient human–machine interaction; see e.g., Baehrens et al. (2010) and Hansen et al. (2011) for early studies in this vein. Finally, bringing the concepts of XAI to other types of models (Lundberg et al., 2020) or ML tasks (Kauffmann et al., 2019) remains an active area of research.

Acknowledgements This work was supported by the German Ministry for Education and Research (BMBF) as BIFOLD – Berlin Institute for the Foundations of Learning and Data (ref. 01IS18025A and ref. 01IS18037A). KRM also received support from the Institute of Information & Communications Technology Planning

& Evaluation (IITP) grants funded by the Korea Government (No. 2019-0-00079, Artificial Intelligence Graduate School Program, Korea University).

References

Alber, Maximilian, Lapuschkin, Sebastian, Seegerer, Philipp, Hägele, Miriam, Schütt, Kristof T., Montavon, Grégoire, Samek, Wojciech, Müller, Klaus-Robert, Dähne, Sven, and Kindermans, Pieter-Jan. 2019. iNNvestigate neural networks! *Journal of Machine Learning Research*, **20**(93), 1–8.

Anders, Christopher J., Neumann, David, Marinc, Talmaj, Samek, Wojciech, Müller, Klaus-Robert, and Lapuschkin, Sebastian. 2020. XAI for analyzing and unlearning spurious correlations in ImageNet. *Proc. ICML 2020 Workshop – XXAI: Extending Explainable AI Beyond Deep Models and Classifiers*.

Antol, Stanislaw, Agrawal, Aishwarya, Lu, Jiasen, Mitchell, Margaret, Batra, Dhruv, Zitnick, C. Lawrence, and Parikh, Devi. 2015. VQA: Visual question answering. Pages 2425–2433 of: *Proc. International Conference on Computer Vision*.

Arjona-Medina, Jose A., Gillhofer, Michael, Widrich, Michael, Unterthiner, Thomas, Brandstetter, Johannes, and Hochreiter, Sepp. 2019. RUDDER: Return decomposition for delayed rewards. Pages 13566–13577 of: *Advances in Neural Information Processing Systems*.

Arras, Leila, Montavon, Grégoire, Müller, Klaus-Robert, and Samek, Wojciech. 2017a. Explaining recurrent neural network predictions in sentiment snalysis. Pages 159–168 of: *Proc. EMNLP'17 Workshop on Computational Approaches to Subjectivity, Sentiment & Social Media Analysis (WASSA)*.

Arras, Leila, Horn, Franziska, Montavon, Grégoire, Müller, Klaus-Robert, and Samek, Wojciech. 2017b. "What is relevant in a text document?": An interpretable machine learning approach. *PLoS ONE*, **12**(7), e0181142.

Arras, Leila, Osman, Ahmed, Müller, Klaus-Robert, and Samek, Wojciech. 2019a. Evaluating recurrent neural network explanations. Pages 113–126 of: *Proc. ACL'19 BlackboxNLP Workshop: Analyzing and Interpreting Neural Networks for NLP*.

Arras, Leila, Arjona-Medina, José, Widrich, Michael, Montavon, Grégoire, Gillhofer, Michael, Müller, Klaus-Robert, Hochreiter, Sepp, and Samek, Wojciech. 2019b. Explaining and interpreting LSTMs. Pages 211–238 of: *Explainable AI: Interpreting, Explaining and Visualizing Deep Learning*. Lecture Notes in Computer Science, vol. 11700.

Bach, S., Binder, A., Montavon, G., Klauschen, F., Müller, K.-R., and Samek, W. 2015. On pixel-wise explanations for non-linear classifier decisions by layer-wise relevance propagation. *PLoS ONE*, **10**(7), e0130140.

Baehrens, David, Schroeter, Timon, Harmeling, Stefan, Kawanabe, Motoaki, Hansen, Katja, and Müller, Klaus-Robert. 2010. How to explain individual classification decisions. *Journal of Machine Learning Research*, **11**, 1803–1831.

Bahdanau, Dzmitry, Cho, Kyunghyun, and Bengio, Yoshua. 2014. Neural machine translation by jointly learning to align and translate. ArXiv preprint arXiv:1409.0473.

Baldi, Pierre, Sadowski, Peter, and Whiteson, Daniel. 2014. Searching for exotic particles in high-energy physics with deep learning. *Nature Communications*, **5**, 4308.

Balduzzi, David, Frean, Marcus, Leary, Lennox, Lewis, J.P., Ma, Kurt Wan-Duo, and McWilliams, Brian. 2017. The shattered gradients problem: If RESNETs are the answer, then what is the question? Pages 342–350 of: *Proc. 34th International Conference on Machine Learning*.

Bau, David, Zhou, Bolei, Khosla, Aditya, Oliva, Aude, and Torralba, Antonio. 2017. Network dissection: Quantifying interpretability of deep visual representations. Pages 6541–6549 of: *Proc. IEEE Conference on Computer Vision and Pattern Recognition*.

Chang, Chun-Hao, Creager, Elliot, Goldenberg, Anna, and Duvenaud, David. 2018. Explaining image classifiers by counterfactual generation. ArXiv preprint arXiv:1807.08024.

Cho, Kyunghyun, van Merrienboer, Bart, Gulcehre, Caglar, Bahdanau, Dzmitry, Bougares, Fethi, Schwenk, Holger, and Bengio, Yoshua. 2014. Learning phrase representations using RNN encoder–decoder for statistical machine translation. Pages 1724–1734 of: *Proc. 2014 Conference on Empirical Methods in Natural Language Processing*.

Cireşan, Dan, Meier, Ueli, Masci, Jonathan, and Schmidhuber, Jürgen. 2011. A committee of neural networks for traffic sign classification. Pages 1918–1921 of: *Proc. International Joint Conference on Neural Networks*.

Devlin, Jacob, Chang, Ming-Wei, Lee, Kenton, and Toutanova, Kristina. 2018. BERT: Pre-training of deep bidirectional transformers for language understanding. ArXiv preprint arXiv:1810.04805.

Ding, Yanzhuo, Liu, Yang, Luan, Huanbo, and Sun, Maosong. 2017. Visualizing and understanding neural machine translation. Pages 1150–1159 of: *Proc. 55th Annual Meeting of the Association for Computational Linguistics*.

Dombrowski, Ann-Kathrin, Alber, Maximillian, Anders, Christopher, Ackermann, Marcel, Müller, Klaus-Robert, and Kessel, Pan. 2019. Explanations can be manipulated and geometry is to blame. Pages 13567–13578 of: *Advances in Neural Information Processing Systems*.

Doshi-Velez, Finale, and Kim, Been. 2017. Towards a rigorous science of interpretable machine learning. ArXiv preprint arXiv:1702.08608.

Eberle, Oliver, Büttner, Jochen, Kräutli, Florian, Müller, Klaus-Robert, Valleriani, Matteo, and Montavon, Grégoire. 2021. Building and interpreting deep similarity models. *IEEE Transactions on Pattern Analysis & Machine Intelligence*.

Esteva, Andre, Kuprel, Brett, Novoa, Roberto A., Ko, Justin, Swetter, Susan M., Blau, Helen M., and Thrun, Sebastian. 2017. Dermatologist-level classification of skin cancer with deep neural networks. *Nature*, **542**(7639), 115.

Fong, Ruth C., and Vedaldi, Andrea. 2017. Interpretable explanations of black boxes by meaningful perturbation. Pages 3429–3437 of: *Proc. IEEE Conference on Computer Vision and Pattern Recognition*.

Goodman, Bryce, and Flaxman, Seth. 2017. European Union regulations on algorithmic decision-making and a "right to explanation". *AI Magazine*, **38**(3), 50–57.

Goyal, Yash, Khot, Tejas, Summers-Stay, Douglas, Batra, Dhruv, and Parikh, Devi. 2017. Making the V in VQA matter: Elevating the role of image understanding in visual question answering. In: *Proc. IEEE Conference on Computer Vision and Pattern Recognition*.

Greff, Klaus, Srivastava, Rupesh K., Koutník, Jan, Steunebrink, Bas R., and Schmidhuber, Jürgen. 2017. LSTM: A search space odyssey. *IEEE Transactions on Neural Networks and Learning Systems*, **28**(10), 2222–2232.

Guyon, Isabelle, and Elisseeff, André. 2003. An introduction to variable and feature selection. *Journal of Machine Learning Research*, **3**, 1157–1182.

Hannun, Awni Y., Rajpurkar, Pranav, Haghpanahi, Masoumeh, Tison, Geoffrey H., Bourn, Codie, Turakhia, Mintu P., and Ng, Andrew Y. 2019. Cardiologist-level arrhythmia detection and classification in ambulatory electrocardiograms using a deep neural network. *Nature Medicine*, **25**(1), 65.

Hansen, Katja, Baehrens, David, Schroeter, Timon, Rupp, Matthias, and Müller, Klaus-Robert. 2011. Visual interpretation of kernel-based prediction models. *Molecular Informatics*, **30**(9), 817–826.

Hochreiter, Sepp, and Schmidhuber, Jürgen. 1997. Long short-term memory. *Neural Computation*, **9**(8), 1735–1780.

Horst, Fabian, Lapuschkin, Sebastian, Samek, Wojciech, Müller, Klaus-Robert, and Schöllhorn, Wolfgang I. 2019. Explaining the unique nature of individual gait patterns with deep learning. *Scientific Reports*, **9**, 2391.

Johnson, Justin, Hariharan, Bharath, van der Maaten, Laurens, Fei-Fei, Li, Zitnick, C. Lawrence, and Girshick, Ross B. 2017a. CLEVR: A diagnostic dataset for compositional language and elementary visual reasoning. Pages 1988–1997 of: *Proc. IEEE Conference on Computer Vision and Pattern Recognition*.

Johnson, Justin, Hariharan, Bharath, van der Maaten, Laurens, Hoffman, Judy, Fei-Fei, Li, Lawrence Zitnick, C., and Girshick, Ross. 2017b. Inferring and executing programs for visual reasoning. In: *Proc. IEEE International Conference on Computer Vision (ICCV)*.

Jurmeister, Philipp, Bockmayr, Michael, Seegerer, Philipp, Bockmayr, Teresa, Treue, Denise, Montavon, Grégoire, Vollbrecht, Claudia, Arnold, Alexander, Teichmann, Daniel, Bressem, Keno, Schüller, Ulrich, von Laffert, Maximilian, Müller, Klaus-Robert, Capper, David, and Klauschen, Frederick. 2019. Machine learning analysis of DNA methylation profiles distinguishes primary lung squamous cell carcinomas from head and neck metastases. *Science Translational Medicine*, **11**(509).

Kauffmann, Jacob, Esders, Malte, Montavon, Grégoire, Samek, Wojciech, and Müller, Klaus-Robert. 2019. From clustering to cluster explanations via neural networks. ArXiv preprint arXiv:1906.07633.

Kauffmann, Jacob, Müller, Klaus-Robert, and Montavon, Grégoire. 2020. Towards explaining anomalies: a deep Taylor decomposition of one-class models. *Pattern Recognition*, **101**, 107198.

Kim, Been, Wattenberg, Martin, Gilmer, Justin, Cai, Carrie, Wexler, James, Viegas, Fernanda, and Sayres, Rory. 2018. Interpretability beyond feature attribution: Quantitative testing with concept activation vectors (TCAV). Pages 2668–2677 of: *Proc. International Conference on Machine Learning*.

Kohlbrenner, Maximilian, Bauer, Alexander, Nakajima, Shinichi, Binder, Alexander, Samek, Wojciech, and Lapuschkin, Sebastian. 2020. Towards best practice in explaining neural network decisions with LRP. Pages 1–7 of: *Proc. IEEE International Joint Conference on Neural Networks*.

Lapuschkin, Sebastian, Binder, Alexander, Montavon, Grégoire, Müller, Klaus-Robert, and Samek, Wojciech. 2016a. Analyzing classifiers: Fisher vectors and deep neural networks. Pages 2912–2920 of: *Proc. IEEE Conference on Computer Vision and Pattern Recognition*.

Lapuschkin, Sebastian, Binder, Alexander, Montavon, Grégoire, Müller, Klaus-Robert, and Samek, Wojciech. 2016b. The LRP toolbox for artificial neural networks. *Journal of Machine Learning Research*, **17**(1), 3938–3942.

Lapuschkin, Sebastian, Wäldchen, Stephan, Binder, Alexander, Montavon, Grégoire, Samek, Wojciech, and Müller, Klaus-Robert. 2019. Unmasking Clever Hans predictors and assessing what machines really learn. *Nature Communications*, **10**, 1096.

Li, Jiwei, Monroe, Will, and Jurafsky, Dan. 2016. Understanding neural networks through representation erasure. ArXiv preprint arXiv:1612.08220.

Lu, Chaochao, and Tang, Xiaoou. 2015. Surpassing human-level face verification performance on LFW with GaussianFace. Pages 3811–3819 of: *Proc. 29th AAAI Conference on Artificial Intelligence*.

Lundberg, Scott M., and Lee, Su-In. 2017. A unified approach to interpreting model predictions. Pages 4765–4774 of: *Advances in Neural Information Processing Systems*.

Lundberg, Scott M., Erion, Gabriel, Chen, Hugh, DeGrave, Alex, Prutkin, Jordan M., Nair, Bala, Katz, Ronit, Himmelfarb, Jonathan, Bansal, Nisha, and Lee, Su-In. 2020. From local explanations to global understanding with explainable AI for trees. *Nature Machine Intelligence*, **2**(1), 2522–5839.

Macdonald, Jan, Wäldchen, Stephan, Hauch, Sascha, and Kutyniok, Gitta. 2019. A rate-distortion framework for explaining neural network decisions. ArXiv preprint arXiv:1905.11092.

Mascharka, D., Tran, P., Soklaski, R., and Majumdar, A. 2018. Transparency by design: closing the gap between performance and interpretability in visual reasoning. Pages 4942–4950 of: *Proc. IEEE Conference on Computer Vision and Pattern Recognition*.

Mayr, Andreas, Klambauer, Günter, Unterthiner, Thomas, and Hochreiter, Sepp. 2016. DeepTox: toxicity prediction using deep learning. *Frontiers in Environmental Science*, **3**, 80.

Mnih, Volodymyr, Kavukcuoglu, Koray, Silver, David, Rusu, Andrei A., Veness, Joel, Bellemare, Marc G., Graves, Alex, Riedmiller, Martin, Fidjeland, Andreas K., Ostrovski, Georg, et al. 2015. Human-level control through deep reinforcement learning. *Nature*, **518**(7540), 529–533.

Montavon, Grégoire. 2019. Gradient-based vs. propagation-based explanations: an axiomatic comparison. Pages 253–265 of: *Explainable AI: Interpreting, Explaining and Visualizing Deep Learning*. Lecture Notes in Computer Science, vol. 11700. Springer.

Montavon, Grégoire, Lapuschkin, Sebastian, Binder, Alexander, Samek, Wojciech, and Müller, Klaus-Robert. 2017. Explaining nonlinear classification decisions with deep Taylor decomposition. *Pattern Recognition*, **65**, 211–222.

Montavon, Grégoire, Samek, Wojciech, and Müller, Klaus-Robert. 2018. Methods for interpreting and understanding deep neural networks. *Digital Signal Processing*, **73**, 1–15.

Montavon, Grégoire, Binder, Alexander, Lapuschkin, Sebastian, Samek, Wojciech, and Müller, Klaus-Robert. 2019. Layer-wise relevance propagation: An overview. Pages 193–209 of: *Explainable AI: Interpreting, Explaining and Visualizing Deep Learning*. Lecture Notes in Computer Science, vol. 11700. Springer.

Moravčík, Matej, Schmid, Martin, Burch, Neil, Lisý, Viliam, Morrill, Dustin, Bard, Nolan, et al. 2017. DeepStack: Expert-level artificial intelligence in heads-up no-limit poker. *Science*, **356**(6337), 508–513.

Osman, Ahmed, Arras, Leila, and Samek, Wojciech. 2020. Towards ground truth evaluation of visual explanations. ArXiv preprint arXiv:2003.07258.

Poerner, Nina, Schütze, Hinrich, and Roth, Benjamin. 2018. Evaluating neural network explanation methods using hybrid documents and morphosyntactic agreement. Pages 340–350 of: *Proc. 56th Annual Meeting of the Association for Computational Linguistics*.

Reyes, Esteban, Estévez, Pablo A., Reyes, Ignacio, Cabrera-Vives, Guillermo, Huijse, Pablo, Carrasco, Rodrigo, and Forster, Francisco. 2018. Enhanced rotational invariant convolutional neural network for supernovae detection. Pages 1–8 of: *Proc. International Joint Conference on Neural Networks*.

Ribeiro, Marco Tulio, Singh, Sameer, and Guestrin, Carlos. 2016. Why should I trust you?: Explaining the predictions of any classifier. Pages 1135–1144 of: *Proc. ACM International Conference on Knowledge Discovery and Data Mining*.

Robnik-Šikonja, Marko, and Bohanec, Marko. 2018. Perturbation-based explanations of prediction models. Pages 159–175 of: *Human and Machine Learning*, J. Zhou and F. Chen (eds). Springer.

Ruff, Lukas, Kauffmann, Jacob R., Vandermeulen, Robert A., Montavon, Grégoire, Samek, Wojciech, Kloft, Marius, Dietterich, Thomas G., and Müller, Klaus-Robert. 2021. A unifying review of deep and shallow anomaly dtection. *Proceedings of the IEEE*, **109**, 756–795.

Samek, Wojciech, and Müller, Klaus-Robert. 2019. Towards explainable artificial intelligence. Pages 5–22 of: *Explainable AI: Interpreting, Explaining and Visualizing Deep Learning*. Lecture Notes in Computer Science, vol. 11700. Springer.

Samek, Wojciech, Binder, Alexander, Montavon, Grégoire, Lapuschkin, Sebastian, and Müller, Klaus-Robert. 2017. Evaluating the visualization of what a deep neural network has learned. *IEEE Transactions on Neural Networks and Learning Systems*, **28**(11), 2660–2673.

Samek, Wojciech, Montavon, Grégoire, Vedaldi, Andrea, Hansen, Lars Kai, and Müller, Klaus-Robert. 2019. *Explainable AI: Interpreting, explaining and visualizing deep learning*. Lecture Notes in Computer Science, vol. 11700. Springer.

Samek, Wojciech, Montavon, Grégoire, Lapuschkin, Sebastian, Anders, Christopher J., and Müller, Klaus-Robert. 2020. Toward interpretable machine learning: Transparent deep neural networks and beyond. ArXiv preprint arXiv:2003.07631.

Santoro, Adam, Raposo, David, Barrett, David G., Malinowski, Mateusz, Pascanu, Razvan, Battaglia, Peter, and Lillicrap, Tim. 2017. A simple neural network module for relational reasoning. Pages 4967–4976 of: *Advances in Neural Information Processing Systems*.

Schütt, Kristof T., Arbabzadah, Farhad, Chmiela, Stefan, Müller, Klaus R., and Tkatchenko, Alexandre. 2017. Quantum-chemical insights from deep tensor neural networks. *Nature Communications*, **8**, 13890.

Shrikumar, Avanti, Greenside, Peyton, Shcherbina, Anna, and Kundaje, Anshul. 2016. Not just a black box: Learning important features through propagating activation differences. ArXiv preprint arXiv:1605.01713.

Silver, David, Huang, Aja, Maddison, Chris J., Guez, Arthur, Sifre, Laurent, Van Den Driessche, George, et al. 2016. Mastering the game of Go with deep neural networks and tree search. *Nature*, **529**(7587), 484–489.

Silver, David, Schrittwieser, Julian, Simonyan, Karen, Antonoglou, Ioannis, Huang, Aja, Guez, Arthur, Hubert, Thomas, Baker, Lucas, Lai, Matthew, Bolton, Adrian, et al. 2017. Mastering the game of Go without human knowledge. *Nature*, **550**(7676), 354–359.

Simonyan, Karen, and Zisserman, Andrew. 2014. Very deep convolutional networks for large-scale image recognition. ArXiv preprint arXiv:1409.1556.

Simonyan, Karen, Vedaldi, Andrea, and Zisserman, Andrew. 2013. Deep inside convolutional networks: Visualising image classification models and saliency maps. ArXiv preprint arXiv:1312.6034.

Smilkov, Daniel, Thorat, Nikhil, Kim, Been, Viégas, Fernanda, and Wattenberg, Martin. 2017. Smoothgrad: removing noise by adding noise. ArXiv preprint arXiv:1706.03825.

Sundararajan, Mukund, Taly, Ankur, and Yan, Qiqi. 2017. Axiomatic attribution for deep networks. Pages 3319–3328 of: *Proc. International Conference on Machine Learning*.

Swartout, William R., and Moore, Johanna D. 1993. Explanation in Second Generation Expert Systems. Pages 543–585 of: *Second Generation Expert Systems*. Springer.

Thomas, Armin W., Heekeren, Hauke R., Müller, Klaus-Robert, and Samek, Wojciech. 2019. Analyzing neuroimaging data through recurrent deep learning models. *Frontiers in Neuroscience*, **13**, 1321.

von Lilienfeld, O. Anatole, Müller, Klaus-Robert, and Tkatchenko, Alexandre. 2020. Exploring chemical compound space with quantum-based machine learning. *Nat. Rev. Chem.*, **4**, 347—-358.

Warnecke, Alexander, Arp, Daniel, Wressnegger, Christian, and Rieck, Konrad. 2020. Evaluating explanation methods for deep learning in security. Pages 158–174 of: *Proc. 2020 IEEE European Symposium on Security and Privacy*.

Weller, Adrian. 2019. Transparency: Motivations and challenges. Pages 23–40 of: *Explainable AI: Interpreting, Explaining and Visualizing Deep Learning*. Lecture Notes in Computer Science, vol. 11700. Springer.

Yang, Yinchong, Tresp, Volker, Wunderle, Marius, and Fasching, Peter A. 2018. Explaining therapy predictions with layer-wise relevance propagation in neural networks. Pages 152–162 of: *Proc. IEEE International Conference on Healthcare Informatics*.

Yang, Zichao, He, Xiaodong, Gao, Jianfeng, Deng, Li, and Smola, Alexander J. 2016. Stacked attention networks for image question answering. Pages 21–29 of: *Proc. IEEE Conference on Computer Vision and Pattern Recognition*.

Yeom, Seul-Ki, Seegerer, Philipp, Lapuschkin, Sebastian, Wiedemann, Simon, Müller, Klaus-Robert, and Samek, Wojciech. 2019. Pruning by explaining: A novel criterion for deep neural network pruning. ArXiv preprint arXiv:1912.08881.

Zeiler, Matthew D., and Fergus, Rob. 2014. Visualizing and understanding convolutional networks. Pages 818–833 of: *Proc. ECCV 2014*.

Zhang, J., Lin, Z.L., Brandt, J., Shen, X., and Sclaroff, S. 2018. Top-down neural attention by excitation backprop. *International Journal of Computer Vision*, **126**, 1084–1102.

Zintgraf, Luisa M., Cohen, Taco S., Adel, Tameem, and Welling, Max. 2017. Visualizing deep neural network decisions: Prediction difference analysis. In: *Proc. International Conference on Learning Representations*.

6

Stochastic Feedforward Neural Networks: Universal Approximation

Thomas Merkh and Guido Montúfar

Abstract: In this chapter we take a look at the universal approximation question for stochastic feedforward neural networks. In contrast with deterministic neural networks, which represent mappings from a set of inputs to a set of outputs, stochastic neural networks represent mappings from a set of inputs to a set of probability distributions over the set of outputs. In particular, even if the sets of inputs and outputs are finite, the class of stochastic mappings in question is not finite. Moreover, while for a deterministic function the values of all output variables can be computed independently of each other given the values of the inputs, in the stochastic setting the values of the output variables may need to be correlated, which requires that their values are computed jointly. A prominent class of stochastic feedforward networks which has played a key role in the resurgence of deep learning is the class of deep belief networks. The representational power of these networks has been studied mainly in the generative setting as models of probability distributions without an input, or in the discriminative setting for the special case of deterministic mappings. We study the representational power of deep sigmoid belief networks in terms of compositions of linear transformations of probability distributions, Markov kernels, which can be expressed by the layers of the network. We investigate different types of shallow and deep architectures, and the minimal number of layers and units per layer that are sufficient and necessary for the network to be able to approximate any given stochastic mapping from the set of inputs to the set of outputs arbitrarily well. The discussion builds on notions of probability sharing and mixtures of product distributions, focusing on the case of binary variables and conditional probabilities given by the sigmoid of an affine map. After reviewing existing results, we present a detailed analysis of shallow networks and a unified analysis for a variety of deep networks. Most of the results were previously unpublished or are new.

6.1 Introduction

Obtaining detailed comparisons between deep and shallow networks remains a topic of theoretical and practical importance as deep learning continues to grow in popularity. The success of deep networks exhibited in many recent applications has sparked much interest in such comparisons (Larochelle et al., 2007; Bengio, 2009; Delalleau and Bengio, 2011; Pascanu et al., 2014; Montúfar et al., 2014; Mhaskar and Poggio, 2016; Eldan and Shamir, 2016; Poggio et al., 2017; Lu et al., 2017; Raghu et al., 2017; Yarotsky, 2017, 2018; Bölcskei et al., 2019; Gribonval et al., 2019) and in the development of the theory of deep architectures. Despite the acclaim, guidelines for choosing the most appropriate model for a given problem have remained elusive. One approach to obtaining such guidance is to analyze the representational and approximation capabilities of different types of architectures. The representational power of neural networks poses a number of interesting and important questions, even if it might not capture other important and complex aspects that impact the performance in practice. In particular, we note that the choice of network architecture defines a particular parametrization of the representable functions, which in turn has an effect on the shape of the parameter optimization landscape.

This chapter examines one aspect of this subject matter; namely, how do deep and shallow stochastic feedforward networks compare in terms of the number of computational units and parameters that are sufficient to approximate a target stochastic function to a given accuracy? In contrast with deterministic neural networks, which represent mappings from a set of inputs to a set of outputs, stochastic neural networks represent mappings from a set of inputs to a set of probability distributions over the set of outputs. As such, stochastic networks can be used to model the probability distribution of a given set of training examples. This type of problem, which is an instance of parametric density estimation, is a core problem in statistics and machine learning. When trained on a set of unlabeled examples, a stochastic network can learn to map an internal hidden variable to new examples which follow a similar probability distribution to that of the training examples. They can also be trained to generate examples which follow probability distributions conditioned on given inputs. For instance, the input might specify a value "cat" or "dog", and the outputs could be images of the corresponding animals. Generative modeling is a very active area of research in contemporary machine learning. In recent years, a particularly popular approach to generative modeling is the generative adversarial network (Goodfellow et al., 2014) and its many variants. The distinguishing property of this approach is that the training loss is formulated in terms of the ability of a discriminator to tell apart the generated examples and the training examples. Aside from utilizing this particular type of loss, these models are implemented in the same general way, as a sequence of mappings that take an internal source to values in a desired domain. The distinguishing property of stochastic neural networks is that each layer can implement randomness. Learning stochastic feedforward networks has been an important topic of research for years (Neal, 1990; Ngiam et al., 2011; Tang and Salakhutdinov, 2013; Raiko et al., 2014; Lee et al., 2017). Stochastic neural networks have found applications not only as generative models, but also in unsupervised feature learning (Hinton and Salakhutdinov, 2006; Ranzato et al., 2007), semantic hashing (Salakhutdinov and Hinton, 2009), and natural language understanding (Sarikaya et al., 2014), among others. Unsupervised training with stochastic networks can be used as a parameter initialization strategy for subsequent supervised learning, which was a key technique in the rise of deep learning in the decade after 2000 (Hinton et al., 2006; Bengio et al., 2007; Bengio, 2009).

We study the representational power of stochastic feedforward networks from a class that is known as Bayesian sigmoid belief networks (Neal, 1992). These are special types of directed graphical models, also known as Bayesian networks (Lauritzen, 1996; Pearl, 1988). We consider a spectrum of architectures (network topologies) in relation to universal approximation properties. When viewing networks as approximators of elements from a specific class, they can be quantified and compared by measures such as the worst-case error for the class. If a sufficiently large network is capable of approximating all desired elements with arbitrary accuracy, it can be regarded as a *universal approximator*. The question of whether a certain network architecture is capable of universal approximation and, if so, how many computational units and trainable parameters suffice, has been studied for a variety of stochastic networks (see, e.g., Sutskever and Hinton, 2008; Le Roux and Bengio, 2010; Bengio and Delalleau, 2011; Montúfar and Ay, 2011; Montúfar et al., 2011; Montúfar, 2014a; Montúfar et al., 2015; Montúfar, 2014b, 2015; Montúfar and Rauh, 2017; Montúfar, 2015).

Most of the existing works on the representational power of stochastic feedforward networks focus on the generative setting with no inputs, modeling a single probability distribution over the outputs, or the discriminative setting modeling a deterministic mapping from inputs to outputs. Models of stochastic functions, which are also referred to as Markov kernels or conditional probability distributions, are more complex than models of probability distributions. Rather than a single probability distribution, they need to approximate a probability distribution for each possible input. Universal approximation in this context inherently requires more complexity as compared with generative models with no inputs. There is also a wider variety of possible network architectures, each with virtually no guidance on how one compares with another. Nonetheless, as we will see, the question of the universal approximation of Markov kernels can be addressed using similar tools as those previously developed for studying the universal approximation of probability distributions with deep belief networks (Sutskever and Hinton, 2008; Le Roux and Bengio, 2010; Montúfar and Ay, 2011; Montúfar, 2014b). We will also draw on unpublished studies of shallow stochastic feedforward networks (Montúfar, 2015).

The overall idea of universal approximation that we consider here is as follows. For each possible input $\mathbf{x} \in \{0,1\}^d$ to the network, there will be a target conditional distribution $p(\cdot \mid \mathbf{x})$ over the outputs $\mathbf{y} \in \{0,1\}^s$, which the network attempts to learn. Note that while there is only a finite number $(2^s)^{2^d}$ of deterministic mappings from inputs to outputs, there is a continuum $(\Delta_{\{0,1\}^s})^{2^d}$ of mappings from inputs to probability distributions over outputs, where $\Delta_{\{0,1\}^s}$ is the $(2^s - 1)$-dimensional simplex of probability distributions over $\{0,1\}^s$. As the number of hidden units of the network grows, the network gains the ability to better approximate the target conditional distributions. At a certain threshold, the model will have sufficient complexity to approximate each conditional distribution with arbitrarily high precision. The precise threshold is unknown except in special cases, and thus upper bounds for universal approximation are generally used to quantify a network's representational capacity. Since feedforward networks operate sequentially, each layer can be seen as a module that is able to implement certain operations that share or diffuse the probability mass away from the distribution at the previous layer and toward the target distribution. This is referred to as *probability mass sharing*. Depending on the size of the layers, the types of possible operations varies. The composition of operations layer by layer is a key difference between deep and shallow networks.

We prove sufficiency bounds for universal approximation with shallow networks and with a spectrum of deep networks. The proof methods for the deep and shallow cases differ in important ways owing to the compositional nature of deep architectures. This is especially so when restrictions are imposed on the width of the hidden layers. We extend the ideas put forth by Sutskever and Hinton (2008), Le Roux and Bengio (2010), and Montúfar and Ay (2011), where universal approximation bounds were proven for deep belief networks. Our main results can be stated as follows.

- *A shallow sigmoid stochastic feedforward network with d binary inputs, s binary outputs, and a hidden layer of width $2^d(2^{s-1} - 1)$ is a universal approximator of Markov kernels.*

- *There exists a spectrum of deep sigmoid stochastic feedforward networks with d binary inputs, s binary outputs, and $2^{d-j}(2^{s-b} + 2^b - 1)$ hidden layers of width $2^j(s+d-j)$ that are universal approximators of Markov kernels. Here $b \sim \log_2(s)$, and the overall shape of each network is controlled by $j \in \{0,1,\ldots,d\}$. Moreover, each of these networks can be implemented with a minimum of $2^d(2^s - 1)$ trainable parameters.*

- *For the networks in the previous item, if both the trainable and non-trainable* *parameters are restricted to have absolute values at most α, the approximation error for any target kernel can be bounded in infinity norm by $1 - \sigma(\frac{\alpha}{2}(d+s))^N + 2\sigma(-\frac{\alpha}{2}(d+s))$, where N is the total number of units of the network and σ is the standard logistic sigmoid function.*

The chapter is organized as follows. In §6.2 we discuss previous works for context and in §6.3 we consider preliminary notions and fix notation. Then, in §6.4 we present an analysis of shallow networks; the proofs are contained in §6.5. In §6.6 we give the main results, describing universal approximation with a spectrum of deep networks and approximation with bounded weights. The proofs of these results are to be found in §6.7. Next, in §6.8 we discuss the lower bounds for universal approximation. Afterward, a brief comparison between architectures and numerical experiments is given in §6.9. Lastly, §6.10 offers a conclusion and avenues for future research.

6.2 Overview of Previous Works and Results

The universal approximation property has been studied in a variety of contexts in the past. The seminal work of Cybenko (1989) and Hornik et al. (1989) showed that deterministic multilayer feedforward networks with at least one sufficiently large hidden layer are universal approximators over a certain class of Borel measurable functions. An overview on universal approximation for deterministic networks was provided by Scarselli and Tsoi (1998). The case of stochastic functions was not covered by this analysis, and was studied later. Soon after Hinton et al. (2006) introduced a practical technique for training deep architectures, universal approximation for deep belief networks (DBNs) was shown by Sutskever and Hinton (2008). They found that a DBN consisting of $3(2^s - 1) + 1$ layers of width $s + 1$ is sufficient for approximating any distribution $p \in \Delta_s$ arbitrarily well. This sufficiency bound was improved upon twice, first by Le Roux and Bengio (2010), then by Montúfar and Ay (2011). The former introduced the idea of using Gray codes to overlap probability sharing steps, thereby reducing the number of layers down to $\sim 2^s/s$, each having width s. The latter further reduced the number of layers to $2^{s-1}/(s-b)$, with $b \sim \log_2(s)$, by improving previous results on the representational capacity of restricted Boltzmann machines (RBMs) and probability-sharing theorems. It is interesting to note that still further improvements have been made on the representational capabilities of RBMs (Montúfar and Rauh, 2017), but it remains unclear whether universal approximation bounds for DBNs can benefit from such improvements. For a recent review of results on RBMs, see Montúfar (2018).

Several stochastic networks in addition to DBNs have been shown to be universal approximators. The undirected counterpart to DBNs, called a deep Boltzmann machine (DBM), was proven to be a universal approximator even if the hidden layers are restricted to have at most the same width as the output layer (Montúfar, 2014a). Here it was shown that DBMs could be analyzed similarly to feedforward networks under certain parameter regimes. This result verifies the intuition that undirected graphical models are in some well-defined sense at least as powerful as their directed counterparts. For shallow stochastic networks, universal approximation bounds have been obtained for feedforward networks, which will be discussed next, and for undirected networks called conditional restricted Boltzmann machines (CRBMs) (Montúfar et al., 2015). Both such architectures are capable of universal approximation and have similar sufficiency bounds. We note that not every network architecture is capable of providing universal approximation. For example, it is known that for an RBM, DBN, or DBM to be a universal approximator of distributions over $\{0, 1\}^s$, the hidden layer immediately before the visible layer must have at least $s - 1$ units (Montúfar, 2014a). In fact, if s is odd, at least s units are needed (Montúfar and Morton, 2015). In addition, necessary bounds for universal approximation exist for all of the previously mentioned architectures, though such bounds are generally harder to refine. Except for very small models, there exists a gap between the known necessary bounds and the sufficiency bounds. Last, it was recently shown that deterministic feedforward networks with hidden layer width at most equal to the input dimension are unable to capture functions with bounded level sets (Johnson, 2019). Such discoveries exemplify the importance of analyzing the approximation capabilities of different network architectures.

As already mentioned in the introduction, the representational power of discriminative models has been studied previously. In particular, the representation of deterministic functions from $\{0, 1\}^d \rightarrow \{0, 1\}$, known as Boolean functions, by logical circuits or threshold gates has been studied for many years. Shannon (1949) showed that almost all d-input Boolean functions require a logic circuit of size at least $(1 - o(1))2^d/d$. Lupanov (1956) showed that every d-input Boolean function can be expressed by a logic circuit of size at most $(1 + o(1))2^d/d$. Other works on the representation of Boolean functions include Brunato and Battiti (2015); Huang et al. (2006); Muroga (1971); Neciporuk (1964); Wenzel et al. (2000). A particularly interesting result by Hastad and Goldmann (1991) shows that, when the depth of a threshold circuit is restricted, some Boolean functions require exponentially more units to be represented.

Rojas (2003) showed that a sufficiently deep stack of perceptrons where each layer is connected to the input and feeds forward a single bit of information is capable of learning any d-input Boolean function. The equivalent network without skip connections to the input would be a network of width $d + 1$. In that work it was pointed out that there is a direct trade-off between the width and depth of the network, and this idea will surface again in the analysis of deep networks that follows. Le Roux and Bengio (2010) showed that a sigmoid belief network with $2^{d-1}+1$ layers of width d is sufficient for representing any deterministic function $f\colon \{0,1\}^d \to \{0,1\}$. This was achieved by showing that the parameters of one layer can be chosen to map a single vector to some fixed $\mathbf{h}_0 \in \{0,1\}^d$. Then, considering two classes of vectors, those for which $f(\mathbf{h}) = 0$ and those for which $f(\mathbf{h}) = 1$, one may choose to map the smaller of the two classes of vectors to $\mathbf{h}_0$. This can be done in 2^{d-1} layers or less, and then the last layer can correctly label the inputs depending on whether the network mapped them to $\mathbf{h}_0$. This process differs from that to be discussed in that these networks are not learning multivariate conditional distributions for each input, but rather labeling each input 0 or 1. While for a deterministic function the values of all output variables can be computed independently of each other given the values of the inputs, in the stochastic setting the values of the output variables may be correlated, which requires that their values are computed jointly.

6.3 Markov Kernels and Stochastic Networks

6.3.1 Binary Probability Distributions and Markov Kernels

Let $s \in \mathbb{N}$ and consider the set of vectors $\{0,1\}^s$ of cardinality 2^s. A probability distribution over the set $\{0,1\}^s$ is a vector $p \in \mathbb{R}^{2^s}$ with non-negative entries p_i, $i \in \{1,\dots,2^s\}$ that add to one. The entries correspond to the probabilities $p(\mathbf{y})$ that this distribution assigns to each $\mathbf{y} \in \{0,1\}^s$. The set of all such probability distributions is the set

$$\Delta_s := \left\{ p \in \mathbb{R}^{2^s} : \sum_{i=1}^{2^s} p_i = 1,\ p_i \geq 0 \text{ for } i = 1,2,\dots,2^s \right\}. \tag{6.1}$$

This set is a simplex of dimension $2^s - 1$. The vertices of Δ_s are point distributions which assign full probability mass to a single $\mathbf{y} \in \{0,1\}^s$ and no mass to $\{0,1\}^s \setminus \mathbf{y}$. Such distributions are denoted $\delta_{\mathbf{y}}$ and are sometimes referred to as *deterministic* because there is no uncertainty in them. The support of a distribution $p \in \Delta_s$ is denoted by $\mathrm{supp}(p)$ and is the set of the vectors in $\{0,1\}^s$ to which p assigns non-zero probability. The support set of a deterministic distribution is a singleton. A probability model $\mathcal{M}$ is just a subset of Δ_s. If a model $\mathcal{M} \subseteq \Delta_s$ satisfies $\overline{\mathcal{M}} = \Delta_s$ then $\mathcal{M}$ is said to have the universal approximation property. Here $\overline{\mathcal{M}}$ refers to the closure of $\mathcal{M}$ in the Euclidean topology.

A stochastic map or Markov kernel with input space $\{0,1\}^d$ and output space $\{0,1\}^s$ is a map $P\colon \{0,1\}^d \to \Delta_s$. Such a Markov kernel can be seen as a $2^d \times 2^s$ matrix with non-negative entries and with rows that sum to 1. The ith row is the probability distribution over $\{0,1\}^s$ corresponding to the ith input. The set of all

Markov kernels is written as

$$\Delta_{d,s} := \left\{ P \in \mathbb{R}^{2^d \times 2^s} : P_{ij} \geq 0, \sum_{j=1}^{2^s} P_{ij} = 1 \text{ for all } i = 1, 2, \ldots, 2^d \right\}. \quad (6.2)$$

One can see that $\Delta_{d,s}$ is the 2^d-fold Cartesian product of Δ_s and thus is a polytope of dimension $2^d(2^s - 1)$. A model of Markov kernels $\mathcal{N}$ is simply a subset of $\Delta_{d,s}$. If a model $\mathcal{N}$ fills this polytope, meaning $\overline{\mathcal{N}} = \Delta_{d,s}$, it is said to be a universal approximator of Markov kernels.

An important class of probability distributions is that of the factorizable or independent distributions, for which the probability of observing a joint state $\mathbf{z} \in \{0,1\}^d$ is just the product of the probabilities of observing each state $z_j \in \{0,1\}$, $j = 1, \ldots, d$, individually. These distributions can be written as

$$p(\mathbf{z}) = \prod_{j=1}^{d} p_{z_j}(z_j) = \prod_{j=1}^{d} p_j^{z_j}(1 - p_j)^{1-z_j}, \text{ for all } \mathbf{z} = (z_1, \ldots, z_d) \in \{0,1\}^d, \quad (6.3)$$

where p_{z_j} is a probability distribution over $\{0,1\}$ and $p_j = p_{z_j}(z_j = 1) \in [0,1]$ is the probability of the event $z_j = 1$, for $j = 1, \ldots, d$. We denote the set of all factorizable distributions of d binary variables, of the form given above, by $\mathcal{E}_d$. The Hamming distance $\|a - b\|_H$ between two vectors a and b is the number of positions where a and b differ. One notable property of $\mathcal{E}_d$ is that if $\mathbf{x}', \mathbf{x}'' \in \{0,1\}^d$ have Hamming distance $\|\mathbf{x}' - \mathbf{x}''\|_H = 1$ then *any* probability distribution $p \in \Delta_d$ with $\text{supp}(p) = \{\mathbf{x}', \mathbf{x}''\}$ is in $\mathcal{E}_d$.

Certain configurations of binary vectors will be important in our analysis. The set of d-bit binary vectors can be visualized as the vertex set of the d-dimensional hypercube. If $\mathbf{x}', \mathbf{x}'' \in \{0,1\}^d$ have Hamming distance $\|\mathbf{x}' - \mathbf{x}''\|_H = 1$, they form an edge of the d-cube. For this reason, they are sometimes referred to as an *edge pair*. A codimension $0 \leq j \leq d$ face of the d-cube consists of the 2^{d-j} vectors having the same j bits in common.

6.3.2 Stochastic Feedforward Networks

We consider stochastic networks known as Bayesian sigmoid belief networks (Neal, 1992), which are Bayesian networks (Pearl, 1988; Lauritzen, 1996) with conditional distributions taking the form of a logistic sigmoid function applied to a linear combination of the parent variables. Details can be found in (Saul et al., 1996) and (Bishop, 2006, Section 8.1).

Each unit of the network represents a random variable and edges capture dependencies between variables. In our discussion, all of the units of the network are binary. The graphs are directed and acyclic, so that the units can be arranged into a sequence of layers. We will focus on the case where consecutive layers are fully connected and there are no intralayer or skip connections. The units in each layer are conditionally independent of the state of the units in the previous layer. Figure 6.5 shows an example of such an architecture.

We denote the binary inputs by $\mathbf{x} \in \{0,1\}^d$, and the outputs by $\mathbf{y} \in \{0,1\}^s$. The network's computational units take states in $\{0,1\}$ with activation probabilities given by the sigmoid function applied to an affine transformation of the previous layer's values. Specifically, given a state $\mathbf{h}^{l-1} \in \{0,1\}^{m_{l-1}}$ of the m_{l-1} units in layer $l-1$, the jth unit of the lth layer *activates*, i.e. it takes state $h^l_j = 1$, with probability

$$p(h^l_j = 1 \mid \mathbf{h}^{l-1}) = \sigma(\mathbf{W}^l_j \mathbf{h}^{l-1} + b^l_j) = \frac{1}{1 + e^{-(\mathbf{W}^l_j \mathbf{h}^{l-1} + b^l_j)}}. \tag{6.4}$$

Here $\mathbf{W}^l_j \in \mathbb{R}^{1 \times m_{l-1}}$ is a row vector of weights and $b^l_j \in \mathbb{R}$ is a bias. The weights and biases of all units in layer l are collected in a matrix $\mathbf{W}^l \in \mathbb{R}^{m_l} \times \mathbb{R}^{m_{l-1}}$ and a vector $\mathbf{b}^l = (b^l_1, \ldots, b^l_{m_l}) \in \mathbb{R}^{m_l}$. We denote the parameters (weights and biases) of the entire network collectively by θ. Note that the inverse of the sigmoid function σ is known as the *logit* function $\sigma^{-1}(x) = \log\left(\frac{x}{1-x}\right) = \log(x) - \log(1-x)$. The units in layer l are conditionally independent of the state $\mathbf{h}^{l-1}$ of the units in the preceding layer. The probability of observing state $\mathbf{h}^l = (h^l_1, \ldots, h^l_{m_l}) \in \{0,1\}^{m_l}$ at layer l given $\mathbf{h}^{l-1}$ is

$$p(\mathbf{h}^l \mid \mathbf{h}^{l-1}) = \prod_{j=1}^{m_l} \sigma(\mathbf{W}^l_j \mathbf{h}^{l-1} + b^l_j)^{h^l_j} \left(1 - \sigma(\mathbf{W}^l_j \mathbf{h}^{l-1} + b^l_j)\right)^{1-h^l_j}. \tag{6.5}$$

Given an input $\mathbf{x}$, the conditional distribution of all units in a network with $L+2$ layers (including input and output layers) can be written as

$$p(\mathbf{h}^1, \mathbf{h}^2, \ldots, \mathbf{h}^L, \mathbf{y} \mid \mathbf{x}) = p(\mathbf{y} \mid \mathbf{h}^L) p(\mathbf{h}^L \mid \mathbf{h}^{L-1}) \cdots p(\mathbf{h}^1 \mid \mathbf{x}). \tag{6.6}$$

By marginalizing over the hidden layers, which are all the layers other than the input and output layers, one obtains the conditional distribution of the output given the input as

$$p(\mathbf{y} \mid \mathbf{x}) = \sum_{\mathbf{h}^1} \cdots \sum_{\mathbf{h}^L} p(\mathbf{y} \mid \mathbf{h}^L) p(\mathbf{h}^L \mid \mathbf{h}^{L-1}) \cdots p(\mathbf{h}^1 \mid \mathbf{x}). \tag{6.7}$$

In particular, a network with fixed parameters represents a Markov kernel in $\Delta_{d,s}$. When we allow the network's parameter θ to vary arbitrarily, we obtain the set of all Markov kernels in $\Delta_{d,s}$ that are representable by the particular network architecture. The architecture is fully determined by the number of layers and the sizes $m_1, \ldots, m_L$ of the hidden layers. We call a network *shallow* if $L = 1$, and *deep* if $L > 1$.

We denote by $F_{d,s} \subseteq \Delta_{d,s}$ the set of all Markov kernels that can be represented by a network module of the form (6.5) with an input layer of size d and an output layer of size s, with no hidden layers. Networks with $L > 1$ can be seen as the composition of $L + 1$ such network modules. We denote by $F_{d,m_1,...,m_L,s} :=$ $F_{m_L,s} \circ F_{m_L-1,m_L} \circ \cdots \circ F_{m_1,m_2} \circ F_{d,m_1} \subseteq \Delta_{d,s}$ the set of all Markov kernels of the form (6.7) representable by a network architecture with an input layer of size d, hidden layers of size m_l for $l = 1, \ldots, L$, and an output layer of size s.

The general task in practice for our feedforward stochastic network is to learn a conditional distribution $p^*(\cdot \mid \mathbf{x})$ for each given input $\mathbf{x}$. In other words, when providing the network with input $\mathbf{x}$, the goal is to have the outputs $\mathbf{y}$ distributed according to some target distribution $p^*(\cdot \mid \mathbf{x})$. We will be interested in the question of which network architectures have the universal approximation property, meaning that they are capable of representing *any* Markov kernel in $\Delta_{d,s}$ with arbitrarily high accuracy.

Our analysis builds on previous works discussing closely related types of stochastic networks. For completeness, we now provide the definition of those networks. A restricted Boltzmann machine (RBM) with m hidden and d visible binary units is a probability model in Δ_d consisting of the distributions

$$p(\mathbf{x}) = \sum_{\mathbf{h} \in \{0,1\}^m} \frac{1}{Z(\mathbf{W}, \mathbf{b}, \mathbf{c})} \exp(\mathbf{x}^\top \mathbf{W} \mathbf{h} + \mathbf{x}^\top \mathbf{b} + \mathbf{h}^\top \mathbf{c}), \quad \text{for all } \mathbf{x} \in \{0,1\}^d, \quad (6.8)$$

where $\mathbf{W} \in \mathbb{R}^{d \times m}$, $\mathbf{b} \in \mathbb{R}^d$, $\mathbf{c} \in \mathbb{R}^m$ are weights and biases, and Z is defined in such a way that $\sum_{\mathbf{x} \in \{0,1\}^d} p(\mathbf{x}) = 1$ for any choice of the weights and biases. This is an undirected graphical model with hidden variables. A deep belief network (DBN) is a probability model constructed by composing a restricted Boltzmann machine and a Bayesian sigmoid belief network as described above. Such a DBN represents probability distributions of the form

$$p(\mathbf{y}) = \sum_{\mathbf{x} \in \{0,1\}^d} p(\mathbf{y} \mid \mathbf{x}) p(\mathbf{x}), \quad \text{for all } \mathbf{y} \in \{0,1\}^s, \quad (6.9)$$

where $p(\mathbf{y} \mid \mathbf{x})$ is a conditional probability distribution of the form (6.7) and $p(\mathbf{x})$ is a probability distribution of the form (6.8).

6.4 Results for Shallow Networks

In the case of shallow networks, which have an input layer, a single hidden layer, and an output layer, as shown in Figure 6.1, we are interested in the smallest size of hidden layer which will provide for a universal approximation capacity. The results in this section are taken from a technical report (Montúfar, 2015), with a few adjustments.

The shallow network $F_{d,m,s} = F_{m,s} \circ F_{d,m}$ has a total of $dm + m + sm + s$ free parameters. We will also consider a restricted case where the second module has fixed weights, meaning that we fix $R \in F_{m,s}$ and consider the composition

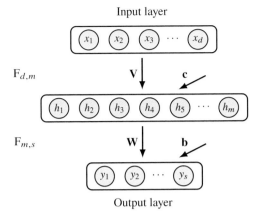

Figure 6.1 Feedforward network with a layer of d input units, a layer of m hidden units, and a layer of s output units. Weights and biases are $(\mathbf{V}, \mathbf{c})$ for the hidden layer, and $(\mathbf{W}, \mathbf{b})$ for the output layer.

$R \circ F_{d,m}$, which has only $dm + m$ free parameters. By comparing the number of free parameters and the dimension of $\Delta_{d,s}$, which is $2^d(2^s - 1)$, it is possible to obtain (see Theorem 6.21 in §6.8) the following lower bound on the minimal number of hidden units that suffices for universal approximation:

Proposition 6.1. *Let $d \geq 1$ and $s \geq 1$.*

- *If there is an $R \in \overline{F_{m,s}}$ with $R \circ \overline{F_{d,m}} = \Delta_{d,s}$ then $m \geq \frac{1}{(d+1)} 2^d(2^s - 1)$.*
- *If $\overline{F_{d,m,s}} = \Delta_{d,s}$ then $m \geq \frac{1}{(s+d+1)}(2^d(2^s - 1) - s)$.*

In the following, we will bound the minimal number of hidden units of a universal approximator from above. First we consider the case where the output layer has fixed weights and biases. Then we consider the case where all weights and biases are free parameters.

6.4.1 Fixed Weights in the Output Layer

Theorem 6.2. *Let $d \geq 1$ and $s \geq 1$. A shallow sigmoid stochastic feedforward network with d inputs, m units in the hidden layer, s outputs, and fixed weights and biases in the output layer is a universal approximator of Markov kernels in $\Delta_{d,s}$ whenever $m \geq 2^{d-1}(2^s - 1)$.*

The theorem will be shown by constructing $R \in \overline{F_{m,s}}$ such that $R \circ \overline{F_{d,m}} = \Delta_{d,s}$ whenever $m \geq \frac{1}{2} 2^d(2^s - 1)$. In view of the lower bound from Proposition 6.1, this upper bound is tight at least when $d = 1$.

When there are no input units, i.e., $d = 0$, we may set $F_{0,m} = \mathcal{E}_m$, the set of factorizable distributions of m binary variables (6.3), which has m free parameters, and $\Delta_{0,s} = \Delta_s$, the set of all probability distributions over $\{0,1\}^s$. Theorem 6.2 generalizes to this case as:

Proposition 6.3. *Let $s \geq 2$. There is an $R \in \overline{F_{m,s}}$ with $R \circ \overline{\mathcal{E}_m} = \Delta_s$ whenever $m \geq 2^s - 1$.*

This bound is always tight, since the network uses exactly $2^s - 1$ parameters to approximate every distribution from Δ_s arbitrarily well. For $s = 1$, one hidden unit is sufficient and necessary for universal approximation.

6.4.2 Trainable Weights in the Output Layer

When we allow for trainable weights and biases in both layers, we obtain a slightly more compact bound:

Theorem 6.4. *Let $d \geq 1$ and $s \geq 2$. A shallow sigmoid stochastic feedforward network with d inputs, m units in the hidden layer, and s outputs is a universal approximator of kernels in $\Delta_{d,s}$ whenever $m \geq 2^d(2^{s-1} - 1)$.*

This bound on the number of hidden units is slightly smaller than that obtained for fixed weights in the output layer. However, it always leaves a gap in the corresponding parameter-counting lower bound.

As before, we can also consider the setting where there are no input units, $d = 0$, in which case the units in the hidden layer may assume an arbitrary product distribution, $F_{0,m} = \mathcal{E}_m$. In this case we obtain:

Proposition 6.5. *Let $s \geq 1$. Then $\overline{F_{m,s}} \circ \overline{\mathcal{E}_m} = \Delta_s$, whenever $m \geq 2^{s-1} - 1$.*

For $s = 1$, the bias of the output unit can be adjusted to obtain any desired distribution, and hence no hidden units are needed. For $s = 2$, a single hidden unit, $m = 1$, is sufficient and necessary for universal approximation, so that the bound is tight. For $s = 3$, three hidden units are necessary (Montúfar and Morton, 2015, Proposition 3.19), so that the bound is tight in this case also.

6.5 Proofs for Shallow Networks

We first give an outline of the proofs and then proceed with the analysis, first for the case of fixed weights in the output layer and then for the case of trainable weights in the output layer. Our strategy for proving Theorems 6.2 and 6.4 can be summarized as follows:

- First we show that the first layer of $F_{d,m,s}$ can approximate Markov kernels arbitrarily well, which fixes the state of some units, depending on the input, and

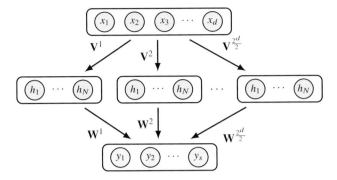

Figure 6.2 Illustration of the construction used in our proof. Each block of hidden units is active on a distinct subset of possible inputs. The output layer integrates the activities of the block that was activated by the input, and produces corresponding activities of the output units.

has an arbitrary product distribution over the states of the other units. The idea is illustrated in Figure 6.2.

- Then we show that the second layer can approximate arbitrarily well deterministic kernels whose rows are copies of the point measures from Δ_S, ordered in an appropriate way with respect to the different inputs. Note that the point measures are the vertices of the simplex Δ_S.
- Finally, we show that the set of product distributions of each block of hidden units is mapped to the convex hull of the rows of the kernel represented by the second layer, which is Δ_S.
- The output distributions of distinct sets of inputs is modeled individually by distinct blocks of hidden units, and so we obtain the universal approximation of Markov kernels.

The goal of our analysis is to construct the individual pieces of the network so that they are as compact as possible. Lemma 6.6 will provide a trick that allows us to use each block of units in the hidden layer for a pair of distinct input vectors at the same time. This allows us to halve the number of hidden units that would be needed if each input had an individual block of active hidden units. Similarly, Lemma 6.11 gives a way of producing mixture components at the output layer that are more flexible than simple point measures. This comes at the expense of allowing only one input per hidden block, but it allows us to nearly halve the number of hidden units per block, for only a slight reduction in the total number of hidden units.

6.5.1 *Fixed Weights in the Output Layer*

The First Layer

We start with the following lemma.

Lemma 6.6. *Let* $x', x'' \in \{0,1\}^d$ *differ in only one entry, and let* q', q'' *be any two distributions on* $\{0,1\}$. *Then* $F_{d,1}$ *can approximate the following arbitrarily well:*

$$p(\cdot \mid x) = \begin{cases} q', & \text{if } x = x' \\ q'', & \text{if } x = x'' \\ \delta_0, & \text{otherwise} \end{cases}.$$

Proof Given the input weights and bias, $V \in \mathbb{R}^{1 \times d}$ and $c \in \mathbb{R}$, for each input $x \in \{0,1\}^d$ the output probability is given by

$$p(z = 1 \mid x) = \sigma(Vx + c). \tag{6.10}$$

Since the two vectors $x', x'' \in \{0,1\}^d$ differ in only one entry, they form an edge pair E of the d-dimensional unit cube. Let $l \in [d] := \{1, \ldots, d\}$ be the entry in which they differ, with $x'_l = 0$ and $x''_l = 1$. Since E is a face of the cube, there is a supporting hyperplane of E. This means that there are $\tilde{V} \in \mathbb{R}^{1 \times d}$ and $\tilde{c} \in \mathbb{R}$ with $\tilde{V}x + \tilde{c} = 0$ if $x \in E$ and $\tilde{V}x + \tilde{c} < -1$ if $x \in \{0,1\}^d \setminus E$. Let $\gamma' = \sigma^{-1}(q'(z = 1))$ and $\gamma'' = \sigma^{-1}(q''(z = 1))$. We define $c = \alpha\tilde{c} + \gamma'$ and $V = \alpha\tilde{V} + (\gamma'' - \gamma')e_l^\top$. Then, as $\alpha \to \infty$,

$$Vx + c = \begin{cases} \gamma', & \text{if } x = x' \\ \gamma'', & \text{if } x = x'' \\ -\infty, & \text{otherwise} \end{cases}.$$

Substituting this into (6.10) proves the claim. □

Given any binary vector $x = (x_1, \ldots, x_d) \in \{0,1\}^d$, let $\text{dec}(x) := \sum_{i=1}^d 2^{i-1}x_i$ be its integer representation. Using the previous lemma, we obtain the following.

Proposition 6.7. *Let* $N \geq 1$ *and* $m = 2^{d-1}N$. *For each* $x \in \{0,1\}^d$, *let* $p(\cdot \mid x)$ *be an arbitrary factorizing distribution from* $\mathcal{E}_N$. *The model* $F_{d,m}$ *can approximate the following kernel from* $\Delta_{d,m}$ *arbitrarily well:*

$$P(h \mid x) = \delta_0(h^0) \cdots \delta_0(h^{\lfloor \text{dec}(x)/2 \rfloor - 1}) p(h^{\lfloor \text{dec}(x)/2 \rfloor} \mid x)$$
$$\times \delta_0(h^{\lfloor \text{dec}(x)/2 \rfloor + 1}) \cdots \delta_0(h^{2^{d-1}-1}), \quad \text{for all } h \in \{0,1\}^m, x \in \{0,1\}^d,$$

where $h^i = (h_{Ni+1}, \ldots, h_{N(i+1)})$ *for all* $i \in \{0, 1, \ldots, 2^{d-1} - 1\}$.

Proof We divide the set $\{0,1\}^d$ of all possible inputs into 2^{d-1} disjoint pairs with successive decimal values. The ith pair consists of the two vectors x with $\lfloor \text{dec}(x)/2 \rfloor = i$, for all $i \in \{0, \ldots, 2^{d-1} - 1\}$. The kernel P has the property that, for the ith input pair, all output units are inactive with probability one, except those with index $Ni + 1, \ldots, N(i + 1)$. Given a joint distribution q let q_j denote the corresponding marginal distribution on the states of the jth unit. By Lemma 6.6, we can set

$$P_{Ni+j}(\cdot \mid \mathbf{x}) = \begin{cases} p_j(\cdot \mid \mathbf{x}), & \text{if } \text{dec}(\mathbf{x}) = 2i \\ p_j(\cdot \mid \mathbf{x}), & \text{if } \text{dec}(\mathbf{x}) = 2i + 1 \\ \delta_0, & \text{otherwise} \end{cases}$$

for all $i \in \{0, \ldots, 2^{d-1} - 1\}$ and $j \in \{1, \ldots, N\}$. □

The Second Layer

For the second layer we will consider deterministic kernels. Given a binary vector $\mathbf{z}$, let $l(\mathbf{z}) := \lceil \log_2(\text{dec}(\mathbf{z}) + 1) \rceil$ denote the largest j where $z_j = 1$. Here we set $l(0, \ldots, 0) = 0$. Given an integer $l \in \{0, \ldots, 2^s - 1\}$, let $\text{bin}_s(l)$ denote the s-bit representation of l; that is, the vector with $\text{dec}(\text{bin}_s(l)) = l$. Lastly, when applying any scalar operation to a vector, such as subtraction by a number, it should be understood as being performed pointwise on each vector element.

Lemma 6.8. *Let $N = 2^s - 1$. The set $\mathrm{F}_{N,s}$ can approximate the following deterministic kernel arbitrarily well:*

$$Q(\cdot \mid \mathbf{z}) = \delta_{\text{bin}_s \, l(\mathbf{z})}(\cdot), \quad \text{for all } \mathbf{z} \in \{0, 1\}^N.$$

In words, the $\mathbf{z}$th row of Q indicates the largest non-zero entry of the binary vector $\mathbf{z}$. For example, for $s = 2$ we have $N = 3$ and

$$Q = \begin{array}{c} \\ \end{array} \begin{matrix} 00 & 01 & 10 & 11 & \\ \begin{pmatrix} 1 & & & \\ & 1 & & \\ & & 1 & \\ & & 1 & \\ & & & 1 \\ & & & 1 \\ & & & 1 \\ & & & 1 \end{pmatrix} & \begin{matrix} 000 \\ 001 \\ 010 \\ 011 \\ 100 \\ 101 \\ 110 \\ 111 \end{matrix} \end{matrix}.$$

Proof of Lemma 6.8 Given the input and bias weights, $\mathbf{W} \in \mathbb{R}^{s \times N}$ and $\mathbf{b} \in \mathbb{R}^s$, for each input $\mathbf{z} \in \{0, 1\}^N$ the output distribution is the product distribution $p(\mathbf{y} \mid \mathbf{z}) = \frac{1}{z(\mathbf{Wz}+\mathbf{b})} \exp(\mathbf{y}^\top (\mathbf{Wz} + \mathbf{b}))$ in $\mathcal{E}_s$ with parameter $\mathbf{Wz} + \mathbf{b}$. If $\text{sgn}(\mathbf{Wz} + \mathbf{b}) = \text{sgn}(\mathbf{x} - \frac{1}{2})$ for some $\mathbf{x} \in \{0, 1\}^s$ then the product distribution with parameters $\alpha(\mathbf{Wz} + \mathbf{b})$, $\alpha \to \infty$, tends to $\delta_{\mathbf{x}}$. We need to show only that there is a choice of $\mathbf{W}$ and $\mathbf{b}$ with $\text{sgn}(\mathbf{Wz} + \mathbf{b}) = \text{sgn}(f(\mathbf{z}) - \frac{1}{2})$, $f(\mathbf{z}) = \text{bin}_s(l(\mathbf{z}))$, for all $\mathbf{z} \in \{0, 1\}^N$. That is precisely the statement of Lemma 6.9 below. □

We used the following lemma in the proof of Lemma 6.8. For $l = 0, 1, \ldots, 2^s - 1$,

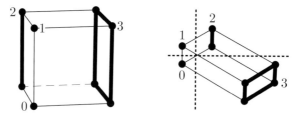

Figure 6.3   Illustration of Lemma 6.9 for $s = 2$, $N = 2^s - 1 = 3$. There is an arrangement of s hyperplanes which divides the vertices of a $(2^s - 1)$-dimensional cube as $0|1|2, 3|4, 5, 6, 7| \cdots |2^{2^s-2}, \ldots, 2^{2^s-1} - 1$.

the lth orthant of $\mathbb{R}^s$ is the set of all vectors $\mathbf{r} \in \mathbb{R}^s$ with strictly positive or negative entries and $\mathrm{dec}(\mathbf{r}_+) = l$, where $\mathbf{r}_+$ indicates the positive entries of $\mathbf{r}$.

Lemma 6.9. *Let $N = 2^s - 1$. There is an affine map $\{0, 1\}^N \to \mathbb{R}^s; \mathbf{z} \mapsto \mathbf{Wz} + \mathbf{b}$, sending $\{\mathbf{z} \in \{0, 1\}^N : l(\mathbf{z}) = l\}$ to the lth orthant of $\mathbb{R}^s$, for all $l \in \{0, 1, \ldots, N\}$.*

Proof   Consider the affine map $\mathbf{z} \mapsto \mathbf{Wz} + \mathbf{b}$, where $\mathbf{b} = -(1, \ldots, 1)^\top$ and the lth column of $\mathbf{W}$ is $2^{l+1}(\mathrm{bin}_s(l) - \frac{1}{2})$ for all $l \in \{1, \ldots, N\}$. For this choice, $\mathrm{sgn}(\mathbf{Wz} + \mathbf{b}) = \mathrm{sgn}(\mathrm{bin}_s(l(\mathbf{z})) - \frac{1}{2})$ lies in the lth orthant of $\mathbb{R}^s$. $\square$

Lemma 6.9 is illustrated in Figure 6.3 for $s = 2$ and $N = 2^s - 1 = 3$. As another example, for $s = 3$ the affine map can be defined as $\mathbf{z} \mapsto \mathbf{Wz} + \mathbf{b}$, where

$$b = \begin{pmatrix} -1 \\ -1 \\ -1 \end{pmatrix} \quad \text{and} \quad W = \begin{pmatrix} 2 & -4 & 8 & -16 & 32 & -64 & 128 \\ -2 & 4 & 8 & -16 & -32 & 64 & 128 \\ -2 & -4 & -8 & 16 & 32 & 64 & 128 \end{pmatrix}.$$

Proposition 6.10. *Let $N = 2^s - 1$ and let Q be defined as in Lemma 6.8. Then $Q \circ \mathcal{E}_N = \Delta_s^+$, the interior of Δ_s consisting of all strictly positive distributions.*

Proof   Consider a strictly positive product distribution $p \in \mathcal{E}_N$ with $p(\mathbf{z}) = \prod_{i=1}^N p_i^{1-z_i}(1 - p_i)^{z_i}$ for all $\mathbf{z} \in \{0, 1\}^N$. Then $p^\top Q \in \Delta_s$ is the vector $q = (q_0, q_1, \ldots, q_N)$ with entries $q_0 = p(\mathbf{0}) = \prod_{j=1}^N p_j$ and

$$q_i = \sum_{\mathbf{z}: l(\mathbf{z})=i} p(\mathbf{z})$$

$$= \sum_{z_1, \ldots, z_{i-1}} \left(\prod_{k<i} p_k^{1-z_k}(1 - p_k)^{z_k} \right)(1 - p_i)\left(\prod_{j>i} p_j \right)$$

$$= (1 - p_i) \prod_{j>i} p_j,$$

for all $i = 1, \ldots, N$. Therefore

$$\frac{q_i}{q_0} = \frac{1 - p_i}{p_i} \frac{1}{\prod_{j=1}^{i-1} p_j} \qquad \text{for all } i = 1, \ldots, N. \tag{6.11}$$

Since $(1 - p_i)/p_i$ can be made arbitrary in $(0, \infty)$ by choosing an appropriate p_i, independently of p_j, for $j < i$, the quotient q_i/q_0 can be made arbitrary in $(0, \infty)$ for all $i \in \{1, \ldots, N\}$. This implies that q can be made arbitrary in Δ_s^+. In fact, each $p \in \mathcal{E}_N \cap \Delta_N^+$ is mapped uniquely to one $q \in \Delta_s^+$. $\qquad \square$

Proof of Theorem 6.2 The statement follows from Propositions 6.7 and 6.10. $\qquad \square$

6.5.2 Trainable Weights in the Second Layer

In order to prove Theorem 6.4 we use the same construction of the first layer as in the previous section, except that we use one block of hidden units for each input vector. The reason for not using a single block for a pair of inputs is that now the second layer will contribute to the modeling of the output distribution in a way that depends on the specific input of the block. For the second layer we will use the following refinement of Lemma 6.8.

Lemma 6.11. *Let $s \geq 2$ and $N = 2^{s-1} - 1$. The set $\mathrm{F}_{N,s}$ can approximate the following kernels arbitrarily well:*

$$Q(\cdot \mid \mathbf{z}) = \lambda_{\mathbf{z}} \delta_{\text{bin}_s \, 2l(\mathbf{z})}(\cdot) + (1 - \lambda_{\mathbf{z}}) \delta_{\text{bin}_s \, 2l(\mathbf{z})+1}(\cdot), \quad \textit{for all } \mathbf{z} \in \{0,1\}^N,$$

where $\lambda_{\mathbf{z}}$ are certain (not mutually independent) weights in $[0, 1]$. Given any $r_l \in \mathbb{R}_+$, $l \in \{0, 1, \ldots, N\}$, it is possible to choose the $\lambda_{\mathbf{z}}$ such that

$$\frac{\sum_{\mathbf{z}: \, l(\mathbf{z})=l} \lambda_{\mathbf{z}}}{\sum_{\mathbf{z}: \, l(\mathbf{z})=l} (1 - \lambda_{\mathbf{z}})} = r_l, \quad \textit{for all } l \in \{0, 1, \ldots, N\}.$$

In words, the $\mathbf{z}$th row of Q is a convex combination of the indicators of $2l(\mathbf{z})$ and $2l(\mathbf{z}) + 1$, and, furthermore, the total weight assigned to $2l$ relative to $2l + 1$ can be made arbitrary for each l. For example, for $s = 3$ we have $N = 3$ and

$$Q = \begin{array}{c} \\ \\ \\ \\ \\ \\ \\ \\ \end{array} \begin{pmatrix} \lambda_{000} & (1-\lambda_{000}) & & & & & & \\ & & \lambda_{001} & (1-\lambda_{001}) & & & & \\ & & & & \lambda_{010} & (1-\lambda_{010}) & & \\ & & & & \lambda_{011} & (1-\lambda_{011}) & & \\ & & & & & & \lambda_{100} & (1-\lambda_{100}) \\ & & & & & & \lambda_{101} & (1-\lambda_{101}) \\ & & & & & & \lambda_{110} & (1-\lambda_{110}) \\ & & & & & & \lambda_{111} & (1-\lambda_{111}) \end{pmatrix} \begin{array}{l} 000 \\ 001 \\ 010 \\ 011 \\ 100 \\ 101 \\ 110 \\ 111 \end{array}.$$

The sum of all weights in any given even-numbered column can be made arbitrary, relative to the sum of all weights in the column right next to it, for all $N + 1$ such pairs of columns simultaneously.

Proof of Lemma 6.11   Consider the sets $Z_l = \{z \in \{0,1\}^N : l(\mathbf{z}) = l\}$, for $l = 0, 1, \ldots, N$. Let $\mathbf{W}' \in \mathbb{R}^{(s-1) \times N}$ and $\mathbf{b}' \in \mathbb{R}^{s-1}$ be the input weights and biases defined in Lemma 6.8. We define $\mathbf{W}$ and $\mathbf{b}$ by appending a row $(\mu_1, \ldots, \mu_N)$ above $\mathbf{W}'$ and an entry μ_0 above $\mathbf{b}'$.

If $\mu_j < 0$ for all $j = 0, 1, \ldots, N$ then $\mathbf{z} \mapsto \mathbf{Wz} + \mathbf{b}$ maps Z_l to the $2l$th orthant of $\mathbb{R}^s$, for each $l = 0, 1, \ldots, N$.

Consider now some arbitrary fixed choice of μ_j, for $j < l$. Choosing $\mu_l < 0$ with $|\mu_l| > \sum_{j<l} |\mu_l|$, Z_l is mapped to the $2l$th orthant. If $\mu_l \to -\infty$ then $\lambda_{\mathbf{z}} \to 1$ for all $\mathbf{z}$ with $l(\mathbf{z}) = l$. As we increase μ_l to a sufficiently large positive value, the elements of Z_l gradually are mapped to the $(2l + 1)$th orthant. If $\mu_l \to \infty$ then $(1 - \lambda_{\mathbf{z}}) \to 1$ for all $\mathbf{z}$ with $l(\mathbf{z}) = l$. By continuity, there is a choice of μ_l such that

$$\frac{\sum_{\mathbf{z}: \, l(\mathbf{z})=l} \lambda_{\mathbf{z}}}{\sum_{\mathbf{z}: \, l(\mathbf{z})=l} (1 - \lambda_{\mathbf{z}})} = r_l.$$

Note that the images of Z_j, for $j < l$, are independent of the ith columns of $\mathbf{W}$ for all $i = l, \ldots, N$. Hence changing μ_l does not have any influence on the images of Z_l, nor on $\lambda_{\mathbf{z}}$ for $\mathbf{z}: l(\mathbf{z}) < l$. Tuning μ_i sequentially, starting with $i = 0$, we obtain a kernel that approximates any Q of the claimed form arbitrarily well.   □

Let Q_s^N be the collection of kernels described in Lemma 6.11.

Proposition 6.12. *Let $s \geq 2$ and $N = 2^{s-1} - 1$. Then $Q_s^N \circ \mathcal{E}_N = \Delta_s^+$.*

Proof   Consider a strictly positive product distribution $p \in \mathcal{E}_N$ with $p(\mathbf{z}) = \prod_{i=1}^N p_i^{1-z_i}(1-p_i)^{z_i}$ for all $\mathbf{z} \in \{0,1\}^N$. Then $p^\top Q \in \Delta_s$ is a vector $(q_0, q_1, \ldots, q_{2N+1})$ whose entries satisfy $q_0 + q_1 = p(\mathbf{0}) = \prod_{j=1}^N p_j$ and

$$q_{2i} + q_{2i+1} = (1 - p_i) \prod_{j>i} p_j,$$

for all $i = 1, \ldots, N$. As in the proof of Proposition 6.10, this implies that the vector $(q_0+q_1, q_2+q_3, \ldots, q_{2N}+q_{2N+1})$ can be made arbitrary in Δ_{s-1}^+. This is irrespective of the coefficients $\lambda_0, \ldots, \lambda_N$. Now all we need to show is that we can make q_{2i} arbitrary relative to q_{2i+1} for all $i = 0, \ldots, N$.

We have

$$q_{2i} = \sum_{\mathbf{z}:\, l(\mathbf{z})=i} \lambda_{\mathbf{z}} p(\mathbf{z})$$

$$= \left(\sum_{\mathbf{z}:\, l(\mathbf{z})=i} \lambda_{\mathbf{z}} \left(\prod_{k<i} p_k^{1-z_k} (1-p_k)^{z_k} \right) \right) (1-p_i) \left(\prod_{j>i} p_j \right),$$

and

$$q_{2i+1} = \sum_{\mathbf{z}:\, l(\mathbf{z})=i} (1 - \lambda_{\mathbf{z}}) p(\mathbf{z})$$

$$= \left(\sum_{\mathbf{z}:\, l(\mathbf{z})=i} (1 - \lambda_{\mathbf{z}}) \left(\prod_{k<i} p_k^{1-z_k} (1-p_k)^{z_k} \right) \right) (1-p_i) \left(\prod_{j>i} p_j \right).$$

Therefore,

$$\frac{q_{2i}}{q_{2i+1}} = \frac{\sum_{\mathbf{z}:\, l(\mathbf{z})=i} \lambda_{\mathbf{z}} \left(\prod_{k<i} p_k^{1-z_k} (1-p_k)^{z_k} \right)}{\sum_{\mathbf{z}:\, l(\mathbf{z})=i} (1 - \lambda_{\mathbf{z}}) \left(\prod_{k<i} p_k^{1-z_k} (1-p_k)^{z_k} \right)}.$$

By Lemma 6.11 it is possible to choose all $\lambda_{\mathbf{z}}$ arbitrarily close to zero for all $\mathbf{z}$ with $l(\mathbf{z}) = i$ and have them transition continuously to values arbitrarily close to one (independently of the values of $\lambda_{\mathbf{z}}$, $\mathbf{z}$: $l(\mathbf{z}) \neq i$). Since all p_k are strictly positive, this implies that the quotient $\frac{q_{2i}}{q_{2i+1}}$ takes all values in $(0, \infty)$ as the $\lambda_{\mathbf{z}}$, $\mathbf{z}$: $l(\mathbf{z}) = i$, transition from zero to one. □

Proof of Theorem 6.4 This follows from a direct modification of Proposition 6.7, so that it has a hidden block per input vector, and Proposition 6.12. □

6.5.3 Discussion of the Proofs for Shallow Networks

We have proved upper bounds on the minimal size of shallow sigmoid stochastic feedforward networks that can approximate any stochastic function with a given number of binary inputs and outputs arbitrarily well. By our analysis, if all parameters of the network are free, $2^d(2^{s-1} - 1)$ hidden units suffice but, if only the parameters of the first layer are free, $2^{d-1}(2^s - 1)$ hidden units suffice.

It is interesting to compare these results with what is known about the universal approximation of Markov kernels by the undirected stochastic networks known as conditional restricted Boltzmann machines. For those networks, Montúfar et al. (2015) showed that $2^{d-1}(2^s - 1)$ hidden units suffice; if the number d of input units is large enough, $\frac{1}{4}2^d(2^s - 1 + \frac{1}{30})$ suffice. A more recent work (Montúfar and Rauh,

2017) showed that an RBM is a universal approximator as soon as

$$m \geq \frac{2(\log(v) + 1)}{(v + 1)} 2^v - 1,$$

where $v = d + s$; such an RBM has a smaller asymptotic behavior. In the case of no input units, our bound $2^{s-1} - 1$ equals the bound for RBMs from Montúfar et al. (2011) but is larger than the bound from Montúfar and Rauh (2017). It has been observed that undirected networks can represent many kernels that can be represented by feedforward networks, especially when these are not too stochastic (Montúfar et al., 2015; Montúfar, 2014a). Verifying the tightness of the bounds remains an open problem, as well as a detailed comparison of directed and undirected architectures.

6.6 Results for Deep Networks

We now consider networks with multiple layers of hidden units, i.e., $L > 1$. Since the dimension of $\Delta_{d,s}$ is $2^d(2^s - 1)$, a lower bound on the number of trainable parameters that a model needs for universal approximation is $2^d(2^s - 1)$. Details on this are provided in §6.8. The following theorem provides sufficient conditions for a spectrum of deep architectures to be universal approximators.

Theorem 6.13. *Let $d, s \in \mathbb{N}$, and assume that $s = 2^{b-1} + b$ for some $b \in \mathbb{N}$. Then a deep sigmoid stochastic feedforward network with d binary inputs and s binary outputs is a universal approximator of Markov kernels in $\Delta_{d,s}$ if it contains $2^{d-j}(2^{s-b} + 2^b - 1)$ hidden layers, each consisting of $2^j(s + d - j)$ units, for any $j \in \{0, 1, 2, \ldots, d\}$.*

We note that the indicated upper bounds on the width and depth hold for the universal approximation of $\Delta_{d,s'}$ for any $s' \leq s$. Moreover, if $j = d$, we can save one layer. We will make use of this in our numerical example in §6.9. One can also use a simplified construction with 2^{d+s-j} hidden layers.

The theorem indicates that there is a spectrum of networks capable of providing universal approximation such that if a network is made narrower, it must become proportionally deeper. The network topology with $j = d$ has depth exponential in s and width exponential in d, whereas $j = 0$ has depth exponential in d and s, but width exponential only in $d + s$. See Figure 6.4 for an illustration of how j affects the different network properties and shape. There may exist a spectrum of networks bridging the gap between the shallow universal approximators from §6.4 which have width exponential in d and s and only one hidden layer, and the $j = d$ case, although no formal proof has been established.

When considered as fully connected, the networks described in Theorem 6.13

vary greatly in their numbers of parameters. However, we will see that each of them can be implemented with the same minimal number of trainable parameters, equal to the dimension of $\Delta_{d,s}$. For the narrowest case $j = 0$, each input vector is carried to a specific block of hidden layers which create the corresponding output distribution; this is then passed downwards until the output layer. When $j > 0$ it will be shown that the first layer can divide the input space into 2^j sets, each to be handled by its own parallel section of the network. Each of the 2^j sections can be thought of as running side by side and non-interacting, meanwhile creating the corresponding output distributions of the 2^{d-j} different inputs. In the widest case, $j = d$, each input is processed by its own parallel section of the network and $2^s/(2(s-b))+2(s-b)-1$ hidden layers are sufficient for creating the corresponding output distribution, which resembles the the bound for deep belief networks (Montúfar and Ay, 2011).

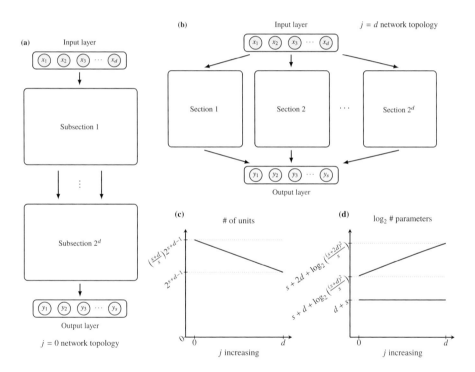

Figure 6.4 (a) The deepest narrowest network architecture, $j = 0$. Here, there is a single section consisting of 2^d subsections stacked on top of each other. (b) The widest deep architecture $j = d$. Here, there are 2^d sections placed in parallel, each consisting of a single subsection. (c) A plot of how the number of units scales as a function of j, for fixed s, d. (d) A log-scale plot of how the total number of network parameters scales with j; the lowest horizontal line shows the log of the rounded number of trainable parameters in our construction, which is independent of j.

In some special instances, small reductions in size are possible. For instance, in the widest network topology considered, where $j = d$, universal approximation can be done with one layer less.

6.6.1 Parameter Count

If we are to consider the networks as being fully connected and having all weight and bias parameters trainable, the number of parameters grows exponentially with j as

$$|\theta_{\text{full}}| = O\left(\frac{2^{s+d+j}(s + d - j)^2}{2(s - \log_2(s))}\right),$$

suggesting that the deepest topology where $j = 0$ is the most efficient universal approximator considered. The number of units for these networks linearly decreases with j as

$$\# \text{ of units} = O\left(\frac{2^{s+d}(s + d - j)}{2(s - \log_2(s))}\right),$$

meaning that the widest topology, where $j = d$, uses the least number of units. However, if one counts only the parameters that cannot be fixed prior to training according to the construction that we provide below in §6.7, one obtains

$$|\theta_{\text{trainable}}| = 2^d(2^s - 1).$$

Each of the network topologies has the hidden units organized into 2^j sections and a total of 2^d subsections, each with $2^s - 1$ trainable parameters. The first hidden layer and the output layer have fixed parameters. Each of the trainable parameters controls exactly one entry in the Markov kernel; the number of parameters is also necessary for universal approximation of $\Delta_{d,s}$, as we will show below in §6.8.

6.6.2 Approximation with Finite Weights and Biases

The quality of approximation provided in our construction depends on the magnitudes of the network parameters. If this is allowed to increase unboundedly, a universal approximator will be able to approximate any Markov kernel with arbitrary accuracy. If the parameters are only allowed to have a certain maximal magnitude, the approximation is within an error bound described in the following theorem.

Theorem 6.14. *Let $\epsilon \in (0, 1/2^s)$ and consider a target kernel p^* in the nonempty set $\Delta_{d,s}^\epsilon := \{P \in \Delta_{d,s} : \epsilon \leq P_{ij} \leq 1 - \epsilon \text{ for all } i, j\}$. There is a choice of the network parameters, bounded in absolute value by $\alpha = 2m\sigma^{-1}(1 - \epsilon)$, where*

$m = \max\{j, s + (d - j)\} \le d + s$, *such that the conditional probabilities* $p(\mathbf{y} \mid \mathbf{x})$
generated by the network are uniformly close to the target values, according to

$$|p(\mathbf{y} \mid \mathbf{x}) - p^*(\mathbf{y} \mid \mathbf{x})| \le 1 - (1 - \epsilon)^N + \epsilon, \quad \text{for all } \mathbf{x} \in \{0, 1\}^d, \mathbf{y} \in \{0, 1\}^s,$$

where N *is the total number of units in the network excluding input units. If one
considers an arbitrary target kernel* p^*, *the error bound increases by* ϵ.

The proof of Theorem 6.14 is presented in §6.7.4 after the proof of Theorem 6.13. It depends on explicit error bounds for the probability-sharing steps to be discussed next.

6.7 Proofs for Deep Networks

The proof naturally splits into three steps. The first step shows that the first layer is capable of dividing the input space into 2^j disjoint sets of 2^{d-j} input vectors, sending each set to a different parallel-running section of the network. The 2^{d-j} vectors in the τth set will activate the τth section, while the other sections take state zero with probability one. Second, it is shown that each of the 2^j sections is capable of approximating the conditional distributions for the corresponding 2^{d-j} inputs. The last step explicitly determines the parameters needed to copy the relevant units from the last hidden layer to the output layer.

6.7.1 Notation

The integer j dictates the network's topology. This index can be any number in $\{0, 1, 2, \ldots, d\}$. For an input vector $\mathbf{x}$, we denote the r through r' bits by $\mathbf{x}_{[r,r']}$. The target conditional probability distribution given the input $\mathbf{x}$ is denoted by $p^*(\cdot \mid \mathbf{x})$. The joint state of all units in the lth hidden layer is denoted by $\mathbf{h}^l$. The state of the rth unit of the lth layer is denoted by h^l_r. If a range is provided as superscript (subscript), it refers to a range of layers (units), i.e., $\mathbf{h}^{[l,l+2]}$ refers to the hidden layers $\mathbf{h}^l, \mathbf{h}^{l+1}, \mathbf{h}^{l+2}$. The integer $\tau = 1, 2, \ldots, 2^j$ is an index specifying a *block* of units in a layer. Each block consists of $s + d - j$ consecutive units. The τth block of units in a given layer comprises those indexed from $(\tau - 1)(s + d - j) + 1$ to $\tau(s + d - j)$. The state of the τth block of units of hidden layer l is $\mathbf{h}^l_{(\tau)} := \mathbf{h}^l_{[(\tau-1)(s+d-j)+1, \tau(s+d-j)]}$. If a block *activates*, this means that it can take a state other than the zero vector with non-zero probability. If the block is *inactive*, it will take the zero state with arbitrarily high probability. Owing to their different functions in what follows, it is useful to denote by $\mathbf{a}^l_{(\tau)}$ and $\mathbf{b}^l_{(\tau)}$ the first s and the last $d - j$ units of the τth block at the lth layer. The first unit of $\mathbf{a}^l_{(\tau)}$ is denoted as $\mathbf{a}^l_{(\tau),1}$; it plays an important role in the first layer of the network.

For the second part of the proof, we will first show that $L = 2^{s+d-j}$ hidden layers suffice, and then refine this bound. Thus the focus will be on the entire τth *section* of hidden units. The τth section comprises the units in the τth block over all the hidden layers, written without a superscript as $\mathbf{h}_{(\tau)} := \mathbf{h}_{(\tau)}^{[1,2^{s+d-j}]}$. Each section is broken into subsections, indexed by $q = 1, 2, \ldots, 2^{d-j}$. The qth subsection of the τth section is $\mathbf{h}_{(\tau)}^{(q)} := \mathbf{h}_{(\tau)}^{[(q-1)2^s+1, q2^s]}$. Lastly, each subsection of the network will have a Gray code associated with it, i.e., a sequence of binary vectors in which subsequent vectors differ in only one bit. In actuality, since each subsection will be capable of performing not just one but rather multiple tasks per layer, it will have a set of partial Gray codes associated with it, to be defined in the following. See Figure 6.5 for an illustration of the notation described here.

6.7.2 Probability Mass Sharing

For fixed weights and a given input, a width-m layer of the network will exhibit a marginal distribution $p \in \Delta_m$. A subsequent width-m layer determines a particular mapping of p to another distribution $p' \in \Delta_m$. For certain choices of the parameters, this mapping transforms p in such a way that a fraction of the mass of a given state $\mathbf{g} \in \{0,1\}^m$ is transferred to some other state $\hat{\mathbf{g}} \in \{0,1\}^m$, so that $p'(\hat{\mathbf{g}}) = p(\hat{\mathbf{g}}) + \lambda p(\mathbf{g})$, $p'(\mathbf{g}) = (1 - \lambda)p(\mathbf{g})$, and $p'(\mathbf{z}) = p(\mathbf{z})$ for all other states $\mathbf{z}$. This mapping is referred to as probability mass sharing, and was exploited in the works of Sutskever and Hinton (2008), Le Roux and Bengio (2010), andMontúfar and Ay (2011). One important takeaway from these works is that probability mass sharing in one layer is restrictive, and the states $\mathbf{g}$ and $\hat{\mathbf{g}}$ need to stand in a particular relation to each other, e.g., as Hamming neighbors. Montúfar and Morton (2012) gave a description of the mappings that are expressible by the individual layers of a Bayesian sigmoid belief network. In the following we describe ways in which probability mass sharing is possible.

We define Gray codes and partial Gray codes, as they will be useful in discussion of probability mass sharing sequences. A *Gray code* G for s bits is a sequence of vectors $\mathbf{g}_i \in \{0,1\}^s$, $i = 1, \ldots, 2^s$, such that $\|\mathbf{g}_i - \mathbf{g}_{i-1}\|_H = 1$ for all $i \in \{2, \ldots, 2^s\}$, and $\bigcup_i \{\mathbf{g}_i\} = \{0,1\}^s$. One may visualize such a code as tracing a path along the edges of an s-cube without ever returning to the same vertex but covering all the vertices. A *partial Gray code* S_i for s bits is a sequence of vectors $S_{i,j} \in \{0,1\}^s$, $j = 1, \ldots, r \leq 2^s$, such that $\|S_{i,j} - S_{i,j-1}\|_H = 1$ for all $j \in \{1, \ldots, r\}$. We will be interested in collections of partial Gray codes which contain the same number of vectors and which partition $\{0,1\}^s$. In the analysis, subsections of the network will activate to the values of different partial Gray codes with appropriate probabilities.

The first proposition states that, when considering two consecutive layers $l - 1$

Input layer

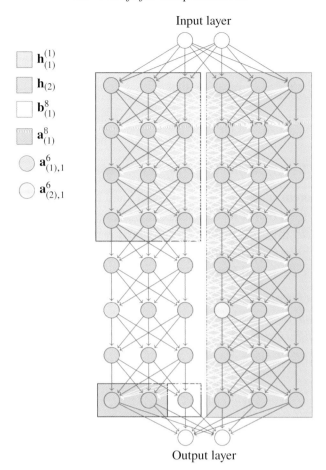

Output layer

Figure 6.5 The network architecture from Theorem 6.13 for $j = 1$, with $d = 2$ inputs and $s = 2$ outputs. The figure exemplifies the notation defined in §6.7.1. The white connections (which are present also in the white section of the figure) are set to zero, separating the hidden units into 2^{d-j} parallel running sections. Here there are two sections indexed by $\tau = 1, 2$, and in each section there are two subsections indexed by $q = 1, 2$. The network has 2^d subsections in total when they are added across all sections. Each output vector is generated with an appropriate conditional probability, given the input vector $\mathbf{x}$, by mapping the input through a corresponding sequence of states of $\mathbf{a}_{(\tau)}$ with appropriate probabilities; information about the input is preserved throughout the hidden layers by $\mathbf{b}_{(\tau)}$.

and l, there exists a weight vector $\mathbf{W}_i^l$ and bias b_i^l such that h_i^l will be a copy of h_i^{l-1} with arbitrarily high probability. See Sutskever and Hinton (2008, Section 3.2) or Le Roux and Bengio (2010, Section 3.3) for equivalent statements.

Proposition 6.15. *Fix $\epsilon \in (0, 1/2)$ and $\alpha = \log(1 - \epsilon) - \log(\epsilon)$. Choose the ith row of weights $\mathbf{W}_i^l$ such that $W_{ii}^l = 2\alpha$ and $W_{ij}^l = 0$ for $j \neq i$, and choose the ith bias*

$b_i^l = -\alpha$. Then $\Pr(h_i^l = h_i^{l-1} \mid \mathbf{h}^{l-1}) = (1 - \epsilon)$ *for all* $\mathbf{h}^{l-1}$. *Letting* $\alpha \to \infty$ *allows the unit to copy the state of a unit in the previous layer with arbitrarily high probability.*

Proof   For the given choice of weights and bias, the total input to the ith unit in layer l will be $2\alpha h_i^{l-1} - \alpha$, meaning that

$$\Pr(h_i^l = 1 \mid \mathbf{h}^{l-1}) = \begin{cases} \sigma(\alpha) & \text{when } h_i^{l-1} = 1 \\ \sigma(-\alpha) & \text{when } h_i^{l-1} = 0. \end{cases} \tag{6.12}$$

Since $\alpha = \sigma^{-1}(1 - \epsilon)$, one has that $\Pr(h_i^l = h_i^{l-1} \mid \mathbf{h}^{l-1}) = (1 - \epsilon)$.   □

The next theorem states that the weights $\mathbf{W}_i^l$ and bias b_i^l of the ith unit in layer l may be chosen such that if $\mathbf{h}^{l-1}$ matches any of two pre-specified vectors $\mathbf{g}$ and $\hat{\mathbf{g}}$ in $\{0,1\}^m$ then h_i^l flips h_i^{l-1} with a pre-specified probability. Otherwise, if $\mathbf{h}^{l-1}$ is not $\mathbf{g}$ or $\hat{\mathbf{g}}$, the bit is copied with arbitrarily high probability. This corresponds to Theorem 2 of Le Roux and Bengio (2010), adjusted to our notation.

Theorem 6.16 (Theorem 2 of Le Roux and Bengio, 2010). *Consider two adjacent layers* $l - 1$ *and* l *of width* m. *Consider two vectors* $\mathbf{g}$ *and* $\hat{\mathbf{g}}$ *in* $\{0,1\}^m$ *with* $\|\mathbf{g} - \hat{\mathbf{g}}\|_H = 1$, *differing in entry* j. *Fix two probabilities* $\rho, \hat{\rho} \in (0,1)$ *and a tolerance* $\epsilon \in (0, 1/2)$. *For any* $i \neq j$, *there exist* $(\mathbf{W}_i^l, b_i^l)$ *with absolute values at most* $\alpha = 2m(\sigma^{-1}(1 - \epsilon))$ *such that*

$$\Pr(h_i^l = 1 \mid \mathbf{h}^{l-1} = \mathbf{g}) = \rho_\epsilon,$$
$$\Pr(h_i^l = 1 \mid \mathbf{h}^{l-1} = \hat{\mathbf{g}}) = \hat{\rho}_\epsilon;$$

otherwise,

$$\Pr(h_i^l = h_i^{l-1} \mid \mathbf{h}^{l-1} \neq \mathbf{g}, \hat{\mathbf{g}}) = 1 - \epsilon.$$

Here $\rho_\epsilon = \max\{\epsilon, \min\{\rho, 1 - \epsilon\}\}$. *If we fix a maximum parameter magnitude* α *instead of a tolerance then we can substitute* $\epsilon = 1 - \sigma(\alpha/2m)$.

This theorem allows to have a given vector $\mathbf{g} \in \{0,1\}^m$ map at the subsequent layer to itself or to a Hamming adjacent vector $\mathbf{g}' \in \{0,1\}^m$ with a pre-specified probability ρ, with

$$\Pr(\mathbf{h}^l = \mathbf{g} \mid \mathbf{h}^{l-1} = \mathbf{g}) = \rho_\epsilon(1 - \epsilon)^{m-1}, \tag{6.13}$$
$$\Pr(\mathbf{h}^l = \mathbf{g}' \mid \mathbf{h}^{l-1} = \mathbf{g}) = (1 - \rho_\epsilon)(1 - \epsilon)^{m-1}, \tag{6.14}$$

and

$$\Pr(\mathbf{h}^l = \mathbf{h}^{l-1} \mid \mathbf{h}^{l-1} \neq \mathbf{g}) = (1 - \epsilon)^m, \tag{6.15}$$

where ϵ can be made arbitrarily small if the maximum magnitude of weights and biases, $\alpha = 2m(\sigma^{-1}(1 - \epsilon))$, is allowed to grow to infinity. This mapping is referred to as a *probability mass sharing step*, or a sharing step for short. This in turn allows the transfer of probability mass around the m-cube, one vertex at a layer, until the correct probability mass resides on each binary vector, to the given level of accuracy. The sharing path follows a Gray code, each pair of consecutive vectors having Hamming distance one.

In fact, the theorem allows us to overlay multiple sharing paths, so long as the Gray codes are sufficiently separated. A collection of partial codes satisfying this requirement and covering the set of binary strings is described in the following theorem, which is Lemma 4 of Montúfar and Ay (2011).

Theorem 6.17 (Lemma 4 of Montúfar and Ay, 2011). *Let $m = \frac{2^b}{2} + b, b \in \mathbb{N}, b \geq 1$. There exist $2^b = 2(m - b)$ sequences S_i, $1 \leq i \leq 2^b$, composed of length-m binary vectors $S_{i,k}$, $1 \leq k \leq 2^{m-b}$, satisfying the following:*

(i) *$\{S_1, \ldots, S_{2^b}\}$ is a partition of $\{0,1\}^m$.*
(ii) *The vectors $S_{1,1}, \ldots, S_{2^b,1}$ share the same values in their last $m - b$ bits.*
(iii) *The vector $(0, \ldots, 0)$ is the last element $S_{1,2^{m-b}}$ of the first sequence.*
(iv) *For all $i \in \{1, \ldots, 2^b\}$ and $k \in \{1, \ldots, 2^{m-b} - 1\}$, we have $\|S_{i,k}, S_{i,k+1}\|_H = 1$.*
(v) *For all $i, r \in \{1, \ldots, 2^b\}$ such that $i \neq r$ and, for all $k \in \{1, \ldots, 2^{m-b} - 1\}$, the bit switched between $S_{i,k}$ and $S_{i,k+1}$ and the bit switched between $S_{r,k}$ and $S_{r,k+1}$ are different, unless $\|S_{i,k} - S_{r,k}\|_H = 1$.*

This theorem describes a schedule that allows for probability to be shared from $2(m - b)$ vectors per layer, starting from the vectors $S_{i,1}$, $i = 1, \ldots, 2(m - b)$. For every layer l, if $\mathbf{h}^{l-1}$ matches $S_{i,l-1}$, probability mass will be shared onto $S_{i,l}$, for each $i = 1, \ldots, 2(m - b)$, and it will be copied unchanged otherwise. The accuracy of the transition probabilities depends on the maximum allowed magnitudes of the weights and biases, similarly to equation (6.15).

6.7.3 Universal Approximation

The First Layer

The first step of the proof focuses on the flexibility of the first layer of the network. For fixed d, s, j, there are $2^j (s + d - j)$ units in $\mathbf{h}^1$ belonging to 2^j consecutive blocks, indexed by $\tau = 1, \ldots, 2^j$.

Within each block, set the parameters according to Proposition 6.15 to copy the last $d - j$ bits of the input $\mathbf{x}$, so that $\mathbf{b}^1_{(\tau)} = \mathbf{x}_{[j+1,d]}$ with probability $(1 - \epsilon)^{j-d}$ and parameters of magnitude no more than $\alpha = 2\sigma^{-1}(1 - \epsilon)$.

Within each block, $\mathbf{a}^1_{(\tau)}$ will activate with probability close to one for exactly 2^{d-j} inputs $\mathbf{x}$. This can be done by setting the parameters of the first unit $\mathbf{a}^1_{(\tau),1}$ of each block in such a way that the unit takes state 1 only if the first j bits of $\mathbf{x}$ agree with the number τ of the block. This is formalized in the following lemma. The remainder units $a^1_{(\tau),i}$, $i = 2, \ldots, s$, are set to take the zero state with probability $1 - \epsilon$, by choosing their weights to be zero and bias equal to $-\sigma^{-1}(1 - \epsilon)$.

Lemma 6.18. *Fix* $\tau \in \{1, 2, \ldots, 2^j\}$ *and* $\epsilon \in (0, 1/2)$. *Let*

$$S = \left\{ \mathbf{x} \in \{0, 1\}^d : \left\lfloor \frac{\mathrm{int}(\mathbf{x})}{2^{d-j}} \right\rfloor + 1 = \tau \right\}.$$

Then there exist weights $\mathbf{W} \in \mathbb{R}^{1 \times d}$ *and biases* $b \in \mathbb{R}$ *for the first unit of the* τ*th block having absolute values at most* $\alpha = 2d\sigma^{-1}(1 - \epsilon)$, *such that*

$$\Pr\left(a^1_{(\tau),1} = 1 \mid \mathbf{x}\right) = \begin{cases} 1 - \epsilon, & \mathbf{x} \in S \\ \epsilon, & \mathbf{x} \notin S. \end{cases} \tag{6.16}$$

Proof The probability of unit $a^1_{(\tau),1}$ activating is given by

$$\Pr\left(a^1_{(\tau),1} = 1 \mid \mathbf{x}\right) = \sigma(\mathbf{W}\mathbf{x} + b). \tag{6.17}$$

Note that S is the set of length-d binary vectors whose first j bits equal the length-j binary vector $\mathbf{g}$ with integer representation τ. Geometrically, S is a $(d - j)$-dimensional face of the d-hypercube. In turn, there exists an affine hyperplane in $\mathbb{R}^d$ separating S from $\{0, 1\}^d \setminus S$. For instance, we may choose $\mathbf{W} = \gamma(2(\mathbf{g} - \frac{1}{2}), \mathbf{0})^\top$ and $b = \gamma(\|\mathbf{g}\|_1 - \frac{1}{2})$, which gives $\mathbf{W}\mathbf{x} + b = \frac{1}{2}\gamma$ for all $\mathbf{x} \in S$ and $\mathbf{W}\mathbf{x} + b \leq -\frac{1}{2}\gamma$ for all $\notin S$. Choosing $\gamma = 2\sigma^{-1}(1 - \epsilon)$ yields the claim. $\qquad\square$

Note that $\mathbf{x} \in S$ is equivalent to $\mathbf{x}_{[1,j]} = \mathbf{g}$, where $\mathbf{g}$ is the j-bit representation of τ. Following (6.13)–(6.15), the second bit can also be activated, as

$$\Pr\left(a^1_{(\tau),2} = 1 \mid \mathbf{x}\right) = \begin{cases} \rho_\epsilon, & \mathbf{x}_{[1,j]} = \mathbf{g} \\ \epsilon, & \mathbf{x}_{[1,j]} \neq \mathbf{g} \end{cases}, \tag{6.18}$$

for any chosen $\rho \in [0, 1]$. We will be able to use this type of initialization to save one layer when $j = d$, where there is only one subsection per section.

The Hidden Layers

In the second part of our construction, the focus is restricted to individual sections of the network, having width $s + (d - j)$ and $L = 2^{d-j}(2^{s-b} + 2(s - b) - 1)$ layers. To prevent separate sections from interfering with one another, set all weights between the units in sections τ and τ' to zero, for all $\tau' \neq \tau$. The τth section will only be contingent upon its parameters and $\mathbf{h}^1_{(\tau)}$, which can be regarded as the input to the section. Each section is responsible for approximating the target conditional distributions of 2^{d-j} inputs. Each section should be thought of as consisting of 2^{d-j} subsections in sequence, each consisting of $2^{s-b} + 2(s - b) - 1$ consecutive layers.

Each subsection is responsible for approximating the target conditional distribution of a single input $\mathbf{x}$. The first layer of any subsection copies the state from the previous layer, except for the very first subsection, which we described above. Subsection q will be "activated" if $\mathbf{a}^l_{(\tau)} = (1,0,\ldots,0)$ and $\mathbf{b}^l_{(\tau)}$ takes the specific value $\mathrm{bin}_{d-j}(q)$, where l is the first layer of the subsection. When a subsection is activated, it will carry out a sequence of sharing steps to generate the output distribution. This can be achieved in 2^s layers by applying a single sharing step per layer, with schedule given by a Gray code with initial state $(1,0,\ldots,0)$ and final state $(0,\ldots,0)$. If only single sharing steps are used then the parameters which need to be trainable are biases. Alternatively, we can arrange for the first $2(s-b)$ layers of the subsection to conduct probability sharing to distribute the mass of $\mathbf{a}^l_{(\tau)} = (1,0,\ldots,0)$ across the initial states $S_{i,1}$, $i = 1,\ldots,2(s-b)$, of the partial Gray codes from Theorem 6.17. Following this, the subsection overlays the $2^b = 2(s-b)$ sequences of sharing steps with the schedule from Theorem 6.17, to generate the output distribution. When the subsection is not activated, it copies the incoming vector downwards until its last layer.

By the construction one can see that if $\mathbf{a}^l_{(\tau)} = \mathbf{0}$, probability mass is never transferred away from this state, meaning that the last hidden layer of the section takes the state $\mathbf{a}^L_{(\tau)} = \mathbf{0}$ with probability close to one. Therefore the blocks of the final hidden layer will be distributed as

$$\mathbf{a}^L_{(\tau)} \sim \begin{cases} p^*(\cdot \mid \mathbf{x}), & \text{if } \left(\lfloor \frac{\mathrm{int}(\mathbf{x})}{2^{d-j}} \rfloor + 1\right) = \tau \\ \delta_{\mathbf{0}}, & \text{otherwise.} \end{cases} \qquad (6.19)$$

We can obtain a slight improvement when $j = d$ and there is only one subsection per section. In this case, we can set two of the initial states $S_{i,1}$, $i = 1,\ldots,2(s-b)$, as $(1,0,0,\ldots,0)$ and $(1,1,0,\ldots,0)$. We initialize the first hidden layer by (6.18), which allows us to place probabilities ρ_ϵ and $1 - \rho_\epsilon$ on these two states and so to save one of the $2(s-b)$ sharing steps that are used to initialize the partial Gray codes.

The Output Layer

The third and final step of the proof specifies how the last layer of the network will copy the relevant block of the final hidden layer in such a way that the output layer exhibits the correct distribution. To this end, we just need the ith unit of the output layer to implement an **or** gate over the ith bits of all blocks, for $i = 1,\ldots,s$. This can be achieved, with probability $1 - \epsilon$, by setting the the bias of each output unit as $-\alpha$, and the weight matrix $\mathbf{W} \in \mathbb{R}^{s \times 2^j(s+d-j)}$ of the output layer as

$$\mathbf{W} = \alpha \left(I_s \mid Z \mid I_s \mid Z \mid \cdots \mid I_s \mid Z \right), \qquad (6.20)$$

where I_s is the $s \times s$ identity matrix, Z is the $s \times (d - j)$ zero matrix, and $\alpha = 2\sigma^{-1}(1 - \epsilon)$. This concludes the proof of Theorem 6.13.

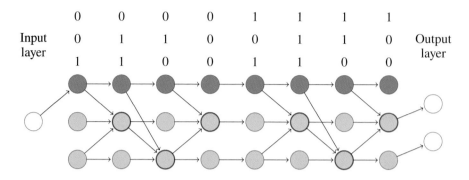

Figure 6.6 The narrow network topology for $d = 1$, $s = 2$, $j = 0$, where only one probability-sharing step is utilized per layer, and the Gray codes specifying them are shown. This network is a universal approximator of Markov kernels in $\Delta_{1,2}$. The units shown in blue will copy the input state throughout the network. The first hidden layer of the network will either be "100" or "101" depending on the input. If it is the former, only the first subsection $\mathbf{h}^{[1,4]}$ will perform probability mass sharing, resulting in $\mathbf{h}^4$ distributed as $p^*(\cdot \,|\, x = 0)$. If it is the latter, probability mass sharing will only occur in $\mathbf{h}^{[5,8]}$. Only the non-zero weights are shown. This network requires only six trainable parameters, which are all biases, indicated by the bold outlined units.

Example 6.19. Consider the case where $d = 1$ and $s = 2$ and the simple sharing scheme uses a Gray code. The narrowest case where $j = 0$ is a network consisting of $2 \times 2^2 = 8$ layers, each of width $2 + 1$. There is only one section, and it consists of two subsections, one for each possible input. The first subsection is responsible for approximating $p^*(\cdot \,|\, \mathbf{x} = 0)$ and the second for $p^*(\cdot \,|\, \mathbf{x} = 1)$. See Figure 6.6 for an illustration of the network and the Gray codes used to specify the sharing steps.

6.7.4 Error Analysis for Finite Weights and Biases

The proof construction demonstrates that we may conduct sequential probability sharing steps according to Gray codes which specify a unique path from every $\mathbf{x}$ to every $\mathbf{y}$. Given an input $\mathbf{x}$, the path generating $\mathbf{y}$ will occur with probability $p^*(\mathbf{y} \,|\, \mathbf{x})$ as the size of the parameters becomes infinitely large. If the magnitude of the parameters is bounded by $\alpha = 2m(\sigma^{-1}(1 - \epsilon))$ and we consider a target kernel $P \in \Delta_{d,s}^\epsilon := \{P \in \Delta_{d,s} : \epsilon \le P_{ij} \le 1 - \epsilon \text{ for all } i, j\}$, we may utilize Theorem 6.16 to compute bounds on the probability of the path intended to generate $\mathbf{y}$. Any other paths from $\mathbf{x}$ to $\mathbf{y}$ will have a low probability. The details are as follows.

Proof of Theorem 6.14   Fix an $\epsilon \in (0, 1/2^s)$ and $p^* \in \Delta_{d,s}^\epsilon$. Suppose that a network from Theorem 6.13 has L hidden layers of width m. Without loss of generality, assume that $\mathbf{y} = \mathbf{g}^r$ for some $r \in \{1, \ldots, 2^s\}$ where the sequence $\{\mathbf{g}^l\}$ is the Gray code defining the sharing steps. Recall that $p(\mathbf{y} \mid \mathbf{x})$ may be written as

$$p(\mathbf{y} \mid \mathbf{x}) = \sum_{\mathbf{h}^1} \cdots \sum_{\mathbf{h}^L} p(\mathbf{y} \mid \mathbf{h}^L) \cdots p(\mathbf{h}^1 \mid \mathbf{x}) = \sum_{\mathbf{h}} p(\mathbf{y} \mid \mathbf{h}^L) \cdots p(\mathbf{h}^1 \mid \mathbf{x}). \quad (6.21)$$

Note that most terms in this sum are $O(\epsilon)$ or smaller when using the proof construction for Theorem 6.13. The one term that is larger than the rest is the term where the hidden layers activate as the sequence $\mathbf{h}^1 = \mathbf{g}^1, \ldots, \mathbf{h}^r = \mathbf{g}^r, \mathbf{h}^{r+1} = \mathbf{g}^r, \ldots, \mathbf{h}^L = \mathbf{g}^r$. In particular, if the parameters in the network were infinitely large, this sequence of hidden layer activations would occur with probability exactly $p^*(\mathbf{y} \mid \mathbf{x})$ by construction. Denote this sequence by T and let $p(\mathbf{y}, T \mid \mathbf{x})$ denote the probability of observing this sequence,

$$p(\mathbf{y}, T \mid \mathbf{x}) :=$$
$$p(\mathbf{y} \mid \mathbf{h}^L = \mathbf{g}^r) p(\mathbf{h}^L = \mathbf{g}^r \mid \mathbf{h}^{L-1} = \mathbf{g}^r) \cdots p(\mathbf{h}^r = \mathbf{g}^r \mid \mathbf{h}^{r-1} = \mathbf{g}^{r-1}) \cdots p(\mathbf{h}^1 = \mathbf{g}^1 \mid \mathbf{x}).$$

When the magnitude of the weights is bounded by $2m\sigma^{-1}(1 - \epsilon)$, Theorem 6.16 provides the error terms for each $p(\mathbf{h}^l = \mathbf{g}^l \mid \mathbf{h}^{l-1} = \mathbf{g}^{l-1})$. Specifically, we have that

$$p(\mathbf{h}^1 = \mathbf{g}^1 \mid \mathbf{x}) = (1 - \epsilon)^m,$$
$$p(\mathbf{h}^2 = \mathbf{g}^2 \mid \mathbf{h}^1 = \mathbf{g}^1) = \rho^{[1]}(1 - \epsilon)^{m-1},$$
$$\vdots \qquad \qquad \vdots$$
$$p(\mathbf{h}^r = \mathbf{g}^r \mid \mathbf{h}^{r-1} = \mathbf{g}^{r-1}) = \rho^{[r-1]}(1 - \epsilon)^{m-1},$$
$$p(\mathbf{h}^{r+1} = \mathbf{g}^r \mid \mathbf{h}^r = \mathbf{g}^r) = (1 - \rho^{[r]})(1 - \epsilon)^{m-1},$$
$$p(\mathbf{h}^{r+2} = \mathbf{g}^r \mid \mathbf{h}^{r+1} = \mathbf{g}^r) = (1 - \epsilon)^m,$$
$$\vdots \qquad \qquad \vdots$$
$$p(\mathbf{h}^L = \mathbf{g}^r \mid \mathbf{h}^{L-1} = \mathbf{g}^r) = (1 - \epsilon)^m,$$
$$p(\mathbf{y} \mid \mathbf{h}^L = \mathbf{g}^r) = (1 - \epsilon)^s,$$

where $\rho^{[l]}$ are the transfer probabilities between layers l and $l + 1$ discussed in Theorem 6.16. We point out that for the output of the network to be $\mathbf{y} = \mathbf{g}^r$, the complementary sharing probability must occur at layer $l = r$, i.e., it is $(1 - \rho^{[r]})$. Additionally, we point out that $p^*(\mathbf{y} \mid \mathbf{x}) = \rho^{[1]}\rho^{[2]} \cdots \rho^{[r-1]}(1 - \rho^{[r]})$. With this, the bound in Theorem 6.14 may be derived as follows:

$$|p(\mathbf{y} \mid \mathbf{x}) - p^*(\mathbf{y} \mid \mathbf{x})| = \left| \sum_{\mathbf{h}^1} \cdots \sum_{\mathbf{h}^L} p(\mathbf{y} \mid \mathbf{h}^L) \cdots p(\mathbf{h}^1 \mid \mathbf{x}) - p^*(\mathbf{y} \mid \mathbf{x}) \right|$$

$$\leq |p(T, \mathbf{y} \mid \mathbf{x}) - p^*(\mathbf{y} \mid \mathbf{x})| + \left| \sum_{(\mathbf{h}^1, \ldots, \mathbf{h}^L) \neq T} p(\mathbf{y} \mid \mathbf{h}^L) \cdots p(\mathbf{h}^1 \mid \mathbf{x}) \right|$$

$$< |p(T, \mathbf{y} \mid \mathbf{x}) - p^*(\mathbf{y} \mid \mathbf{x})| + \epsilon$$

$$= |\rho^{[1]} \cdots \rho^{[r-1]}(1 - \rho^{[r]})(1 - \epsilon)^{mL-r+s} - p^*(\mathbf{y} \mid \mathbf{x})| + \epsilon$$

$$= |p^*(\mathbf{y} \mid \mathbf{x})(1 - \epsilon)^{mL-r+s} - p^*(\mathbf{y} \mid \mathbf{x})| + \epsilon$$

$$= p^*(\mathbf{y} \mid \mathbf{x})|1 - (1 - \epsilon)^{mL-r+s}| + \epsilon$$

$$< 1 - (1 - \epsilon)^{mL-r+s} + \epsilon.$$

In the third line, the second term is upper bounded by ϵ because each term in the sum has at least one factor ϵ and the sum itself cannot be larger than 1. Since $mL - r + s \leq N$, where N is the total number of units in the network excluding the input units, for any $r \in 2^s$, we can uniformly bound the difference in each probability using $1 - (1 - \epsilon)^N$.

It remains to show that if $p^* \in \Delta_{d,s}^\epsilon$ then, for each $\mathbf{x}$, the factorization $p^*(\mathbf{g}^r \mid \mathbf{x}) = \rho^{[1]} \cdots \rho^{[r-1]}(1 - \rho^{[r]})$ has factors in $[\epsilon, 1 - \epsilon]$ for each $\mathbf{g}^r$. Since $p^*(\mathbf{g}^1 \mid \mathbf{x}) = (1 - \rho^{[1]}) \geq \epsilon$, we have that $\rho^{[1]} \leq 1 - \epsilon$. Similarly, since $p^*(\mathbf{g}^2 \mid \mathbf{x}) = \rho^{[1]}(1 - \rho^{[2]}) \geq \epsilon$ and $(1 - \rho^{[2]}) \leq 1$, we have that $\rho^{[1]} \geq \epsilon$. The same argument applies recursively for all r.

Finally, for an arbitrary target kernel $p^* \in \Delta_{d,s}$, one finds an approximation $p^{*,\epsilon} \in \Delta_{d,s}^\epsilon$ with $|p^*(\mathbf{y} \mid \mathbf{x}) - p^{*,\epsilon}(\mathbf{y} \mid \mathbf{x})| \leq \epsilon$ and

$$|p(\mathbf{y} \mid \mathbf{x}) - p^*(\mathbf{y} \mid \mathbf{x})| \leq |p(\mathbf{y} \mid \mathbf{x}) - p^{*,\epsilon}(\mathbf{y} \mid \mathbf{x})| + \epsilon. \qquad \square$$

6.7.5 Discussion of the Proofs for Deep Networks

Since universal approximation was shown for the shallow case, it follows that any stochastic feedforward network of width at least $2^d(2^{s-1} - 1)$ with $s \geq 2$, $d \geq 1$, and $L \geq 1$ hidden layers is a universal approximator. The proof above refines this bound by showing that, as a network is made deeper, it may be made proportionally narrower while still remaining a universal approximator. This proof applies to network topologies indexed by $j \in \{0, 1, \ldots, d\}$, where the shallowest depth occurs when $j = d$; $2^{s-b} + 2(s - b)$ hidden layers is sufficient, with $b \sim \log_2(s)$. This leaves open whether there is a spectrum of networks between the $j = d$ case and the shallow case which are also universal approximators. Beyond the narrow side of the spectrum, where $j = 0$, it is also open whether narrower universal approximators exist. This is due to the proof technique, which relies on information about the input being passed from layer to layer.

We point out that the universal approximation of $\Delta_{d,s}$ requires unbounded parameters. Indeed, if we want to express a conditional probability value of 1 as the product of conditional probabilities expressed by the network then some of these factors need to have entries 1. On the other hand it is clear that a sigmoid unit only approaches the value 1 as its total input tends to infinity, which requires that the parameters tend to infinity. We have provided bounds on the approximation errors when the parameters are bounded in magnitude. However, it is left open whether the universal approximation of kernels in $\Delta_{d,s}^{\epsilon}$, with entries bounded away from 0 and 1, is possible with finite weights. The reason is that our proof technique relies on inducing nearly deterministic behavior in many of the computational units by sending the weights toward infinity. Nonetheless, as shown in our bounds and illustrated in §6.9, most of the approximation quality is already present for moderately sized weights.

The networks that we have discussed here are optimal in the sense that they only utilize $2^d(2^s - 1)$ trainable parameters. This follows from the observation that each probability-mass-sharing step has exactly one parameter that depends on the kernel being approximated. Further improvements on finding more compact universal approximators, in the sense that they have fewer units, may be possible. It remains of interest to determine the tightness of our theorems regarding the number of units. Lower bounds for the width and overall number of parameters of the network can be determined by the information-theoretic and geometric techniques to be discussed next.

6.8 Lower Bounds for Shallow and Deep Networks

6.8.1 Parameter Counting Lower Bounds

The following theorem establishes a lower bound on the number of parameters needed in a network for universal approximation to be possible. It verifies the intuition that the number of trainable parameters of the model needs to be at least as large as the dimension of the set of kernels that we want to approximate arbitrarily well. This result is needed in order to exclude the possibility of the type of lower-dimensional universal approximator that is a space-filling curve.

The proof is based on finding a smooth parametrization of the closure of the model and then applying Sard's theorem (Sard, 1942). We start with the parametrization.

Proposition 6.20. *The closure of the set of kernels* $F_{d,m_1,\ldots,m_L,s} \subseteq \Delta_{d,s}$ *represented by any Bayesian sigmoid belief network can be parametrized in terms of a finite* collection of smooth maps with compact parameter space of the same dimension as the usual parameter space.

Proof Since the composition of units to create a network corresponds to taking matrix products and since marginalization corresponds to adding entries of a matrix, both of which are smooth maps, it suffices to prove the statement for a single unit. Consider the set $F_{m,1}$ of kernels in $\Delta_{m,1}$ represented by a unit with m binary inputs. The usual parametrization takes $w = (w_0, w_1, \ldots, w_m) \in \mathbb{R}^{m+1}$ to the kernel in $\Delta_{m,1}$ given by the 2×2^m matrix

$$\left[\sigma\left(\sum_{j=0}^{m} w_j h_j \right), \sigma\left(- \sum_{j=0}^{m} w_j h_j \right) \right]_{h \in \{1\} \times \{0,1\}^m},$$

where any $h = (h_0, h_1, \ldots, h_m)$ has first entry $h_0 = 1$. We split the parameter space $\mathbb{R}^{m+1}$ into the 2^{m+1} closed orthants. Fix one of the orthants $\mathbb{R}_S^{m+1}$, which is specified by a partition of $\{0, 1, \ldots, m\}$ into a set S of coordinates that are allowed to be negative and a complementary set L of coordinates that are allowed to be positive. Now consider the bijection $w \in \mathbb{R}_S^{m+1} \to [\omega, \gamma] \in (0,1]^{m+1}$ with $\omega_j = \exp(w_j)$ for each $j \in S$ and $\gamma_j = \exp(-w_j)$ for each $j \notin S$. Then

$$\sigma\left(\sum_{j=0}^{m} w_j h_j \right) = \frac{\exp(\sum_{j=0}^{m} w_j h_j)}{\exp(\sum_{j=0}^{m} w_j h_j) + 1}$$

$$= \frac{\prod_{j=0}^{m} \exp(w_j h_j)}{\prod_{j=0}^{m} \exp(w_j h_j) + 1}$$

$$= \frac{\prod_{j \in S} \exp(w_j h_j)}{\prod_{j \in S} \exp(w_j h_j) + \prod_{j \notin S} \exp(-w_j h_j)}$$

$$= \frac{\prod_{j \in S} \omega_j^{h_j}}{\prod_{j \in S} \omega_j^{h_j} + \prod_{j \notin S} \gamma_j^{h_j}}.$$

This defines a smooth map $\psi_S : [0,1]^{m+1} \to \Delta_{m,1}$ (or a finite family of smooth maps over the relative interiors of the faces of $[0,1]^{m+1}$). Since the map ψ_S is continuous and its domain is compact and its co-domain is Hausdorff, the image $\psi_S([0,1]^{m+1})$ is closed. In turn, the union over different orthants $\bigcup_S \psi_S([0,1]^{m+1})$ is a closed set which contains $F_{m,1}$ as a dense subset, so that it is equal to $\overline{F_{m,1}}$. □

Theorem 6.21. *Consider a stochastic feedforward network with d binary inputs and s binary outputs. If the network is a universal approximator of Markov kernels in $\Delta_{d,s}$, then necessarily the number of trainable parameters is at least $2^d(2^s - 1)$.*

The space of Markov kernels is $\Delta_{d,s} = \Delta_s \times \cdots \times \Delta_s$ (2^d times), and has dimension $2^d(2^s - 1)$. This theorem states that at least one parameter is needed per degree of freedom of a Markov kernel.

Proof Consider one of the smooth and closed maps ψ appearing in Proposition 6.20 and denote its input space by $\Omega = [0,1]^k$. Sard's theorem states that the set of critical values of a smooth map is a null set. If the input-space dimension is less than the output-space dimension then every point is a critical point and the image of the map is a null set. Therefore, we conclude that if $\dim(\Omega) = k$ is less than $2^d(2^s - 1)$, the set $\psi(\Omega) = \overline{\psi}(\Omega)$ is a null set. Since the closure of the model is a finite union of such sets, it cannot possibly be a universal approximator if the dimension is of the parameter space is less than indicated. □

6.8.2 Minimum Width

A universal approximator cannot have layers that are too narrow. We can show this by utilizing the data processing-inequality. Another proof uses the combinatorics of the tuples of factorizing distributions represented by a layer of stochastic units.

We start with the approach based on the data-processing inequality. To be precise, consider the mutual information of two discrete random vectors $\mathbf{X}$ and $\mathbf{Y}$, which is defined as

$$\text{MI}(\mathbf{X}; \mathbf{Y}) = H(\mathbf{Y}) - H(\mathbf{Y} \mid \mathbf{X}), \tag{6.22}$$

where $H(\mathbf{Y}) = -\sum_{\mathbf{y}} p(\mathbf{y}) \log p(\mathbf{y})$ stands for the entropy of the probability distribution of $\mathbf{Y}$ and $H(\mathbf{Y} \mid \mathbf{X}) = -\sum_{\mathbf{x}} p(\mathbf{x}) \sum_{\mathbf{y}} p(\mathbf{y} \mid \mathbf{x}) \log p(\mathbf{y} \mid \mathbf{x})$ stands for the conditional entropy of $\mathbf{Y}$ given $\mathbf{X}$. If the state spaces are $\mathcal{X}$ and $\mathcal{Y}$ then the maximum value of the mutual information is $\min\{\log |\mathcal{X}|, \log |\mathcal{Y}|\}$. This value is attained by any joint distribution for which one of the variables is uniformly distributed and its state is fully determined by the observation of the other variable.

The data processing inequality states that if a joint distribution satisfies the Markov chain $p(\mathbf{x}, \mathbf{h}, \mathbf{y}) = p(\mathbf{x})p(\mathbf{h} \mid \mathbf{x})p(\mathbf{y} \mid \mathbf{h})$ then the mutual information behaves monotonically in the sense that $\text{MI}(\mathbf{X}; \mathbf{Y}) \leq \text{MI}(\mathbf{X}; \mathbf{H})$. Note that this inequality is independent of how the conditional distributions are parametrized, and in special cases there might exist stronger inequalities. From this generic inequality we infer the following.

Proposition 6.22. *Consider a sigmoid stochastic feedforward network with d inputs and s outputs. If the network is a universal approximator of Markov kernels in $\Delta_{d,s}$ then each hidden layer has at least $\min\{d, s\}$ units.*

Proof The network is a universal approximator of Markov kernels if and only if the model augmented to include arbitrary probability distributions over the inputs is a universal approximator of joint distributions over inputs and outputs. In view of the data-processing inequality, if any of the hidden layers has less than $\min\{d, s\}$ units then the joint distributions of inputs and outputs represented by the network satisfy non-trivial inequalities regarding the mutual information, meaning that an open non-trivial set of joint distributions is excluded.   □

We can strengthen this result further in the case where the number of inputs is smaller than the number of outputs.

Proposition 6.23. *Consider stochastic feedfoward networks with d inputs and s > d outputs.*

- *If $d \geq 0$ and $s \geq 2$, the last hidden layer of a universal approximator has at least $s - 1$ units when s is even and at least s units when s is odd.*
- *If $d \geq 1$, the last hidden layer of a universal approximator has at least s units.*

Proof   Note that the output distribution is a mixture of the conditional distributions of the output layer given all possible values of the second-to-last layer, all of which are factorizing distributions. Further, note that if a factorizing distribution has support strictly contained in the set of even (or odd) parity strings then it must be a point measure.

Consider $d \geq 0$ and, as a desired output distribution, the uniform distribution on strings of even parity. In order for the the network to represent this, the last kernel needs to contain the 2^{s-1} point measures on even parity strings as rows. In turn, the last hidden layer must have at least $s - 1$ units. The lower bound s results from the fact that the rows of the kernels are not arbitrary product distributions. Indeed, for a module with m input units, the 2^m rows of the kernel are factorizing distributions with shared parameters of the form $\mathbf{Wh} + \mathbf{b}$, $\mathbf{h} \in \{0, 1\}^m$. The parameter vector of a point measure that is concentrated on a given vector $\mathbf{y} \in \{0, 1\}^s$ is a vector on the yth orthant of $\mathbb{R}^s$. The set of parameters $\mathbf{Wh} + \mathbf{b}$, $\mathbf{h} \in \{0, 1\}^m$, intersects all even-parity orthants of $\mathbb{R}^s$ only if $m \geq s$ (see Montúfar and Morton, 2015, Proposition 3.19).

Now consider $d \geq 1$ and, as a desired pair of output distributions for two different inputs, a distribution supported strictly on the even-parity strings and a distribution supported on the odd-parity strings. This requires that the last kernel has all 2^s point measures as rows, and hence at least s inputs.   □

An example of Proposition 6.23 is shown in Figure 6.7.

6.9 A Numerical Example

The previous theory is constructive in the sense that, given a specific Markov kernel $P \in \Delta_{d,s}$, for any choice of the shape coefficient j the parameters are explicitly determined. To validate this for the $d = 2$, $s = 2$ case, 500 Markov kernels in $\Delta_{2,2}$ were generated uniformly at random by sampling from the Dirichlet distribution with parameter 1. For each kernel, a network consisting of the parameters specified

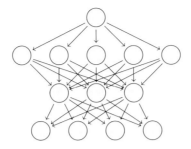

Figure 6.7 By Proposition 6.23, this network is not a universal approximator of $\Delta_{1,4}$, although it has more than $\dim(\Delta_{1,4}) = 32$ parameters.

Table 6.1

10ϵ	α	Error bound of Thm 6.14	E_{avg}	E_{max}
2^{-2}	14.65	0.4160	0.0522	0.1642
2^{-3}	17.47	0.2276	0.0248	0.1004
2^{-4}	20.28	0.1192	0.0134	0.0541
2^{-5}	23.06	0.0610	0.0077	0.0425
2^{-6}	25.84	0.0308	0.0060	0.0306

by the theory above was instantiated. We considered the architecture with $j = d = 2$. As the magnitude of the non-zero parameters grows, the network will converge to the target kernel according to Theorem 6.14.

Let P^* be the target kernel and P the approximation represented by the network (for the relatively small number of variables it could be calculated exactly, but here we calculated it via 25,000 samples of the output for each input). The error is $E = \max_{i,j} |P_{ij} - P^*_{ij}|$. In Table 6.1 we report the average error over 500 target kernels, $E_{avg} = \frac{1}{500} \sum_{k=1}^{500} E_k$ and the maximum error $E_{max} = \max_k E_k$, for the various values of the coefficient ϵ from our theorem, along with the corresponding parameter magnitude bound α, and the error upper bound in Theorem 6.14

$$|p(\mathbf{y} \mid \mathbf{x}) - p^*(\mathbf{y} \mid \mathbf{x})| \leq 1 - (1 - \epsilon)^N + 2\epsilon.$$

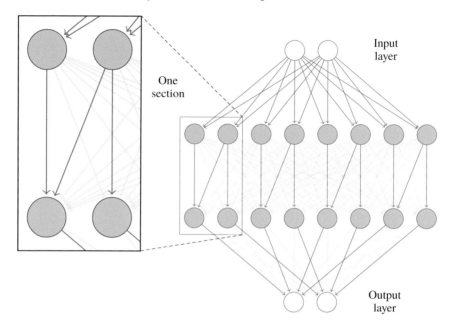

Figure 6.8 The network architecture used in the numerical example of §6.9 to demonstrate our results. The non-zero connections are shown in black. Notice that even within sections the connectivity does not need to be full.

We now describe the explicit construction. Write a given kernel as

$$P = \begin{pmatrix} p(0,0\,|\,0,0) & p(0,1\,|\,0,0) & p(1,0\,|\,0,0) & p(1,1\,|\,0,0) \\ p(0,0\,|\,0,1) & p(0,1\,|\,0,1) & p(1,0\,|\,0,1) & p(1,1\,|\,0,1) \\ p(0,0\,|\,1,0) & p(0,1\,|\,1,0) & p(1,0\,|\,1,0) & p(1,1\,|\,1,0) \\ p(0,0\,|\,1,1) & p(0,1\,|\,1,1) & p(1,0\,|\,1,1) & p(1,1\,|\,1,1) \end{pmatrix}$$

$$= \begin{pmatrix} p_{11} & p_{12} & p_{13} & p_{14} \\ p_{21} & p_{22} & p_{23} & p_{24} \\ p_{31} & p_{32} & p_{33} & p_{34} \\ p_{41} & p_{42} & p_{43} & p_{44} \end{pmatrix}.$$

Given a fixed kernel of this form, the following choices of network parameters will make the network exactly approximate the kernel as we allow the maximum magnitude of the parameters $\alpha \to \infty$.

We consider the widest deep architecture with $j = d$. Since we have $d = 2$ inputs and $s = 2 = 2^{b-1} + b$ outputs, with $b = 1$, the network has

$$2^{d-j}\left(\frac{2^s}{2(s-b)} + 2(s-b) - 1 \right) - 1 = 2$$

hidden layers of width $2^j(s + d - j) = 8$. Here, since $j = d$, we can save one layer in comparison with the general construction. This network consists of $2^j = 4$ independent sections, one for each possible input. See Figure 6.8 for an illustration of the overall network topology.

The sharing schedule of the single subsection of each section follows the $2^b = 2(d - b) = 2$ partial Gray codes

$$S_1 = \begin{pmatrix} S_{1,1} \\ S_{1,2} \end{pmatrix} = \begin{pmatrix} 1 & 0 \\ 0 & 0 \end{pmatrix} \quad \text{and} \quad S_2 = \begin{pmatrix} S_{2,1} \\ S_{2,2} \end{pmatrix} = \begin{pmatrix} 1 & 1 \\ 0 & 1 \end{pmatrix}. \tag{6.23}$$

For a given $0 < \epsilon < 1/4$ we set $\gamma = \sigma^{-1}(1 - \epsilon)$. The parameters have magnitude at most $\alpha = 2m\sigma^{-1}(1 - \epsilon)$, where $m = \max\{j, s + (d - j)\} = 2$. The weights and biases of the first hidden layer are

$$W^1 = \begin{pmatrix} -2\gamma & -2\gamma \\ -\gamma & -\gamma \\ -2\gamma & 2\gamma \\ -2\gamma & 2\gamma \\ 2\gamma & -2\gamma \\ 2\gamma & -2\gamma \\ 2\gamma & 2\gamma \\ \gamma & \gamma \end{pmatrix}, \quad b^1 = \begin{pmatrix} \gamma \\ \sigma^{-1}(p_{12} + p_{14}) \\ -\gamma \\ \sigma^{-1}(p_{22} + p_{24}) - 2\gamma \\ -\gamma \\ \sigma^{-1}(p_{32} + p_{34}) - 2\gamma \\ -3\gamma \\ \sigma^{-1}(p_{41} + p_{44}) - 2\gamma \end{pmatrix}. \tag{6.24}$$

This will map $\mathbf{x} = (0,0)$ to $\mathbf{a}^1_{(1)} = (1,0)$ with probability $(1 - \epsilon)(1 - (p_{12} + p_{14})) = (1 - \epsilon)(p_{11} + p_{13})$ and to $\mathbf{a}^1_{(1)} = (1,1)$ with probability $(1 - \epsilon)(p_{12} + p_{14})$. The other transitions are similar. When $P \in \Delta^\epsilon_{2,2}$, one necessarily has that $\epsilon \le 1/4$; otherwise $\Delta^\epsilon_{2,2}$ would be empty, $p_{ij} \le 1 - 3\epsilon$, and $p_{ij} + p_{ik} \le 1 - 2\epsilon$ for any i, j, k. This in turn would mean that the bias parameters in (6.24) are bounded by 3γ.

The second hidden layer has weights

$$W^2 = \begin{pmatrix} \gamma & \omega_1 & 0 & 0 & 0 & 0 & 0 & 0 \\ 0 & 2\gamma & 0 & 0 & 0 & 0 & 0 & 0 \\ 0 & 0 & \gamma & \omega_2 & 0 & 0 & 0 & 0 \\ 0 & 0 & 0 & 2\gamma & 0 & 0 & 0 & 0 \\ 0 & 0 & 0 & 0 & \gamma & \omega_3 & 0 & 0 \\ 0 & 0 & 0 & 0 & 0 & 2\gamma & 0 & 0 \\ 0 & 0 & 0 & 0 & 0 & 0 & \gamma & \omega_4 \\ 0 & 0 & 0 & 0 & 0 & 0 & 0 & 2\gamma \end{pmatrix}, \tag{6.25}$$

where

$$\omega_i = \sigma^{-1}\left(\frac{p_{i4}}{p_{i2} + p_{i4}}\right) - \sigma^{-1}\left(\frac{p_{i3}}{p_{i1} + p_{i3}}\right), \tag{6.26}$$

for $i = 1, 2, 3, 4$. The second-hidden-layer biases are chosen as

$$
\mathbf{b}^2 = \begin{pmatrix} \sigma^{-1}(p_{13}/(p_{11} + p_{13})) - \gamma \\ -\gamma \\ \sigma^{-1}(p_{23}/(p_{21} + p_{23})) - \gamma \\ -\gamma \\ \sigma^{-1}(p_{33}/(p_{33} + p_{31})) - \gamma \\ -\gamma \\ \sigma^{-1}(p_{43}/(p_{43} + p_{41})) - \gamma \\ -\gamma \end{pmatrix}. \tag{6.27}
$$

This will map $\mathbf{a}^1_{(1)} = (1, 0)$ to $\mathbf{a}^2_{(1)} = (1, 0)$ with probability $p_{13}/(p_{11} + p_{13})(1 - \epsilon)$ and to $\mathbf{a}^2_{(1)} = (0, 0)$ with probability $(1 - p_{13}/(p_{11} + p_{13}))(1 - \epsilon)$. In particular, for input $\mathbf{x} = (0, 0)$ we have

$$
\Pr\left(\mathbf{a}^2_{(1)} = (0, 0), \mathbf{a}^1_{(1)} = (1, 0) \mid \mathbf{x} = (0, 0)\right)
$$
$$
= \left(1 - \frac{p_{13}}{p_{11} + p_{13}}\right)(1 - \epsilon) \cdot (1 - \epsilon)(p_{11} + p_{13}) = p_{11}(1 - \epsilon)^2.
$$

Note that if $\epsilon \leq p_{ij} \leq 1 - \epsilon$ for all i, j, then the factors $p_{13}/(p_{11} + p_{13})$ and $(p_{11} + p_{13})$ are also between ϵ and $1 - \epsilon$. The other transitions are similar.

The weights and biases of the output layer are

$$
\mathbf{W}^3 = \begin{pmatrix} 2\gamma & 0 & 2\gamma & 0 & 2\gamma & 0 & 2\gamma & 0 \\ 0 & 2\gamma & 0 & 2\gamma & 0 & 2\gamma & 0 & 2\gamma \end{pmatrix}, \quad \mathbf{b}^3 = \begin{pmatrix} -\gamma \\ -\gamma \end{pmatrix}. \tag{6.28}
$$

This will map, for example, $\mathbf{h}^2 = (\mathbf{a}^2_{(1)}, \mathbf{a}^2_{(2)}, \mathbf{a}^2_{(3)}, \mathbf{a}^2_{(4)}) = (0, 0, 0, \ldots, 0)$ to $\mathbf{y} = (0, 0)$ with probability $(1 - \sigma(-\gamma))^2 = (1 - \epsilon)^2$. Furthermore, to see that the parameters in (6.26) and (6.27) are bounded by 2γ, we need to show that $\frac{p_{ij}}{p_{ij} + p_{ik}} \leq 1 - \epsilon$ or $1 + \frac{p_{ik}}{p_{ij}} \geq (1 - \epsilon)^{-1}$. The smallest possible $\frac{p_{ik}}{p_{ij}}$ is $\frac{\epsilon}{1 - 3\epsilon}$, and $\frac{1}{1 - \epsilon} \leq 1 + \frac{\epsilon}{1 - 3\epsilon}$ is easily verified for $\epsilon \in (0, 1/4]$.

Note that exactly $2^2(2^2 - 1) = 12$ parameters depend on the values of the target Markov kernel itself, while the other parameters are fixed and depend only on the desired level of accuracy.

6.10 Conclusion

In this chapter we have made advances towards a more complete picture of the representational power of stochastic feedforward networks. We showed that a spectrum of sigmoid stochastic feedforward networks is capable of universal approximation. In the obtained results, a shallow architecture requires fewer hidden units than a deep architecture, while deep architectures achieve the minimum number of trainable parameters necessary for universal approximation. At the extreme of the spectrum discussed is the $j = 0$ case, where a network of width $s + d$ and depth approx $2^{d+s}/2(s - b)$, $b \sim \log_2(s)$, is sufficient for universal approximation. At the other end of the deep spectrum is the $j = d$ case, which can be seen as an intermediate between the $j = 0$ case and the shallow universal approximator since its width is exponential in d and its depth is exponential in s. Further, we obtained bounds on the approximation errors when the network parameters are restricted in absolute value by some $\alpha > 0$. In our construction, the error is then bounded by $1 - (1 - \epsilon)^N + 2\epsilon$ where ϵ is the error of each unit, which is bounded by $\sigma(-\alpha/2(d + s))$.

6.11 Open Problems

Here we collect a few open problems that we believe would be worth developing in the future.

- Determination of the dimension of the set of distributions represented at layer l of a deep stochastic network. In this direction, the dimension of RBMs has been studied previously (Cueto et al., 2010; Montúfar and Morton, 2017).

- Determination of the equations and inequalities that characterize the set of Markov kernels representable by a deep stochastic feedforward network. Work in this direction includes studies of Bayesian networks (Garcia et al., 2005), the RBM with three visible and two hidden binary variables (Seigal and Montúfar, 2018), and naive Bayes models with one hidden binary variable (Allman et al., 2019).

- Obtaining maximum approximation error bounds for a network which is *not* a universal approximator, by measures such as the maximum KL-divergence, and evaluating how the behavior of different network topologies depends on the number of trainable parameters. There is a deal of research in this direction, covering hierarchical graphical models (Matúš, 2009), exponential families (Rauh, 2011), RBMs and DBNs (Le Roux and Bengio, 2008; Montúfar et al., 2011, 2013, 2015). For the RBM with three visible and two hidden units mentioned above, Seigal and Montúfar (2018) obtained the exact value.

- Finding out whether it is possible to obtain more compact families of universal approximators of Markov kernels than those we presented here. We constructed universal approximators with the minimal number of trainable weights, but which include a substantial number of non-zero fixed weights. Is it possible to construct more compact universal approximators with a smaller number of units and non-zero weights? Can we refine the lower bounds for the minimum width and the minimum depth given a maximum width of the hidden layers of a universal approximator? This kind of problem has traditionally been more difficult than refining upper bounds. A few examples are listed in Montúfar and Rauh (2017).

- Our construction uses sparsely connected networks to achieve the minimum possible number of parameters. How does restricting the connectivity of a network affect the distributions it can represent? Are advantages provided by sparsely connected networks over fully connected networks?
- Generalization of the analysis to conditional distributions other than sigmoid and to non-binary variables. Efforts in this direction include the treatment of RBMs with non-binary units (Montúfar and Morton, 2015) and of DBNs with non-binary units (Montúfar, 2014b).
- Another interesting research direction would be to consider the theoretical advantages of stochastic networks in relation to deterministic networks, and to develop more effective techniques for training stochastic networks. In this direction, Tang and Salakhutdinov (2013) discussed multi-modality and combinations of deterministic and stochastic units.

Acknowledgement We thank Nihat Ay for insightful discussions. This project has received funding from the European Research Council (ERC) under the European Union's Horizon 2020 research and innovation programme (grant agreement no. 757983).

References

Allman, Elizabeth S., Cervantes, Hector Baños, Evans, Robin, Hoşten, Serkan, Kubjas, Kaie, Lemke, Daniel, Rhodes, John A., and Zwiernik, Piotr. 2019. Maximum likelihood estimation of the latent class model through model boundary decomposition. *Journal of Algebraic Statistics*, **10**(1).

Bengio, Yoshua. 2009. Learning deep architectures for AI. *Foundations and Trends in Machine Learning*, **2**(1), 1–127.

Bengio, Yoshua, and Delalleau, Olivier. 2011. On the expressive power of deep architectures. Pages 18–36 of: *Algorithmic Learning Theory*, Kivinen, Jyrki, Szepesvári, Csaba, Ukkonen, Esko, and Zeugmann, Thomas (eds). Springer.

Bengio, Yoshua, Lamblin, Pascal, Popovici, Dan, and Larochelle, Hugo. 2007. Greedy layer-wise training of deep networks. Pages 153–160 of: *Advances in Neural Information Processing Systems*, vol. 19, Schölkopf, B., Platt, J. C., and Hoffman, T. (eds).

Bishop, Christopher M. 2006. *Pattern Recognition and Machine Learning* Springer.

Bölcskei, Helmut, Grohs, Philipp, Kutyniok, Gitta, and Petersen, Philipp. 2019. Optimal approximation with sparsely connected deep neural networks. *SIAM Journal on Mathematics of Data Science*, **1**(1), 8–45.

Brunato, Mauro, and Battiti, Roberto. 2015. Stochastic local search for direct training of threshold networks. Pages 1–8 of: *Proc. 2015 International Joint Conference on Neural Networks*.

Cueto, María Angélica, Morton, Jason, and Sturmfels, Bernd. 2010. Geometry of the restricted Boltzmann machine. pages 135–153 of: *Algebraic Methods in Statistics and Probability II*, Viana, M. A. G. and Wynn, H. (eds). Amer. Math Soc.

Cybenko, George. 1989. Approximation by superpositions of a sigmoidal function. *Mathematics of Control, Signals and Systems*, **2**(4), 303–314.

Delalleau, Olivier, and Bengio, Yoshua. 2011. Shallow vs. deep sum-product networks. Pages 666–674 of: *Advances in Neural Information Processing Systems*, vol. 24.

Eldan, Ronen, and Shamir, Ohad. 2016. The power of depth for feedforward neural networks. Pages 907–940 of: *Proc. 29th Annual Conference on Learning Theory*, Feldman, Vitaly, Rakhlin, Alexander, and Shamir, Ohad (eds). Proceedings of Machine Learning Research, vol. 49.

Garcia, Luis David, Stillman, Michael, and Sturmfels, Bernd. 2005. Algebraic geometry of Bayesian networks. *Journal of Symbolic Computation*, **39**(3), 331–355.

Goodfellow, Ian, Pouget-Abadie, Jean, Mirza, Mehdi, Xu, Bing, Warde-Farley, David, Ozair, Sherjil, Courville, Aaron, and Bengio, Yoshua. 2014. Generative adversarial nets. Pages 2672–2680 of: *Advances in Neural Information Processing Systems*, vol. 27.

Gribonval, Rémi, Kutyniok, Gitta, Nielsen, Morten, and Voigtländer, Felix. 2019. Approximation spaces of deep neural networks. ArXiv preprint arXiv:1905.01208.

Hastad, Johan, and Goldmann, Mikael. 1991. On the power of small-depth threshold circuits. *Computational Complexity*, **1**(2), 113–129.

Hinton, Geoffrey E, and Salakhutdinov, Ruslan R. 2006. Reducing the dimensionality of data with neural networks. *Science*, **313**(5786), 504–507.

Hinton, Geoffrey E, Osindero, Simon, and Teh, Yee-Whye. 2006. A fast learning algorithm for deep belief nets. *Neural Computation*, **18**(7), 1527–1554.

Hornik, Kurt, Stinchcombe, Maxwell, and White, Halbert. 1989. Multilayer feedforward networks are universal approximators. *Neural Networks*, **2**(5), 359–366.

Huang, Guang-Bin, Zhu, Qin-Yu, Mao, K. Z., Siew, Chee-Kheong, Saratchandran, Paramasivan, and Sundararajan, Narasimhan. 2006. Can threshold networks be trained directly? *IEEE Transactions on Circuits and Systems II: Express Briefs*, **53**(3), 187–191.

Johnson, Jesse. 2019. Deep, skinny neural networks are not universal aApproximators. In: *Proc. International Conference on Learning Representations*.

Larochelle, Hugo, Erhan, Dumitru, Courville, Aaron, Bergstra, James, and Bengio, Yoshua. 2007. An empirical evaluation of deep architectures on problems with many factors of variation. Pages 473–480 of: *Proc. 24th International Conference on Machine Learning*.

Lauritzen, Steffen L. 1996. *Graphical Models*. Oxford Statistical Science Series. Clarendon Press.

Le Roux, Nicolas, and Bengio, Yoshua. 2008. Representational power of restricted Boltzmann machines and deep belief networks. *Neural Computation*, **20**(6), 1631–1649.

Le Roux, Nicolas, and Bengio, Yoshua. 2010. Deep belief networks are compact universal approximators. *Neural Computation*, **22**(8), 2192–2207.

Lee, Kimin, Kim, Jaehyung, Chong, Song, and Shin, Jinwoo. 2017. Simplified stochastic feedforward neural networks. ArXiv preprint arXiv:1704.03188.

Lu, Zhou, Pu, Hongming, Wang, Feicheng, Hu, Zhiqiang, and Wang, Liwei. 2017. The expressive power of neural networks: A view from the width. Pages 6231–6239 of: *Advances in Neural Information Processing Systems*, vol. 30.

Lupanov, Oleg B. 1956. On rectifier and switching-and-rectifier circuits. *Doklady Academii Nauk SSSR*, **111**(6), 1171–1174.

Matúš, František. 2009. Divergence from factorizable distributions and matroid representations by partitions. *IEEE Transactions on Information Theory*, **55**(12), 5375–5381.

Mhaskar, Hrushikesh N., and Poggio, Tomaso. 2016. Deep vs. shallow networks: An approximation theory perspective. *Analysis and Applications*, **14**(06), 829–848.

Montúfar, Guido. 2014a. Deep narrow Boltzmann machines are universal approximators. In: *Proc. International Conference on Learning Representations*.

Montúfar, Guido. 2014b. Universal approximation depth and errors of narrow belief networks with discrete units. *Neural Computation*, **26**(7), 1386–1407.

Montúfar, Guido. 2015. A comparison of neural network architectures. In: *Proc. Deep Learning Workshop, ICML*.

Montúfar, Guido. 2015. Universal approximation of Markov kernels by shallow stochastic feedforward networks. ArXiv preprint arXiv:1503.07211.

Montúfar, Guido. 2018. Restricted Boltzmann machines: Introduction and review. Pages 75–115 of: *Information Geometry and Its Applications*, Ay, Nihat, Gibilisco, Paolo, and Matúš, František (eds). Springer.

Montúfar, Guido, and Ay, Nihat. 2011. Refinements of universal approximation results for deep belief networks and restricted Boltzmann machines. *Neural Computation*, **23**(5), 1306–1319.

Montúfar, Guido, and Morton, Jason. 2012. Kernels and submodels of deep belief networks. In: *Proc. Deep Learning and Unsupervised Feature Learning Workshop, NIPS*.

Montúfar, Guido, and Morton, Jason. 2015. Discrete restricted Boltzmann machines. *Journal of Machine Learning Research*, **16**, 653–672.

Montúfar, Guido, and Morton, Jason. 2015. When does a mixture of products contain a product of mixtures? *SIAM Journal on Discrete Mathematics*, **29**(1), 321–347.

Montúfar, Guido, and Morton, Jason. 2017. Dimension of marginals of Kronecker product models. *SIAM Journal on Applied Algebra and Geometry*, **1**(1), 126–151.

Montúfar, Guido, and Rauh, Johannes. 2017. Hierarchical models as marginals of hierarchical models. *International Journal of Approximate Reasoning*, **88**, 531–546.

Montúfar, Guido, Rauh, Johannes, and Ay, Nihat. 2011. Expressive power and approximation errors of restricted Boltzmann machines. Pages 415–423 of: *Advances in Neural Information Processing Systems*, vol. 24.

Montúfar, Guido, Rauh, Johannes, and Ay, Nihat. 2013. Maximal information divergence from statistical models defined by neural networks. Pages 759–766 of: *Geometric Science of Information*. Springer.

Montúfar, Guido, Pascanu, Razvan, Cho, Kyunghyun, and Bengio, Yoshua. 2014. On the number of linear regions of deep neural networks. Pages 2924–2932 of: *Advances in Neural Information Processing Systems*, vol. 27.

Montúfar, Guido, Ay, Nihat, and Ghazi-Zahedi, Keyan. 2015. Geometry and expressive power of conditional restricted Boltzmann machines. *Journal of Machine Learning Research*, **16**(1), 2405–2436.

Muroga, Saburo. 1971. *Threshold Logic and its Applications*. Wiley-Interscience.

Neal, Radford M. 1990. Learning stochastic feedforward networks. Technical Report. CRG-TR-90-7, Deptment of Computer Science, University of Toronto.

Neal, Radford M. 1992. Connectionist learning of belief networks. *Artificial Intelligence*, **56**(1), 71–113.

Neciporuk, E.I. 1964. The synthesis of networks from threshold elements. *Problemy Kibernetiki*, **11**, 49–62.

Ngiam, Jiquan, Chen, Zhenghao, Koh, Pang, and Ng, Andrew. 2011. Learning deep energy models. Pages 1105–1112 of: *Proc. 28th International Conference on Machine Learning*.

Pascanu, Razvan, Montúfar, Guido, and Bengio, Yoshua. 2014. On the number of response regions of deep feed forward networks with piece-wise linear activations. In: *Proc. International Conference on Learning Representations*.

Pearl, Judea. 1988. *Probabilistic Reasoning in Intelligent Systems: Networks of Plausible Inference*. Morgan Kaufmann Publishers Inc.

Poggio, Tomaso, Mhaskar, Hrushikesh, Rosasco, Lorenzo, Miranda, Brando, and Liao, Qianli. 2017. Why and when can deep – but not shallow – networks avoid the curse of dimensionality: A review. *International Journal of Automation and Computing*, **14**(5), 503–519.

Raghu, Maithra, Poole, Ben, Kleinberg, Jon, Ganguli, Surya, and Sohl-Dickstein, Jascha. 2017. On the Expressive Power of Deep Neural Networks. Pages

2847–2854 of: *Proc. 34th International Conference on Machine Learning*. Proceedings of Machine Learning Research, vol. 70.

Raiko, Tapani, Berglund, Mathias, Alain, Guillaume, and Dinh, Laurent. 2014. Techniques for learning binary stochastic feedforward neural networks. In: *Proc. International Conference on Learning Representations*.

Ranzato, M., Huang, F. J., Boureau, Y., and LeCun, Y. 2007 (June). Unsupervised learning of invariant feature hierarchies with applications to object recognition. Pages 1–8 of: *Proc. IEEE Conference on Computer Vision and Pattern Recognition*.

Rauh, Johannes. 2011. Finding the maximizers of the information divergence from an exponential family. *IEEE Transactions on Information Theory*, **57**(6), 3236–3247.

Rojas, Raúl. 2003. Networks of width one are universal classifiers. Pages 3124–3127 of: *Proc. International Joint Conference on Neural Networks*, vol. 4.

Salakhutdinov, Ruslan, and Hinton, Geoffrey. 2009. Semantic hashing. *International Journal of Approximate Reasoning*, **50**(7), 969–978.

Sard, Arthur. 1942. The measure of the critical values of differentiable maps. *Bulletin of the American Mathematical Society*, **48**(12), 883–890.

Sarikaya, Ruhi, Hinton, Geoffrey E., and Deoras, Anoop. 2014. Application of deep belief networks for natural language understanding. *IEEE/ACM Transactions on Audio, Speech, and Language Processing*, **22**(4), 778–784.

Saul, Lawrence K., Jaakkola, Tommi, and Jordan, Michael I. 1996. Mean field theory for sigmoid belief networks. *Journal of Artificial Intelligence Research*, **4**(1), 61–76.

Scarselli, Franco, and Tsoi, Ah Chung. 1998. Universal approximation using feedforward neural networks: A survey of some existing methods, and some new results. *Neural Networks*, **11**(1), 15–37.

Seigal, Anna, and Montúfar, Guido. 2018. Mixtures and products in two graphical models. *Journal of Algebraic Statistics*, **9**(1).

Shannon, Claude E. 1949. The synthesis of two-terminal switching circuits. *The Bell System Technical Journal*, **28**(1), 59–98.

Sutskever, Ilya, and Hinton, Geoffrey E. 2008. Deep, narrow sigmoid belief networks are universal approximators. *Neural Computation*, **20**(11), 2629–2636.

Tang, Yichuan, and Salakhutdinov, Ruslan R. 2013. Learning stochastic feedforward neural networks. Pages 530–538 of: *Advances in Neural Information Processing Systems*, vol. 26.

Wenzel, Walter, Ay, Nihat, and Pasemann, Frank. 2000. Hyperplane arrangements separating arbitrary vertex classes in *n*-cubes. *Advances in Applied Mathematics*, **25**(3), 284–306.

Yarotsky, Dmitry. 2017. Error bounds for approximations with deep ReLU networks. *Neural Networks*, **94**, 103–114.

Yarotsky, Dmitry. 2018. Optimal approximation of continuous functions by very deep ReLU networks. Pages 639–649 of: *Proc. 31st Conference On Learning Theory*. Proceedings of Machine Learning Research, vol. 75.

7

Deep Learning as Sparsity-Enforcing Algorithms

A. Aberdam and J. Sulam

Abstract: Over the last few decades sparsity has become a driving force in the development of new and better algorithms in signal and image processing. In the context of the late deep learning zenith, a pivotal work by Papyan et al. showed that deep neural networks can be interpreted and analyzed as pursuit algorithms seeking for sparse representations of signals belonging to a multilayer-synthesis sparse model. In this chapter we review recent contributions showing that this observation is correct but incomplete, in the sense that such a model provides a symbiotic mixture of coupled synthesis and analysis sparse priors. We make this observation precise and use it to expand on uniqueness guarantees and stability bounds for the pursuit of multilayer sparse representations. We then explore a convex relaxation of the resulting pursuit and derive efficient optimization algorithms to approximate its solution. Importantly, we deploy these algorithms in a supervised learning formulation that generalizes feed-forward convolutional neural networks into recurrent ones, improving their performance without increasing the number of parameters of the model.

7.1 Introduction

The search for parsimonious representations is concerned with the identification of a few but fundamental components that explain a particular observable. In signal processing, sparsity has continuously been a driving force in the design of algorithms, transformations, and a plethora of applications in computer vision (see Elad (2010) and references therein).

Broadly speaking, sparse representation modeling assumes that real signals (and among them, images) can be well approximated by a linear combination of only a few elements from a collection of atoms, termed a dictionary. More formally, a signal $\mathbf{x}^{[0]} \in \mathbb{R}^{n_0}$ can be expressed as

$$\mathbf{x}^{[0]} = \mathbf{D}^{[1]}\mathbf{x}^{[1]} + \mathbf{v}, \tag{7.1}$$

where $\mathbf{D}^{[1]} \in \mathbb{R}^{n_0 \times n_1}$ is an overcomplete dictionary ($n_0 < n_1$), $\mathbf{x}^{[1]} \in \mathbb{R}^{n_1}$ is the representations vector, and $\mathbf{v} \in \mathbb{R}^{n_0}$ accounts for measurement noise and model deviations. Importantly, $\mathbf{x}^{[1]}$ has only a few non-zero coefficients, as indicated by the ℓ_0 pseudo-norm, $\|\mathbf{x}^{[1]}\|_0 \leq s_1 \ll n_1$. Over the last two decades, numerous works have studied the problem of estimating such sparse representations for a given dictionary (Mallat and Zhang, 1993; Tropp, 2004, 2006; Blumensath and Davies, 2009), and methods have even been proposed to adaptively find some optimal dictionary for a particular task (Aharon et al., 2006; Mairal et al., 2010). The latter problem, termed *dictionary learning*, has enabled sparse enforcing methods to provide state-of-the-art solutions to a wide variety of problems in signal and image processing (Sulam et al., 2014; Romano et al., 2014; Mairal et al., 2010, 2009) and machine learning (Jiang et al., 2013; Patel et al., 2014; Shrivastava et al., 2014; Mairal et al., 2012).

While convolutional neural networks (CNNs) were developed independently of these ideas (LeCun et al., 1990; Rumelhart et al., 1986), a recent work (Papyan et al., 2017a) has shown that these models can be interpreted as pursuit algorithms enforcing particular sparse priors on the neurons' activations. This observation was formalized in terms of a multilayer and convolutional sparse coding (ML–CSC) model, in which it was proposed that not only should we set $\mathbf{x}^{[0]} = \mathbf{D}^{[1]}\mathbf{x}^{[1]}$ (for a convolutional dictionary $\mathbf{D}^{[1]}$) but also $\mathbf{x}^{[1]}$ should admit a representation by yet another dictionary, $\mathbf{x}^{[1]} = \mathbf{D}^{[2]}\mathbf{x}^{[2]}$, with $\mathbf{x}^{[2]}$ also sparse. Such an assumption can be extended to a number, L, of layers, naturally resulting in a deep sparse model. Under this framework, the forward pass in a CNN – the process of computing the deepest representation from a given input – can be interpreted in terms of nested thresholding operators, resulting in coarse estimations of the underlying sparse representations at different layers. With this understanding, one can resort to well-established theoretical results in sparse approximation (Elad, 2010), together with recent extensions to the convolutional setting (Papyan et al., 2017b), to derive conditions under which the activations computed by convolutional networks are stable (Papyan et al., 2017a).

More broadly, these ideas (first presented in Papyan et al., 2017a, then extended in Sulam et al., 2018, and recently summarized in Papyan et al., 2018) are based on a cascade of *synthesis sparse models* across several layers. While insightful, such constructions lead to a series of baffling issues.

(i) The resulting theoretical guarantees provide recovery bounds that become looser with the network depth.

(ii) The sparsity constraints imposed on the representations seem too stringent. What is more, the cardinality of the representations or activations is bound to grow (i.e., become denser) toward shallower layers.

(iii) While such ideas can be employed to learn a multilayer model on real data (Sulam et al., 2018), the resulting algorithms are still far from achieving the computational efficiency of deep learning models, and it is unclear how practical CNN architectures can be tied to the ML–CSC model.

In this chapter, we first review several works at the intersection of sparse representations and neural networks and then move on to present some recent results (mainly those in Aberdam et al., 2019; Sulam et al., 2018; Romano and Elad, 2018) showing that the above multilayer model admits an alternative (and more useful) interpretation: while such a construction does impose a synthesis sparse prior on the deepest representation, the intermediate representations serve to enforce an *analysis* sparse prior on it. Hence, ML–CSC puts forward a model in which these two complementary ideas (synthesis and analysis) interact in a symbiotic manner. This difference might seem subtle, but its implications are far reaching. We will show that such an interpretation resolves the issues mentioned above, allowing for representations that are *not as sparse* and enabling the development of improved uniqueness and stability guarantees. Moreover, this analysis naturally leads to a problem formulation that is a generalization of the basis pursuit problem in a multilayer setting. Importantly, we will show how the solution to this problem can be approximated by recurrent CNNs.

The remainder of this chapter is organized as follows. In the next section we briefly comment on related works that have explored the interplay between sparse priors and neural networks before reviewing some basic definitions and results needed to expand on the multilayer sparse model in §7.4. We then present a holistic interpretation of this multilayer construction in §7.5, combining synthesis and analysis sparse ideas. The resulting pursuit problem is then analyzed practically in §7.6 by means of a multilayer iterative shrinkage algorithm, before we conclude by commenting in §7.6.1 on ongoing and future research directions.

7.2 Related Work

Neural networks and sparsity have a long and rich history of synergy, and researchers have borrowed elements and insights from one field and have brought interesting results and applications to the other. Though an exhaustive review is beyond the scope of this chapter, we mention here a few important works at the intersection of these fields.

One of the earliest and most notable connections between (biological) neural networks and sparse representations was made by Olshausen and Fields (1996, 1997), showing that an unsupervised approach that maximizes sparsity (i.e., sparse coding) can explain statistical properties of the receptive fields of neurons in the mammalian primary visual cortex. In the machine learning community, early neural networks algorithms were also proposed for maximizing some measure of sparsity in an overcomplete basis through some regularization strategy or built-in nonlinearities (Ranzato et al., 2007, 2008; Lee et al., 2008; Ng *et al.*, 2011); see Goodfellow et al. (2016, Chapter 14) for an overview. Such unsupervised models are broadly known as autoencoders: algorithms that (approximately) compress an input into a *simpler* code, while being able to then decode it. Later work (Makhzani and Frey, 2013) required the activations in *k-sparse* autoencoders to be exactly sparse by means of a hard-thresholding operator. These ideas were extended in Makhzani and Frey (2015), imposing further sparsity constraints and deploying them for image classification in a stacked fashion.

On a different line of work, Gregor and LeCun showed that a particular neural network architecture with skip connections can be trained in a supervised manner to provide approximations to sparse codes resulting from the iterative soft-thresholding algorithm (ISTA) (Gregor and LeCun, 2010). Interestingly, only a few steps (or layers) of their proposed network – coined learned ISTA (LISTA) – suffices to produce accurate solutions, resulting in a much faster inference algorithm for sparse coding. This result has recently attracted considerable interest in the signal processing and machine learning communities, as it provides theoretical analyses and guarantees (Moreau and Bruna, 2017; Giryes et al., 2018; Chen et al., 2018; Liu et al., 2019).

Sparsity continues to be a driving force in the design and analysis of deep neural networks, and it includes ideas from harmonic analysis (Bölcskei et al., 2019; Mallat, 2016) as well as probabilistic models (Patel et al., 2016; Ho et al., 2018). Our approach in this chapter makes further connections between deep learning architectures and a generative sparse multilayer model for natural signals, extending the results in Papyan et al. (2017a). As we will shortly show, this approach enables us to provide theoretical guarantees for particular network architectures, while still improving performance in practical applications over simpler baseline models.

7.3 Background

Let us first review some basic concepts of sparse modeling, and settle the notation for the reminder of the chapter. The problem of retrieving a sparse representation $\mathbf{x}^{[1]}$ for a signal $\mathbf{x}^{[0]}$ and dictionary $\mathbf{D}^{[1]}$ can be formulated in terms of the following optimization problem:

$$\min_{\mathbf{x}^{[1]}} \|\mathbf{x}^{[1]}\|_0 \text{ s.t. } \|\mathbf{x}^{[0]} - \mathbf{D}^{[1]}\mathbf{x}^{[1]}\|_2^2 \le \varepsilon. \tag{7.2}$$

The allowed error, ε, can account for noisy measurements and model deviations, and can be replaced by an equality constraint (i.e., such that $\mathbf{x}^{[0]} = \mathbf{D}^{[1]}\mathbf{x}^{[1]}$) in an ideal case. The problem in (7.2) is non-convex and NP-hard in general, and thus one must resort to approximation algorithms in practice. One family of such methods employs a *greedy* approach by progressively building an estimation of the unknown support, such as matching pursuit (Mallat and Zhang, 1993) or variations thereof (e.g., Pati et al., 1993). A second alternative is to relax the non-convex and non-smooth ℓ_0 pseudo-norm for a convex surrogate, such as the ℓ_1 norm. This relaxation, termed basis pursuit[1], is formulated in its Lagrangian form as

$$\min_{\mathbf{x}^{[1]}} \left(\frac{1}{2}\|\mathbf{x}^{[0]} - \mathbf{D}^{[1]}\mathbf{x}^{[1]}\|_2^2 + \lambda\|\mathbf{x}^{[1]}\|_1 \right), \tag{7.3}$$

where the penalty parameter λ provides a compromise between sparsity and reconstruction error. This formulation has become very popular for sparse coding (Tropp, 2006) because the problem in (7.3) is convex and can be addressed by a large collection of optimization tools: see Boyd and Vandenberghe (2004) and references therein.

The characteristics of the dictionary influence our ability to find solutions to the problems above, and there exist several measures for quantifying the *goodness* of a matrix $\mathbf{D}^{[1]}$. One such notion is the *spark* of the dictionary, $\eta(\mathbf{D}^{[1]})$, defined as the smallest number of linearly dependent columns in $\mathbf{D}^{[1]}$. The spark immediately enables the formulation of uniqueness guarantees, since if there exists a representation $\mathbf{x}^{[1]}$ for a signal $\mathbf{x}^{[0]}$ (i.e., $\mathbf{x}^{[0]} = \mathbf{D}^{[1]}\mathbf{x}^{[1]}$) such that $\|\mathbf{x}^{[1]}\|_0 < \frac{\eta(\mathbf{D}^{[1]})}{2}$, then this solution is necessarily the sparsest solution possible (Donoho and Elad, 2003) to the problem in (7.2) when $\varepsilon = 0$.

From a practical perspective, the mutual coherence $\mu(\mathbf{D}^{[1]})$ is a more useful measure since, unlike the spark, it is trivial to compute. Assuming hereafter that the columns of $\mathbf{D}^{[1]}$ are normalized to unit length ($\|\mathbf{d}_j\|_2 = 1$), the mutual coherence is defined by

$$\mu(\mathbf{D}^{[1]}) = \max_{i \neq j} \left| \mathbf{d}_i^T \mathbf{d}_j \right|. \tag{7.4}$$

One may then bound the spark with the mutual coherence (Donoho and Elad, 2003), as

$$\eta(\mathbf{D}^{[1]}) \geq 1 + \frac{1}{\mu(\mathbf{D}^{[1]})}.$$

In this way, a sufficient condition for uniqueness is to require that

$$\left\|\mathbf{x}^{[1]}\right\|_0 < \frac{1}{2}\left(1 + \frac{1}{\mu(\mathbf{D}^{[1]})}\right).$$

---

[1] More precisely, the problem in (7.3) is a basis pursuit denoising (BPDN) formulation, also known as least the absolute shrinkage and selection operator (LASSO) in the statistical learning community.

As described, this model is commonly referred to as a *synthesis sparsity* model, because the linear operator $\mathbf{D}^{[1]}$ *synthesizes* the signal $\mathbf{x}^{[0]}$ from its representation $\mathbf{x}^{[1]}$. An alternative, slightly more recent version, is that of an *analysis sparse model*, in which it is assumed that real signals can be analyzed by an operator $\mathbf{\Omega} \in \mathbb{R}^{n_1 \times n_0}$, resulting in a representations that is co-sparse (Nam et al., 2013); i.e. $\|\mathbf{\Omega}\mathbf{x}^{[0]}\|_0 \le n_1 - l_1$, where l_1 is the *co-sparsity* level. The corresponding pursuit problem over a variable $\alpha \in \mathbb{R}^{n_0}$,

$$\min_{\alpha} \|\mathbf{x}^{[0]} - \alpha\|_2^2 \text{ such that } \|\mathbf{\Omega}\alpha\|_0 \le n_1 - l_1, \tag{7.5}$$

is NP-complete (Nam et al., 2013), as is the problem in (7.2), and analogous approximation techniques exist. We will combine these two models in a synergetic way later, in §7.5.

These sparse models are typically deployed on small image patches, mainly owing to computational and complexity constraints (Sulam et al., 2016). In order to model large natural images, the synthesis sparse model has been recently studied in a convolutional setting (Papyan et al., 2017b) by constraining the dictionary $\mathbf{D}^{[1]}$ to be a concatenation of circulant banded matrices determined by low-dimensional atoms $\mathbf{d}_i \in \mathbb{R}^{n_d}$. Formally, this model assumes that

$$\mathbf{x}^{[0]} = \sum_{i=1}^{m} \mathbf{d}_i \circledast \mathbf{x}_i^{[1]} + \mathbf{v}, \tag{7.6}$$

where the signal dimension is typically much larger than the dimension of the atoms, $n_0 \gg n_d$, and the corresponding representations (or *feature maps*) $\mathbf{x}_i^{[1]}$ are sparse. When periodic extensions are employed, the expression above can be written equivalently in terms of the redundant matrix $\mathbf{D}^{[1]} \in \mathbb{R}^{n_0 \times n_1}$ and the concatenation of all $\mathbf{x}_i^{[1]}$ into the vector $\mathbf{x}^{[1]}$, resulting in a generative (yet structured) model, $\mathbf{x}^{[0]} = \mathbf{D}^{[1]}\mathbf{x}^{[1]} + \mathbf{v}$.

In this convolutional setting, a local measure of sparsity, or rather *density*, was shown to be more appropriate than the traditional ℓ_0. The work in Papyan et al. (2017b) proposed an $\ell_{0,\infty}$ measure which accounts for the cardinality of the densest *stripe* of $\mathbf{x}^{[1]}$ – the set of coefficients coding for any n_d-dimensional patch in the n_0-dimensional signal $\mathbf{x}^{[0]}$. With these local notions, Papyan et al. (2017b) formulated the convolutional pursuit problem just as in (7.2), though replacing the ℓ_0 norm by the $\ell_{0,\infty}$ norm. Interestingly, the ℓ_1 norm still serves as a surrogate for this density measure, in the sense that the basis pursuit problem in (7.3) is guaranteed to recover the solution to the convolutional pursuit problem for signals that are $\ell_{0,\infty}$-sparse (Papyan et al., 2017b). In order to keep our exposition succinct, we will not dwell on convolutional sparsity any further, though we will mention it again when appropriate.

7.4 Multilayer Sparse Coding

Papyan et al. (2017a) put forward a multilayer extension of sparse models by assuming that, just as $x^{[0]} \approx D^{[1]}x^{[1]}$, the representation $x^{[1]}$ can be further approximated by yet another dictionary $D^{[2]}$ and representation $x^{[2]}$, i.e., $x^{[1]} \approx D^{[2]}x^{[2]}$. This model was first proposed in the context of convolutional sparse representations, under the assumption that all dictionaries are convolutional and that the representations are $\ell_{0,\infty}$-sparse. We will employ the more general multilayer sparse coding (ML–SC) formulation following Aberdam et al. (2019) and state that, given dictionaries $\{D^{[i]}\}_{i=1}^{L}$ of appropriate dimensions, a signal $x^{[0]} \in \mathbb{R}^{n_0}$ admits a representation in terms of the ML–SC model if

$$
\begin{aligned}
x^{[0]} &= D^{[1]}x^{[1]}, & \left\|x^{[1]}\right\|_0 &\leq s_1, \\
x^{[1]} &= D^{[2]}x^{[2]}, & \left\|x^{[2]}\right\|_0 &\leq s_2, \\
&\;\;\vdots \\
x^{[L-1]} &= D^{[L]}x^{[L]}, & \left\|x^{[L]}\right\|_0 &\leq s_L.
\end{aligned}
\tag{7.7}
$$

Denoting the *effective dictionary* from layer i to j as

$$
D^{[i,j]} = D^{[i]}D^{[i+1]} \cdots D^{[j-1]}D^{[j]},
$$

one can concisely[2] write $x^{[0]} = D^{[1,i]}x^{[i]}$, with $\|x^{[i]}\|_0 \leq s_i$, for all $1 \leq i \leq L$.

This construction imposes a synthesis sparsity model on representations at different layers. As such, one can resort to the vast theoretical guarantees for this model (Elad, 2010) and apply them in a layer-by-layer fashion. This enabled Papyan et al. (2017a) to formulate theoretical guarantees for the nested sparse vectors $x^{[i]}$. As an example, we state here the uniqueness guarantees from that work:

Theorem 7.1 (Theorem 4 from Papyan et al., 2017a). *If a set of representations* $\{x^{[i]}\}_{i=1}^{L}$ *exists such that*

$$
x^{[i-1]} = D^{[i]}x^{[i]}, \quad \text{for all } 1 \leq i \leq L
\tag{7.8}
$$

and

$$
\left\|x^{[i]}\right\|_0 = s_i < \frac{1}{2}\left(1 + \frac{1}{\mu(D^{[i]})}\right), \quad \text{for all } 1 \leq i \leq L,
\tag{7.9}
$$

then these representations are the sparsest for the signal $x^{[0]}$.

This result relies on each representation being the sparsest for its respective layer, and thus uniqueness is guaranteed only if all the representations are sparse enough. We should wonder whether we could do better – we will revisit this uniqueness guarantee in §7.5. For the formal proof of this result (as well as those in the following sections), we refer the reader to the respective references.

---

[2] Note that, for simplicity, we employ a slight abuse of notation by denoting $D^{[i,i]} = D^{[i]}$.

7.4.1 ML–SC Pursuit and the Forward Pass

In practice, one is given measurements $\mathbf{x}^{[0]} = \mathbf{x} + \mathbf{v}$, where $\mathbf{x}$ admits a representation in terms of the ML–SC model (with cardinalities s_i), and $\mathbf{v}$ is assumed Gaussian. The corresponding pursuit for the set of L representations, dubbed deep pursuit (Papyan et al., 2017a), seeks to find a set of sparse $\mathbf{x}^{[i]}$ that approximately reconstruct each layer. Formally, this problem is given by:

$$\text{Find } \{\mathbf{x}^{[i]}\}_{i=1}^{L} \text{ such that } \|\mathbf{x}^{[i-1]} - \mathbf{D}^{[i]}\mathbf{x}^{[i]}\|_2^2 \le \varepsilon_i, \quad \|\mathbf{x}^{[i]}\|_0 \le s_i \text{ for all } 1 \le i \le L. \tag{7.10}$$

Arguably the simplest algorithm that can provide an approximate solution to this problem is given in terms of layered thresholding operators. A soft-thresholding operator with threshold β is the scalar function given by

$$\mathcal{T}_\beta(x) = \begin{cases} \text{sign}(x)(|x| - \beta) & \text{if } |x| \ge \beta \\ 0 & \text{if } |x| < \beta. \end{cases} \tag{7.11}$$

Such a soft-thresholding operator results from the proximal of the ℓ_1 norm, employed as a relaxation of the ℓ_0 norm. Alternatively, a hard-thresholding function provides the corresponding proximal for the latter option. With such a function at hand, an estimate for the first representation can be obtained by performing $\hat{\mathbf{x}}^{[1]} = \mathcal{T}_{\beta^{[1]}}(\mathbf{D}^{[1]^T}\mathbf{x}^{[0]})$. Then, one can further compute

$$\hat{\mathbf{x}}^{[i]} = \mathcal{T}_{\beta^{[i]}}(\mathbf{D}^{[i]^T}\hat{\mathbf{x}}^{[i-1]}), \quad \text{for all } 2 \le i \le L. \tag{7.12}$$

The central observation in Papyan et al. (2017a) was that, if a non-negativity assumption is also imposed on the representations, and denoting $\mathbf{W}^{[i]} = \mathbf{D}^{[i]^T}$, such a *layered soft-thresholding algorithm* can be written equivalently in terms of the rectifier linear unit (ReLU), or non-negative projection, $\sigma(x) = \max\{0, x\}$ as

$$\hat{\mathbf{x}}^{[i]} = \sigma(\mathbf{W}^{[i]}\hat{\mathbf{x}}^{[i-1]} + \mathbf{b}^{[i]}), \quad \text{for all } 2 \le i \le L. \tag{7.13}$$

The equivalence is exact when the biases $\mathbf{b}^{[i]}$ are set according to[3] the thresholds $\beta^{[i]}$. In other words, the forward pass algorithm in (7.13) – computing the innermost representation from an input signal (or image) $\mathbf{x}^{[0]}$ through a sequence of affine transformations and the ReLU activation function – can be interpreted as a coarse pursuit seeking to estimate the representations $\mathbf{x}^{[i]}$ for that signal. This is formalized in the following result.

Theorem 7.2 (Stability of the forward pass – layered soft-thresholding algorithm,

---

[3] Note that this expression is more general, in that it allows for different thresholds per atom, than the expression in (7.12). The latter can be recovered by setting every entry in the bias vector equal to $-\beta^{[i]}$.

Papyan et al., 2017a, Theorem 10). *Suppose that an ML–SC signal is contaminated with a bounded noise* $\|\mathbf{v}\|_2 \leq \epsilon_0$, *so that* $\mathbf{x}^{[0]} = \mathbf{D}^{[1,i]}\mathbf{x}^{[i]} + \mathbf{v}$, *and suppose too that*

$$\|\mathbf{x}^{[i]}\|_0 = s_i < \frac{1}{2}\left(1 + \frac{c_i}{\mu(\mathbf{D}^{[i]})}\right) - \frac{\epsilon_{i-1}}{\mu(\mathbf{D}^{[i]})}k_i, \quad \text{for all } 1 \leq i \leq L, \tag{7.14}$$

where $c_i = |\mathbf{x}^{[i]}_{\min}|/|\mathbf{x}^{[i]}_{\max}|$ *and* $k_i = 1/|\mathbf{x}^{[i]}_{\max}|$ *are constants depending on the maximal and minimal absolute values of the non-zero values in* $\mathbf{x}^{[i]}$.

Then, for proper thresholds[4] $\beta^{[i]}$ the layered soft-thresholding algorithm recovers a set of representations $\{\hat{\mathbf{x}}^{[i]}\}_{i=1}^{L}$ with the correct supports and that satisfy

$$\|\mathbf{x}^{[i]} - \hat{\mathbf{x}}^{[i]}\|_2 \leq \epsilon_i = \sqrt{s_i}\left(\epsilon_{i-1} + \beta^{[i]} + \mu(\mathbf{D}^{[i]})k_i^{-1}(s_i - 1)\right), \text{ for all } 1 \leq i \leq L. \tag{7.15}$$

In simple terms, Theorem 7.2 guarantees that, under sparse assumptions on the representations (or activations) $\mathbf{x}^{[i]}$ and small mutual coherence of the dictionaries $\mu(\mathbf{D}^{[i]})$, the vectors computed by the forward pass, $\hat{\mathbf{x}}^{[i]}$, provide approximations to such underlying sparse representations. These estimates $\hat{\mathbf{x}}^{[i]}$ are stable, in the sense that the correct support is recovered and their distance to the original $\mathbf{x}^{[i]}$ is bounded in an ℓ_2 sense. Note that these guarantees based on $\mu(\mathbf{D}^{[i]})$ result from a worst-case scenario analysis, and so they are typically quite pessimistic. Networks satisfying these conditions were constructed in Papyan et al. (2017a). Interestingly, later work (Cisse et al., 2017) showed that enforcing filters to behave like Parseval frames – tightly related to a small mutual coherence – provides improved stability against adversarial attacks. We will comment on this connection later in this chapter.

A result such as Theorem 7.2 is illuminating, as it demonstrates the potential of employing results in sparse approximation to the study of deep learning. The mere application of these guarantees in a layered-synthesis manner provides bounds that become looser with the depth of the network, as can be observed in (7.15), so it is unclear to what extent the layer-wise constraints really contribute to an improved estimation of $\mathbf{x}^{[i]}$ or what their underlying benefit is. Papyan et al. (2017a) also suggested an improvement to the above strategy by replacing simple thresholding with the complete solution to basis pursuit at every layer in a sequential manner, and named it *layered basis pursuit*:

$$\hat{\mathbf{x}}^{[i]} = \arg\min_{\mathbf{x}^{[i]}} \frac{1}{2}\|\hat{\mathbf{x}}^{[i-1]} - \mathbf{D}^{[i]}\mathbf{x}^{[i]}\|_2^2 + \lambda_i\|\mathbf{x}^{[i]}\|_1. \tag{7.16}$$

Unlike the forward pass, this allows recovery of the representations exactly in an ideal (noiseless) setting. Still, note that no global reconstruction is possible in general, as the solution to the above problem yields only approximations $\hat{\mathbf{x}}^{[i-1]} \approx \mathbf{D}^{[i]}\hat{\mathbf{x}}^{[i]}$, and it is thus unclear how to reconstruct $\hat{\mathbf{x}}^{[0]}$ from $\{\hat{\mathbf{x}}^{[i]}\}_{i=1}^{L}$ in a stable way.

---

[4] The proper thresholds depend on the values of the representations $\mathbf{x}^{[i]}$, the mutual coherence of the dictionaries and the noise contamination. Further details can be found in Papyan et al., 2017a, Appendix E.

7.4.2 ML–SC: A Projection Approach

These shortcomings led Sulam et al. (2018) to propose a projection alternative to the deep pursuit problem from (7.10). Given measurements $\mathbf{x}^{[0]} = \mathbf{x} + \mathbf{v}$, they proposed the following optimization problem:

$$\min_{\mathbf{x}^{[i]}} \; \|\mathbf{x}^{[0]} - \mathbf{D}^{[1,L]}\mathbf{x}^{[L]}\|_2^2 \text{ such that } \begin{cases} \mathbf{x}^{[i-1]} = \mathbf{D}^{[i]}\mathbf{x}^{[i]}, & \text{for all } 2 \le i \le L, \\ \|\mathbf{x}^{[i]}\|_0 \le s_i, & \text{for all } 1 \le i \le L. \end{cases}$$

$$(7.17)$$

In words, this seeks to obtain the closest signal $\mathbf{x}$ to the measurements $\mathbf{x}^{[0]}$ that satisfies the model constraints. To solve this problem, one can resort to a global pursuit stage (finding the deepest $\hat{\mathbf{x}}^{[L]}$ that minimizes the ℓ_2 data term) followed by a back-tracking step that ensures the sparsity constraints are met and modifies them otherwise. This scheme has the advantage that the stability bounds for the estimates $\hat{\mathbf{x}}^{[i]}$ do not necessarily increase with the depth of the model (Sulam et al., 2018).

More interestingly, this projection alternative provided a first dictionary learning approach for this multilayer (and convolutional) model. The authors leverage the sparsity of the intermediate dictionaries $\mathbf{D}^{[i]}$ as proxies for the sparsity intermediate representations. Indeed, $\|\mathbf{x}^{[i-1]}\|_0 \le \|\mathbf{D}^{[i,L]}\|_0 \|\mathbf{x}^{[L]}\|_0$, where $\|\mathbf{D}^{[i,L]}\|_0$ counts the maximal number of non-zeros in any column of $\mathbf{D}^{[i,L]}$ – it forms an induced ℓ_0 pseudo-norm. Using this approach, for a collection of N training signals $\mathbf{x}_i^{[0]}$, Sulam et al. (2018) proposed the following multilayer dictionary learning problem:

$$\min_{\mathbf{x}_i^{[L]}, \mathbf{D}^{[l]}} \; \frac{1}{2N} \sum_{i=1}^{N} \|\mathbf{x}_i^{[0]} - \mathbf{D}^{[1,L]}\mathbf{x}_i^{[L]}\|_2^2 + \sum_{l=2}^{L} \lambda^{[l]} \|\mathbf{D}^{[l]}\|_0 + \iota \sum_{l=1}^{L} \|\mathbf{D}^{[l]}\|_F^2 + \lambda \|\mathbf{x}_i^{[L]}\|_1,$$

$$(7.18)$$

explicitly enforcing sparsity on the atoms in all intermediate dictionaries. Such a non-convex problem can be minimized empirically by an alternating minimization approach, solving for $\mathbf{x}_i^{[L]}$ while keeping the dictionaries fixed and then vice versa. Moreover, this can be carried out in an online way, minimizing (7.18) one sample (or a mini-batch of samples) at a time. This is the approach for training such a model on digit images (MNIST), yielding the convolutional multilayer mode shown in Figure 7.1. The features (or representations) that result from this unsupervised learning scheme were also shown to be useful, providing comparable classification performance to competing modern auto-encoder alternatives (Makhzani and Frey, 2013, 2015). Nonetheless, this framework is restricted to sparse dictionaries, and the resulting algorithm does not scale as well as other convolutional network implementations. Such an alternating minimization scheme deviates from traditional autoencoders, which minimize the reconstruction loss through back-propagation.

$\mathbf{D}^{[1]}$ $\mathbf{D}^{[1]}\mathbf{D}^{[2]}$

$\mathbf{D}^{[1]}\mathbf{D}^{[2]}\mathbf{D}^{[3]}$

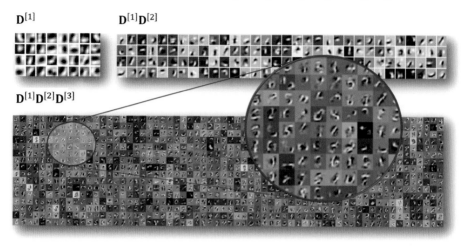

Figure 7.1   A three-layer convolutional model trained on MNIST digits, taken from Papyan et al. (2018).

7.5 The Holistic Way

Both approaches presented above, the layer-wise and the projection alternatives, consist of relatively separate pursuits for each representation layer. As a consequence, in the layer-wise approach the recovery error increases with the network depth (Papyan et al., 2017a), while in the projection case this error is essentially the same as that found using the effective model as a single-layer model (Sulam et al., 2018). These results contradict the intuition that the estimation of the representations in a ML–CS model should improve, since this imposes further constraints than the traditional case. Extra constraints convey additional information, which the previous methods seem to be incapable of leveraging. In this section we offer a holistic perspective that aims to analyze the deep pursuit problem wholly, enforcing all constraints simultaneously. In doing so, we will show that this model imposes a synergetic coupling between synthesis and analysis sparse models, leading to answers to the baffling questions posed previously.

To solve all the constraints in the deep pursuit problem at the same time we shall first rewrite it as a function of the deepest layer. Let us express the intermediate representations as linear functions of $\mathbf{x}^{[L]}$; namely, $\mathbf{x}^{[i-1]} = \mathbf{D}^{[i,L]}\mathbf{x}^{[L]}$. Thus, (7.17) becomes

$$\min_{\mathbf{x}^{[L]}} \|\mathbf{x}^{[0]} - \mathbf{D}^{[1,L]}\mathbf{x}^{[L]}\|_2^2 \text{ such that } \begin{cases} \|\mathbf{x}^{[L]}\|_0 \leq s_L, \\ \|\mathbf{D}^{[i,L]}\mathbf{x}^{[L]}\|_0 \leq s_i, & \text{for all } 2 \leq i \leq L. \end{cases}$$

$$(7.19)$$

Written in this way, it is clear that from a global perspective the effective dictionary

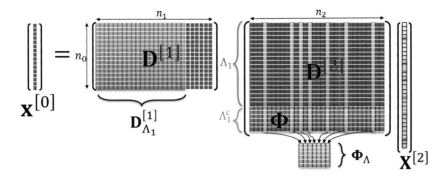

$\mathbf{D}^{[1,L]}$ imposes a synthesis-sparse prior on the deepest representation $\mathbf{x}^{[L]}$. However, there are extra constraints on it: $\mathbf{x}^{[L]}$ should be not only sparse but also produce zeros in the intermediate layers $\mathbf{x}^{[i-1]}$ when multiplied by $\mathbf{D}^{[i,L]}$. In other words, the intermediate dictionaries $\mathbf{D}^{[i,L]}$ act as analysis operators in a co-sparse model, as depicted in Figure 7.2 for a two-layer case.

This particular coupling of both sparse priors sheds light on the dimensionality of the space spanned by the ML–SC model. From a synthesis point of view, an s_L-sparse signal $\mathbf{x}^{[L]}$ lives in a union of s_L-dimensional subspaces. However, and following Figure 7.2, when requiring the intermediate representations to be sparse we are enforcing $\mathbf{x}^{[L]}$ to be orthogonal to certain *rows* from $\mathbf{D}^{[2]}$. Denoting such rows by $\mathbf{\Phi}$, we conclude that $\mathbf{x}^{[2]}$ must be in the kernel of $\mathbf{\Phi}$. Letting Λ denote the support of $\mathbf{x}^{[2]}$, this boils down to the condition that $\mathbf{\Phi}_\Lambda \mathbf{x}^{[2]}_\Lambda = \mathbf{0}$. As shown in Aberdam et al. (2019), this extra constraint reduces the degrees of freedom of the deepest representation, and so the ML–SC signals effectively lies in a union of $(s_L - r)$-dimensional subspaces, where $r = \text{rank}\{\mathbf{\Phi}_\Lambda\}$.

This new understanding of the dimensionality of the signals in the ML–SC model leads to several corollaries. For instance, one can now evaluate whether the model is empty simply by observing the kernel space of $\mathbf{\Phi}_\Lambda$. If this subspace contains only the zero vector (i.e., $s_L \leq r$) then no signal exists satisfying the support constraints. Otherwise, one could sample signals from the model by randomly selecting representations $\mathbf{x}^{[L]}$ in the kernel of $\mathbf{\Phi}_\Lambda$ – easily done through a singular value decomposition. A second relevant conclusion is that the representation layers should not be too sparse, providing more generous bounds. Indeed, under a full-rank assumption for the intermediate dictionaries, every additional zero at any intermediate layer increases r, thus reducing the effective dimension of the signal. This is in sharp contrast to the analysis from §7.4. The previous pursuit schemes required the dictionaries to be sparse in order to satisfy the stringent sparsity constraints. Such a requirement is not needed under this holistic interpretation.

An important consequence of the holistic approach is a significant improvement in uniqueness guarantees. Recall from Theorem 7.1 that in the layered synthesis interpretation, every representation at every layer should be *sparse enough* to be the unique (i.e., sparsest) representation for its respective layer. However, thanks to the analysis–synthesis understanding, the set of representations in an ML–SC model is guaranteed to be unique if the deepest representation satisfies $\|x^{[L]}\|_0 \leq \frac{\eta(D^{[1,L]})-1}{2} + r$. In other words, the traditional bound on the allowed cardinality is extended by r, the rank of Φ_Λ. This is formalized in the following result:

Theorem 7.3 (Aberdam et al., 2019, Theorem 5.1). *Consider an ML–SC signal* $x^{[0]}$ *and a set of dictionaries* $\{D^{[i]}\}_{i=1}^L$. *If a set of representations* $\{x^{[i]}\}_{i=1}^L$ *satisfies*

$$\|x^{[L]}\|_0 = s_L < \frac{1}{2}\left(1 + \frac{1}{\mu(D^{[1,L]})}\right) + r, \tag{7.20}$$

where $r = \text{rank}\{\Phi_\Lambda\}$, *then, for a set of dictionaries* $\{D^{[i]}\}_{i=1}^L$ *in general position,[5], this set is the unique ML–SC representation for* $x^{[0]}$.

Other results can be derived using similar arguments, and we give here one final example from Aberdam et al. (2019). Consider the oracle denoising case, in which the supports of the representations at every layer are known and the goal is to provide an estimate of $\hat{x}^{[i]}$ given noisy measurements $x^{[0]} = D^{[1,i]}x^{[i]} + v$. Assuming Gaussian noise with standard deviation σ_v and disregarding the analysis-sparse prior in the model, one can show that the expected error in the deepest representation is upper bounded as follows:

$$\mathbb{E}\|\hat{x}^{[L]} - x^{[L]}\|_2^2 \leq \frac{\sigma_v^2}{1 - \delta_{s_L}} s_L, \tag{7.21}$$

where δ_{s_L} is the restricted isometry property (RIP) for the effective dictionary $D^{[1,L]}$ and cardinality of s_L. This property measures how far a redundant matrix is from an isometry for sparse vectors, small values being preferred. If one also leverages the information contained in the analysis priors of the intermediate layers, however, one can show that this error is reduced, resulting in:

$$\mathbb{E}\|\hat{x}^{[L]} - x^{[L]}\|_2^2 \leq \frac{\sigma_v^2}{1 - \delta_{s_L}}(s_L - r). \tag{7.22}$$

As it is now clear, this dual prior interpretation provides a significant advantage in

---

[5] The assumption of the dictionaries being in general position – i.e. not containing non-trivial linear dependencies among its rows – follows from the analysis in Nam et al. (2013) and further details can be found in Aberdam et al. (2019). Such an assumption holds for almost every dictionary set in Lebesgue measure.

terms of theoretical guarantees, showing the important benefits of the intermediate sparse representations. How can these theoretical benefits be brought to practice by some pursuit algorithm?

A first answer was provided by Aberdam et al. (2019) who proposed a holistic pursuit that alternates between application of the synthesis priors and of the analysis priors, following a greedy strategy. This algorithm[6] provides recovery guarantees that have the same flavor as those commented on in this section, i.e., an error that is proportional to $s_L - r$. However, such greedy approaches are still far from being scalable and efficient algorithms that can bring these ideas into the practical deep learning world. This is what we study next.

7.6 Multilayer Iterative Shrinkage Algorithms

Our approach to reducing the hard optimization problem from (7.19) to an easier form relies, naturally, on an ℓ_1 relaxation of both synthesis and analysis priors. We propose the following multilayer extension of a basis pursuit problem:

$$\text{ML–BP}: \quad \min_{\mathbf{x}^{[L]}} \frac{1}{2}\|\mathbf{x}^{[0]} - \mathbf{D}^{[1,L]}\mathbf{x}^{[L]}\|_2^2 + \sum_{l=2}^{L} \lambda^{[l-1]}\|\mathbf{D}^{[l,L]}\mathbf{x}^{[L]}\|_1 + \lambda^{[L]}\|\mathbf{x}^{[L]}\|_1.$$

$$(7.23)$$

Note that setting all but the last penalty parameters to zero ($\lambda^{[l]} = 0$ for $1 \leq l < L$, and $\lambda^{[L]} > 0$) results in a traditional ℓ_1 pursuit for the effective model $\mathbf{D}^{[1,L]}$. The problem above is related to other approaches in the compressed sensing literature, such as the analysis lasso (Candes et al., 2010) and robust sparse analysis regularization (Vaiter et al., 2013). Yet the coupling of the synthesis and analysis operators makes ML–BP different from other previous formulations.

The optimization problem in (7.23) is convex, and a wide variety of solvers could be employ to find a minimizer (Boyd and Vandenberghe, 2004). Nonetheless, we are interested in first-order methods that only incur matrix–vector multiplication and entry-wise operations, which scale to large-dimensional problems. Iterative shrinkage algorithms (ISTAs) and their accelerated versions (Fast ISTAs, or FIS-TAs) (Beck and Teboulle, 2009) are attractive, but not directly applicable to problem (7.23). ISTA minimizes the sum of functions $f + g$, where f is convex and L-smooth while g is convex but possible non-smooth, by means of a proximal gradient approach that iterates the updates:

$$\mathbf{x}_{k+1} = \text{prox}_{\frac{1}{L}g}\left(\mathbf{x}_k - \frac{1}{L}\nabla f(\mathbf{x}_k)\right). \quad (7.24)$$

One might consider letting f be the ℓ_2 data term in problem (7.23) and g be the

---

[6] Code is available at https://github.com/aaberdam/Holistic_Pursuit.

sum of the ℓ_1 penalty functions. This, however, is not very useful as calculating the proximal of a sum of functions is problematic (Combettes and Pesquet, 2011).

As an alternative, Sulam et al. (2020) put forward a *proximal gradient-mapping* algorithm. Given functions f and g, the gradient-mapping operator is defined as

$$G_L^{f,g}(\mathbf{x}) = L \left[\mathbf{x} - \mathrm{prox}_{\frac{1}{L}g} \left(\mathbf{x} - \frac{1}{L}\nabla f(\mathbf{x}) \right) \right]. \tag{7.25}$$

This operator is a sort of generalization of gradient, since $G_L^{f,g}(\mathbf{x}_*) = 0$ if and only if $\mathbf{x}_*$ is a minimizer of $f + g$, and $G_L^{f,g}(\mathbf{x}) = \nabla f(\mathbf{x})$ if $g \equiv 0$ (Beck, 2017).

For simplicity, let us consider a two-layer model and the associated pursuit problem

$$\min_{\mathbf{x}^{[2]}} F(\mathbf{x}^{[2]}) \triangleq \underbrace{\frac{1}{2} \| \mathbf{x}^{[0]} - \mathbf{D}^{[1]}\mathbf{D}^{[2]}\mathbf{x}^{[2]} \|_2^2}_{f(\mathbf{D}^{[2]}\mathbf{x}^{[2]})} + \underbrace{\lambda^{[1]} \| \mathbf{D}^{[2]}\mathbf{x}^{[2]} \|_1}_{g_1(\mathbf{D}^{[2]}\mathbf{x}^{[2]})} + \underbrace{\lambda^{[2]} \| \mathbf{x}^{[2]} \|_1}_{g_2(\mathbf{x}^{[2]})}. \tag{7.26}$$

Note that we have chosen to express the overall loss as $F = f + g_1 + g_2$. All the functions are convex, but only f is smooth. With these, the multilayer ISTA (ML–ISTA) from Sulam et al. (2020) employs a sequence of nested proximal gradient mappings. In this way, and employing the auxiliary variable $\mathbf{x}^{[1]} = \mathbf{D}^{[2]}\mathbf{x}^{[2]}$, the updates of ML–ISTA for the problem in (7.26) can be written as:

$$\mathbf{x}_{k+1}^{[2]} = \mathrm{prox}_{tg_2} \left(\mathbf{x}_k^{[2]} - t\mathbf{D}^{[2]^T} G_{1/\rho}^{f,g_1} \left(\mathbf{x}_k^{[1]} \right) \right). \tag{7.27}$$

In the particular case where g_1 and g_2 are the ℓ_1 norms, their prox is the soft-thresholding operator, and so the above update can be written as

$$\mathbf{x}_{k+1}^{[2]} = \mathcal{T}_{t\lambda^{[2]}} \left(\mathbf{x}_k^{[2]} - \frac{t}{\rho} \mathbf{D}^{[2]^T} \left(\mathbf{x}_k^{[1]} - \mathcal{T}_{\rho\lambda^{[1]}}(\mathbf{x}_k^{[1]} - \rho\mathbf{D}^{[1]^T}(\mathbf{D}^{[1]}\mathbf{x}_k^{[1]} - \mathbf{x}^{[0]})) \right) \right). \tag{7.28}$$

Though seemingly intricate, this algorithm simply performs a series of proximal gradient updates per layer, albeit in a global and holistic way, that require only matrix–vector multiplications and entry-wise operators. Moreover, when the dictionaries are convolutional, one can leverage fast GPU implementations to the ML–BP problem on high-dimensional data.

Proximal gradient-mapping algorithms have not been proposed before, let alone analyzed. In fact, by noting that gradient-mapping is, in general, not the gradient of any primitive function, one naturally asks: Does such an update even minimize the problem ML–BP in (7.26)? We give here the convergence result from Sulam et al. (2020), presenting some first theoretical insights. In a nutshell, it states that if the iterates are close enough, in the sense that they are ε-fixed points, $\| \mathbf{x}_{k+1}^{[2]} - \mathbf{x}_k^{[2]} \|^2 < t\varepsilon$, then these iterates can get arbitrarily close to the optimum of $F(\mathbf{x}^{[2]})$ in the function value.

Theorem 7.4 (Sulam et al., 2020, Corollary 2.21). *Suppose that* $\{\mathbf{x}_k^{[2]}\}$ *is the sequence generated by ML–ISTA with* $\rho \in \left(0, \frac{1}{\|\mathbf{D}^{[1]}\|_2^2}\right)$ *and* $t \in \left(0, \frac{4\rho}{3\|\mathbf{D}^{[2]}\|_2}\right)$. *If* $\|\mathbf{x}_{k+1}^{[2]} - \mathbf{x}_k^{[2]}\|_2 \le t\varepsilon$ *then*

$$F(\mathbf{x}_{k+1}^{[2]}) - F_{\text{opt}} \le \eta\varepsilon + (\beta + \kappa t)\rho, \tag{7.29}$$

where η, β *and* κ *are constants not depending on* t, ρ, ϵ.

One can state an analogous result for an accelerated version of the above algorithm, a fast ML–ISTA (Sulam et al., 2020). However, further work is required to provide a complete convergence analysis of these multilayer ISTA approaches that provide convergence rates. In addition, the above result is limited to a two-layer model, and an extension to further layers is not trivial. These questions constitute exciting avenues of current research.

7.6.1 Towards Principled Recurrent Neural Networks

To test the ideas presented in the last two sections in a real data application, and through this tie them to practical implementations of deep neural networks, we propose the following experiment. Train a convolutional ML–SC model in a supervised learning setting for image classification by considering a training set of N pairs of images $\mathbf{x}_i^{[0]}$ and their corresponding labels y_i, i.e., $\{(\mathbf{x}_i^{[0]}, y_i)\}_{i=1}^N$. Denote by $\zeta_\theta(\hat{\mathbf{x}}_i^{[L]})$ a classifier parameterized by θ acting on representations $\hat{\mathbf{x}}_i^{[L]}$, computed from each example $\mathbf{x}_i^{[0]}$. We propose to address the following optimization problem:

$$\min_{\theta, \{\mathbf{D}^{[i]}, \lambda^{[i]}\}} \frac{1}{N} \sum_{i=1}^N \mathcal{L}\left(y_i, \zeta_\theta(\hat{\mathbf{x}}_i^{[L]})\right) \text{ such that} \tag{7.30}$$

$$\hat{\mathbf{x}}_i^{[L]} = \arg\min_{\mathbf{x}^{[L]}} \frac{1}{2}\|\mathbf{x}_i^{[0]} - \mathbf{D}^{[1,L]}\mathbf{x}^{[L]}\|_2^2 + \sum_{i=1}^{L-1} \lambda^{[i]}\|\mathbf{D}^{[i+1,L]}\mathbf{x}^{[L]}\|_1 + \lambda^{[L]}\|\mathbf{x}^{[L]}\|_1.$$

In other words, we employ a classification loss $\mathcal{L}$ (such as the cross-entropy function) to train a classifier $\zeta_\theta(\hat{\mathbf{x}}_i^{[L]})$, where the representation vector $\hat{\mathbf{x}}_i^{[L]}$ is a solution to the multilayer basis pursuit problem. Solving this bi-level problem while computing an exact minimizer of the ML–BP is challenging. However, this difficulty can be alleviated by employing the ML–ISTA iterates as approximations to the representation vectors at different iterations, $(\hat{\mathbf{x}}_i^{[L]})_k$. In this way, we can replace the analytic expressions for such iterates in the loss function $\mathcal{L}$, enabling minimization with respect to the parameters by back-propagation. Notably, this provides a

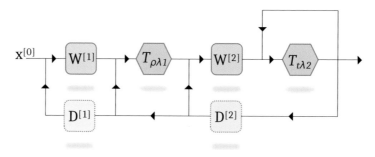

Figure 7.3 Recurrent network interpretation of the ML–ISTA algorithm in (7.28). Note that the filters are given by $\mathbf{W}^{[i]} = \mathbf{D}^{[i]^T}$, and the thresholding operators $\mathcal{T}_\beta$ can be equivalently written in terms of a ReLU activations function, σ, and appropriate biases $\mathbf{b}$. Adapted from Sulam et al. (1980). ©1980 IEEE. Reprinted with permission of IEEE.

learning algorithm that is closer to more traditional autoencoders. Nonetheless, the sparse-promoting norms (at every layer) are made explicit in (7.30). This implies that a pursuit involving a single thresholding operation per layer (such as the forward pass) is sub-optimal, as it will not provide minimizers of the bilevel problem above.

The formulation in (7.30) generalizes feed-forward convolutional neural networks. Indeed, if only one iteration of the ML–ISTA is used (and initially we once again takes $\mathbf{x}_0^{[2]} = 0$, for a two-layer model, for simplicity) we simply compute the representations by

$$\hat{\mathbf{x}}^{[2]} = \mathcal{T}_{t\lambda^{[2]}} \left(\frac{t}{\rho} \mathbf{D}^{[2]^T} \mathcal{T}_{\rho\lambda^{[1]}} \left(\rho \mathbf{D}^{[1]^T} \mathbf{x}^{[0]} \right) \right). \tag{7.31}$$

Once again, denoting the network's filters by $\mathbf{W}^{[i]} = \mathbf{D}^{[i]^T}$ and under a non-negative assumption on the representations $\mathbf{x}^{[i]}$, the above can be written simply as $\hat{\mathbf{x}}^{[2]} = \sigma \left(\frac{t}{\rho} \mathbf{W}^{[2]} \sigma \left(\rho \mathbf{W}^{[1]} \mathbf{x}^{[0]} + \mathbf{b}^{[1]} \right) + \mathbf{b}^{[2]} \right)$, i.e., by computing the forward pass. More generally, however, further iterations of ML–ISTA compute more iterates from the recurrent network in Figure 7.3. Alas, unlike other architectures popular in the deep learning community, such as Resnet (He et al., 2016), Densenet (Huang et al., 2017), these "skip connections" are nothing other than the implementation of an optimization algorithm minimizing the multilayer basis pursuit problem. Importantly, while further iterations of the ML–ISTA effectively implement "deeper" networks, *the number of parameters in the model remains unchanged*.

Before moving onto the numerical demonstration of these algorithms, a comment about the LISTA approach from Gregor and LeCun (2010) is appropriate. Note that in our case the representations are obtained as those estimated by ML–ISTA from (7.27). LISTA, on the other hand, factorizes the update of ISTA into two new matrices, *for a single layer or dictionary,* and it learns those instead. As a result, the number of parameters is doubled. An extension of our approach in the spirit of Gregor and LeCun (2010) should in the first place extend LISTA to the multilayer setting presented in this chapter, and some preliminary results in this direction can be found in Sulam et al. (2020).

We studied the problem in (7.30) for three common datasets: MNIST, SVHN and CIFAR10. For the first two cases, we construct a three layer convolutional neural network with ReLU activations (i.e., employing non-negativity constraints in the representations) followed by a final linear (fully connected) classifier $\zeta_\theta(\mathbf{x})$. For CIFAR10, we implemented an analogous three layer convolutional ML–SC model, and define $\zeta_\theta(\mathbf{x})$ as a three-layer convolutional network with pooling operators.[7] The models were trained with stochastic gradient descent (SGD), without any other optimization tricks (batch normalization, dropout, etc.), so as to provide a clear experimental setting. For the same reason, we excluded from this comparison other – more sophisticated – models that can be trained with these tools. For reference, the reader should note that such state-of-the-art methods obtain around 92%–95% accuracy in the CIFAR10 dataset (Huang et al., 2017). Our goal here is not to provide a best-performing architecture but, rather, to verify the practical validity of the ML–SC model through a pursuit algorithm that serves it better, and to explore the benefits of ML–ISTA over feed-forward networks. Further implementation details can be found in Sulam et al. (2020), and code is provided to reproduce these experiments.[8]

The results are shown in Figure 7.4, which give, for comparison, the networks resulting from applying ML–ISTA and ML–FISTA with, as baseline, a feed-forward CNN. We also include in these experiments the layered basis pursuit approach from (7.16). These four networks (the feed-forward CNN, ML–ISTA, ML–FISTA, and ML–BP) all have exactly the same number of model parameters, namely for dictionaries, bias vectors, and the final classifier. The latter constructions, however, are networks that are *effectively* deeper, as they "unroll" the iterations of different multilayer pursuit algorithms. A natural question is, then, how well would a network with the same depth and general recurrent architecture perform if the parameters (weights) were not tied but rather free to be learned? This is the model denoted by "all free" in Figure 7.4. Somewhat surprisingly, performance does not improve any further, despite – or perhaps because – a significant increase in the numbers of parameters.

---

[7] Note that ML–SC is a linear generative model. As such, in order to include the shift-invariant properties that are important for very heterogeneous images in CIFAR, we included pooling operators in the classifier part.

[8] Code is available at `https://github.com/jsulam/ml-ista`.

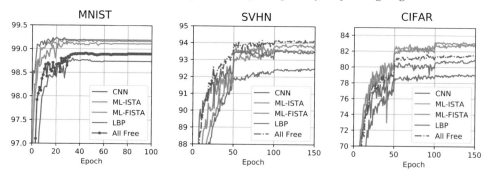

Figure 7.4 Comparison of different architectures on the SVHN dataset, with a feed-forward network as baseline. All networks have the same number of parameters. Adapted from Sulam et al. (1980). © 1980 IEEE. Reprinted, with permission, from IEEE.

7.7 Final Remarks and Outlook

This chapter has two main objectives. The first consists in exploring the new multilayer model for sparse signals, analysing the dimensionality of such sparse representations and briefly presenting some theoretical results regarding uniqueness and stability guarantees. The second objective is to employ this understanding of the ML–SC model to design tractable pursuit formulations, as well as efficient algorithms to solve them. In doing so, we also showed how these first-order algorithms generalise feed-forward CNNs, improving their performance while maintaining the number of parameters in the model constant.

Several exciting research directions exist in both avenues of work. An important question that remains unanswered is the following: how stable are these solutions to the ML–BP problem? Unlike the layered and projections approaches from §7.4, there are currently no bounds known for the distance between the estimates recovered by the ML–ISTA and the original representations generating these signals. Such results would provide stability bounds that depende on the amount of unfoldings of the recurrent network in Figure 7.3 and would have feed-forward networks as a particular case.

A second major issue that we have not explored in this chapter is the *learnability* of the dictionaries in the ML–SC model. How do the model constraints affect or aid the sample complexity of such a model? How would this answer depend on the accuracy of the estimates for the representations $\hat{\mathbf{x}}^{[L]}$? Providing answers to these questions would likely shed light on the sample complexity of particular classes of recurrent network architectures.

As the careful reader might have noticed, the experimental results in the final section reveal something rather curious: modifying the mapping from the input space to the representation space, $\mathcal{A}(\mathbf{x}^{[0]})\colon \mathbb{R}^{n_0} \to \mathbb{R}^{n_L}$, while maintaining the structure of the generative model improved classification when minimizing the supervised loss $\mathcal{L}(y_i, \zeta_\theta(\mathcal{A}(\mathbf{x}_i^{[0]})))$. Why does it happen? What does this imply about the aptitude of the obtained $\hat{\mathbf{x}}_i^{[L]}$ as representations for a signal $\mathbf{x}_i^{[0]}$ in the context of supervised learning? Seeking explanations to this phenomenon, in particular from a learning theory perspective, is also a highly promising avenue of work.

Finally, what else can we learn from ML–SC as a generative model for deep learning? In this sense, improving the stability and robustness of deep classifiers is a clear path. In the theoretical analysis of the model, and of the pursuits involved, we have ignored the fact that the ultimate task was to employ the obtained sparse representations for classification. How do these eventually affect the subsequent classifier? Romano and Elad (2018) studied precisely this point, showing that the stability of the obtained $\hat{\mathbf{x}}_{[L]}$ directly affects the stability of the (linear) classifier acting on them. In particular, they showed that the coherence of the dictionaries in the ML–SC model influences the margin of the final classifier and in turn controls the robustness to adversarial attacks. Further work is required to tie their analysis to the holistic approach presented here in §7.5; this opens exciting research directions.

References

Aberdam, Aviad, Sulam, Jeremias, and Elad, Michael. 2019. Multi-layer sparse coding: The holistic way. *SIAM Journal on Mathematics of Data Science*, **1**(1), 46–77.

Aharon, Michal, Elad, Michael, and Bruckstein, Alfred. 2006. K-SVD: An algorithm for designing overcomplete dictionaries for sparse representation. *IEEE Transactions on Signal Processing*, **54**(11), 4311–4322.

Beck, Amir. 2017. *First-Order Methods in Optimization*. SIAM.

Beck, Amir, and Teboulle, Marc. 2009. A fast iterative shrinkage-thresholding algorithm for linear inverse problems. *SIAM Journal on Imaging Sciences*, **2**(1), 183–202.

Blumensath, Thomas, and Davies, Mike E. 2009. Iterative hard thresholding for compressed sensing. *Applied and Computational Harmonic Analysis*, **27**(3), 265–274.

Bölcskei, Helmut, Grohs, Philipp, Kutyniok, Gitta, and Petersen, Philipp. 2019. Optimal approximation with sparsely connected deep neural networks. *SIAM Journal on Mathematics of Data Science*, **1**(1), 8–45.

Boyd, Stephen, and Vandenberghe, Lieven. 2004. *Convex Optimization*. Cambridge University Press.

Candes, Emmanuel J., Eldar, Yonina C., Needell, Deanna, and Randall, Paige. 2010. Compressed sensing with coherent and redundant dictionaries. ArXiv preprint arXiv:1005.2613.

Chen, Xiaohan, Liu, Jialin, Wang, Zhangyang, and Yin, Wotao. 2018. Theoretical linear convergence of unfolded ista and its practical weights and thresholds. Pages 9061–9071 of: *Advances in Neural Information Processing Systems.*

Cisse, Moustapha, Bojanowski, Piotr, Grave, Edouard, Dauphin, Yann, and Usunier, Nicolas. 2017. Parseval networks: Improving robustness to adversarial examples. Pages 854–863 of: *Proc. 34th International Conference on Machine Learning.*

Combettes, Patrick L., and Pesquet, Jean-Christophe. 2011. Proximal splitting methods in signal processing. Pages 185–212 of: *Fixed-Point Algorithms for Inverse Problems in Science and Engineering.* Springer.

Donoho, David L., and Elad, Michael. 2003. Optimally sparse representation in general (nonorthogonal) dictionaries via ℓ_1 minimization. *Proc. National Academy of Sciences,* **100**(5), 2197–2202.

Elad, Michael. 2010. *Sparse and Redundant Representations – From Theory to Applications in Signal and Image Processing.* Springer.

Giryes, Raja, Eldar, Yonina C., Bronstein, Alex M., and Sapiro, Guillermo. 2018. Tradeoffs between convergence speed and reconstruction accuracy in inverse problems. *IEEE Transactions on Signal Processing,* **66**(7), 1676–1690.

Goodfellow, Ian, Bengio, Yoshua, and Courville, Aaron. 2016. *Deep Learning.* MIT Press. http://www.deeplearningbook.org.

Gregor, Karol, and LeCun, Yann. 2010. Learning fast approximations of sparse coding. Pages 399–406 of: *Proc. 27th International Conference on International Conference on Machine Learning.* Omnipress.

He, Kaiming, Zhang, Xiangyu, Ren, Shaoqing, and Sun, Jian. 2016. Deep residual learning for image recognition. Pages 770–778 of: *Proc. IEEE Conference on Computer Vision and Pattern Recognition.*

Ho, Nhat, Nguyen, Tan, Patel, Ankit, Anandkumar, Anima, Jordan, Michael I., and Baraniuk, Richard G. 2018. Neural rendering model: Joint generation and prediction for semi-supervised learning. ArXiv preprint arXiv:1811.02657.

Huang, Gao, Liu, Zhuang, Weinberger, Kilian Q., and van der Maaten, Laurens. 2017. Densely connected convolutional networks. Page 3 of: *Proceedings of the IEEE Conference on Computer Vision and Pattern Recognition,* vol. 1.

Jiang, Zhuolin, Lin, Zhe, and Davis, Larry S. 2013. Label consistent K-SVD: Learning a discriminative dictionary for recognition. *IEEE Transactions on Pattern Analysis and Machine Intelligence,* **35**(11), 2651–2664.

LeCun, Yann, Boser, Bernhard E., Denker, John S., Henderson, Donnie, Howard, Richard E., Hubbard, Wayne E., and Jackel, Lawrence D. 1990. Handwritten digit recognition with a back-propagation network. Pages 396–404 of: *Advances in Neural Information Processing Systems.*

Lee, Honglak, Ekanadham, Chaitanya, and Ng, Andrew Y. 2008. Sparse deep belief net model for visual area V2. Pages 873–880 of: *Advances in Neural Information Processing Systems.*

Liu, Jialin, Chen, Xiaohan, Wang, Zhangyang, and Yin, Wotao. 2019. ALISTA: Analytic weights are as good as learned weights in LISTA. In: *Proc. International Conference on Learning Representations*.

Mairal, Julien, Bach, Francis, Ponce, Jean, Sapiro, Guillermo, and Zisserman, Andrew. 2009. Non-local sparse models for image restoration. Pages 2272–2279 of: *proc. 12th International Conference on Computer Vision*. IEEE.

Mairal, Julien, Bach, Francis, Ponce, Jean, and Sapiro, Guillermo. 2010. Online learning for matrix factorization and sparse coding. *Journal of Machine Learning Research*, **11**, 19–60.

Mairal, Julien, Bach, Francis, and Ponce, Jean. 2012. Task-driven dictionary learning. *IEEE Transactions on Pattern Analysis and Machine Intelligence*, **34**(4), 791–804.

Makhzani, Alireza, and Frey, Brendan. 2013. K-sparse autoencoders. ArXiv preprint arXiv:1312.5663.

Makhzani, Alireza, and Frey, Brendan J. 2015. Winner-take-all autoencoders. Pages 2791–2799 of: *Advances in Neural Information Processing Systems*.

Mallat, Stéphane. 2016. Understanding deep convolutional networks. *Philosophical Transactions of the Royal Society A: Mathematical, Physical and Engineering Sciences*, **374**(2065), 20150203.

Mallat, Stéphane G, and Zhang, Zhifeng. 1993. Matching pursuits with time–frequency dictionaries. *IEEE Transactions on Signal Processing*, **41**(12), 3397.

Moreau, Thomas, and Bruna, Joan. 2017. Understanding trainable sparse coding via matrix factorization. In: *Proc. International Conference on Learning Representations*.

Nam, Sangnam, Davies, Mike E., Elad, Michael, and Gribonval, Rémi. 2013. The cosparse analysis model and algorithms. *Applied and Computational Harmonic Analysis*, **34**(1), 30–56.

Ng, Andrew, et al. 2011. Sparse autoencoder. CS294A Lecture Notes, Stanford University.

Olshausen, Bruno A., and Field, David J. 1996. Emergence of simple-cell receptive field properties by learning a sparse code for natural images. *Nature*, **381**(6583), 607.

Olshausen, Bruno A., and Field, David J. 1997. Sparse coding with an overcomplete basis set: A strategy employed by V1? *Vision Research*, **37**(23), 3311–3325.

Papyan, Vardan, Romano, Yaniv, and Elad, Michael. 2017a. Convolutional neural networks analyzed via convolutional sparse coding. *Journal of Machine Learning Research*, **18**(1), 2887–2938.

Papyan, Vardan, Sulam, Jeremias, and Elad, Michael. 2017b. Working locally thinking globally: Theoretical guarantees for convolutional sparse coding. *IEEE Transactions on Signal Processing*, **65**(21), 5687–5701.

Papyan, Vardan, Romano, Yaniv, Sulam, Jeremias, and Elad, Michael. 2018. Theoretical foundations of deep learning via sparse representations: A multilayer sparse model and its connection to convolutional neural networks. *IEEE Signal Processing Magazine*, **35**(4), 72–89.

Patel, Ankit B., Nguyen, Minh Tan, and Baraniuk, Richard. 2016. A probabilistic framework for deep learning. Pages 2558–2566 of: *Advances in Neural Information Processing Systems*.

Patel, Vishal M., Chen, Yi-Chen, Chellappa, Rama, and Phillips, P. Jonathon. 2014. Dictionaries for image and video-based face recognition. *Journal of the Optical Society of America A*, **31**(5), 1090–1103.

Pati, Yagyensh Chandra, Rezaiifar, Ramin, and Krishnaprasad, Perinkulam Sambamurthy. 1993. Orthogonal matching pursuit: Recursive function approximation with applications to wavelet decomposition. Pages 40–44 of: *Conference Record of the 27th Asilomar Conference on Signals, Systems and Computers, 1993*. IEEE.

Ranzato, MarcÁurelio, Poultney, Christopher, Chopra, Sumit, LeCun, Yann, et al. 2007. Efficient learning of sparse representations with an energy-based model. Pages 1137–1144 of: *Advances in Neural Information Processing Systems*.

Ranzato, MarcÁurelio, Boureau, Y-Lan, and LeCun, Yann. 2008. Sparse feature learning for deep belief networks. Pages 1185–1192 of: *Advances in Neural Information Processing Systems*.

Romano, Yaniv, and Elad, Michael. 2018. Classification stability for sparse-modeled signals. ArXiv preprint arXiv:1805.11596.

Romano, Yaniv, Protter, Matan, and Elad, Michael. 2014. Single image interpolation via adaptive nonlocal sparsity-based modeling. *IEEE Transactions on Image Processing*, **23**(7), 3085–3098.

Rumelhart, David E., Hinton, Geoffrey E., and Williams, Ronald J. 1986. Learning representations by back-propagating errors. *Nature*, **323**(6088), 533.

Shrivastava, Ashish, Patel, Vishal M., and Chellappa, Rama. 2014. Multiple kernel learning for sparse representation-based classification. *IEEE Transactions on Image Processing*, **23**(7), 3013–3024.

Sulam, J., Aberdam, A., Beck, A. and Elad, M. 1980. On multi-layer basis pursuit, efficient algorithms and convolutional neural networks. *IEEE Transactions on Pattern Analysis and Machine Intelligence*, **42**(8), 1968–1980.

Sulam, Jeremias, Ophir, Boaz, and Elad, Michael. 2014. Image denoising through multi-scale learnt dictionaries. Pages 808–812 of: *Proc. International Conference on Image Processing*. IEEE.

Sulam, Jeremias, Ophir, Boaz, Zibulevsky, Michael, and Elad, Michael. 2016. Trainlets: Dictionary learning in high dimensions. *IEEE Transactions on Signal Processing*, **64**(12), 3180–3193.

Sulam, Jeremias, Papyan, Vardan, Romano, Yaniv, and Elad, Michael. 2018. Multilayer convolutional sparse modeling: Pursuit and dictionary learning. *IEEE Transactions on Signal Processing*, **66**(15), 4090–4104.

Sulam, Jeremias, Aberdam, Aviad, Beck, Amir, and Elad, Michael. 2020. On multi-layer basis pursuit, efficient algorithms and convolutional neural networks.

IEEE Transactions on Pattern Recognition and Machine Intelligence, **42**(8), 1968–1980.

Tropp, Joel A. 2004. Greed is good: Algorithmic results for sparse approximation. *IEEE Transactions on Information theory*, **50**(10), 2231–2242.

Tropp, Joel A. 2006. Just relax: Convex programming methods for identifying sparse signals in noise. *IEEE Transactions on Information Theory*, **52**(3), 1030–1051.

Vaiter, Samuel, Peyré, Gabriel, Dossal, Charles, and Fadili, Jalal. 2013. Robust sparse analysis regularization. *IEEE Transactions on Information Theory*, **59**(4), 2001–2016.

8

The Scattering Transform

Joan Bruna

Abstract: In this chapter we present scattering representations, a signal representation built using wavelet multiscale decompositions with a deep convolutional architecture. Its construction highlights the fundamental role of geometric stability in deep learning representations, and provides a mathematical basis to study convolutional neural networks (CNNs). We describe its main mathematical properties, its applications to computer vision, speech recognition and physical sciences, as well as its extensions to Lie groups and non-Euclidean domains. Finally, we discuss recent applications to the modeling of high-dimensional probability densities.

8.1 Introduction

Understanding the success of deep learning in challenging data domains, such as computer vision, speech recognition or natural language processing, remains a major unanswered question that requires a tight integration of different theoretical aspects of the learning algorithm: approximation, estimation and optimization. Amongst the many pieces responsible for such success, an important element comes from the extra structure built into the neural architecture as a result of the input signal structure. Images, sounds and text are signals defined over low-dimensional domains such as grids or their continuous Euclidean counterparts. In these domains one can articulate specific priors of data distributions and tasks, which are leveraged in neural networks through convolutional layers.

This requires developing a signal processing theory of deep learning. In order to gain a mathematical understanding of the interplay between geometric properties of the input domain and convolutional architectures, in this chapter we set aside the optimization and data-adaptivity pieces of the puzzle and take an axiomatic approach to building high-dimensional signal representations with prescribed properties that make them amenable to complex recognition and classification tasks.

The first step is to develop the notion of geometric stability (§8.2). In essence,

338

a signal representation defined on a metric domain is geometrically stable if small perturbations in the metric structure result in small changes in the output features. In Euclidean domains, geometric stability can be expressed in terms of diffeomorphisms, which model many naturally occurring transformations in computer vision and speech recognition, such as changes in viewpoint, local translations or musical pitch transpositions.

Stability with respect to the action of diffeomorphisms is achieved by separating scales, leading to multiscale signal decompositions. Section 8.3 describes scattering representations on the Euclidean translation group. First introduced in Mallat (2012), they combine wavelet multiscale decompositions with pointwise modulus activation functions. We describe their main mathematical properties and applications to computer vision. Scattering transforms are natural generalizations of multiscale representations of stochastic processes, in which classical high-order polynomial moments are replaced by stable non-linear transforms. Section 8.4 reviews stochastic scattering representations and their main applications to multifractal analysis.

Euclidean scattering representations serve as a mathematical basis for studying CNNs on image and audio domains. In many areas of physical and social sciences, however, data are rarely defined over regular Euclidean domains. As it turns out, one can extend the formalism of geometric stability and wavelet scattering representations in two important directions: first, to more general Lie groups of transformations (§8.5), and then to graphs and manifolds (§8.5.3).

We conclude this chapter by focusing on two important applications of scattering representations. Thanks to their ability to capture key geometrical properties of high-dimensional signals with stability guarantees, they may be used in unsupervised learning to perform high-dimensional density estimation and implicit modeling, as described in §8.6.

8.2 Geometric Stability

This ection describes the notion of geometric stability in signal representations. We begin with the Euclidean setting (§8.2.1), where this stability is expressed in terms of diffeomorphisms of the signal domain. We discuss how to extend this notion to general metric domains in §8.2.3, and then highlight the limitations of several standard high-dimensional signal representations in regards to geometric stability (§8.2.4).

8.2.1 Euclidean Geometric Stability

Consider a compact d-dimensional Euclidean domain $\Omega = [0,1]^d \subset \mathbb{R}^d$ on which square-integrable functions $\mathbf{x} \in L^2(\Omega)$ are defined (for example, in image analysis applications, images can be thought of as functions on the unit square $\Omega = [0,1]^2$). We consider a generic supervised learning setting, in which an unknown function $f: L^2(\Omega) \to \mathcal{Y}$ is observed on a training set $\{\mathbf{x}_i \in L^2(\Omega), f_i = f(\mathbf{x}_i)\}_{i \in I}$. In the vast majority of computer vision and speech analysis tasks, the unknown function f satisfies crucial regularity properties expressed in terms of the signal domain Ω.

Global translation invariance. Let $\mathcal{T}_v \mathbf{x}(u) = \mathbf{x}(u - v)$, with $u, v \in \Omega$, be a *translation operator*[1] acting on functions $\mathbf{x} \in L^2(\Omega)$. Our first assumption is that the function f is either *invariant*, i.e., $f(\mathcal{T}_v \mathbf{x}) = f(\mathbf{x})$ for any $\mathbf{x} \in L^2(\Omega)$ and $v \in \Omega$, or *equivariant*, i.e., $f(\mathcal{T}_v \mathbf{x}) = \mathcal{T}_v f(\mathbf{x})$, with respect to translations, depending on the task. Translation invariance is typical in object classification tasks, whereas equivariance arises when the output of the model is a space in which translations can act upon (for example, in problems of object localization, semantic segmentation, or motion estimation).

The notions of global invariance and equivariance can be easily extended to other transformation groups beyond translations. We discuss in §8.5 one such extension, to the group of rigid motions generated by translations and rotations in Ω.

However, global invariance is not a strong prior in the face of high-dimensional estimation. Ineed, global transformation groups are typically low dimensional; in particular, in signal processing, they often correspond to subgroups of the affine group $\mathrm{Aff}(\Omega)$, with dimension $O(d^2)$. A much stronger prior may be defined by specifying how the function f behaves under geometric perturbations of the domain which are 'nearby' these global transformation groups.

Local deformations and scale separation. In particular, given a smooth vector field $\tau: \Omega \to \Omega$, a deformation by τ acts on $L^2(\Omega)$ as $\mathbf{x}_\tau(u) := \mathbf{x}(u - \tau(u))$. Deformations can model local translations, changes in viewpoint, rotations and frequency transpositions (Bruna and Mallat, 2013) and have been extensively used as models of image variability in computer vision (Jain et al., 1996; Felzenszwalb et al., 2010; Girshick et al., 2014). Most tasks studied in computer vision are not only translation invariant/equivariant but also stable with respect to local deformations (Mallat, 2016; Bruna and Mallat, 2013). In tasks that are translation invariant, the above prior may be expressed informally as

$$|f(\mathbf{x}_\tau) - f(\mathbf{x})| \approx \|\tau\|, \tag{8.1}$$

---

[1] Assuming periodic boundary conditions to ensure that the operation is well defined over $L^2(\Omega)$.

for all $\mathbf{x}, \tau$. Here, $\|\tau\|$ measures the distance of the associated diffeomorphism $\varphi(u) := u - \tau(u)$ to the translation group; we will see in the next section how to specify this metric in the space of diffeomorphisms. In other words, the target to be predicted does not change much if the input image is slightly deformed. In tasks that are translation equivariant, we have $|f(\mathbf{x}_\tau) - f_\tau(\mathbf{x})| \approx \|\tau\|$ instead. The deformation stability property is much stronger than that of global invariance, since the space of local deformations has high dimensionality, as opposed to the group of global invariants.

Besides this deformation stability, another key property of target functions arising from the physical world is that long-range dependences may be broken into multiscale local interaction terms, leading to hierarchical models in which the spatial resolution is progressively reduced. To illustrate this principle, denote by

$$q(z_1, z_2; v) = \text{Prob}(\mathbf{x}(u) = z_1 \text{ and } \mathbf{x}(u + v) = z_2) \tag{8.2}$$

the joint distribution of two image pixels at an offset v from each other, where we have assumed a stationary statistical model for natural images (hence q does not depend upon the location u). In presence of long-range dependencies, this joint distribution will not be separable for any v. However, the deformation stability prior states that $q(z_1, z_2; v) \approx q(z_1, z_2; v(1 + \epsilon))$ for small ϵ. In other words, whereas long-range dependencies do indeed exist in natural images and are critical to object recognition, they can be captured and downsampled at different scales.

This principle of stability with respect to local deformations has been exploited in the computer vision community in models other than CNNs, for instance, deformable-parts models (Felzenszwalb et al., 2010), as we will review next. In practice, the Euclidean domain Ω is discretized using a regular grid with n points; the translation and deformation operators are still well-defined so the above properties hold in the discrete setting.

8.2.2 Representations with Euclidean Geometric Stability

Motivated by the previous geometric stability prior, we are interested in building signal representations that are compatible with such a prior. Specifically, suppose our estimation for f, the target function, takes the form

$$\hat{f}(\mathbf{x}) := \langle \Phi(\mathbf{x}), \theta \rangle, \tag{8.3}$$

where $\Phi \colon L^2(\Omega) \to \mathbb{R}^K$ corresponds to the signal representation and $\theta \in \mathbb{R}^K$ to the classification or regression coefficients, respectively. In a CNN, one would associate Φ with the operator that maps the input to the final hidden layer, and θ with the final output layer of the network.

The linear relationship between $\Phi(\mathbf{x})$ and $\hat{f}(\mathbf{x})$ above implies that geometric stability in the representation is sufficient to guarantee a predictor which is also geometrically stable. Indeed, if we assume that

$$\text{for all } \mathbf{x}, \tau \,, \; \|\Phi(\mathbf{x}) - \Phi(\mathbf{x}_\tau)\| \lesssim \|\mathbf{x}\|\|\tau\| \,, \tag{8.4}$$

then by Cauchy–Schwarz, it follows that

$$|\hat{f}(\mathbf{x}) - \hat{f}(\mathbf{x}_\tau)| \le \|\theta\|\|\Phi(\mathbf{x}) - \Phi(\mathbf{x}_\tau)\| \lesssim \|\theta\|\|\mathbf{x}\|\|\tau\| \,.$$

This motivates the study of signal representations where one can certify (8.4), while ensuring that Φ captures enough information that $\|\Phi(\mathbf{x}) - \Phi(\mathbf{x}')\|$ is large whenever $|f(\mathbf{x}) - f(\mathbf{x}')|$ is large. In this setting, a notorious challenge to achieving (8.4) while keeping enough discriminative power in $\Phi(\mathbf{x})$ is to transform the high-frequency content of $\mathbf{x}$ in such a way that it becomes stable.

In recognition tasks, one may want to consider not only geometric stability but also stability with respect to the Euclidean metric in $L^2(\Omega)$:

$$\text{for all } \mathbf{x}, \mathbf{x}' \in L^2(\Omega), \quad \|\Phi(\mathbf{x}) - \Phi(\mathbf{x}')\| \lesssim \|\mathbf{x} - \mathbf{x}'\| \,. \tag{8.5}$$

This stability property ensures that additive noise in the input will not drastically change the feature representation.

The stability desiderata (8.4) and (8.5) may also be interpreted in terms of robustness to adversarial examples (Szegedy et al., 2014). Indeed, the general setup of adversarial examples consists in producing small perturbations $\mathbf{x}'$ of a given input $\mathbf{x}$ (measured by appropriate norms) such that $|\langle\Phi(\mathbf{x}) - \Phi(\mathbf{x}'), \theta\rangle|$ is large. Stable representations certify that those adversarial examples cannot be obtained with small additive or geometric perturbations.

8.2.3 Non-Euclidean Geometric Stability

Whereas Euclidean domains may be used to model many signals of interest, such as images, videos or speech, a wide range of high-dimensional data across the physical and social sciences is naturally defined on more general geometries. For example, signals measured on social networks have rich geometrical structure, encoding locality and multiscale properties, yet they have a non-Euclidean geometry. An important question is thus how to extend the notion of geometrical stability to more general domains.

Deformations provide the natural framework for describing geometric stability in Euclidean domains, but their generalization to non-Euclidean, non-smooth domains is not straightforward. Let $\mathbf{x} \in L^2(X)$ be a signal defined on a domain X. If X is embedded into a low-dimension Euclidean space $\Omega \subset \mathbb{R}^d$, such as a 2-surface within a three-dimensional space, then one can still define meaningful deformations on X via *extrinsic* deformations of Ω. Indeed, if $\tau \colon \mathbb{R}^d \to \mathbb{R}^d$ is a smooth field with

$\varphi(v) = v - \tau(v)$ the corresponding diffeomorphism (assuming $\|\tau\| < 1/2$), then we can define $\mathbf{x}_\tau \in L^2(\mathcal{X}_\tau)$ as

$$\mathbf{x}_\tau(u) := \mathbf{x}(\varphi^{-1}(u)), \quad u \in \mathcal{X}.$$

Such deformation models were studied in Kostrikov et al. (2018) with applications in surface representation in which the notion of geometric stability relies on its ambient Euclidean structure.

In more general applications, however, we may be interested in intrinsic notions of geometric stability that do not necessarily rely on a pre-existing low-dimensional embedding of the domain. The change of variables $\varphi(u) = u - \tau(u)$ defining the deformation can be seen as a perturbation of the Euclidean metric in $L^2(\mathbb{R}^d)$. Indeed,

$$\langle \mathbf{x}_\tau, \mathbf{y}_\tau \rangle_{L^2(\mathbb{R}^d,\mu)} = \int_{\mathbb{R}^d} \mathbf{x}_\tau(u)\mathbf{y}_\tau(u)d\mu(u) = \int_{\mathbb{R}^d} \mathbf{x}(u)\mathbf{y}(u)|I - \nabla\tau(u)|d\mu(u)$$

$$= \langle \mathbf{x}, \mathbf{y} \rangle_{L^2(\mathbb{R}^d,\tilde{\mu})},$$

with $d\tilde{\mu}(u) = |I - \nabla\tau(u)|d\mu(u)$ and $|I - \nabla\tau(u)| \approx 1$ if $\|\nabla\tau\|$ is small, where I is the identity. Therefore, a possible way to extend the notion of deformation stability to general domains $L^2(\mathcal{X})$ is to think of $\mathcal{X}$ as a metric space and reason in terms of the stability of $\Phi\colon L^2(\mathcal{X}) \to \mathbb{R}^K$ to *metric changes* in $\mathcal{X}$. This requires a representation that can be defined on generic metric spaces, as well as a criterion for comparing how close two metric spaces are to each other. We will describe a general approach for discrete metric spaces that is based on diffusion operators in §8.5.3.

8.2.4 *Examples*

Kernel Methods

Kernel methods refer to a general theory in the machine learning framework, whose main purpose consists in embedding data in a high-dimensional space, in order to express complex relationships in terms of linear scalar products.

For a generic input space $\mathcal{Z}$ (which can be thought of as $\mathcal{Z} = L^2(\mathcal{X})$, corresponding to the previous discussion), a *feature map* $\Phi\colon \mathcal{Z} \longrightarrow \mathcal{H}$ maps data into a Hilbert space $\mathcal{H}$ with the reproducing property: for each $f \in \mathcal{H}$ and $\mathbf{x} \in \mathcal{Z}$, $f(\mathbf{x}) = \langle f, \Phi(\mathbf{x}) \rangle$. Linear classification methods access the transformed data $\Phi(\mathbf{x})$ only through scalar products of the form (Shawe-Taylor and Cristianini, 2004)

$$\langle \Phi(\mathbf{x}), \Phi(\mathbf{x}') \rangle .$$

Rather than building the mapping explicitly, the popular 'kernel trick' exploits Mercer's theorem. This theorem states that a continuous, symmetric and positive definite kernel $K\colon \mathcal{Z} \times \mathcal{Z} \to \mathbb{R}$ defines an integral operator of $L^2(\mathcal{Z})$, which diagonalizes in an orthonormal basis (Minh et al., 2006) $\{\phi_n\}_n$ of $L^2(\mathcal{Z})$, with non-negative eigenvalues. As a result, $K(\mathbf{x}, \mathbf{x}')$ admits a representation

$$K(\mathbf{x}, \mathbf{x}') = \sum_{n \geq 1} \lambda_n \phi_n(\mathbf{x}) \phi_n(\mathbf{x}'),$$

which yields

$$K(\mathbf{x}, \mathbf{x}') = \langle \Phi(\mathbf{x}), \Phi(\mathbf{x}') \rangle,$$

with $\Phi(\mathbf{x}) = (\lambda_n^{1/2} \phi_n(\mathbf{x}))_n$. For kernel methods it is thus sufficient to construct positive definite kernels K on $\mathcal{Z}^2$ in order to extend linear classification tools to more complex relationships.

Despite their success and effectiveness in a number of machine learning tasks, the high-dimensional embeddings induced by kernel methods do not automatically enjoy stability with respect to additive noise or deformations. The kernel needs to be chosen accordingly. *Convolutional kernels networks* (Mairal et al., 2014; Bietti and Mairal, 2019a) have been developed to capture geometric stability properties and to offer empirical performance competitive with modern deep architectures. These kernels contrast with another recent family, that of *neural tangent kernels* (Jacot et al., 2018), which linearize a generic deep architecture around its parameter initialization but which do not offer the same amount of geometric stability (Bietti and Mairal, 2019b).

Power Spectra, Autocorrelation and Registration Invariants

Translation invariant representations can be obtained from registration, auto-correlation or Fourier modulus operators. However, the resulting representations are not Lipschitz continuous to deformations.

A representation $\Phi(\mathbf{x})$ is translation invariant if it maps global translations, $\mathbf{x}_c(u) = \mathbf{x}(u - c)$, with $c \in \mathbb{R}^d$, of any function $x \in L^2(\mathbb{R}^d)$ to the same image:

$$\text{for all } \mathbf{x} \in L^2(\mathbb{R}^d), \text{ for all } c \in \mathbb{R}^d, \quad \Phi(\mathbf{x}_c) = \Phi(\mathbf{x}). \tag{8.6}$$

The Fourier transform modulus is an example of a translation invariant representation. Let $\hat{x}(\omega)$ be the Fourier transform of $\mathbf{x}(u) \in L^2(\mathbb{R}^d)$. Since $\widehat{x_c}(\omega) = e^{-ic.\omega} \hat{x}(\omega)$, it follows that $|\widehat{x_c}| = |\hat{x}|$ does not depend upon c.

A Fourier modulus is translation invariant and stable to additive noise, but unstable to small deformations at high frequencies (Mallat, 2012), as is illustrated with the following dilation example. Let $\tau(u) = su$ denote a linear displacement field, where $|s|$ is small, and let $\mathbf{x}(u) = e^{i\xi u}\theta(u)$ be a modulated version of a low-pass window $\theta(u)$. Then the dilation $\mathbf{x}_\tau(u) = L[\tau]\mathbf{x}(u) = \mathbf{x}((1 + s)u)$ moves the central frequency of $\hat{\mathbf{x}}$ from ξ to $(1 + s)\xi$. If $\sigma_\theta^2 = \int |\omega|^2 |\hat{\theta}(\omega)|^2 \, d\omega$ measures the frequency spread of θ then

$$\sigma_x^2 = \int |\omega - \xi|^2 |\hat{x}(\omega)|^2 d\omega = \sigma_\theta^2,$$

and

$$\sigma_{x_\tau}^2 = (1+s)^{-d} \int (\omega - (1+s)\xi)^2 |\hat{x}((1+s)^{-1}\omega)|^2 d\omega$$

$$= \int |(1+s)(\omega - \xi)|^2 |\hat{x}(\omega)|^2 d\omega = (1+s)^2 \sigma_x^2.$$

It follows that if the distance between the central frequencies of $\mathbf{x}$ and $\mathbf{x}_\tau$, $s\xi$, is large compared with their frequency spreads, $(2+s)\sigma_\theta$, then the frequency supports of $\mathbf{x}$ and $\mathbf{x}_\tau$ are nearly disjoint and hence

$$|||\hat{\mathbf{x}}_\tau| - |\hat{\mathbf{x}}||| \sim ||\mathbf{x}||,$$

which shows that $\Phi(\mathbf{x}) = |\hat{\mathbf{x}}|$ is not Lipschitz continuous to deformations, since ξ can be arbitrarily large.

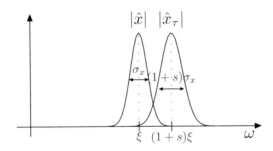

Figure 8.1 Dilation of a complex bandpass window. If $\xi \gg \sigma_x s^{-1}$ then the supports are nearly disjoint.

The autocorrelation of $\mathbf{x}$,

$$R_{\mathbf{x}}(v) = \int \mathbf{x}(u)\mathbf{x}^*(u - v)\, du,$$

is also translation invariant: $R_{\mathbf{x}} = R_{\mathbf{x}_c}$. Since $R_{\mathbf{x}}(v) = \mathbf{x} \star \overline{\mathbf{x}}(v)$, with $\overline{\mathbf{x}}(u) = \mathbf{x}^*(-u)$, it follows that $\widehat{R_{\mathbf{x}}}(\omega) = |\hat{x}(\omega)|^2$. The Plancherel formula thus proves that it has the same instabilities as a Fourier transform:

$$||R_{\mathbf{x}} - R_{\mathbf{x}_\tau}|| = (2\pi)^{-1} \left|\left| |\hat{\mathbf{x}}|^2 - |\hat{\mathbf{x}}_\tau|^2 \right|\right|.$$

Besides deformation instabilities, the Fourier modulus and the autocorrelation lose too much information. For example, a Dirac $\delta(u)$ and a linear chirp e^{iu^2} are two signals having Fourier transforms whose moduli are equal and constant. Very different signals may not be discriminated from their Fourier moduli.

A canonical invariant (Keysers et al., 2007; Soatto, 2009) $\Phi(\mathbf{x}) = \mathbf{x}(u - a(\mathbf{x}))$ registers $\mathbf{x} \in \mathbf{L}^2(\mathbb{R}^d)$ with an anchor point $a(\mathbf{x})$, which is translated when $\mathbf{x}$ is translated:

$$a(\mathbf{x}_c) = a(\mathbf{x}) + c .$$

It thus defines a translation invariant representation: $\Phi \mathbf{x}_c = \Phi \mathbf{x}$. For example, the anchor point may be a filtered maximum $a(\mathbf{x}) = \arg\max_u |\mathbf{x} \star h(u)|$, for some filter $h(u)$. A canonical invariant $\Phi \mathbf{x}(u) = \mathbf{x}(u - a(\mathbf{x}))$ carries more information than a Fourier modulus, and characterizes $\mathbf{x}$ up to a global absolute position (Soatto, 2009). However, it has the same high-frequency instability as a Fourier modulus transform. Indeed, for any choice of anchor point $a(\mathbf{x})$, applying the Plancherel formula proves that

$$\|\mathbf{x}(u - a(\mathbf{x})) - \mathbf{x}'(u - a(\mathbf{x}'))\| \geq (2\pi)^{-1} \|\,|\hat{\mathbf{x}}(\omega)| - |\hat{\mathbf{x}}'(\omega)|\,\| .$$

If $\mathbf{x}' = \mathbf{x}_\tau$, the Fourier transform instability at high frequencies implies that $\Phi \mathbf{x} = \mathbf{x}(u - a(\mathbf{x}))$ is also unstable with respect to deformations.

8.3 Scattering on the Translation Group

This section reviews the scattering transform on the translation group and its mathematical properties. In §8.3.1 we discuss windowed scattering transforms and its construction from Littlewood–Paley wavelet decompositions. In §8.3.2 we introduce the scattering metric and review the scattering energy conservation property, and in §8.3.3 we describe the Lipschitz continuity property of scattering transforms with respect to deformations. Section 8.3.4 presents algorithmic aspects and implementation, and finally §8.3.5 illustrates scattering properties in computer vision applications.

8.3.1 Windowed Scattering Transform

A wavelet transform is defined by dilating a mother wavelet $\psi \in \mathbf{L}^2(\mathbb{R}^d)$ with scale factors $\{a^j\}_{j \in \mathbb{Z}}$ for $a > 1$. In image processing applications one usually sets $a = 2$, whereas audio applications need smaller dilation factors, typically $a \leq 2^{1/8}$. Wavelets can be not only dilated but also rotated along a discrete rotation group G of $\mathbb{R}^d$. As a result, a dilation by a^j and a rotation by $r \in G$ of ψ produce

$$\psi_{a^j r}(u) = a^{-dj}\psi(a^{-j}r^{-1}u) . \tag{8.7}$$

Wavelets are thus normalized in $\mathbf{L}^1(\mathbb{R}^d)$, so that $\|\psi_{a^j r}\|_1 = \|\psi\|_1$, which means that their Fourier transforms satisfy $\hat{\psi}_{a^j r}(\omega) = \hat{\psi}(a^j r \omega)$. In order to simplify notation, we write $\lambda = a^j r \in a^{\mathbb{Z}} \times G$ and $|\lambda| = a^j$ and define $\psi_\lambda(u) = a^{-dj} \psi(\lambda^{-1} u)$. This notation will be used throughout the rest of the chapter.

Scattering operators can be defined for general mother wavelets, but of particular interest are the complex wavelets that can be written as

$$\psi(u) = e^{i \eta u} \theta(u) ,$$

where θ is a lowpass window whose Fourier transform is real and has a bandwidth of the order of π. As a result, after a dilation and a rotation, $\hat{\psi}_\lambda(\omega) = \hat{\theta}(\lambda \omega - \eta)$ is centered at $\lambda^{-1} \eta$ and has a support size proportional to $|\lambda|^{-1}$. In §8.3.4 we shall specify the wavelet families used in all numerical experiments.

A Littlewood–Paley wavelet transform is a redundant representation which computes the following filter bank, without subsampling:

$$\text{for all } u \in \mathbb{R}^d \text{ and } \lambda \in a^{\mathbb{Z}} \times G, \quad W_\lambda \mathbf{x}(u) = \mathbf{x} \star \psi_\lambda(u) = \int \mathbf{x}(v) \psi_\lambda(u - v) \, dv . \quad (8.8)$$

If $\mathbf{x}$ is real and the wavelet is chosen such that $\hat{\psi}$ is also real then $W_{-\lambda} \mathbf{x} = W_\lambda \mathbf{x}^*$, which implies that in this case one can assimilate a rotation r with its negative version $-r$ into an equivalence class of positive rotations $G^+ = G/\{\pm 1\}$.

A wavelet transform with a finite scale 2^J considers only the subbands λ satisfying $|\lambda| \le 2^J$. The low frequencies which are not captured by these wavelets are recovered by a lowpass filter ϕ_J whose spatial support is proportional to 2^J: $\phi_J(u) = 2^{-dJ} \phi(2^{-J} u)$. The wavelet transform at scale 2^J thus consists of the filter bank

$$\mathcal{W}_J \mathbf{x} = \{\mathbf{x} \star \phi_J, (W_\lambda \mathbf{x})_{\lambda \in \Lambda_J}\} ,$$

where $\Lambda_J = \{a^j r : r \in G^+, |\lambda| \le 2^J\}$. Its norm is defined as

$$\|\mathcal{W}_J \mathbf{x}\|^2 = \|\mathbf{x} \star \phi_J\|^2 + \sum_{\lambda \in \Lambda_J} \|W_\lambda \mathbf{x}\|^2 .$$

Thus $\mathcal{W}_J$ is a linear operator from $\mathbf{L}^2(\mathbb{R}^d)$ to a product space generated by copies of $\mathbf{L}^2(\mathbb{R}^d)$. It defines a frame of $\mathbf{L}^2(\mathbb{R}^d)$, whose bounds are characterized by the following Littlewood–Paley condition:

Proposition 8.1. *If there exists $\epsilon > 0$ such that, for almost all $\omega \in \mathbb{R}^d$ and all $J \in \mathbb{Z}$,*

$$1 - \epsilon \le |\hat{\phi}(2^J \omega)|^2 + \frac{1}{2} \sum_{j \le J} \sum_{r \in G} |\hat{\psi}(2^j r \omega)|^2 \le 1 ,$$

then $\mathcal{W}_J$ is a frame with bounds given by $1 - \epsilon$ and 1:

$$(1 - \epsilon)\|\mathbf{x}\|^2 \leq \|\mathcal{W}_J\mathbf{x}\|^2 \leq \|\mathbf{x}\|^2, \quad \mathbf{x} \in \mathbf{L}^2(\mathbb{R}^d). \tag{8.9}$$

In particular, this Littlewood–Paley condition implies that $\hat{\psi}(0) = 0$ and hence that the wavelet must have at least a vanishing moment. When $\epsilon = 0$, the wavelet decomposition preserves the Euclidean norm and we say that it is unitary.

Wavelet coefficients are not translation invariant but translate as the input is translated, and their average $\int W_\lambda \mathbf{x}(u)\, du$ does not produce any information since wavelets have zero mean. A translation invariant measure which is also stable to the action of diffeomorphisms can be extracted out of each wavelet sub-band λ, by introducing a non-linearity which restores a non-zero, informative, average value. This is for instance achieved by computing the complex modulus and averaging the result:

$$\int |\mathbf{x} \star \psi_\lambda|(u)\, du. \tag{8.10}$$

Although many other choices of non-linearity are algorithmically possible, the complex modulus preserves the signal energy and enables overall energy conservation; see the next section, and finally in §8.7, how half-rectified alternatives provide further insights into the signal through the phase harmonics.

The information lost by the averaging in (8.10) is recovered by a new wavelet decomposition $\{|\mathbf{x} \star \psi_\lambda| \star \psi_{\lambda'}\}_{\lambda' \in \Lambda_J}$ of $|\mathbf{x} \star \psi_\lambda|$, which produces new invariants by iterating the same procedure. Let $U[\lambda]\mathbf{x} = |\mathbf{x} \star \psi_\lambda|$ denote the wavelet modulus operator corresponding to the subband λ. Any sequence $p = (\lambda_1, \lambda_2, \ldots, \lambda_m)$ defines a *path*, i.e., the ordered product of non-linear and non-commuting operators

$$U[p]\mathbf{x} = U[\lambda_m] \cdots U[\lambda_2]\, U[\lambda_1]\mathbf{x} = |\cdots \||\mathbf{x} \star \psi_{\lambda_1}| \star \psi_{\lambda_2}| \cdots | \star \psi_{\lambda_m}|,$$

with $U[\emptyset]\mathbf{x} = \mathbf{x}$.

As with frequency variables, path variables $p = (\lambda_1, \ldots, \lambda_m)$ can be manipulated in a number of ways. The scaling and rotation by $a^l g \in a^{\mathbb{Z}} \times G^+$ of a path p is denoted by $a^l g p = (a^l g \lambda_1, \ldots, a^l g \lambda_m)$, and the concatenation of two paths is written as $p + p' = (\lambda_1, \ldots, \lambda_m, \lambda'_1, \ldots, \lambda'_{m'})$.

Many applications in image and audio recognition require representations that are locally translation invariant, but which keep spatial or temporal information beyond a certain scale 2^J. A windowed scattering transform computes a locally translation invariant representation by applying a low-pass filter at scale 2^J with $\phi_{2^J}(u) = 2^{-2J}\phi(2^{-J}u)$.

Definition 8.2. For each path $p = (\lambda_1, \ldots, \lambda_m)$ with $\lambda_i \in \Lambda_J$ and $\mathbf{x} \in \mathbf{L}^1(\mathbb{R}^d)$ we

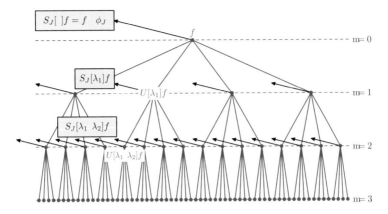

Figure 8.2 Convolutional structure of the windowed scattering transform. Each layer is computed from the previous one by applying a wavelet modulus decomposition U to each envelope $U[p]\mathbf{x}$. The outputs of each layer are obtained via a low-pass filter ϕ_J.

define the windowed scattering transform as

$$S_J[p]\mathbf{x}(u) = U[p]\mathbf{x} \star \phi_{2^J}(u) = \int U[p]\mathbf{x}(v)\phi_{2^J}(u - v)\, dv .$$

A scattering transform has the structure of a convolutional network, but its filters are given by wavelets instead of being learned. Thanks to this structure, the resulting transform is locally translation invariant and stable to deformations, as will be discussed in §8.3.3. The scattering representation enjoys several appealing properties that are described in the following subsections.

8.3.2 Scattering Metric and Energy Conservation

The windowed scattering representation is obtained by cascading a basic propagator operator,

$$\mathcal{U}_J\mathbf{x} = \{\mathbf{x} \star \phi_J, (U[\lambda]\mathbf{x})_{\lambda \in \Lambda_J}\} . \tag{8.11}$$

The first layer of the representation applies $\mathcal{U}_J$ to the input function, whereas successive layers are obtained by applying $\mathcal{U}_J$ to each output $U[p]\mathbf{x}$. Since $U[\lambda]U[p] = U[p + \lambda]$ and $U[p]\mathbf{x} \star \phi_J = S_J[p]\mathbf{x}$, it follows that

$$\mathcal{U}_J U[p]\mathbf{x} = \{S_J[p]\mathbf{x}, (U[p + \lambda]\mathbf{x})_{\lambda \in \Lambda_J}\} . \tag{8.12}$$

If Λ_J^m denotes the set of paths of length or *order m*, it follows from (8.12) that the $(m+1)$th layer, given by Λ_J^{m+1}, is obtained from the previous layer via the propagator $\mathcal{U}_J$. We denote by $\mathcal{P}_J$ the set of paths of any order up to scale 2^J, $\mathcal{P}_J = \bigcup_m \Lambda_J^m$.

The propagator $\mathcal{U}_J$ is non-expansive since the wavelet decomposition $\mathcal{W}_J$ is non-expansive, from (8.9), and the modulus is also non-expansive. As a result,

$$\|\mathcal{U}_J\mathbf{x} - \mathcal{U}_J\mathbf{x}'\|^2 = \|\mathbf{x} \star \phi_J - \mathbf{x}' \star \phi_J\|^2 + \sum_{\lambda \in \Lambda_J} \||W_\lambda \mathbf{x}| - |W_\lambda \mathbf{x}'|\|^2 \leq \|\mathbf{x} - \mathbf{x}'\|^2 .$$

Moreover, if the wavelet decomposition is unitary then the propagator $\mathcal{U}_J$ is also unitary.

For any path set Ω, the Euclidean norm defined by the scattering coefficients $S_J[p]$, $p \in \Omega$, is

$$\|S_J[\Omega]\mathbf{x}\|^2 = \sum_{p \in \Omega} \|S_J[p]\mathbf{x}\|^2 .$$

Since $S_J[\mathcal{P}_J]$ is constructed by cascading the non-expansive operator $\mathcal{U}_J$, it follows that $S_J[\mathcal{P}_J]$ is also non-expansive:

Proposition 8.3. *The windowed scattering transform is non-expansive:*

$$\text{for all } \mathbf{x}, \mathbf{x}' \in \mathbf{L}^2(\mathbb{R}^d), \qquad \|S_J[\mathcal{P}_J]\mathbf{x} - S_J[\mathcal{P}_J]\mathbf{x}'\| \leq \|\mathbf{x} - \mathbf{x}'\| . \qquad (8.13)$$

The windowed scattering thus defines a metric which is continuous with respect to the $\mathbf{L}^2(\mathbb{R}^d)$ Euclidean metric, and thus is stable to additive noise.

Let us now consider the case where the wavelet decomposition is unitary, i.e., $\epsilon = 0$ in (8.9). One can easily verify by induction on the path order $m = |p|$ that

$$\text{for all } m, \quad \|\mathbf{x}\|^2 = \sum_{|p| < m} \|S_J[p]\mathbf{x}\|^2 + \sum_{|p| = m} \|U[p]\mathbf{x}\|^2 .$$

This decomposition expresses the signal energy $\|\mathbf{x}\|^2$ in terms of coefficients captured by the first m layers of the scattering network and a residual energy $\mathcal{R}_{J,\mathbf{x}}(m) := \sum_{p \in \mathcal{P}_J : |p| = m} \|U[p]\mathbf{x}\|^2$. An important question with practical implications is how to understand the energy decay $\mathcal{R}_{J,\mathbf{x}}(m)$ as m grows, since this determines how many layers of processing are effectively needed to represent the input. In particular, the scattering representation is energy preserving if $\lim_{m \to \infty} \mathcal{R}_{J,\mathbf{x}}(m) = 0$.

This was established, under mild assumptions on the wavelet decomposition, for the univariate case $\mathbf{x} \in L^2(\mathbb{R})$ in Waldspurger (2017):

Theorem 8.4 (Waldspurger, 2017, Theorem 3.1). *Let $\{\psi_j\}_{j \in \mathbb{Z}}$ be a family of wavelets satisfying the Littlewood–Paley condition (8.9) and such that*

$$\text{for all } j, \omega > 0, \quad |\hat{\psi}_j(-\omega)| \leq |\hat{\psi}_j(\omega)|,$$

with strict inequality for each ω for at least one scale. Finally, we assume for some $\epsilon > 0$ that

$$\hat{\psi}(\omega) = O(|\omega|^{1+\epsilon}) .$$

Then, for any $J \in \mathbb{Z}$, there exists $r > 0$, $a > 1$ such that for all $m \geq 2$ and $f \in L^2(\mathbb{R})$ it holds that

$$\mathcal{R}_{J,\mathbf{x}}(m) \leq \|\mathbf{x}\|^2 - \|\mathbf{x} \star \chi_{ra^m}\|^2, \tag{8.14}$$

where χ_s is the Gaussian window $\chi_s(t) = \sqrt{\pi}s \exp(-(\pi st)^2)$.

In particular, this result establishes energy conservation, owing to the square integrability of $\hat{\mathbf{x}} \in L^2(\mathbb{R})$. But, importantly, it also provides a quantitative rate at which the energy decays within the network: the energy in the input signal carried by frequencies around 2^k disappears after $O(k)$ layers, leading to exponential energy decay. An earlier version of the energy conservation was established in Mallat (2012) for general input dimensions but under more restrictive admissibility conditions for the wavelet, and without the rate of convergence.

A similar energy conservation result, also with an exponential convergence rate, has been established for extensions of the scattering transform where the wavelet decomposition is replaced by other frames. Czaja and Li (2017) studied energy conservation for *uniform covering* frames, obtaining exponential convergence too. Wiatowski et al. (2017) generalized this result to more general frames that are also allowed to vary from one layer to the next.

8.3.3 Local Translation Invariance and Lipschitz Continuity with Respect to Deformations

The windowed scattering metric defined in the previous section is non-expansive, which gives stability to additive perturbations. In this subsection we review its geometric stability to the action of deformations, and its asymptotic translation invariance, as the localization scale 2^J increases.

Each choice of such a localization scale defines a metric

$$d_J(\mathbf{x}, \mathbf{x}') := \|S_J[\mathcal{P}_J]\mathbf{x} - S_J[\mathcal{P}_J]\mathbf{x}'\|.$$

An induction argument over the non-expansive Littlewood–Paley property (8.9) shows that the limit of d_J as $J \to \infty$ is well defined, thanks to the following non-expansive property:

Proposition 8.5 (Mallat, 2012, Proposition 2.9). *For all $\mathbf{x}, \mathbf{x}' \in \mathbf{L}^2(\mathbb{R}^d)$ and $J \in \mathbb{Z}$,*

$$\|S_{J+1}[\mathcal{P}_{J+1}]\mathbf{x} - S_{J+1}[\mathcal{P}_{J+1}]\mathbf{x}'\| \leq \|S_J[\mathcal{P}_J]\mathbf{x} - S_J[\mathcal{P}_J]\mathbf{x}'\|.$$

As a result, the sequence $(\|S_J[\mathcal{P}_J]\mathbf{x} - S_J[\mathcal{P}_J]\mathbf{x}'\|)_J$ is positive and non-increasing as J increases, and hence it converges.

In fact, under mild assumptions, this limit metric is translation invariant:

Theorem 8.6 (Mallat, 2012, Theorem 2.10). *Let $x_v(u) = x(u - v)$. Then for admissible scattering wavelets satisfying the assumptions of Theorem 8.4 it holds that*

$$\text{for all } \mathbf{x} \in \mathbf{L}^2(\mathbb{R}^d), \ c \in \mathbb{R}^d, \quad \lim_{J \to \infty} \|S_J[\mathcal{P}_J]x - S_J[\mathcal{P}_J]x_v\| = 0 \tag{8.15}$$

for $d = 1$.

Remark 8.7. This result is proved in Mallat (2012) for general dimensions d under stronger assumptions on the wavelets (admissibility condition (2.28) in Mallat, 2012). However, these stronger assumptions can be made unnecessary, by extending the result in Waldspurger (2017) to arbitrary d.

Remark 8.8. Wiatowski and Bölcskei (2017) described an interesting extension of Theorem 8.6 which holds for more general decomposition frames than wavelets that is based on the notion of *vertical* translation invariance. This refers to the asymptotic translation invariance enjoyed by mth-layer coefficients of the network, as m grows.

The translation invariance of the overall representation is based on two fundamental properties: (i) the equivariance of wavelet modulus decomposition operators with respect to translation, $\mathcal{U}_J \mathcal{T}_v \mathbf{x} = \mathcal{T}_v \mathcal{U}_J \mathbf{x}$, and (ii) the invariance provided by the local averaging operator $A_J \mathbf{x} := \mathbf{x} \star \phi_J$. Indeed, scattering coefficients up to order m are obtained by composing $\mathcal{U}_J$ up to m times followed by A_J. It follows that the translation invariance measured at order m is expressed as

$$\|S_J[\Lambda_J^m]\mathcal{T}_v\mathbf{x} - S_J[\Lambda_J^m]\mathbf{x}\| = \|A_J\mathcal{T}_vU[\Lambda_J^m]\mathbf{x} - A_JU[\Lambda_J^m]\mathbf{x}\|$$
$$\leq \|U[\Lambda_J^m]\mathbf{x}\| \|A_J\mathcal{T}_v - A_J\| .$$

As well as asymptotic translation invariance, the windowed scattering transform defines a stable metric with respect to the action of diffeomorphisms, which can model non-rigid deformations. A diffeomorphism maps a point $u \in \mathbb{R}^d$ to $u - \tau(u)$, where $\tau(u)$ is a vector displacement field satisfying $\|\nabla\tau\|_\infty < 1$, where $\|\nabla\tau\|$ is the operator norm. As described in §8.2.1, it acts on functions $\mathbf{x} \in \mathbf{L}^2(\mathbb{R}^d)$ by composition: $\mathbf{x}_\tau(u) = \mathbf{x}(u - \tau(u))$. The following central theorem computes an upper bound of $\|S_J[\mathcal{P}_J]\mathbf{x}_\tau - S_J[\mathcal{P}_J]\mathbf{x}\|$. For that purpose, we assume an admissible scattering wavelet,[2] and define the auxiliary norm

$$\|U[\mathcal{P}_J]\mathbf{x}\|_1 = \sum_{m \geq 0} \|U[\Lambda_J^m]\mathbf{x}\| .$$

---

[2] Again, as mentioned in Remark 8.7, such admissible wavelet conditions can be relaxed by extending the energy conservation results from Waldspurger (2017).

Theorem 8.9 (Mallat, 2012, Theorem 2.12). *There exists C such that every $\mathbf{x} \in \mathbf{L}^2(\mathbb{R}^d)$ with $\|U[\mathcal{P}_J]\mathbf{x}\|_1 < \infty$ and $\tau \in C^2(\mathbb{R}^d)$ with $\|\nabla\tau\|_\infty \leq 1/2$ satisfy*

$$\|S_J[\mathcal{P}_J]\mathbf{x}_\tau - S_J[\mathcal{P}_J]\mathbf{x}\| \leq C\|U[\mathcal{P}_J]\mathbf{x}\|_1 K(\tau), \tag{8.16}$$

with

$$K(\tau) = 2^{-J}\|\tau\|_\infty + \|\nabla\tau\|_\infty \max\left(1, \log\frac{\sup_{u,u'} |\tau(u) - \tau(u')|}{\|\nabla\tau\|_\infty}\right) + \|H\tau\|_\infty,$$

and, for all $m \geq 0$, if $\mathcal{P}_{J,m} = \bigcup_{n<m} \Lambda_J^n$ then

$$\|S_J[\mathcal{P}_{J,m}]\mathbf{x}_\tau - S_J[\mathcal{P}_{J,m}]\mathbf{x}\| \leq Cm\|\mathbf{x}\|K(\tau). \tag{8.17}$$

This theorem shows that a diffeomorphism produces in the scattering domain an error bounded by a term proportional to $2^{-J}\|\tau\|_\infty$, which corresponds to the local translation invariance, plus a deformation error proportional to $\|\nabla\tau\|_\infty$. Whereas rigid translations $\mathcal{T}_v$ commute with all the convolutional or pointwise operators defining the scattering representation, non-rigid deformations no longer commute with convolutions. The essence of the proof is thus to control the *commutation error* between the wavelet decomposition and the deformation. If $\mathcal{L}_\tau$ denotes the deformation operator $\mathcal{L}_\tau\mathbf{x} = \mathbf{x}_\tau$, Mallat (2012) proved that

$$\|[\mathcal{W}_J, \mathcal{L}_\tau]\| = \|\mathcal{W}_J \mathcal{L}_\tau - \mathcal{L}_\tau \mathcal{W}_J\| \lesssim \|\nabla\tau\|,$$

thanks to the scale-separation properties of wavelet decompositions.

The norm $\|U[\mathcal{P}_J]\mathbf{x}\|_1$ measures the decay of the scattering energy across depth. Again, in the univariate case it was shown in Waldspurger (2017) that

$$\text{for all } m, \qquad \|U[\Lambda_J^m]\mathbf{x}\| \leq \left(\int |\hat{\mathbf{x}}(\omega)|^2 h_m(\omega)\, d\omega\right)^{1/2},$$

with $h_m(\omega) = 1 - \exp(-2(\omega/(ra^m))^2)$ and $a > 1$. Denote by

$$\mathcal{F} = \left\{\mathbf{x}; \int |\hat{\mathbf{x}}(\omega)|^2 \log(1 + |\omega|)\, d\omega < \infty\right\}$$

the space of functions whose Fourier transform is square integrable against a logarithmic scaling. This corresponds to a logarithmic Sobolev class of functions having an average modulus of continuity in $\mathbf{L}^2(\mathbb{R}^d)$. In that case, for $\mathbf{x} \in \mathcal{F}$, we have:

Proposition 8.10. *If $\mathbf{x} \in \mathcal{F}$ then $\|U[\mathcal{P}_J]\mathbf{x}\|_1 < \infty$.*

This implies that the geometric stability bound from Theorem 8.9 applies to such functions, with an upper bound that does not blow up with depth. When $\mathbf{x}$ has compact support, the following corollary shows that the windowed scattering metric is Lipschitz continuous under the action of diffeomorphisms:

Corollary 8.11 (Mallat, 2012, Corollary 2.15). *For any compact set* $\Omega \subset \mathbb{R}^d$ *there exists C such that, for all* $\mathbf{x} \in \mathbf{L}^2(\mathbb{R}^d)$ *supported in* Ω *with* $\|U[\mathcal{P}_J]\mathbf{x}\|_1 < \infty$ *and for all* $\tau \in C^2(\mathbb{R}^d)$ *with* $\|\nabla\tau\|_\infty \leq 1/2$, *it holds that*

$$\|S_J[\mathcal{P}_{J,m}]\mathbf{x}_\tau - S_J[\mathcal{P}_{J,m}]\mathbf{x}\| \leq C\|U[\mathcal{P}_J]\mathbf{x}\|_1 \left(2^{-J}\|\tau\|_\infty + \|\nabla\tau\|_\infty + \|H\tau\|_\infty\right).$$
$$(8.18)$$

The translation error term, proportional to $2^{-J}\|\tau\|_\infty$, can be reduced to a second-order error term, $2^{-2J}\|\tau\|_\infty^2$, by considering a first-order Taylor approximation of each $S_J[p]\mathbf{x}$ (Mallat, 2012).

As mentioned earlier, Czaja and Li (2017) and Wiatowski and Bölcskei (2017) developed extensions of scattering representations by replacing scattering wavelets with other decomposition frames, also establishing deformation stability bounds. However, an important difference between these results and Theorem 8.9 is that no bandlimited assumption is made on the input signal $\mathbf{x}$, but rather the weaker condition that $\|U[\mathcal{P}_J]\mathbf{x}\|_1 < \infty$. For appropriate wavelets leading to exponential energy decay, such a quantity is bounded for $\mathbf{x} \in L^1 \cap L^2$. Finally, another relevant work that connects the above geometric stability results with kernel methods is Bietti and Mairal (2019a), in which a convolutional kernel is constructed that enjoys provable deformation stability.

8.3.4 Algorithms

We now describe algorithmic aspects of the scattering representation, in particular the choice of scattering wavelets and the overall implementation as a specific CNN architecture.

Scattering Wavelets

The Littlewood–Paley wavelet transform of $\mathbf{x}$, $\{\mathbf{x} \star \psi_\lambda(u)\}_\lambda$, defined in (8.8), is a redundant transform with no orthogonality property. It is stable and invertible if the wavelet filters $\hat{\psi}_\lambda(\omega)$ cover the whole frequency plane. On discrete images, to avoid aliasing, one should capture frequencies only in the circle $|\omega| \leq \pi$ inscribed in the image frequency square. Most camera images have negligible energy outside this frequency circle.

As mentioned in §8.3.1, one typically considers near-analytic wavelets, meaning that $|\hat{\psi}(-\omega)| \ll |\hat{\psi}(\omega)|$ for ω lying on a predefined half-space of $\mathbb{R}^2$. The reason is hinted at in Theorem 8.4, namely the complex envelope of analytic wavelets is smoother than that of a real wavelet, and therefore more energy will be captured at earlier layers of the scattering representation.

Let $u \cdot u'$ and $|u|$ denote the inner product and norm in $\mathbb{R}^2$. A Morlet wavelet ψ

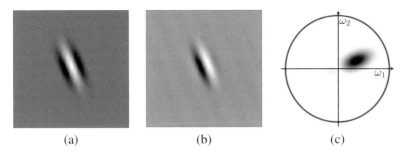

Figure 8.3 Complex Morlet wavelet. (a) Real part of $\psi(u)$. (b) Imaginary part of $\psi(u)$. (c) Fourier modulus $|\hat{\psi}(\omega)|$.

is an example of a complex wavelet given by

$$\psi(u) = \alpha \left(e^{iu \cdot \xi} - \beta \right) e^{-|u|^2/(2\sigma^2)},$$

where $\beta \ll 1$ is adjusted so that $\int \psi(u)\, du = 0$. Its real and imaginary parts are nearly quadrature phase filters. Figure 8.3 shows the Morlet wavelet, with $\sigma = 0.85$ and $\xi = 3\pi/4$, as used in all classification experiments. The Morlet wavelet ψ shown in Figure 8.3 together with $\phi(u) = \exp(-|u|^2/(2\sigma^2))/(2\pi\sigma^2)$ for $\sigma = 0.7$ satisfies (8.9) with $\epsilon = 0.25$.

Cubic spline wavelets constitute an important family of unitary wavelets satisfying the Littlewood–Paley condition (8.9) with $\epsilon = 0$. They are obtained from a cubic-spline orthogonal Battle–Lemairé wavelet, defined from the conjugate mirror filter (Mallat, 2008)

$$\hat{h}(\omega) = \sqrt{\frac{S_8(\omega)}{2^8 S_8(2\omega)}}, \qquad \text{with } S_n(\omega) = \sum_{k=-\infty}^{\infty} \frac{1}{(\omega + 2k\pi)^n},$$

which in the case $n = 8$ simplifies to the expression

$$S_8(2\omega) = \frac{5 + 30\cos^2(\omega) + 30\sin^2(\omega)\cos^2(\omega)}{1052^8 \sin^8(\omega)}$$

$$+ \frac{70\cos^4(\omega) + 2\sin^4(\omega)\cos^2(\omega) + \frac{2}{3}\sin^6(\omega)}{105 \times 2^8 \sin^8(\omega)}.$$

In two dimensions, $\hat{\psi}$ is defined as a separable product in frequency polar coordinates $\omega = |\omega|\eta$, where η is a unit vector:

$$\text{for all } |\omega|,\ \eta \in \mathbb{R}^+ \times S^1, \quad \hat{\psi}(\omega) = \hat{\psi}_1(|\omega|)\gamma(\eta),$$

with γ designed such that

$$\text{for all } \eta, \quad \sum_{r \in G^+} |\gamma(r^{-1}\eta)|^2 = 1.$$

Figure 8.4 shows the corresponding two-dimensional filters obtained with spline wavelets on setting both $\hat{\psi}_1$ and γ to be cubic splines.

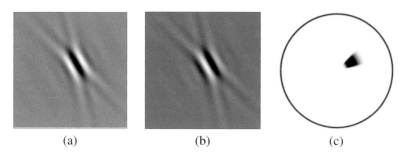

(a)   (b)   (c)

Figure 8.4 Complex cubic spline wavelet. (a) Real part of $\psi(u)$. (b) Imaginary part of $\psi(u)$. (c) Fourier modulus $|\hat{\psi}(\omega)|$.

Fast Scattering Computations with Scattering Convolutional Network

A scattering representation is implemented with a CNN having a very specific architecture. As opposed to standard CNNs, output scattering coefficients are produced by each layer as opposed to just the last layer. Filters are not learned from the data but are predefined wavelets. If $p = (\lambda_1, \ldots, \lambda_m)$ is a path of length m then the windowed scattering coefficients $S_J[p]\mathbf{x}(u)$ of order m are computed at layer m of a convolution network which is specified.

We will describe a fast scattering implementation over frequency-decreasing paths, where most of the scattering energy is concentrated. A frequency-decreasing path $p = (2^{-j_1}r_1, \ldots, 2^{-j_m}r_m)$ satisfies $0 < j_k \leq j_{k+1} \leq J$. If the wavelet transform is computed over K rotation angles then the total number of frequency-decreasing paths of length m is $K^m \binom{J}{m}$. Let N be the number of pixels of the image x. Since ϕ_{2^J} is a low-pass filter scaled by 2^J, $S_J[p]\mathbf{x}(u) = U[p]\mathbf{x} \star \phi_{2^J}(u)$ is uniformly sampled at intervals $\alpha 2^J$, with $\alpha = 1$ or $\alpha = 1/2$. Each $S_J[p]\mathbf{x}$ is an image with $\alpha^{-2}2^{-2J}N$ coefficients. The total number of coefficients in a scattering network of maximum depth $\overline{m}$ is thus

$$P = N\alpha^{-2} 2^{-2J} \sum_{m=0}^{\overline{m}} K^m \binom{J}{m}. \tag{8.19}$$

If $\overline{m} = 2$ then $P \simeq \alpha^{-2} N 2^{-2J} K^2 J^2/2$. It decreases exponentially when the scale 2^J increases.

Algorithm 8.1 describes the computations of scattering coefficients on sets $\mathcal{P}_{\downarrow}^m$ of frequency-decreasing paths of length $m \leq \overline{m}$. The initial set $\mathcal{P}_{\downarrow}^0 = \{\emptyset\}$ corresponds to the original image $U[\emptyset]\mathbf{x} = \mathbf{x}$. Let $p + \lambda$ be the path which begins at p and ends at $\lambda \in \mathcal{P}$. If $\lambda = 2^{-j}r$ then $U[p + \lambda]\mathbf{x}(u) = |U[p]\mathbf{x} \star \psi_\lambda(u)|$ has energy at frequencies mostly below $2^{-j}\pi$. To reduce computations we can thus subsample this convolution at intervals $\alpha 2^j$, with $\alpha = 1$ or $\alpha = 1/2$ to avoid aliasing.

Algorithm 8.1 Fast Scattering Transform

> **for** $m = 1$ to $\overline{m}$ **do**
>> **for all** $p \in \mathcal{P}_\downarrow^{m-1}$ **do**
>>> Output $S_J[p]\mathbf{x}(\alpha 2^J n) = U[p]\mathbf{x} \star \phi_{2^J}(\alpha 2^J n)$
>> **end for**
>> **for all** $p + \lambda_m \in \mathcal{P}_\downarrow^m$ with $\lambda_m = 2^{-j_m} r_m$ **do**
>>> Compute
>>> $$U[p + \lambda_m]\mathbf{x}(\alpha 2^{j_m} n) = |U[p]\mathbf{x} \star \psi_{\lambda_m}(\alpha 2^{j_m} n)|$$
>> **end for**
> **end for**
> **for all** $p \in \mathcal{P}_\downarrow^{\max}$ **do**
>> Output $S_J[p]\mathbf{x}(\alpha 2^J n) = U[p]\mathbf{x} \star \phi_{2^J}(\alpha 2^J n)$
> **end for**

At layer m there are $K^m \binom{J}{m}$ propagated signals $U[p]\mathbf{x}$ with $p \in \mathcal{P}_\downarrow^m$. They are sampled at intervals $\alpha 2^{j_m}$ which depend on p. One can verify by induction on m that layer m has a total number of samples equal to $\alpha^{-2} (K/3)^m N$. There are also $K^m \binom{J}{m}$ scattering signals $S[p]\mathbf{x}$ but they are subsampled by 2^J and thus have many fewer coefficients. The number of operations to compute each layer is therefore driven by the $O((K/3)^m N \log N)$ operations needed to compute the internal propagated coefficients using FFTs. For $K > 3$, the overall computational complexity is thus $O((K/3)^{\overline{m}} N \log N)$.

The package Kymatio (Andreux et al., 2018) provides a modern implementation of scattering transforms leveraging efficient GPU-optimized routines.

8.3.5 Empirical Analysis of Scattering Properties

To illustrate the properties of scattering representations, let us describe a visualization procedure. For a fixed position u, windowed scattering coefficients $S_J[p]\mathbf{x}(u)$ of order $m = 1, 2$ are displayed as piecewise constant images over a disk representing the Fourier support of the image $\mathbf{x}$. This frequency disk is partitioned into sectors $\{\Omega[p]\}_{p \in \mathcal{P}^m}$ indexed by the path p. The image value is $S_J[p]\mathbf{x}(u)$ on the frequency sectors $\Omega[p]$, as shown in Figure 8.5.

For $m = 1$, the scattering coefficient $S_J[\lambda_1]\mathbf{x}(u)$ depends upon the local Fourier transform energy of $\mathbf{x}$ over the support of $\hat{\psi}_{\lambda_1}$. Its value is displayed over a sector $\Omega[\lambda_1]$ which approximates the frequency support of $\hat{\psi}_{\lambda_1}$. For $\lambda_1 = 2^{-j_1} r_1$, there are

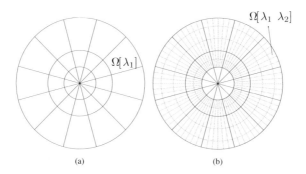

Figure 8.5   To display scattering coefficients, the disk covering the image frequency support is partitioned into sectors $\Omega[p]$, which depend upon the path p. (a): For $m = 1$, each $\Omega[\lambda_1]$ is a sector rotated by r_1 which approximates the frequency support of $\hat{\psi}_{\lambda_1}$. (b): For $m = 2$, all $\Omega[\lambda_1, \lambda_2]$ are obtained by subdividing each $\Omega[\lambda_1]$.

K rotated sectors located in an annulus of scale 2^{-j_1}, corresponding to each $r_1 \in G$, as shown by Figure 8.5(a). Their areas are proportional to $\|\psi_{\lambda_1}\|^2 \sim K^{-1} 2^{-j_1}$.

The second-order scattering coefficients $S_J[\lambda_1, \lambda_2]\mathbf{x}(u)$ are computed with a second wavelet transform, which performs a second frequency subdivision. These coefficients are displayed over frequency sectors $\Omega[\lambda_1, \lambda_2]$ which subdivide the sectors $\Omega[\lambda_1]$ of the first wavelets $\hat{\psi}_{\lambda_1}$, as illustrated in Figure 8.5(b). For $\lambda_2 = 2^{-j_2}r_2$, the scale 2^{j_2} divides the radial axis and the resulting sectors are subdivided into K angular sectors corresponding to the different values of r_2. The scale and angular subdivisions are adjusted so that the area of each $\Omega[\lambda_1, \lambda_2]$ is proportional to $\||\psi_{\lambda_1}| \star \psi_{\lambda_2}\|^2$.

A windowed scattering S_J is computed with a cascade of the wavelet modulus operators $\mathcal{U}$ defined in (8.11), and its properties thus depend upon the wavelet transform properties. In §§8.3.3 and 8.3.2 conditions were given for wavelets to define a scattering transform that is non-expansive and preserves the signal norm. The scattering energy conservation shows that $\|S_J[p]\mathbf{x}\|$ decreases quickly as the length of p increases, and is non-negligible only over a particular subset of frequency-decreasing paths. Reducing computations to these paths defines a convolution network with many fewer internal and output coefficients.

Theorem 8.4 shows that the energy captured by the mth layer of the scattering convolutional network, $\sum_{|p|=m} \|S_J[p]x\|^2$, converges to 0 as $m \to \infty$. This scattering energy conservation also proves that the more sparse the wavelet coefficients, the more energy propagates to deeper layers. Indeed, when 2^J increases, one can verify that, at the first layer, $S_J[\lambda_1]\mathbf{x} = |\mathbf{x} \star \psi_{\lambda_1}| \star \phi_{2^J}$ converges to $\|\phi\|^2 \|\mathbf{x} \star \psi_{\lambda}\|_1^2$. The more sparse $\mathbf{x} \star \psi_{\lambda}$, the smaller $\|\mathbf{x} \star \psi_{\lambda}\|_1$ and hence the more energy is propagated to deeper layers to satisfy the global energy conservation of Theorem 8.4.

Figure 8.6 shows two images having same first-order scattering coefficients, but

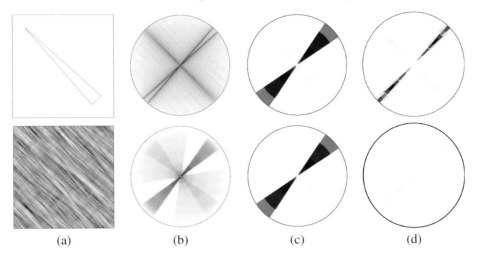

(a)   (b)   (c)   (d)

Figure 8.6 (a) Two images $x(u)$. (b) Fourier modulus $|\hat{x}(\omega)|$. (c) First-order scattering coefficients $S_J x[\lambda_1]$ displayed over the frequency sectors of Figure 8.5(a). They are the same for both images. (d) Second-order scattering coefficients $S_J x[\lambda_1, \lambda_2]$ over the frequency sectors of Figure 8.5(b). They are different for each image.

the top image is piecewise regular and hence has wavelet coefficients which are much more sparse than those of the uniform texture at the bottom. As a result the top image has second-order scattering coefficients of larger amplitude than those of the bottom image. Higher-order coefficients are not displayed because they have negligible energy. For typical images, as in the CalTech101 dataset (Fei-Fei et al., 2004), Table 8.1 shows that the scattering energy has an exponential decay as a function of the path length m. The scattering coefficients are computed with cubic spline wavelets, which define a unitary wavelet transform and satisfy the scattering admissibility condition for energy conservation. As expected, the energy of the scattering coefficients converges to 0 as m increases, and it is already below 1% for $m \geq 3$.

The propagated energy $\|U[p]\mathbf{x}\|^2$ decays because $U[p]\mathbf{x}$ is a progressively lower-frequency signal as the path length increases. Indeed, each modulus computes a regular envelope of oscillating wavelet coefficients. The modulus can thus be interpreted as a non-linear 'demodulator' which pushes the wavelet coefficient energy towards lower frequencies. As a result, an important portion of the energy of $U[p]\mathbf{x}$ is then captured by the low-pass filter ϕ_{2^J}, which outputs $S_J[p]\mathbf{x} = U[p]\mathbf{x} \star \phi_{2^J}$. Hence less energy is propagated to the next layer.

Another result is that the scattering energy propagates only along a subset of frequency-decreasing paths. Since the envelope $|\mathbf{x} \star \psi_\lambda|$ is more regular than $\mathbf{x} \star \psi_\lambda$, it follows that $|\mathbf{x} \star \psi_\lambda(u)| \star \psi_{\lambda'}$ is non-negligible only if $\psi_{\lambda'}$ is located at lower frequencies than ψ_λ and, hence, if $|\lambda'| < |\lambda|$. Iterating on wavelet modulus

Table 8.1 *Percentage of energy* $\sum_{p \in \mathcal{P}^m_{\downarrow}} \|S_J[p]\mathbf{x}\|^2/\|\mathbf{x}\|^2$ *of scattering coefficients on frequency-decreasing paths of length m, with dependence upon J. These average values are computed on the Caltech-101 database, with zero mean and unit variance images.*

J	m = 0	m = 1	m = 2	m = 3	m = 4	m ≤ 3
1	95.1	4.86	–	–	–	99.96
2	87.56	11.97	0.35	–	–	99.89
3	76.29	21.92	1.54	0.02	–	99.78
4	61.52	33.87	4.05	0.16	0	99.61
5	44.6	45.26	8.9	0.61	0.01	99.37
6	26.15	57.02	14.4	1.54	0.07	99.1
7	0	73.37	21.98	3.56	0.25	98.91

operators thus propagates the scattering energy along frequency-decreasing paths $p = (\lambda_1, \ldots, \lambda_m)$ where $|\lambda_k| < |\lambda_{k-1}|$ for $1 \leq k < m$. We denote by $\mathcal{P}^m_{\downarrow}$ the set of frequency-decreasing (or equivalently scale-increasing) paths of length m. The scattering coefficients along other paths have a negligible energy. This is verified by Table 8.1, which shows not only that the scattering energy is concentrated on low-order paths, but also that more than 99% of the energy is absorbed by frequency-decreasing paths of length $m \leq 3$. Numerically, it is therefore sufficient to compute the scattering transform along frequency-decreasing paths. It defines a much smaller convolution network. In §8.3.4 we will show that the resulting coefficients are computed with $O(N \log N)$ operations.

Signal recovery versus energy conservation. Preserving energy does not imply that the signal information is preserved. Since a scattering transform is calculated by iteratively applying $\mathcal{U}$, inverting S_J requires inverting $\mathcal{U}$. The wavelet transform $\mathcal{W}$ is a linear invertible operator, so inverting $\mathcal{U}z = \{z \star \phi_{2^J}, |z \star \psi_\lambda|\}_{\lambda \in \mathcal{P}}$ amounts to recovering the complex phases of wavelet coefficients removed by the modulus. The phases of the Fourier coefficients cannot be recovered from their moduli, but wavelet coefficients are redundant, as opposed to Fourier coefficients. For particular wavelets, it has been proved that the phases of the wavelet coefficients can indeed be recovered from their moduli, and that $\mathcal{U}$ has a continuous inverse (Waldspurger, 2012).

Still, one cannot invert S_J exactly because we discard information when computing the scattering coefficients $S_J[p]\mathbf{x} = U[p]\mathbf{x} \star \phi_{2^J}$ of the last layer $\mathcal{P}^{\overline{m}}$. Indeed, the propagated coefficients $|U[p]\mathbf{x} \star \psi_\lambda|$ of the next layer are eliminated, because they are not invariant and have negligible total energy. The number of such coefficients

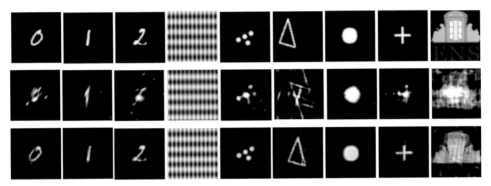

Figure 8.7 Signal reconstruction from scattering coefficients $S_J\mathbf{x}$ with $J = \log N$. Top: original images. Middle: reconstruction from only first-order coefficients. Bottom: reconstruction using first- and second-order coefficients.

is larger than the total number of scattering coefficients kept at previous layers. Initializing the inversion by setting these small coefficients to zero produces an error. This error is further amplified as the inversion of $\mathcal{U}$ progresses across layers from $\overline{m}$ to 0.

Yet, under some structural assumptions on the signal $\mathbf{x}$, it is possible to recover the signal from its scattering coefficients $\mathbf{z} = S_J\mathbf{x}$. For instance, if $\mathbf{x}$ admits a sparse wavelet decomposition, Bruna and Mallat (2018) showed that important geometrical information of $\mathbf{x}$ is preserved in $S_J\mathbf{x}$. Figure 8.7 illustrates signal recovery using either $m = 1$ or $m = 2$ with $J = \log N$. The recovery is obtained using gradient descent on the energy $E(\mathbf{x}) = \|S_J\mathbf{x} - \mathbf{z}\|^2$ as will be described in §8.6. In this case, first-order scattering provides a collection of ℓ_1 norms $\{\|\mathbf{x} \star \psi_\lambda\|_1\}_\lambda$, which recover the overall regularity of the signal but fail to reconstruct its geometry. Adding second-order coefficients results in $O(\log N^2)$ coefficients and substantially improves the reconstruction quality. In essence, the sparsity in these images creates no scale interactions on a large subset of scattering coefficients, which reduces the loss of information caused by the removal of the wavelet phases.

For natural images with weaker sparsity, Figure 8.8 shows reconstructions from second-order scattering coefficients for different values of J, using the same recovery algorithm. When the scale 2^J is such that the number of scattering coefficients is comparable with the dimensionality of $\mathbf{x}$, we observe good perceptual quality. When $\dim(S_J\mathbf{x}) \ll \dim(\mathbf{x})$, the scattering coefficients define an underlying generative model based on a microcanonical maximum entropy principle, as will be described in §8.6.

Figure 8.8 Samples from $\Omega_{J,\epsilon}$ for different values of J using the gradient descent algorithm described in §8.6.3. Top row: original images. Second row: $J = 3$. Third row: $J = 4$. Fourth row: $J = 5$. Fifth row: $J = 6$. The visual quality of the reconstruction is nearly perfect for $J = 3$ and degrades for larger values of J.

8.3.6 Scattering in Modern Computer Vision

Thanks to their provable deformation stability and ability to preserve important geometric information, scattering representations are suitable as feature extractors in many computer vision pipelines.

First demonstrated in Bruna and Mallat (2013) on handwritten digit classification and texture recognition, scattering-based image classification models have been further developed in Oyallon and Mallat (2015), Oyallon et al. (2017), and Oyallon et al. (2018b), by extending the wavelet decomposition to other transformation groups (see §8.5) and by integrating them within CNN architectures as preprocessing stages.

In particular, the results from Oyallon et al. (2018b) demonstrate that the geometric priors of scattering representations provide a better trade-off than data-driven models in the small-training regime, where large-capacity CNNs tend to overfit.

Even first-order scattering coefficients may be used to ease inference and learning within CNN pipelines, as demonstrated in Oyallon et al. (2018a).

Also, let us mention models that are hybrids between fully structured scattering networks and fully trainable CNNs. Jacobsen et al. (2016) proposed the learning of convolutional filters in the wavelet domain, leveraging the benefits of multiscale decompositions. Cohen and Welling (2016a,b) and Kondor and Trivedi (2018) added group convolution of the joint scattering representation of §8.5 to the CNNs, significantly improving the sample complexity. Finally, Zarka et al. (2020) achieved Res-Net performance on Imagenet by combining scattering operators with learned channel-wise 1×1 convolutions.

8.4 Scattering Representations of Stochastic Processes

This section reviews the definitions and basic properties of the expected scattering of random processes (Mallat, 2012; Bruna et al., 2015a). First, we prove a version of scattering mean-squared consistency for orthogonal Haar scattering in §8.4.1.

8.4.1 Expected Scattering

If $(X(t))_{t \in \mathbb{R}}$ is a stationary process or has stationary increments, meaning that $\delta_s X(t) = X(t) - X(t - s)$ is stationary for all s, then $X \star \psi_\lambda$ is also stationary, and taking the modulus preserves stationarity. It follows that, for any path $p = (\lambda_1, \ldots, \lambda_m) \in \mathcal{P}_\infty$, the process

$$U[p]X = |\cdots|X \star \psi_{\lambda_1}| \star \cdots| \star \psi_{\lambda_m}|$$

is stationary, hence its expected value does not depend upon the spatial position t.

Definition 8.12. Let $X(t)$ be a stochastic process with stationary increments. The expected scattering of X is defined for all $p \in \mathcal{P}_\infty$ by

$$\overline{S}X(p) = \mathbb{E}(U[p]X) = \mathbb{E}(|\cdots|X \star \psi_{\lambda_1}| \star \cdots| \star \psi_{\lambda_m}|) .$$

The expected scattering defines a representation for the process $X(t)$ which carries information on high-order moments of $X(t)$, as we shall see later. It also defines a metric between stationary processes, given by

$$\|\overline{S}X - \overline{S}Y\|^2 := \sum_{p \in \mathcal{P}_\infty} |\overline{S}X(p) - \overline{S}Y(p)|^2 .$$

The scattering representation of $X(t)$ is estimated by computing a windowed scattering transform of a realization $\mathbf{x}$ of $X(t)$. If $\Lambda_J = \{\lambda = 2^j : 2^{-j} > 2^{-J}\}$ denotes the set of scales smaller than J, and $\mathcal{P}_J$ is the set of finite paths $p = (\lambda_1, \ldots, \lambda_m)$

with $\lambda_k \in \Lambda_J$ for all k, then the windowed scattering at scale J of a realization $\mathbf{x}(t)$ is

$$S_J[\mathcal{P}_J]\mathbf{x} = \{U[p]\mathbf{x} \star \phi_J, \, p \in \mathcal{P}_J\}. \tag{8.20}$$

Since $\int \phi_J(u) \, du = 1$, we have $\mathbb{E}(S_J[\mathcal{P}_J]X) = \mathbb{E}(U[p]X) = \bar{S}X(p)$, so S_J is an unbiased estimator of the scattering coefficients contained in $\mathcal{P}_J$. When the wavelet ψ satisfies the Littlewood–Paley condition (8.9), the non-expansive nature of the operators defining the scattering transform implies that $\bar{S}$ and $S_J[\mathcal{P}_J]$ are also non-expansive, similarly to the deterministic case covered in Proposition 8.3:

Proposition 8.13. *If X and Y are finite second-order stationary processes then*

$$\mathbb{E}(\|S_J[\mathcal{P}_J]X - S_J[\mathcal{P}_J]Y\|^2) \leq \mathbb{E}(|X - Y|^2), \tag{8.21}$$

$$\|\bar{S}X - \bar{S}Y\|^2 \leq \mathbb{E}(|X - Y|^2), \tag{8.22}$$

in particular

$$\|\bar{S}X\|^2 \leq \mathbb{E}(|X|^2). \tag{8.23}$$

The $\mathbf{L}^2(\mathbb{R}^d)$ energy conservation theorem, 8.4, yields an equivalent energy conservation property for the mean-squared power:

Theorem 8.14 (Waldspurger, 2017, Theorem 5.1). *Under the same assumptions on scattering wavelets as in Theorem 8.4, and if X is stationary, then*

$$\mathbb{E}(\|S_J[\mathcal{P}_J]X\|^2) = \mathbb{E}(|X|^2). \tag{8.24}$$

The expected scattering coefficients are estimated with the windowed scattering $S_J[p]X = U[p]X \star \psi_J$ for each $p \in \mathcal{P}_J$. If $U[p]X$ is ergodic, $S_J[p]X$ converges in probability to $\bar{S}X(p) = \mathbb{E}(U[p]X)$ when $J \to \infty$. A process $X(t)$ with stationary increments is said to have a mean squared consistent scattering if the total variance of $S_J[\mathcal{P}_J]X$ converges to zero as J increases:

$$\lim_{J \to \infty} \mathbb{E}(\|S_J[\mathcal{P}_J]X - \bar{S}X\|^2) = \sum_{p \in \mathcal{P}_J} \mathbb{E}(|S_J[p]X - \bar{S}X(p)|^2) = 0. \tag{8.25}$$

This condition implies that $S_J[\mathcal{P}_J]X$ converges to $\bar{S}X$ with probability 1. Mean-squares consistent scattering is observed numerically on a variety of processes, including Gaussian and non-Gaussian fractal processes. It was conjectured in Mallat (2012) that Gaussian stationary processes X whose autocorrelation R_X is in $\mathbf{L}^1$ have a mean squared consistent scattering.

Consistency of orthogonal Haar scattering. We show a partial affirmative answer of the above conjecture, by considering a specific scattering representation built from discrete orthogonal real Haar wavelets. Consider $(X_n)_{n \in \mathbb{Z}}$, a stationary process defined over discrete time steps. The orthogonal Haar scattering transform S_J^{H} maps 2^J samples of X_n into 2^J coefficients, defined recursively as

$$
\begin{aligned}
x^{0,k} &= X_k, \quad k = 0, \ldots, 2^J - 1, \\
x^{j,k} &= \frac{1}{2}(x^{j-1,2k} + x^{j-1,2k+1}), \\
x^{j,k+2^{J-j}} &= \frac{1}{2}|x^{j-1,2k} - x^{j-1,2k+1}|, \quad 0 < j \le J, k = 0, \ldots, 2^{J-1} - 1, \\
S_J^{\mathrm{H}} X &:= (x^{J,k}; k = 0, \ldots, 2^J - 1).
\end{aligned}
$$
(8.26)

This representation thus follows a multiresolution analysis (MRA) (Mallat, 1999) but also decomposes the details at each scale, after applying the modulus non-linearity. It is easy to verify by induction that (8.26) defines an orthogonal trans-formation that preserves energy: $\|S_J^{\mathrm{H}} \mathbf{x}\| = \|\mathbf{x}\|$. However, in contrast with the Littlewood–Paley wavelet decomposition, orthogonal wavelets are defined from downsampling operators, and therefore the resulting scattering representation S_J^{H} is not translation invariant when $J \to \infty$. We have the following consistency result:

Theorem 8.15 (Bruna, 2019). *The progressive Haar Scattering operator S_J^{H} is consistent in the class of compactly supported linear processes, in the sense that*

$$
\lim_{J \to \infty} \mathbb{E}(\|S_J^{\mathrm{H}} X - \mathbb{E} S_J^{\mathrm{H}} X\|^2) = 0 \,,
$$
(8.27)

for stationary processes X which can be represented as $X = W \star h$, where W is a white noise and h is compactly supported.

As a consequence of Theorem 8.14, mean-squared consistency implies an ex-pected scattering energy conservation:

Corollary 8.16. *For admissible wavelets as in Theorem 8.14, $S_J[\mathcal{P}_J]X$ is mean-squared consistent if and only if*

$$
\|\bar{S}X\|^2 = \mathbb{E}(|X|^2) \,.
$$

The expected scattering coefficients depend upon normalized high-order mo-ments of X. If one expresses $|U[p]X|^2$ as

$$
|U[p]X(t)|^2 = \mathbb{E}(|U[p]X|^2)(1 + \epsilon(t)) \,,
$$

then, assuming $|\epsilon| \ll 1$, a first-order approximation

$$
U[p]X(t) = \sqrt{|U[p]X(t)|^2} \approx \mathbb{E}(|U[p]X|^2)^{1/2}(1 + \epsilon/2)
$$

yields

$$
U[p + \lambda]X = |U[p]X \star \psi_\lambda| \approx \frac{\||U[p]X|^2 \star \psi_\lambda\|}{2\mathbb{E}(|U[p]X|^2)^{1/2}} \,,
$$

thus showing that $\overline{S}X(p) = \mathbb{E}(U[p]X)$ for $p = (\lambda_1, \ldots, \lambda_m)$ depends upon normalized moments of X of order 2^m, determined by the cascade of wavelet sub-bands λ_k. As opposed to a direct estimation of high moments, scattering coefficients are computed with a non-expansive operator which allows consistent estimation with few realizations. This is a fundamental property which enables texture recognition and classification from scattering representations (Bruna, 2013).

The scattering representation is related to the sparsity of the process through the decay of its coefficients $\overline{S}X(p)$ as the order $|p|$ increases. Indeed, the ratio of the first two moments of X,

$$\rho_X = \frac{\mathbb{E}(|X|)}{\mathbb{E}(|X|^2)^{1/2}}$$

gives a rough measure of the fatness of the tails of X.

For each p, the Littlewood–Paley unitarity condition satisfied by ψ gives

$$\mathbb{E}(|U[p]X|^2) = \mathbb{E}(U[p]X)^2 + \sum_\lambda \mathbb{E}(|U[p + \lambda]X|^2),$$

which yields

$$1 = \rho_{U[p]X} + \frac{1}{\mathbb{E}(|U[p]X|^2)} \sum_\lambda \mathbb{E}(|U[p + \lambda]X|^2). \qquad (8.28)$$

Thus, the fraction of energy that is trapped at a given path p is given by the relative sparsity $\rho_{U[p]X}$.

This relationship between sparsity and scattering decay across the orders is of particular importance for the study of point processes, which are sparse in the original spatial domain, and for regular image textures, which are sparse when decomposed in the first level UX of the transform. In particular, the scattering transform can easily discriminate between white noises of different sparsity, such as Bernouilli and Gaussian.

The autocovariance of a real stationary process X is denoted

$$RX(\tau) = \mathbb{E}\Big(\big(X(x) - \mathbb{E}(X)\big) \big(X(x - \tau) - \mathbb{E}(X)\big) \Big).$$

Its Fourier transform $\widehat{R}X(\omega)$ is the power spectrum of X. Replacing X by $X \star \psi_\lambda$ in the energy conservation formula (8.24) implies that

$$\sum_{p \in \mathcal{P}_J} \mathbb{E}(|S_J[p + \lambda]X|^2) = \mathbb{E}(|X \star \psi_\lambda|^2). \qquad (8.29)$$

These expected squared wavelet coefficients can also be written as a filtered integration of the Fourier power spectrum $\widehat{R}X(\omega)$:

$$\mathbb{E}(|X \star \psi_\lambda|^2) = \int \widehat{R}X(\omega) |\hat{\psi}(\lambda^{-1}\omega)|^2 \, d\omega. \qquad (8.30)$$

These two equations prove that summing the scattering coefficients recovers the power spectrum integral over each wavelet's frequency support, which depends only upon second-order moments of X. However, the scattering coefficients $\overline{S}X(p)$ depend upon moments of X up to the order 2^m if p has length m. Scattering coefficients can thus discriminate textures having same second-order moments but different higher-order moments.

8.4.2 Analysis of Stationary Textures with Scattering

In §8.4.1 we showed that the scattering representation can be used to describe stationary processes, in such a way that high-order moment information is captured and estimated consistently with few realizations.

Image textures can be modeled as realizations of stationary processes $X(u)$. The Fourier spectrum $\widehat{R}_X(\omega)$ is the Fourier transform of the autocorrelation

$$R_X(\tau) = \mathbb{E}\big([X(u) - \mathbb{E}(X)][X(u - \tau) - \mathbb{E}(X)]\big) .$$

Despite the importance of spectral methods, the Fourier spectrum is often not sufficient to discriminate image textures because it does not take into account higher-order moments.

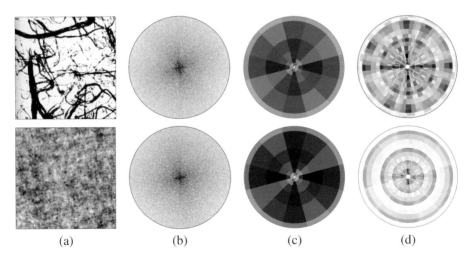

(a) (b) (c) (d)

Figure 8.9 Two different textures having the same Fourier power spectrum. (a) Textures $X(u)$. Upper, Brodatz texture; lower, Gaussian process. (b) Same estimated power spectrum $\widehat{R}X(\omega)$. (c) Nearly the same scattering coefficients $S_J[p]X$ for $m = 1$ and 2^J equal to the image width. (d) Different scattering coefficients $S_J[p]X$ for $m = 2$.

The discriminative power of scattering representations is illustrated using the two textures in Figure 8.9, which have the same power spectrum and hence the same second-order moments. The scattering coefficients $S_J[p]X$ are shown for $m = 1$ and

$m = 2$ with the frequency tiling illustrated in Figure 8.5. The ability to discriminate the upper process X_1 from the lower, X_2, is measured by the scattering distance normalized by the variance:

$$\rho(m) = \frac{\|S_J X_1[\Lambda_J^m] - \mathbb{E}(S_J X_2[\Lambda_J^m])\|^2}{\mathbb{E}(\|S_J X_2[\Lambda_J^m] - \mathbb{E}(S_J X_2[\Lambda_J^m])\|^2)}.$$

For $m = 1$, the scattering coefficients mostly depend upon second-order moments and are thus nearly equal for both textures. One can indeed verify numerically that $\rho(1) = 1$ so the textures cannot be distinguished using first-order scattering coefficients. In contrast, scattering coefficients of order 2 are highly dissimilar because they depend on moments up to order 4, and $\rho(2) = 5$. A scattering representation of stationary processes includes second- and higher-order moment descriptors of stationary processes, which discriminates between such textures.

The windowed scattering $S_J[\mathcal{P}_J]X$ estimates scattering coefficients by averaging wavelet modulus over a support of size proportional to 2^J. If X is a stationary process, we saw in §8.4.1 that the expected scattering transform $\bar{S}X$ is estimated using the windowed scattering

$$S_J[\mathcal{P}_J]X = \{U[p]X \star \phi_J, \quad p \in \mathcal{P}_J\}.$$

This estimate is called mean-squared consistent if its total variance over all paths converges:

$$\lim_{J \to \infty} \sum_{p \in \mathcal{P}_J} \mathbb{E}(|S_J[p]X - \bar{S}X(p)|^2) = 0.$$

Corollary 8.16 showed that mean-squared consistency is equivalent to

$$\mathbb{E}(|X|^2) = \sum_{p \in \mathcal{P}_\infty} |\bar{S}X(p)|^2,$$

which in turn is equivalent to

$$\lim_{m \to \infty} \sum_{p \in \mathcal{P}_\infty, \, |p|=m} \mathbb{E}(|U[p]X|^2) = 0. \qquad (8.31)$$

If a process $X(t)$ has a mean-squared consistent scattering, then one can recover the scaling law of its second moments with scattering coefficients:

Proposition 8.17. *Suppose that $X(t)$ is a process with stationary increments such that $S_J X$ is mean-squared consistent. Then*

$$\mathbb{E}(|X \star \psi_j|^2) = \sum_{p \in \mathcal{P}_\infty} |\bar{S}X(j + p)|^2. \qquad (8.32)$$

Table 8.2 *Percentage decay of the total scattering variance* $\sum_{p\in\mathcal{P}_J} \mathbb{E}(|S_J[p]X - \overline{S}X(p)|^2)/E(|X|^2)$ *as a function of J, averaged over the Brodatz dataset. Results obtained using cubic spline wavelets.*

$J = 1$	$J = 2$	$J = 3$	$J = 4$	$J = 5$	$J = 6$	$J = 7$
85	65	45	26	14	7	2.5

Table 8.3 *Percentage of expected scattering energy* $\sum_{p\in\Lambda_\infty^m} |\overline{S}X(p)|^2$, *as a function of the scattering order m, computed with cubic spline wavelets, over the Brodatz dataset.*

$m = 0$	$m = 1$	$m = 2$	$m = 3$	$m = 4$
0	74	19	3	0.3

For a large class of ergodic processes, including most image textures, it is observed numerically that the total scattering variance $\sum_{p\in\mathcal{P}_J} \mathbb{E}(|S_J[p]X - \overline{S}X(p)|^2)$ decreases to zero when 2^J increases. Table 8.2 shows the decay of the total scattering variance, computed on average over the Brodatz texture dataset.

Corollary 8.16 showed that this variance decay then implies that

$$\|\overline{S}X\|^2 = \sum_{m=0}^{\infty} \sum_{p\in\Lambda_\infty^m} |\overline{S}X(p)|^2 = \mathbb{E}(|X|^2) \, .$$

Table 8.3 gives the percentage of the expected scattering energy $\sum_{p\in\Lambda_\infty^m} |\overline{S}X(p)|^2$ carried by paths of length m, for textures in the Brodatz database. Most of the energy is concentrated in paths of length $m \leq 3$.

8.4.3 Multifractal Analysis with Scattering Moments

Many physical phenomena exhibit irregularities at all scales, as illustrated by the canonical example of turbulent flow or Brownian motion. Fractals are mathematical models of stochastic processes that express such a property through scale-invariance symmetries of the form

$$\text{for all } s > 0, \quad \{X(st): t \in \mathbb{R}\} \overset{d}{=} A_s \cdot \{X(t): t \in \mathbb{R}\} \, . \tag{8.33}$$

In other words, the law of stochastic processes is invariant under time dilation, up to a scale factor. Here A_s denotes a random variable independent of X that controls the strength of the irregularity of sample trajectories of $X(t)$. Fractional Brownian motions are the only Gaussian processes satisfying (8.33) with $A_s := s^H$, where $H = 0.5$ corresponds to the standard Wiener process.

   Fractals can be studied from wavelet coefficients through the distribution of point-wise Hölder exponents (Doukhan et al., 2002). Moments of order q define a scaling exponent $\zeta(q)$ such that

$$\mathbb{E}[|X \star \psi_j|^q] \simeq 2^{j\zeta(q)}, \quad \text{as } j \to -\infty.$$

This characteristic exponent provides rich information about the process; in particular, the curvature of $\zeta(q)$ measures the presence of different Hölder exponents within a realization and can be interpreted as a measure of *intermittency*. Intermittency is an ill-defined mathematical notion that is used in physics to describe those irregular bursts of large amplitude variations appearing for example in turbulent flows (Yoshimatsu et al., 2011). Multiscale intermittency appears in other domains such as network traffic, financial time series, and geophysical and medical data.

   Intermittency is created by heavy-tail processes, such as Lévy processes. It produces large, if not infinite, polynomial moments of degree greater than 2, and empirical estimations of second-order moments have a large variance. These statistical instabilities can be reduced by calculating the expected values of non-expansive operators in mean-squared norm, which reduces the variance of empirical estimation. Scattering moments are computed with such a non-expansive operator.

   In Bruna et al. (2015a), it was shown that second-order scattering moments provide robust estimation of such intermittency through the following renormalisation scheme. In the univariate case, we consider, for each $j, j_1, j_2 \in \mathbb{Z}$,

$$\tilde{S}X(j) := \frac{\mathbb{E}[|X \star \psi_j|]}{\mathbb{E}[|X \star \psi_0|]}, \qquad \tilde{S}X(j_1, j_2) = \frac{\mathbb{E}[||X \star \psi_{j_1}| \star \psi_{j_2}|]}{\mathbb{E}[|X \star \psi_{j_1}|]}. \tag{8.34}$$

This renormalized scattering can be estimated by substituting into both numerator and denominator the windowed scattering estimators (8.20). These renormalized scattering moments capture both self-similarity and intermittence, as illustrated by the following result.

Proposition 8.18 (Bruna et al., 2015a, Proposition 3.1). *Let $X(t)$ be a self-similar process* (8.33) *with stationary increments. Then, for all $j_1 \in \mathbb{Z}$,*

$$\tilde{S}X(j_1) = 2^{j_1 H}, \tag{8.35}$$

and, for all $(j_1, j_2) \in \mathbb{Z}^2$,

$$\tilde{S}X(j_1, j_2) = \overline{\tilde{S}\tilde{X}}(j_2 - j_1) \text{ with } \tilde{X}(t) = \frac{|X \star \psi(t)|}{\mathbb{E}(|X \star \psi|)}. \tag{8.36}$$

Moreover, the discrete curvature $\zeta(2) - 2\zeta(1)$ satisfies

$$2^{j(\zeta(2)-2\zeta(1))} \simeq \frac{\mathbb{E}(|X \star \psi_j|^2)}{\mathbb{E}(|X \star \psi_j|)^2} \geq 1 + \sum_{j_2=-\infty}^{+\infty} |\tilde{S}X(j, j_2)|^2 . \tag{8.37}$$

This proposition illustrates that second-order scattering coefficients $\tilde{S}X(j_1, j_2)$ of self-similar processes are only functions of the difference $j_2 - j_1$, which can be interpreted as a stationarity property across scales. Moreover, it follows from (8.37) that if $\sum_{j_2=-\infty}^{+\infty} \tilde{S}X(j, j_2)^2 \simeq 2^{j\beta}$ as $j \to -\infty$ with $\beta < 0$, then $\zeta(2) - 2\zeta(1) < 0$. Therefore, the decay of $\tilde{S}X(j, j + l)$ with l (or absence thereof) captures a rough measure of intermittency. Figure 8.10 illustrates the behavior of normalized scattering coefficients for three representative processes: Poisson point processes, fractional Brownian motion, and a Mandelbrot cascade. The asymptotic decay of the scattering moments clearly distinguishes the different intermittent behaviors. Bruna et al. (2015a) explore the applications of such scattering moments to perform model selection in real-world applications, such as turbulent flows and financial time series.

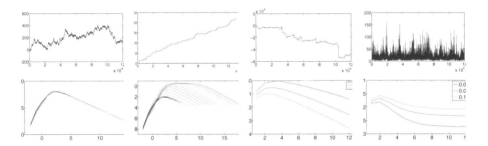

Figure 8.10 Upper row: Realizations of a Brownian motion, a Poisson point process, a Lévy process and a multifractal random cascade. Lower row: the corresponding normalized second-order coefficients.

8.5 Non-Euclidean Scattering

Scattering representations defined over the translation group are extended to other global transformation groups by defining Littlewood–Paley wavelet decompositions on non-Euclidean domains with group convolutions. Wavelet decompositions can also be defined on domains lacking global symmetries, such as graphs and manifolds. In this section we present this formalism and discuss several applications.

8.5.1 Joint versus Separable Scattering

Let us consider the question of building a signal representation $\Phi(\mathbf{x})$ that is invariant under the action of a certain transformation group G acting on $\mathbf{L}^2(\mathbb{R}^d)$:

$$G \times \mathbf{L}^2(\mathbb{R}^d) \to \mathbf{L}^2(\mathbb{R}^d),$$

$$(g, \mathbf{x}) \mapsto \mathbf{x}_g \ .$$

The signal representation Φ is G-invariant if $\Phi(\mathbf{x}_g) = \Phi(\mathbf{x})$ for all $g \in G$, and G-equivariant if $\Phi(\mathbf{x}_g) = (\Phi(\mathbf{x}))_g$; that is, G acts on the image of Φ respecting the axioms of a group action.

Now, suppose that the group G admits a factorization as a *semidirect* product of two subgroups G_1, G_2:

$$G = G_1 \rtimes G_2 \ .$$

This means that G_1 is a normal subgroup of G and that each element $g \in G$ can be uniquely written as $g = g_1 g_2$, with $g_i \in G_i$. It is thus tempting to leverage group factorizations to build invariants to complex groups by combining simpler invariants and equivariants as building blocks.

Suppose that Φ_1 is G_1-invariant and G_2-equivariant, and Φ_2 is G_2-invariant. Then $\bar{\Phi} := \Phi_2 \circ \Phi_1$ satisfies, for all $(g_1, g_2) \in G_1 \rtimes G_2$,

$$\bar{\Phi}(\mathbf{x}_{g_1 g_2}) = \Phi_2((\Phi_1(\mathbf{x}))_{g_2}) = \Phi_2(\Phi_1(\mathbf{x})) = \bar{\Phi}(\mathbf{x}) \ ,$$

showing that we can effectively build larger invariants by composing simpler invariants and equivariants.

However, such a compositional approach comes with a loss of discriminative power (Sifre and Mallat, 2013). Indeed, whereas a group can be factorized into smaller groups, the group action that acts on the data is seldom separable, as illustrated in Figure 8.11. In the case of images $\mathbf{x} \in \mathbf{L}^2(\mathbb{R}^2)$, an important example comes from the action of general affine transformations of $\mathbb{R}^2$. This motivates the construction of joint scattering representations in the roto-translation group, to be discussed next.

8.5.2 Scattering on Global Symmetry Groups

We illustrate the ideas from §8.5.1 with the construction of a scattering representation over the roto-translation group for images, as developed in Sifre and Mallat (2013) and Oyallon and Mallat (2015), for the Heisenberg group of frequency transpositions (Andén and Mallat, 2014; Andén et al., 2018), and for SO(3) in quantum chemistry (Hirn et al., 2017; Eickenberg et al., 2017). In essence, these representations adapt the construction in §8.3 by defining appropriate wavelet decompositions over the roto-translation group.

Figure 8.11 From Sifre and Mallat (2013). The left and right textures are not discriminated by a separable invariant along rotations and translations, but can be discriminated by a joint invariant.

Roto-translation group. The roto-translation group is formed by pairs $g = (v, \alpha) \in \mathbb{R}^2 \times SO(2)$ acting on $u \in \Omega$ as follows:

$$(g, u) \mapsto g \cdot u := v + R_\alpha u,$$

where R_α is a rotation of the plane by an angle α. One can easily verify that the set of all pairs (v, α) forms a group $G_{\mathrm{Rot}} \simeq \mathbb{R}^2 \rtimes SO(2)$, with group multiplication defined as

$$(v_1, \alpha_1) \cdot (v_2, \alpha_2) = (v_1 + R_{\alpha_1} v_2, \alpha_1 + \alpha_2).$$

The group acts on images $\mathbf{x}(u)$ by the usual composition: $\mathbf{x}_g := \mathbf{x}(g^{-1} \cdot u)$.

Wavelet decompositions over a compact group are obtained from group convolutions, defined as weighted averages over the group. Specifically, if $\tilde{\mathbf{x}} \in L^2(G)$ and $h \in L^1(G)$, the *group convolution* of $\mathbf{x}$ with the filter h is

$$\tilde{\mathbf{x}} \star_G h(g) := \int_G \mathbf{x}_g h(g^{-1}) \, d\mu(g). \tag{8.38}$$

Here μ is the uniform Haar measure over G. One can immediately verify that group convolutions are the only linear operators which are equivariant with respect to the group action: $\tilde{\mathbf{x}}_{g'} \star_G h(g) = \tilde{\mathbf{x}} \star_G h((g')^{-1} \cdot g)$ for all $g, g' \in G$.

Given an input $\mathbf{x}(u)$, $u \in \Omega \subset \mathbb{R}^2$, we consider first a wavelet decomposition over the translation group $W_1 = \{\psi_{j,\theta}\}_{\theta \in SO(2), j \in \mathbb{Z}}$, with the dilations and rotations of a given mother wavelet. The corresponding propagated wavelet modulus coefficients become

$$U_1(\mathbf{x})(p_1) = |\mathbf{x} \star \psi_{j_1, \theta_1}|(u), \quad \text{with } p_1 := (u, j_1, \theta_1).$$

The vector of the coefficients is equivariant with respect to translations, since it is defined through spatial convolutions and pointwise non-linearities. We can verify that it is also equivariant with respect to rotations, since

$$U_1(r_\alpha \mathbf{x})(u, j_1, \theta_1) = U_1(\mathbf{x})(r_{-\alpha} u, j_1, \theta_1 - \alpha).$$

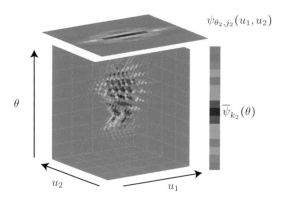

Figure 8.12 From Sifre and Mallat (2013). A wavelet defined on the roto-translation group, displayed in the 3D domain defined by positions u_1, u_2 and angles θ.

In summary, the first layer U_1 is G_{Rot}-equivariant, $U_1(\mathbf{x}_g) = [U_1(\mathbf{x})]_g$, with group action on the coefficients $g \cdot p_1 = (g \cdot u, j_1, \theta_1 - \alpha)$, for $g = (v, \alpha) \in G_{\mathrm{Rot}}$.

While the original scattering operator from §8.3 would now propagate each sub-band of $U_1\mathbf{x}$ independently using the same wavelet decomposition operator, roto-translation scattering now considers a joint wavelet decomposition W_2 defined over functions of G_{Rot}. Specifically, $W_2 = \{\Psi_\gamma\}_\gamma$ is a collection of wavelets defined in $L^1(G_{\mathrm{Rot}})$. In Sifre and Mallat (2013) and Oyallon and Mallat (2015) these wavelets are defined as separable products of spatial wavelets defined in $\Omega \subset \mathbb{R}^2$ with 1D wavelets defined in SO(2). Figure 8.12 illustrates one such Ψ_γ.

Importantly, the geometric stability and energy conservation properties described in §§8.3.2 and 8.3.3 carry over the roto-translation scattering (Mallat, 2012; Oyallon and Mallat, 2015). As discussed earlier, addressing the invariants jointly or separately gives different discriminability trade-offs. Some numerical applications greatly benefit from the joint representatation, in particular texture recognition under large viewpoint variability (Sifre and Mallat, 2013).

Time–frequency scattering. Joint scattering transforms also appear naturally in speech and audio processing, to leverage interactions of the signal energy at different time–frequency scales. The successful recognition of audio signals requires stability to small time-warps as well as frequency transpositions. Similarly to the previous example, where the input $\mathbf{x}(u)$ was 'lifted' to a function over the roto-translation group with appropriate equivariance properties, in the case of audio signals this initial lifting is carried out by the so-called *scalogram*, which computes a Littlewood–Paley wavelet decomposition mapping a time series $x(t)$ to a two-dimensional function $\mathbf{z}(t, \lambda) = |\mathbf{x} \star \psi_\lambda(t)|$ (Andén and Mallat, 2014). The time–frequency interactions in $\mathbf{z}$ can be captured by a joint wavelet decomposition

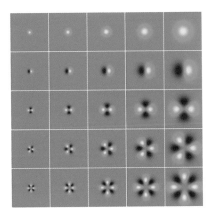 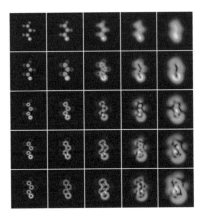

Figure 8.13 From Eickenberg et al. (2017). Left: Real parts of 2D solid harmonic wavelets. Cartesian slices of 3D spherical harmonic wavelets yield similar patterns. Right: Solid harmonic wavelet moduli $S[j, l, 1](\rho x)(u) = |\rho x \star \psi_j|(u)$ for a molecule ρx. The interference patterns at the different scales are reminiscent of molecular orbitals obtained in, e.g., density functional theory.

frame, leading to state-of-the-art classification and synthesis on several benchmarks (Andén et al., 2018).

Solid harmonic scattering for quantum chemistry Building representations of physical systems with rotational and translational invariance and stability to deformations is of fundamental importance across many domains, since these symmetries are present in many physical systems. Specifically, Hirn et al. (2017) and Eickenberg et al. (2017) studied scattering representations for quantum chemistry, by considering a wavelet decomposition over SO(3). Such a wavelet decomposition is constructed in the spectral domain, and given by spherical harmonics. The resulting scattering representation enjoys provable roto-translational invariance and stability under small deformations, and leads to state-of-the-art performance in the regression of molecular energies (Eickenberg et al., 2017). Figure 8.13 illustrates the 'harmonic' wavelets as well as the resulting scattering coefficients for some molecules.

8.5.3 Graph Scattering

In §8.5.2 we described invariant representations of functions defined over a *fixed* domain with *global* symmetries. Despite being of fundamental importance in physics, global symmetries are lacking in many systems in other areas of science, such as networks, surface meshes, or proteins. In those areas, one is rather interested in local symmetries, and often the domain is variable as well as the measurements over that domain.

Invariance and Stability in Graphs

In this context, graphs are flexible data structures that enable general metric structures and the modeling of non-Euclidean domains. The main ingredients of the scattering transform can be generalized using tools from computational harmonic analysis on graphs. As described in §8.2.3, the Euclidean treatment of deformations as changes of variables in the signal domain $\Omega \subset \mathbb{R}^d$, $u \mapsto \varphi_\tau(u) = u - \tau(u)$, can now be seen more generally as a change of metric, from an original metric domain X to a deformed metric domain X_τ.

We shall thus focus on deformations on the underlying graph domain, while keeping the same function-mapping, i.e., we model deformations as a change in the underlying graph support and analyze how this affects the interaction between the function mapping and the graph. Similarly to the group scattering constructions of §8.5.2, defining scattering representations for graphs amounts to defining wavelet decompositions with appropriate equivariance and stability and with averaging operators providing the invariance.

Consider a weighted undirected graph $G = (V, E, W)$ with $|V| = n$ nodes, edge set E and adjacency matrix $W \in \mathbb{R}^{n \times n}$, with $W_{i,j} > 0$ if and only if $(i, j) \in E$. In this context, the natural notion of invariance is given by permutations acting simultaneously on nodes and edges. Let us define $G_\pi = (\tilde{V}, \tilde{E}, \tilde{W})$ such that there exists a permutation $\pi \in S_n$ with $\tilde{v}_i = v_{\pi(i)}$, $(\tilde{i}, \tilde{j}) \in \tilde{E}$ if and only if $(\pi(i), \pi(j)) \in E$ and $\tilde{W} = \Pi W \Pi^\top$, where $\Pi \in \{0, 1\}^{n \times n}$ is the permutation matrix associated with π. Many applications require a representation Φ such that $\Phi(\mathbf{x}; G) = \Phi(\mathbf{x}_\pi, G_\pi) = \Phi(\mathbf{x}, G)$ for all π.

Previously, Littlewood–Paley wavelets were designed in connection with a non-expansive operator $\|W\| \le 1$ with small commutation error with respect to deformations: $\|[W, \mathcal{L}_\tau]\| \lesssim \|\nabla \tau\|$. The first task is to quantify the metric perturbations X_τ induced by deforming the graph.

Diffusion Metric Distances

A weighted undirected graph $G = (V, E, W)$ with $|V| = n$ nodes, edge set E and adjacency matrix $W \in \mathbb{R}^{n \times n}$ defines a diffusion process A on its nodes that is given in its symmetric form by the normalized adjacency

$$\overline{W} := D^{-1/2} W D^{-1/2}, \quad \text{with } D = \text{diag}(d_1, \dots, d_n), \tag{8.39}$$

where $d_i = \sum_{(i,j) \in E} W_{i,j}$ denotes the degree of node i. Denote by $\mathbf{d} = W\mathbf{1}$ the degree vector containing d_i in the ith element. By construction, $\overline{W}$ is well localized in space (it is non-zero only where there is an edge connecting nodes), it is self-adjoint and it satisfies $\|\overline{W}\| \leq 1$, where $\|\overline{W}\|$ is the operator norm. It is convenient to assume that the spectrum of A (which is real and discrete since $\overline{W}$ is self-adjoint and finite dimensional) is non-negative. Since we shall be taking powers of $\overline{W}$, this will avoid folding negative eigenvalues into positive ones. For that purpose, we adopt so-called *lazy diffusion*, given by $T := \frac{1}{2}(I + \overline{W})$. We will use this diffusion operator to define both a multiscale wavelet filter bank and a low-pass average pooling, leading to the diffusion scattering representation.

This diffusion operator can be used to construct a metric on G. So-called *diffusion maps* (Coifman and Lafon, 2006; Nadler et al., 2006) measure distances between two nodes $x, x' \in V$ in terms of their associated diffusion at time s: $d_{G,s}(x, x') = \|T_G^s \delta_x - T_G^s \delta_{x'}\|$, where δ_x is a vector with all zeros except for a unit in position x. This diffusion metric can be now used to define a distance between two graphs G, G'. Assuming first that G and G' have the same size, the simplest formulation is to compare the diffusion metrics generated by G and G' up to a node permutation:

Definition 8.19. Let $G = (V, E, W)$, $G' = (V', E', W')$ have the same size $|V| = |V'| = n$. The normalized diffusion distance between graphs G, G' at time $s > 0$ is

$$d^s(G, G') := \inf_{\Pi \in \Pi_n} \|(T_G^s)^*(T_G^s) - \Pi^\top (T_{G'}^s)^*(T_{G'}^s)\Pi\| = \inf_{\Pi \in \Pi_n} \|T_G^{2s} - \Pi^\top T_{G'}^{2s}\Pi\|,$$
(8.40)

where Π_n is the space of $n \times n$ permutation matrices.

The diffusion distance is defined at a specific time s. As s increases, this distance becomes weaker,[3] since it compares points at later stages of diffusion. The role of time is thus to select the smoothness of the 'graph deformation', just as $\|\nabla \tau\|$ measures the smoothness of the deformation in the Euclidean case. For convenience, we write $d(G, G') = d^{1/2}(G, G')$ and use the distance at $s = 1/2$ as our main deformation measure. The quantity d defines a distance between graphs (seen as metric spaces) and yields a stronger topology than other alternatives such as the Gromov–Hausdorff distance, defined as

$$d_{\mathrm{GH}}^s(G, G') = \inf_{\Pi} \sup_{x, x' \in V} \left| d_G^s(x, x') - d_{G'}^s(\pi(x), \pi(x')) \right|$$

with $d_G^s(x, x') = \|T_G^t(\delta_x - \delta_{x'})\|_{L^2(G)}$. Finally, we are considering for simplicity only the case where the sizes of G and G' are equal, but Definition 8.19 can be naturally extended to compare variable-sized graphs by replacing permutations by soft correspondences (see Bronstein et al., 2010).

Our goal is to build a stable and rich representation $\Phi_G(\mathbf{x})$. The stability property is stated in terms of the diffusion metric above: for a chosen diffusion time s, for all

---

[3] In the sense that it defines a weaker topology, i.e., $\lim_{m \to \infty} d^s(G, G_m) \to 0 \Rightarrow \lim_{m \to \infty} d^{s'}(G, G_m) = 0$ for $s' > s$, but not vice versa.

$\mathbf{x} \in \mathbb{R}^n$, $G = (V, E, W)$, $G' = (V', E', W')$ with $|V| = |V'| = n$, we require that

$$\|\Phi_G(\mathbf{x}) - \Phi_{G'}(\mathbf{x})\| \lesssim \|\mathbf{x}\| d(G, G') . \qquad (8.41)$$

This representation can be used to model both signals and domains, or just domains G, by considering a prespecified $\mathbf{x} = f(G)$ such as the degree, or by marginalizing from an exchangeable distribution $\Phi_G = \mathbb{E}_{\mathbf{x} \sim Q} \Phi_G(\mathbf{x})$.

The motivation of (8.41) is two-fold: on the one hand, we are interested in applications where the signal of interest may be measured in dynamic environments that modify the domain, e.g., in measuring brain signals across different individuals. On the other hand, in other applications, such as building generative models for graphs, we may be interested in representing the domain G itself. A representation from the adjacency matrix of G needs to build invariance with respect to node permutations, while capturing enough discriminative information to separate different graphs. In particular, and similarly to Gromov-Hausdorff distance, the definition of $d(G, G')$ involves a matching problem between two kernel matrices, which defines an NP-hard combinatorial problem. This further motivates the need for efficient representations Φ_G of graphs that can efficiently tell two graphs apart, and such that $\ell(\theta) = \|\Phi_G - \Phi_{G(\theta)}\|$ can be used as a differentiable loss for training generative models.

Diffusion Wavelets

Diffusion wavelets (Coifman and Lafon, 2006) provide a simple framework to define a multi-resolution analysis from powers of a diffusion operator defined on a graph, and they are stable to diffusion metric changes.

Let $\lambda_0 \geq \lambda_1 \geq \cdots \geq \lambda_{n-1}$ denote the eigenvalues of an operator A in decreasing order. Defining $\mathbf{d}^{1/2} = (\sqrt{d_1}, \ldots, \sqrt{d_n})$, one can easily verify that the normalized square-root degree vector $\mathbf{v} = \mathbf{d}^{1/2}/\|\mathbf{d}^{1/2}\|_2 = \mathbf{d}/\|\mathbf{d}\|_1$ is the eigenvector with associated eigenvalue $\lambda_0 = 1$. Also, note that $\lambda_{n-1} = -1$ if and only if G has a connected component that is non-trivial and bipartite (Chung and Graham, 1997).

Following Coifman and Lafon (2006), we construct a family of multiscale filters by exploiting the powers of the diffusion operator T^{2^j}. We define

$$\psi_0 := I - T, \quad \psi_j := T^{2^{j-1}}(I - T^{2^{j-1}}) = T^{2^{j-1}} - T^{2^j}, \quad j > 0 . \qquad (8.42)$$

This corresponds to a graph wavelet filter bank with optimal spatial localization. Graph diffusion wavelets are localized both in space and frequency, and favor a spatial localization, since they can be obtained with only two *filter coefficients*, namely $h_0 = 1$ for diffusion $T^{2^{j-1}}$ and $h_1 = -1$ for diffusion T^{2^j}. The finest scale ψ_0 corresponds to one-half of the normalized Laplacian operator

$$\psi_0 = \frac{1}{2}\Delta = \frac{1}{2}(I - D^{-1/2}WD^{-1/2}),$$

here seen as a temporal difference in a diffusion process, seeing each diffusion step (each multiplication by Δ) as a time step. The coarser scales ψ_j capture temporal differences at increasingly spaced diffusion times. For $j = 0, \ldots, J_n - 1$, we consider the linear operator

$$
\begin{aligned}
\mathcal{W} : L^2(G) &\rightarrow (L^2(G))^{J_n}, \\
\mathbf{x} &\mapsto (\psi_j \mathbf{x})_{j=0,\ldots,J_n-1},
\end{aligned}
\tag{8.43}
$$

which is the analog of the wavelet filter bank in the Euclidean domain. Whereas several other options exist for defining graph wavelet decompositions (Rustamov and Guibas, 2013; Gavish et al., 2010), we consider here wavelets that can be expressed with few diffusion terms, favoring spatial over frequential localization, for stability reasons that will become apparent next. We choose dyadic scales for convenience, but the construction is analogous if one replaces scales 2^j by $\lceil \gamma^j \rceil$, for any $\gamma > 1$, in (8.42). If the graph G exhibits a *spectral gap*, i.e., $\beta_G = \sup_{i=1,\ldots n-1} |\lambda_i| < 1$, the linear operator $\mathcal{W}$ defines a stable frame.

Proposition 8.20 (Gama et al., 2018, Prop 4.1). *For each n, let $\mathcal{W}$ define the diffusion wavelet decomposition (8.43) and assume that $\beta_G < 1$. Then there exists a constant $0 < C(\beta)$, depending only on β, such that for any $\mathbf{x} \in \mathbb{R}^n$ satisfying $\langle \mathbf{x}, \mathbf{v} \rangle = 0$, it holds that*

$$
C(\beta)\|\mathbf{x}\|^2 \leq \sum_{j=0}^{J_n-1} \|\psi_j \mathbf{x}\|^2 \leq \|\mathbf{x}\|^2.
\tag{8.44}
$$

This proposition thus provides the Littlewood–Paley bounds of $\mathcal{W}$, which control the ability of the filter bank to capture and amplify the signal $\mathbf{x}$ along each 'frequency'. We note that diffusion wavelets are neither unitary nor analytic and therefore do not preserve energy. However, the frame bounds in Proposition 8.20 provide lower bounds on the energy lost. They also inform us about how the spectral gap β determines the appropriate diffusion scale J: the maximum of $p(u) = (u^r - u^{2r})^2$ is at $u = 2^{-1/r}$, thus the cutoff r_* should align with β as $r_* = -1/\log_2 \beta$, since larger values of r capture energy in a spectral range where the graph has no information. Therefore, the maximum scale can be adjusted to be

$$
J = \lceil 1 + \log_2 r_* \rceil = 1 + \left\lceil \log_2 \left(\frac{-1}{\log_2 \beta} \right) \right\rceil.
$$

Diffusion Scattering

Recall that the Euclidean scattering transform is constructed by cascading three building blocks: a wavelet decomposition operator, a pointwise modulus activation function, and an averaging operator. Following the procedure for Euclidean scattering, given a graph G and $\mathbf{x} \in L^2(G)$ we define an analogous diffusion scattering transform $S_G(\mathbf{x})$ by cascading three building blocks: the wavelet decomposition operator $\mathcal{W}$, a pointwise activation function ρ, and an average operator A which extracts the average over the domain. The average over a domain can be interpreted as the diffusion at infinite time, thus $A\mathbf{x} = \lim_{t\to\infty} T^t \mathbf{x} = \langle \mathbf{v}, \mathbf{x}\rangle$. More specifically, we consider a first-layer transformation given by

$$S_G[\Lambda_1]\mathbf{x}) = A\rho\mathcal{W}\mathbf{x} = \{A\rho\psi_j\mathbf{x}\}_{0\le j\le J_n-1}, \qquad (8.45)$$

followed by second-order coefficients

$$S_G[\Lambda_2]\mathbf{x}) = A\rho\mathcal{W}\rho\mathcal{W}\mathbf{x} = \{A\rho\psi_{j_2}\rho\psi_{j_1}\mathbf{x}\}_{0\le j_1,j_2\le J_n-1}, \qquad (8.46)$$

and so on. The representation obtained from m layers of such a transformation is thus

$$S_{G,m}(\mathbf{x}) = \{A\mathbf{x}, S_G[\Lambda_1](\mathbf{x}),\ldots,S_G[\Lambda_m](\mathbf{x})\} = \{A(\rho\mathcal{W})^k\mathbf{x}\,;\ k = 0,\ldots,m-1\}. \qquad (8.47)$$

Stability and Invariance of Diffusion Scattering

The scattering transform coefficients $S_G(\mathbf{x})$ obtained after m layers are given by (8.47), for a low-pass operator A such that $A\mathbf{x} = \langle \mathbf{v}, \mathbf{x}\rangle$.

The stability of diffusion wavelets with respect to small changes of the diffusion metric can be leveraged to obtain a resulting diffusion scattering representation with prescribed stability, as shown by the following theorem.

Theorem 8.21 (Gama et al., 2018, Theorem 5.3). *Let $\beta_- = \min(\beta_G,\beta_{G'})$ and $\beta_+ = \max(\beta_G,\beta_{G'})$ and assume $\beta_+ < 1$. Then, for each $k = 0,\ldots,m-1$, the following holds:*

$$\|S_{G,m}(\mathbf{x}) - S_{G',m}(\mathbf{x})\|^2$$

$$\le \sum_{k=0}^{m-1} \left[\left(\frac{2}{1-\beta_-}\,d(G,G')\right)^{1/2} + k\sqrt{\frac{\beta_+^2(1+\beta_+^2)}{(1-\beta_+^2)^3}}\,d(G,G')\right]^2 \|\mathbf{x}\|^2$$

$$\lesssim m\,d(G,G')\|\mathbf{x}\|^2 \quad \text{if } d(G,G') \ll 1. \qquad (8.48)$$

This result shows that the closer two graphs are in terms of the diffusion metric, the closer will be their scattering representations. The constant is given by topological properties, the spectral gaps of G and G', as well as design parameters and the number of layers m. We observe that, as the stability bound grows, the smaller the spectral gap becomes, as is the case when more layers are considered. The spectral gap is tightly linked with diffusion processes on graphs, and thus it does emerge from the choice of a diffusion metric. Graphs with values of β closer to 1 exhibit weaker diffusion paths, and thus a small perturbation on the edges of these graphs would lead to a larger diffusion distance. We also note that the spectral gap appears in our upper bounds, but it is not necessarily sharp. In particular, the spectral gap is a poor indication of stability in regular graphs, and we believe that our bound can be improved by leveraging the structural properties of regular domains.

Finally, we note that the size of the graphs under comparison impacts the stability result inasmuch as it impacts the distance measure $d(G, G')$. A similar scattering construction was developed in Zou and Lerman (2020), where the authors established stability with respect to a graph measure that depends on the spectrum of the graph through both eigenvectors and eigenvalues. More specifically, it is required that the spectrum becomes more concentrated as the graphs grow. However, in general, it is not straightforward to relate the topological structure of the graph to its spectral properties.

As mentioned above, the stability is computed with a metric $d(G, G')$ which is stronger than might be expected. This metric is permutation invariant, in analogy with the rigid translation invariance in the Euclidean case, and stable with respect to small perturbations around permutations. Recently, Gama et al. (2019) extended the previous stability analysis to more general wavelet decompositions, using a *relative* notion of deformation. Figure 8.14 illustrates the performance of graph scattering operators on several graph signal processing tasks. Moreover, Gao et al. (2019) developed a similar scattering representation for graphs, achieving state-of-the-art results on several graph classification tasks. The extension of (8.48) to weaker metrics, using e.g. multiscale deformations, is an important open question.

Unsupervised Haar Scattering on Graphs

A particularly simple wavelet representation on graphs – which avoids any spectral decomposition – is given by Haar wavelets (Gavish et al., 2010). Such wavelets were used in the first work, Chen et al. (2014), that extended scattering representations to graphs. Given an undirected graph $G = (V, E)$, an *orthogonal Haar scattering* transform is obtained from a multiresolution approximation of G. Let $G_0 := G$. In the dyadic case $|V| = 2^J$, this transform is defined as a hierarchical partition $\{V_{j,n}\}_{j,n}$ of G of the form

$$V_{0,i} = \{i\}, \ i \le 2^J; \quad V_{j+1,i} = V_{j,a_i} \sqcup V_{j,b_i}, \ i = 1 \le 2^{J-j-1},$$

where the pairings (a_i, b_i) are connected in the induced subsampled graph $G_j = (V_j, E_j)$, of size $|V_j| = 2^{J-j}$, whose vertices are precisely $V_j := \{V_{j,i}\}_i$ and whose edges are inherited recursively from G_{j-1}: $(i, i') \in E_j$ if and only if there exists $\bar{e} = (\bar{i}, \bar{i}') \in E_{j-1}$ with $\bar{i} \in V_{j,i}$ and $\bar{i}' \in V_{j,i'}$.

Let $\mathbf{x} \in l^2(G)$. By rearranging the pairings sequentially, the resulting orthogonal

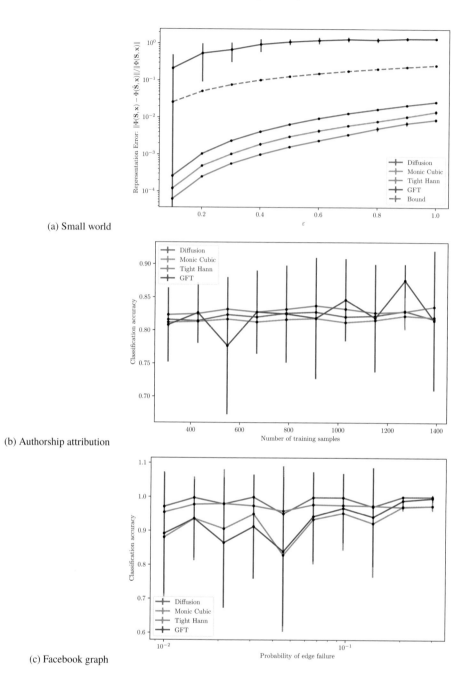

(a) Small world

(b) Authorship attribution

(c) Facebook graph

Figure 8.14 From Gama et al. (2019). (a): Difference in representation between signals defined using the original graph scattering S_G and $S_{G'}$ corresponding to the deformed graph, as a function of the perturbation size $d(G, G')$. (b), (c): Classification accuracy as a function of perturbation for an authorship attribution graph and a Facebook graph, respectively.

Haar scattering representation $S_J \mathbf{x}$ is defined recursively as

$$S_0 \mathbf{x}(i, 0) := \mathbf{x}(i), \quad i = 1, \ldots, 2^J$$

$$S_{j+1} \mathbf{x}(i, 2q) := S_j \mathbf{x}(a_i, q) + S_j \mathbf{x}(b_i, q), \quad (8.49)$$

$$S_{j+1} \mathbf{x}(i, 2q + 1) := |S_j(a_i, q) - S_j(b_i, q)|, \quad i = 1, \ldots, 2^{J-j-1}, \ q = 2^j.$$

One easily verifies (Chen et al., 2014; Cheng et al., 2016) that the resulting transformation preserves the number, 2^J, of coefficients, and is contractive and unitary up to a normalization factor $2^{J/2}$. However, since the multiresolution approximation defines an orthogonal transformation, the resulting orthogonal scatering coefficients are not permutation invariant. In order to recover an invariant representation, it is thus necessary to average an ensemble of orthogonal transforms using different multiresolution approximations. Nevertheless, the main motivation in Chen et al. (2014); Cheng et al. (2016) was to perform graph scattering on domains with unknown (but presumed) graph connectivity structure. In that case, the sparsity of scattering coefficients was used as a criterion to find the optimal multiresolution approximation, resulting in state-of-the-art performance on several graph classification datasets.

8.5.4 Manifold Scattering

In the previous sections we have seen some instances of extending scattering representations to non-Euclidean domains, including compact Lie groups and graphs. Such extensions (which in fact also apply to the wider class of convolutional neural network architectures; see Bronstein et al. (2017) for an in-depth review) can be understood through the lens of the spectrum of differential operators, in particular the Laplacian. Indeed, the Laplacian operator encapsulates the symmetries and stability requirements that we have been manipulating so far, and can be defined across many different domains.

In particular, if $\mathcal{M}$ denotes a compact, smooth Riemannian manifold without boundary, one can define the Laplace–Beltrami operator Δ in $\mathcal{M}$ as the divergence of the manifold gradient. In these conditions, $-\Delta$ is self-adjoint and positive semidefinite; therefore its eigenvectors define an orthonormal basis of $L^2(\mathcal{M}, \mu)$, where μ is the uniform measure on $\mathcal{M}$. Expressing any $f \in L^2(\mathcal{M})$ in this basis amounts to computing a 'Fourier transform' on $\mathcal{M}$. Indeed, the Laplacian operator in $\mathbb{R}^d$ is precisely diagonal in the standard Euclidean Fourier basis. Convolutions in the Euclidean case can be seen as linear operators that diagonalize in the Fourier basis or equivalently that commute with the Laplacian operator. A natural generalization of convolutions to non-Euclidean domains $\mathcal{M}$ thus formally sees them as linear operators that commute with the Laplacian defined in $\mathcal{M}$ (Bruna et al., 2013;

Bronstein et al., 2017). Specifically, if $\{\varphi_k\}_k$ are the eigenvectors of Δ and $\Lambda :=$ $\{\lambda_k\}_k$ its eigenvalues, a function of *spectral multipliers* $\eta: \Lambda \to \mathbb{R}$ defines a kernel in $\mathcal{M}$:

$$K_\eta(u, v) = \sum_k \eta(\lambda_k)\varphi_k(u)\varphi_k(v), \quad u, v \in \mathcal{M},$$

and a 'convolution' from its corresponding integral operator:

$$
\begin{aligned}
L^2(\mathcal{M}) &\to L^2(\mathcal{M}) \\
\mathbf{x} &\mapsto (T_\eta\mathbf{x})(u) = \int K_\eta(u, v)\mathbf{x}(v)\mu(dv).
\end{aligned}
\tag{8.50}
$$

Perlmutter et al. (2018) used this formalism to build scattering representations on Riemannian manifolds, by defining Littlewood–Paley wavelet decompositions from appropriately chosen spectral multipliers $(\eta_j)_j$. The resulting scattering representation is shown to be stable to additive noise and to smooth diffeomorphisms of $\mathcal{M}$.

8.6 Generative Modeling with Scattering

In this section we discuss applications of scattering representation to build high-dimensional generative models. Data priors defined from the scattering representation enjoy geometric stability and may be used as models for stationary processes or to regularize ill-posed inverse problems.

8.6.1 Sufficient Statistics

Defining probability distributions of signals $\mathbf{x}(u) \in \mathbf{L}^2(\mathbb{R}^d)$ is a challenging task due to the curse of dimensionality and the lack of tractable analytic models of 'real' data. A powerful way for approaching this challenge is via the principle of maximum entropy: construct probability models that are maximally regular while satisfying a number of constraints given by a vector $\Phi(\mathbf{x}) \in \mathbb{R}^K$ of sufficient statistics that is fitted to the available data. When $\Phi(\mathbf{x}) = \mathbf{xx}^\top$ consists of covariance measurements, the resulting maximum entropy model is a Gaussian process, and when $\Phi(\mathbf{x})$ computes local potentials one obtains Markov random fields instead. In either case, one is quickly confronted with fundamental challenges, either statistical (exponential sample complexity for powerful statistical models, or large bias in small parametric ones) or computational, coming from the intractability of computing partition functions and sampling in high dimensions.

The sufficient statistics in a maximum entropy model capture our prior information about 'what matters' in the input data. In this subsection, we shall explore maximum entropy models where the sufficient statistics are given by scattering representations. Depending on the localization scale 2^J, two distinct regimes emerge. For fixed and relatively small scales J, windowed scattering representations provide local statistics that are nearly invertible, and help regularize ill-posed inverse problems (§8.6.4). As $J \to \infty$, expected scattering moments may be used to define models for stationary processes (§8.6.5).

Thanks to the scattering mean-squared consistency discussed in §8.4, we can circumvent the aforementioned challenges of maximum entropy models with the so-called *microcanonical* models from statistical physics, to be described in §8.6.2. In both regimes an important algorithmic component will be solving a problem of the form $\min_{\mathbf{x}} \|S(\mathbf{x}) - y\|$. We discuss a gradient descent strategy for that purpose in §8.6.3.

8.6.2 *Microcanonical Scattering Models*

First, suppose that we wish to characterize a probability distribution μ over input signals $\mathbf{x} \in \mathcal{D} = \mathbf{L}^2(\mathbb{R}^d)$, from the knowledge that $S_J(\mathbf{x}) \approx y$. In this setup, we could think of y as being an empirical average

$$y = \frac{1}{n} \sum_{i=1}^{n} S_J(\mathbf{x}_i),$$

where $\mathbf{x}_i$ are training samples that are conditionally independent and identically distributed.

Recall that the differential entropy of a probability distribution μ which admits a density $p(\mathbf{x})$ relative to the Lebesgue measure is

$$H(\mu) := -\int p(\mathbf{x}) \log p(\mathbf{x}) \, d\mathbf{x}. \tag{8.51}$$

In the absence of any other source of information, the classic macrocanonical model from Boltzmann and Gibbs, μ^{ma}, has density p_{ma} at maximum entropy, conditioned on $\mathbb{E}_{p_{\mathrm{ma}}}(S_J(\mathbf{x})) = y$. However, a microcanonical model replaces the expectation constraint with an empirical constraint of the form $\|S_J(\mathbf{x}) - y\| \le \epsilon$ for small, appropriately chosen, ϵ.

Despite being similar in appearance, microcanonical and macrocanonical models have profound differences. On the one hand, under appropriate conditions, macrocanonical models may be expressed as Gibbs distributions of the form

$$p_{\mathrm{ma}}(\mathbf{x}) = \frac{e^{\langle \theta, S_J(\mathbf{x}) \rangle}}{Z_\theta},$$

where Z_θ is the normalizing constant or partition function and θ is a vector of

Lagrange multipliers enforcing the expectation constraint. Unfortunately, this vector has no closed-form expression in terms of estimable quantities in general, and needs to be adjusted using MCMC (Wainwright et al., 2008). On the other hand, microcanonical models have compact support. However, under mild ergodicity assumptions on the underlying data-generating process, one can show that both models become asymptotically equivalent via the Boltzmann equivalence principle (Dembo and Zeitouni, 1993) as $J \to \infty$, although microcanonical models may exist even when their macrocanonical equivalents do not (Bruna and Mallat, 2018; Chatterjee, 2017). Also, estimating microcanonical models does not require the costly estimation of Lagrange multipliers.

Microcanonical models. The microcanonical set of width ϵ associated with y is

$$\Omega_{J,\epsilon} = \{x \in \mathcal{D} : \|S_J(x) - y\| \le \epsilon\}.$$

A maximum entropy microcanonical model $\mu^{\mathrm{mi}}(J, \epsilon, y)$ was defined by Boltzmann as the maximum entropy distribution supported in $\Omega_{J,\epsilon}$. If we assume conditions which guarantee that S_J preserves energy (§8.3.2), then we can verify that $\Omega_{J,\epsilon}$ is a compact set. It follows that the maximum entropy distribution has a uniform density $p_{d,\epsilon}$:

$$p_{d,\epsilon}(x) := \frac{1_{\Omega_{J,\epsilon}}(x)}{\int_{\Omega_{J,\epsilon}} dx}. \tag{8.52}$$

Its entropy is therefore the logarithm of the volume of $\Omega_{J,\epsilon}$:

$$H(p_{d,\epsilon}) = -\int p_{d,\epsilon}(x) \log p_{d,\epsilon}(x)\, dx = \log\left(\int_{\Omega_{J,\epsilon}} dx\right). \tag{8.53}$$

The scale J corresponds to an important trade-off in this model, as illustrated in the case where $y = S_J(\bar{x})$ represent measurements coming from a single realization. When J is small, as explained in §8.3.4, the number of scattering coefficients is larger than the input dimension, and thus one may expect $\Omega_{J,\epsilon}$ to converge to a single point $\bar{x}$ as $\epsilon \to 0$. As J increases, the system of equations $S_J(x) = S_J(\bar{x})$ becomes under-constrained, and thus $\Omega_{J,\epsilon}$ will be a non-singular set. Figure 8.8 illustrates this on a collection of input images. The entropy of the microcanonical model thus grows with J. It was proved in Bruna and Mallat (2018) that under mild assumptions the entropy is an *extensive* quantity, meaning that its growth is of the same order as 2^J, the support of the representation.

The appropriate scale J needs to balance two opposing effects. On the one hand, we want S_J to satisfy a concentration property to ensure that typical samples from the unknown data distribution μ are included in $\Omega_{J,\epsilon}$ with high probability, and hence are typical for the microcanonical measure μ^{mi}. On the other hand, the sets $\Omega_{J,\epsilon}$ must not be too large in order to avoid having elements of $\Omega_{J,\epsilon}$ – and hence typical samples of μ^{mi} – which are not typical for μ. To obtain an accurate microcanonical model, the scale J must define microcanonical sets of minimum volume, while satisfying a concentration property akin to (8.25); see Bruna and Mallat (2018, Section 2.1) for further details. In particular, this implies that the only data distributions that admit a valid microcanonical model as J increases are ergodic, stationary textures, where spatial averages converge to the expectation. Bruna and Mallat (2018) developed microcanonical models built from scattering representations, showing the ability of such representations to model complex stationary phenomena such as Ising models, point processes and natural textures with tractable sample complexity. We will illustrate scattering microcanonical models for such textures in §8.6.5. In essence, these models need to sample from the uniform measure of sets of the form $\{\mathbf{x}; \|S(\mathbf{x}) - y\| \leq \epsilon\}$. We describe next how to solve this efficiently using gradient descent.

8.6.3 Gradient Descent Scattering Reconstruction

Computing samples of a maximum entropy microcanonical model is typically done with MCMC algorithms or Langevin dynamics (Creutz, 1983), which is computationally expensive. Microcanonical models computed with alternative projections and gradient descents have been implemented to sample texture synthesis models (Heeger and Bergen, 1995; Portilla and Simoncelli, 2000; Gatys et al., 2015).

We will consider microcanonical gradient descent models obtained by transporting an initial measure towards a microcanonical set, using gradient descent with respect to the distance to the microcanoncal ensemble. Although this gradient descent sampling algorithm does not in general correspond to the maximum entropy microcanonical model, it preserves many symmetries of the maximum entropy microcanonical measure, and has been shown to converge to the microcanonical set for appropriate choices of energy vector (Bruna and Mallat, 2018).

We transport an initial measure μ_0 towards a measure supported in a microcanonical set $\Omega_{J,\epsilon}$, by iteratively minimizing

$$E(\mathbf{x}) = \frac{1}{2}\|S_J(\mathbf{x}) - y\|^2 \qquad (8.54)$$

with mappings of the form

$$\varphi_n(\mathbf{x}) = \mathbf{x} - \kappa_n \nabla E(\mathbf{x}) = \mathbf{x} - \kappa_n \partial S_J(\mathbf{x})^\top (S_J(\mathbf{x}) - y), \qquad (8.55)$$

where κ_n is the gradient step at each iteration n.

Given an initial measure μ_0, the measure update is

$$\mu_{n+1} := \varphi_{n,\#}\mu_n, \qquad (8.56)$$

with the standard pushforward measure $f_\#(\mu)[\mathcal{A}] = \mu[f^{-1}(\mathcal{A})]$ for any μ-measurable set $\mathcal{A}$, where $f^{-1}(\mathcal{A}) = \{x; f(x) \in \mathcal{A}\}$.

Samples from μ_n are thus obtained by transforming samples $\mathbf{x}_0$ from μ_0 with the mapping $\bar{\varphi} = \varphi_n \circ \varphi_{n-1} \circ \cdots \circ \varphi_1$. It corresponds to n steps of a gradient descent initialized with $\mathbf{x}_0 \sim \mu_0$:

$$\mathbf{x}_{l+1} = \mathbf{x}_l - \kappa_l \partial S_J(\mathbf{x}_l)^\top (S_J(\mathbf{x}_l) - y).$$

Bruna and Mallat (2018) studied the convergence of the gradient descent measures μ_n for general choices of sufficient statistics including scattering vectors. Even if the μ_n converge to a measure supported in a microcanonical set $\Omega_{J,\epsilon}$, in general they do not converge to a maximum entropy measure on this set. However, the next theorem proves that if μ_0 is a Gaussian measure of i.i.d. Gaussian random variables then they have a large class of common symmetries with the maximum entropy measure. Let us recall that a symmetry of a measure μ is a linear invertible operator L such that, for any measurable set $\mathcal{A}$, $\mu[L^{-1}(\mathcal{A})] = \mu[\mathcal{A}]$. A linear invertible operator L is a symmetry of Φ_d if for all $\mathbf{x} \in \mathcal{D}$, $S_J(L^{-1}\mathbf{x}) = S_J(\mathbf{x})$. It preserves volumes if its determinant satisfies $|\det L| = 1$. It is orthogonal if $L^t L = LL^t = I$ and we say that it preserves a stationary mean if, $L\mathbf{1} = \mathbf{1}$ for $\mathbf{1} = (1,\ldots,1) \in \mathbb{R}^\ell$.

Theorem 8.22 (Bruna and Mallat, 2018, Theorem 3.4). (i) *If L is a symmetry of S_J which preserves volumes then it is a symmetry of the maximum entropy microcanonical measure.*

(ii) *If L is a symmetry of S_J and of μ_0 then it is a symmetry of μ_n for any $n \geq 0$.*

(iii) *Suppose that μ_0 is a Gaussian white noise measure of d i.i.d. Gaussian random variables. Then, if L is a symmetry of Φ_d which is orthogonal and preserves a stationary mean, it is a symmetry of μ_n for any $n \geq 0$.*

The initial measure μ_0 is chosen so that it has many symmetries in common with Φ_d and hence the gradient descent measures have many symmetries in common with a maximum entropy measure. A Gaussian measure of i.i.d. Gaussian variables of mean m_0 and σ_0 is a maximum entropy measure conditioned by a stationary mean and variance. It is uniform over spheres, which guarantees that it has a large group of symmetries.

Observe that periodic shifts are linear orthogonal operators and preserve a stationary mean. The following corollary applies property (iii) of Theorem 8.22 to prove that the μ_n are circular-stationary.

Corollary 8.23 (Bruna and Mallat, 2018, Corollary 3.5). *When $J \to \infty$ then S_J is invariant with respect to periodic shift. Therefore if μ_0 is a Gaussian white noise then μ_n is circular-stationary for $n \geq 0$.*

8.6.4 *Regularising Inverse Problems with Scattering*

Ill-posed inverse problems attempt to estimate an unknown signal $\mathbf{x}$ from noisy, possibly non-linear and under-determined measurements $\mathbf{y} = \mathcal{G}\mathbf{x} + w$, where w models the additive noise. A natural Bayesian perspective is to consider the maximum-a-posteriori (MAP) estimate, given by

$$\hat{\mathbf{x}} \in \arg\max p(\mathbf{x}|\mathbf{y}) = \arg\max p(\mathbf{x}) \cdot p(\mathbf{y}|\mathbf{x}) = \arg\max \log p(\mathbf{x}) + \log p(\mathbf{y}|\mathbf{x}).$$

Under a Gaussian noise assumption, $-\log p(\mathbf{y}|\mathbf{x})$ takes the familiar form $C\|\mathbf{y} - \mathcal{G}\mathbf{x}\|^2$. Regularizing inverse problems using microcanonical scattering generative models thus amounts to choosing a prior $\log p(\mathbf{x})$ of the form

$$\|S_J(\mathbf{x}) - \mathbf{z}\|^2,$$

where $\mathbf{z}$ can be adjusted using a training set.

If μ denotes the underlying data-generating distribution of signals $\mathbf{x}$, such a prior implicitly assumes that scattering coefficients $S_J(\mathbf{x})$, are concentrated around $\mathbf{x} \sim \mu$. In some applications, however, μ may not enjoy such ergodocity properties, in which case one can also consider a microcanonical 'amortised' prior that is allowed to depend on the scattering coefficients of the measurements. The resulting estimator thus becomes

$$\hat{\mathbf{x}} \in \arg\min_{\mathbf{x}} \|\mathcal{G}\mathbf{x} - \mathbf{y}\|^2 + \beta\|S_J\mathbf{x} - MS_J\mathbf{y}\|^2 a, \tag{8.57}$$

M being a linear operator learned by solving a linear regression of pairs $(S_J\mathbf{x}_i, S_J\mathbf{y}_i)_i$ in the scattering domain and where $\{\mathbf{x}_i, \mathbf{y}_i\}_i$ is a training set of input–output pairs.

This estimator differs from typical data-driven estimators that leverage supervised training in inverse problems using CNNs. More specifically, given a trainable model $\mathbf{x}_\theta = \Phi(\mathbf{y}; \theta)$, one considers

$$\hat{\mathbf{x}}_{\text{CNN}} = \mathbf{x}_{\theta^*}, \quad \text{where } \theta^* \in \arg\min_{\theta} \sum_i \|\mathbf{x}_i - \Phi(\mathbf{y}_i; \theta)\|^2. \tag{8.58}$$

See Adler and Öktem (2018); Zhang et al. (2017); Jin et al. (2017) for recent surveys on data-driven models for imaging inverse problems. Despite their phenomenal success across many inverse problems, such estimators suffer from the so-called 'regression-to-the-mean' phenomenon, in which the model is asked to predict a specific input $\mathbf{x}_i$ from potentially many plausible signals explaining the same observations $\mathbf{y}_i$; this leads to an estimator that averages all such plausible solutions, thus losing high-frequency and texture information. Instead, the scattering mircocanonical estimator (8.57) learns a linear operator using the scattering metric, which leverages the stability of the scattering transform to small deformations in order to avoid the regression-to-the-mean of baseline estimators.

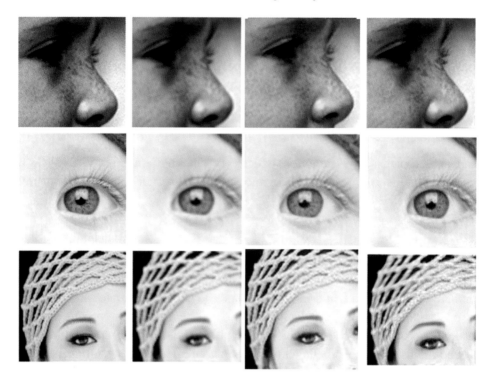

Figure 8.15 Comparison of single-image super-resolution using scattering microcanonical prior and pure data-driven models, for a linear model (leading to spline interpolation) and for a CNN model from Dong et al. (2014). From left to right: original iamge, linear model, CNN model, and scattering model.

The estimator (8.57) was studied in Bruna et al. (2015b) using localized scattering, in the context of single-image super-resolution, and in Dokmanić et al. (2016) for other imaging inverse problems from, e.g., tomography. In all cases, the gradient descent algorithm from §8.6.3 was employed. Figure 8.15 compares the resulting estimates with spline interpolation and with estimators of the form (8.58).

Generative networks as inverse problems with scattering transforms. Angles and Mallat (2018) considered a variant of the microcanonical scattering model, by replacing the gradient descent sampling scheme of §8.6.3 with a learned deep convolutional network *generator*, which learns to map a vector of scattering coefficients $\mathbf{z} = S_J(\mathbf{x})$ back to $\mathbf{x}$. Deep generative models such as variational autoencoders (Kingma and Welling, 2014; Rezende et al., 2014) or GANs (Goodfellow et al., 2014) consider two networks, an *encoder* and a *decoder*. The encoder maps the data to a latent space with prescribed probability density, e.g. a standard Gaussian distribution, and the decoder maps it back to reconstruct the input. In this context, the scattering transform S_J may be used as an encoder on appropriate data distributions, thanks to its ability to linearize small deformations and 'Gaussianize' the input distribution (Angles and Mallat, 2018).

Finally, in Andreux and Mallat (2018) the authors used the time–frequency joint scattering transform of §8.5.2 and the learned decoder from Angles and Mallat (2018) for the generation and transformation of musical sounds.

8.6.5 *Texture Synthesis with Microcanonical Scattering*

An image or an audio texture is usually modeled as the realization of a stationary process. A texture model computes an approximation of this stationary process given a single realization, and texture synthesis then consists in calculating new realizations from this stochastic model.

Since in general the original stochastic process is not known, perceptual comparisons are the only criteria that can be used to evaluate a texture synthesis algorithm. Microcanonical models can be considered as texture models computed from an energy function $S_J(\mathbf{x})$ which concentrates close to its mean.

Geman and Geman (1984) introduced macrocanonical models based on Markov random fields. These provide good texture models as long as these textures are realizations of random processes having no long-range correlations. Several approaches were then introduced to incorporate long-range correlations. Heeger and Bergen (1995) captured texture statistics through the marginal distributions obtained by filtering images with oriented wavelets. This approach wasgeneralized by the macrocanonical frame model of Zhu et al. (1998), based on marginal distributions of filtered images. The filters are optimized by minimizing the maximum entropy conditioned by the marginal distributions. Although the Cramer–Wold theorem proves that enough marginal probability distributions characterize any random vector defined over $\mathbb{R}^d$, the number of such marginals is typically intractable which limits this approach. Portilla and Simoncelli (2000) made important improvements to these texture models using wavelet transforms. They captured the correlation of the modulus of wavelet coefficients with a covariance matrix which defines an energy vector $\Phi_d(x)$. Although they used a macrocanonical maximum entropy formalism, their algorithm computes a microcanonical estimation from a single realization with alternate projections as opposed to a gradient descent.

Excellent texture syntheses have recently been obtained with deep convolutional neural networks. In Gatys et al. (2015), the authors considered a deep VGG convolutional network, trained on a large-scale image classification task. The energy vector is defined as the spatial cross-correlation values of feature maps at every layer of the VGG networks. This energy vector is calculated for a particular texture image. Texture syntheses of very good perceptual quality are calculated with a

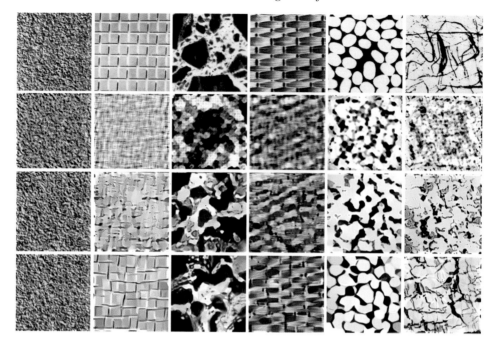

Figure 8.16 Examples of microcanonical texture synthesis using different vectors of sufficient statistics. From top to bottom: original samples, Gaussian model, first-order scattering and second-order scattering.

gradient descent microcanonical algorithm initialized on random noise. However, the dimension of this energy vector is larger than the dimension of the input image. These estimators are therefore not statistically consistent and have no asymptotic limit.

Figure 8.16 displays examples of textures from the Brodatz dataset synthesized using the scattering microcanonical model from Bruna and Mallat (2018), and gives a comparison of the effects of using either only first-order scattering coefficients or only covariance information. Although qualitatively better than these alternatives, deep convolutional networks reproduce image and audio textures with even better perceptual quality than that of scattering coefficients (Gatys et al., 2015), but use over 100 times more parameters. Much smaller models providing similar perceptual quality can be constructed with wavelet phase harmonics for audio signals (Mallat et al., 2018) or images (Zhang and Mallat, 2021); these capture alignment of phases across scales. However, understanding how to construct low-dimensional multiscale energy vectors for approximating random processes remains mostly an open problem.

8.7 Final Remarks

The aim of this was to provide chapter a comprehensive overview of scattering representations, more specifically to motivate their role in the puzzle of understanding the effectiveness of deep learning.

In the context of high-dimensional learning problems involving geometric data, beating the curse of dimensionality requires exploiting as many geometric priors as possible. In particular, good signal representations should be stable with respect to small metric perturbations of the domain, expressed as deformations in the case of natural images. Scattering representations, through their constructive approach to building such stability, reveal the role of convolutions, depth and scale that underpins the success of CNN architectures.

We have focused mostly on the theoretical aspects of the scattering representation, and some of its ramifications beyond the context of computer vision and learning. That said, logically we could not cover all application areas nor some of the recent advances, especially the links with turbulence analysis and other non-linear PDEs in physics, or applications to financial time series (Leonarduzzi et al., 2019), or video. Another important aspect that we did not address is the role of the non-linear activation function. All our discussion has focused on the complex modulus, but recent related work (Mallat et al., 2018) considered the half-rectification case through the notion of 'phase harmonics', of which the modulus can be seen as the 'fundamental', complemented by higher harmonics.

Despite the above points, the inherent limitation of a scattering theory in explaining deep learning is precisely that it does not consider the dynamical aspects of learning. Throughout numerous computer vision benchmarks, one systematically finds a performance gap between hand-designed scattering architectures and their fully trained counterparts, as soon as datasets become sufficiently large. The ability of CNNs to interpolate high-dimensional data while seemingly avoiding the curse of dimensionality remains an essential ability that scattering-based models currently lack. Hybrid approaches such as those outlined in Oyallon et al. (2018b) hold the promise of combining the interpretability and robustness of scattering models with the data-fitting power of large neural networks.

References

Adler, Jonas, and Öktem, Ozan. 2018. Learned primal–dual reconstruction. *IEEE Transactions on Medical Imaging*, **37**(6), 1322–1332.

Andén, Joakim, and Mallat, Stéphane. 2014. Deep scattering spectrum. *IEEE Transactions on Signal Processing*, **62**(16), 4114–4128.

Andén, Joakim, Lostanlen, Vincent, and Mallat, Stéphane. 2018. Classification with joint time–frequency scattering. ArXiv preprint arXiv:1807.08869.

Andreux, Mathieu, and Mallat, Stéphane. 2018. Music generation and transformation with moment matching–scattering inverse networks. Pages 327–333 of: *Proc. International Society for Music Retrieval Conference*.

Andreux, Mathieu, Angles, Tomás, Exarchakis, Georgios, Leonarduzzi, Roberto, Rochette, Gaspar, Thiry, Louis, Zarka, John, Mallat, Stéphane, Belilovsky, Eugene, Bruna, Joan, et al. 2018. Kymatio: Scattering transforms in Python. *J. Machine Learning Research*, **21**(60), 1–6.

Angles, Tomás, and Mallat, Stéphane. 2018. Generative networks as inverse problems with scattering transforms. In *Proc. International Conference on Learning Representations*.

Bietti, Alberto, and Mairal, Julien. 2019a. Group invariance, stability to deformations, and complexity of deep convolutional representations. *J. Machine Learning Research*, **20**(1), 876–924.

Bietti, Alberto, and Mairal, Julien. 2019b. On the inductive bias of neural tangent kernels. In *Proc. 33rd Neural Information Processing Systems*, pp. 12873–12884.

Bronstein, Alexander M., Bronstein, Michael M., Kimmel, Ron, Mahmoudi, Mona, and Sapiro, Guillermo. 2010. A Gromov–Hausdorff framework with diffusion geometry for topologically-robust non-rigid shape matching. *International Journal of Computer Vision*, **89**(2–3), 266–286.

Bronstein, Michael M., Bruna, Joan, LeCun, Yann, Szlam, Arthur, and Vandergheynst, Pierre. 2017. Geometric deep learning: Going beyond Euclidean data. *IEEE Signal Processing Magazine*, **34**(4), 18–42.

Bruna, J., and Mallat, S. 2013. Invariant scattering convolution networks. *Trans. Pattern Analysis and Machine Intelligence*, **35**(8), 1872–1886.

Bruna, Joan. 2013. *Scattering Representations for Recognition*. Ph.D. thesis, Ecole Polytechnique.

Bruna, Joan. 2019. Consistency of Haar scattering. Preprint.

Bruna, Joan, and Mallat, Stéphane. 2018. Multiscale sparse microcanonical models. ArXiv preprint arXiv:1801.02013.

Bruna, Joan, Zaremba, Wojciech, Szlam, Arthur, and LeCun, Yann. 2013. Spectral networks and locally connected networks on graphs. *Proc. International Conference on Learning Representations*.

Bruna, Joan, Mallat, Stéphane, Bacry, Emmanuel, Muzy, Jean-François, et al. 2015a. Intermittent process analysis with scattering moments. *Annals of Statistics*, **43**(1), 323–351.

Bruna, Joan, Sprechmann, Pablo, and LeCun, Yann. 2015b. Super-resolution with deep convolutional sufficient statistics. In *Proc. International Conference on Learning Representations*.

Chatterjee, Sourav. 2017. A note about the uniform distribution on the intersection of a simplex and a sphere. *Journal of Topology and Analysis*, **9**(4), 717–738.

Chen, Xu, Cheng, Xiuyuan, and Mallat, Stéphane. 2014. Unsupervised deep Haar scattering on graphs. Pages 1709–1717 of: *Advances in Neural Information Processing Systems*.

Cheng, Xiuyuan, Chen, Xu, and Mallat, Stéphane. 2016. Deep Haar scattering networks. *Information and Inference*, **5**, 105–133.

Chung, Fan, and Graham, R. K. 1997. *Spectral Graph Theory*. American Mathematical Society.

Cohen, Taco, and Welling, Max. 2016a. Group equivariant convolutional networks. Pages 2990–2999 of: *Proc. International Conference on Machine Learning*.

Cohen, Taco S., and Welling, Max. 2016b. Steerable CNNs. In: *Proc. International Conference on Learning Representations*.

Coifman, Ronald R., and Lafon, Stéphane. 2006. Diffusion maps. *Applied and Computational Harmonic Analysis*, **21**(1), 5–30.

Creutz, Michael. 1983. Microcanonical Monte Carlo simulation. *Physical Review Letters*, **50**(19), 1411.

Czaja, Wojciech, and Li, Weilin. 2017. Analysis of time–frequency scattering transforms. *Applied and Computational Harmonic Analysis*, **47**(1), 149–171.

Dembo, A., and Zeitouni, O. 1993. *Large Deviations Techniques and Applications*. Jones and Bartlett Publishers.

Dokmanić, Ivan, Bruna, Joan, Mallat, Stéphane, and de Hoop, Maarten. 2016. Inverse problems with invariant multiscale statistics. ArXiv preprint arXiv:1609.05502.

Dong, Chao, Loy, Chen Change, He, Kaiming, and Tang, Xiaoou. 2014. Learning a deep convolutional network for image super-resolution. Pages 184–199 of: *Proc. European Conference on Computer Vision*. Springer.

Doukhan, P., Oppenheim, G., and Taqqu, M. (eds.) 2002. *Theory and Applications of Long-Range Dependence*. Birkhauser.

Eickenberg, Michael, Exarchakis, Georgios, Hirn, Matthew, and Mallat, Stéphane. 2017. Solid harmonic wavelet scattering: Predicting quantum molecular energy from invariant descriptors of 3D electronic densities. Pages 6540–6549 of: *Advances in Neural Information Processing Systems*.

Fei-Fei, L., Fergus, R., and Perona, P. 2004. Learning generative visual models from few training examples: An incremental Bayesian approach tested on 101 object categories. *Proc. IEEE Conference on Computer Vision and Pattern Recognition*.

Felzenszwalb, Pedro F., Girshick, Ross B., McAllester, David, and Ramanan, Deva. 2010. Object detection with discriminatively trained part-based models. *Trans. Pattern Analysis and Machine Intelligence*, **32**(9), 1627–1645.

Gama, Fernando, Ribeiro, Alejandro, and Bruna, Joan. 2018. Diffusion scattering transforms on graphs. In *Proc. International Conference on Learning Representations*.

Gama, Fernando, Bruna, Joan, and Ribeiro, Alejandro. 2019. Stability of graph scattering transforms. Pages 8038–8048 of: *Advances in Neural Information Processing Systems* **32**.

Gao, Feng, Wolf, Guy, and Hirn, Matthew. 2019. Geometric scattering for graph data analysis. Pages 2122–2131 of: *Proc. International Conference on Machine Learning*.

Gatys, Leon, Ecker, Alexander S, and Bethge, Matthias. 2015. Texture synthesis using convolutional neural networks. Pages 262–270 of: *Advances in Neural Information Processing Systems*.

Gavish, Matan, Nadler, Boaz, and Coifman, Ronald R. 2010. Multiscale wavelets on trees, graphs and high dimensional data: Theory and applications to semi supervised learning. In: *Proc. International Conference on Machine Learning*.

Geman, Stuart, and Geman, Donald. 1984. Stochastic relaxation, Gibbs distributions, and the Bayesian restoration of images. *IEEE Transactions on Pattern Analysis and Machine Intelligence*, 721–741.

Girshick, Ross, Donahue, Jeff, Darrell, Trevor, and Malik, Jitendra. 2014. Rich feature hierarchies for accurate object detection and semantic segmentation. Pages 580–587 of: *Proc. IEEE Conference on Computer Vision and Pattern Recognition*.

Goodfellow, Ian, Pouget-Abadie, Jean, Mirza, Mehdi, Xu, Bing, Warde-Farley, David, Ozair, Sherjil, Courville, Aaron, and Bengio, Yoshua. 2014. Generative adversarial nets. Pages 2672–2680 of: *Advances in Neural Information Processing Systems*.

Heeger, David J., and Bergen, James R. 1995. Pyramid-based texture analysis/synthesis. Pages 229–238 of: *Proc. 22nd ACM Conference on Computer Graphics and Interactive Techniques*.

Hirn, Matthew, Mallat, Stéphane, and Poilvert, Nicolas. 2017. Wavelet scattering regression of quantum chemical energies. *Multiscale Modeling & Simulation*, **15**(2), 827–863.

Jacobsen, Jorn-Henrik, van Gemert, Jan, Lou, Zhongyu, and Smeulders, Arnold W. M. 2016. Structured receptive fields in CNNs. Pages 2610–2619 of: *Proc. IEEE Conference on Computer Vision and Pattern Recognition*.

Jacot, Arthur, Gabriel, Franck, and Hongler, Clément. 2018. Neural tangent kernel: Convergence and generalization in neural networks. Pages 8571–8580 of: *Advances in Neural Information Processing Systems*.

Jain, Anil K., Zhong, Yu, and Lakshmanan, Sridhar. 1996. Object matching using deformable templates. *IEEE Transactions on Pattern Analysis and Machine Intelligence*, **18**(3), 267–278.

Jin, Kyong Hwan, McCann, Michael T., Froustey, Emmanuel, and Unser, Michael. 2017. Deep convolutional neural network for inverse problems in imaging. *IEEE Transactions on Image Processing*, **26**(9), 4509–4522.

Keysers, D., Deselaers, T., Gollan, C., and Hey, N. 2007. Deformation models for image recognition. *IEEE Transactions on Pattern Analysis and Machine Intelligence*.

Kingma, Diederik P., and Welling, Max. 2014. Auto-encoding variational Bayes. In: *Proc. International Conference on Learning Representations*.

Kondor, Risi, and Trivedi, Shubhendu. 2018. On the generalization of equivariance and convolution in neural networks to the action of compact groups. Pages 2747–2755 of: *Proc. International Conference on Machine Learning*.

Kostrikov, Ilya, Bruna, Joan, Panozzo, Daniele, and Zorin, Denis. 2018. Surface networks. Pages 2540–2548 of: *Proc. IEEE Conference on Computer Vision and Pattern Recognition*.

Leonarduzzi, Roberto, Rochette, Gaspar, Bouchaud, Jean-Phillipe, and Mallat, Stéphane. 2019. Maximum-entropy scattering models for financial time series. Pages 5496–5500 of: *proc. IEEE International Conference on Acoustics, Speech and Signal Processing*.

Mairal, Julien, Koniusz, Piotr, Harchaoui, Zaid, and Schmid, Cordelia. 2014. Convolutional kernel networks. Pages 2627–2635 of: *Advances in Neural Information Processing Systems*.

Mallat, Stéphane. 1999. *A Wavelet Tour of Signal Processing*, first edition. Academic Press.

Mallat, Stéphane. 2008. *A Wavelet Tour of Signal Processing*, second edition. Academic Press.

Mallat, Stéphane. 2012. Group invariant scattering. *Communications in Pure and Applied Mathematics*, **65**(10), 1331–1398.

Mallat, Stéphane. 2016. Understanding deep convolutional networks. *Philosophical Transactions of the Royal Society A*, **374**(2065).

Mallat, Stéphane, Zhang, Sixin, and Rochette, Gaspar. 2018. Phase harmonics and correlation invariants in convolutional neural networks. ArXiv preprint arXiv:1810.12136.

Minh, H., Niyogi, P., and Yao, Y. 2006. Mercer's Theorem, Feature Maps and Smoothing. In *Proc. Computational Learning Theory Conference*.

Nadler, Boaz, Lafon, Stéphane, Coifman, Ronald R., and Kevrekidis, Ioannis G. 2006. Diffusion maps, spectral clustering and reaction coordinates of dynamical systems. *Applied and Computational Harmonic Analysis*, **21**(1), 113–127.

Oyallon, Edouard, and Mallat, Stéphane. 2015. Deep roto-translation scattering for object classification. Pages 2865–2873 of: *Proc. IEEE Conference on Computer Vision and Pattern Recognition*.

Oyallon, Edouard, Belilovsky, Eugene, and Zagoruyko, Sergey. 2017. Scaling the scattering transform: Deep hybrid networks. Pages 5618–5627 of: *Proc. IEEE International Conference on Computer Vision*.

Oyallon, Edouard, Belilovsky, Eugene, Zagoruyko, Sergey, and Valko, Michal. 2018a. Compressing the Input for CNNs with the first-order scattering transform. Pages 301–316 of: *Proc. European Conference on Computer Vision*.

Oyallon, Edouard, Zagoruyko, Sergey, Huang, Gabriel, Komodakis, Nikos, Lacoste-Julien, Simon, Blaschko, Matthew B., and Belilovsky, Eugene. 2018b. Scattering networks for hybrid representation learning. *IEEE Transactions on Pattern Analysis and Machine Intelligence*, **41**(9), 2208–2221.

Perlmutter, Michael, Wolf, Guy, and Hirn, Matthew. 2018. Geometric scattering on manifolds. ArXiv preprint arXiv:1812.06968.

Portilla, Javier, and Simoncelli, Eero P. 2000. A parametric texture model based on joint statistics of complex wavelet coefficients. *International Journal of Computer Vision*, **40**(1), 49–70.

Rezende, Danilo Jimenez, Mohamed, Shakir, and Wierstra, Daan. 2014. Stochastic backpropagation and variational inference in deep latent Gaussian models. Pages 1278–1286 of: *Proc. International Conference on Machine Learning*.

Rustamov, Raif, and Guibas, Leonidas J. 2013. Wavelets on graphs via deep learning. Pages 998–1006 of: *Advances in Neural Processing Systems* **26**.

Shawe-Taylor, J., and Cristianini, N. 2004. *Kernel Methods for Pattern Analysis*. Cambridge University Press.

Sifre, L., and Mallat, S. 2013. Rotation, scaling and deformation invariant scattering for texture discrimination. In: *Proc. IEEE Conference on Computer Vision and Pattern Recognition*.

Soatto, S. 2009. Actionable information in vision. *Proc. Proc. International Conference on Computer Vision*.

Szegedy, Christian, Zaremba, Wojciech, Sutskever, Ilya, Bruna, Joan, Erhan, Dumitru, Goodfellow, Ian, and Fergus, Rob. 2014. Intriguing properties of neural networks. In: *Proc. International Conference on Learning Representations*.

Wainwright, Martin J., Jordan, Michael I., et al. 2008. Graphical models, exponential families, and variational inference. *Foundations and Trends in Machine Learning*, **1**(1–2), 1–305.

Waldspurger, I. 2012. Recovering the phase of a complex wavelet transform. CMAP, Ecole Polytechnique, Technical Report.

Waldspurger, Irène. 2017. Exponential decay of scattering coefficients. Pages 143–146 of: *Proc. International Conference on Sampling Theory and Applications*.

Wiatowski, Thomas, and Bölcskei, Helmut. 2017. A mathematical theory of deep convolutional neural networks for feature extraction. *IEEE Transactions on Information Theory*, **64**(3), 1845–1866.

Wiatowski, Thomas, Grohs, Philipp, and Bölcskei, Helmut. 2017. Energy propagation in deep convolutional neural networks. *IEEE Transactions on Information Theory*, **64**(7), 4819–4842.

Yoshimatsu, K., Schneider, K., Okamoto, N., Kawahura, Y., and Farge, M. 2011. Intermittency and geometrical statistics of three-dimensional homogeneous magnetohydrodynamic turbulence: A wavelet viewpoint. *Physics of Plasmas*, **18**, 092304.

Zarka, John, Guth, Florentin, and Mallat, Stéphane. 2020. Separation and concentration in deep networks. In: *proc. International Conference on Learning Representations*.

Zhang, Kai, Zuo, Wangmeng, Gu, Shuhang, and Zhang, Lei. 2017. Learning deep CNN denoiser prior for image restoration. Pages 3929–3938 of: *Proc. IEEE Conference on Computer Vision and Pattern Recognition*.

Zhang, Sixin, and Mallat, Stephane. 2021. Wavelet phase harmonic covariance models of stationary processes. *Applied Computational and Harmonic Analysis*, **53**, 199–230.

Zhu, Song Chun, Wu, Yingnian, and Mumford, David. 1998. Filters, random fields and maximum entropy (FRAME): Towards a unified theory for texture modeling. *International Journal of Computer Vision*, **27**(2), 107–126.

Zou, D., and Lerman, G. 2020. Graph convolutional neural networks via scattering. *Applied and Computational Harmonic Analysis*, **49**(3), 1046–1074.

9

Deep Generative Models and Inverse Problems

Alexandros G. Dimakis

Abstract: Deep generative models have been recently proposed as modular data-driven priors to solve inverse problems. Linear inverse problems involve the reconstruction of an unknown signal (e.g. a tomographic image) from an underdetermined system of noisy linear measurements. Most results in the literature require that the reconstructed signal has some known structure, e.g. it is sparse in some known basis (usually Fourier or wavelet). Such prior assumptions can be replaced with pre-trained deep generative models (e.g. generative adversarial networks (GANs) and variational autoencoders (VAEs)) with significant performance gains. This chapter surveys this rapidly evolving research area and includes empirical and theoretical results in compressed sensing for deep generative models.

9.1 Introduction

In his seminal paper, Claude Shannon (1948) laid out the foundations of information theory by establishing two fundamental theorems: one for the ultimate limits of compressing a source of information and one for communicating reliably over a noisy channel. The implications of these results have since developed into two sub-areas of information theory: the study of compression (called source coding) and the study of protection from noise (called channel coding). Both settings rely critically on probabilistic models: the former for modeling information sources (e.g. images, text, video) of what we want to compress, the latter for modeling noise (e.g. random bit flips, Gaussian noise) or whatever we want to protect against. Channel coding has had a tremendous impact on real-world applications, since all wired and wireless communication systems rely on innovations such as Reed–Solomon codes, turbo codes, LDPC codes and more recently polar codes. In contrast, source coding has influenced the practice of data compression somewhat less, with a few notable exceptions (e.g. for lossless compression). Image, audio and video compression standards have been informed by source coding principles, but the impact of the theory has been arguably smaller than that of channel coding.

I attribute this discrepancy to the degree of simplicity of the involved models relative to the physical processes they try to capture. For channel coding, toy mathematical models (e.g. additive white Gaussian noise or the random independent dropping of packets) capture real noisy systems *well enough* to inform the design of channel codes. For sources, however, modeling images as independent pixels or local Markov chains seems to be insufficient to capture critical aspects of the problem. The central challenge is to invent more expressive models for representing high-dimensional distributions.

The difficulty, simply put, is that to represent a joint probability distribution over n variables (say pixels of an image), even if each pixel is binary, requires $2^n - 1$ parameters. Therefore, to efficiently represent n dependent variables, some type of *structure* must be postulated to reduce this exponential complexity. A tremendous volume of research in probability theory, statistical physics, information theory, signal processing and machine learning has been addressing this very question.

9.2 How to Tame High Dimensions

Three types of structure are described here. The first two are classical and well studied but still many fundamental questions remain open. The third is newer, known empirically to be very powerful, and significantly less studied.

9.2.1 Sparsity

For the first prominent family of models for high-dimensional data it is assumed that the modeled vectors are *sparse* in a known basis. The well-studied field of compressed sensing considers linear inverse problems under sparsity assumptions.

The goal is to recover a high-dimensional vector from a small number of linear projections (measurements). If there is no noise in the observed projections, the inverse problem then is to find the sparsest vector that satisfies a set of given linear equations, a problem that is computationally intractable (NP-complete). If the measurements are noisy, one has to solve a linear regression problem where the number of samples is smaller than the number of parameters but the unknown model is sparse. This is, again, an NP-hard problem and the natural approximation algorithm is to relax the ℓ_0 sparsity constraint to an ℓ_1-regularized linear regression called Lasso (Tibshirani, 1996).

Remarkably, under natural assumptions for the projections (the measurement matrix, in compressed sensing nomenclature) this ℓ_1 relaxation provably yields the required sparsest solution. Such conditions include the restricted isometry property

(RIP) or the related restricted eigenvalue condition (REC)(see e.g. Tibshirani, 1996; Candes et al., 2006; Donoho, 2006; Bickel et al., 2009). There is a vast literature on sparsity and high-dimensional problems, including various recovery algorithms, as well as on generalizations of RIP for other vector structures; see e.g. Bickel et al. (2009), Negahban et al. (2009), Agarwal et al. (2010), Loh and Wainwright (2011), Bach et al. (2012), and Baraniuk et al. (2010). Wainwright (2019) provides a comprehensive and rigorous exposition of this area.

It should be emphasized that models built on sparsity have been tremendously successful for modeling high-dimensional data such audio, images and video. Sparsity (e.g. in the discrete cosine transform (DCT) or wavelet domains) plays the *central* role in most real-world lossy compression standards such as JPEG (Wallace, 1992), JPEG-2000 (Marcellin et al., 2000) and MPEG (Manjunath et al., 2002).

9.2.2 Conditional Independence

The second prominent family of models postulates that the joint probability distribution satisfies some *conditional independence* conditions. This leads to graphical models, factor graphs, Bayesian networks and Markov random fields. Distributions in these frameworks *factorize* according to an undirected or directed graph, which represents these conditional independences. For example, fully independent random variables correspond to an empty graph, while Markov chains correspond to path graphs. Markov random fields and Bayesnets (also called undirected and directed graphical models, respectively) are well-studied families of high-dimensional distributions, and there is an array of tools for performing learning and statistical inference for them; see e.g., Koller et al. (2009), Wainwright et al. (2008), and Jordan (2003).

These models are not very frequently used for modeling sources such as images or video, but they have played a central role in communications and channel coding. Low-density parity-check (LDPC) codes are distributions modeled by sparse factor graphs, a type of graphical model (Gallager, 1962; Richardson and Urbanke, 2008). Here, graphical models are used not to describe noise, but rather to design high-dimensional distributions of the codewords used. Belief propagation, the inference algorithm used for decoding LDPC codes, is central for graphical model inference and has been independently discovered in various forms in coding theory (Gallager, 1962) and artificial intelligence (Pearl, 1982). See also Kschischang et al. (2001) for the remarkable connections between belief propagation, sum-product, the Viterbi algorithm and the fast Fourier transform (FFT). Also, belief propagation can be seen as a form of approximate variational inference; see Wainwright et al. (2008), Blei et al. (2017).

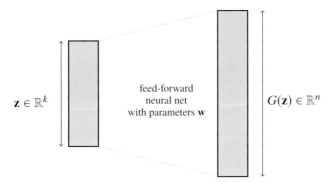

Figure 9.1   A deep generative model is a function $G(\mathbf{z})$ that takes a low-dimensional random vector $\mathbf{z}$ in $\mathbb{R}^k$ and produces a high-dimensional sample $G(\mathbf{z}) \in \mathbb{R}^n$. The function is usually a convolutional neural network and is therefore continuous and differentiable almost everywhere. For invertible generative models, the dimension of the latent code is the same as the ambient dimension, i.e. $k = n$ and an explicit likelihood can be efficiently computed for each given output.

9.2.3 Deep Generative Models

The central tool considered in this chapter is the third family of models for high-dimensional distributions, which we call *deep generative models*. These models do not rely on conditional independence or sparsity, but rather are described by a deterministic function $G(\mathbf{z})$ from a low-dimensional space $\mathbb{R}^k$ to $\mathbb{R}^n$. This function is called a *generator* or *decoder* and is in practice represented by a feed-forward neural network with weights $\mathbf{w}$ that are trained from data. To obtain a probability distribution over the high-dimensional ambient space $\mathbb{R}^n$, one can seed the generator with a random latent vector $\mathbf{z}$, usually drawn from a zero-mean isotropic Gaussian, $\mathcal{N}(0, I_{k \times k})$. Remarkably, these generator functions can be trained to transform simple randomness into highly structured randomness and to capture natural signals with unprecedented quality.

We group deep generative models into the following categories:

  (i)   Generative adversarial networks (GANs);
 (ii)   Variational auto-encoders (VAEs);
(iii)   Invertible generative models (also called normalizing flows);
(iv)   Untrained generative models.

We emphasize that compressed sensing and inverse problems on general manifolds have been studied in great depth previously; see e.g. Hegde et al. (2008), Baraniuk and Wakin (2009), and Eftekhari and Wakin (2015). Also, reconstruction algorithms that exploit structure beyond sparsity have been investigated as model-based compressed sensing (Baraniuk et al., 2010). What is new here is the specific parametrization of these models using feed-forward neural networks and the novel methods used for training these generators.

9.2.4 GANs and VAEs

To train a deep generative model, one optimizes its parameters **w** in an unsupervised way, given samples from the true data distribution. The goal is that the output distribution produced by the neural network is *close* to the observed data distribution. Depending on how one measures distance between distributions and how one approximates the solution of this optimization problem, we are led into different types of deep generative models.

Two primary examples are variational auto-encoders (VAEs) (Kingma and Welling, 2013), which are trained using variational inference techniques, and generative adversarial networks (GANs) (Goodfellow et al., 2014), which are trained by defining a zero-sum game between a player who is setting the parameters **w** of G_w, and another player who is setting the parameters of another neural network, called the discriminator. The goal of the latter is to set the parameters of the discriminator network in such a way that this network distinguishes as well as possible between samples generated by the generator and samples generated by the true distribution. The goal of the former is to fool the discriminator. Empirically, deep generative models have shown impressive performance in generating complex high-dimensional signals; e.g. BigGAN can produce near-photorealistic images from Imagenet classes (Brock et al., 2019).

Understanding deep generative models and improving their performance has received a great deal of attention across many disciplines including theoretical computer science, machine learning, statistics and information theory. One of the major challenges in training GANs, is a phenomenon called *mode collapse*, which refers to a lack of diversity of the generated samples: the generative model essentially overfits to a subset of the training data; see e.g.Metz et al. (2017), and Arora et al. (2018). Many approaches have been proposed to prevent mode collapse that include different ways of training GANs, such as BiGAN (Donahue et al., 2016) and adversarially learned nference, ALI, (Dumoulin et al., 2016), Wasserstein loss training (Arjovsky et al., 2017; Gulrajani et al., 2017; Sanjabi et al., 2018), Blackwell-inspired packing (Lin et al., 2017) and ideas from linear quadratic control (Feizi et al., 2017). Significant challenges remain in understanding theoretically what distributions GANs actually learn; see e.g. Arora et al. (2017a,b, 2018) and Liu et al. (2017).

These deep generative models (including VAEs and GANs) are called *implicit* since they do not provide tractable access to likelihoods (Mohamed and Lakshminarayanan, 2016; Huszár, 2017). Instead, implicit generative models are easy to sample from, and more importantly to *compute subgradients of samples with respect to model parameters*. The optimization algorithms used for training and inference are crucially using subgradients with respect to these model parameters.

9.2.5 Invertible Generative Models

Another family of deep generative models that is attracting significant interest is *invertible generative models* or *normalizing flows*; see, e.g., Dinh et al. (2016), Gomez et al. (2017), and Kingma and Dhariwal (2018). In these models, the dimension of the latent code $\mathbf{z}$ is the same as the ambient dimension, i.e. $k = n$. As before, the high-dimensional distribution is created by transforming a simple Gaussian $\mathbf{z}$ by means of a complex transformation parametrized by a differentiable neural network. The additional constraint is that the transformation $G(\mathbf{z})$ must be invertible. Further, for some of these models, called normalizing flows, it is tractable to compute the Jacobian of the transformation and hence easily to compute likelihoods, for any given point $G(\mathbf{z}) \in \mathbb{R}^n$.

These models do not represent data in a lower-dimensional space and hence do not offer dimensionality reduction. However, they have the advantage that an explicit likelihood can be easily computed for any given data point. Furthermore, every generated high-dimensional sample $G(\mathbf{z})$ corresponds to a unique $\mathbf{z}$ which can be efficiently computed, since the generative mapping is invertible by construction. Invertible generative models offer several advantages: likelihoods make these models easy to use for inverse problems, circumventing many of the difficulties we will be discussing for other models. Furthermore, there are recent invertible models such as Glow (Kingma and Dhariwal, 2018) that achieve excellent image quality for human faces and also generalize very well into other natural images. Asim et al. (2019) proposed the use of invertible generative models for solving inverse problems and showed excellent performance using Glow that outperformed GANs that were introduced for inverse problems by Bora et al. (2017).

One shortcoming of current invertible generative models is the high training effort required. The Glow model (Kingma and Dhariwal, 2018) was trained on 256×256 human faces using 40 GPUs for two weeks, which is significantly more compared with GANs that can now achieve higher resolution generation for more diverse datasets; see Odena (2019). Significant ongoing work is currently progressing the state of the art for both GANs and Invertible models, so this landscape is changing.

9.2.6 Untrained Generative Models

The final family that we discuss involves what are called *untrained* generative models. These are deep neural prior distributions that can be used to solve inverse problems even without a large dataset and a pre-trained generative model. Deep image prior (DIP) (Ulyanov et al., 2017) was the first such model; it was initially proposed for denoising and inpainting but it can be easily extended to solve general inverse problems (Van Veen et al., 2018). We also mention a closely related technique called the deep decoder, which was proposed in Heckel and Hand (2018).

In DIP-based schemes, a convolutional deep generative model (e.g. DCGAN) is initialized with random weights; these weights are subsequently optimized to make the network produce an output as close to the target image as possible. In the general case any inverse problem with a differentiable forward operator (Van Veen et al., 2018), the weights are updated through gradient descent to explain the measurements. This procedure is applied directly into one image, using no prior information. The prior is enforced only by the fixed convolutional structure of the generator neural network.

Generators used in DIP are typically[1] over-parameterized , i.e. the number of network weights is much larger compared to the output dimension. For this reason DIP can overfit to noise if run for too many iterations or not carefully regularized (see Ulyanov et al., 2017; Van Veen et al., 2018). Therefore, the design effort lies in designing the architecture and also using early stopping and other regularization techniques as we will discuss.

We continue with showing how all these generative models can be used to solve inverse problems.

9.3 Linear Inverse Problems Using Deep Generative Models

We will start with a linear inverse problem, i.e. reconstructing an unknown vector $\mathbf{x}^* \in \mathbb{R}^n$ after observing $m < n$ linear measurements, $\mathbf{y}$ of its entries, possibly with added noise:

$$\mathbf{y} = \mathbf{A}\mathbf{x}^* + \mathbf{e}.$$

Here $\mathbf{A} \in \mathbb{R}^{m \times n}$ is the measurement matrix and $\mathbf{e} \in \mathbb{R}^m$ is the noise. Even without the noise term, this is an underdetermined system of linear equations with infinitely many solutions that explain the measurements. We must therefore make a modeling assumption for the unknown vector, and so the problem of modeling high-dimensional data appears.

The field of compressed sensing started with the structural assumption that the vector $\mathbf{x}^*$ is k-sparse in some known basis (or approximately k-sparse). Finding the sparsest solution to an underdetermined system of linear equations is NP-hard, but nevertheless, convex optimization can provably recover the true sparse vector $\mathbf{x}^*$ if the matrix $\mathbf{A}$ satisfies conditions such as the restricted isometry property (RIP) or

---

[1] For a non-overparametrized untrained generative model, see Heckel and Hand (2018).

the related restricted eigenvalue condition (REC) (Tibshirani, 1996; Candes et al., 2006; Donoho, 2006; Bickel et al., 2009).

The key idea is to change this structural assumption and model the unknown vector $\mathbf{x}^*$ as being in (or near) the range of a pre-trained deep generative model. This is called the CSGM (compressed sensing with generative models) framework proposed in Bora et al. (2017), and assumes that there exists a hidden latent vector $\mathbf{z}^*$ such that:

$$\mathbf{x}^* = G(\mathbf{z}^*).$$

We know the measurement matrix $\mathbf{A}$, the measurement vector $\mathbf{y} = \mathbf{A}\,G(\mathbf{z}^*)$ and want to reconstruct $\mathbf{z}^*$ or equivalently $\mathbf{x}^* = G(\mathbf{z}^*)$. The deep generative model $G(\mathbf{z})$ is assumed to be known and fixed.

The CSGM algorithm searches the latent space for explaining the measurements, i.e. solves the following minimization problem with gradient descent:

$$\min_{\mathbf{z}} \|\mathbf{A}\,G(\mathbf{z}) - \mathbf{y}\|^2. \tag{9.1}$$

In words, we are searching for a (low-dimensional) vector $\mathbf{z}$ such that the generated image $G(\mathbf{z})$, after it has been measured using $\mathbf{A}$, agrees with the observed measurements $\mathbf{y}$.

The optimization problem (9.1) is non-convex and further, for generative models with four or more layers, is known to be NP-hard (Lei et al., 2019). One natural algorithm starts with a random initial vector $\mathbf{z}_0$, evaluates the gradient of the loss function with respect to $\mathbf{z}$ using back-propagation, and uses standard gradient-descent-based optimizers in the latent $\mathbf{z}$ space. If the optimization procedure terminates at $\hat{\mathbf{z}}$, our reconstruction for $\mathbf{x}^*$ is $G(\hat{\mathbf{z}})$. We define the measurement error to be $\|\mathbf{A}G(\hat{\mathbf{z}}) - \mathbf{y}\|^2$ and the reconstruction error to be $\|G(\hat{\mathbf{z}}) - \mathbf{x}^*\|^2$.

Empirically, gradient descent performs very well in solving problem (9.1), even from random initializations. In simple experiments with a known ground truth, gradient descent very frequently found the global optimum of this non-convex problem in a few hundred iterations. Furthermore, Bora et al. (2017) showed that this method can significantly outperform the standard reconstruction algorithms that rely on sparsity (in DCT or a wavelet domain) for natural images. An example of reconstructions using CSGM versus Lasso is shown in Figure 9.3.

9.3.1 Reconstruction from Gaussian Measurements

Following a standard benchmark in compressed sensing, we create an linear inverse problem that involves making $\mathbf{A}$ to be a matrix with random independent Gaussian entries with zero mean and standard deviation $1/m$. Each entry of the noise vector

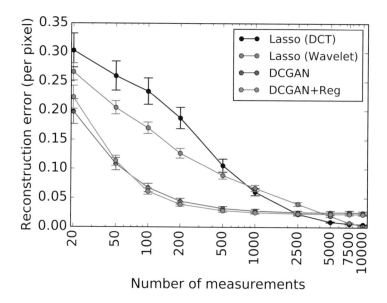

Figure 9.2 A comparison of the performance of CSGM using a DCGAN prior with baselines that rely on sparsity. The plot shows the per-pixel reconstruction error as the number of measurements is varied. The vertical bars indicate 95% confidence intervals. Figure taken from Bora et al. (2017).

η is also i.i.d. Gaussian. We compared the performance of different sensing algorithms qualitatively and quantitatively. For quantitative comparison, we used the reconstruction error $\|\hat{x} - x^*\|^2$, where $\hat{x}$ is the reconstructed signal estimate of x^*. In all cases the results were shown on a held-out test set, unseen by the generative model at training time.

In these experiments, the optimization problem (9.1) was solved using the Adam optimizer (Kingma and Ba, 2014), with a learning rate of 0.1 and a few random restarts. In Figure 9.2, we show the reconstruction error as the number of measurements both for Lasso and for CSGM is varied. As can be seen, CSGM with a DCGAN prior (for $k = 100$) produces reasonable reconstructions with as few as 500 measurements, while the output of the baseline algorithms is quite blurry. If the number of measurements increases, the benefits of the stronger prior diminish and CSGM performance saturates. For more than 5000 measurements, Lasso gives a better reconstruction since the generative model has produced the best approximation in its range and further measurements no longer improve performance. In this regime, a more powerful generative model is needed, possibly increasing the latent code dimension $k > 100$ to obtain better performance in a high-measurement regime.

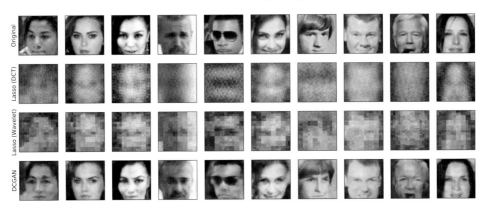

Figure 9.3 Reconstruction results using $m = 500$ measurements (of $n = 12,288$ dimensional human face images). We show original images (top row), reconstructions by Lasso with DCT basis (second row), Lasso with wavelet basis (third row), and our algorithm (last row). Here the measurement process was performed by taking $\mathbf{A}$ to be a random matrix with IID Gaussian entries with zero mean and standard deviation of $1/m$, a standard compressed sensing measurement process. The generative model used in our algorithm was trained on CelebA, a human face dataset, but all the reported results are on images from a hold-out test set and hence were unseen by the generative model at training time. Figure from Bora et al. (2017).

9.3.2 Optimization Challenges

From a theoretical standpoint, a key complication is the loss of information due to projection onto the rows of $\mathbf{A}$. The work of Bora et al. (2017) obtained conditions for the measurement matrix under which a minimizer $\hat{z}$ of (9.1) guarantees that $G(\hat{z})$ is itself as close as possible to the true unknown signal $\mathbf{x}^*$. The obtained condition generalizes the restricted egenvalue condition (REC) (Bickel et al., 2009; Negahban et al., 2009; Agarwal et al., 2010) developed for classical compressed sensing. Specifically, Bora et al. (2017) defined an REC for vectors generated by a generative model and showed that a matrix with random Gaussian entries will satisfy this property if the number of measurements scales as $O(k \log L)$. Here, L is the Lipschitz constant of the generative model, which can be easily bounded by a quantity that scales exponentially in the depth of the network and in the maximum neuron weight values.

This framework analyzes the exact solution to the minimization of (9.1), while in practice this was approximated using gradient descent. Subsequently, Hand and Voroninski (2017) obtained theoretical guarantees for the performance of gradient descent for non-convex problem under the assumption that the generative model has weights $\mathbf{w}$ that are random and independent. The surprising result is that gradient descent will provably solve this non-convex optimization problem if the generative model has sufficiently expansion, i.e. every layer is approximately a $\log k$ factor larger than the previous layer. Daskalakis et al. (2020) improved this result and demonstrated similar guarantees with only a constant factor expansion in the layer sizes.

We also note that some recent works have considered different reconstruction algorithms, beyond gradient descent, for projecting onto the range of a generative model. We mention Lei et al. (2019), who invert a generative model one layer after another, and also some other work (Fletcher et al., 2018; Pandit et al., 2019) in which was proposed an approximate message-passing (AMP) inference algorithm for these inference problems. Most real generators do not have expansive layers (especially in the final layers), so theoretically extending the result (Hand and Voroninski, 2017) for non-expansive architectures remains as an important mathematical open problem. In addition, relaxing the random generator weight assumption and analyzing different measurement matrices remain to be investigated.

9.3.3 Extending the Range of the Generator

Perhaps the central limitation of using low-dimensional deep priors (e.g. GANs and VAEs) for inverse problems is that the low dimensionality of their latent space impedes the reconstruction of images that lie outside their generated manifold. To mitigate this issue, one natural idea is to model the final image as the sum of an image in the range of a generator plus a sparse deviation (Dhar et al., 2018). This idea showed significant performance gains over CSGM and has subsequently been generalized to internal representations of the generator which were allowed to deviate from their realizable values through a technique called intermediate layer optimization (ILO) (Daras et al., 2021); see Figures 9.4 and 9.5. This technqiue extends the set of signals that can be reconstructed by allowing sparse deviations from the range of intermediate layers of the generator. Correctly regularizing intermediate layers is crucial when solving inverse problems, to avoid overfitting to the measurements (Daras et al., 2021).

9.3.4 Non-Linear Inverse Problems

The final research direction that I would like to mention involves extending the use of deep generative priors to non-linear measurements. In this case, the unknown true vector $x^* \in \mathbb{R}^n$ is passed through a non-linear measurement operator $A: \mathbb{R}^n \to \mathbb{R}^m$ (also called the forward operator). The measurements $y \in \mathbb{R}^m$ are then observed, possibly with added noise:

$$y = A[x^*] + e.$$

If the forward operator A is differentiable then the previous method can be applied: define the loss function $loss(z) = \|A[G(z)] - y\|^2$ and minimize it iteratively

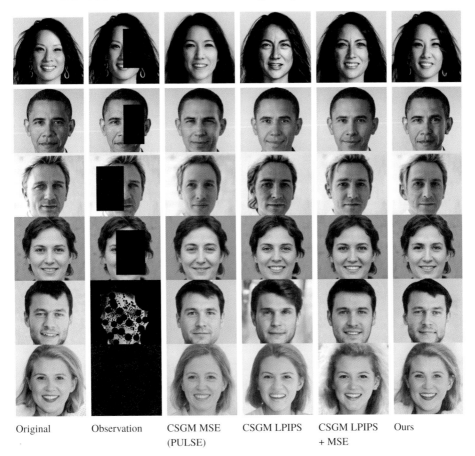

Original	Observation	CSGM MSE (PULSE)	CSGM LPIPS	CSGM LPIPS + MSE	Ours

Figure 9.4 Results on the inpainting task. Rows 1, 2, 3 and 5 are real images (outside of the test set, collected from the web) while rows 4 and 6 are StyleGAN-2 generated images. Column 2: the first five images have masks that were chosen to remove important facial features. The last row is an example of randomized inpainting, i.e. a random 1% of the total pixels is observed. Columns 3–5: reconstructions using the CSGM (Bora et al., 2017) algorithm with the StyleGAN-2 generator and the optimization setting described in PULSE (Menon et al., 2020). While PULSE only applies to super-resolution, it was extended using MSE, LPIPS and a joint MSE + LPIPS loss.. The experiments of Columns 3–5 form an ablation study of the benefits of each loss function. Column 6: reconstructions with ILO (ours). As shown, ILO consistently gives better reconstructions of the original image. Also, many biased reconstructions can be corrected with ILO. In the last two rows, recovery of the image is still possible from very few pixel observations using our method. Figure from Daras et al. (2021).

using gradient descent or some other optimization method. A useful non-linear inverse problem is phase retrieval (Candes et al., 2015a,b) and the generative prior framework has been extended to this problem (Hand et al., 2018).

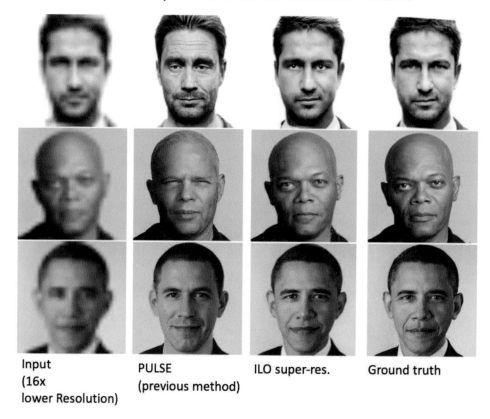

Input
(16x
lower Resolution)

PULSE
(previous method)

ILO super-res.

Ground truth

Figure 9.5   Results on super-resolution using intermediate layer Optimization (ILO) (with a StyleGAN2 prior) versus the highly influential PULSE baseline (also using the StyleGAN2 prior and the CSGM framework). As shown, ILO can significantly mitigate biases in reconstructions. It should be emphasized that both PULSE and ILO use the same training prior (i.e. the same training data) and there is no need for a characterization involving biases that must be corrected. ILO simply makes the reconstruction algorithm more flexible and less reliant on its prior. Figure from Daras et al. (2021).

9.3.5 Inverse Problems with Untrained Generative Priors

As discussed above, deep generative models are very powerful priors since they can capture various nuances of real signals. However, training a deep generative model for some types of data is difficult since it requires a large number of examples and careful neural network design. While this has been achieved for various types of images, e.g. the human faces of CelebA (Liu et al., 2015) via DCGAN (Radford et al., 2015), it remains challenging for other datasets, e.g. medical images (Wolterink et al., 2017; Schlegl et al., 2017; Nie et al., 2017; Schlemper et al., 2017). Untrained generative models provide a way of circumventing this problem.

Ulyanov et al. (2017) proposed a deep image prior (DIP), which uses *untrained* convolutional neural networks to solve various imaging problems such as denoising and inpainting. Further, Van Veen et al. (2018) generalized this to any inverse problem with a differentiable forward operator.

Assume, as before, that some measurements of an unknown vector $\mathbf{x}^* \in \mathbb{R}^n$ are observed through a differentiable forward operator $\mathbf{A}\colon \mathbb{R}^n \to \mathbb{R}^m$ to obtain measurements $\mathbf{y} \in \mathbb{R}^m$:

$$\mathbf{y} = \mathbf{A}[\mathbf{x}^*] + \mathbf{e}.$$

In contrast with the previous discussion, we do not assume that we have some good generative model for $\mathbf{x}^*$. Instead, we start with a deep generative convolutional network (e.g. DCGAN topology) and initialize it with *random* weights $\mathbf{w}_0$. We also select some random input noise $\mathbf{z}_0 \in \mathbb{R}^k$. Clearly, the signal generated with this random input and random weights $G_{\mathbf{w}_0}(\mathbf{z}_0)$ will have nothing to do with $\mathbf{x}^*$.

The DIP approach is to minimize *over weights* $\mathbf{w}$, to find some that explain the measurements while keeping the input fixed at $\mathbf{z}_0$. In other words, we aim to optimize over $\mathbf{w}$ so that $\mathbf{A}[G_{\mathbf{w}^*}(\mathbf{z}_0)]$ matches the measurements $\mathbf{y}$. Hence, CS-DIP (Van Veen et al., 2018) solves the following optimization problem:

$$\mathbf{w}^* = \operatorname*{argmin}_{\mathbf{w}} \|\mathbf{y} - \mathbf{A}G_{\mathbf{w}}(\mathbf{z}_0)\|^2. \tag{9.2}$$

This is, of course, a non-convex problem because $G_{\mathbf{w}}(\mathbf{z}_0)$ is a non-convex function of $\mathbf{w}$. Still, we can use gradient-based optimizers for any generative model and measurement process that is differentiable. Remarkably, this procedure, if stopped early produces natural signals, due to the convolutional structure of the generator G. The convolutional network structure alone, provides a good prior for reconstructing images (Ulyanov et al., 2017). In CS-DIP (Van Veen et al., 2018) various simple regularization techniques were also deployed, including total variation (Rudin et al., 1992; Liu et al., 2018) and hence the final optimization problem becomes:

$$\mathbf{w}^* = \operatorname*{argmin}_{\mathbf{w}} \|\mathbf{y} - \mathbf{A}\, G_{\mathbf{w}}(\mathbf{z}_0)\|^2 + R(\mathbf{w}). \tag{9.3}$$

The specific design of the regularizer can range from total variation (Liu et al., 2018) to a combination of data-driven regularizers (Van Veen et al., 2018) and early stopping (see also Gilton et al., 2019). These techniques improve the performance, but even without any of them, DIP priors are surprisingly good models for natural images.

Van Veen et al. (2018) established theoretically that DIP can fit any measurements to zero error with gradient descent, in the over-parametrized regime for a single layer under technical conditions. It is expected that over-parametrized neural networks can fit any signal, but the fact that gradient descent can provably solve this non-convex problem to a global optimum is interesting and provides theoretical justification for early stopping. Empirically, CS-DIP outperforms other untrained methods in many cases. Figure 9.6 shows that CS-DIP achieves good reconstruction results for a retinopathy inverse problem where no known generative models are available. It should be emphasized that methods that leverage pre-trained deep generative models perform better (Bora et al., 2017; Asim et al., 2019), but require large datasets of ground truth images.

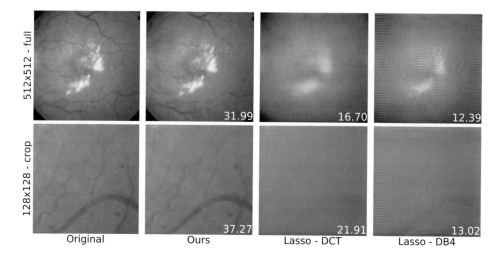

Figure 9.6 Reconstruction of retinopathy medical images from random Gaussian measurements using CS-DIP. This was done by performing compressed sensing using *untrained* convolutional neural networks. In CS-DIP, a convolutional neural network generator (DCGAN) is initialized with random weights which are subsequently optimized using gradient descent to make the network produce an output that explains the measurements as well as possible. The values in the lower right of the reconstructed images denote the PSNR (dB). Figure from Van Veen et al. (2018).

9.4 Supervised Methods for Inverse Problems

Finally, I mention briefly another large family of deep learning techniques for solving inverse problems: supervised methods. If a large dataset of paired measurements and reconstructions is available, a supervised method simply trains an inversion network to go from measurements to reconstructions. Numerous optimization and regularization ideas have been proposed that build on this fundamental framework. With enough training data, end-to-end supervised methods frequently outperform the unsupervised methods discussed in this chapter; see Tian et al. (2020), Sun et al. (2020), and Tripathi et al. (2018) for denoising; Sun and Chen (2020) and

Yang et al. (2019) for super-resolution; and Yu et al. (2019), Liu et al. (2019) for inpainting.

The main disadvantages of solving inverse problems with supervised methods are: (i) separate training is required for each forward problem; (ii) there is significant fragility to forward operator changes (robustness issues) (Darestani et al., 2021; Ongie et al., 2020); and (iii) it is much easier to modify the loss function or the forward operator in an interactive way for unsupervised techniques. This makes it possible for experts to adaptively modify reconstructed imaging parameters as desired, something frequently done in practice. I would also like to point out the recent taxonomy of deep learning techniques for inverse problems (Ongie et al., 2020) that organizes the significant volume of deep learning methods into supervised and unsupervised methods, depending on the setting.

Conclusions and Outlook

I have argued that deep generative models are a third important family of high-dimensional priors, in addition to sparsity and graphical models. The data-driven nature of these priors allows them to leverage massive training datasets and hence to outperform simpler models. This also leads to numerous theoretical problems to do with learning and inference which take new mathematical forms for feed-forward neural networks priors. Further, inverse problems can be solved even with untrained neural networks (e.g. with deep image prior or the deep decoder) which are suitable for inverse problems when very little training data are available.

As a final note, I would like to mention the rapid progress in designing and training deep generative models. The new family of score-based generative models (Song et al., 2021) and the probabilistic models closely related to diffusion (Sohl-Dickstein et al., 2015; Ho et al., 2020) are demonstrating remarkable performance in terms of generation, ease of training and use in inverse problems even as I finalize this chapter. I would like to emphasize one significant benefit of the presented unsupervised framework for solving inverse problems: that of modularity. One can download pre-trained generators (score-based generators, GANs or any other feed-forward generator), apply the techniques discussed in this chapter, and get increasingly better results. The massive dataset and computational resources used to train the generators are easily leveraged for solving all types of inverse problems by separating the forward operator from the natural signal modeling problem. Owing to this modularity, I expect that deep generative models will have a significant role for numerous inverse problems, as powerful data-driven priors of natural signals.

Acknowledgements and Funding Information

This research has been supported by NSF Grants CCF 1934932, AF 1901292, 2008710, 2019844, and the NSF IFML 2019844 award, as well as research gifts from Western Digital, Interdigital, WNCG and MLL, and computing resources from TACC and the Archie Straiton Fellowship.

References

Agarwal, Alekh, Negahban, Sahand, and Wainwright, Martin J. 2010. Fast global convergence rates of gradient methods for high-dimensional statistical recovery. Pages 37–45 of: *Advances in Neural Information Processing Systems*.

Arjovsky, Martin, Chintala, Soumith, and Bottou, Léon. 2017. Wasserstein GAN. ArXiv preprint arXiv:1701.07875.

Arora, Sanjeev, Ge, Rong, Liang, Yingyu, Ma, Tengyu, and Zhang, Yi. 2017a. Generalization and equilibrium in generative adversarial nets (GANs). In: *Proc. 34th International Conference on Machine Learning*.

Arora, Sanjeev, Risteski, Andrej, and Zhang, Yi. 2017b. Theoretical limitations of encoder–decoder GAN architectures. ArXiv preprint arXiv:1711.02651.

Arora, Sanjeev, Risteski, Andrej, and Zhang, Yi. 2018. Do GANs learn the distribution? Some theory and empirics. In: *Proc. International Conference on Learning Representations*.

Asim, Muhammad, Ahmed, Ali, and Hand, Paul. 2019. Invertible generative models for inverse problems: Mitigating representation error and dataset bias. ArXiv preprint arXiv:1905.11672.

Bach, Francis, Jenatton, Rodolphe, Mairal, Julien, Obozinski, Guillaume, et al. 2012. Optimization with sparsity-inducing penalties. *Foundations and Trends in Machine Learning*, **4**(1), 1–106.

Baraniuk, Richard G., and Wakin, Michael B. 2009. Random projections of smooth manifolds. *Foundations of Computational Mathematics*, **9**(1), 51–77.

Baraniuk, Richard G., Cevher, Volkan, Duarte, Marco F., and Hegde, Chinmay. 2010. Model-based compressive sensing. *IEEE Transactions on Information Theory*, **56**(4), 1982–2001.

Bickel, Peter J., Ritov, Ya'cov, Tsybakov, Alexandre B., et al. 2009. Simultaneous analysis of Lasso and Dantzig selector. *Annals of Statistics*, **37**(4), 1705–1732.

Blei, David M., Kucukelbir, Alp, and McAuliffe, Jon D. 2017. Variational inference: A review for statisticians. *Journal of the American Statistical Association*, **112**(518), 859–877.

Bora, Ashish, Jalal, Ajil, Price, Eric, and Dimakis, Alexandros G. 2017. Compressed sensing using generative models. In: *Proc. International Conference on Machine Learning*.

Brock, Andrew, Donahue, Jeff, and Simonyan, Karen. 2019. *Large scale GAN training for high fidelity natural image synthesis*. ArXiv preprint arXiv:1809.11096

Candes, Emmanuel J., Romberg, Justin K., and Tao, Terence. 2006. Stable signal recovery from incomplete and inaccurate measurements. *Communications on Pure and Applied Mathematics*, **59**(8), 1207–1223.

Candes, Emmanuel J., Eldar, Yonina C., Strohmer, Thomas, and Voroninski, Vladislav. 2015a. Phase retrieval via matrix completion. *SIAM Review*, **57**(2), 225–251.

Candes, Emmanuel J., Li, Xiaodong, and Soltanolkotabi, Mahdi. 2015b. Phase retrieval via Wirtinger flow: Theory and algorithms. *IEEE Transactions on Information Theory*, **61**(4), 1985–2007.

Daras, Giannis, Dean, Joseph, Jalal, Ajil, and Dimakis, Alexandros G. 2021. Intermediate layer optimization for inverse problems using deep generative models. In: *Proc. International Conference on Machine Learning*.

Darestani, Mohammad Zalbagi, Chaudhari, Akshay, and Heckel, Reinhard. 2021. Measuring robustness in deep learning based compressive sensing. ArXiv preprint arXiv:2102.06103.

Daskalakis, Constantinos, Rohatgi, Dhruv, and Zampetakis, Emmanouil. 2020. Constant-expansion suffices for compressed sensing with generative priors. Pages 13917–13926 of: *Advances in Neural Information Processing Systems*, **33**.

Dhar, Manik, Grover, Aditya, and Ermon, Stefano. 2018. Modeling sparse deviations for compressed sensing using generative models. Pages 1214–1223 of: *Proc. International Conference on Machine Learning*.

Dinh, Laurent, Sohl-Dickstein, Jascha, and Bengio, Samy. 2016. Density estimation using real NVP. ArXiv preprint arXiv:1605.08803.

Donahue, Jeff, Krähenbühl, Philipp, and Darrell, Trevor. 2016. Adversarial feature learning. ArXiv preprint arXiv:1605.09782.

Donoho, David L. 2006. Compressed sensing. *IEEE Transactions on Information Theory*, **52**(4), 1289–1306.

Dumoulin, Vincent, Belghazi, Ishmael, Poole, Ben, Lamb, Alex, Arjovsky, Martin, Mastropietro, Olivier, and Courville, Aaron. 2016. Adversarially learned inference. ArXiv preprint arXiv:1606.00704.

Eftekhari, Armin, and Wakin, Michael B. 2015. New analysis of manifold embeddings and signal recovery from compressive measurements. *Applied and Computational Harmonic Analysis*, **39**(1), 67–109.

Feizi, Soheil, Suh, Changho, Xia, Fei, and Tse, David. 2017. Understanding GANs: The LQG setting. ArXiv preprint arXiv:1710.10793.

Fletcher, Alyson K., Rangan, Sundeep, and Schniter, Philip. 2018. Inference in deep networks in high dimensions. Pages 1884–1888 of: *Proc. IEEE International Symposium on Information Theory*. IEEE.

Gallager, Robert. 1962. Low-density parity-check codes. *IRE Transactions on Information Theory*, **8**(1), 21–28.

Gilton, Davis, Ongie, Greg, and Willett, Rebecca. 2019. Neumann networks for inverse problems in imaging. ArXiv preprint arXiv:1901.03707.

Gomez, Aidan N., Ren, Mengye, Urtasun, Raquel, and Grosse, Roger B. 2017. The reversible residual network: Backpropagation without storing activations. Pages 2214–2224 of: *Advances in Neural Information Processing Systems*.

Goodfellow, Ian, Pouget-Abadie, Jean, Mirza, Mehdi, Xu, Bing, Warde-Farley, David, Ozair, Sherjil, Courville, Aaron, and Bengio, Yoshua. 2014. Generative adversarial nets. Pages 2672–2680 of: *Advances in Neural Information Processing Systems*.

Gulrajani, Ishaan, Ahmed, Faruk, Arjovsky, Martin, Dumoulin, Vincent, and Courville, Aaron C. 2017. Improved training of Wasserstein GANs. Pages 5769–5779 of: *Advances in Neural Information Processing Systems*.

Hand, Paul, and Voroninski, Vladislav. 2017. Global guarantees for enforcing deep generative priors by empirical risk. ArXiv preprint arXiv:1705.07576.

Hand, Paul, Leong, Oscar, and Voroninski, Vlad. 2018. Phase retrieval under a generative prior. Pages 9136–9146 of: *Advances in Neural Information Processing Systems*.

Heckel, Reinhard, and Hand, Paul. 2018. Deep decoder: Concise image representations from untrained non-convolutional networks. ArXiv preprint arXiv:1810.03982.

Hegde, Chinmay, Wakin, Michael, and Baraniuk, Richard. 2008. Random projections for manifold learning. Pages 641–648 of: *Advances in Neural Information Processing Systems*.

Ho, Jonathan, Jain, Ajay, and Abbeel, Pieter. 2020. Denoising diffusion probabilistic models. ArXiv preprint arXiv:2006.11239.

Huszár, Ferenc. 2017. Variational inference using implicit distributions. ArXiv preprint arXiv:1702.08235.

Jordan, Michael I. 2003. *An Introduction to Probabilistic Graphical Models.* `https://people.eecs.berkeley.edu/~jordan/prelims/`

Kingma, Diederik, and Ba, Jimmy. 2014. Adam: A method for stochastic optimization. ArXiv preprint arXiv:1412.6980.

Kingma, Diederik P., and Welling, Max. 2013. Auto-encoding variational bayes. ArXiv preprint arXiv:1312.6114.

Kingma, Durk P., and Dhariwal, Prafulla. 2018. Glow: Generative flow with invertible 1×1 convolutions. Pages 10215–10224 of: *Advances in Neural Information Processing Systems*.

Koller, Daphne, Friedman, Nir, and Bach, Francis. 2009. *Probabilistic Graphical Models: Principles and Techniques.* MIT Press.

Kschischang, Frank R., Frey, Brendan J., Loeliger, Hans-Andrea, et al. 2001. Factor graphs and the sum–product algorithm. *IEEE Transactions on Information Theory*, **47**(2), 498–519.

Lei, Qi, Jalal, Ajil, Dhillon, Inderjit S., and Dimakis, Alexandros G. 2019. Inverting deep generative models, one layer at a time. ArXiv preprint arXiv:1906.07437.

Lin, Zinan, Khetan, Ashish, Fanti, Giulia, and Oh, Sewoong. 2017. PacGAN: The power of two samples in generative adversarial networks. ArXiv preprint arXiv:1712.04086.

Liu, Hongyu, Jiang, Bin, Xiao, Yi, and Yang, Chao. 2019. Coherent semantic attention for image inpainting. *Proc. International Conference on Computer Vision.*

Liu, Jiaming, Sun, Yu, Xu, Xiaojian, and Kamilov, Ulugbek S. 2018. Image restoration using total variation regularized deep image prior. ArXiv preprint arXiv:1810.12864.

Liu, Shuang, Bousquet, Olivier, and Chaudhuri, Kamalika. 2017. Approximation and convergence properties of generative adversarial learning. Pages 5551–5559 of: *Advances in Neural Information Processing Systems.*

Liu, Ziwei, Luo, Ping, Wang, Xiaogang, and Tang, Xiaoou. 2015 (December). Deep learning face attributes in the wild. In: *Proc. International Conference on Computer Vision.*

Loh, Po-Ling, and Wainwright, Martin J. 2011. High-dimensional regression with noisy and missing data: Provable guarantees with non-convexity. Pages 2726–2734 of: *Advances in Neural Information Processing Systems.*

Manjunath, Bangalore S., Salembier, Philippe, and Sikora, Thomas. 2002. *Introduction to MPEG-7: Multimedia Content Description Interface.* Vol. 1. John Wiley & Sons.

Marcellin, Michael W., Gormish, Michael J., Bilgin, Ali, and Boliek, Martin P. 2000. An overview of JPEG-2000. Pages 523–541 of: *Proc. Data Compression Conference.*

Menon, Sachit, Damian, Alexandru, Hu, Shijia, Ravi, Nikhil, and Rudin, Cynthia. 2020. PULSE: Self-supervised photo upsampling via latent space exploration of generative models. *Proc. Conference on Computer Vision and Pattern Recognition.*

Metz, Luke, Poole, Ben, Pfau, David, and Sohl-Dickstein, Jascha. 2017. Unrolled generative adversarial networks. In: *Proc. International Conference on Learning Representations.*

Mohamed, Shakir, and Lakshminarayanan, Balaji. 2016. Learning in implicit generative models. ArXiv preprint arXiv:1610.03483.

Negahban, Sahand, Yu, Bin, Wainwright, Martin J., and Ravikumar, Pradeep K. 2009. A unified framework for high-dimensional analysis of m-estimators with decomposable regularizers. Pages 1348–1356 of: *Advances in Neural Information Processing Systems.*

Nie, Dong, Trullo, Roger, Lian, Jun, Petitjean, Caroline, Ruan, Su, Wang, Qian, and Shen, Dinggang. 2017. Medical image synthesis with context-aware generative adversarial networks. Pages 417–425 of: *Proc. International Conference on Medical Image Computing and Computer-Assisted Intervention.*

Odena, Augustus. 2019. Open questions about generative adversarial networks. *Distill,* **4**(4), e18.

Ongie, Gregory, Jalal, Ajil, Metzler, Christopher A., Baraniuk, Richard G., Dimakis, Alexandros G, and Willett, Rebecca. 2020. Deep learning techniques for inverse problems in imaging. *IEEE Journal on Selected Areas in Information Theory*, **1**(1), 39–56.

Pandit, Parthe, Sahraee, Mojtaba, Rangan, Sundeep, and Fletcher, Alyson K. 2019. Asymptotics of map inference in deep networks. ArXiv preprint arXiv:1903.01293.

Pearl, Judea. 1982. Reverend Bayes on inference engines: A distributed hierarchical approach. Pages 133–136 of: *Proc. AAAI Conference on Artifical Intelligence*.

Radford, Alec, Metz, Luke, and Chintala, Soumith. 2015. Unsupervised representation learning with deep convolutional generative adversarial networks. ArXiv preprint arXiv:1511.06434.

Richardson, Tom, and Urbanke, Ruediger. 2008. *Modern Coding Theory*. Cambridge University Press.

Rudin, Leonid I., Osher, Stanley, and Fatemi, Emad. 1992. Nonlinear total variation based noise removal algorithms. *Physica D: Nonlinear Phenomena*, **60**(1-4), 259–268.

Sanjabi, Maziar, Ba, Jimmy, Razaviyayn, Meisam, and Lee, Jason D. 2018. Solving approximate Wasserstein GANs to stationarity. ArXiv preprint arXiv:1802.08249.

Schlegl, Thomas, Seeböck, Philipp, Waldstein, Sebastian M., Schmidt-Erfurth, Ursula, and Langs, Georg. 2017. Unsupervised anomaly detection with generative adversarial networks to guide marker discovery. Pages 146–157 of: *Proc. International Conference on Information Processing in Medical Imaging*.

Schlemper, Jo, Caballero, Jose, Hajnal, Joseph V., Price, Anthony N, and Rueckert, Daniel. 2017. A deep cascade of convolutional neural networks for dynamic MR image reconstruction. *IEEE Transactions on Medical Imaging*, **37**(2), 491–503.

Shannon, Claude E. 1948. A mathematical theory of communication. *The Bell system Technical Journal*, **27**(3), 379–423.

Sohl-Dickstein, Jascha, Weiss, Eric, Maheswaranathan, Niru, and Ganguli, Surya. 2015. Deep unsupervised learning using nonequilibrium thermodynamics. Pages 2256–2265 of: *Proc. International Conference on Machine Learning*.

Song, Yang, Sohl-Dickstein, Jascha, Kingma, Diederik P., Kumar, Abhishek, Ermon, Stefano, and Poole, Ben. 2021. Score-based generative modeling through stochastic differential equations. In: *Proc. International Conference on Learning Representations*.

Sun, Wanjie, and Chen, Zhenzhong. 2020. Learned image downscaling for upscaling using content adaptive resampler. *IEEE Transactions on Image Processing*, **29**, 4027–4040.

Sun, Yu, Liu, Jiaming, and Kamilov, Ulugbek S. 2020. Block coordinate regularization by denoising. *IEEE Transactions on Computational Imaging*, **6**, 908–921.

Tian, Chunwei, Fei, Lunke, Zheng, Wenxian, Xu, Yong, Zuo, Wangmeng, and Lin, Chia-Wen. 2020. Deep learning on image denoising: An overview. *Neural Networks*, **131**(November), 251–275.

Tibshirani, Robert. 1996. Regression shrinkage and selection via the lasso. *Journal of the Royal Statistical Society. Series B (Methodological)*, 267–288.

Tripathi, Subarna, Lipton, Zachary C., and Nguyen, Truong Q. 2018. Correction by projection: Denoising images with generative adversarial networks. ArXiv preprint arXiv:1803.04477.

Ulyanov, Dmitry, Vedaldi, Andrea, and Lempitsky, Victor. 2017. Deep image prior. ArXiv preprint arXiv:1711.10925.

Van Veen, David, Jalal, Ajil, Price, Eric, Vishwanath, Sriram, and Dimakis, Alexandros G. 2018. Compressed sensing with deep image prior and learned regularization. ArXiv preprint arXiv:1806.06438.

Wainwright, Martin J. 2019. *High-Dimensional Statistics: A Non-Asymptotic Viewpoint*. Vol. 48. Cambridge University Press.

Wainwright, Martin J., Jordan, Michael I., et al. 2008. Graphical models, exponential families, and variational inference. *Foundations and Trends in Machine Learning*, **1**(1–2), 1–305.

Wallace, Gregory K. 1992. The JPEG still picture compression standard. *IEEE Transactions on Consumer Electronics*, **38**(1), xviii–xxxiv.

Wolterink, Jelmer M., Leiner, Tim, Viergever, Max A., and Išgum, Ivana. 2017. Generative adversarial networks for noise reduction in low-dose CT. *IEEE Transactions on Medical Imaging*, **36**(12), 2536–2545.

Yang, Wenming, Zhang, Xuechen, Tian, Yapeng, Wang, Wei, Xue, Jing-Hao, and Liao, Qingmin. 2019. Deep learning for single image super-resolution: A brief review. *IEEE Transactions on Multimedia*, **21**(12), 3106–3121.

Yu, Jiahui, Lin, Zhe, Yang, Jimei, Shen, Xiaohui, Lu, Xin, and Huang, Thomas. 2019. Free-form image inpainting with gated convolution. *Proc. International Conference on Computer Vision*.

10

Dynamical Systems and Optimal Control Approach to Deep Learning

Weinan E, Jiequn Han, Qianxiao Li

Abstract: We give a short and concise review of the dynamical system and control theory approach to deep learning. From the viewpoint of dynamical systems, the back-propagation algorithm in deep learning becomes a simple consequence of the variational equations in ODEs. From the viewpoint of control theory, deep learning is a case of mean-field control in that all the agents share the same control. As an application, we discuss a new class of algorithms for deep learning based on Pontryagin's maximum principle in control theory.

10.1 Introduction

Deep learning is at present the most successful machine learning tool for a wide variety of tasks ranging from computer vision (Deng et al., 2009), to scientific computing (Han et al., 2018a; E et al., 2017) to molecular modeling (Han et al., 2018b; Zhang et al., 2018a,b). From a mathematical viewpoint, its multilayer compositional structure puts deep learning into a quite different category from other machine learning models, and for this reason there is a need for different kinds of algorithms as well as a different mathematical framework for understanding deep learning. One such example is the back-propagation algorithm, which plays a key role in deep learning. Another, related, example is the control theory approach to deep learning, put forward already in LeCun (1989). Both are quite unique to deep learning. In this chapter, we examine the mathematical structure behind these ideas and we discuss recent efforts to design new training algorithms using them.

The first point we will discuss is that one can think about the continuous (in time) analogs of deep neural networks, and this will allow us to make use of the theory and numerical algorithms for ODEs. This simple idea was first put forward in E (2017) and has become popular under the name of "neural ODEs" (Chen et al., 2018) (see also Haber and Ruthotto, 2017; Ruthotto and Haber, 2018; Sonoda and Murate, 2019; Lu et al., 2017). In light of this, the back-propagation algorithm becomes a natural development of the well-known variational equation for ODEs.

The second issue we will examine is the control theory viewpoint of deep learning. It turns out that, though intuitively very clear, making this approach rigorous is non-trivial since the problem falls into the category of "mean-field control" in that all agents share the same control. This forms a loose parallel with mean-field games (E et al., 2019a), in which the input-label samples play the roles of agents and the control (consisting of trained weights) is determined by some collective behavior of these samples or agents. As such, the state space becomes infinite dimensional and the associated Hamilton–Jacobi–Bellman (HJB) equation becomes highly non-trivial. For this reason, we will not dwell on the HJB approach to this mean-field control problem. Instead, we will focus on the maximum principle approach initiated by E et al. (2019a). As an application of these ideas, we will discuss a new class of training algorithm motivated by the maximum principle. In this algorithm, one solves a coupled forward–backward problem, but the optimization, in the form of the maximization of Hamiltonian functions, is done layer-wise. Note that the standard back-propagation algorithm is a special case where the Hamiltonian maximizations are performed by one step of gradient ascent. One advantage of considering this more general class of algorithms is that other methods, such as L-BFGS (Liu and Nocedal, 1989), can be used to perform this layer-wise optimization, leading to novel algorithms with different properties (Li et al., 2017). Another advantage of this approach is that it applies equally well to the case when the weights live on discrete spaces. This is useful for developing principled training algorithms for quantized neural networks, in which the weights are restricted to take values in a finite set, e.g. binary and ternary networks (Li and Hao, 2018).

10.1.1 The Problem of Supervised Learning

In supervised learning, the object of interest is a target function f^*, where $f: \mathbb{R}^d \to \mathbb{R}^1$; f^* is defined by f together with a probability distribution μ_0 on $\mathbb{R}^d$. We are given a data set $S = \{(x_j, y_j)\}_{j=1}^{n}$, where the x_j are sampled from a probability distribution μ_0, $y_j = f^*(x_j)$. In principle one should also allow the presence of measurement noise in y_j, but here we will focus on the case without measurement noise. Our task is to approximate f^* on the basis of the information in S. Generally speaking, supervised learning strategies consist of the following components:

- The construction of some "hypothesis space" (a space of functions) $\mathcal{H}_m$. Here m is roughly the dimension of $\mathcal{H}_m$ or the number of free parameters that describe a function in the hypothesis space.

- Minimization of the "empirical risk",

$$\hat{R}_n = \frac{1}{n} \sum_{j=1}^{n} \Phi(f(\boldsymbol{x}_j), y_j) = \frac{1}{n} \sum_{j=1}^{n} \Phi(f(\boldsymbol{x}_j), f^*(\boldsymbol{x}_j)),$$

where $f \in \mathcal{H}_m$. Here, Φ denotes the loss function, e.g., mean square loss could correspond to $\Phi(y, y') := (y - y')^2$.

Notice immediately that what we really want to minimize is the "population risk",

$$\mathcal{R} = \mathbb{E}\Phi(f(\boldsymbol{x}), f^*(\boldsymbol{x})) = \int_{\mathbb{R}^d} \Phi(f(\boldsymbol{x}), f^*(\boldsymbol{x}))d\mu_0(\boldsymbol{x}).$$

Whether the minimizers of these two risk functions are close to each other is a central problem in machine learning.

An important issue is how to choose the hypothesis space. The simplest choice is the space of linear functions, $\mathcal{H}_m = \{f(\boldsymbol{x}) = \boldsymbol{\beta} \cdot \boldsymbol{x} + \beta_0, \boldsymbol{\beta} \in \mathbb{R}^d, \beta_0 \in \mathbb{R}\}$. This is the case in linear regression. A slight extension is the generalized linear model, $\mathcal{H}_m = \{f(\boldsymbol{x}) = \sum_{k=1}^{m} c_k \phi_k(\boldsymbol{x}), c_k \in \mathbb{R}\}$. Here $\{\phi_k\}$ is a set of linearly independent functions. A shallow neural network with one hidden layer corresponds to the case when $\mathcal{H}_m = \{f(\boldsymbol{x}) = \sum_{k=1}^{m} a_k \sigma(\boldsymbol{b}_k \cdot \boldsymbol{x} + c_k), a_k, c_k \in \mathbb{R}, \boldsymbol{b}_k \in \mathbb{R}^d\}$, where σ is some non-linear function, called the activation function, e.g. $\sigma(z) = \max(z, 0)$, the ReLU (rectified linear unit) activation function . In this view, deep neural networks (DNN) correspond to the case when the hypothesis space consists of compositions of functions of the form above:

$$f(\boldsymbol{x}, \boldsymbol{\theta}) = \boldsymbol{W}_L \sigma \circ (\boldsymbol{W}_{L-1} \sigma \circ (\cdots \sigma \circ (\boldsymbol{W}_0 \boldsymbol{x}))), \qquad \boldsymbol{\theta} = (\boldsymbol{W}_0, \boldsymbol{W}_1, \ldots, \boldsymbol{W}_L).$$

Here "$\circ$" means that the non-linear function σ is applied to each component of the argument vector, the $\boldsymbol{W}_i$ are matrices (note that we have adopted the standard abuse of notation and have omitted the constant term; $\boldsymbol{W}_0 \boldsymbol{x}$ should really be an affine function instead of a linear function). The trick is to find the right set of functions that are rich enough to approximate accurately the target function but simple enough that the task of finding the best approximation is manageable.

10.2 ODE Formulation

An interesting way of constructing functions is through the flow map of an ODE system. This viewpoint was first proposed in E (2017) and later in Chen et al. (2018). Consider the following ODEs in $\mathbb{R}^d$:

$$\frac{dz_t}{dt} = f(z_t \cdot \boldsymbol{\theta}_t), \quad z_0(\boldsymbol{x}) = \boldsymbol{x}. \tag{10.1}$$

The solution at time t is denoted by $z_t(x)$. We say that $x \to z_t(x)$ is the flow map at time t following the dynamics (10.1), and so the flow map implicitly depends on $\theta \equiv \{\theta_t : t \in [0, T]\}$. Fixing a time horizon T, we can define the hypothesis space through the different flow maps obtained by choosing different values for θ and α:

$$\mathcal{H}_m = \{\alpha \cdot z_T(\cdot), \; \alpha \in \mathbb{R}^d, \theta \in L^\infty\}. \tag{10.2}$$

How should we choose the functional form of f? One reasonable strategy is to choose the simplest non-linear function in some sense and $f(z, \theta) = \sigma \circ (\theta z)$ is arguably such a choice. Here only a fixed scalar non-linear function enters into the construction; all the parameters are in the linear transformation θ.

A DNN can be understood as the discrete form of the formalism discussed above. The structures before the output layer can be viewed as a discrete dynamical system in the feature space. In this case, the matrices θ do not have to be square matrices and a change of dimensionality is allowed in the dynamical system.

A byproduct of the ODE formulation is that the back-propagation algorithm in deep learning becomes the direct analog of the variational equation for ODEs. To see this, note that if we define the matrix $V_t := \nabla_{z_t} z_T$ then we can derive a variational equation for the evolution of V_t in the form

$$\dot{V}_t = -\nabla_z f(z_t, \theta_t) V_t, \qquad V_T = I. \tag{10.3}$$

This equation describes the effects of perturbations in z_t on the final state z_T, from which one can then use the chain rule to obtain gradients with respect to each θ_t. In fact, the variational equation (10.3) is simply the back-propagation of the derivatives with respect to the hidden states. See Li et al. (2017) and E et al. (2019a) for further discussions of this connection and the role of variational equations in the optimality conditions.

10.3 Mean-Field Optimal Control and Pontryagin's Maximum Principle

It is natural to think of deep learning as an optimal control problem: choosing the best control θ to minimize the risk. Although this viewpoint was formulated by LeCun (1989), the full mathematical theory was only established much later in E et al. (2019a). The subtlety lies in the fact that this is not an ordinary control problem, but a mean-field control problem. As was shown in E et al. (2019a), the associated HJB equation should be formulated on the Wasserstein space, which is an infinite-dimensional space of probability measures. We will not discuss the HJB equation here since it is quite technical and requires a considerable amount of new notations. Instead, we will focus on the maximum principle viewpoint in control theory and discuss algorithms that are based on the maximum principle.

Consider a set of admissible controls or training weights $\Theta \subseteq \mathbb{R}^m$. In typical deep learning, Θ is taken as the whole space $\mathbb{R}^m$, but here we consider the more general case where Θ can be constrained. To cast the deep learning problem as a control problem, it is helpful to consider the more general setting where a regularization term is added to the objective function. The population risk minimization problem in deep learning can hence be posed as the following *mean-field optimal control problem*

$$\inf_{\boldsymbol{\theta} \in L^\infty([0,T],\Theta)} J(\boldsymbol{\theta}) := \mathbb{E}_{\mu_0} \left[\Phi(z_T, y) + \int_0^T L(z_t, \boldsymbol{\theta}_t)dt \right], \quad \text{subject to (10.1)}.$$

(10.4)

Note that here we have simplified the set-up slightly by absorbing α, assuming it is constant, into Φ, so that the latter is now a function from $\mathbb{R}^d \times \mathbb{R}^l$ to $\mathbb{R}^l$. Also, we now denote by μ_0 the joint distribution of the input-label pair (x, y). The term "mean-field" highlights the fact that $\boldsymbol{\theta}$ is shared by a whole population, and the optimal control must depend on the law of the input-target random variables. Note that the law of z_t does not enter the forward equations explicitly (unlike e.g. McKean–Vlasov control Carmona and Delarue, 2015), and hence our forward dynamics are not explicitly in mean-field form. We also refer to E et al. (2019a) for a discussion on batch-normalized dynamical systems which possess explicit mean-field dynamics.

The empirical risk minimization problem can be posed as a sampled optimal control problem

$$\inf_{\boldsymbol{\theta} \in L^\infty([0,T],\Theta)} J(\boldsymbol{\theta}) := \frac{1}{n} \sum_{i=1}^n \left[\Phi(z_T^i, y^i) + \int_0^T L(z_t^i, \boldsymbol{\theta}_t)dt \right],$$

(10.5)

$$\text{subject to } \dot{z}_t^i = f(z_t^i, \boldsymbol{\theta}_t), \quad 1 = 1, \ldots, n,$$

where $\{x^i, y^i\}$ are i.i.d. samples from μ_0. The solutions of sampled optimal control problems are typically random variables. Note that this is a special case of (10.4) with μ_0 replaced by the empirical measure $\{x^i, y^i\}$.

It is likely that, to obtain optimal error control, one should add an n-dependent coefficient in front of the regularization term (see E et al., 2019b). At the moment, this theory is not yet complete. Therefore, here, we will neglect such a dependence.

10.3.1 Pontryagin's Maximum Principle

One of the most powerful tools in control theory is the maximum principle discovered by Pontryagin (PMP); see Boltyanskii et al. (1960) and Pontryagin (1987). This maximum principle is amazingly general: for example it applies to cases when the set of controls is discrete.

To begin with, we define the *Hamiltonian* $H: [0,T] \times \mathbb{R}^d \times \mathbb{R}^d \times \Theta \to \mathbb{R}$ given by

$$H(z,p,\theta) := p \cdot f(z,\theta) - L(z,\theta).$$

Theorem 10.1 (Mean-field PMP). *Suppose that f is bounded, f, L are continuous in θ and f, L, Φ are continuously differentiable with respect to z. Suppose further that the distribution μ_0 has bounded support. Let $\theta^* \in L^\infty([0,T],\Theta)$ be a solution of (10.4) in the sense that $J(\theta^*)$ attains the infimum. Then there exist absolutely continuous stochastic processes z^*, p^* such that*

$$
\begin{aligned}
\dot{z}_t^* &= f(z_t^*,\theta_t^*), & z_0^* &= x, & (10.6)\\
\dot{p}_t^* &= -\nabla_z H(z_t^*,p_t^*,\theta_t^*), & p_T^* &= -\nabla_z \Phi(z_T^*,y), & (10.7)\\
\mathbb{E}_{\mu_0} H(z_t^*,p_t^*,\theta_t^*) &\geq \mathbb{E}_\mu H(z_t^*,p_t^*,\theta), & \text{for all } \theta \in \Theta & \quad \text{a.e. } t \in [0,T], & (10.8)
\end{aligned}
$$

where $(x,y) \sim \mu_0$ are random variables.

This is a simple generalization of the usual Pontryagin maximum principle (for which the expectation is absent; see e.g. Athans and Falb, 2013, Bertsekas, 1995, and Liberzon, 2012) to the learning setting, and the proof can be found in E et al. (2019a). The PMP can be regarded as a generalization of the Karush–Kuhn–Tucker (KKT) conditions for non-linear constrained optimization to non-smooth (in θ) and mean-field settings. Indeed, we can view (10.4) as a non-linear program over the function space $L^\infty([0,T],\Theta)$ where the constraint is the ODE (10.1). In this sense, the co-state process p^* plays the role of a continuous-time analogue of Lagrange multipliers. The key difference between the PMP and the KKT conditions (besides the lack of inequality constraints on the state) is the Hamiltonian maximization condition (10.19), which is stronger than a typical first-order condition that assumes smoothness with respect to θ (e.g. $\nabla_\theta \mathbb{E}_{\mu_0} H = 0$). In particular, the PMP says that $\mathbb{E}_{\mu_0} H$ is not only stationary, but globally maximized at an optimal control – which is a much stronger statement if the averaged Hamiltonian is not concave. Moreover, the PMP makes minimal assumptions on the parameter space Θ; it holds even when f is non-smooth with respect to θ, or worse, when Θ is a discrete subset of $\mathbb{R}^m$.

The three simultaneous equations in Theorem 10.1 allow us to solve for the unknowns z^*, p^*, θ^* simultaneously as a function of t. In this sense, the resulting optimal control θ^* is *open-loop* and is not in a feedback form $\theta_t^* = g(t,z_t^*)$ for some control function g. The latter is of closed-loop type and is typically obtained from dynamic programming and the Hamilton–Jacobi–Bellman formalism (Bellman, 2013). In this sense, the PMP gives a weaker control. However, open-loop solutions are sufficient for neural network applications, where the trained weights and biases are fixed and depend only on the layer number and not explicitly on the inputs and hidden states at the times when inferences are made.

10.4 Method of Successive Approximations

10.4.1 Extended Pontryagin Maximum Principle

We now discuss the development of novel training algorithms based on the PMP. For practical purposes we are always dealing with empirical risk minimization, where μ_0 is an empirical measure induced by samples. Thus, we can simplify the notation by concatenating all the x^i and y^i into a pair of long vectors (x, y) and redefining $(f, \ldots, f)$ as f. Consequently, the expectations in (10.4) (or the sum in (10.5)) can now be ignored and x, y can be considered deterministic.

It turns out that for the purpose of designing efficient algorithms with error control, it is useful to introduce an extended version of the maximum principle, by applying similar ideas to augmented Lagrangians (Hestenes, 1969). This extended maximum principle was introduced in Li et al. (2017). Fix some $\rho > 0$ and introduce the augmented Hamiltonian

$$\tilde{H}(z, p, \theta, v, q) := H(z, p, \theta) - \frac{1}{2}\rho\|v - f(z, \theta)\|^2 - \frac{1}{2}\rho\|q + \nabla_z H(z, p, \theta)\|^2. \quad (10.9)$$

Then we have the following set of alternative necessary conditions for optimality:

Proposition 10.2 (Extended PMP). *Suppose that $\theta^* \in L^\infty([0,T], \Theta)$ is a solution to the optimal control problem (10.5) (with the concatenated notation described above). Then there exists an absolutely continuous co-state process p^* such that the tuple $(z_t^*, p_t^*, \theta_t^*)$ satisfies the necessary conditions*

$$\dot{z}_t^* = \nabla_p \tilde{H}(z_t^*, p_t^*, \theta_t^*, \dot{z}_t^*, \dot{p}_t^*), \qquad\qquad z_0^* = x, \qquad\qquad (10.10)$$

$$\dot{p}_t^* = -\nabla_z \tilde{H}(z_t^*, p_t^*, \theta_t^*, \dot{z}_t^*, \dot{p}_t^*), \qquad\qquad p_T^* = -\nabla_z \Phi(z_T^*, y), \qquad (10.11)$$

$$\tilde{H}(z_t^*, p_t^*, \theta_t^*, \dot{z}_t^*, \dot{p}_t^*) \geq \tilde{H}(z_t^*, p_t^*, \theta, \dot{z}_t^*, \dot{p}_t^*), \qquad \theta \in \Theta, \quad t \in [0,T]. \quad (10.12)$$

The proof can be found in Li et al. (2017). Compared with the usual PMP, the extended PMP is a weaker necessary condition. However, the advantage is that maximizing $\tilde{H}$ naturally penalizes errors in the Hamiltonian dynamical equations, which is useful for ensuring convergence of the successive approximation type of algorithms, which we now discuss.

10.4.2 The Basic Method of Successive Approximation

Here again we will focus on the continuous-in-time setting, but one should note that the algorithm can also be formulated in a discrete setting, which is the case for the deep neural networks used in practice. In the optimal control literature, there are many methods for the numerical solution of the PMP, including two-point boundary value problem methods (Bryson, 1975; Roberts and Shipman, 1972), and collocation methods (Betts, 1988) coupled with general non-linear programming techniques (Bertsekas, 1999; Bazaraa et al., 2013). See Rao (2009) for a review. Most of these methods concern the small-scale problems typically encountered in control applications (e.g. trajectory optimization of spacecraft) and do not scale well to modern machine learning problems with a large number of state and control variables. One exception is the method of successive approximations (MSA) (Chernousko and Lyubushin, 1982), which is an iterative method based on alternating propagation and optimization steps.

Observe that (10.6) is simply the equation

$$\dot{z}_t^* = f(z_t^*, \theta_t^*)$$

and is independent of the co-state p^*. Therefore, we may proceed in the following manner. First, we make an initial guess of the optimal control $\theta^0 \in L^\infty([0,T], \Theta)$. For each $k = 0, 1, 2, \ldots$, we first solve (10.6),

$$\dot{z}_t = f(z_t, \theta_t^k), \qquad z_0 = x, \tag{10.13}$$

for $\{z_t\}$, which then allows us to solve (10.7),

$$\dot{p}_t = -\nabla_z H(z_t, p_t, \theta_t^k), \qquad p_T = -\nabla \Phi(z_T, y) \tag{10.14}$$

to get $\{p_t\}$. Finally, we use the maximization condition (10.8) to set

$$\theta_t^{k+1} = \underset{\theta \in \Theta}{\mathrm{argmax}}\, H(z_t, p_t, \theta)$$

for $t \in [0, T]$. The algorithm is summarized in Algorithm 10.1.

Now, MSA consists of two major components: the forward–backward Hamiltonian dynamics (Steps 4, 5) and the maximization for the optimal parameters at each time (Step 6). An important feature of MSA is that the Hamiltonian maximization step is decoupled for each $t \in [0, T]$. In the language of deep learning, the optimization step is decoupled for different layers and only the Hamiltonian ODEs (Steps 3, 4 of Algorithm 10.1) involve propagation through the layers. This allows the parallelization of the maximization step, which is typically the most time-consuming step.

Although it can been shown that the basic MSA converges for a restricted class of linear quadratic regulators (Aleksandrov, 1968), in general it tends to diverge, especially if a bad initial θ^0 is chosen (Aleksandrov, 1968; Chernousko and Lyubushin, 1982). Our goal is to modify the basic MSA to control its divergent behavior. Before we do so, it is important to understand why the MSA diverges and, in particular, the relationship between the maximization step in Algorithm 10.1 and the empirical risk minimization problem (10.5).

Algorithm 10.1 Basic method of successive approximations

1: **procedure** BASIC MSA
2: Initialize $k = 0$, $\theta^0 \in L^\infty([0,T],\Theta)$
3: **while** Stopping criterion not satisfied **do**
4: $\quad \{z_t : t \in [0,T]\} \leftarrow$ solution of $\dot{z}_t = f(z_t, \theta_t^k)$, $\quad z_0 = x \quad \triangleright$ Solve state equation

5: $\quad \{p_t : t \in [0,T]\} \leftarrow$ solution of $\dot{p}_t = -\nabla_z H(z_t, p_t, \theta_t^k)$, $\quad p_T = -\nabla_z \Phi(z_T, y)$
$\qquad\qquad \triangleright$ Solve co-state equation
6: $\quad \theta_t^{k+1} \leftarrow \mathrm{argmax}_{\theta \in \Theta}\, H(z_t, p_t, \theta)$, $\quad t \in [0,T] \quad \triangleright$ Maximize Hamiltonian
7: $\quad k \leftarrow k + 1$
8: **return** θ^k

For each $\theta \in L^\infty([0,T],\Theta)$, recall that we are minimizing

$$J(\theta) := \Phi(z_T^\theta, y) + \int_0^T L(z_t^\theta, \theta_t)\,dt,$$

where $\{z_t^\theta\}$, satisfying (10.13) with parameters θ, Φ, is the empirical risk function. We show in the following lemma the relationship between the values of J and the Hamiltonian maximization step. We start by making the following assumptions.

(A1) Φ is twice continuously differentiable in z, with Φ and $\nabla\Phi$ satisfying a Lipschitz condition in z, i.e. there exists $K > 0$ such that

$$|\Phi(z, y) - \Phi(z', y)| + \|\nabla\Phi(z, y) - \nabla\Phi(z', y)\| \leq K\|z - z'\|$$

for all z, $z' \in \mathbb{R}^d$ and $y \in \mathbb{R}$.

(A2) $f(\cdot, \theta)$ is twice continuously differentiable in z, with f, $\nabla_z f$ satisfying a Lipschitz condition in z uniformly in θ and t, i.e. there exists $K > 0$ such that

$$\|f(z, \theta) - f(z', \theta)\| + \|\nabla_z f(z, \theta) - \nabla_z f(z', \theta)\|_2 \leq K\|z - z'\|$$

for all $z, z' \in \mathbb{R}^d$ and $t \in [0,T]$, where $\|\cdot\|_2$ denotes the induced 2-norm.

With these assumptions, we have the following estimate.

Lemma 10.3. *Suppose that* (A1)–(A2) *hold. Then there exists a constant $C > 0$ such that for any $\theta, \phi \in L^\infty([0,T],\Theta)$,*

$$J(\phi) \leq J(\theta) - \int_0^T \Delta_{\phi,\theta} H(t)\, dt + C \int_0^T \|f(z_t^\theta, \phi_t) - f(z_t^\theta, \theta_t)\|\, dt$$

$$+ C \int_0^T \|\nabla_z(z_t^\theta, p_t^\theta, \phi_t) - \nabla_z H(z_T^\theta, p_t^\theta, \theta_t)\|^2\, dt,$$

Algorithm 10.2 Extended method of successive approximations

1: **procedure** EXTENDED MSA (Hyper-parameter: ρ)
2: Initialize $k = 0$, $\theta^0 \in L^\infty([0,T],\Theta)$
3: **while** Stopping criterion not satisfied **do**
4:   $\{z_t : t \in [0,T]\} \leftarrow$ solution of $\dot{z}_t = f(z_t, \theta_t^k)$, $z_0 = x$ ▷ Solve state equation

5:   $\{p_t : t \in [0,T]\} \leftarrow$ solution of
    $\dot{p}_t = -\nabla_z H(z_t, p_t, \theta_t^k)$, $p_T = -\nabla_z \Phi(z_T, y)$ ▷ Solve co-state equation
6:   $\theta_t^{k+1} \leftarrow \text{argmax}_{\theta \in \Theta}\, \tilde{H}(z_t, p_t, \theta, \dot{z}_t, \dot{p}_t)$, $t \in [0,T]$
                 ▷ Maximize extended Hamiltonian

7:   $k \leftarrow k + 1$
8: **return** θ^k

---

where z^θ, p^θ satisfy (10.13), (10.14) respectively and $\Delta H_{\phi,\theta}$ denotes the change in Hamiltonian:

$$\Delta H_{\phi,\theta} := H(z_t^\theta, p_t^\theta, \phi_t) - H(z_t^\theta, p_t^\theta, \theta_t).$$

See Li et al. (2017) for the proof of this lemma. Lemma 10.3 says that the Hamiltonian maximization step in MSA (Step 6 in Algorithm 10.1) is in some sense the optimal descent direction for J. However, the last two terms on the right-hand side indicates that this descent can be nullified if substituting ϕ for θ incurs too much error in the Hamiltonian dynamics (Steps 4, 5 in Algorithm 10.1). In other words, the last two integrals measure the degree to which the Hamiltonian dynamics (10.6), (10.18) are satisfied, and can be viewed as feasibility conditions, when one replaces θ by ϕ. Thus, we may call these *feasibility errors*. The divergence of the basic MSA happens when these feasibility errors dominate the descent due to Hamiltonian maximization. The controlling of feasibility errors is the motivation for developing the extended PMP and the extended MSA.

10.4.3 Extended Method of Successive Approximation

The extended MSA can be understood as an application of the basic MSA not to the original PMP but to the extended PMP introduced in Li et al. (2017), where the terms with ρ regularize the feasibility errors. Hence, we have Algorithm 10.2.

Define

$$\mu_k := \int_0^T \Delta H_{\theta^{k+1},\theta^k}(t) \geq 0.$$

If $\mu_k = 0$, then from the Hamiltonian maximization step (10.12) we must have

$$0 = -\mu_k \leq \frac{1}{2}\rho \int_0^T \|f(z_t^{\theta^k}, \theta_t^{k+1}) - f(z_t^{\theta^k}, \theta_t^k)\|^2 \, dt$$

$$- \frac{1}{2}\rho \int_0^T \|\nabla_z H(z_t^{\theta^k}, p_t^{\theta^k}, \theta_t^{k+1}) - \nabla_z H(z_t^{\theta^k}, p_t^{\theta^k}, \theta_t^k)\|^2 \, dt$$

$$\leq 0$$

and so

$$\max_\theta \tilde{H}(z_t^{\theta^k}, p_t^{\theta^k}, 0, \dot{z}_t^{\theta^k}, \dot{p}_t^{\theta^k}) = \tilde{H}(z_t^{\theta^k}, p_t^{\theta^k}, \theta_k, \dot{z}_t^{\theta^k}, \dot{p}_t^{\theta^k}),$$

i.e., $(z^{\theta^k}, p^{\theta^k}, \theta^k)$ satisfies the extended PMP. In other words, the quantity $\mu_k \geq 0$ measures the distance from a solution of the extended PMP, and if it equals 0, then we have a solution. The following result gives a sufficient condition for the convergence of μ_k.

Theorem 10.4. *Assume that the conditions in Lemma 10.3 hold and let $\theta^0 \in L^\infty([0,T], \Theta)$ be any initial measurable control with $J(\theta^0) < +\infty$. Assume also that $\inf_{\theta \in L^\infty([0,T], \Theta)} J(\theta) > -\infty$. Then, for ρ large enough, we have from Algorithm 10.2,*

$$J(\theta^{k+1}) - J(\theta^k) \leq -D\mu_k.$$

for some constant $D > 0$ and

$$\lim_{k \to 0} \mu_k = 0;$$

i.e., the extended MSA algorithm converges to the set of solutions of the extended PMP.

Since the proof is quite simple and informative, we reproduce it here from Li et al. (2017).

Proof   Using Lemma 10.3 with $\theta \equiv \theta^k$, $b\phi \equiv \theta^{k+1}$, we have

$$J(\theta^{k+1}) - J(\theta^k) \leq \mu_k + C \int_0^T \|f(z_t^{\theta^k}, \theta_t^{k+1}) - f(z_t^{\theta^k}, \theta_t^k)\|^2 \, dt$$

$$+ C \int_0^T \|\nabla_z H(z_t^{\theta^k}, p_t^{\theta^k}, \theta_t^{k+1}) - \nabla_z H(z_t^{\theta^k}, p_t^{\theta^k}, \theta_t^k)\|^2 \, dt.$$

From the Hamiltonian maximization step in Algorithm 10.2, we know that

$$H(z_t^{\theta^k}, p_t^{\theta^k}, \theta_t^k) \leq H(z_t^{\theta^k}, p_t^{\theta^k}, \theta_t^{k+1}) + \frac{1}{2}\rho\|f(z_t^{\theta^k}, \theta_t^{k+1}) - f(z_t^{\theta^k}, \theta_t^k)\|^2$$

$$- \frac{1}{2}\rho\|\nabla_z H(z_t^{\theta^k}, p_t^{\theta^k}, \theta_t^{k+1}) - \nabla_z H(z_t^{\theta^k}, p_t^{\theta^k}, \theta_t^k)\|^2.$$

Hence we have

$$J(\boldsymbol{\theta}^{k+1}) - J(\boldsymbol{\theta}^k) \le -\left(1 - \frac{2C}{\rho}\right)\mu_k.$$

Pick $\rho > 2C$; then we indeed have $J(\boldsymbol{\theta}^{k+1}) - J(\boldsymbol{\theta}^k) \le -D\mu_k$ with $D = \left(1 - \frac{2C}{\rho}\right) > 0$. Moreover, we can rearrange and sum the above expression to get

$$\sum_{k=0}^{M} \mu_k \le D^{-1}(J(\boldsymbol{\theta}^0) - J(\boldsymbol{\theta}^{M+1})) \le D^{-1}\left[J(\boldsymbol{\theta}^0) - \inf_{\boldsymbol{\theta} \in L^\infty([0,T],\Theta)} J(\boldsymbol{\theta})\right]$$

and hence $\sum_{k=0}^{\infty} \mu_k < +\infty$, which implies $\mu_k \to 0$. $\qquad\square$

In an actual implementation of Algorithm 10.2, one can solve the forward and backward equations using standard numerical integration methods (e.g. the forward Euler method, as in Li et al., 2017). On the other hand, the Hamiltonian maximization step deserves some discussion. Note that if we replace this step by a gradient ascent step in the Hamiltonian, in essence we recover (at least for the case of $\rho = 0$) classical back-propagation with a gradient descent algorithm. In Li et al. (2017), a different option was proposed where the Hamiltonian maximization is performed using the L-BFGS method; it was shown that the resulting algorithm enjoys certain advantages over the usual back-propagation with gradient descent method, such as faster initial descent and a lesser likelihood of being trapped near flat regions of the loss function.

Another instance for which the MSA occurs useful is when the Hamiltonian maximization step admits a closed-form solution. This is the case for quantized neural networks, where the weight space Θ is finite, e.g. $\Theta = \{+1, -1\}^m$ (a binary network) or $\Theta = \{+1, 0, -1\}^m$ (a ternary network). In this case, one can exploit explicit solutions of the Hamiltonian maximization to design efficient optimization algorithms. The reader is referred to Li and Hao (2018) for details. Novel algorithms based on the maximum principles have also found applications in distributed optimization (Parpas and Muir, 2019) and adversarial training (Zhang et al., 2019).

10.4.4 Discrete PMP and Discrete MSA

So far, we have focused on a continuous-time idealization of the deep learning problem and its theoretical and algorithmic consequences. It is thus a natural question to ask how much of this holds in the discrete setting. Below, we briefly discuss the optimal control viewpoint in the discrete-time setting and some known theoretical results in this direction. For simplicity, we shall stick to the empirical risk minimization setting, but these statements also hold for a general setting with explicit consideration of stochasticity.

In the discrete setting, $T \in \mathbb{Z}_+$ now denotes the number of layers and, in place of the ODE (10.1), we have the feed-forward dynamical system

$$z_{t+1} = f_t(z_t, \theta_t), \qquad t = 0, 1, \ldots, T - 1,$$
$$z_0 = x.$$

$$(10.15)$$

We will now consider the case when the dimensions of $z_t \in \mathbb{R}^{d_t}$ and $\theta_t \in \Theta_t$ depend on and can vary with layers t. Also, we allow the feed-forward function f_t to vary with t. This framework now encompasses most deep neural networks employed in practice. The empirical learning problem then takes the form

$$\min_{\theta} J(\theta) := \Phi(z_T, y) + \sum_{t=0}^{T-1} L_t(z_t, \theta_t)$$

$$(10.16)$$

subject to:

$$z_{t+1} = f_t(z_t, \theta_t), \qquad t = 0, \ldots, T - 1.$$

It turns out that, even in the discrete case, one indeed has a Pontryagin's maximum principle, albeit with some additional caveats. This was first proved in Halkin (1966) and we reproduce a simplified statement below.

Theorem 10.5 (Discrete PMP). *Let f_t and Φ be sufficiently smooth in z. Assume further that for each t and $z \in \mathbb{R}^{d_t}$, the sets $\{f_t(z, \theta): \theta \in \Theta_t\}$ and $\{L_t(z, \theta): \theta \in \Theta_t\}$ are convex. Then there exist co-state processes, $p^* := \{p_t^*: t = 0, \ldots, T\}$, such that the following hold for $t = 0, \ldots, T - 1$:*

$$z_{t+1}^* = f(z_t^*, \theta_t^*), \qquad\qquad z_0 = x, \qquad\qquad (10.17)$$
$$p_t^* = \nabla_z H_t(z_t^*, p_{t+1}^*, \theta_t^*), \qquad p_T^* = -\nabla\Phi(x_T^*, y), \qquad (10.18)$$
$$H_t(z_t^*, p_{t+1}^*, \theta_t^*) \geq H_t(z_t^*, p_{t+1}^*, \theta), \quad \text{for all } \theta \in \Theta_t, \quad t = 0, \ldots, T - 1, \quad (10.19)$$

where the Hamiltonian function is given by

$$H_t(z, p, \theta) := p \cdot f_t(z, \theta) - \frac{1}{S} L_t(z, \theta).$$

$$(10.20)$$

The precise statement of Theorem 10.5 involves explicit smoothness assumptions and additional technicalities (such as the inclusion of an abnormal multiplier). We refer the reader to Li et al. (2017) and the original proof (Halkin, 1966) for a thorough discussion of these issues.

Compared with the continuous-time PMP, the striking additional assumption in Theorem 10.5 is the convexity of the sets $\{f_t(z, \theta): \theta \in \Theta_t\}$ and $\{L_t(z, \theta): \theta \in \Theta_t\}$ for each fixed z. Note that this is in general unrelated to the convexity, in the sense of functions of L_t with respect to either z or θ. For example, the scalar function $f(z, \theta) = \theta^3 \sin(z)$ is evidently non-convex in both arguments, but $\{f(z, \theta): \theta \in \mathbb{R}\}$

is convex for each z. On the other hand $\{\theta z : \theta \in \{-1, 1\}\}$ is non-convex because here we have a non-convex admissible set. The convexity assumptions place some mild restrictions on the types of neural network structures to which this result can apply.

Let us first assume that the admissible sets Θ_t are convex. Then, the assumption with respect to L_t is not restrictive since most regularizers (e.g. ℓ_1, ℓ_2) satisfy it. Let us consider the convexity of $\{f_t(z, \theta) : \theta \in \Theta_t\}$. In classical feed-forward neural networks, there are two types of layers: trainable and non-trainable.

Suppose layer t is non-trainable (e.g. $f(z_t, \theta_t) = \sigma(z_t)$ where σ is a non-linear activation function); then for each z the set $\{f_t(z, \theta) : \theta \in \Theta_t\}$ is a singleton, and hence trivially convex. On the other hand, in trainable layers, f_t is usually affine in θ. This includes fully connected layers, convolution layers and batch normalization layers (Ioffe and Szegedy, 2015). In these cases, as long as the admissible set Θ_t is convex, the convexity assumption is again satisfied. Residual networks also satisfy the convexity constraint if one introduces auxiliary variables (see Li and Hao, 2018, Appendix A.1). When the set Θ_t is not convex then it is not generally true that the PMP constitutes necessary conditions. Nevertheless, even in cases where the PMP does not hold, an error estimate similar to Lemma 10.3 can be derived, on the basis of which efficient training algorithms can be developed (Li and Hao, 2018). Finally, we remark that in the continuous-time case, the convexity condition can be removed due to the "convexifying" effect of integration with respect to time (Halkin, 1966; Warga, 1962). Hence, the convexity condition is purely an artifact of discrete-time dynamical systems.

10.5 Future Work

A very important issue is to analyze the generalization error in deep neural network models. To do so, one has to be careful about choosing the right regularization term, as was suggested in the work of E et al. (2019b). It is also of great interest to formulate similar continuous-in-time, control theory, or game theory models for other networks such as GANs (generative adversarial network) or autoencoders.

References

Vladimir V. Aleksandrov (1968). On the accumulation of perturbations in the linear systems with two coordinates. *Vestnik MGU*, **3**, 67–76.

Michael Athans and Peter L. Falb (2013). *Optimal Control: An Introduction to the Theory and its Applications*. Courier Corporation.

Mokhtar S. Bazaraa, Hanif D. Sherali, and Chitharanjan M. Shetty (2013). *Nonlinear Programming: Theory and Algorithms*. John Wiley & Sons.

Richard Bellman (2013). *Dynamic Programming*. Courier Corporation.

Dimitri P. Bertsekas (1995). *Dynamic Programming and Optimal Control, volume 1*. Athena Scientific.

Dimitri P. Bertsekas (1999). *Nonlinear Programming*. Athena Scientific.

John T. Betts (1988). Survey of numerical methods for trajectory optimization. *Journal of Guidance Control and Dynamics*, **21**(2), 193–207.

Vladimir Grigor'evich Boltyanskii, Revaz Valer'yanovich Gamkrelidze and Lev Semenovich Pontryagin (1960). The theory of optimal processes. I. The maximum principle. *Izv. Akad. Nauk SSSR. Ser. Mat.*, **24**, 3–42.

Arthur Earl Bryson (1975). *Applied Optimal Control: Optimization, Estimation and Control*. CRC Press.

René Carmona and François Delarue (2015). Forward–backward stochastic differential equations and controlled McKean–Vlasov dynamics. *Annals of Probability*, **43**(5), 2647–2700.

Tian Qi Chen, Yulia Rubanova, Jesse Bettencourt, and David K. Duvenaud (2018). Neural ordinary differential equations. In *Advances in Neural Information Processing Systems* **31**, 6572–6583.

Felix L. Chernousko and Alexey A. Lyubushin (1982). Method of successive approximations for solution of optimal control problems. *Optimal Control Applications and Methods*, **3**(2), 101–114.

Jia Deng, Wei Dong, Richard Socher, Li-Jia Li, Kai Li, and Li Fei-Fei (2009). ImageNet: A large-scale hierarchical image database. In: *Proc. Computer Vision and Pattern Recognition*.

Weinan E (2017). A proposal on machine learning via dynamical systems. *Communications in Mathematics and Statistics*, **5**(1), 1–11.

Weinan E, Jiequn Han, and Arnulf Jentzen (2017). Deep learning-based numerical methods for high-dimensional parabolic partial differential equations and backward stochastic differential equations. *Communications in Mathematics and Statistics*, **5**(4), 349–380.

Weinan E, Jiequn Han, and Qianxiao Li (2019a). A mean-field optimal control formulation of deep learning. *Research in the Mathematical Sciences*, **6**(1). 10.

Weinan E, Chao Ma, and Qingcan Wang (2019b). *A priori* estimates for the population risk for residual networks. Submitted.

Eldad Haber and Lars Ruthotto (2017). Stable architectures for deep neural networks. *Inverse Problems*, **34**(1), 014004.

Hubert Halkin (1966). A maximum principle of the Pontryagin type for systems described by nonlinear difference equations. *SIAM Journal on Control*, **4**(1), 90–111.

Jiequn Han, Arnulf Jentzen, and Weinan E (2018a). Solving high-dimensional partial differential equations using deep learning. *Proceedings of the National Academy of Sciences*, **115**(34), 8505–8510.

Jiequn Han, Linfeng Zhang, Roberto Car, and Weinan E (2018b). Deep potential: A general representation of a many-body potential energy surface. *Communications in Computational Physics*, **23** (3), 629–639.

Magnus R. Hestenes. Multiplier and gradient methods (1969). *Journal of Optimization Theory and Applications*, **4**(5), 303–320.

Sergey Ioffe and Christian Szegedy (2015). Batch normalization: accelerating deep network training by reducing internal covariate shift. Pages 448–456 of: *Proc. International Conference on Machine Learning*.

Yann LeCun (1989). A theoretical framework for back-propagation. In: *Proc. 1988 Connectionist Models Summer School*, vol. 1 D. Touretzky, G. Hinton and T. Sejnowski (eds). Morgan Kauffman, pp. 21–28.

Qianxiao Li and Shuji Hao (2018). An optimal control approach to deep learning and applications to discrete-weight neural networks. Pages 2985–2994 of: *Proc. International Conference on Machine Learning*.

Qianxiao Li, Long Chen, Cheng Tai, and Weinan E (2017). Maximum principle based algorithms for deep learning. *Journal of Machine Learning Research*, **18**(1), 5998–6026.

Daniel Liberzon (2012). *Calculus of Variations and Optimal Control Theory: A Concise Introduction*. Princeton University Press.

Dong C. Liu and Jorge Nocedal (1989). On the limited memory BFGS method for large scale optimization. *Mathematical Programming*, **45**(1), 503–528.

Yiping Lu, Aoxiao Zhong, Quanzheng Li, and Bin Dong (2017). Beyond finite layer neural networks: Bridging deep architectures and numerical differential equations. ArXiv 1710.10121.

Panos Parpas and Corey Muir (2019). Predict globally, correct locally: Parallel-in-time optimal control of neural networks. ArXiv 1902.02542.

Lev S. Pontryagin (1987). *Mathematical Theory of Optimal Processes*. CRC Press.

Lars Ruthotto and Eldad Haber (2018). Deep neural networks motivated by partial differential equations. ArXiv 1804.04272.

Anil V. Rao (2009). A survey of numerical methods for optimal control. *Advances in the Astronautical Sciences*, **135**(1), 497–528.

Sanford M. Roberts and Jerome S. Shipman (1972). Two-point boundary value problems: Shooting methods. *SIAM Rev.*, **16**(2), 265–266.

Sho Sonoda and Noboru Murata (2019). Transport analysis of infinitely deep neural network. *Journal of Machine Learning Research*, **20**(1), 31–82.

Jack Warga (1962). Relaxed variational problems. *Journal of Mathematical Analysis and Applications*, **4**(1), 111–128.

Dinghuai Zhang, Tianyuan Zhang, Yiping Lu, Zhanxing Zhu, and Bin Dong (2019). You only propagate once: Accelerating adversarial training via maximal principle. ArXiv 1905.00877.

Linfeng Zhang, Jiequn Han, Han Wang, Roberto Car, and Weinan E (2018a). Deep potential molecular dynamics: A scalable model with the accuracy of quantum mechanics. *Physical Review Letters*, **120**(14), 143001.

Linfeng Zhang, Jiequn Han, Han Wang, Wissam Saidi, Roberto Car, and Weinan
    E (2018b). End-to-end symmetry preserving inter-atomic potential energy
    model for finite and extended systems. In: *Advances in Neural Information
    Processing Systems* **31**, 4441–4451.

11

Bridging Many-Body Quantum Physics and Deep Learning via Tensor Networks

Yoav Levine, Or Sharir, Nadav Cohen and Amnon Shashua

Abstract: Deep network architectures have exhibited an unprecedented ability to encompass the convoluted dependencies which characterize hard learning tasks such as image classification or speech recognition. However, some key questions regarding deep learning architecture design have no adequate theoretical answers. In the seemingly unrelated field of many-body physics, there is a growing need for highly expressive computational schemes that are able to efficiently represent highly entangled many-particle quantum systems. In this chapter, we describe a tensor network (TN) based common language that has been established between the two disciplines, which allows for bidirectional contributions. By showing that many-body wave functions are structurally equivalent to mappings of convolutional and recurrent networks, we can construct their TN descriptions and bring forth quantum entanglement measures as natural quantifiers of dependencies modeled by such networks. Accordingly, we propose a novel entanglement-based deep learning design scheme that sheds light on the success of popular architectural choices made by deep learning practitioners and suggests new practical prescriptions. In the other direction, we identify the fact that an inherent re-use of information in prominent deep learning architectures is a key trait distinguishing them from standard TN-based wave function representations. Therefore, we employ a TN manifestation of information re-use and construct TNs corresponding to deep recurrent networks and overlapping convolutional networks. This allows us to demonstrate theoretically that these architectures are powerful enough to represent highly entangled quantum systems polynomially more efficiently than the previously employed restricted Boltzmann machines. We thus provide theoretical motivation to shift trending neural-network-based wave function representations closer to state-of-the-art deep learning architectures.

11.1 Introduction

Machine learning and many-body physics are distinct scientific disciplines; however, they share a common need for the efficient representation of highly expressive multivariate function classes. In the former, the function class of interest describes the dependencies required for performing a modern machine learning task and in the latter it captures the entanglement of the many-body quantum system under examination.

In the physics domain, a prominent approach for simulating many-body quantum systems makes use of their entanglement properties in order to construct tensor network (TN) architectures that aptly model them. Though this method is successful in modeling one-dimensional (1D) systems through the matrix product state (MPS) TN (Fannes et al., 1992; Perez-García et al., 2007), it still faces difficulties in modeling two-dimensional (2D) systems due to their intractability (Verstraete and Cirac, 2004; Orús, 2014).

In the machine learning domain, deep network architectures have enabled unprecedented results in recent years (Krizhevsky et al., 2012; Simonyan and Zisserman, 2014; Szegedy et al., 2015; He et al., 2016; Sutskever et al., 2011; Graves et al., 2013; Bahdanau et al., 2014; Amodei et al., 2016), owing to their ability to efficiently capture intricate dependencies in complex data sets. However, despite their popularity in science and industry, formal understanding of these architectures is limited. Specifically, the question of why the multivariate function families induced by common deep learning architectures successfully capture the dependencies brought forth by challenging machine learning tasks, is largely open.

The applications of TN in machine learning include optimizations of an MPS to perform learning tasks (Stoudenmire and Schwab, 2016; Han et al., 2017) and unsupervised preprocessing of the data set via tree TNs (Stoudenmire, 2017). Inspired by recent achievements in machine learning, quantum wave function representations based on fully connected neural networks and restricted Boltzmann machines (RBMs), which represent relatively mature deep learning constructs, have recently been suggested (Carleo and Troyer, 2017; Saito, 2017; Deng et al., 2017a; Gao and Duan, 2017; Carleo et al., 2018; Cai and Liu, 2018). Consequently, RBMs have been shown as being able to support high entanglement with a number of parameters that is linear in the number of quantum particles in 2D (Deng et al., 2017b), as opposed to thequadratic dependence required in 2D fully connected networks.

In this chapter, we describe a TN-based approach for modeling the deep learning architectures that are at the forefront of recent empirical successes. Thus, we establish a bridge that facilitates an interdisciplinary transfer of results and tools, and allows us to address the abovementioned needs of both fields. First, we import concepts from quantum physics that enable us to obtain new results in the rapidly

evolving field of deep learning theory. In the opposite direction, we obtain TN man-
ifestations of provably powerful deep learning principles, which help us to establish
the benefits of employing such principles for the representation of highly entangled
quantum systems.

We begin in §11.2 by providing a brief introduction to the computational challenges which many-body quantum physicists face. We present the relevant concepts
and tools, namely, many-body wave-functions, quantum entanglement, and tensor networks. Next, in §11.3 we identify an equivalence between the tensor-based
form of a many-body wave function and the function realized by convolutional
arithmetic circuits (ConvACs) (Cohen et al., 2016b; Cohen and Shashua, 2016,
2017) and single-layered recurrent arithmetic circuits (RACs) (Levine et al., 2017;
Khrulkov et al., 2018). These are representatives of two prominent deep learning architecture classes: convolutional networks, commonly operating over spatial inputs
and used for tasks such as image classification; and recurrent networks, commonly
operating over temporal inputs and used for tasks such as speech recognition.[1]
Given the above equivalence, we construct a tree TN representation of the ConvAC
architecture and an MPS representation of the RAC architecture (Figure 11.4), and
show how entanglement measures (Plenio and Virmani, 2007) quantify, in an natural way, the ability of the multivariate function realized by such networks to model
dependencies.

Consequently, we are able to demonstrate in §11.4 how the common practice,
in many-body physics, of entanglement-based TN architecture selection can be
readily converted into a methodological approach for matching the architecture of
a deep network to a given task. Specifically, our construction allows the translation
of derived bounds on the maximal entanglement represented by an arbitrary TN
(Cui et al., 2016) into machine learning terms. We thus obtain novel quantum-
physics inspired practical guidelines for the task-tailored architecture design of
deep convolutional networks.

The above analysis highlights a key principle separating powerful deep learning
architectures from common TN-based representations, namely, the re-use of information. Specifically, in the ConvAC architecture, which can be shown to be described by a tree TN, the convolutional windows have 1×1 receptive fields and therefore do not spatially overlap when slid across the feature maps. In contrast, state-of-
the-art convolutional networks involve larger convolution kernels (e.g. 3×3), which
therefore overlap during calculation of the convolution (Krizhevsky et al., 2012;
Simonyan and Zisserman, 2014). Such overlapping architectures inherently involve
the re-use of information, since the same activation is used for the calculation of
several adjacent activations in the subsequent layer. Similarly, unlike the shallow

---

[1] See a similar analysis of the more recent self-attention architecture class, which has advanced the field of
natural language processing, in Levine et al. (2020).

recurrent network, which can be shown to be described by an MPS TN, state-of-the-art deep recurrent networks inherently involve information re-use (Graves et al., 2013).

Relying on the above observation, we employ in §11.5 a duplication method for representing information re-use within the standard TN framework, reminiscent of that introduced in the context of categorical TN states (Biamonte et al., 2011). Accordingly, we are able to present new TN constructs that correspond to deep recurrent and overlapping convolutional architectures (Figures 11.8 and 11.9). We thus obtain the tools to examine the entanglement scaling of powerful deep networks. Specifically, we prove that deep recurrent networks support entanglement which corresponds to critical quantum systems in 1D, and that overlapping convolutional networks can support arbitrary entanglement scaling in 1D and in 2D (see §11.2.2 for the definition of entanglement scaling).

Our analysis shows that the number of parameters required for supporting highly entangled systems scales as the square root of the number of particles in 2D overlapping convolutional networks. Therefore, we can demonstrate that these networks not only allow tractable access to 2D quantum systems of sizes unattainable by current TN-based approaches but also are polynomially more efficient in representing highly entangled 2D systems in comparison with previously suggested neural-network wave function representations. We thus establish the formal benefits of employing state-of-the-art deep learning principles for many-body wave function representation (which have recently inspired corresponding empirical achievements; see Sharir et al., 2020), and we suggest a practical framework for implementing and investigating these architectures within the standard TN platform.

11.2 Preliminaries – Many-Body Quantum Physics

In this section we succinctly outline relevant efforts in the numerical investigation of many-body quantum phenomena that have been carried out in the condensed matter physics community over the past few decades. This field addresses physical systems composed of many interacting quantum particles, as is the case in nearly all materials in nature (a few grams of any material contain of the order of 10^{23} atoms). The quantum properties governing the interactions between the particles give rise to to highly non-intuitive phenomena, such as magnetism, superconductivity, and more, that are observed on a macroscopic scale. The analytical and computational methods that have been developed to solve problems in atomic and nuclear physics do not scale well for a large number of particles, and are unable to account for the observed many-body phenomena or to predict emergent properties. Therefore, a numerical toolbox has been developed with the intention of harnessing modern computational power for probing these, until recently, unattainable natural properties.

Our analysis, presented subsequently in §§11.3–11.4, draws inspiration from concepts and tools developed in the field of many-body quantum physics, which is considerably more mature than the field of deep learning theory. With that said, the established connections also contribute in the other direction: in §11.5 we rely on recent theoretical advances in deep learning theory and provide novel contributions to the effort of investigating interacting many-body quantum systems.

A secondary goal of this section is to provide a ramp-up regarding basic concepts in tensor analysis and many-body quantum physics that are necessary for following our analyses. We begin in §11.2.1 by describing the concept of many-body quantum wavevfunctions, and then move on to present the notion of quantum entanglement and its measures in §11.2.2. Finally, in §11.2.3 we give a short introduction to TNs – a numerical tool employed for modeling many-body quantum systems – and discuss its strengths and limitations.

11.2.1 The Many-Body Quantum Wave Function

We provide below a short introduction to the notation used by physicists when describing quantum mechanical properties of a many-body system. We follow relevant derivations in Preskill (1998) and Hall (2013), referring the interested reader to these sources for a more comprehensive mathematical introduction to quantum mechanics.

A complete description of a quantum system is given in quantum mechanics by its *wave function*, alternatively referred to as its *state*. We limit our discussion to states which reside in finite-dimensional Hilbert spaces, as these are at the heart of the analogies that we draw with deep learning architectures. The quantum state is simply a vector in such a space. Besides being of interest to us, these spaces have also been extensively investigated in the physics community. For example, the spin component of a spinful particle's wave function resides in a finite-dimensional Hilbert space.

Physicists employ the 'ket' notation, in which a vector ψ is denoted by $|\psi\rangle \in \mathcal{H}$. The Hilbert space $\mathcal{H}$ has an inner product denoted by $\langle\phi|\psi\rangle$, which maps a pair of vectors in $\mathcal{H}$ to a scalar. A 'bra' notation, $\langle\phi|$, is used for the 'dual vector', which formally is a linear mapping between vectors to scalars, defined as $|\psi\rangle \mapsto \langle\phi|\psi\rangle$. We can intuitively think of a 'ket' as a column vector and 'bra' as a row vector.

One can represent a general single-particle state $|\psi\rangle \in \mathcal{H}_1$, where $\dim(\mathcal{H}_1) = M$, as a linear combination of some orthonormal basis vectors:

$$|\psi\rangle = \sum_{d=1}^{M} v_d |\hat{\psi}_d\rangle, \qquad (11.1)$$

where $\mathbf{v} \in \mathbb{C}^M$ is the vector of coefficients compatible with the basis $\{|\hat{\psi}_d\rangle\}_{d=1}^M$ of $\mathcal{H}_1$, each entry of which can be calculated by the projection: $v_d = \langle \hat{\psi}_d | \psi \rangle$.

We extend the discussion to the many-body case of N particles, each corresponding to a local Hilbert space $\mathcal{H}_j$ for $j \in [N]$ such that, for all j, $\dim(\mathcal{H}_j) = M$. Denoting an orthonormal basis of the local Hilbert space by $\{|\hat{\psi}_d\rangle\}_{d=1}^M$, the many-body wave function $|\psi\rangle \in \mathcal{H} = \otimes_{j=1}^N \mathcal{H}_j$ can be written as

$$|\psi\rangle = \sum_{d_1,\ldots,d_N=1}^M \mathcal{A}_{d_1,\ldots,d_N} |\hat{\psi}_{d_1,\ldots,d_N}\rangle, \tag{11.2}$$

where $|\hat{\psi}_{d_1,\ldots,d_N}\rangle := |\hat{\psi}_{d_1}\rangle \otimes \cdots \otimes |\hat{\psi}_{d_N}\rangle$ is a basis vector of the M^N-dimensional many-body Hilbert space $\mathcal{H}$, and the *coefficient tensor* $\mathcal{A}$ is the generalization of the above coefficients vector to the many-body case.

A *tensor* may be thought of as a multi-dimensional array. The *order* of a tensor is defined to be the number of indexing entries in the array, which are referred to as *modes*. The *dimension* of a tensor in a particular mode is defined as the number of values that may be taken by the index in that mode. The coefficient tensor $\mathcal{A}$ is a tensor of order N and dimension M in each mode $j \in [N] := \{1,\ldots,N\}$; its entries are denoted $\mathcal{A}_{d_1,\ldots,d_N}$, where the index in each mode takes values between 1 and the dimension, $d_j \in [M]$.

As per its definition, the number of entries in the coefficient tensor is exponential in the number of quantum particles. This is in fact the reason why many-body quantum systems cannot be handled by the analytical and computational tools developed for other fields in quantum physics that involve only a small number of particles. However, even when attempting to extract relevant information by an arbitrarily powerful computer program, solutions for systems of over 100 particles would be unattainable as they require more coefficients than the number of atoms in the universe. In what appears to be an unsurpassable barrier, interesting quantum phenomena can be observed only for systems of sizes much larger than 100. In the following subsection, we obtain tools for discussing 'lucky' natural traits that, despite the above, allow physicists to escape this exponential curse of dimensionality and achieve meaningful insights regarding many-body quantum systems.

11.2.2 Quantum Entanglement Measures

We present below the concept of *quantum entanglement* that is widely used by physicists as a quantifier of dependencies in a many-body quantum system. One of the fathers of quantum mechanics, Erwin Schrödinger, defined entanglement as "the characteristic trait of quantum mechanics, the one that enforces its entire departure from classical lines of thought" (Schrödinger, 1935). In the last few decades, entanglement has played a key role in understanding emergent quantum many-body phases of matter. Following the formal definition, which directly relates to the many-body wave function above discussed, we will elaborate on the entanglement properties that have been examined by many-body physicists.

Consider a partition of a system of N particles, labeled by integers $[N] := \{1, \dots, N\}$, which splits it into two disjoint subsystems $A \cup B = [N]$. Let $\mathcal{H}^A$ and $\mathcal{H}^B$ be the Hilbert spaces in which the many body wave functions of the particles in subsystems A and B reside, respectively, with $\mathcal{H} \cong \mathcal{H}^A \otimes \mathcal{H}^B$. The many-body wave function in (11.2) can be now written as:

$$|\psi\rangle = \sum_{\alpha=1}^{\dim(\mathcal{H}^A)} \sum_{\beta=1}^{\dim(\mathcal{H}^B)} (\llbracket \mathcal{A} \rrbracket_{A,B})_{\alpha,\beta} |\psi_\alpha^A\rangle \otimes |\psi_\beta^B\rangle, \tag{11.3}$$

where $\{|\psi_\alpha^A\rangle\}_{\alpha=1}^{\dim(\mathcal{H}^A)}$ and $\{|\psi_\beta^B\rangle\}_{\beta=1}^{\dim(\mathcal{H}^B)}$ are bases for $\mathcal{H}^A$ and $\mathcal{H}^B$, respectively,[2] and $\llbracket \mathcal{A} \rrbracket_{A,B}$ is the *matricization of $\mathcal{A}$ with respect to the partition (A, B)*, which is essentially the rearrangement of the tensor elements as a matrix whose rows correspond to A and columns to B.[3] Let us denote the maximal rank of $\llbracket \mathcal{A} \rrbracket_{A,B}$ by $r := \min(\dim(\mathcal{H}^A), \dim(\mathcal{H}^B))$. A singular value decomposition of $\llbracket \mathcal{A} \rrbracket_{A,B}$ results in the following form (also referred to as the Schmidt decomposition):

$$|\psi\rangle = \sum_{\alpha=1}^{r} \lambda_\alpha |\phi_\alpha^A\rangle \otimes |\phi_\alpha^B\rangle, \tag{11.4}$$

where $\lambda_1 \geq \cdots \geq \lambda_r$ are the singular values of $\llbracket \mathcal{A} \rrbracket_{A,B}$, and $\{|\phi_\alpha^A\rangle\}_{\alpha=1}^r$, $\{|\phi_\alpha^B\rangle\}_{\alpha=1}^r$ are r vectors in new bases for $\mathcal{H}^A$ and $\mathcal{H}^B$, respectively, obtained by the decomposition.

Equation (11.4) represents the N-particle wave function in terms of a sum of tensor products between its two disjoint parts. Each summand in (11.4) is a separable state with respect to the partition (A, B), which represents the fact that there is no quantum dependency between these two subsystems. Essentially, the *measure of entanglement with respect to the partition (A, B)* is a quantity that represents the difference between the state in question and a state that is separable with respect to this partition.

There are several different quantum entanglement measures. The entanglement entropy (Vedral and Plenio, 1998) is one such measure; it is defined as:[4] $S_{A,B} = -\sum_\alpha |\lambda_\alpha|^2 \ln |\lambda_\alpha|^2$. The minimal entanglement entropy, $S = 0$, is achieved when

---

[2] It is possible to write $|\psi_\alpha^A\rangle = |\psi_{d_{a_1}}\rangle \otimes \cdots \otimes |\psi_{d_{a_{|A|}}}\rangle$ and $|\psi_\beta^B\rangle = |\psi_{d_{b_1}}\rangle \otimes \cdots \otimes |\psi_{d_{b_{|B|}}}\rangle$ with the matricization mapping from $A := \{a_1, \dots, a_{|A|}\}$ to α and from $B := \{b_1, \dots, b_{|B|}\}$ to β.

[3] Specifically, $\llbracket \mathcal{A} \rrbracket_{A,B}$, is the $M^{|A|} \times M^{|B|}$ matrix containing the entries of $\mathcal{A}$ such that $\mathcal{A}_{d_1,\dots,d_N}$ is placed in the row whose index is $1 + \sum_{t=1}^{|A|} (d_{i_t} - 1) M^{|A|-t}$ and the column whose index is $1 + \sum_{t=1}^{|B|} (d_{j_t} - 1) M^{|B|-t}$.

[4] $|\psi\rangle$ is conventionally chosen to be normalized so that the singular values satisfy $\sum_\alpha |\lambda_\alpha|^2 = 1$. This can be relaxed and the entropy may be defined on the normalized singular values.

the rank of $[\![\mathcal{A}]\!]_{A,B}$ is 1. When $[\![\mathcal{A}]\!]_{A,B}$ is fully ranked, the entanglement entropy obtains its maximal value of $\ln(r)$ (upon normalization of the singular values).

Another measure of entanglement is the geometric measure, defined as the L^2 distance of $|\psi\rangle$ from the set of separable states, $\min_{|\psi^{\mathrm{sp}(A,B)}\rangle} |\langle\psi^{\mathrm{sp}(A,B)}|\psi\rangle|^2$; it can be shown (e.g., Cohen and Shashua, 2017) to be

$$D = \sqrt{1 - \frac{|\lambda_1|^2}{\sum_{\alpha=1}^{r} |\lambda_\alpha|^2}}.$$

A final measure of entanglement we mention is the Schmidt number, which is simply the rank of $[\![\mathcal{A}]\!]_{A,B}$. i.e., the number of its non-zero singular values. All these measures are minimal for states which are separable with respect to the partition (A, B) and increase when the quantum dependency between sub-systems A and B is more complicated.

To connect the abstract notion of entanglement with condensed matter problems currently being investigated, we describe a partition commonly employed by many-body physicists to examine the entanglement properties of an N-particle system in d dimensions. For this partition, A is taken to be a small contiguous subsystem of size $|A| \ll N/2$, and B is taken to be its complement (see Figure 11.1a). In this setting, one asks how the entanglement measures scale as the size of subsystem A is gradually varied.

We denote by A_{lin} the typical size of subsystem A along each dimension (also referred to as its linear dimension). If the entanglement entropy with respect to the partition A, B scales as subsystem A's d-dimensional volume, i.e., $S_{A,B} \propto (A_{\mathrm{lin}})^d$, then the entire N-particle system is said to exhibit *volume-law entanglement scaling*. This is referred to as a highly entangled scenario, since it implies that each particle in subsystem A exhibits a quantum dependency on particles in subsystem B (see Figure 11.1b). If, in contrast, the entanglement entropy scales as subsystem A's d-dimensional area, i.e., $S_{A,B} \propto (A_{\mathrm{lin}})^{d-1}$, then the N-particle system is said to exhibit *area-law entanglement scaling*. In this scenario, qualitatively, the entanglement is short range and therefore only particles at the boundary between subsystems A and B are entangled (see Figure 11.1c).

If one were to randomize a many-body wave function (i.e., choose a random coefficients tensor $\mathcal{A}$), a state obeying volume-law entanglement scaling will be obtained with probability 1. Stated differently, besides a set of states of measure 0 within the many-body Hilbert space, all states exhibit volume-law entanglement scaling. Luckily – or owing to some yet-to-be explained fundamental low-dimensional quality of nature – some actual many-body systems of interest are members of this negligible set and follow sub-volume law entanglement scaling. In the following subsection we present a leading numerical approach for simulating such systems.

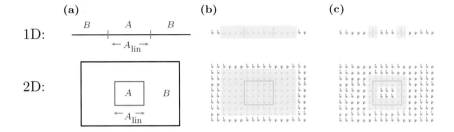

Figure 11.1 (a) A typical partition considered in entanglement scaling – A is a small contiguous subsystem of linear dimension A_{lin} and B is its complement. (b) Volume-law entanglement scaling implies that all quantum particles in subsystem A (again defined by the square outline) are entangled with those of B (the red area marks the interacting particles). (c) Area-law entanglement scaling implies that only particles in the boundary between the subsystems are entangled.

11.2.3 Tensor Networks

Directly storing the entries of a general order-N tensor, though very efficient in lookup time (all the entries are stored 'waiting' to be called upon), is very costly in storage, being exponential in N, which, as discussed above, is not feasible. A tradeoff can be employed in which only a polynomial amount of parameters is kept while the lookup time increases. Namely, some calculation has to be performed in order to obtain the entries of $\mathcal{A}_{d_1,...,d_N}$.[5] The TN tool is a graphical representation of such a calculation; it amounts to a compact representation of a high-order tensor in terms of inner products of lower-order tensors. Its graphical description allows physicists to construct TN architectures which are straightforwardly compliant with the entanglement characterizing the state to be represented. We now provide a brief introduction to TNs, followed by some remarks on the expressive abilities and shortcomings of common TNs.

Introduction to Tensor Networks

A TN is essentially a weighted graph, where each node corresponds to a low-order tensor, whose order is equal to the degree of the node in the graph. Accordingly, the edges emanating out of a node, also referred to as its legs, represent the different modes of the corresponding low-order tensor. The weight of each edge in the graph, also referred to as its bond dimension, is equal to the dimension of the appropriate tensor mode. In accordance with the relation between the mode, dimension, and index of a tensor presented in §11.2.1, each edge in a TN is represented by an index that runs between 1 and its bond dimension. Figure 11.2a shows three examples: (1) a vector, which is a tensor of order 1, is represented by a node with one leg; (2)

---

[5] It is noteworthy that, for a given tensor, there is no guarantee that the number of parameters can be actually reduced. This is dependent on its rank and on how well the decomposition fits the tensor's dependencies.

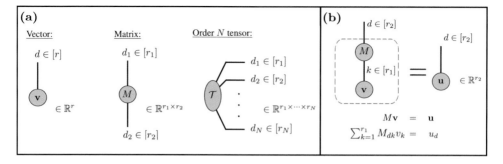

Figure 11.2   A quick introduction to tensor Nnetworks (TNs). (a) Tensors in the TN are represented by nodes. The degree of the node corresponds to the order of the tensor represented by it. (b) A matrix multiplying a vector in TN notation. The contracted index k, which connects two nodes, is summed over, which is not the case for the open index d. The number of open indices equals the order of the tensor represented by the entire network. All the indices receive values that range between 1 and their bond dimension. The contraction is indicated by the dashed line.

a matrix, which is a tensor of order 2, is represented by a node with two legs; (3) accordingly, a tensor of order N is represented in the TN as a node with N legs.

We move on to present the connectivity properties of a TN. Edges which connect two nodes in the TN represent an operation between the two corresponding tensors. An index which represents such an edge is called a contracted index, and the operation of contracting that index is in fact a summation over all the values it can take. An index representing an edge with one loose end is called an open index. The tensor represented by the entire TN, whose order is equal to the number of open indices, can be calculated by summing over all the contracted indices in the network.

An example of the contraction of a simple TN is depicted in Figure 11.2b. There, a TN corresponding to the operation of multiplying a vector $\mathbf{v} \in \mathbb{R}^{r_1}$ by a matrix $M \in \mathbb{R}^{r_2 \times r_1}$ is obtained by summing over the only contracted index, k. As there is only one open index, d, the result of contracting the network is an order-1 tensor (a vector), $\mathbf{u} \in \mathbb{R}^{r_2}$, which satisfies $\mathbf{u} = M\mathbf{v}$. Though below we use the contraction of indices in more elaborate TNs, this operation can be essentially viewed as a generalization of matrix multiplication.

Entanglement in Common Tensor Networks

A quantitative connection exists between a TN representing a quantum state and that state's entanglement scaling (Cui et al., 2016). Essentially, for fixed bond dimensions (that are independent of subsystem A's size), the weight of the minimal cut in the TN weighted graph which separates subsystems A and B is an upper bound on the entanglement scaling of any state representable by this TN. Tensor networks in current use include the matrix product state (MPS), tree TN, and multiscale

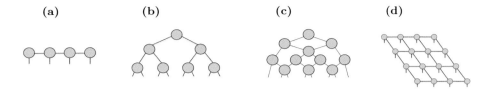

Figure 11.3 Common TNs. In 1D: (a) MPS; (b) tree; (c) MERA. In 2D: (d) PEPS.

entanglement renormalization ansatz (MERA) in 1D; and the projected entangled pair state (PEPS) in 2D (see Figure 11.3). In these TNs, the decomposition of a high-order tensor into a set of sparsely interconnected lower-order tensors, allows the representation of an order-N tensor by a number of parameters that is linear in N. Therefore, systems containing thousands of interacting quantum particles can be simulated and many-body quantum phenomena can be investigated. As can be easily be seen by applying the above minimal-cut considerations, MPS and PEPS TNs are able to efficiently represent area-law entanglement scaling in 1D and 2D, respectively. The MERA TN is more powerful, as it is able to efficiently represent a logarithmic dependence on subsystem A's volume, which in 1D is referred to as a *logarithmic correction to the area-law entanglement scaling.*

Given the bounds on their entanglement scaling, the above TNs are far from being powerful enough to represent most states in the Hilbert space, which obey volume-law scaling. In fact, in order to represent such highly entangled states, one would need to employ TNs with exponential bond dimensions, rendering them impractical. Despite this, the unlikely existence of natural many-body systems which exhibit low entanglement has rendered the tool of TNs very fruitful in the past decade. Matrix product state TNs are employed for investigating 1D systems deep within a gapped quantum phase, such as Ising spin-chains in their ferromagnetic phase (a proxy for magnetism), as these exhibit area-law entanglement scaling (Hastings, 2007). In contrast, MERA TNs are used in order to investigate phase transition properties, such as on the critical point of Ising spin-chains between the ferromagnetic and normal phases, since at this point the system's entanglement scaling has a logarithmic correction. In 2D the situation is more difficult, as PEPS TNs are restricted to area-law entanglement scaling while at the same time they suffer from intractability, which gravely harms their performance.

Despite the relative success of TNs in addressing many-body systems (mainly in 1D), researchers are seeking practical means to go beyond sub-volume-law limitations and to have numerical access to highly entangled systems in 1D, 2D, and even 3D. Restricted Boltzmann machine (RBM) based wave function representations have recently been shown to demonstrate such abilities (Deng et al., 2017b); however the number of parameters they require is incompatible with current optimization approaches. In contrast, our analysis below (§11.5) shows that deep convolutional networks have the potential to decrease significantly the number of parameters required for modeling highly entangled systems, connecting state-of-the-art methods in deep learning with the difficult task of probing quantum many-body phenomena.

11.3 Quantum Wave Functions and Deep Learning Architectures

In the previous section we introduced the relevant tools and described some of the remaining challenges in modern many-body quantum physics research. In the following, we tie these to the emerging field of deep learning theory, in §§11.3–11.4 harnessing the tools that have been developed, and in §11.5 addressing contemporary needs. The presented analyses are further detailed in Levine et al. (2017, 2018, 2019).

We begin by showing the structural equivalence between a many-body wave function and the function which a deep learning architecture implements over its inputs. The convolutional and recurrent networks described below have been analyzed to date via tensor decompositions (Kolda and Bader, 2009; Hackbusch, 2012), which are compact high-order tensor representations based on linear combinations of *outer products* between low-order tensors. The presented equivalence to wave functions, suggests the slightly different algebraic approach manifested by TNs (see §11.2.3); ths approach uses a compact representation of a high-order tensor through contractions (or *inner products*) among lower-order tensors. Accordingly, we provide TN constructions of the deep learning architectures that we examine.

11.3.1 Convolutional and Recurrent Networks as Wave Functions

We consider a convolutional network referred to as a convolutional arithmetic circuit (ConvAC) (Cohen et al., 2016b; Cohen and Shashua, 2016, 2017). This deep convolutional network operates similarly to the ConvNets that have typically been employed in practice (Krizhevsky et al., 2012; Simonyan and Zisserman, 2014), only with linear activations and product pooling instead of the more common nonlinear activations and max out pooling. In a ConvAC, depicted in Figure 11.4a, each layer consists of a linear convolution operation followed by a spatial decimation (pooling) operation, which is carried out by multiplying neighboring activations. Proof methodologies related to ConvACs have been extended to common ConvNets (Cohen and Shashua, 2016), and from an empirical perspective, ConvACs work well in many practical settings (Sharir et al., 2016; Cohen et al., 2016a).

Analogously, we examine a class of recurrent networks referred to as recurrent arithmetic circuits (RACs) (Levine et al., 2017; Khrulkov et al., 2018). These

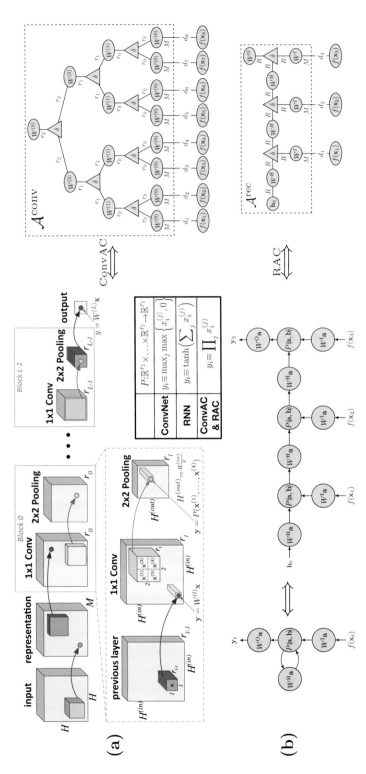

Figure 11.4 (a) The ConvAC (Cohen et al., 2016b), which has convolution kernels of size 1×1, linear activations, and product pooling operations (P is an element-wise multiplication operation), is equivalent to a tree TN (presented for the case of $N = 8$ in its 1D form for clarity). The triangular δ-tensors impose the same-channel pooling trait as the ConvAC. The matrices in the tree TN host the ConvAC's convolutional weights, and the bond dimensions at each tree level $i \in [L]$ are equal to the number of channels in the corresponding layer of the ConvAC, also referred to as its width, denoted r_i. This fact allows us to translate a min-cut result on the TN into practical conclusions regarding pooling geometry and layer widths in convolutional networks. (b) The shallow RAC (Levine et al., 2017), which merges the hidden state of the previous time step with new incoming data via the multiplicative integration operation, is equivalent to an MPS TN (presented for the case of $N = 3$). The matrices W^I, W^H, and W^O, are the RAC's input, hidden, and output weight matrices, respectively. The δ-tensors correspond to the multiplicative integration property of RACs. In (11.5), we write down the output of the RAC after N time steps.

networks employ linear activations but otherwise share the architectural features of standard recurrent networks, where information from previous time-steps is mixed with current incoming data via a multiplicative integration operation (Wu et al., 2016; Sutskever et al., 2011) (see Figure 11.4b). It has been experimentally demonstrated that the conclusions reached by analyses of the above arithmetic circuits extend to commonly used networks (Cohen and Shashua, 2017; Levine et al., 2018; Sharir and Shashua, 2018; Khrulkov et al., 2018).

In the convolutional case, we consider tasks in which the network is given an N-pixel input image, $X = (\mathbf{x}_1^{[0]}, \ldots, \mathbf{x}_N^{[0]})$ (e.g., image classification). In the recurrent case, we focus on tasks in which the network is given a sequential input $\{\mathbf{x}_t^{[0]}\}_{t=1}^N$ (e.g. speech recognition). The output of a ConvAC/single-layered RAC was shown to obey:

$$y(\mathbf{x}_1^{[0]}, \ldots, \mathbf{x}_N^{[0]}) = \sum_{d_1, \ldots, d_N = 1}^{M} \mathcal{A}_{d_1, \ldots, d_N}^{\text{conv/rec}} \prod_{j=1}^{N} f_{d_j}(\mathbf{x}_j^{[0]}), \tag{11.5}$$

where $\{f_d\}_{d=1}^{M}$ are linearly independent representation functions, which form an initial mapping of each input $\mathbf{x}_j^{[0]}$ to a vector $(f_1(\mathbf{x}_j^{[0]}), \ldots, f_M(\mathbf{x}_j^{[0]}))^{\mathsf{T}} \in \mathbb{R}^M$. The tensors $\mathcal{A}^{\text{conv}}$ and $\mathcal{A}^{\text{rec}}$ that define the computation of the ConvAC and RAC, have been analyzed to date via the hierarchical tucker (Hackbusch and Kühn, 2009) and tensor train (Oseledets, 2011) decompositions, respectively. Their entries are polynomials in the appropriate network's convolutional weights (Cohen et al., 2016b) or recurrent weights (Levine et al., 2017; Khrulkov et al., 2018), and their N indices respectively correspond to the N spatial or temporal inputs.

Considering N-particle quantum states with a local Hilbert space $\mathcal{H}_j$ of dimension M for $j \in [N]$, (11.5) is equivalent to the inner product,

$$y(\mathbf{x}_1^{[0]}, \ldots, \mathbf{x}_N^{[0]}) = \langle \psi^{\text{product}}(\mathbf{x}_1^{[0]}, \ldots, \mathbf{x}_N^{[0]}) | \psi^{\text{conv/rec}} \rangle, \tag{11.6}$$

with the ket state corresponding to the convolutional/recurrent network's operation (see §11.2.1 for a defintion of the many-body quantum wave function),

$$| \psi^{\text{conv/rec}} \rangle = \sum_{d_1, \ldots, d_N = 1}^{M} \mathcal{A}_{d_1, \ldots, d_N}^{\text{conv/rec}} | \hat{\psi}_{d_1, \ldots, d_N} \rangle, \tag{11.7}$$

and the product state (which exhibits no entanglement with respect to any partition) corresponding to the inputs,

$$| \psi^{\text{product}}(\mathbf{x}_1^{[0]}, \ldots, \mathbf{x}_N^{[0]}) \rangle = \sum_{d_1, \ldots, d_N = 1}^{M} \prod_{j=1}^{N} f_{d_j}(\mathbf{x}_j^{[0]}) | \hat{\psi}_{d_1, \ldots, d_N} \rangle, \tag{11.8}$$

where $| \hat{\psi}_{d_1, \ldots, d_N} \rangle$ is some orthonormal basis of the many-body Hilbert space $\mathcal{H} =$

$\otimes_{j=1}^N \mathcal{H}_j$. In this structural equivalence, the N inputs to the deep learning architecture (e.g., pixels in an input image or syllables in an input sentence) are analogous to the N particles. Since the unentangled product state[6] $|\psi^{\text{product}}(\mathbf{x}_1^{[0]}, \ldots, \mathbf{x}_N^{[0]})\rangle$ can be associated with some local preprocessing of the inputs, all the information regarding input dependencies that the network is able to model is effectively encapsulated in $\mathcal{A}^{\text{conv/rec}}$, which by definition also holds the entanglement structure of the state $|\psi^{\text{conv/rec}}\rangle$ (see §11.2.2).

11.3.2 Tensor Network Representations of Convolutional and Recurrent Networks

In order to investigate the properties of the convolutional or recurrent weights tensors, and in light of their above connection with quantum wave functions, we examine their form in TN language (see §11.2.3 for an introduction to TNs). In Figure 11.4a, we present the TN corresponding to $\mathcal{A}^{\text{conv}}$. The depth of this tree TN is equal to the depth of the convolutional network, L, and the circular 2-legged tensors represent matrices holding the convolutional weights of each layer $i \in [L]$, denoted $W^{(i)}$. Accordingly, the bond dimension of the TN edges comprising each tree level $i \in [L]$ is equal to the number of channels in the corresponding layer of the convolutional network, r_i, referred to as the layer's width. The 3-legged triangles in the tree TN represent δ_{jkl} tensors (equal to 1 if $j = k = l$ and 0 otherwise), which correspond to the prevalent 'same-channel pooling' decimation procedure.

In Figure 11.4b we present the TN corresponding to $\mathcal{A}^{\text{rec}}$. In this MPS-shaped TN, the circular 2-legged tensors represent matrices holding the input, hidden, and output weights, respectively denoted W^{I}, W^{H}, and W^{O}. The δ-tensors correspond to the multiplicative integration trait of the RAC.

11.4 Deep Learning Architecture Design via Entanglement Measures

The structural connection between many-body wave functions and functions realized by convolutional and recurrent networks, (11.5) and (11.6) above, creates an opportunity to employ well-established tools and insights from many-body physics for the design of these deep learning architectures. We begin this section by showing that quantum entanglement measures extend the means previously used for quantifying dependencies modeled by deep learning architectures. Then, inspired by common condensed matter physics practice, we rely on the TN descriptions of the above architectures and propose a novel methodology for principled deep network design.

---

[6] The underlying tensor of this state, given entry-wise by $\mathcal{A}_{d_1,\ldots,d_N}^{\text{product}} := \prod_{j=1}^N f_{d_j}(\mathbf{x}_j^{[0]})$, is of rank 1. Therefore, any entanglement measure defined on it (see §11.2.2) would be minimal.

11.4.1 Dependencies via Entanglement Measures

In Cohen and Shashua (2017), the algebraic notion of the separation rank is used as a tool for measuring dependencies modeled between two disjoint parts of a deep convolutional network's input. Let (A, B) be a partition of $[N]$. The separation rank of $y(\mathbf{x}_1^{[0]}, \ldots, \mathbf{x}_N^{[0]})$ with respect to (A, B) is defined as the minimal number of multiplicatively separable (with respect to (A, B)) summands that together give y. For example, if y is separable with respect to (A, B) then its separation rank is 1 and it models there being no dependency between the inputs of A and those of B.[7] The higher the separation rank, the stronger the dependency modeled between sides of the partition (Beylkin and Mohlenkamp, 2002). Remarkably, due to the equivalence in (11.6), the separation rank of the function realized by a ConvAC or a single-layered RAC, (11.5), with respect to a partition (A, B) is equal to the Schmidt entanglement measure of $|\psi^{\text{conv/rec}}\rangle$ with respect to (A, B).[8] As per their definitions (see §11.2.2), the logarithm of the Schmidt entanglement measure upper-bounds the state's entanglement entropy with respect to (A, B).

The analysis of separation ranks, now extended to entanglement measures, brings forth a principle for designing a deep learning architecture intended to perform a task specified by certain dependencies – the network should be designed such that these dependencies can be modeled, i.e., partitions that split dependent regions should have a high entanglement entropy. This connection places the analysis of dependencies as a key ingredient in the proper harnessing of the inductive bias when constructing a deep network architecture. For example, in a natural image, pixels which are closer to each other are more correlated than far away pixels. Therefore, the relevant partition to favor when the inputs are natural images is the *interleaved partition*, presented in Figure 11.5a, which splits the image in a checkerboard manner such that A is composed of the pixels located in blue positions and B is composed of the pixels located in yellow positions. This partition will split many pixels which are correlated to one another. Intuitively, this dependency manifests itself in the following manner: given an image composed only of the pixels in the blue positions, one would have a good idea of how to complete the missing parts. Thus, for natural images, constructing the network so that it supports exponentially high entanglement measures for the interleaved partition is preferable.

Similarly, if the input is composed of symmetric images, such as human face images, one expects pixels positioned symmetrically around the middle to be highly correlated. Accordingly, constructing the network such that it supports exponentially high entanglement measures for the *left–right partition*, shown in Figure 11.5b,

---

[7]   In a statistical setting, where $f(\cdot)$ is a probability density function, separability with respect to (A, B) corresponds to statistical independence between the inputs from A and B.

[8]   The equivalence of the Schmidt entanglement measure and the separation rank follows from the linear independence of the representation functions.

(a) **(b)**

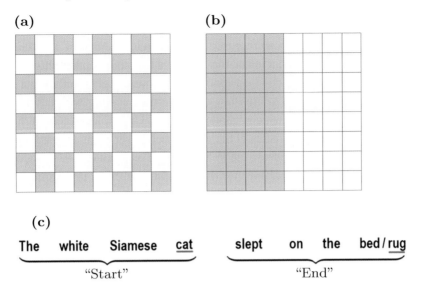

(c)

The   white   Siamese   <u>cat</u>   slept   on   the   bed / <u>rug</u>

"Start"   "End"

Figure 11.5   For convolutional networks, an illustration of (a) an interleaved partition and (b) a left–right partition. The network should support high entanglement measures with respect to the left-right partition for it to be able to model intricate dependencies between the two sides of the image (e.g., for face images), and with respect to the interleaved partition if one wishes to do so for neighboring pixels (e.g., for natural images). In §11.4 we show how this control over the inductive bias of the convolutional network can be achieved by adequately tailoring the number of channels in each of its layers. (c) For recurrent networks, high entanglement with respect to the Start–End partition implies that the network is able to represent functions which model long-term memory, i.e., intricate dependencies between the beginning and end of the input sequence. In the depicted 'next-word prediction task' example, in order to correctly predict the word **rug** the network must be able to represent some convoluted function involving the two subsets 'Start' and 'End'. Levine et al. (2017) employed the TN construction of recurrent networks presented above and proved that deep recurrent networks have a combinatorially large Start–End entanglement relative to their shallow counterparts, thus providing theoretical grounds for an empirically widely observed phenomenon (Hermans and Schrauwen, 2013).

is advisable in this case. Otherwise, the network's expressive ability to capture required long-range dependencies is hindered. As for recurrent networks, they should be able to integrate data from different time steps. Specifically, in order to translate long sentences or answer elaborate questions, their expressive ability to model long-term dependencies between the beginning and ending of the input sequence is of interest – see the toy example in Figure 11.5c. Therefore, the recurrent network should ideally support high entanglement with respect to the partition separating the first inputs from the later inputs, referred to as the *Start–End partition* (Levine et al., 2017).

11.4.2 *Quantum-Physics-Inspired Control of Inductive Bias*

When physicists choose a TN to represent the coefficient tensor of a certain wave function, the entanglement characterizing the wave function is taken into consideration and the network which can best model it is chosen (e.g., simulating a system with logarithmic corrections to area-law entanglement scaling with a MERA TN rather than with an MPS TN, which cannot model it). Thus, understanding the interparticle dependency characteristics of the wave function serves as a prior knowledge that helps restrict the hypothesis space to a suitable TN architecture. In accordance with the analogies discussed above, we draw inspiration from this approach, as it represents a 'healthy' process of first quantifying the key dependencies that the network is required to model, and then constructing the network appropriately. This is in effect a control over the inductive bias of the network.

The TN constructions of convolutional and recurrent networks in Figure 11.4 allow us to investigate means of matching the inductive bias to given input dependencies. In the following theorem, we translate a known result on the quantitative connection between quantum entanglement and TNs (Cui et al., 2016) into bounds on dependencies supported by the above deep learning architectures:

Theorem 11.1 (Proof in Levine et al., 2018). *Let y be the function computed by a ConvAC/single-layered RAC, (11.5), with $\mathcal{A}^{\text{conv/rec}}$ represented by the TNs in Figure 11.4. Let (A, B) be any partition of $[N]$. Assume that the channel numbers (equivalently, bond dimensions) are all powers of the same integer.[9] Then, the maximal entanglement entropy with respect to (A, B) supported by the convolutional or recurrent network is equal to the weight of the minimal cut separating A from B in the TN representing $\mathcal{A}^{\text{conv/rec}}$, where the weight of each edge is the logarithm of its bond dimension.*

Theorem 11.1 not only provides us with theoretical observations regarding the role that the number of channels in each layer fulfills in the overall expressiveness of a deep network, but also entails practical implications for the construction of a deep network architecture when there is prior knowledge regarding the task at hand. If one wishes to construct a deep learning architecture that is expressive enough to model intricate dependencies according to some partition (A, B), it is advisable to design the network so that all the cuts separating A from B in the corresponding TN have high weights.

To get a grasp of what can be understood from the theoretical results, consider 1D partitions similar in essence to the left–right partition and the interleaved partition depicted in Figure 11.5. For a TN representing a depth-L ConvAC network (Figure 11.4a) it is simple to see that the minimal weight of a cut with respect to

---

[9] See (Levine et al., 2018) for a treatment of a general channel numbers setting.

the left–right partition, $W^{\text{left-right}}$, obeys

$$W^{\text{left-right}} = \min(r_{L-1}, r_{L-2}, \ldots, r_i^{2^{(L-2-l)}}, \ldots, r_0^{N/4}, M^{N/2}), \qquad (11.9)$$

whereas the minimal weight of a cut with respect to the interleaved partition, $W^{\text{interleaved}}$, is guaranteed to be exponential in the number of pixels N:

$$W^{\text{interleaved}} = \min(r_0^{N/4}, M^{N/2}). \qquad (11.10)$$

It is worth noting that these minimal cut values are a direct consequence of the contiguous pooling scheme in the convolutional network. The exponential value of $W^{\text{interleaved}}$ explains the success of commonly employed networks with contiguous pooling windows – they are able to model short-range dependencies in natural data sets (this was established also in Cohen and Shashua (2017) by using a separation-rank-based approach).

The above are two examples that bring forth indications for the following 'rule of thumb'. If one is interested in modeling elaborate dependencies between pixels from opposite ends of an image, such those characterizing face images for example, we see from the expression in (11.9) that a small number of channels in deep layers can create an undesired 'shortcut' which harms the expressiveness of the network in a way that prevents it from modeling the required dependencies. In this case, it is advisable to keep more parameters in the deeper layers in order to obtain a higher entanglement measure for the required partition. However, if one is interested in modeling only short-range dependencies, and one knows that the typical input to the network will not exhibit relevant long-range dependencies, it is advisable to concentrate more parameters (in the form of more channels) in the lower levels, as it raises the entanglement measure with respect to the partition which corresponds to the short-range dependencies.

The two partitions analyzed above represent two extreme cases of the shortest- and longest-ranged dependencies. However, the min-cut result in Theorem 11.1 applies to any partition of the inputs, so that implications regarding the channel numbers can be drawn for any intermediate length scale of dependencies. The relevant layers that contribute to the min-cut between partitions (A, B) for which both A and B have contiguous segments of a certain length ξ can be easily identified – the minimal cut with respect to such a partition (A, B) may only include the channel numbers $M, r_0, \ldots, r_{\lceil \log_2 \xi \rceil}$. This is in fact a generalization of the treatment above with $\xi = 1$ for the interleaved partition and $\xi = N/2$ for the left–right partition. Any cut which includes edges in higher levels is guaranteed to have a higher weight than the minimal cut, as, in addition, it will have to include a cut of edges in the lower levels in order for a separation between A and B to actually take place. This can be understood by flow considerations in the graph underlying this tree TN – a cut that

Figure 11.6 Samples of the randomly positioned MNIST digits to be classified in the global task (upper panels) and the local task (lower panels).

is located above a certain sub-branch can not assist in cutting the flow between the A and B vertices that reside in that sub-branch.

For a dataset with features of characteristic size D (e.g., in a 2D digit classification task it is the size of the digits that are to be classified), such partitions of length scales $\xi < D$ are guaranteed to separate different parts of a feature placed in any input location. However, in order to perform the classification task of this feature correctly, an elaborate function modeling a strong dependence between different parts of it must be realized by the network. As discussed above, this means that a high measure of entanglement with respect to such a partition must be supported by the network, and now we are able to describe this measure of entanglement in terms of a min-cut in the TN graph.

We accompanied this understanding by corroborating experiments exemplifying that the theoretical findings, established above for the deep ConvAC, apply to a regular ConvNet architecture which involves the more common ReLU activations and average or max pooling. Two tasks were designed, one with a short characteristic length, to be referred to as the 'local task', and the other with a long characteristic length, to be referred to as the 'global task'. Both tasks were based on the MNIST dataset (LeCun et al., 1998) and consisted of 64×64 black background images on top of which resized binary MNIST images were placed in random positions. For the local task, the MNIST images were shrunk to small 8×8 images while for the global task they were enlarged to size 32×32. In both tasks the digit was to be identified correctly with a label $0, \ldots, 9$. See Figure 11.6 for a sample of images from each task.

We designed two different networks that tackle these two tasks, with ReLU activation and max pooling, which differ in the channel ordering – in the 'wide-base' network they are wider in the beginning and narrow down in the deeper layers while in the 'wide-tip' network they follow the opposite trend. Specifically, we set a parameter r to determine each pair of such networks according to the following scheme:

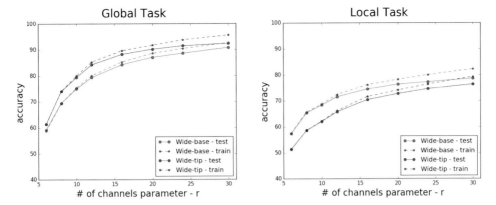

Figure 11.7 Results of applying deep convolutional rectifier networks with max pooling to the global and local classification tasks. Two channel arrangement geometries were evaluated: 'wide-tip', which supports modeling dependencies between far away regions; and 'wide-base', which puts the focus on dependencies between regions that are close to each other. Each channel arrangement geometry outperforms the other on a task which exhibits fitting dependencies, demonstrating how prior knowledge regarding a task at hand may be used to tailor the inductive bias through appropriate channel arrangements. Furthermore, these results demonstrate that the theoretical conclusions following Theorem 11.1, obtained for a ConvAC, extend to the common ConvNet architecture which involves ReLU activations and max pooling.

- wide-base: $[10; 4r; 4r; 2r; 2r; r; r; 10]$
- wide-tip: $[10; r; r; 2r; 2r; 4r; 4r; 10]$

The channel numbers from left to right go from input to output. The channel numbers were chosen to be gradually increased or decreased in iterations of two layers at a time as a tradeoff – we wanted the network to be reasonably deep but not to have too many different channel numbers, in order to resemble conventional channel choices. The parameter count for both configurations is identical: $10 \cdot r + r \cdot r + r \cdot 2r + 2r \cdot 2r + 2r \cdot 4r + 4r \cdot 4r + 4r \cdot 10 = 31r^2 + 50r$.

A result compliant with our theoretical expectation was achieved, as shown in Figure 11.7 – the 'wide-base' network outperforms the 'wide-tip' network in the local classification task, and the converse occurs in the global classification task. In natural images it may be hard to point out a single most important length scale D; however, the conclusions presented above can be viewed as an incentive to better characterize the input dependencies which are most relevant to the task at hand.

In the above we have described practical insights regarding deep convolutional network design, in the form of architecture selection (the pooling scheme) and resource allocation (choosing layer widths). Before concluding this section, we mention two additional theoretical results regarding the expressive power of deep learning architectures that can be obtained by using the TN framework. First, Levine et al. (2018) showed that such TN-based analyses can straightforwardly lead to reproduction of the exponential depth efficiency in convolutional networks, shown originally in Cohen et al. (2016b). The second result relates to the recurrent network case. We recall the discussion regarding entanglement with respect to the Start–End partition as a surrogate for long-term memory in recurrent networks (Figure 11.5c). Since the TN corresponding to a single-layered RAC has the form of an MPS (Figure 11.4b), the minimal weight of a cut with respect to the Start–End partition is trivially equal to the logarithm of the number of channels in the hidden recurrent unit, R. We thus obtain that by adding parameters to the RAC one may only linearly increase its ability to model long-term dependencies, as reflected by the Start–End Schmidt entanglement measure. Levine et al. (2017) employed the TNs tool and demonstrated that the Start–End Schmidt entanglement measure increases polynomially with the number of parameters for deep recurrent networks, thus providing a first-of-its-kind theoretical assertion for the widely observed empirical phenomenon of depth-enhanced long-term memory in recurrent networks.

In conclusion, inspired by entanglement-based TN architecture selection for many-body wave functions, novel deep learning outcomes can be found.

11.5 Power of Deep Learning for Wave Function Representations

In this section we provide a novel quantitative analysis of the ability of deep learning architectures to model highly entangled many-body systems, as detailed in Levine et al. (2019). We consider successful extensions to the above-presented architectures, in the form of deep recurrent networks and overlapping convolutional networks. These extensions, presented below (Figures 11.8 and 11.9), are seemingly 'innocent' – they introduce a linear growth in the number of parameters and their computation remains tractable. Despite this, both are empirically known to enhance performance (Krizhevsky et al., 2012; Graves et al., 2013), and have been shown theoretically to introduce a boost in network expressivity (Sharir and Shashua, 2018; Levine et al., 2017). As demonstrated below, both deep recurrent and overlapping convolutional architectures inherently involve information re-use, where a single activation is duplicated and sent to several subsequent calculations along the network computation.

We pinpoint this re-use of information along the network as a key element differentiating powerful deep learning architectures from the standard TN representations employed in many-body physics. Though data duplication is generally unachievable in the language of TNs, we circumvent this restriction and construct TN equivalents of the above networks, which may be viewed as deep-learning inspired enhancements of MPS and tree TNs. We are thus able to translate expressivity results on the above networks into super-area-law lower bounds on the entanglement scaling that can be supported by them (see §11.2.2 for the definition of entanglement scaling).

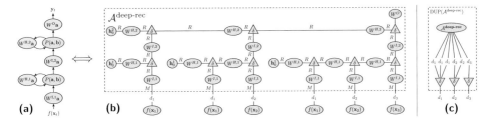

Figure 11.8 (a) A deep recurrent network is represented by a concise and tractable computation graph, which employs information re-use (two arrows emanating from a single node). (b) In TN language, deep RACs (Levine et al., 2017) are represented by a 'recursive MPS' TN structure (presented for the case of $N = 3$), which makes use of input duplication to circumvent the inherent inability of TNs to model information re-use. This novel tractable extension to an MPS TN supports logarithmic corrections to the area-law entanglement scaling in 1D (Theorem 11.2). (c) Given the high-order tensor $\mathcal{A}^{\text{deep-rec}}$ with duplicated external indices, presented in (b), the process of obtaining a dup-tensor $\text{DUP}(\mathcal{A}^{\text{deep-rec}})$ that corresponds to $|\psi^{\text{deep-rec}}\rangle$, (11.13), involves a single δ-tensor (operating here similarly to the copy-tensor in Biamonte et al., 2011) per unique external index.

Our results indicate that these successful deep learning architectures are natural candidates for joining the recent efforts regarding neural-network-based wave function representations, currently focused mainly on RBMs. As a by product, our construction suggests new TN architectures, which enjoy an equivalence to tractable deep learning computation schemes and surpass the traditionally used expressive TNs in representable entanglement scaling.

11.5.1 Entanglement Scaling of Deep Recurrent Networks

Beginning with recurrent networks, an architectural choice that has been shown empirically to yield enhanced performance in sequential tasks (Graves et al., 2013; Hermans and Schrauwen, 2013), and recently proven to bring forth a significant advantage in network long-term memory capacity (Levine et al., 2017), is the addition of adding more layers, i.e., deepening (see Figure 11.8a). The construction of a TN which matches the calculations of a deep RAC is less trivial than that of the shallow case, since the output vector of each layer at every time-step is re-used and sent to two different calculations – as an input to the next layer up and as a hidden vector for the next time step. This operation of duplicating data, which is easily achieved in any practical setting, is actually impossible to represent in the framework of TNs (see Claim 1 in Levine et al., 2017). However, the form of a TN representing a deep recurrent network may be attained by a simple 'trick' – duplication of the input data itself, so that each instance of a duplicated intermediate vector is generated by a separate TN branch. This technique yields the 'recursive-MPS' TN construction of deep recurrent networks, depicted in Figure 11.8b.

It is noteworthy that owing to these external duplications, the tensor represented by a deep RAC TN, written $\mathcal{A}^{\text{deep-rec}}$, does not immediately correspond to an N-particle wave function, as the TN has more than N external edges. However, when considering the operation of the deep recurrent network over inputs comprised solely of standard basis vectors, $\{\hat{e}^{(i_j)}\}_{j=1}^N$ ($i_j \in [M]$), with identity representation functions,[10] we may write the function realized by the network in a form analogous to that of (11.6):

$$y\left(\hat{e}^{(i_1)}, \dots, \hat{e}^{(i_N)}\right) = \langle \psi^{\text{product}}\left(\hat{e}^{(i_1)}, \dots, \hat{e}^{(i_N)}\right) | \psi^{\text{deep-rec}}\rangle, \tag{11.11}$$

where in this case the product state simply satisfies

$$|\psi^{\text{product}}\left(\hat{e}^{(i_1)}, \dots, \hat{e}^{(i_N)}\right)\rangle = |\hat{\psi}_{d_1, \dots, d_N}\rangle, \tag{11.12}$$

i.e., some orthonormal basis element of the many-body Hilbert space $\mathcal{H}$, and the state representing the deep recurrent network's operation obeys

$$|\psi^{\text{deep-rec}}\rangle := \sum_{d_1, \dots, d_N = 1}^{M} \text{DUP}(\mathcal{A}^{\text{deep-rec}})_{d_1, \dots, d_N} |\hat{\psi}_{d_1, \dots, d_N}\rangle, \tag{11.13}$$

where $\text{DUP}(\mathcal{A}^{\text{deep-rec}})$ is the N-indexed sub-tensor of $\mathcal{A}^{\text{deep-rec}}$ that holds the values of the latter when the duplicated external indices are equal; it is referred to as the dup-tensor. Figure 11.8c shows the TN calculation of $\text{DUP}(\mathcal{A}^{\text{deep-rec}})$, which makes use of δ-tensors for external index duplication, similarly to the operation of the copy-tensors applied on boolean inputs in Biamonte et al. (2011). The resulting TN resembles other TNs that can be written using copy-tensors to duplicate their external indices, such as those representing string bond states (Schuch et al., 2008) and entangled plaquette states (Mezzacapo et al., 2009) (also referred to as correlator product states; see Changlani et al., 2009), both recently shown to generalize RBMs (Glasser et al., 2018; Clark, 2018).

Effectively, since (11.11–11.13) dictate that

$$y\left(\hat{e}^{(i_1)}, \dots, \hat{e}^{(i_N)}\right) = \text{DUP}(\mathcal{A}^{\text{deep-rec}})_{i_1, \dots, i_N}, \tag{11.14}$$

under the above conditions the deep recurrent network represents the N-particle wave function $|\psi^{\text{deep-rec}}\rangle$. In the following theorem we show that the maximum entanglement entropy of a 1D state $|\psi^{\text{deep-rec}}\rangle$ modeled by such a deep recurrent network increases logarithmically with sub-system size:

Theorem 11.2 (Proof in Levine et al., 2019). *Let y be the function computing the output after N time steps of an RAC with two layers and R hidden channels per*

---

[10] This scenario of representing inputs to an RNN as 'one-hot' vectors is actually quite common in sequential tasks; see e.g., Graves (2013).

layer (Figure 11.8a), with 'one-hot' inputs and M identity representation functions,
(11.11). Let $\mathcal{A}^{\text{deep-rec}}$ be the tensor represented by the TN corresponding to y (Fig-
ure 11.8b) and $\text{DUP}(\mathcal{A}^{\text{deep-rec}})$ the matching N-indexed dup-tensor (Figure 11.8c).
Let (A, B) be a partition of $[N]$ such that $|A| \leq |B|$ and $B = \{1, \ldots, |B|\}$.[11] Then the
maximal entanglement entropy with respect to (A, B) supported by $\text{DUP}(\mathcal{A}^{\text{deep-rec}})$
is lower bounded by

$$\log \left\{ \binom{\min\{R, M\} + |A| - 1}{|A|} \right\} \propto \log\{|A|\}. \tag{11.15}$$

The above theorem implies that the entanglement scaling representable by a deep RAC is similar to that of the multiscale entanglement renormalization ansatz (MERA) TN (Vidal, 2007), which is also linear in $\log\{|A|\}$. Indeed, in order to model wave functions with such logarithmic corrections to the area-law entanglement scaling in 1D, which cannot be efficiently represented by an MPS TN (e.g., in the case of ground states of critical systems), a common approach is to employ the MERA TN. Theorem 11.2 demonstrates that the 'recursive MPS' in Figure 11.8b, which corresponds to the deep-recurrent network's tractable computation graph in Figure 11.8a, constitutes a competing enhancement to the MPS TN that supports similar logarithmic corrections to the area-law entanglement scaling in 1D.

We have thus established the motivation for the inclusion of deep recurrent networks in the recent effort to achieve wave function representations in neural networks. Due to the tractability of the deep recurrent network, calculation of the represented wave function amplitude would be efficient, and stochastic sampling techniques for optimization such as in Carleo and Troyer (2017), which cannot be used for optimizing a MERA TN, become available.

11.5.2 Entanglement Scaling of Overlapping Convolutional Networks

Moving to convolutional networks, state-of-the-art architectures make use of convolution kernels of size $K \times K$, where $K > 1$ (Krizhevsky et al., 2012; Simonyan and Zisserman, 2014). This architectural trait, which implies that the kernels spatially overlap when slid across the feature maps during computation, has been shown to yield an exponential enhancement in network expressivity (Sharir and Shashua, 2018). An example of such an architecture is the overlapping ConvAC depicted in Figure 11.9a. It is important to notice that the overlap in convolution kernels automatically results in information re-use, since a single activation is being used for computing several neighboring activations in the following layer. As above, such

---

[11] We focus on the case where A is located to the right of B for proof simplicity; numerical simulations of the network in Figure 11.8 with randomized weight matrices indicate that the lower bound in Theorem 11.2 holds for all other locations of A.

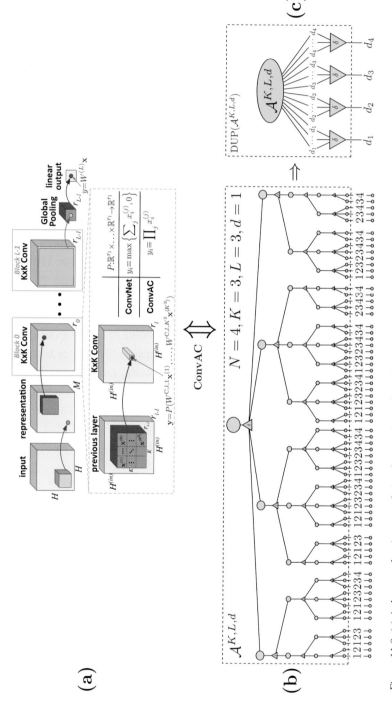

Figure 11.9 (a) A deep overlapping convolutional network, in which the convolution kernels are of size $K \times K$, with $K > 1$. This results in information re-use since each activation in layer $i \in [L]$ is part of the calculations of several adjacent activations in layer $l + 1$. (b) The TN corresponding to the calculation of the overlapping ConvAC (Sharir and Shashua, 2018) in the 1D case when the convolution kernel size is $K = 3$, the network depth is $L = 3$, and its spatial extent is $N = 4$. As in the case of deep recurrent networks, the inherent re-use of information in the overlapping convolutional network results in the duplication of external indices and a recursive TN structure. This novel tractable extension to a tree TN supports volume-law entanglement scaling until the linear dimension of the represented system exceeds the order LK (Theorem 11.3). For legibility, $j \in [4]$ stands for d_j in this figure. (c) The TN representing the calculation of the dup-tensor $\mathrm{DUP}(\mathcal{A}^{K,L,d})$, which corresponds to $|\psi^{\mathrm{overlap\text{-}conv}}\rangle$, (11.17).

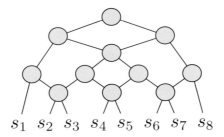

Figure 11.10 A 1D MERA TN with open boundary conditions for the case $N = 8$. The loops in this TN render the computation of its inner product with a product state (analogous to its tensor entry computation, required for wave function amplitude sampling) intractable for large system sizes.

re-use of information poses a challenge to the straightforward TN description of overlapping convolutional networks. We employ an input duplication technique similar to that used for deep recurrent networks, in which all instances of a duplicated vector are generated in separate TN branches. This results in a complex-looking TN representing the computation of the overlapping ConvAC, presented in Figure 11.9b (in 1D form, with $j \in [4]$ representing d_j for legibility).

Comparing the ConvAC TN in Figure 11.9b and the MERA TN in Figure 11.10, it is evident that the many-body physics and deep learning communities have effectively elected competing mechanisms in order to enhance the naive decimation/coarse graining scheme represented by a tree TN. The MERA TN introduces loops which entail the intractability of straightforward wave-function amplitude computation, yet facilitate properties of interest such as automatic normalization. In contrast, overlapping-convolutional networks employ information re-use, resulting in a compact and tractable computation of the amplitude of the wave function in question.

Owing to the input duplications, the tensor represented by the TN of the overlapping ConvAC of depth L with kernel size K^d in d spatial dimensions, denoted $\mathcal{A}^{K,L,d}$, has more than N external edges and does not correspond to an N-particle wave function. When considering the operation of the overlapping ConvAC over standard basis inputs, $\{\hat{e}^{(i_j)}\}_{j=1}^{N}$, with identity representation functions, we obtain a form similar to the above:

$$y\left(\hat{e}^{(i_1)}, \ldots, \hat{e}^{(i_N)}\right) = \langle \psi^{\text{product}}\left(\hat{e}^{(i_1)}, \ldots, \hat{e}^{(i_N)}\right) | \psi^{\text{overlap-conv}} \rangle, \qquad (11.16)$$

where the product state is a basis element of the many-body Hilbert space $\mathcal{H}$, as in

(11.12), and

$$|\psi^{\text{overlap-conv}}\rangle := \sum_{d_1,\ldots,d_N=1}^{M} \text{DUP}(\mathcal{A}^{K,L,d})_{d_1,\ldots,d_N} |\hat{\psi}_{d_1,\ldots,d_N}\rangle. \qquad (11.17)$$

The dup-tensor $\text{DUP}(\mathcal{A}^{K,L,d})$ is the N-indexed sub-tensor of $\mathcal{A}^{K,L,d}$ that hold the values of the latter when the duplicated external indices are equal (see its TN calculation in Figure 11.9c). Equations (11.16) and (11.17) imply that, under the above conditions, the overlapping ConvAC represents the dup-tensor, which corresponds to the N-particle wave-function $|\psi^{\text{overlap-conv}}\rangle$. Relying on results regarding the expressiveness of overlapping-convolutional architectures (Sharir and Shashua, 2018), we examine the entanglement scaling of a state $|\psi^{\text{overlap-conv}}\rangle$ modeled by such a network:

Theorem 11.3 (Proof in Levine et al., 2019). *Let y be the function computing the output of the depth-L, d-dimensional overlapping ConvAC with convolution kernels of size K^d (Figure 11.9a) for $d = 1, 2$, with 'one-hot' inputs and identity representation functions, (11.16). Let $\mathcal{A}^{K,L,d}$ be the tensor represented by the TN corresponding to y (Figure 11.9b) and $\text{DUP}(\mathcal{A}^{K,L,d})$ be the matching N-indexed dup-tensor (Figure 11.9c). Let (A, B) be a partition of $[N]$ such that A is of size A_{lin} in $d = 1$ and $A_{\text{lin}} \times A_{\text{lin}}$ in $d = 2$ (A_{lin} is the linear dimension of the subsystem), with $|A| \leq |B|$. Then, the maximal entanglement entropy with respect to (A, B) modeled by $\text{DUP}(\mathcal{A}^{K,L,d})$ obeys*

$$\Omega\left(\min\left\{(A_{\text{lin}})^d, LK\,(A_{\text{lin}})^{d-1}\right\}\right).$$

Thus, an overlapping convolutional network with L layers supports volume-law entanglement scaling: $(A_{\text{lin}})^d$, for systems of linear size $A_{\text{lin}} < LK$. Practically, overlapping-convolutional networks with common characteristics of e.g. kernel size $K = 5$ and depth $L = 20$, can support the entanglement of any 2D system of interest up to sizes 100×100, which are unattainable by competing intractable approaches (Gull et al., 2013; Chen et al., 2013; Lubasch et al., 2014; Zheng and Chan, 2016; Liu et al., 2017; LeBlanc et al., 2015).

Moreover, the result in Theorem 11.3 indicates a significant advantage in modeling the volume-law entanglement scaling of deep convolutional networks relative to the competing veteran neural-network-based approaches. These new approaches promised to grant tractable access to 2D systems that cannot be modeled by 2D TNs, since they render the computation of wave function amplitudes tractable and therefore stochastic-sampling-based optimization techniques can be employed, even for large 2D systems. However, in order to represent volume-law entanglement in a 2D system of N particles, fully connected networks require a number of network parameters that scales as $O(N^2)$ (Saito, 2017; Cai and Liu, 2018), while RBMs require $O(N)$ parameters (Carleo and Troyer, 2017; Deng et al., 2017b). In contrast, since the number of parameters in 2D overlapping convolutional networks is proportional to LK^2, the above volume-law condition, $A_{\mathrm{lin}} < LK$, implies the following corollary of Theorem 11.3.

Corollary 11.4. *The number of overlapping convolutional network parameters required for modeling volume-law entanglement scaling in a 2D system of N particles, scales as $O(\sqrt{N})$.*

Therefore, these networks have a clear polynomial advantage in resource efficiency over the fully connected networks and RBMs used previously. Thus, deep convolutional networks have the potential to provide access to highly entangled 2D systems of sizes unattainable by the competing veteran neural-network-based approaches, and to shed light on currently unreachable quantum phenomena.

Finally, the result in Theorem 11.3 applies to a network with no spatial decimation (pooling) in its first L layers, such as that employed in, e.g., Oord et al. (2016) and van den Oord et al. (2016). In Levine et al. (2019), a result analogous to that of Theorem 11.3 is proven for overlapping networks that integrate pooling layers in between convolution layers. In this case the volume-law entanglement scaling is limited to system sizes under a cut-off equal to the convolution kernel size K, which is small in common convolutional network architectures. Practically, this suggests the use of overlapping convolutional networks without pooling operations for modeling highly entangled states, and the use of overlapping convolutional networks that include pooling for modeling states that obey area-law entanglement scaling.

11.6 Discussion

The TN constructions of prominent deep learning architectures that we have presented, serve as a bidirectional bridge for the transfer of concepts and results between the two domains. In one direction, it allows us to convert well-established tools and approaches from many-body physics into new deep learning insights. An identified structural equivalence between many-body wave functions and the functions realized by non-overlapping convolutional and shallow recurrent networks brings forth the use of entanglement measures as well-defined quantifiers of a network's ability to model dependencies in the inputs. Via the TN construction of the above networks, in the form of tree and MPS TNs (Figure 11.4), we have made use of a quantum physics result which bounds the entanglement represented by a generic TN (Cui et al., 2016) in order to propose a novel deep learning architecture design scheme. We were thus able to suggest principles for parameter allocation along the network (the layer widths) and the choice of network connectivity (i.e., the pooling geometry), which have been shown to correspond to a network's ability to model dependencies of interest. Notably, Levine et al. (2020) used similar tools for analyzing the relation between layer width and network depth in self-attention architectures, which have recently become the standard in natural language processing.

In the opposite direction, we constructed TNs corresponding to powerful enhancements of the above architectures, in the form of deep recurrent networks and overlapping convolutional networks. These architectures, which stand at the forefront of recent deep learning achievements, inherently involve the re-use of information along network computation. In order to construct their TN equivalents, we employed a method of index duplications, resulting in recursive MPS (Figure 11.8) and tree TNs (Figure 11.9). This method allowed us to demonstrate how a tensor corresponding to an N-particle wave function can be represented by the above architectures, and thus makes available the investigation of their entanglement scaling properties.

Relying on a result which established that depth has a combinatorially enhancing effect on long-term memory capacity in recurrent networks (Levine et al., 2017), we showed that deep recurrent networks support logarithmic corrections to the area-law entanglement scaling in 1D. Similarly, by translating a recent result which shows that overlapping convolutional networks are exponentially more expressive than their non-overlapping counterparts (Sharir and Shashua, 2018), we showed that such architectures support volume-law entanglement scaling for systems of linear sizes smaller than LK (where L is the network depth and K is the convolution kernel size) and area-law entanglement scaling for larger systems. Our results show that overlapping convolutional networks are polynomially more efficient for modeling highly entangled states in 2D than competing neural-network-based representations.

Our treatment addressed the expressivity of deep learning architectures in the context of modeling many-body wave-functions, ensuring their a priori ability to support sufficient entanglement scaling. Once this is established, one must be able to optimize them efficiently, which means finding the correct parameters for describing the wave function of interest. In this regard, our proposed architectures do not differ greatly from recently employed neural-network architectures, which are optimized by tractable computations of overlaps with product states, allowing for optimization techniques that use stochastic sampling (see, e.g., Carleo and Troyer (2017) or the more recent work of Sharir et al. (2020) that optimize convolutional networks for modeling ground states). Overlapping convolutional networks are advantageous relative to previously employed RBMs in this aspect as well. Equations (11.16) and (11.17) show that the deep network in Figure 11.9 computes a wave function amplitude per inserted spin configuration. The computational cost of this operation is $O(NL)$ versus $O(N^2)$ for computing wave function amplitudes using RBMs. Moreover, the demonstrated polynomial efficiency of these deep networks in representing 2D volume-law entanglement, together with the locality of the convolution computation relative to the long range of RBMs, can provide a further boost in optimization speed. When implemented on graphical processing units (GPUs), which have substantially speeded up deep networks in recent years, there are significant runtime advantages to having low memory together with local operations.

The view that we have established, of entanglement measures as quantifiers of dependencies supported by deep networks, indicates that this connection may help shed light on the question of characteristic dependencies in machine learning datasets. Physicists often have a clear understanding of the entanglement properties of the many-body system they wish to represent, which assists them in choosing an adequate TN architecture to represent it. In the machine learning domain, dependencies in natural data sets are yet to be adequately characterized. Empirical evidence suggests that the mutual information in various natural datasets such as English Wikipedia, works of Bach, the human genome, etc., decays polynomially with a critical exponent similar in value to that of the critical Ising model (Lin and Tegmark, 2016). Our results show that deep learning architectures can support the entanglement scaling of such critical systems. A future quantification of the 'characteristic entanglement' in natural data sets may shed light on the empirical success of deep learning architectures, and it may suggest further task-specific design principles such as those brought forth in this work. Overall, we believe that the bidirectional bridge presented in this work can help bring quantum many-body physics research and state-of-the-art machine learning approaches one step closer together.

References

Amodei, Dario, Ananthanarayanan, Sundaram, Anubhai, Rishita, Bai, Jingliang, Battenberg, Eric, Case, Carl, et al. 2016. Deep speech 2: End-to-end speech recognition in english and mandarin. Pages 173–182 of: *Proc. International Conference on Machine Learning*.

Bahdanau, Dzmitry, Cho, Kyunghyun, and Bengio, Yoshua. 2014. Neural machine translation by jointly learning to align and translate. ArXiv preprint arXiv:1409.0473.

Beylkin, Gregory, and Mohlenkamp, Martin J. 2002. Numerical operator calculus in higher dimensions. *Proceedings of the National Academy of Sciences*, **99**(16), 10246–10251.

Biamonte, Jacob D., Clark, Stephen R., and Jaksch, Dieter. 2011. Categorical tensor network states. *AIP Advances*, **1**(4), 042172.

Cai, Zi, and Liu, Jinguo. 2018. Approximating quantum many-body wave functions using artificial neural networks. *Physical Review B*, **97**(3), 035116.

Carleo, Giuseppe, and Troyer, Matthias. 2017. Solving the quantum many-body problem with artificial neural networks. *Science*, **355**(6325), 602–606.

Carleo, Giuseppe, Nomura, Yusuke, and Imada, Masatoshi. 2018. Constructing exact representations of quantum many-body systems with deep neural networks. ArXiv preprint arXiv:1802.09558.

Changlani, Hitesh J., Kinder, Jesse M., Umrigar, Cyrus J., and Chan, Garnet Kin-Lic. 2009. Approximating strongly correlated wave functions with correlator product states. *Physical Review B*, **80**(24), 245116.

Chen, K.-S., Meng, Zi Yang, Yang, S.-X., Pruschke, Thomas, Moreno, Juana, and Jarrell, Mark. 2013. Evolution of the superconductivity dome in the two-dimensional Hubbard model. *Physical Review B*, **88**(24), 245110.

Clark, Stephen R. 2018. Unifying neural-network quantum states and correlator product states via tensor networks. *Journal of Physics A: Mathematical and Theoretical*, **51**(13), 135301.

Cohen, Nadav, and Shashua, Amnon. 2016. Convolutional rectifier networks as generalized tensor decompositions. In: *Proc. International Conference on Machine Learning*.

Cohen, Nadav, and Shashua, Amnon. 2017. Inductive bias of deep convolutional networks through pooling geometry. In: *Proc. 5th International Conference on Learning Representations*.

Cohen, Nadav, Sharir, Or, and Shashua, Amnon. 2016a. Deep SimNets. In: *Proc. IEEE Conference on Computer Vision and Pattern Recognition*.

Cohen, Nadav, Sharir, Or, and Shashua, Amnon. 2016b. On the expressive power of deep learning: A tensor analysis. In: *Proc. Conference On Learning Theory*.

Cui, Shawn X., Freedman, Michael H., Sattath, Or, Stong, Richard, and Minton, Greg. 2016. Quantum max-flow/min-cut. *Journal of Mathematical Physics*, **57**(6), 062206.

Deng, Dong-Ling, Li, Xiaopeng, and Das Sarma, S. 2017a. Machine learning topological states. *Physical Review B*, **96**(Nov), 195145.

Deng, Dong-Ling, Li, Xiaopeng, and Das Sarma, S. 2017b. Quantum entanglement in neural network states. *Physical Review X*, **7**(May), 021021.

Fannes, Mark, Nachtergaele, Bruno, and Werner, Reinhard F. 1992. Finitely correlated states on quantum spin chains. *Communications in Mathematical Physics*, **144**(3), 443–490.

Gao, Xun, and Duan, Lu-Ming. 2017. Efficient representation of quantum many-body states with deep neural networks. *Nature Communications*, **8**(1), 662.

Glasser, Ivan, Pancotti, Nicola, August, Moritz, Rodriguez, Ivan D., and Cirac, J. Ignacio. 2018. Neural-network quantum states, string-bond states, and chiral topological states. *Physical Review X*, **8**(Jan), 011006.

Graves, Alex. 2013. Generating sequences with recurrent neural networks. ArXiv preprint arXiv:1308.0850.

Graves, Alex, Mohamed, Abdel-Rahman, and Hinton, Geoffrey. 2013. Speech recognition with deep recurrent neural networks. Pages 6645–6649 of: *Proc.*

IEEE International Conference on Acoustics, Speech and Signal Processing. IEEE.

Gull, Emanuel, Parcollet, Olivier, and Millis, Andrew J. 2013. Superconductivity and the pseudogap in the two-dimensional Hubbard model. *Physical Review Letters*, **110**(21), 216405.

Hackbusch, Wolfgang. 2012. *Tensor Spaces and Numerical Tensor Calculus.* Springer Science & Business Media.

Hackbusch, Wolfgang, and Kühn, Stefan. 2009. A new scheme for the tensor representation. *Journal of Fourier Analysis and Applications*, **15**(5), 706–722.

Hall, Brian C. 2013. *Quantum Theory for Mathematicians.* Springer.

Han, Zhao-Yu, Wang, Jun, Fan, Heng, Wang, Lei, and Zhang, Pan. 2017. Unsupervised generative modeling using matrix product states. ArXiv preprint arXiv:1709.01662.

Hastings, Matthew B. 2007. An area law for one-dimensional quantum systems. *Journal of Statistical Mechanics: Theory and Experiment*, **2007**(08), P08024.

He, Kaiming, Zhang, Xiangyu, Ren, Shaoqing, and Sun, Jian. 2016. Deep residual learning for image recognition. Pages 770–778 of: *Proc. IEEE Conference on Computer Vision and Pattern Recognition*.

Hermans, Michiel, and Schrauwen, Benjamin. 2013. Training and analysing deep recurrent neural networks. Pages 190–198 of: *Advances in Neural Information Processing Systems*.

Khrulkov, Valentin, Novikov, Alexander, and Oseledets, Ivan. 2018. Expressive power of recurrent neural networks. In: *Proc. 6th International Conference on Learning Representations*.

Kolda, Tamara G., and Bader, Brett W. 2009. Tensor decompositions and applications. *SIAM Review*, **51**(3), 455–500.

Krizhevsky, Alex, Sutskever, Ilya, and Hinton, Geoffrey E. 2012. ImageNet Classification with Deep Convolutional Neural Networks. Pages 1097–1105 of: *Advances in Neural Information Processing Systems*, **25**.

LeBlanc, J. P. F., Antipov, Andrey E., Becca, Federico, Bulik, Ireneusz W., Chan, Garnet Kin-Lic, Chung, Chia-Min, Solutions of the two-dimensional Hubbard model: Benchmarks and results from a wide range of numerical algorithms. *Physical Review X*, **5**(4), 041041.

LeCun, Yann, Cortes, Corinna, and Burges, Christopher J. C. 1998. *The MNIST Database of Handwritten Digits*.

Levine, Yoav, Sharir, Or, and Shashua, Amnon. 2017. On the long-term memory of deep recurrent networks. ArXiv preprint arXiv:1710.09431.

Levine, Yoav, Yakira, David, Cohen, Nadav, and Shashua, Amnon. 2018. Deep learning and quantum entanglement: Fundamental connections with implications to network design. In: *Proc. 6th International Conference on Learning Representations*.

Levine, Yoav, Sharir, Or, Cohen, Nadav, and Shashua, Amnon. 2019. Quantum entanglement in deep learning architectures. *Physical Review Letters*, **122**(6), 065301.

Levine, Yoav, Wies, Noam, Sharir, Or, Bata, Hofit, and Shashua, Amnon. 2020. Limits to depth efficiencies of self-attention. Pages 22640–22651 of: *Advances in Neural Information Processing Systems*, **33**.

Lin, Henry W., and Tegmark, Max. 2016. Critical behavior from deep dynamics: A hidden dimension in natural language. ArXiv preprint arXiv:1606.06737.

Liu, Wen-Yuan, Dong, Shao-Jun, Han, Yong-Jian, Guo, Guang-Can, and He, Lixin. 2017. Gradient optimization of finite projected entangled pair states. *Physical Review B*, **95**(19), 195154.

Lubasch, Michael, Cirac, J. Ignacio, and Banuls, Mari-Carmen. 2014. Algorithms for finite projected entangled pair states. *Physical Review B*, **90**(6), 064425.

Mezzacapo, Fabio, Schuch, Norbert, Boninsegni, Massimo, and Cirac, J. Ignacio. 2009. Ground-state properties of quantum many-body systems: Entangled-plaquette states and variational Monte Carlo. *New Journal of Physics*, **11**(8), 083026.

Oord, Aaron van den, Kalchbrenner, Nal, and Kavukcuoglu, Koray. 2016. Pixel recurrent neural networks. ArXiv preprint arXiv:1601.06759.

Orús, Román. 2014. A practical introduction to tensor networks: Matrix product states and projected entangled pair states. *Annals of Physics*, **349**, 117–158.

Oseledets, Ivan V. 2011. Tensor-train decomposition. *SIAM Journal on Scientific Computing*, **33**(5), 2295–2317.

Perez-García, David, Verstraete, Frank, Wolf, Michael M., and Cirac, J. Ignacio. 2007. Matrix product state representations. *Quantum Information and Computation*, **7**(5-6), 401–430.

Plenio, Martin B, and Virmani, Shashank. 2007. An introduction to entanglement measures. *Quantum Information and Computation*, **7**(1), 001–051.

Preskill, John. 1998. Lecture Notes for Physics 229: Quantum Information and Computation. *California Institute of Technology*.

Saito, Hiroki. 2017. Solving the Bose–Hubbard model with machine learning. *Journal of the Physical Society of Japan*, **86**(9), 093001.

Schrödinger, Erwin. 1935. Discussion of probability relations between separated systems. *Mathematical Proceedings of the Cambridge Philosophical Society*, **31**, 555–563.

Schuch, Norbert, Wolf, Michael M., Verstraete, Frank, and Cirac, J. Ignacio. 2008. Simulation of quantum many-body systems with strings of operators and Monte Carlo tensor contractions. *Physical Review Letters*, **100**(4), 040501.

Sharir, Or, and Shashua, Amnon. 2018. On the expressive power of overlapping architectures of deep learning. In: *Proc. 6th International Conference on Learning Representations*.

Sharir, Or, Tamari, Ronen, Cohen, Nadav, and Shashua, Amnon. 2016. Tractable generative convolutional arithmetic circuits. ArXiv preprint arXiv:1610.04167.

Sharir, Or, Levine, Yoav, Wies, Noam, Carleo, Giuseppe, and Shashua, Amnon. 2020. Deep autoregressive models for the efficient variational simulation of many-body quantum systems. *Physical Review Letters*, **124**(January), 020503.

Simonyan, Karen, and Zisserman, Andrew. 2014. Very deep convolutional networks for large-scale image recognition. ArXiv preprint arXiv:1409.1556.

Stoudenmire, E. Miles. 2017. Learning relevant features of data with multi-scale tensor networks. ArXiv preprint arXiv:1801.00315.

Stoudenmire, Edwin, and Schwab, David J. 2016. Supervised learning with tensor networks. Pages 4799–4807 of: *Advances in Neural Information Processing Systems*, **29**.

Sutskever, Ilya, Martens, James, and Hinton, Geoffrey E. 2011. Generating text with recurrent neural networks. Pages 1017–1024 of: *Proc. 28th International Conference on Machine Learning*.

Szegedy, Christian, Liu, Wei, Jia, Yangqing, Sermanet, Pierre, Reed, Scott, Anguelov, Dragomir, Erhan, Dumitru, Vanhoucke, Vincent, and Rabinovich, Andrew. 2015. Going deeper with convolutions. In: *Proc. IEEE Conference on Computer Vision and Pattern Recognition*.

van den Oord, Aaron, Kalchbrenner, Nal, Espeholt, Lasse, Vinyals, Oriol, Graves, Alex, et al. 2016. Conditional image generation with pixelcnn decoders. Pages 4790–4798 of: *Advances in Neural Information Processing Systems*.

Vedral, Vlatko, and Plenio, Martin B. 1998. Entanglement measures and purification procedures. *Physical Review A*, **57**(3), 1619.

Verstraete, Frank, and Cirac, J. Ignacio. 2004. Renormalization algorithms for quantum-many body systems in two and higher dimensions. ArXiv preprint cond-mat/0407066.

Vidal, Guifre. 2007. Entanglement renormalization. *Physical Review Letters*, **99**(22), 220405.

Wu, Yuhuai, Zhang, Saizheng, Zhang, Ying, Bengio, Yoshua, and Salakhutdinov, Ruslan R. 2016. On multiplicative integration with recurrent neural networks. Pages 2856–2864 of: *Advances in Neural Information Processing Systems*.

Zheng, Bo-Xiao, and Chan, Garnet Kin-Lic. 2016. Ground-state phase diagram of the square lattice Hubbard model from density matrix embedding theory. *Physical Review B*, **93**(3), 035126.